Our Minds, Our Memories

Enhancing Thinking and Learning at All Ages

Jeanne Ellis Ormrod

Emerita, University of Northern Colorado

Boston   Columbus   Indianapolis   New York   San Francisco   Upper Saddle River
Amsterdam   Cape Town   Dubai   London   Madrid   Milan   Munich   Paris   Montreal   Toronto
Delhi   Mexico City   Sao Paulo   Sydney   Hong Kong   Seoul   Singapore   Taipei   Tokyo

Editor-in-Chief: Paul Smith
Editorial Assistant: Matthew Buchholz
Vice President, Director of Marketing: Margaret Waples
Marketing Manager: Joanna Sabella
Production Editor: Annette Joseph
Editorial Production Service: TexTech International
Manufacturing Buyer: Megan Cochran
Electronic Composition: TexTech International
Interior Design: Deborah Schneck
Cover Designer: Elena Sidorova

Library of Congress Cataloging-in-Publication Data

Ormrod, Jeanne Ellis.
   Our minds, our memories : enhancing thinking and learning at all ages / Jeanne Ellis Ormrod.
      p. cm.
   Includes bibliographical references and index.
   ISBN-13: 978-0-13-701343-2 (alk. paper)
   ISBN-10: 0-13-701343-4 (alk. paper)
   1. Learning.   2. Learning—Physiological aspects.   3. Memory.   I. Title.
   LB1060.O75 2011
   370.15'23—dc22

                                        2010033244

10 9 8 7 6 5 4 3 2 1   RRD-VA   14 13 12 11 10

www.pearsonhighered.com

ISBN-10: 0-13-701343-4
ISBN-13: 978-0-13-701343-2

About the Author

Jeanne Ellis Ormrod received her A.B. degree in psychology from Brown University and her M.S. and Ph.D. degrees in educational psychology from The Pennsylvania State University. She earned licensure in school psychology through postdoctoral work at Temple University and the University of Colorado at Boulder and has worked as a middle school geography teacher and school psychologist. She was Professor of Educational Psychology at the University of Northern Colorado until 1998 and is now Professor Emerita in UNC's School of Psychological Sciences. Her "Emerita" status means that she has officially retired from university duties, but she can't imagine ever *really* retiring. She remains an avid reader of psychological and educational research, stays in touch with many of her professional colleagues around the world, and continues to update her popular college textbooks in human learning, educational psychology, and research methodologies. She currently lives in New Hampshire with her husband Richard.

Contents

Chapter **3**

We're Builders, Not Sponges: Learning as Sense Making   25

Chapter **4**

**We Can't Have It All: A Simple Model of the Human Memory
System   46**

Chapter 7

Thinking about Thinking: Metacognition   128

Chapter 8

Common Sense Isn't Always Sensible: Reasoning and Critical Thinking   151

Chapter 9

**Applying the Old to the New: Transfer, Problem Solving,
and Creativity   184**

Chapter 10

**Becoming a More Intelligent Thinker and Learner: Acquiring
Productive Perspectives and Habits   215**

Chapter **11**

Enhancing Minds and Memories: The Big Picture   247

Preface

In my many conversations with friends, relatives, and students over the years, I've learned that people often have misconceptions about how they learn and remember—and also about how they *don't* learn and remember—new information and skills. Some of my friends and relatives have needlessly fretted that they were experiencing early symptoms of Alzheimer's disease. Some of my students have been convinced that they were irreparably stupid or, at the very least, had "really bad math genes."

Our minds are hardly the complete records of events that some people think they are or should be, and they can't always do the things we'd like them to do. Although in some ways our minds are quite flawed, in other ways they accomplish far more than anything a video camera, tape recorder, or obsessive-compulsive stenographer could do.

My purpose in writing this book is to share what researchers have learned about what our very human minds and memories can and cannot do for us. Within the past few decades, psychologists and neurophysiologists have uncovered many small "truths" about how—and also how *well*—human beings think and remember. In these pages I've condensed their findings into larger, more general "truths." I've intentionally *not* included details about most of the research studies on which I've based various principles and recommendations. However, you can track down many of these studies by using the tiny endnote numbers scattered liberally throughout the text, which will direct you to particular sources in the reference list at the end of the book. I'm a researcher myself, and so I'm not one to depart much from the facts as researchers currently know them.

I've written this book for a broad audience—students, professional educators and clinicians, people who provide training in the business world, and the general public. In nine of my eleven chapters I translate what psychologists have learned about thinking, learning, and memory into general recommendations in *Thinking Smart* and *Helping Others Think Smart* sections. In eight chapters I also include *Teaching Tips* sections with more concrete suggestions, most of which are applicable to instruction for virtually any age-group—children, adolescents, college students, working adults, or retired folks.

I've tried to strike a balance between everyday language and the psychological lingo central to an understanding of human learning and memory. I hope that I've successfully walked that narrow tightrope.

Acknowledgments

Any readers who are familiar with my earlier publications may notice that I've drawn some parts of this book from my *Human Learning* book and other parts (such as most of the exercises) from my *Educational Psychology* and *Essentials of Educational Psychology* books. But much of what appears within these pages is either new or reframed for a broader audience.

Despite a title page that lists me as sole author, many people have contributed to this book in significant ways. Most importantly, I must thank the individuals listed in the references, whose research and theories have provided a solid foundation for the ideas and suggestions I present here. As I've written the book, I've been able to stand on the shoulders of giants and see much greater distances than I possibly could have seen otherwise.

Two editors have also been critical partners along my writing journey. My editor for almost two decades, Kevin Davis, supported the book from the time it was just a tiny seed in my mind, and when my schedule finally allowed me to pursue this project, he encouraged the seed to grow. With Kevin's promotion to greater responsibilities at Pearson Education, Paul Smith embraced the project just as enthusiastically as Kevin had and suggested that I read, of all things, a certain history textbook to get some creative ideas for my table of contents. Paul was right—the book definitely got my creative juices flowing.

I'm most appreciative, too, of the reviewers who've helped me improve the book in many small but important ways. Two dear friends and neighbors, Debby Grubbs and Lorelei Chernyshov, read my first drafts of Chapters 1 through 5 and gave me the woman-on-the-street vantage point I needed to tweak the text a bit. Also, numerous colleagues in distant places read the first drafts of Chapters 1 through 10 and offered suggestions that have strengthened the book considerably: Nadine Butcher Ball, Maryville University; Angela Humphrey Brown, Piedmont College; Joshua Dickinson, Jefferson Community College; Joyce Edwards, Duxbury Public Schools (Massachusetts);

Kathryn A. Egawa, Seattle Public Schools (Washington); Kimberly Rombach, State University of New York, Cortland; Anna Valtcheva, State University of New York, Albany; Karen L. Westberg, University of St. Thomas; and three anonymous reviewers as well.

To all of the individuals I've just mentioned, I say a hearty "Thank you." I couldn't have done it without you.

J. E. O.

What You Don't Know (about Knowing) Can Hurt You: Common Misconceptions about Thinking and Memory

I can't believe I forgot that important meeting today. I know I learned the Pythagorean theorem in high school math, so how come I can't remember what it is? And where in the world did I put my car keys??!! I must be losing my mind.

If these questions sound familiar, you're a normal human being. And you're almost certainly *not* losing your mind. Instead, the problem is that you don't really *know* your mind.

In my many years of experience teaching college students about learning and memory, I've discovered that, by and large, human beings know very little about how their minds work. Even many well-educated adults have little idea about what the human brain is equipped—and not equipped—to do for them.

So how much do *you* know? The following true-or-false quiz can give you an idea.

Check It Out: **A Short Quiz**

Decide whether each of the following statements is true (T) or false (F). The answers will follow immediately after the quiz. Don't peek!

1. The human brain saves virtually all of the information it encounters. T   F

2. Some people are predominantly left-brain thinkers, whereas others are largely right-brain thinkers. T   F

3. The human brain is physiologically mature by age 15 or 16. T   F

4. Things in short-term memory typically last less than a minute. T   F

5. The best way to remember a new fact is to repeat it over and over very quickly—say, within the first 20 or 30 seconds after seeing or hearing it. T   F

6. Taking notes on a lecture makes the lecture easier to remember. T   F

7. People themselves are usually the best judges of what they do and don't know. T   F

Let's take these items one by one.

1. *The human brain saves virtually all of the information it encounters.* Given what researchers have learned about the brain, this statement is almost certainly *false.* Most of the things our eyes, ears, noses, and other senses detect in the outside world probably register temporarily in our brains. But much of the information we get from our environment—such as the quiet hum of a nearby fan and the gentle pressure of our chairs on our backs and thighs as we sit at our desks—is of little use to us. Especially if we don't pay attention to it, such information vanishes fairly quickly.

Even when we *do* pay attention to things, we don't necessarily need to keep them forever. Why would you need to remember the telephone number of a florist you called last week or the specific items you ordered at a fast-food restaurant on this date two years ago? But certainly some things are important to hold onto over the long run. The trick is to take control over what we remember and what we can reasonably leave in the dust.

2. *Some people are predominantly left-brain thinkers, whereas others are largely right-brain thinkers.* This one, too, is *false.* The two halves, or hemispheres, of the brain have somewhat different specialties, but they continually communicate and collaborate in tackling even the simplest of tasks. People have

unique strengths, of course—for instance, some are mathematically gifted, others are talented artists—and such strengths undoubtedly reflect differences in certain, very specific areas of the brain. But for all intents and purposes, there is no such thing as left-brain or right-brain thinking.

3. *The human brain is physiologically mature by age 15 or 16.* This is another *false* one. As you'll discover in Chapter 2, the brain continues to develop in important ways in late adolescence and early adulthood. For example, the part of the brain immediately behind the forehead, known as the *prefrontal cortex*, undergoes changes well into the 20-something years. These late-coming changes in the prefrontal cortex enable young adults to plan ahead and control their impulses much more so than they did in their teenage years.

4. *Things in short-term memory typically last less than a minute.* This statement is *true*. Surprised? Many people think of short-term memory as being a place where they save things they need to remember for a few days or weeks—say, things they need to remember for an important exam. But to psychologists, information in short-term memory typically lasts for less than *half* a minute. Anything that lasts considerably longer than this is usually in *long-term* memory. Even long-term memory isn't necessarily forever, as you'll learn in Chapter 4.

5. *The best way to remember a new fact is to repeat it over and over very quickly—say, within the first 20 or 30 seconds after seeing or hearing it.* This one is *false*. Simply repeating something over and over in a short time span, especially if we do so mindlessly, can help us with *short-term* memory. For instance, it can help us remember a telephone number long enough to dial it. But if we truly want to keep the information for the long haul, we need to do something more with it—in particular, to make sense of it in some way.

6. *Taking notes on a lecture makes the lecture easier to remember.* Yes, this is *true*, and for at least two reasons. First, we're more likely to remember something if we pay attention to it, and taking notes on a lecture helps us keep our attention on what we're hearing. When we don't take notes in, say, a lecture or committee meeting, it's all too easy for our minds to wander; although we're physically in the same room as those who are speaking, mentally we're somewhere else entirely.

A second advantage of taking notes is that they provide an external record of what we've heard. As noteworthy and memorable as new tidbits of information may seem to us when we first hear them, they're apt to become less memorable as days go by, especially if we don't do something significant with them in the meantime. Most good "rememberers" have external "memories" as well as internal ones, in the forms of lecture notes, to-do lists, calendar and alarm functions on their cell phones, and so on.

7. *People themselves are usually the best judges of what they do and don't know.* Nope, this one is definitely *false*. For example, two eyewitnesses to a crime or accident may both be quite confident about what they've observed and yet give conflicting accounts that cannot possibly both be right. And many high school and college students think that if they've spent a long time studying a textbook chapter, they must know its contents very well. However, if they've spent most of their study time inefficiently (perhaps by "reading" while thinking about something else altogether or by mindlessly copying definitions), they may know far less than they think they do.

If you answered all seven quiz items correctly, congratulations—maybe you don't need to read any further. But if you missed a few, you still have a lot to learn about how your mind works, even though it's been your constant companion for . . . how long? 15 years? 25 years? 40? 60? Even longer? In any case, it's been with you since Day One—Mother Nature's birthday present. It's about time you got to know it better.

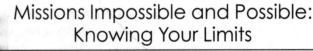

Missions Impossible and Possible: Knowing Your Limits

When I talk about the *brain* in this book, I'm talking about the actual physical hardware that resides inside your skull, between your ears. When I speak of the *mind*, I'm apt to be talking about the psychological phenomena the brain enables: thought processes, knowledge, beliefs, and so on. As we explore the nature of human thinking and memory, we'll examine research findings about both physical and psychological phenomena. But the first step is to get a general idea of what our physical brains and psychological minds are able to do for us. We'll start with our limitations—what we *cannot* do—and then look at what we *can* do, often very effectively.

We Aren't Video Cameras or Tape Recorders

Wouldn't it be wonderful if our brains could record everything we see and hear? Need to remember the name of that miracle drug you saw advertised on

TV? Just fast-forward through your mental "video" for the time period when you were watching television last night. Want to recall something a biology teacher once said about trilobites? Just rewind your mental "tape recording" to the teacher's lecture on fossils three years ago.

Hmm, no, that would involve a lot of fast-forwarding and rewinding—pretty time-consuming, even if we do it mentally rather than physically. And you'll probably never have a use for most of the advertisements and academic trivia you've consumed over the years. Mother Nature apparently figured these things out a long time ago, and so she gave us equipment that's a bit more practical.

We're Pattern Detectors and Summarizers

Rather than learn and remember every trivial detail in our environments, we seem to be predisposed to look for patterns and summarize what we've observed. As an example of what I mean, try the following exercise.

Check It Out: A Breeze, a Rock, and Some Ants

Carefully read all of the sentences that follow in List 1. After you've finished reading them, I'll give you a second list of sentences and ask you to identify those that you previously saw in List 1.

LIST 1

1. The breeze blowing from the sea stirred the air.
2. The tiny hut was at the edge of the woods.
3. The ants ate the sweet jelly.
4. The breeze stirred the air.
5. The rock rolled down the mountain.
6. The warm breeze blowing from the sea stirred the air.
7. The ants ate the jelly.
8. The rock that rolled down the mountain crushed the tiny hut.
9. The ants in the kitchen ate the jelly that was on the table.

10. The warm breeze stirred the air.

11. The ants ate the sweet jelly that was on the table.

12. The sweet jelly was on the table.

13. The rock crushed the tiny hut at the edge of the woods.

14. The evening air was heavy.

15. The rock crushed the hut.

16. The warm breeze stirred the heavy evening air.

17. The jelly was sweet.

18. The rock crushed the tiny hut.

Now cover the list of statements with a sheet of paper. Look at the sentences that follow in List 2. Some of the sentences are exactly the same, word for word, as sentences in List 1; others are new ones. Mark sentences you've previously seen as "old"; mark the others as "new."

LIST 2

1. The breeze blowing from the sea stirred the heavy evening air.	old	new
2. The ants in the kitchen ate the jelly.	old	new
3. The rock that rolled down the mountain crushed the hut.	old	new
4. The hut was at the edge of the woods.	old	new
5. The breeze stirred the heavy evening air.	old	new
6. The ants in the kitchen ate the sweet jelly that was on the table.	old	new
7. The warm breeze blowing from the sea stirred the air.	old	new
8. The ants ate the jelly that was on the table.	old	new
9. The rock crushed the hut at the edge of the woods.	old	new
10. The warm breeze blowing from the sea stirred the heavy evening air.	old	new
11. The rock that rolled down the mountain crushed the hut at the edge of the woods.	old	new
12. The breeze was blowing from the sea.	old	new

13. The ants ate the sweet jelly that was on the table.	old	new
14. The warm breeze was blowing from the sea.	old	new
15. The rock that rolled down the mountain crushed the tiny hut at the edge of the woods.	old	new
16. The ants were in the kitchen.	old	new
17. The rock that rolled down the mountain crushed the tiny hut.	old	new
18. The ants in the kitchen ate the sweet jelly.	old	new

Did you find this task to be more difficult than you initially thought it might be? In fact, only *three* sentences in List 2 are old ones: Items 7, 13, and 17. (They appear in List 1 as Items 6, 11, and 8, respectively.) The other fifteen are new ones.

In a classic experiment, John Bransford and Jeffrey Franks[1] gave such a task to college students, who erroneously "recognized" most of the new sentences as being ones they had seen before. The students were especially likely to "recognize" sentences that best summarized the information they had previously read—in particular, these three items in List 2:

6. The ants in the kitchen ate the sweet jelly that was on the table.

10. The warm breeze blowing from the sea stirred the heavy evening air.

15. The rock that rolled down the mountain crushed the tiny hut at the edge of the woods.

Our tendency to look for patterns and integrate details into general summaries pervades much of what we mentally do as we interact with our environment. For example, after reading a novel, we can typically remember major characters and the overall plot but not the blow-by-blow and nitty-gritty of each page. After traveling through new territory, we're apt to describe its topography in general terms—"farm country," "narrow, windy roads"— rather than describe each and every edifice and turn in the road. And when we think about people in our lives, we're more likely to think about their general physical and personal traits—"she's outgoing," "he loves to tell jokes"—than to recall their every action and utterance.

We're Also Meaning Makers

As human beings, we seem determined to make some sort of *sense* of our experiences. To see what I mean, try the next exercise.

Check It Out: **What Is It?**

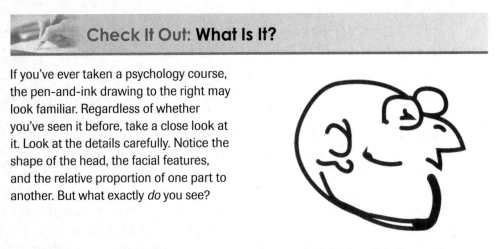

If you've ever taken a psychology course, the pen-and-ink drawing to the right may look familiar. Regardless of whether you've seen it before, take a close look at it. Look at the details carefully. Notice the shape of the head, the facial features, and the relative proportion of one part to another. But what exactly *do* you see?

Source: Figure from "The Role of Frequency in Developing Perceptual Sets" by B. R. Bugelski and D. A. Alampay, 1961, *Canadian Journal of Psychology, 15,* p. 206. Copyright 2010, Canadian Psychological Association. Permission granted for use of material.

Did you see a picture of a mouse or rat, or did you see a bald-headed man? The drawing isn't a very good picture of *anything;* too many details have been left out. Despite the missing pieces, people usually do make some sort of sense of the drawing.

Some things we simply take at face value—grass is green, the sky is blue, the mail usually arrives around lunch time—without questioning the whys or wherefores. But we human beings seem to want to find meaning in many aspects of our lives. I'm not talking about such existential issues as whether God exists or what ultimate reason (if any) there is for our being on this planet. Instead, I'm talking about making sense of day-to-day events. *Why won't my car start? Why was Mary so irritable yesterday? How come I got a C on that research paper when I worked so hard on it?* Such questions occupy a good deal of our mental energy.

We don't always reach consensus among ourselves, of course. For instance, we might disagree about why Mary was irritable yesterday. Maybe we did something to annoy her, but maybe, instead, she wasn't feeling well or was distressed about events earlier in the day. Maybe she wasn't feeling angry or sad at all: What we perceived to be an irritable woman was actually someone who was deep in thought about, say, why her car wouldn't start.

And what about the C on that research paper? The teacher who graded the paper may have perceived it to be a disorganized mess or an overly simplistic treatment of a complex topic. We, on the other hand, might interpret the C to reflect the teacher's careless or capricious grading practices ("I'll bet he didn't even read it," "She's never liked me anyway").

Rarely, then, do we remember things exactly as we've experienced them. We're constantly summarizing the things we've seen and heard and imposing our interpretations on them. Do we summarize and interpret accurately? Sometimes yes, but sometimes . . . well, not so much.

To fully understand the workings of the human mind, we need to know something about the physical hardware with which it operates. I present the basics of brain physiology and functioning in the next chapter. You might be tempted to skip that chapter—"too technical," you might think, or "I studied that stuff a long time ago"—but it's a short one, and I'm willing to bet that you'll gain helpful new insights about what is, without question, the most "human" part of your body.

CHAPTER 2

Billions upon Billions of Brain Cells: The Hardware of Thinking and Learning

The brain is an incredibly complicated mechanism that includes several *trillion* cells. Written numerically, each of those trillions is 1,000,000,000,000 brain cells, virtually all of which are microscopic in size—presenting a daunting task to even the most energetic and diligent of researchers who study the brain. Fortunately, recent advances in technology have been kind to brain researchers, who now have a variety of devices and research methods that are beginning to reveal how the brain functions under varying circumstances. I'll start with the most basic components of the brain: neurons and glial cells.

Gray Anatomy: Neurons and Their Synapses

A *neuron* is a cell in the body that specializes in receiving and transmitting messages. Some neurons in the brain receive information from elsewhere in the body, others synthesize and interpret the information, and still others send messages back to the rest of the body, telling it how to respond to its present circumstances. Experts estimate that a typical adult human has approximately 100 billion neurons. Neurons are brownish-grayish in color and so are sometimes collectively called *gray matter*.

Neurons vary somewhat in shape and size but have several features in common (see Figure 2.1). First, like other cells in the body, they have a *cell body,*

Figure 2.1
Neurons and Their Interconnections

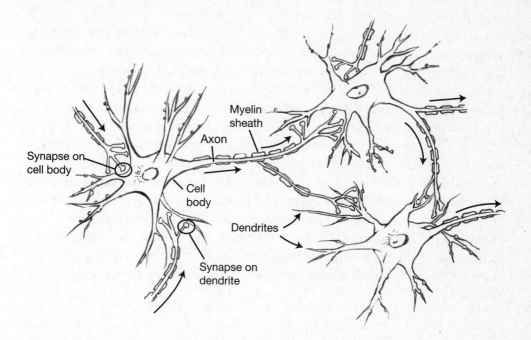

which contains the cell's nucleus and is responsible for the cell's health and well-being. They also have a number of branchlike structures called *dendrites,* which receive messages from other neurons. And they have an *axon,* a long, armlike structure that transmits information to still other neurons. For some (but not all) neurons, much of the axon has a white, fatty coating called a *myelin sheath.*

When a neuron's dendrites are stimulated either by a particular sensory organ or (for most neurons) by one or more *other* neurons, the dendrites become electrically charged. If the total charge reaches a certain level, the neuron "fires," sending an electrical impulse along its axon, which may, in turn, stimulate neurons farther along the pipeline to fire. If the axon has a myelin sheath, the impulse travels along it quite rapidly because it leaps from one gap in the myelin to the next, almost as if it were playing leap frog. If the axon doesn't have a myelin sheath, the impulse travels more slowly.

Curiously, however, neurons don't actually touch one another. Instead, their axons send messages to their neighbors across tiny spaces known as *synapses.* When an electrical impulse reaches the end of a neuron's axon, it signals the release of chemicals known as *neurotransmitters.* These chemicals travel across the neuron's synapses with other neurons and stimulate the dendrites or (occasionally) cell bodies of those neurons.

Different neurons specialize in different kinds of neurotransmitters. Perhaps in your readings about health, fitness, or related topics, you've seen references to dopamine, epinephrine, norepinephrine, or serotonin. All of these are neurotransmitters, and each of them may play a unique role in the brain. Brain researchers suspect that schizophrenia and other serious psychiatric disorders may sometimes be the result of abnormal levels of certain neurotransmitters.[1]

Any single neuron may have synaptic connections with hundreds or even thousands of other neurons.[2] Some neurotransmitters increase the level of electrical activity in the neurons they stimulate, whereas others reduce the level of electrical activity. Whether a particular neuron fires, then, is the result of how much it is "encouraged" and "discouraged" by its many neighbors. Many researchers have proposed that the physiological basis for learning and memory lies in changes in interconnections among neurons—in particular, in the formation of new synapses or in the strengthening or weakening of existing ones.[3]

White Matter Also Matters: Glial Cells

Accompanying neurons are perhaps one to five trillion *glial cells,* which are whitish in color and collectively known as *white matter.* All of that seemingly "empty" space between the neurons depicted in Figure 2.1 isn't empty at all; it's chock-full of glial cells of various shapes and sizes.

Glial cells appear to serve a variety of specialized functions. Some act as a clean-up crew for unwanted garbage in the brain. Others are "nutritionists" that control blood flow to neurons or "doctors" that tend to infections and injuries. Still others provide the myelin sheath of which I just spoke—the axon coating that enhances the efficiency of many neurons.

Recently some researchers have begun to speculate that certain star-shaped glial cells known as *astrocytes* are just as important as neurons—possibly even more important—in learning and memory. In human beings, astrocytes outnumber neurons by at least 10 to 1—a ratio much larger than that for, say, mice and rats—and they have innumerable chemically mediated connections with one another and with neurons. Astrocytes appear to have considerable control over what neurons do and don't do and how much neurons communicate with one another.[4]

Can we say precisely what roles neurons and astrocytes play in learning and memory? Not at this point, no. For now we'll have to be content with the knowledge that we human beings have many, many, many, *many* brain cells with which to work as we go about our daily business.

The Brain's Division of Labor (Not as Much as You Might Think): Parts of the Brain and Their Specialties

Groups of neurons and glial cells in different parts of the brain seem to specialize in different things. Structures in the lower and middle parts of the brain specialize in essential physiological processes (such as breathing and heart rate), simple body movements (such as walking and riding a bicycle), and basic perceptual skills (such as coordinating eye movements and diverting attention to potentially life-threatening situations).

Complex, conscious thinking takes place primarily in the *cortex,* which rests on the top and sides of the brain like a thick, bumpy toupee (see Figure 2.2). The portion of the cortex located near the forehead, known as the *prefrontal cortex,* is largely in charge of many sophisticated thinking processes, including sustained attention, reasoning, planning, decision making, coordination of complex activities, and inhibition of nonproductive thoughts and behaviors. But other parts of the cortex are important as well—for instance, they're actively involved in interpreting visual, spatial, and auditory information, and they serve as a general repository for our accumulated knowledge about the world.

And Rather Than *Either/Or:* The Two Hemispheres of the Brain

Oddly enough, the left half, or *hemisphere,* of the brain is largely responsible for controlling the right side of the body, and vice versa. Also, the left and right hemispheres of the cortex seem to have somewhat different cognitive

Figure 2.2
Cortex of the Human Brain

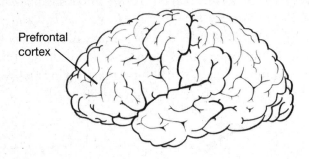

Prefrontal
cortex

specialties. In most people, the left hemisphere takes the lead in producing
and understanding language. For instance, researchers have pinpointed one
particular area of the left hemisphere that plays a major role in speech
production and another area that is critical for understanding speech. Reading
and mathematical calculation skills also seem to be heavily dependent on the
left hemisphere. In contrast, the right hemisphere is more dominant in visual
and spatial tasks, such as perceiving shapes, locating objects in space,
mentally manipulating visual images, recognizing faces and facial expressions,
interpreting people's body language, drawing, and painting. And in general,
the left side is more apt to handle details, whereas the right side is better suited
for integrating those details—that is, for seeing the big picture.[5]

Not all of us have left and right hemispheres that are specialized in the
ways I've just described. For instance, the left hemisphere is the primary
language hemisphere for more than 90% of right-handed individuals but for
only about 60% of left-handed folks. People differ, too, in how "one-sidedly"
they tackle various tasks. Some people regularly think in a fairly balanced,
two-sided manner. Others, however, seem to rely on one hemisphere more than
the other for particular tasks, with the left side being more active in some
circumstances and the right one being more active in others.[6]

Regardless of which hemisphere does what, the two hemispheres
constantly collaborate in day-to-day tasks. Let's take language comprehension
as an example. The left hemisphere handles such basics as syntax and word
meanings, but it seems to interpret what it hears and reads quite literally. The
right hemisphere is better able to consider multiple meanings and take context

into account. Hence, it is more likely to detect sarcasm, irony, metaphors, and puns. Without your right hemisphere, you would find no humor in the following joke, which I've often seen on the Internet:

> A woman gives birth to identical twin boys. Because she and her husband have very little money, they regretfully decide that they must give up their babies for adoption. A Spanish couple adopts one baby and names him Juan. An Egyptian couple adopts the other and names him Amal. Several years later the Spanish couple sends the woman a picture of Juan.
> "Ah," she says wistfully, "I wish I had a picture of Amal as well."
> "But honey," her husband responds, "they're identical twins. If you've seen Juan, you've seen Amal."

Okay, so it's a corny joke—a real groaner, actually. And it works only if you recognize that it's a twist of the common expression "If you've seen one, you've seen them all"—a connection you're most likely to make in your right hemisphere.

Not only are the two hemispheres in regular contact, but the various parts of the brain *all* communicate constantly with one another. Recall a point I made earlier: Neurons have synapses with many, many other neurons. Essentially, learning or thinking about virtually anything tends to be *distributed* across many parts of the brain. Even a single piece of information—for example, your street address, telephone number, or birthday—is probably stashed away in your head in a distributed manner.[7]

Contrary to popular belief, then, we rarely think exclusively in one part of the brain or even in one hemisphere. Except in cases of serious brain injuries or certain surgical procedures that disconnect the two hemispheres (usually to control debilitating epileptic seizures), there is virtually no such thing as "left-brain" or "right-brain" thinking.[8]

Tots and Teens Are Still a Bit Green: How the Brain Changes with Age

A second widespread misconception about the brain is that it reaches full maturity within the first few years of life. Actually, Mother Nature takes more than 20 years to complete her handiwork. We now look at changes in the brain at various points along its developmental journey.

Building the Foundation: The Prenatal Period

About 25 days after conception, the brain first emerges as a tiny tube. The tube grows longer and begins to fold inward to make pockets, which gradually develop into the brain's major parts. Many glial cells and neurons quickly form and reproduce in the inner part of the tube. The rate at which new brain cells form is astonishing. For example, between the 5th and 20th weeks of prenatal development, approximately 50,000 to 100,000 new neurons form per second.[9] In fact, the great majority of the neurons a person will ever have are formed during this time.

In the second trimester of the mother's pregnancy, glial cells and neurons migrate to various locations. On arrival, neurons send out dendrites and axons in an effort to form synapses with one another, with glial cells supporting the neurons in their connection-making efforts. Those neurons that make contact with one another survive and begin to take on particular functions, whereas those that do not (about half of them) die off.[10] Such deaths are not to be mourned, however. Programming human beings to overproduce neurons is apparently Mother Nature's way of ensuring that the developing brain will have a sufficient number with which to work. The excess ones are unnecessary and can quite reasonably wither away.

Adapting to the Local Environment: Infancy and Early Childhood

At birth, the human brain is about one-fourth the size it will be in adulthood, but by age 3 it reaches three-fourths of its future adult size.[11] Several important developmental processes occur during the few years of life to make the brain more serviceable in the world in which it finds itself. All of these processes are driven largely by genetics—by the instructions-for-brain-assembly that a child has inherited at conception.

Accompanying birth is a virtual explosion of new astrocytes, followed soon thereafter by the rapid formation of many new synapses.[12] Neurons sprout new dendrites going every which way, and so they come into contact with a great many of their neighbors. Thanks to this process of *synaptogenesis,* young children have many more synapses than adults do. Eventually, the rapid proliferation of synapses comes to a halt. Exactly when it does so varies for different parts of the brain. For example, synapses reach their peak in areas of the cortex that handle vision and hearing within the first year, but they continue to increase in the prefrontal cortex until age 2 or 3.[13]

As children encounter a wide variety of stimuli and experiences in their daily lives, some synapses come in quite handy and are used repeatedly. Other synapses are largely irrelevant and useless, and these gradually fade away in a process known as *synaptic pruning*. In some areas of the brain, the period of intensive synaptic pruning occurs fairly early—for instance, in the preschool or early elementary years. In other areas, it begins later and continues until well into adolescence.[14]

Why do our brains create a great many synapses, only to eliminate a sizable proportion of them later on? In the case of synapses, more isn't necessarily better. Researchers speculate that by generating more synapses than we'll ever need, we have the potential to adapt to a wide variety of conditions and circumstances. As we encounter certain regularities in our environment, we find that some synaptic connections aren't consistent with what we typically encounter in the world or with how we typically need to respond to it. In fact, effective learning and behaving require not only that we think and do certain things but also that we *not* think and do *other* things—in other words, that we inhibit certain thoughts and actions.[15] Synaptic pruning, then, may be Mother Nature's way of making our brains more efficient.

A third process further enhances the brain's ability to respond to the world quickly and efficiently. As you should recall, the axons of some neurons are covered with a myelin sheath, which greatly speeds up the rate with which an electrical charge travels along the axon. When neurons first form, they have no myelin. The process of coating their axons, known as *myelination*, occurs gradually over time. Some myelination begins near the end of the prenatal period, especially in parts of the brain that handle skills necessary for basic survival. However, much of it occurs in the first few years after birth, with different areas becoming myelinated in a predictable sequence. Myelination accounts for a sizable proportion of the brain's postnatal increase in size.[16]

Fine-Tuning the System: Middle Childhood, Adolescence, and Early Adulthood

Especially in the cortex, synaptic pruning continues into the middle childhood and adolescent years, and myelination continues into the twenties or beyond.[17] Several parts of the brain, especially those that play key roles in thinking and

"Hmm, I have an hour to write a 10-page research paper for my geography class. What can I write about?"

Thanks, in part, to brains that are physiologically still works-in-progress, adolescents aren't always very good at planning ahead.

learning, increase significantly in size from middle childhood until late adolescence or adulthood.[18] The prefrontal cortex continues to mature during late adolescence and early adulthood, enhancing the abilities to plan ahead, maintain attention for lengthy periods, and control impulses.[19]

With puberty comes changes in hormone levels (such as in estrogen and testosterone), and these hormones affect the continuing maturation of various brain structures. Puberty-related hormonal changes may also affect the production and effectiveness of neurotransmitters, as it appears that the levels of some neurotransmitters (such as serotonin and dopamine) change in adolescence.[20] If a particular hormone or neurotransmitter is abnormally high or low at this point, something can go seriously awry in brain functioning. For example, many serious psychiatric conditions, such as schizophrenia and bipolar disorder, often don't appear until adolescence or early adulthood. These disorders seem to be caused, at least in part, by abnormal brain structures or neurotransmitter levels—abnormalities that often don't emerge, or at least don't have much effect, until after puberty.[21]

Learning New Tricks as Old Dogs: Middle Age and the Senior Years

For many years it was common "knowledge" that all the neurons we would ever own are produced during the first few weeks of the prenatal period. Recently, however, researchers have found that some new neurons appear throughout our lives in a particular structure of the brain known as the *hippocampus*. There are actually two of these structures, one located on each side of the brain, and they are invariably involved in creating new memories. New neurons are possibly also formed in certain areas of the cortex. Ongoing learning experiences appear to enhance the young neurons' survival rate, maturation, and ability to connect with older neighbors. Regular physical exercise also helps the young neurons survive and thrive.[22]

And let's not forget those astrocytes that some researchers now believe to be centrally involved in our thinking and learning. Although Mother Nature is a bit stingy with the new neurons she gives us after birth, she's quite generous with astrocytes. Throughout our lifetimes our brains continually generate many new astrocytes, and those astrocytes often divide to create even more astrocytes. Astrocyte division seems to be especially common when we learn new things.[23]

New and challenging learning experiences in adulthood sometimes lead to noticeable changes in certain areas of the brain—noticeable, at least, to researchers who can hook us up to high-tech equipment that allows them to see what's going on inside our heads. For example, adults who become skillful jugglers show increased activity in certain parts of the cortex, and years of experience driving a taxi lead to significant changes within the hippocampus.[24] There's no question about it: Old dogs definitely *can* learn new tricks.

All is not rosy in middle and old age, however. Beginning in the thirties, we very gradually begin to lose some of that myelin of which I spoke earlier. And in later adulthood, the prefrontal cortex loses some of its ability to coordinate and control our thoughts and actions. As a result of such changes, our reaction times on physical and mental tasks increase, and we learn new information and skills at somewhat slower rates.[25]

But unless our brains are overcome by Alzheimer's disease or another seriously debilitating condition, they never go into lockdown mode. They're always able to learn and remember new things, even in the nineties and beyond.

 ## Enhancing Brainpower

The human brain is arguably the most complex and sophisticated of Mother Nature's biological creations, but it needs regular care to keep it working at its best. We can do many things to keep both our own and other people's brains functioning at maximum capacity. In *Thinking Smart* sections in this and the following chapters, I offer suggestions for how you might use your own brain and mind more effectively. In the *Helping Others Think Smart* sections, I suggest ways that you might apply what you're learning about the human brain and mind in education, clinical practice, other helping professions, and your day-to-day dealings with other people. Beginning in Chapter 3, I also include *Teaching Tips* sections written specifically for educators.

THINKING SMART

In recent years, research findings have consistently pointed to three general strategies for keeping our physical brains in tip-top shape.

▶ ***Continually seek out new challenges and learning opportunities.*** You can best keep your brain in good working order by regularly engaging in intellectually stimulating activities. Certainly a full-time, challenging profession can do this for you. But in your retirement years you should continue to be mentally active—perhaps by attending lectures on interesting topics, running for a local government office, debating current political and social issues with friends, or learning Swahili. It's important, too, to continue to learn new skills. It's never too late to learn how to knit, juggle, or play the banjo. Even playing cognitively challenging video games can have positive effects.[26]

As you grow older, your mantra must be *Use it or lose it.* Couch-potato-hood is a no-no. A lifestyle that consistently involves mentally stimulating and challenging activities will not only enrich the quality of your life but will also reduce the chances that you experience the debilitating symptoms of Alzheimer's disease and other cognitive declines in old age.[27]

▶ ***Stay physically active.*** Physical exercise also appears to be good for brain health, especially if it includes aerobic activities that keep the cardiovascular system in good working order.[28] As a 60-something-year-old myself, I play racquetball at least three times a week. I also begin each workday by meeting my neighbors at a nearby stop sign, from which we fast-walk a regular two-mile route. Not only has this routine improved my walking speed and cardiovascular system, but it also keeps me in the loop regarding the latest neighborhood gossip.

▶ *Get plenty of sleep.* You undoubtedly know that a good night's sleep improves mental alertness and can help you ward off germs that intend to do you harm. But sleep has an additional benefit as well. In particular, it helps to firm up your memories of information and events you've encountered during the day, rendering them more memorable over the long run.[29] (I'll talk more about this process of *consolidation* in Chapter 6.)

HELPING OTHERS THINK SMART

Many well-meaning individuals have drawn unwarranted inferences from what researchers have learned about the brain and its functioning. For instance, they've offered strategies and programs for "teaching to the right brain." And they've told parents that infants and toddlers need intensively stimulating activities in academics, athletics, and the arts to prevent the loss of the many synapses that the brain generates in the first three years of life. Such recommendations are *not* based on the facts. As we've seen in this chapter, virtually all mental tasks, even very simple ones, involve both brain hemispheres. And the loss of synapses that begins with a vengeance in the preschool years is a normal and *essential* process through which children's brains become increasingly efficient with age. In fact, many advanced cognitive abilities—for instance, abilities to think logically and abstractly about complex issues—emerge only after most synaptic pruning has already taken place.

Brain research is still in its early stages, but here are several suggestions I can offer with confidence.

▶ *Provide enriching environments for young children, but don't overdo it.* Certain kinds of stimulation in the early years are absolutely critical for children's brain development. For example, when children are born with cataracts that prevent normal vision, early surgery is essential. If the cataracts are removed before age 2, children develop relatively normal vision. But if surgery is postponed until age 5 or older, children remain functionally blind in whichever eye was affected.[30]

Early exposure to some form of human language is also critical. Children who have little or no exposure to at least one language in the first few years of life often have trouble acquiring language later on, even when given intensive language instruction. *Spoken* language isn't a requirement, however. Children who have been completely deaf from birth or soon thereafter often show normal language development in *sign language* if family members and others use it as the primary means of communicating with them.[31]

The kinds of stimulation I've just described are, of course, pervasive in most young children's lives, and so we can usually take them more or less for granted. But more preplanned, structured forms of stimulation can be beneficial as well. For example, high-quality child care and preschool programs frequently lead to gains in intelligence and other cognitive abilities. Such programs are most effective when they're tailored to children's existing abilities and interests.[32]

However, bombarding small children with constant or intense stimulation is *not* advisable. Infants, toddlers, and preschoolers can handle only so much information—and certainly only so much *new* information—at any one time. Furthermore, pushing them into overly challenging activities—such as those more suitable for, say, a 10-year-old—can cause stress, depression, and, in some cases, physical harm.[33] With young children, then, moderation is the key.

▶ *Provide enriching environments for older children and adolescents as well.* The first few years of childhood are important, to be sure, but so are the later ones. For example, gains made in enriching preschool programs may peter out unless children continue to have stimulating experiences during the school years. Educators and policymakers shouldn't put all of their eggs in one age-specific basket. Nurturance of children's mental growth must be a long-term enterprise.[34]

Earlier I mentioned the importance of exposing children to at least one language early in their lives. The window of opportunity for learning a *second* language remains open throughout life, but learning it before adulthood has certain advantages.[35] Typically, children learn how to pronounce a second language flawlessly only if they study it before midadolescence or, better still, even earlier. Children may also have an easier time mastering complex structural aspects of a second language—for instance, unusual grammatical constructions—when they're immersed in the language within the first 5 to 10 years of life.

Early exposure to a second language seems to be most advantageous if the second language is phonetically and structurally very different from the first. For example, a native English speaker benefits more from an early start in Japanese or Arabic than from an early start in, say, Spanish or German. Regardless of the timing, learning two languages instead of one results in greater brain development in areas related to language.[36]

▶ *Help adolescents plan ahead and make appropriate choices.* Remember, brain development isn't complete until early adulthood, especially in the prefrontal cortex—that center of long-term planning and impulse control. Adolescents often live for the moment, and they tend to make choices based on emotions ("This will be fun!") rather than on logic ("Hmm, this isn't likely to end well"). Adolescent risk taking is most common in social contexts, where having fun is typically a high priority and it's easy to get swept away by what peers are doing or suggesting.[37]

It's not enough to lecture adolescents about the hazards of tobacco, alcohol, drugs, and premarital sex. When they're with peers, they will rarely give such messages a second thought—they're apt to throw caution to the wind and common sense out the door. Certainly parents, teachers, and other adults can't keep tabs on teenagers every second of the day. But they *can* create environments that channel teens' risk-taking tendencies into safe activities—structured athletic events, after-prom parties, and so on. And, of course, parents must provide reasonable guidance and supervision regarding their children's activities before and after school.

Adolescents often need help with long-term planning even when no risk taking is involved. Many teens need assistance with strategies for staying on top of their schoolwork and other obligations—for instance, creating to-do lists for each day's homework assignments and notes-to-self for things that need to be completed later in the week. Paper calendars and cell phone calendar functions are useful for helping their owners keep track of due dates for large, lengthy projects. Many teenagers cope with *really* large projects (such as teacher-assigned term papers and end-of-semester portfolios) in the least productive way possible—by procrastinating. A little guidance about how to break seemingly overwhelming tasks into smaller, more manageable pieces, each with a self-imposed due date, can better enable teens to take these tasks in stride.[38]

▶ *Be optimistic that people of all ages have considerable potential to learn new things.* People often become quite proficient in topics or skills they don't begin to tackle until they're adults. For example, I didn't begin to play racquetball until I was in graduate school, didn't study Spanish until I was in my forties, and am learning more and more my about area of expertise—learning and memory— with every passing year. As a 60-something-year-old, I'm *still* learning the ins and outs of my cell phone, but little by little I'm getting the hang of it.

From a physiological standpoint, the brain's ability to adapt to changing circumstances—that is, its ability to *learn*—continues throughout the life span. For most topics and skills, there is no single "best" or "only" time to learn.

CHAPTER 3

We're Builders, Not Sponges: Learning as Sense Making

When I reflect on my days as a high school student, I think about how I used to study, or at least *tried* to study, and I shudder. Although I was a reasonably good student, my ideas about how I could best learn were incredibly naive. For example, I remember sitting on my bed "reading" my history textbook at night: My eyes dutifully went down each page, focusing briefly on every line, but my mind was miles away. After completing a reading assignment, I often couldn't remember a thing I had read, yet I had the crazy notion that my supposed "knowledge" of history would somehow rise to the surface at test time. It didn't.

We do seem to soak up some information in a relatively mind*less* fashion.[1] For example, if bees and wasps sting us often enough, we're apt to learn that they can be pretty nasty critters, and such knowledge will lead some of us to shriek and run away at their approach. (My husband thinks such behavior is ridiculous, but personally I find it quite sensible. And in any case, I can't control myself.)

For information we want to use consciously and deliberately—such as material in a history textbook—it's a different story altogether. In such instances, we must be more mind*ful*. As I mentioned in Chapter 1, we're not video cameras or tape recorders. Instead, we're meaning makers—we *construct* rather than absorb knowledge about our environment—and constructing knowledge involves active mental work.

Sensing versus Sense Making: Sensation Does Not Equal Perception

By *sensation,* I mean a body's physiological responses to stimulation from the physical world. By *perception,* I mean the *meaning*—the interpretation— we impose on that stimulation. When a certain physical object is in your line of sight, light waves bounce off it and hit the retinas of your eyes, giving you a certain visual sensation. But, in addition, you might *perceive* the object as a friend who is walking toward you. On a dark, cloudy afternoon, the sound waves resulting from a lightning bolt reach your ears, causing the sensation of sound that you perceive to be thunder. As you walk past a bakery, certain chemicals drift up your nostrils, and you perceive the aroma of freshly baked bread.

At any given time, our interpretation of the environment (perception) is usually both less and more than the information we actually receive from the environment (sensation). Perception is *less* than sensation because we cannot possibly interpret all of the information that bombards our senses at any particular moment. Right now, as you're looking at this book, light waves are bouncing off the page and hitting the light-sensitive cells in your retinas. At the same time, you may also be receiving light waves from a table at which you're working, a carpet on the floor, and pictures on the walls. Your ears are probably receiving numerous sound waves, perhaps from a radio, a nearby conversation, an air conditioner, or traffic outside your window. Perhaps a certain smell is drifting through the air, or a certain taste from your last meal lingers in your mouth. And, of course, your body can feel the gentle touch of your clothing, the pressure of the chair on which you're sitting, and perhaps an itch or sore spot on an arm or leg. It is neither necessary nor possible for you to interpret *all* of these sensations, so you will attend to some of them and ignore the others.

But perception is also much *more* than sensation, because the immediate, here-and-now stimulation we receive from our environment doesn't begin to give us all the information we need to make sense of our world. Almost invariably we take some of the sensory tidbits we receive and combine them with things we've previously learned about the world to construct a reasonable mental picture of what's going on around us.[2] Let's look at some specific examples of this perception-is-more-than-sensation idea in both vision and audition.

What You See Isn't Exactly What You Get: Sense Making in Vision

Close one eye for a few seconds and look around with the other. What your open eye is giving you is a relatively complete picture of whatever is in your line of sight, right? No, in fact, there's a huge gap in what your eye is actually seeing. A sizable area of each retina, just slightly off center, doesn't see anything at all. This particular area, known as the *blind spot,* is dedicated to the optic nerve, which sends information from the eye to the brain. Fortunately, each eye can usually cover for the other eye's blind spot.

Our eyes are blind in a second way as well. Rather than maintain a steady gaze, they continually make tiny jumps from one point of focus to another, taking periodic "snapshots" of what is visually out there. These jumps in focus, or *saccades,* occur four or five times a second, and our eyes are essentially blind during each one. If we receive only four or five snapshots of visual information per second, our visual world should appear jerky and erratic, much as an old-time movie does. The fact that we instead see smooth-flowing motion is due, in large part, to the mental "filling in" that our minds provide as they interpret visual sensations.

Even if our eyes functioned 100% of the time, they would usually give us an incomplete picture of our physical world. For example, imagine that you walk into a bookstore and see a store clerk behind the counter. You probably sense only the clerk's head and upper torso, yet you perceive an entire person. You assume that the clerk has a humanlike lower torso and two human legs, and you mentally fill in some reasonable ones. You would be quite surprised if you saw a very different lower body—say, that of a miniature giraffe—as the clerk emerged from behind the counter.

We can often make sense of our visual world with only a very small amount of information, as you can discover in the following exercise.

Check It Out: Three Faces

Look at the three black-and-white figures on the next page. What do you see in each one? Most people perceive the figure on the left to be that of a woman's face, even though many of her features are missing. Enough features are visible—an eye, parts of the nose, mouth, chin, and hair—that you can construct a meaningful perception from them. Is enough information available in the other two figures for you to construct two more faces? Construction of a face from the figure on the right may take you a while, but it can be done.

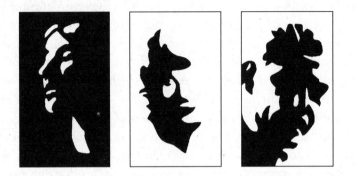

Source: Figures from "Age in the Development of Closure Ability in Children" by C. M. Mooney, 1957, *Canadian Journal of Psychology, 11,* p. 220. Copyright 2010, Canadian Psychological Association. Permission granted for use of material.

Objectively speaking, the three configurations of black splotches, and especially the two rightmost ones, leave a lot to the imagination. The woman in the middle is missing half of her face, and the man on the right is missing the top of his head. Yet knowing what human faces typically look like may have been enough to enable you to mentally add the missing features and perceive complete pictures. Curiously, once you have constructed faces from the figures, they then seem quite obvious. If you were to close this book now and not pick it up again for a month or more, you would probably see the faces almost immediately, even if you had had considerable difficulty perceiving them originally.

Thanks to the constructive nature of our visual perception, we can sometimes find multiple meanings in visual stimuli. The mouse–man drawing in Chapter 1 is a good example. We first use the various pieces of the drawing to build one interpretation—perhaps a bald-headed man with a pronounced overbite—and then recombine the pieces for a very different interpretation.

We often make assumptions about what we don't see and can be quite surprised when reality contradicts them.

Did You Say What I *Think* You Said?
Sense Making in Audition

What our ears actually sense can leave much to be desired as well, especially when we're listening to other people's speech. For example, let's say that you're in a noisy room and hear someone say:

I –an't –ear a thing in –is –lace!

Although you haven't heard everything the person said, you may have enough information to perceive the sentence:

I can't hear a thing in this place!

Even when you do hear everything the speaker says, what you *really* hear is a continuousstreamofsoundwaves rather than . . . separate . . . words . . . spoken . . . like . . . this. Only when you're familiar with the particular language you're listening to can you mentally divide the one long sound you actually sense into separate words. For instance, you can easily understand the following sentence when you hear it:

I read a book.

even though the identical sentence in Mandarin Chinese would give you trouble:

Wǒkànshū.

To an individual fluent in Mandarin Chinese but not in English, the situation would be reversed; that person would "hear" this:

Ireadabook.

and this:

Wǒ kàn shū.

The constructive nature of auditory perception enables us to make sense of speech even when the speaker has a foreign accent that distorts certain speech sounds. For example, when I was in graduate school, one of my apartment mates was Kikuko, a young Japanese woman who, despite being fluent in English, often confused the *L* and *R* sounds. (Different languages make different distinctions among various sounds in human speech; Japanese treats these two sounds as the same sound.) I quickly learned to make mental adjustments in response to Kikuko's mispronunciations. When she bragged of running ten "raps" at the gym, I knew she really meant *laps*. And when she spoke of looking for her "umblella" before heading off to class, I reasonably guessed that she thought it might rain later in the day.

The Whole Is More Than the Sum of Its Parts: Constructing Knowledge

Not only do we strive to make sense of what we're seeing and hearing in our immediate environment, but we're also predisposed to make sense of the larger picture—that is, to make sense of the world as a whole and of our place within it. We take the pieces of information we get from our environment and use them to construct a general understanding of what's happening. As a simple example, try the next exercise.

Check It Out: **Rocky**

Read the following passage *one time only:*

> Rocky slowly got up from the mat, planning his escape. He hesitated a moment and thought. Things were not going well. What bothered him most was being held, especially since the charge against him had been weak. He considered his present situation. The lock that held him was strong but he thought he could break it. He knew, however, that his timing would have to be perfect. Rocky was aware that it was because of his early roughness that he had been penalized so severely—much too severely from his point of view. The situation was becoming frustrating; the pressure had been grinding on him for too long. He was being ridden unmercifully. Rocky was getting angry now. He felt he was ready to make his move. He knew that his success or failure would depend on what he did in the next few seconds.[3]

Now summarize what you've just read in two or three sentences.

What did you think the passage was about? A prison escape? A wrestling match? Or perhaps something else altogether? The passage provides numerous facts but also leaves a lot unsaid. For instance, it tells us nothing about where Rocky was, what kind of lock was holding him, or why timing was of the utmost importance. Yet you were probably able to use the information the passage *does* include to construct a reasonable understanding of Rocky's situation.

Different people often interpret the same situation differently, in part because they each bring unique prior experiences, knowledge, and beliefs to the situation. For example, when the Rocky passage was used in an experiment with college students, physical education majors frequently interpreted it as a wrestling match, but music education majors (most of whom had little or no knowledge of wrestling) were more likely to think it was about a prison break.[4]

To say that we're predisposed to make sense of our world is an understatement. It's probably more accurate to say that we're *driven* to make sense of it.[5] For instance, preschoolers ask a lot of *why* and *how* questions ("Why is the sky blue?" "How does a telephone call know which house to go to?"). Many adolescents spend long hours puzzling over social matters ("When Anthony called me a 'brainiac,' did he mean that as a compliment or an insult?" "How can Angela be so popular when she's such a bitch?!"). And many adults impose their own, often very different interpretations on current social and political

events ("Providing universal health care is a moral imperative" "No, it's not—
it's just another example of the government trying to take over our lives!").

Some situations are cut-and-dried, with little room for diverse perspectives.
We can all agree that grass is green and Paris is the capital of France. But
many situations are ambiguous, giving us insufficient information to draw a
this-is-definitely-the-way-things-are conclusion. The "Rocky" passage is one
example; the mouse–man drawing in Chapter 1 is another. So, too, are many
of our social interactions with friends and colleagues and many political events
on the national and international scenes. The more ambiguous the situation,
the more likely we are to impose our own, unique interpretation based on our
own, unique collection of prior knowledge and beliefs.

Two Heads Can Be Better Than One: Knowledge Construction as a Social Enterprise

Sometimes we work with others, rather than alone, to make sense of situations
and events. For example, teenage girls may swap unflattering stories about a
popular but snobby classmate and jointly conclude that, yes, she really is a
despicable human being. College students might create a study group in an
attempt to better understand a poorly written and confusing textbook. Adults
of a particular political persuasion may convene either formally or informally
to identify the "good" or "bad" in current government leaders and policies.

Some joint sense-making efforts continue over lengthy time periods. Many
of humankind's most important sense-making accomplishments have occurred
over the course of many years, decades, or centuries. Through such disciplines
as mathematics, science, history, economics, and psychology, people have
gradually developed concepts (for instance, *pi* [π], *molecule,* and *revolution*)
and theories (for instance, *supply-and-demand* and *constructive processes in
perception*) that can reasonably explain certain aspects of the world and its
inhabitants. Our predecessors' works of fiction, music, and art help us impose
meaning on the world as well—for example, by trying to capture the thoughts
and feelings that characterize human experience.

To the extent that different groups of people create different mechanisms
(different concepts, theories, works of art, and so on) to help them make sense
of their physical and psychological experiences, they will inevitably see the

world in different ways.[6] Thus we must note the very important role that culture plays in knowledge construction. Members of any single cultural group are apt to share a certain *worldview*—a general set of beliefs and assumptions about how things are and should be—that is passed from one generation to the next. Following are examples of beliefs and assumptions that a worldview might encompass:

- Life and the universe came into being through random acts of nature *or,* instead, as part of a divine plan and purpose.

- Human beings are at the mercy of the forces of nature *or* should strive to master the forces of nature *or* must learn to live in harmony with nature.

- People's successes and failures in life are the result of their own actions *or* divine intervention *or* fate *or* random occurrences.

- People are most likely to enhance their well-being by relying on scientific principles and logical reasoning processes *or* by seeking guidance from authority figures.[7]

People's worldviews influence their understandings of a wide variety of phenomena. For example, some people interpret a hurricane not as the unfortunate result of natural meteorological forces but instead as divine punishment for their own or other people's wrongdoings. When people read newspaper articles about the appropriateness or inappropriateness of prayer in public schools, some view the trend away from prayer as a sign of "progress" toward greater religious freedom, but others view the same trend as a "decline" that reflects abandonment of the country's religious heritage. And Native American high school students often struggle with a science curriculum that explores how human beings can manipulate and gain control over natural events, rather than focusing on how people might strive to accept and live in harmony with nature as it is.[8]

Bastard Cities and Spaceship Skies: Misconstructing "Knowledge"

When my daughter Tina was in fourth grade, she came home one day complaining about a song she was learning in the school choir. "It has bad words in it, Mom," she told me. I was quite surprised to learn that she was talking about the song "America the Beautiful," but then she recited the guilty line from the second verse:

All the bastard cities gleam.

After my initial, horrified reaction to the richness of my daughter's vocabulary (which I'm hoping I hid well beneath my smiling, motherly face), I patiently explained that the line in question was actually "Alabaster cities gleam" and told her what *alabaster* means. Two weeks later, the rest of the family went to hear Tina's choir performing in concert. As the children began to sing "America the Beautiful," my 6-year-old son Alex turned to me and whispered, "Why are they singing about spaceship skies?" He was, of course, referring to the first line of the song: "O beautiful for spacious skies." Alex had never heard the word *spacious* before, but *spaceship* was a frequent word in his world of science fiction cartoons. Likewise, Tina was unfamiliar with *alabaster,* but . . . well, enough said.

When we construct our understandings of the world around us, there is, of course, no guarantee that we'll construct appropriate ones. Even the most educated of us are apt to have certain misconceptions—certain beliefs that are inconsistent with well-validated and thus reasonably accurate explanations of worldly phenomena and events. You probably uncovered some of your misconceptions about human thinking when you took my short quiz in Chapter 1. You might have a few misconceptions about your physical world as well. Here's another short quiz that can help you find out.

Check It Out: **Fact or Fiction?**

Decide whether each of the following statements is true (T) or false (F).

1. Any moving object has some kind of force acting on it.   T   F

2. Rivers always flow from north to south.   T   F

3. Human vision involves some sort of physical energy moving
   outward from the eye toward the object being looked at.   T   F

4. If an astronaut were to open the hatch while traveling in outer space,
   he or she would be sucked out by the vacuum that exists in space. T   F

5. Heavy objects fall faster than light objects.   T   F

6. The Great Lakes of North America contain saltwater.　　　　T　　F

7. The four seasons of the year are the result of the earth being closer to or farther from the sun at different points in its orbit.　　　T　　F

I'm guessing that you appropriately marked some of these as false. But to get a perfect score of 100%, you would have to have marked *all* of them as false. Here's the real scoop on the seven items:

1. After an object is initially set in motion, force is needed only to *change* its speed or direction. In a vacuum and away from any gravity-exerting physical body, a moving object keeps going at the same speed and in the same direction indefinitely—the principle of inertia at work.

2. Rivers flow from higher elevation to lower elevation. For example, in Africa, the Nile River flows north into the Mediterranean.

3. For vision to occur, light rays must travel from the object to the eye, *not* from the eye to the object.

4. After opening the hatch, the astronaut would be blown out by the air inside the spacecraft. A vacuum has no force with which to suck objects toward it.

5. Heavy objects and light objects fall at the same rate unless other forces, such as air resistance, differentially affect them. For example, feathers tend to fall more slowly than most other objects only because they encounter significant air resistance as they fall.

6. All five Great Lakes are freshwater lakes.

7. The seasons of the year are the result of the earth's tilt relative to the sun as it revolves around the sun. For example, in June, the Northern Hemisphere is tilted toward the sun and gets the full brunt of the sun's rays, while the Southern Hemisphere is tilted away from the sun, gets less sunlight per square foot or meter than at other times of the year, and so has winter. In December, it's vice versa: The Southern Hemisphere is tilted toward the sun, and the Northern Hemisphere is tilted away from it.

If you got a less-than-perfect score, don't feel bad: You're in the company of many well-educated adults.[9]

Our misconceptions come from a variety of places. In many instances they arise out of our own well-intentioned efforts to make sense of what we observe. For example, our belief that any moving object must have a force acting on it undoubtedly comes from our everyday experiences. If we want to push a heavy object across the room, we need to keep pushing it or else—thanks to considerable friction between it and the floor beneath it—it will immediately stop where it is.

Our society and culture can also foster misconceptions. For instance, if you began this book thinking that some people are "left-brain" thinkers and others are "right-brain" thinkers, you had undoubtedly seen or heard references to this common misconception in the media. And many oldie-but-goodie cartoons that continue to play on television humorously misrepresent the findings of physicists and archaeologists. For instance, when Wile E. Coyote chases Roadrunner off a cliff, he doesn't start to fall until he realizes that there's nothing holding him up, and the Flintstones regularly cavort with dinosaurs that, in fact, died out more than 60 million years before early humans roamed the earth. Unfortunately, sometimes teachers, textbook authors, and other authority figures pass along misconceptions as well.[10]

Regardless of their origins, our existing misconceptions about the world can wreak havoc on our ability to correctly understand and learn new things.[11] Remember, we use our prior "knowledge" about the world to help us make sense of new information and events. If that prior "knowledge" is incorrect, we'll construct distorted interpretations—possibly downright *wrong* interpretations—of what we're seeing and hearing. As an example, consider a high school student named Barry, whose physics class was studying the idea that an object's weight does *not*, in and of itself, affect the speed at which the object falls. Students were asked to build egg containers that would keep eggs from breaking when dropped from a third-floor window. Then, on a predetermined day, some students dropped their eggs while others recorded the time it took for each egg to reach the ground. Convinced that heavier objects fall faster, Barry had added several nails to his egg's container. Yet when he dropped it, classmates timed its fall at 1.49 seconds, a time very similar to that for other students' lighter containers. Rather than acknowledge that light and heavy objects fall at the same rate, Barry explained the result by rationalizing that "people weren't timing real good."[12]

In the vast majority of situations, our prior knowledge is essential for helping us understand and respond appropriately to our current surroundings. We certainly can't start from scratch every day in making sense of the innumerable new events in our lives. But occasionally the things we know—or rather, the things we *think* we know—are a curse rather than a blessing.

Making Good Sense

At this point, we've only skimmed the surface of how our minds work. Even so, we can draw some implications for thinking smart and helping others think smart.

THINKING SMART

Our species is, without a doubt, the most intelligent and adaptable one on the planet. Furthermore, by regularly passing along what we've learned to the generations that follow us, we gradually become even *more* intelligent and adaptable. But we're also fallible—we can misperceive, misinterpret, misunderstand, and mis*learn.* Here are several suggestions for keeping all those *mis*-es to a minimum.

▶ ***Actively use what you already know—especially what you're sure you correctly know—to help you make sense of new events.*** For everyday situations, you're apt to do this routinely, without much thought. For example, imagine yourself going to a new fast-food restaurant in your town—let's call it Burger Bill's. From your previous experiences at McDonald's, Taco Bell, Kentucky Fried Chicken, and so on, you know that you probably need to do several things at Burger Bill's that you probably *wouldn't* do at a more traditional restaurant:

- Immediately go up to the counter to place your order—if you instead sit down at a table, no one's going to wait on you.

- Look for your possible food options on signs beside or behind the counter—there probably isn't a paper menu to be found anywhere.

- Pay for your food before you get it—you're not likely to get it otherwise.

- Look for forks, napkins, and condiments at a separate counter off to the side—people behind the counter won't necessarily give you these things.

- After you've finished your meal, throw your paper goods and any unfinished food into a trash bin located somewhere inside the restaurant—restaurant staff and other customers will think you're an inconsiderate slob if you don't.

Any time you go into a new fast-food restaurant, you probably do these things without really thinking about them. You're making good use of your prior knowledge.

Yet many of us often *don't* draw on our prior knowledge when we're trying to make sense of more academic information—say, things we're studying in school. For instance, how often have you read a history book without trying to make sense of why things happened as they did? Why did Columbus's crew threaten to revolt after so many days on the open sea? Why did President Harry Truman decide to drop an atomic bomb on Hiroshima in 1945 when he knew full well how much destruction it might cause? You can draw on your knowledge of common human emotions and motives to make sense of these things. For example, members of Columbus's crew were undoubtedly frightened that they would never see their families again, and Truman worried that World War II might drag on interminably—and cause even more destruction—if he didn't do something drastic.

And what about geography? Do you think of this discipline as being a matter of just learning and remembering where things are on a map? Instead, speculate about why things might be located where they are. For example, Paris, the capital of France, is located on the River Seine, which flows northwest into the English Channel. Why is the capital there, rather than, say, in the French Alps or along the Mediterranean coast? What advantages might its location on a river have had for early Frenchmen? What advantages might that *particular* location on the Seine have had?

Such active, intentional sense making can sometimes take considerable mental work—and I do mean *work*—especially if a teacher or textbook doesn't help you much with the process. But for reasons you'll discover in Chapter 5, it's well worth the effort if you really want new information to stick with you for any length of time.

▶ ***Try to keep an open mind about what you're actually seeing and hearing.*** Although it's usually helpful to relate new information and events to previous experiences, you must remember that the things you know about the world—or rather, the things you *think* you know about it—aren't necessarily completely accurate. As you read or hear new information, then, constantly ask yourself, "Is this consistent with what I already know and believe? If not, how is it different? Can I resolve the inconsistency in some way? Might what I currently believe about this topic actually be *wrong?*"

Keeping an open mind is much easier said than done. Over the course of human history, people's close-mindedness has led to many needless conflicts— and a mind-boggling amount of pain and suffering—among individuals and cultural groups. It can be incredibly difficult to abandon existing beliefs even in the face of a great deal of compelling evidence to the contrary. We'll return to this last point in our discussion of critical thinking in Chapter 8, where we'll explore the issue in more depth.

▶ ***Get other people's perspectives.*** You can often make better sense of new phenomena and events when you seek out information from others. In some cases, this involves reading what experts have to say about the matter, perhaps in a book or on reputable Internet websites. In other cases, it involves getting together with others who may be as in-the-dark as you are and jointly trying to pull the various pieces of information you all have into a meaningful, sensible whole.

When you seek out other people's perspectives, it's important that you don't limit yourself to like-minded individuals. On the contrary, you should also get perspectives very different from your own, especially when controversial issues are involved. There are often two sides—sometimes many more than two—that have some legitimacy and must be taken into account.

As I write this book in the United States in the first half of 2010, a variety of issues—universal health care, a sputtering economy, a war in Afghanistan, a disastrous oil spill in the Gulf of Mexico, and so on—are all stirring up a very passionate American public. Unfortunately, many citizens are talking only with other people whose opinions are similar to their own. Thus, the "sense" they make of new information related to these topics simply confirms and amplifies their current beliefs, and groups adhering to differing points of view become increasingly polarized over time.

▶ ***Never trust yourself completely.*** Try as you might to be objective in your appraisals of new situations, your prior beliefs—including your general world-views about how things are "supposed to be"—invariably infiltrate your thinking. Each and every one of us must be willing to admit this to ourselves: We could be wrong.

HELPING OTHERS THINK SMART

Whether you're a parent, a teacher, a clinician, or simply a citizen who's eager to work for the betterment of others, you'll continually encounter situations in which you might help other people make sense of their world and experiences. Here I offer three general strategies, with more specific ones to follow in the first of my *Teaching Tips* boxes:

▶ ***Encourage and answer children's "why" and "how" questions.*** The incessant questions that young children ask ("Why you doing that?" "How come you wear that helmet when you drive your motorcycle?") can get bothersome after a while. But they typically reflect children's genuine desire to make sense of their world and expand on their understandings of what causes what and why things are the way they are.[13]

▶ ***Encourage dialogue about complex issues.*** In general, people construct more complete and accurate understandings of multifaceted topics when they talk about these topics with others.[14] In addition to exposing people to perspectives very different from their own, a healthy dialogue can have benefits such as these:

- People must clarify and organize their thoughts well enough to explain and justify their understandings.

- People tend to extend and expand on what they've learned—for example, by drawing logical inferences and thinking of new examples and applications.

- People may discover flaws and inconsistencies in their own thinking, thereby identifying gaps in their understanding.[15]

▶ ***Offer alternative explanations and perspectives to people whose reasoning reflects misconceptions or counterproductive interpretations.*** People of all ages are apt to have understandings and beliefs that aren't accurate or productive—perhaps about scientific phenomena, current events on the national or international scene, or the implications of a certain ballot initiative in an upcoming election. And people may occasionally misinterpret what others have said or done in social situations ("I can't believe he called me 'green'— how *insulting!*"). Oftentimes people appreciate getting feedback that steers their thinking in more useful directions ("He meant *green* in the sense that you're conserving valuable environmental resources—it was a compliment, not an insult").

Obviously, you must be tactful whenever you suggest that someone isn't interpreting events as they can productively be interpreted. And in spite of your best efforts, you may find that some people cling stubbornly to counter-productive understandings even when confronted with mountains of evidence to the contrary. Perhaps these understandings are consistent with certain religious teachings or worldviews. Perhaps they comprise core beliefs of a certain social group or political party. And some folks are simply reluctant to admit—even to themselves—that they might occasionally be wrong about something.[16]

As human beings, we have an incredible capacity to construct complex meanings and understandings from many tiny, separate pieces of information. But our minds are hardly objective, dispassionate entities that operate independently of the rest of us. Instead, they work in close collaboration with—and are often subservient to—our goals, motives, and emotions.

Teaching Tips

Provide guided opportunities for firsthand observation and experimentation. By observing, interacting, and experimenting with the objects around them, children and adults alike can discover many characteristics of the world on their own. For example, by playing with sand and water, preschoolers can learn valuable lessons about water flow and erosion. By playing games with balls and bats, older children gain insights into force and gravity. By experimenting with various media—watercolors, oil paints, clay, and so on—students of any age can acquire new ways of expressing themselves through the visual arts.

But for many situations, the operative word in this recommendation is *guided.* It's all too easy for students to misconstrue what they see—for instance, to express awe that cave dwellers tamed and rode the huge dinosaurs they see in a natural history museum or, as Barry did, to chalk up the equally rapid falls of light and heavy objects to the fact that "people weren't timing real good." It's important, then, to help students interpret their observations appropriately—for instance, to help them connect what they see to well-established scientific concepts and principles.[17]

◤ **Share experts' accumulated wisdom regarding physical and social phenomena.** Although it's sometimes beneficial to have students discover basic principles for themselves, it's also important to present experts' views—the concepts, principles, theories, and so on that our society has developed to explain the physical and psychological aspects of human experience.[18] Students are most likely to construct a productive view of the world when they have the benefit of experiencing the world firsthand *and* the benefit of learning how experts have come to interpret human experience. For example, students can learn a great deal about various biological species and fragile ecosystems—and are likely to acquire positive attitudes toward science—when firsthand observations in class or on field trips are accompanied by scientific explanations of the phenomena at hand.[19]

You don't always need to present commonly accepted wisdom in a didactic, this-is-how-it-is manner, however. Through appropriate questions, hints, and suggestions, you can sometimes lead students to derive appropriate interpretations of objects and events *on their own.* Teacher Katherine Maria took this approach in a series of discussions with 6-year-old Jennifer about the nature of gravity. Katherine had been trying to help Jennifer understand that people and objects in the southern hemisphere don't fall off the earth just because, from the standpoint of someone looking at a globe, they are located on the earth's "bottom" side. Katherine reported the following interaction between Jennifer (J) and herself (K) to show the progress Jennifer was making in her understanding of gravity:

> I used [an] inflatable globe and a figure stuck to the lower part of South America to explain to Jennifer that I had visited this place and had not fallen off the earth. We then had [this] discussion . . . :
>
> **K:** What would happen if there was a hole in the earth and this person (the figure stuck to South America) dropped a ball through it?
>
> **J:** People might think that if you dropped a rock into the hole it might go back out.
>
> **K:** Why would they think that?
>
> **J:** Because it's at the bottom of the earth. . . . They think that maybe the gravity did that.
>
> **K:** But what does gravity pull you toward?
>
> **J:** Down.

> **K:** (sticking the figure on the top of the inflatable globe): If you're standing here, where is down?

Jennifer points her finger in a downward direction. I move the figure to the South Pole.

> **K:** But suppose this was you. If you were here, where is down?

Jennifer points to a spot in the middle of the globe.

> **K:** Yeah, so it's pulling toward the?
>
> **J:** Middle.
>
> **K:** Right. So where would the rock end up then?
>
> **J:** In the middle.[20]

Identify and vigorously address existing misconceptions about school topics. You can better help students acquire accurate understandings of a topic when you first know—and when they, too, know—what their *mis*understandings are.[21] For example, recall that our first order of business in Chapter 1 was to look at misconceptions you might have about thinking and memory—misconceptions about left-brain–right-brain thinking, the typical duration of short-term memory, and so on. It was important to get those out in the open so that we could tackle them head on.

Students are more likely to revise their current misconceptions when they not only are aware of these misconceptions but also are genuinely motivated to acquire more accurate understandings. Researchers have found numerous strategies to be helpful in raising students' awareness of erroneous beliefs about academic topics and motivating them to acquire more productive ones:

- Ask challenging questions that lead students to discover weaknesses in their current beliefs.

- Ask students to make predictions about what they think will happen in classroom experiments; possibly have students vote regarding different possible outcomes.

- Present phenomena that students cannot adequately explain with their existing understandings.

- Ask students to provide several explanations for a puzzling phenomenon and to discuss the pros and cons of each one.

- Show how one explanation of an event or phenomenon is more plausible—that is, it makes more sense—than others.

■ When students' current understandings have a partly-right–partly-wrong quality, build on the things they understand correctly.

■ Have students apply the new, more accurate perspectives to real-life situations and problems.

■ When pointing out errors or weaknesses in students' reasoning or beliefs, preserve their self-esteem—for instance, by acknowledging that their existing beliefs are logical and consistent with many common experiences.

■ Monitor what students say and write for persistent misconceptions.[22]

■ **Create conditions for productive whole-class and small-group discussions.** Certainly not all children and adolescents—and not all adult students, for that matter—have the personal characteristics and social skills they need to participate appropriately in class discussions about academic topics. You're more likely to have productive student discussions if you anticipate some of the things that can occasionally go wrong. Here are several things to be on the lookout for:

■ Some students may have insufficient communication skills to help others understand their thinking.

■ Some students may be so anxious about making a bad impression on their peers ("Everyone will think I'm dumb") that they have trouble focusing on the overall discussion.

■ Students of high social status may dominate discussions, with others acquiescing to the dominant students' opinions and suggestions.

■ Students may pass along misconceptions that their classmates willingly accept.

■ Students may become annoyed or frustrated and begin to "tune out" if they perceive a discussion to be going in irrelevant or counterproductive directions.

■ If students believe that authority figures are invariably the best source of knowledge, they may see little purpose in discussing controversial issues with classmates.[23]

With such concerns in mind, I offer the following recommendations for ensuring productive dialogues:

■ Communicate the message that understanding a topic at the end of a discussion is more important than having the "correct" answer at the beginning of the discussion.

■ Point out that not all issues have a single "right" answer or way of looking at things.

■ Encourage students to be open to considering diverse perspectives—in other words, to "agree to disagree."

■ Give students guidance about how to behave; for example:

  ● Encourage everyone to participate and listen to others' ideas.

  ● Build on one another's ideas whenever possible.

  ● Be respectful of other students' feelings.

  ● Focus not on winning but on resolving the issue in the best possible way.

■ Have students first discuss a topic in small groups—enabling everyone to voice and gain support for particular ideas and opinions—and then bring students together for a whole-class discussion.

■ Monitor both the content and behaviors of small-group discussions and take corrective actions if necessary.

■ Bring the discussion to some kind of closure that helps students tie together what they've learned—for instance, by identifying and summarizing the key issues that students have raised.[24]

We Can't Have It All: A Simple Model of the Human Memory System

Most of us who own personal computers don't have a clue about how their underlying hardware works. Nor do we necessarily know much, if anything, about the programming-language underpinnings of the software we use for balancing checkbooks, sending and receiving e-mail, surfing the Internet, and so on. We know only how to *use* our computers and their software—and that's okay, as long as we know how to use these things effectively.

In Chapter 2 we looked a bit at the inner workings of our brains—that is, our hardware. We now begin our exploration of an important mental software package that depends on the hardware: the interconnected group of mechanisms known as the *human memory system*. My goal in this and subsequent chapters is not to provide an exhaustive explanation of your memory system's many intricacies but rather to help you get a good sense of what this mental software can—when used to full advantage—do for you.

I must caution you not to take my computer-hardware-and-software analogy too far, however. As you'll discover, although a computer typically operates in a one-thing-predictably-leads-to-another fashion, the human mind is rarely so straightforward and dependable.

Adopting Some Computer Lingo: Storage, Encoding, and Retrieval

When psychologists first began studying human memory in earnest in the 1960s, many hypothesized that the human mind was computerlike in nature. Accordingly, they began using early computer terminology to describe certain basic mental functions. For instance, they used the term *storage* to refer to the process of "putting" information in memory. If you can put this fact in your head:

The author of this book, Jeanne Ormrod, was born on August 22nd.

and if you can keep it there for any length of time—say, until August 22nd of next year—you are *storing* the information.

As we store information in memory, we usually modify it in some way—a process known as *encoding*. Encoding often involves changing the *form* of the information. For example, I once had a combination lock with the combination 22-8-14. I quickly learned the first two numbers by encoding them as "the day and month of my birthday" (no, I wasn't born in 1914). In this case, I changed numerical information into a verbal form. Encoding may also involve *adding to* new information using our existing knowledge about the world. For example, consider this information:

Jeanne Ormrod was born in Providence, Rhode Island.

Reading this fact, you might conclude that I grew up speaking English and that I am a U.S. citizen—inferences you might store along with the information I actually gave you. Yet another encoding process is one of *simplifying* new information, usually by remembering its general gist or meaning rather than all the nitty-gritty details. For example, as you read this book, you are, I hope, learning and remembering its main ideas—such as the constructive nature of perception and learning—but it's highly unlikely that you could recall any single paragraph word for word.

Finally, when we "find" information we have stored in our heads at an earlier time, we are engaging in *retrieval*. The following exercise shows retrieval at work.

Check It Out: **Retrieval Practice**

See how quickly you can answer each of the following questions:

1. What is your name?

2. What is the capital of France?

3. In what year did Christopher Columbus first sail across the Atlantic Ocean to reach the New World?

4. When talking about appetizers at a party, we sometimes use a French term instead of the word *appetizer*. What is that French term and how is it spelled?

As you probably noticed when you tried to answer these questions, retrieving some kinds of information from memory—your name, for example—is quick and easy. Other things—perhaps the capital of France (Paris) and the year of Columbus's first voyage (1492)—can be retrieved only after a bit of thought and effort. Still other pieces of information, even though you may have stored them in memory at one time, may be almost impossible to recall. Perhaps the correct spelling of *hors d'oeuvre* falls into this category.

Computers and computer software packages are typically designed with easy retrieval in mind: If a computer has the correct spelling of *hors d'oeuvre* in its database, you'll probably be able to find it when you need it. But in human memory, retrieval is never guaranteed. Sometimes we find the things we've previously stored, but sometimes we don't. Certainly I'm hoping that, come mid-August, you'll retrieve the date of my birthday and send me a tasteful card. I get cards from very few of my readers, however. I'm guessing that most of them don't retrieve this important piece of information when it might come in handy. An alternative hypothesis—one I try not to think about—is that my readers *do* retrieve my birth date and inexplicably choose to ignore such a momentous occasion.

Very Short, Short, and Longer: Three (Possibly Distinct) Components of Memory

In our modern way of life, we are constantly bombarded with information. For example, consider the hundreds of items a typical adult receives in the mail each year, including packages, letters, bills, brochures, catalogs, and credit card offers. Do you open, examine, and respond to every piece of mail? Probably not. If you're like me, you look closely at only a few key items, such as packages, personal letters, bills, and a few miscellaneous things that catch your eye. You may inspect other items long enough to know you don't need them. You may discard some items without even opening them.

Mother Nature has endowed us with a memory system that seems to function very much as many of us do when we sort through our mail each day. To deal effectively with our complex world, we need to know what information is important to learn and remember and what information we can reasonably cast aside as "junk mail."

Psychologists don't completely agree about the exact nature of human memory. But many have suggested that it has three components that hold information for different lengths of time: sensory memory, working memory, and long-term memory. A model of memory that includes these components is shown in Figure 4.1. Please note that we are *not* necessarily talking about three separate parts of the brain here. The model of memory I describe in this chapter has been derived largely from research studies of how human beings typically remember—and don't remember—various aspects of their environment, rather than from research on brain anatomy.

Figure 4.1
A Possible Model of the Human Memory System

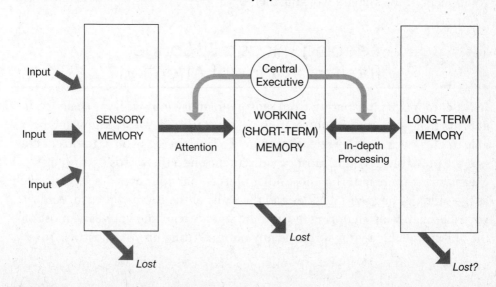

Just for a Moment: Sensory Memory

If you have ever played at night with a lighted sparkler—one of those metal sticks that, when lit, emits fiery sparks at one end for a minute or two—then you've seen the tail of light that follows the sparkler as you wave it about. If you have ever daydreamed during a lecture, you may have noticed that when you tune back in to the lecture, you can still "hear" the three or four words that were spoken just *before* you started paying attention again. The sparkler's tail and the words that linger are not floating out there in the environment. Instead, they're recorded in your sensory memory.

Sensory memory is the component of the human memory system that holds the information we receive—*input*—in more or less its original, *un*encoded form. Thus, visual input is stored in a visual form, auditory input in an auditory form, and so on.[1] Sensory memory can hold a great deal of information, possibly everything about our environment that our bodies detect.

That's the good news. The bad news is that information stored in sensory memory doesn't last very long.[2] Visual information (what we see) probably lasts for less than a second. For example, I can never spell out my entire first name (Jeanne) with a sparkler: The *J* always fades before I get to the first *n*, no matter how quickly I move the sparkler through the air. Auditory information (what we hear) probably lasts a bit longer, perhaps for two or three seconds. To keep information for any time at all, then, we need to move it to the next component of the system: working memory.

Keeping Things a Bit Longer: The Importance of Attention

In order to move information from sensory memory into working memory, it appears that—at least for information we want to *consciously* know and be able to use—we must pay attention to it.[3] For instance, as you read this book, you are probably devoting most of your attention to the words on the page. Meanwhile, you're ignoring most other objects that your eyes are sensing, such as the wrinkles on your knuckles and the walls of the room you've in. And you're probably also ignoring most of the sounds reaching your ears, most of the objects touching your skin, and any odors drifting up your nostrils. Your memory system has quickly discarded those many aspects of your world that you haven't been paying attention to. You've probably lost them forever.

Paying attention involves directing not only our eyes, ears, and other relevant sensory organs but also our *minds* toward whatever we need to learn and remember. For example, perhaps when you were reading my description of the brain in Chapter 2, your eyes were moving down each page while you were thinking about something altogether different—maybe an argument you had with a friend earlier in the day or a high-paying job you recently saw advertised in the newspaper. If so, what did you remember from Chapter 2? Probably not very much. Although your eyes were focused on each and every page, you weren't *mentally* attending to the words in front of you.

Actually, in at least one sensory modality—hearing—it's possible to focus our attention without having to orient our sensory organs in any particular direction. Imagine yourself at a cocktail party at which numerous conversations are going on simultaneously. You can usually focus in on just one of those conversations and ignore all the others. The speaker you attend to may or may not be the one toward which your eyes and ears are physically "aimed." Possibly you're listening to the person standing directly in front of you. But if that person has been rambling on for more than an hour about the trouble he has growing rhubarb, you may instead tune in to a more interesting conversation a few feet to your right or left. Even though you may be looking directly at the rhubarb grower and nodding in mock agreement, your attention is somewhere else altogether. But heaven help you if the rhubarb guy asks you a question that requires more than a simple smile and nod in response.

One reason we don't remember something we've seen or heard, then, is that we never really paid attention to it. For example, if you've been sitting in a committee meeting with your mind on something completely unrelated to the topic of conversation, you might say that you "forgot" what other committee members said, or you might say that you "didn't hear" what they said in the first place. The reality of the situation is somewhere in between: The conversation reached your sensory memory but never made it to your working memory.

Big, Bold, Bouncy, and Bizarre: Physical Factors That Capture Our Attention

Certain kinds of objects and events tend to draw our attention, whereas other kinds do not.[4] For example, which of the following letters first draw your eye?

A B c d E f g

You probably noticed the *B* and *E* before the other letters because of their larger size. Our attention tends to be drawn to large objects—a principle that newspaper publishers apply when they typeset front-page headlines in large letters and that advertisers take advantage of when they put potentially unenticing information in fine print.

More intense stimuli, such as bright colors and loud noises, also attract our attention—a fact that toy manufacturers capitalize on when they use bright colors in the toys they produce. So, too, do moving objects stand out in a crowd of more stationary ones. And stimuli that are new or unusual are hard to ignore, as you can see in the next exercise.

Check It Out: **Four Women**

Look briefly at the four women to the right, and then answer the question below.

Now for the question: At which woman did you look the longest?

You probably found yourself attending more to the woman on the right than to the other three. A woman with two heads and three legs is not someone you see every day.

Finally, objects that don't make sense within their context tend to capture our attention. For example, read this sentence:

I took a walk to the rabbit this morning.

Did you spend a greater amount of time looking at the word *rabbit* than at the other words? There's nothing the least bit unusual about the word *rabbit*— it's a perfectly ordinary word—but it's incongruous with the rest of the sentence.

Personal Significance and Passion: Psychological Factors That Sustain Our Attention

The characteristics I just described may capture our attention for the short run, but they don't necessarily keep it very long. We can look only so long at brightly colored packages and oddly placed words before they lose our interest. In contrast, things we find especially meaningful and relevant to our own lives—things that have personal significance for us—can hold our attention for a considerable time period.[5] For example, when we sit in front of a turned-on television set with an open book in our lap, the thing we attend to—the TV or the book—depends in large part on which one is more closely related to our motives at the time. If the book is interesting or if we need to know its contents well for an exam the following day, we might very well attend to the book. But if a popular situation comedy or a cliff-hanging soap opera is playing on TV, or if the book is dry and unenticing, we may very well forget that the book is even in the same room.

Our emotions come into the mix as well. Events with strong emotional associations usually attract and hold our attention.[6] For instance, in our culture, a nude body flashing through a crowded room is apt to catch the eye of just about everyone present. Events are especially compelling when they are relevant to our own lives *and* stir up strong feelings—perhaps because they make us angry or perhaps because they threaten our self-esteem.

A Bottleneck in the System: Attention's Limited Capacity

Learning and memory would be a lot easier, you might think, if we didn't have to choose certain things to pay attention to, but could instead attend to everything we capture in our sensory memories. Unfortunately, it turns out that our attention is very "narrow-minded." You can see a classic example of this fact in the next exercise.

Check It Out: **The Peter–Paul Goblet**

Look at the figure to the right. At first glance, you probably see a white goblet. But if you look at the black spaces on either side of the goblet, you should also be able to see two silhouettes ("Peter" and "Paul") staring at each other.

Now see if you can focus on both the goblet and the two silhouettes at *exactly* the same time, so that you can simultaneously see the *details* of both the goblet and the silhouettes. Can you do it?

Although you may have found that you could very quickly shift your focus from the goblet to the faces and back to the goblet again, chances are that you couldn't capture the *details* of both the goblet and the faces at exactly the same time. The Peter–Paul goblet illustrates a phenomenon known as *figure–ground*: As we focus in on the details of an object (the *figure*), we cannot simultaneously inspect whatever we're not paying attention to (that is, the background, or *ground*). We may notice a few salient characteristics of the ground, such as color, but more precise information is apt to escape us.

To explain the figure–ground phenomenon, some early psychologists proposed that people can pay attention to only one thing at a time—hence the difficulty most folks have in attending to both the goblet and the faces simultaneously. But now consider a situation in which you're driving your car while also carrying on a conversation with a friend. Certainly you're attending to two things at once: the road and the conversation. To account for such a situation, most psychologists now describe attention as having a *limited capacity*, such that the number of things we can pay attention to at any given time depends on how much thought is required for each one.[7] If you're engaging in a difficult activity, such as learning how to drive a car with a standard transmission, you may very well need to devote your full attention to that activity. However, if you're doing something more habitual or automatic, such as using a standard transmission after years of driving experience, you can easily devote some attention to one or more other things. Many tasks, such as driving, become increasingly automatic over time, therefore requiring less and less of our attention (I'll say more about this point in Chapter 6). Even so, when people carry on a conversation while driving—say, on a cell phone—they have slower reaction times and are less likely to notice traffic signals.[8]

Attention's limited capacity means that we must be quite selective about the information we focus on, and we must ignore (and so lose) a lot of the information we receive. As frustrating as it may sometimes seem, we simply cannot attend to—and so cannot remember—all the juicy tidbits our environment might send our way.

Where the Action Is: Working (Short-Term) Memory

Working memory is the component of our memory system in which we hold attended-to information for a short time while we try to make sense of it. More generally, it's where our "thinking" occurs. For example, working memory is where we think about the content of a lecture, try to decipher a confusing textbook passage, or solve a problem. Basically, this is the component that does most of the mental work of the memory system—hence its name, *working* memory. Whatever our *consciousness* is—and psychologists continue to debate the exact nature of human consciousness—this is probably where it is housed.

To get a bit technical for a moment, I should note that, rather than being a single entity, working memory probably has several components for holding and working with different kinds of information—for example, visual information, auditory information, and the underlying meanings of events—as well as a component that integrates multiple kinds of information. Remember a point I made in Chapter 2: Thinking about virtually anything involves many parts of the brain. Typically these various parts work together seamlessly.

Information that makes its way to working memory doesn't last very long unless we consciously continue to work with it in some manner—hence its alternative name *short-term* memory. If we simply pay attention to something and then don't do anything further with it, it's apt to linger somewhere between 5 and 20 seconds. In some instances, it may simply fade away from neglect. Alternatively, it may be replaced—"bumped out," as one of my professors used to say—by new input.[9] For example, for many years I shared my home not only with my husband but also with our three children, a dog, and two cats, and in such conditions I found myself being frequently interrupted in the middle of tasks. If I had a batch of cookies in the oven and one kid asked me to help search for a misplaced object—and then dog Tobey asked to go out to do his "business"—my cookies were very likely to be pushed from my working memory until I was confronted with new environmental input: The smell of something burning. My husband called me absentminded, but I knew better. My mind was definitely present, but its working component had moved from cookies to more pressing concerns.

The Head of the Head: The Central Executive

Many psychologists suggest that one of working memory's key functions is that of *central executive* for the memory system. This central executive oversees the flow of information throughout the system, selecting and controlling our thoughts and behaviors and inhibiting those that might be counterproductive. To a considerable degree, mental processes associated with the central executive appear to be located in the prefrontal cortex of the brain—that part just behind our foreheads. As you should recall from Chapter 2, this part of the brain continues to mature over the course of childhood, adolescence, and early adulthood. With age, then, the central executive increasingly takes charge and becomes increasingly effective.[10]

Look once again at the model of memory shown in Figure 4.1. Notice how an arrow goes from the central executive part of working memory to the "attention" arrow. One important role our central executive plays is to decide what we should pay attention to. Attention and working memory appear to be closely linked in the brain. Some psychologists propose that attention is actually a *part* of working memory, although the jury is still out on this issue.[11]

Another (or Maybe the Same) Bottleneck:
The Limited Capacity of Working Memory

Like attention, working memory has a limited capacity. (If attention and working memory are one and the same, as some psychologists suggest, we are talking about the *same* limited capacity.) Exactly how much can we typically hold in working memory at once? The classic digit-span test in the following exercise can give you an idea. The exercise is easier to do if you give the test to someone else—perhaps a friend or family member. But if you cover up the seven test items—perhaps with your hand or a piece of scrap paper—until you need to look at each one, you can give it to yourself.

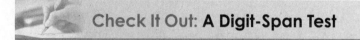

Check It Out: **A Digit-Span Test**

Each of the seven items below presents a series of numbers. The first has three numbers, the second has four, the third has five, and so on, with the final item having nine numbers. Read the sequence of numbers in Item A aloud, pausing for about a second between each number. Then cover the numbers and ask your "guinea pig"—either your accomplice or yourself—to write down the numbers *in order* on a sheet of paper. Follow the same procedure with Items B through G.

A.   2 9 7
B.   7 6 2 8
C.   3 9 4 1 5
D.   9 1 6 3 8 2
E.   7 4 5 1 9 3 8
F.   3 5 8 6 1 2 4 9
G.   5 1 8 9 3 4 2 7 6

Once the test is complete, score your guinea pig's responses to each item. For a response to be correct, all of the numbers in the series must be present and in their original order.

How did your guinea pig do? Adults typically do well with a 6- or 7-digit sequence but then begin to forget one or more numbers after that. Using a digit-span test like this one, a psychologist working in the 1950s estimated working memory's capacity as the *magical number seven, plus or minus two*— that is, people can hold from five to nine units of information in working memory at one time, with the average number being about seven.[12]

It turns out that this early estimate of 7 ± 2 was too simple. The number of pieces of information we can hold in working memory depends on how much information each piece includes and whether we can easily make associations among two or more pieces.[13] For example, we can more easily remember a series of nine numbers if we *chunk* them into three larger units, perhaps by saying "5 1 8" very quickly, then "9 3 4," and then "2 7 6." And we might more easily remember "chair desk book lamp" than "7 6 2 8." Ultimately it's probably impossible to identify a particular, exact capacity of working memory.

Furthermore, there seems to be a trade-off between how much information we can hold and how much we need to think about it. To see what I mean, put your elementary math skills to work for a minute in the next exercise.

Check It Out: A Division Problem

Try computing the answer to this division problem *in your head.* Once you've looked at the problem, cover the page and don't look back at it until you've solved the problem.

$$59\,\overline{)49{,}383}$$

Notice that the problem has only seven digits—an amount that, as you just learned, many adults can remember in a digit-span test. But did you find yourself "losing" some of the digits while you were trying to solve the problem? Did you ever arrive at the correct answer of 837? Most people can't solve a division problem with this many digits unless they write the problem on paper. The fact is, working memory just doesn't have enough space both to hold all of that information *and* to perform mathematical calculations on it. Without paper and pencil or some other external form of information storage to assist us, we can actively hold and think about only a very small amount of material at once.

Extending the Life of "Short-Term": Maintenance Rehearsal

Imagine that you need to call an acquaintance about an important matter. You don't have this person's telephone number recorded in your cell phone, and so you put your phone down and look for a telephone book. You eventually find one in another room and locate the number you need. You pay attention to the number, so it is presumably in your working memory. But now you realize that don't have your cell phone with you—you've left it elsewhere during your search for the phone book. You have no paper and pencil handy. How do you remember your friend's number until you can return to your cell phone and place your call?

If you're like most people, you probably repeat it to yourself over and over. This process, known as *maintenance rehearsal,* can keep information "fresh" in working memory for as long as you're willing to continue talking to yourself. But once you stop, the number disappears fairly quickly.

Maintenance rehearsal can be quite handy *if* the item to be remembered is quite small and *if* we don't have anything more pressing to think about in the interim. For instance, I use it when I need to remember to mail a few bills at the post office on my way home from the gym—often this is because I've forgotten to mail them on my way *to* the gym. When I first started using maintenance rehearsal for this purpose, I would begin repeating the word *mail* over and over to myself as soon as I got into my car at the gym, and I wouldn't stop until I reached the post office and mailed my letters. This procedure got pretty tedious after a while—the post office is about two miles from the gym, so I was having to say "mail" over and over about a gazillion times. My strategy now is to begin singing the song "Ninety-Nine Bottles of Beer on the Wall" but replacing the words "on the wall" with "in the mail." If you're familiar with the song, you know that one bottle falls in each verse, so you have one less bottle in the following verse. Singing the song isn't much more fun than incessantly saying "mail," but it works every time. I'm usually at about eighty bottles by the time I get to the post office, and once I pop those bills in the mailbox, I can—thank goodness—shut up.

Keeping Things Even Longer: Connecting the New with the Old

Mindless repetition can be an effective way of keeping information in working memory, but it's *not* a terribly good way to get things into long-term memory and keep them there. Instead, we can best save information for the long run if we connect it with things we already know. For example, when I once gave a digit-span test to my undergraduate psychology class, a varsity football player named Dave easily remembered all of the items, including the 9-digit sequence:

5 1 8 9 3 4 2 7 6

In fact, he claimed he could have remembered an even longer list of digits without much trouble. When I asked him how he remembered the 9-digit string, he told me this:

Well, "51" is Jason, a guy who played center during my freshman year. "89" is Jeff, a wide receiver from my roommate's hometown. "34" is

John, a current running back on my team—well, his number has changed, but I always think of him as "34." "2" is another Dave (not me), who's a wide receiver. And "76" is my good friend Dan. My number is 75, and so Dan's locker is next to mine.

By attaching the numbers to things he already knew—that is, by giving them *meaning*—Dave wasn't just keeping them in his working memory, he was also storing them in his long-term memory.

The mental processes we use to put information into long-term memory and keep it there are many and varied—so much so that I devote the next two chapters to them. But for now you should know two important points about long-term memory storage. Look once again at the model of memory depicted in Figure 4.1. Notice how the arrow between working memory and long-term memory points in both directions. The process of storing new information in long-term memory usually involves drawing on "old" information already stored there—hence temporarily pulling the old information into working memory. Also notice the thinner arrow going from the central executive to the two-way arrow. We often have considerable conscious control over how we "put" things in long-term memory. This is fortunate, because it means that by intentionally doing certain things—both physically and mentally—we can improve our ability to learn and remember important information for the long haul.

Long but Not Necessarily Forever: Long-Term Memory

As should be obvious from its name, long-term memory holds information much longer than working memory does—perhaps a day, a week, a month, a year, or a lifetime. Long-term memory is where we store our general knowledge about the world, recollections of prior experiences, and things we've learned in school (perhaps the capital of France or the correct spelling of *hors d'oeuvre*). It's also where we store knowledge about how to perform various behaviors, such as how to ride a bicycle, swing a baseball bat, and surf the Internet. Long-term memory seems to be able to hold as much information as we need to keep there. There is probably no such thing as someone "running out of room."

I should note that I'm using the terms *information* and *knowledge* loosely here to include things that aren't necessarily based in reality. For example, some of long-term memory's contents might be misconceptions about the physical world (see Chapter 3 for examples), distorted beliefs about certain individuals in one's social world ("Joe Schmoe is an arrogant, deceitful, self-centered so-and-so"), and deep-rooted stereotypes and prejudices regarding certain racial, ethnic, or religious groups.

That Reminds Me . . . : The Interconnectedness of Long-Term Memory

Much of the knowledge stored in long-term memory is interconnected, such that when we retrieve one piece of information, we almost automatically think of one or more other pieces of information.[14] The next exercise can show you how some of your own long-term memory is organized.

 Check It Out: Train of Thought

Get a pen or pencil and a piece of paper. In just a moment you will read a common, everyday word. As soon as you read it, write down the first word that comes into your head. Then write down the first word that *that* word reminds you of. Continue writing down the first word that each successive word brings to mind until you've generated a list of 10 words.

Ready? Here is the word to get your mind rolling:

beach

Once you've completed your list of 10 words, examine it carefully. It should give you an idea of what ideas are associated with what other ideas in your long-term memory.

Here is the list that I constructed using the same procedure and my own long-term memory:

sand

castle

king

queen

Elizabeth

England

London

theater

Hair

nude

Some of my associations might be similar to yours. For example, beach–sand and king–queen are common associates. Others might be unique to me. For instance, the last five items on my list reflect my trip to London in my college days, when I attended a different theater production every night. The most memorable of the productions was the musical *Hair,* in which several actors briefly appeared nude—quite a shocking and memorable sight in 1969.

Virtually every piece of information we have in long-term memory is probably directly or indirectly connected with every other piece. Sometimes, of course, it may take us a very long train of thought to get from *beach* to, say, *spreadsheet*. But recall a point I made in Chapter 2: Most neurons in the brain have synaptic connections with hundreds or thousands of other neurons. Presumably many of these synapses account for the organized nature of long-term memory.

A Rose Is a Rose Is a Rose: How Information Is Encoded in Long-Term Memory

Take a minute and think about a rose. What things come to mind? Perhaps words such as *flower, red, beautiful, long-stemmed,* or *expensive* pop into your head. Perhaps you can picture what a rose looks like or recall how it smells. Perhaps you can even feel a thorn prick your finger as you imagine yourself reaching out to clip a rose from its bush.

Information in long-term memory appears to be encoded in a number of ways. Some of it is encoded as actual *words*. The poem "Roses are red, violets are blue" is a good example. Other information is stored as *images* that retain certain physical characteristics, such as how they look, sound, or smell. For instance, if you think about a rose, you can probably form a mental picture of a red or white one, and you might be able to conjure up a roselike smell. Still other information is stored as *procedures*—as things you must do either physically or mentally as you tackle certain tasks. For example, you probably know what sequence of steps you would take to clip a rose from a thorny rose bush. Finally, a good deal of information in long-term memory is stored as *meanings*—as general understandings of the basic essences of certain objects and events. Knowing that roses are beautiful and bring you joy . . . possibly such words don't adequately express the thoughts and feelings that roses elicit for you.

The many forms that information takes in long-term memory are probably all intertwined—we don't compartmentalize words into one "box," procedures into another, and sounds and smells into two others.[15] When you think of roses, you're apt to think of many things about them, perhaps including what they look like, how they smell, where you might find them blooming in your neighborhood, and how you can safely pick them without pricking yourself.

You Don't Know Everything You Know: Explicit versus Implicit Knowledge

How do you grow flowers from a packet of flower seeds? You can probably describe the process with some detail, explaining that you need to put the seeds in soil, make sure they have plenty of sunlight, water them regularly, and so on. But how do you move your legs when you skip? How do you keep your balance when you ride a bicycle? Such questions are more difficult to answer: Even though such activities are probably second nature to you, you really can't put your finger on exactly what you do when you engage in them.

Psychologists make a distinction between *explicit knowledge*—knowledge we can easily recall and explain—and *implicit knowledge*—knowledge we can't consciously recall or explain but that nevertheless affects our behavior. Long-term memory includes both kinds of knowledge. Sometimes people have little or no conscious awareness that they've learned something, yet what they've learned clearly shows up in their actions. For example, all of us acquire some implicit knowledge when we learn our first language: We can produce grammatically correct sentences even though we can't explain how we do it.[16]

Knowledge can be so "dim" that it affects us only in very subtle ways. For example, when 9-year-old children look at pictures of classmates from their preschool days, they may have no conscious recollection of some of them, but their physiological responses indicate that they *do* recognize these children at some level.[17] As another example, when college students are asked to specify which direction well-known cultural images face—for instance, when students in England are asked which way Queen Elizabeth faces on a 10-pence coin, and when students in Japan are asked on which side the cartoon character Hello Kitty wears her bow on her head—they can rarely tell you. However, when forced to choose between the correct orientation and its mirror image, they guess correctly about 65 to 80% of the time—hardly stellar performance, but certainly better than chance.[18]

Many of our general beliefs about the world and ourselves also seem to have an implicit, below-the-surface quality. For example, some of the worldviews that lead us to interpret day-to-day events in particular ways—perhaps as random occurrences, on the one hand, or as divinely meted-out consequences for our deeds and misdeeds, on the other—may lie largely outside of conscious awareness. And as we'll discover in the discussion of epistemic beliefs in Chapter 7, we're likely to have implicit beliefs about what it means to *learn* something—perhaps to memorize a set of discrete facts, on the one hand, or to truly understand how all of the facts hang together in a meaningful whole, on the other—and these beliefs can have a huge impact on how effectively we actually *do* learn.

How Long Is "Long"? The Duration of Long-Term Memory

Psychologists haven't yet come to consensus about the duration of long-term memory. Some believe that once information is stored there, it remains there permanently and that any "forgetting" is simply a retrieval problem. Others instead believe that information can vanish from long-term memory through a variety of forgetting processes—processes that may or may not kick in, depending on how the information was initially stored and how often it is used (more about these points in Chapter 6). Ultimately, although some information may remain in long-term memory for long periods, there is probably no way to show conclusively that *all* information stored there remains permanently. All I can truthfully say is that things in long-term memory last a lot longer than they do in working memory. This isn't a very satisfying answer to the question, I know, but it's the best I can offer given the current status of research findings.

The "Active" Mind: Complicating the Simple Model of Memory

Recall the subtitle of this chapter: "A Simple Model of the Human Memory System." Alas, the model is a bit *too* simple, and it almost certainly overcompartmentalizes the nature of human memory. We've already noted that attention may possibly be a *part* of working memory, rather than the separate process depicted in Figure 4.1. Furthermore, research yields mixed results about whether working memory and long-term memory are distinctly different entities.[19] Some psychologists have proposed that working memory and long-term memory simply reflect different levels of *activation* within different parts of a single memory storage mechanism. According to this view, all information stored in memory is in either an active or an inactive state. *Active* information, which may include both incoming information and information previously stored in memory, is what we are currently paying attention to and thinking about—information I've previously described as being in working memory. As our attention shifts, other pieces of information in memory become activated, and the previously activated information gradually becomes *inactive*. The bulk of information stored in memory is in an inactive state, such that we are not consciously aware of it—this is information I've previously described as being in long-term memory.

Although the three-component model I've presented in this chapter isn't perfect—and it clearly doesn't give us the whole story on how memory works—it can help us remember some key characteristics of human memory. For example, the model highlights the critical role of *attention* in learning, the *limited capacity* of attention and working memory, the *interconnectedness* of the knowledge we acquire, and the importance of *relating new information to things previously learned*.

Making the Most of a Limited Capacity

You'll find many recommendations for enhancing long-term memory in later chapters. Here I offer recommendations for getting the most out of two other aspects of the human memory system—attention and working memory—that, by their very nature, place an upper limit on how much we can learn and remember in the first place.

THINKING SMART

What we've discovered about attention and working memory in this chapter has at least three implications for effectively acquiring new knowledge and skills.

> ***Identify your priorities for learning.*** As you've discovered, you can handle only so much information at any one time, and so you must be selective. If you're a student, you're not going to remember all the details presented in lectures and textbooks. If you're an employee of a large corporation, you're not going to remember every memo that crosses your desk or the name of every fellow staff member you might briefly meet at an office party. Effective learners focus on the things they know are in some way important for them and try not to worry about a lot of the "junk mail" that comes their way.

> ***Keep your mind—in particular, your attention—on new things you need to remember.*** This is sometimes easier said than done, as human minds do love to wander.[20] Let's face it, your internal life—the one inside your head—can occasionally be more interesting than your external life. One simple strategy, which can be quite helpful in remembering the names of people you've just been introduced to, is to repeat the information as soon as you've heard it ("Jeanne Ormrod . . . hmm, I've never heard that surname before . . . is it Scandinavian?").[21]
>
> Another effective strategy—especially for a lengthy lecture, boring committee meeting, or any other information-packed event that seems to drag on interminably—is to take copious notes. Taking notes is useful for keeping track of information over the long run, of course, but it also serves a more immediate purpose: It can help you keep your attention where it needs to be.[22]
>
> It's important, too, that you keep yourself well rested and well fed. We humans don't do well attention-wise if we're sleepy or our blood sugar is low. As a general rule, the best diet is one consisting mostly of vegetables, fruits, and proteins. However, on occasions when staying alert is essential despite little or no sleep the night before, I find that a medium-sized chocolate chip cookie can help me stay focused for an hour or two.

> ***Use appropriate physical tools to assist your working memory.*** Remember that exercise in which you almost certainly couldn't solve a long division problem in your head? Over the years our species has developed a variety of techniques for helping us physically extend our working memories into the outside

world—first, by drawing pictures in the dirt, later by using paper and pencil, and more recently by using calculators, computers, and other technological aids. Through such tools, you can physically keep track of some of the things you need to think about so that you have enough room in working memory to actually *think about them*.

HELPING OTHERS THINK SMART

Following are several suggestions for applying what you've just learned about the human memory system in your work with other people.

▶ ***Grab and keep people's attention.*** There's an old saying, "You can lead a horse to water, but you can't make him drink." My corollary is "The horse can't possibly drink if you don't at least lead him to the water." Helping people focus their attention on important information is the first step in helping them learn it: It gets them to the water trough. Following are three general strategies for capturing and keeping people's attention:

- Don't just lecture; include activities that keep people mentally engaged—short hands-on experiments, small-group discussions, challenging problem-solving tasks, and so on.

- Ask questions that people must respond to, either individually or as a group.

- In general, create a stimulating situation in which people *want* to pay attention.[23]

I provide more specific suggestions in the upcoming *Teaching Tips* section.

▶ ***Give guidance about the most important things to learn and remember.*** Despite the best of intentions, people don't always know what things are most important for them to remember. For example, many high school and college students are so concerned about remembering specific facts in their textbooks that they lose track of the main ideas. Even very experienced adult learners often have trouble separating the wheat from the chaff, especially if they don't know the subject matter very well.[24]

You can signal important information in a variety of ways. For example, if you're speaking to a group, you might write key points on a whiteboard or list them as a series of bullets in a PowerPoint presentation. If you're writing a lengthy piece of text for others to learn from, you might <u>underline</u> or **boldface**—or **<u>both</u>**—important phrases and sentences. And—duh!—simply telling people what you hope they will learn and remember can make quite a difference.[25]

▶ ***Repeat yourself a bit.*** No matter how captivating you are, other people's attention will occasionally drift away from what you're telling or showing them. (Be honest, now—hasn't your mind occasionally drifted away from my words in this book?) A certain amount of repetition, especially when important ideas are at stake, is always good practice. Such repetition doesn't need to *appear* repetitive, however. For example, you might say the same idea in several different ways, write it on a whiteboard, and illustrate it with numerous examples. Occasionally returning to the idea in different contexts is also valuable—not only will this help people remember the idea but it also increases the odds that they will *use* the idea at times when they need it (more on this last point in Chapter 9).

▶ ***Be realistic about how much others can learn within a limited time period.*** Pacing is critical here. But pacing doesn't mean . . . speaking . . . at . . . a . . . ridiculously . . . slow . . . speed. Instead, it means striking an appropriate balance between presenting new information and giving people a chance to *do* something with the information—to make sense of it, think about how it is similar to and/or different from things they already know and believe, consider how they might apply it, and so on. Doing such things with new information doesn't just accommodate the limited capacity of people's working memories. It also helps them store the information in their long-term memories. We'll look more closely at effective long-term memory storage processes in the next chapter.

Teaching Tips

▶ **Identify in specific, concrete terms what you want students to learn and be able to do.** Especially at the secondary and postsecondary levels, students frequently encounter more information in classroom lessons and textbooks than they can possibly store in long-term memory within a reasonable time period. In such situations, students often have trouble deciding which things are important and which things are not. For example, they may focus their attention on interesting but trivial details at the expense of less exciting but more important ideas. They may zero in on obvious tidbits, such as what a teacher writes on the board or what a textbook author puts in *italics* or **boldface,** without regard for how those tidbits fit into the overall scheme of things. Or they may look at equations they see in a scientific proof without also looking at verbal explanations of the equations. Compounding the problem is the fact that teachers themselves often disagree about what aspects of a topic are most important to learn and remember.[26]

Perhaps the most effective strategy for helping students distinguish between important and nice-to-know-but-not-essential material is to give them objectives for a unit, lesson, or reading assignment. When they know what you want them to accomplish, they can make more informed decisions about how to focus their efforts and allocate their study time.[27] Following are three commonly cited guidelines for formulating and communicating classroom objectives:

- Describe objectives not in terms of what you will do during instruction, but rather in terms of what *students* should be able to do at the *end* of instruction.

- When identifying objectives for a single lesson or short unit, identify specific behaviors that will reflect accomplishment of the objectives.

- When identifying objectives for a longer time period—for a semester, perhaps—list a few abstract outcomes (for instance, "exhibit good listening skills," "interpret various kinds of maps," "apply principles of physics to real-world problems") and give examples of specific behaviors that reflect each one.[28]

Plan lessons and activities that capture and maintain students' attention. Classrooms are usually lively environments in which many objects and events compete for students' attention. Students' attention will almost inevitably wander off-topic at one time or another—perhaps to a classmate's behavior across the room, to doodles in their notebooks, or to their thoughts about plans for the upcoming weekend. But several strategies can help keep students' attention where it should be for most of the time:

- Model your own excitement and enthusiasm about classroom topics.

- Relate lessons and assignments to students' personal lives and individual interests.

- Address topics about which many students are likely to be interested (animals, popular music, diverse cultural practices, etc.).

- Occasionally incorporate novelty, fantasy, and mystery into lessons and procedures.

- Vary your instructional methods, using a mixture of explanations, class discussions, in-class demonstrations, and so on.

- Provide opportunities for students to respond actively to the subject matter, perhaps by manipulating and experimenting with physical objects, creating new inventions, discussing controversial issues, or teaching something they've learned to classmates.

- Encourage students to identify with historical figures or fictional characters and to imagine what these people might have been thinking or feeling.

- Ask questions that all students must answer, perhaps by requiring everyone to respond with hand votes or preprinted *true* and *false* response cards.

- Provide frequent breaks from sedentary tasks, especially when working with young children.

- Seat easily distracted students near you.

- Perhaps most important, *don't* ask students to engage in activities with little long-term benefit—memorizing trivial facts for no good reason, reading material that is clearly beyond students' comprehension level, and so on.[29]

As should be clear from some of these recommendations, students are more likely to pay attention when you give them reasons to *want* to pay attention.

Keep in mind that students can think about and remember only a limited amount of information at any one time. In my experience as a teacher educator, I've found that novice teachers are often overly optimistic about how much students can learn and remember in a short timeframe. Many new teachers make the mistake of presenting too much information too quickly, and their students' working memories simply can't keep up.

Working memory capacity increases a little bit over the course of childhood and adolescence—but only a *very* little bit.[30] The bottom line is that, regardless of age, students can handle only very small amounts of information in their working memories at once. Here are several strategies for helping students work effectively with their limited working memory capacities:

- Pace any presentation of important new information slowly enough that students have time to mentally process it all.

- Intersperse new ideas with examples, applications, and memory refreshers about related ideas that students already know.

- Illustrate verbal explanations with *simple* visuals; avoid information overload in visual aids.

- When a new procedure involves multiple steps, provide a written set of instructions to which students can refer.

- Encourage students to use pencil and paper, a dry-erase board, a laptop computer, or some other external means of keeping track of the details they're thinking about.[31]

Encourage students to take notes, and teach them how to take good ones. On average, students who take notes learn and remember things more effectively than students who don't.[32] One likely reason is that the note-taking process enhances students' ability to keep their attention on the topic at hand. Another is that, by writing what they hear or see, students must encode the information in at least some minimal way. And, of course, given that students often don't have time to think about any particular idea *in depth* during class time, notes serve as an external storage mechanism—an out-of-body long-term memory, if you will—for information presented in class.

The effectiveness of note taking depends on the type of notes taken. Students' class notes are more useful when they're fairly detailed records of the information that students need to remember.[33] Unfortunately, many students take poor-quality notes—even at the college level—perhaps because they've been given little or no guidance about *how* to take notes. Here are a few simple things you can do to improve the quality and completeness of students' notes:

- Write important ideas on the board (students are more likely to write down the things their teacher writes).

- Emphasize and repeat major themes and principles; perhaps even give such explicit guidance as, "Be sure to include this point in your notes."

- Provide a general organizational framework—perhaps a skeletal outline or a compare-and-contrast matrix—that can guide students in their note taking.[34]

Consider giving students access to reference materials during classroom assessments. When it's important that students learn and remember information for the long haul, you may want students to have only one resource—their own long-term memories—as they complete a test or other assessment activity. But I can't emphasize this point enough: The human memory system isn't geared for absorbing and retaining fact after fact after fact. Especially if your primary objective is for students to locate, analyze, or apply information—rather than commit it to memory—it may be quite appropriate to let students use certain reference materials as they work. In some instances, such materials might be dictionaries, atlases, or magazine articles. In other cases, they might be student-constructed and teacher-approved "cheat sheets"—perhaps all of their class notes or perhaps 3-by-5 index cards on which they can write certain facts or formulas they think they might need.

CHAPTER 5

Making "Long-Term" *Truly* Long Term: Long-Term Memory Storage Processes

As you discovered in Chapter 4, storing things effectively in long-term memory typically involves making some sort of connection between new information and the knowledge and beliefs we have previously stored there. Often we make such connections quickly and with little effort. For example, as you're walking down the street, you might run into two people whom you immediately recognize as your friends George and Martha. The following day you can easily recall that you saw George and Martha on the street, so you have obviously stored this information in your long-term memory.

At other times storing things effectively in long-term memory can be quite a challenge. To see what I mean, try this simple exercise.

Check It Out: **Two Letter Strings**

Study each of the following strings of letters until you can remember them perfectly:

AIIRODFMLAWRS   FAMILIARWORDS

Both strings are 13 letters long, and both contain exactly the same letters. Which string was easier to learn? No doubt you will agree that the second list was easier because you could relate it to words you already know—in this case, the words *familiar words.*

I'm willing to bet that you got the point of my exercise fairly quickly and didn't even bother to learn the first string. If you *did* try to learn it, you probably devised some sort of strategy to help you remember it. For instance, perhaps you saw the word *air*—albeit with an extra *i*—at the beginning, and perhaps you saw the word *lawyers*—albeit missing the *ye*—at the end.

People who learn and remember information effectively tend to be *strategic.* That is, they intentionally call up certain mental processes—certain *learning strategies*—that can help them relate new ideas to things they already know. In this chapter I describe one strategy that doesn't work very well for the long run and then several others that are far more effective.

 ## The Least Strategic Strategy: Rehearsal

You should recall from the preceding chapter that maintenance rehearsal—repeating something over and over—can help us keep information in working memory indefinitely. It's a great way to remember a telephone number long enough to dial it or some bills you need to mail as you drive by the post office.

However, repeating something over and over within a short timeframe—say, within the course of a few seconds or few minutes—is usually *not* a good way to get things into long-term memory and keep them there. This strategy, which psychologists simply call *rehearsal,* is especially *in*effective if all we do is repeat information in an unaltered, verbatim fashion, because we don't make those critical connections with things we already know. For example, in the preceding exercise, did you use rehearsal in a half-hearted attempt to learn the letter string AIIRODFMLAWRS? If so, how many of the letters actually "stuck"? Probably not very many.

Rehearsal is an easy, relatively mindless strategy, and thus it's one of the first learning strategies children use.[1] Many adolescents and adults use it as well, sometimes because they mistakenly believe it's the best way to remember something and sometimes because they don't know what else to do instead. As a high school student, I occasionally used rehearsal when I had trouble remembering something I would be tested on—perhaps when I needed to know a complicated formula, a verbatim definition, or a list of seemingly unrelated items. I would continue to repeat the information to myself as test papers were distributed and then immediately write it in the margin so it would be there for me when I needed it.

Verbally rehearsing information is probably better than not doing anything, and it may be one of the few strategies we can use when we have little prior knowledge to draw on to help us make sense of what we're trying to remember. If we repeat something often enough, it might eventually sink in.[2] However, the process is slow, laborious, and not much fun. Furthermore, for reasons you'll discover in Chapter 6, when we use only rehearsal to store something, we often have trouble recalling it later on.[3]

 ## Increasing the Odds That You Keep What You Get: Effective Strategies

Researchers have identified several effective strategies for encoding and storing things in long-term memory. The five I describe here aren't necessarily mutually exclusive—to some extent they overlap, and in any case, the more the merrier. But I tease them apart here so that you can better understand each of them.

Intentional Sense Making: Meaningful Learning

When I was in high school, two female friends and I took a class in Mandarin Chinese at the local boys' boarding school (I'll leave it to you to decide what our motives might have been). The class met from 4:00 p.m. to 6:00 p.m. every Monday and Thursday afternoon. We typically took a 5-minute break midway through each class session, and by that time of the day my friends and I were often feeling a bit punchy. One day when we took our break, we had just learned that the Chinese word for *we* was pronounced somewhat like "wah-mun" but written in our textbooks as *wŏmen*. (The mark over the *o* is a tone mark, indicating in this case that one's voice should go down and then up while pronouncing the "wo" syllable.) As usual, the three of us began our break by heading for the ladies' restroom. Seeing the word "WOMEN" on the door, I exclaimed, "Aha! This is the door that *we* use." A few weeks later, our class learned that the word for *door* was pronounced a bit like "mun" but spelled in our texts as *mén*. During the break that day I shared another insight with my friends: The door marked "MEN" was "the *door* we *don't* use." It's been more than 40 years since I studied Chinese, and I don't recall very much of it. But two words have remained indelibly in my long-term memory: *wǒmen* means "we" and *mén* means "door."

We learn and remember things much more effectively when we intentionally try to make sense of them, and sense making invariably involves relating new information to things we already know. By relating new information to knowledge already stored in our long-term memories, we find *meaning* in the information. Hence, this process is frequently called *meaningful learning*. It is also what we're referring to when we talk about *understanding* or *comprehension*.

Meaningful learning appears to facilitate both storage and retrieval: We store information more easily in long-term memory, and we recall it more quickly. As an example, try the next exercise.

Check It Out: **The Procedure**

Read the following passage and see how much of it you can remember.

The procedure is actually quite simple. First you arrange things into different groups. Of course, one pile may be sufficient depending on how much there is to do. If you have to go somewhere else due to lack of facilities that is the next step, otherwise you are pretty well set. It is important not to overdo things. That is, it is better to do too few things at once than too many. In the short run this may not seem important, but complications can easily arise. A mistake can be expensive as well. At first the whole procedure will seem complicated. Soon, however, it will become just another facet of life. It is difficult to foresee any end to the necessity for this task in the immediate future, but then one never can tell. After the procedure is completed one arranges the materials into different groups again. Then they can be put into their appropriate places. Eventually they will be used once more and the whole cycle will then have to be repeated. However, that is part of life.[4]

Now read the passage again, this time with the knowledge that it describes the process of washing clothes.

Possibly you realized the first time through that the passage is about doing laundry. If you didn't realize this the first time—and many people don't—you would probably have trouble recalling what seem to be an unrelated set of facts. In a study with college students, people who knew the topic of the passage remembered twice as much as those who had no topic with which to connect things.[5]

We can also store nonverbal material more easily when it has meaning for us. To see what I mean, try another exercise.

Check It Out: **Droodles**

Study each of the two pictures to the right until you can reproduce them accurately from memory.

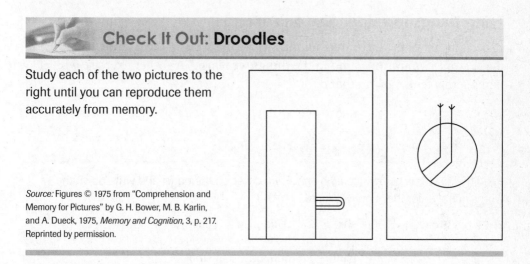

Source: Figures © 1975 from "Comprehension and Memory for Pictures" by G. H. Bower, M. B. Karlin, and A. Dueck, 1975, *Memory and Cognition*, 3, p. 217. Reprinted by permission.

Do you think you could draw the pictures from memory a week from now? If so, your good memory for the drawings was probably due to the fact that you imposed some sort of meaning on them—perhaps *a very short man playing a trombone in a telephone booth* and *an early bird who caught a very strong worm.*[6]

Relating new information to *ourselves* can have a particularly dramatic effect on learning.[7] For example, in another study of meaningful learning, college students were given a list of 40 adjectives and asked to respond to one of four questions about each adjective:

1. Does it have big letters?

2. Does it rhyme with _____?

3. Does it mean the same as _____?

4. Does it describe you?

Then, unexpectedly, the students were asked to remember as many adjectives as they could. If the students were initially asked to consider only superficial characteristics of the words (Questions 1 and 2), they remembered very few of them—on average, 3 to 7%. If they had to think about the meanings of the words (Question 3), they remembered, on average, 13%. But if they were asked to relate the word to themselves (Question 4), their recall jumped to 30%.[8]

Tying Things Together: Organization

Especially as we get older, we humans seem to have a natural tendency to make some connections among the things we learn.[9] Another exercise will let you see this tendency firsthand.

Check It Out: Twelve Words

Read the 12 words below *one time only.* Then cover up the page, and write down the words in the order they come to mind.

shirt	table	hat
carrot	bed	squash
pants	potatoes	stool
chair	shoe	bean

In what order did you recall the words? Chances are that you did *not* recall them in the order in which you read them. Probably, instead, you recalled them category by category—maybe the clothing items first, then the furniture, and then the veggies.

In general, we learn and remember a body of new information more easily when we pull it together into a logical structure of some kind—a process known as *organization*.[10] One way, of course, is to put related pieces of information into discrete categories, as you probably just did in the "Twelve Words" exercise. Another way is to identify interrelationships—for instance, this-causes-that and this-is-an-example-of-that relationships—among the various pieces of information. Still a third way is to pull things together into an overall gist or general summary. This is presumably what you did in the second exercise in Chapter 1, when you read the many sentences about a sea breeze, a rolling rock, and jelly-eating ants.

Going Well Beyond: Elaboration

In order to make meaningful sense of information, and perhaps also to organize it in some way, we often need to expand on the information using things we've previously learned about the world. This process of embellishing on new information to make it more memorable is called *elaboration*. For instance, I'm willing to bet that you engage in elaboration as you do the next exercise.

Check It Out: John

Read this paragraph *one time only:*

> John was feeling bad today so he decided to go see the family doctor. He checked in with the doctor's receptionist, and then looked through several medical magazines that were on the table by his chair. Finally the nurse came and asked him to take off his clothes. The doctor was very nice to him. He eventually prescribed some pills for John. Then John left the doctor's office and headed home.[11]

What things does the paragraph actually tell you? What gaps in information did you need to fill so that you could make sense of it?

You probably had no trouble understanding the paragraph because you have been to a doctor's office yourself and know what events those visits usually include. You can therefore fill in a number of details that the passage doesn't tell you. For example, you reasonably inferred that John had to *travel* to the doctor's office, although the story omits this essential step. Likewise, you probably concluded that John took off his clothes in the examination room, *not* in the waiting room, even though the story never makes it clear where John did his striptease.

Generally speaking, the more we elaborate on new information—that is, the more we use what we already know to help us understand and interpret the new information—the more effectively we can store and remember it.[12] But elaboration has its downsides. First, we often have trouble distinguishing between what we actually saw or heard and our elaborations of it.[13] Second, we may impose incorrect interpretations that we then think of as "truth."[14] For example, my son Jeff tells me that when he first heard the expression "losing my voice" in elementary school, he inferred that this loss of voice is something that happens to everyone sooner or later—that people are born with a finite amount of "voice" that they eventually use up. So as not to waste his own supply, he would mouth the words, rather than actually sing them, during his weekly choir sessions at school.

You might think of elaboration as *learning between the lines.* Most of the time it's quite helpful. But occasionally it can lead to those misconceptions of which I spoke in Chapter 3.

A Picture Might Be Worth a Thousand Words: Visual Imagery

By *visual imagery,* I mean forming mental "pictures" that capture some of the physical features of what we actually see or might see. Are you a good imager? Now might be a good time to find out.

Check It Out: **Revisiting the Droodles**

Without looking back at the Droodles exercise you did in our discussion of meaningful learning earlier in the chapter, draw as much of the two pictures as you can remember in the two boxes below. If you're having trouble remembering what drawings I'm talking about, it might help if I remind you that one of them involved a short man in a telephone booth and the other involved a bird and hypothetical worm.

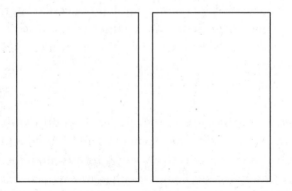

Once you have finished, compare your drawings with the originals. How accurate and complete were you? Were the proportions about right? Did you recall all of the details—for instance, did you remember that the "bird feet" had three "claws" on each one?

We humans differ considerably in our ability to use visual imagery. Some of us form images quickly and easily, whereas others form them slowly and with difficulty.[15]

Visual imagery can be a very powerful means of storing information in long-term memory. For most of us, memory for visual information is better than it is for strictly verbal information.[16] We do even better when we get information in *both* verbal and visual forms, rather than in only one form or the other.[17] If need be, we can create our *own* visual images. In fact, many of us routinely form visual images when we read novels that describe certain characters' physical qualities or history books that depict certain events in vivid detail.[18]

But even if we're good visualizers, our visual images are apt to be imprecise representations of external objects, with many details omitted, blurry, or distorted by our general knowledge of what objects typically look like.[19] Accordingly, visual imagery isn't always dependable when we need to recall something with precision. For example, when I was writing about the Peter–Paul goblet in Chapter 4, I needed to spell the word *silhouette*. My mental image of this word, which was something of this nature

silhouette

left much to be desired. To make sure I spelled the word correctly, then, I had to look it up in the dictionary.

Lighting Mental Fires: Hot Cognition

One important way in which we humans are distinctly different from computers is that when we encounter new situations and events, we often *feel* about them as much as we *think* about them. The parts of the brain that underlie our thinking processes have many interconnections with those parts that underlie various emotions, and so our thoughts about a particular topic can be quite difficult to disentangle from our feelings.[20]

When our thoughts and memories become emotionally charged, we're experiencing *hot cognition*. For example, we might get excited when we read about advances in science that could lead to effective treatments for spinal cord injuries, cancer, AIDS, or mental illness. We're likely to feel sad and disheartened when we see news reports about the desperate living conditions of survivors of floods or famines in distant parts of the world. And we get angry when we learn about large-scale genocides carried out in, say, Rwanda or Darfur in recent years.

Getting a bit hot and bothered about new information has definite benefits. We're more likely to pay attention to information that has emotional overtones. We're also more likely to think about it for extended periods and to repeatedly elaborate on it. And over the long run, we can usually recall information with high emotional content more easily than we can recall relatively nonemotional information.[21] (We'll examine a possible exception to this last point—repression of very traumatic memories—in Chapter 6.)

Occasionally new information gets us riled up for a very different reason: It contradicts something we know or strongly believe to be true. Such information can cause us considerable mental discomfort—a phenomenon known as *cognitive dissonance*. This dissonance can be either a help or a hindrance, depending on how we address it. If we try to keep an open mind and be objective, it can help us examine, reevaluate, and possibly revise certain misconceptions we have about a topic. But if we're bound and determined to cling to what we currently "know" to be true about the matter, we'll be quite eager to ignore or discredit the new information.[22] Certainly the new information might be incorrect. But then again, it might not.

It's important to emphasize here that hot cognition means getting emotional about the content of the subject matter we're trying to learn. It does *not* mean getting overly emotional about our ability to learn and remember it. The latter situation involves *anxiety*—that feeling of uneasiness and apprehension we're apt to have about a situation when we're not sure what its outcome will be. Getting a teensy bit anxious about learning something can spur us into action so that we actually do learn it. For instance, if we know we have an important exam on the horizon—say, a test in a college class or an exam we need to pass in order to become an attorney or teacher—a touch of anxiety will ensure that we read the necessary books, attend the necessary classes, and so on. But a great deal of anxiety works against us. Our limited-capacity working memories are so consumed with our worries ("How can I possibly remember all this stuff??!! And what will become of me if I don't??!!") that there's very little "room" left over to focus on what we're trying to pay attention to and make sense of.[23]

The Rich Get Richer: Long-Term Memory's Snowball Effect

Although the things we currently know and believe can sometimes interfere with effective storage of new information in long-term memory, by and large the more we know, the more easily we can learn and remember new things. For example, people who know a lot about baseball or basketball can remember more new facts about those sports and more about what happened in a particular game than can people who are relatively uninformed about the sports.[24] And experts at the game of chess can remember the locations of chess pieces on a chessboard more accurately than chess novices, but only when the placement of pieces is logical within the framework of an actual game.[25]

In general, people who have a large body of information already stored in long-term memory have more ideas to which they can relate their new experiences and so can more easily engage in such processes as meaningful learning and elaboration. People who lack relevant knowledge must resort to rehearsal and other relatively mindless strategies for remembering things. In other words, the rich (in knowledge) get richer, and the poor stay relatively poor. To switch to a snowball metaphor, a small (in knowledge) snowball gets exponentially larger as it rolls down a hill of information and gathers an increasing number of tidbits with every rotation. When the snowball gets *very* large—that is, when it reflects true *expertise* about a topic—it typically includes many interconnections among concepts and ideas, enabling its owner to think flexibly about the topic and solve problems creatively and productively.[26]

Yet it isn't enough that we have the knowledge we need to make sense of new situations and events. We must also be *aware* that some of our existing knowledge is relevant. In other words, the new information and the relevant prior knowledge must both be in working memory at the same time so that we can make the appropriate connections.[27] Without that critical juxtaposition of the new and the old, we might needlessly resort to mindless repetition of things that would make a great deal of sense if we simply gave them some thought.

Making Sense of Nonsense: Mnemonics

What if we really *don't* have the knowledge we need to make sense of new information? Why is *Au* the chemical symbol for gold? Why must we turn screws clockwise—instead of counterclockwise—in order to tighten them? Why is Augusta the capital of the state of Maine? It turns out that *Au* is short for the Latin word for gold, *aurum*. It's physically easier for right-handed people to turn screws clockwise rather than counterclockwise (as if you lefties didn't already have enough to complain about). And I'm sure that early Mainers had a perfectly good reason for making Augusta the state capital, rather than, say, Portland or Bar Harbor.

We don't necessarily know the underlying origins and logic of all the facts we need to learn and remember. And let's face it, there probably *isn't* any rhyme or reason to some of them.

When we have trouble connecting new information to things we already know, special memory tricks—*mnemonics*—can be immensely helpful.[28] Here I describe three categories of mnemonics—verbal mediation, the keyword method, and superimposed meaningful structures—that I personally have found most useful.

The Principal Is My Pal: Verbal Mediation

Imagine you are trying to learn that the German word *Handschuh* means *glove*. Playing off how the word sounds phonetically, you might remember this word by thinking of a glove as a "shoe for the hand." Such a mnemonic is an example of a *verbal mediator*—a word or phrase that creates a logical connection, or bridge, between two pieces of information. Verbal mediators can be quite handy for remembering such paired pieces of information as foreign language words and their English meanings, chemical elements and their symbols, countries and their capitals, and words and their spellings. For instance, when my daughter Tina was in high school, she remembered the chemical symbol for gold—Au—by thinking "'*Ay, you* stole my *gold* watch!" Following are additional examples:

Information to Be Learned	Verbal Mediator
Quito is the capital of Ecuador.	*Mosquitoes* are at the *equator*.
The word *principal* (a school administrator) ends with the letters *pal* (not *ple*).	The *principal* is my *pal*.
The *humerus* bone is the large arm bone above the elbow.	The *humorous* bone is just above the *funny* bone.
Amendment 2 to the U.S. Constitution is the right to bear arms.	A *bear* has *two arms*.

Love Is a Suit of Armor: The Keyword Method

Like verbal mediation, the keyword method facilitates learning and memory
        a connection between two things. This technique is especially
    en there is no logical verbal mediator to fill the gap—for example,
    is no obvious sentence or phrase to relate a foreign language word
    sh meaning. The keyword method involves two steps, which we can
    sing the Spanish word *amor* and its English meaning, *love:*

    y a concrete object to represent each piece of information. The
    can be either a commonly used symbol (in this case, a heart to
    lize *love)* or a sound-alike word (in this case, a suit of armor to
    represent *amor).* Such objects are *keywords.*

2. Form a visual image—a mental picture—of the two objects interacting or
   in some other way interconnected. For example, to remember that *amor*
   means *love,* we might picture a knight in a suit of armor with a huge red
   heart painted on his chest.

Especially for people who can easily form and remember visual images, the
keyword method can be highly effective. You can try it out in the next exercise.

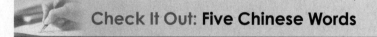

Check It Out: **Five Chinese Words**

Try learning the five Mandarin Chinese words on the next page by forming the visual
images I describe. Don't worry about remembering the tone marks over the words.

Chinese Word	English Meaning	Image
fáng	house	Picture a *house* with *fangs* growing on its roof and walls.
mén	door	Picture a restroom *door* with the word *MEN* painted on it.
ké	guest	Picture someone giving someone else (the *guest*) a *key* to the house.
fàn	food	Picture a plate of *food* being cooled by a *fan*.
shū	book	Picture a *shoe* with a *book* sticking out of it.

Now find something else to do for a couple of minutes. Stand up and stretch, get a glass of water, or use the restroom. But be sure to come back to your reading in just a minute or two.

. . .

Now that you're back, cover the list of Chinese words, English meanings, and visual images. Then try to remember what each word means:

ké   fàn   mén   fáng   shū

Did the Chinese words remind you of the visual images you stored? Did the images, in turn, help you remember the English meanings? You may have remembered all five words easily, or you may have remembered only one or two. As I mentioned earlier, people differ in their ability to use visual imagery.

The keyword method is certainly not limited to learning foreign language vocabulary words. Here are additional examples of how you might use it to remember seemingly arbitrary facts:

Information to Be Learned	Visual Image
Augusta is the capital of Maine.	Picture *a gust of* wind blowing through a horse's *mane*.
Tchaikovsky composed "Swan Lake."	Picture a *swan* swimming on a *lake*, wearing a *tie* and *cough*ing.
Ponce de Leon was the first European to explore what is now the state of Florida.	Picture a *lion pouncing* on a map of *Florida*. For an extra flourish (especially if you don't know Florida's distinctive shape), add palm trees to the map.

Remembering that Tchaikovsky composed "Swan Lake" and that Ponce de Leon was the first European to explore Florida.

When the "Mites" Go Up, the "Tites" Come Down: Superimposed Meaningful Structures

One of my memories from my years as an undergraduate psychology major is being required to learn the 12 cranial nerves: olfactory, optic, oculomotor, trochlear, trigeminal, abducens, facial, auditory, glossopharyngeal, vagus, spinal accessory, and hypoglossal. It isn't the nerves themselves that I remember (I had to look them up so that I could list them for you) but rather how difficult it was to learn them all in their correct order. I had little luck drilling the list into my thick skull (I was using the tried-and-not-so-true method of rehearsal) until a friend passed along this mnemonic:

On old Olympus's towering top, a Finn and German
viewed some hops.

Notice that the first letters of the words in the sentence correspond with the first letters of the 12 cranial nerves: Just like in the list of nerves, the first three words in the sentence begin with *O*, the next two begin with *T*, and so on. And the sentence, though a bit strange, is fairly easy to remember because of the structure provided by its rhythm and rhyme.

"On old Olympus" illustrates a mnemonic I call a *superimposed meaningful structure*. The technique is simple: We impose a familiar structure on the body of information to be learned. That structure can be a sentence, story, common poetic meter, acronym, or anything else we're familiar with. For instance, during a trip to England, I stumbled on a catchy poem for remembering the kings and queens of England, beginning with King William I and ending with Queen Elizabeth II. An Internet search gave me several variations, but here's the gist of it:

> Willie, Willie, Harry, Steve,
> Harry, Dick, John, Harry three.
> Edward one, two, three, Dick two,
> Harrys four five six, then who?
> Edwards four, five, Dick the Bad,
> Harrys twain and Ned the lad.
> Mary, Bessie, James the vain,
> Charlie, Charlie, James again.
> William and Mary, Anna Gloria,
> Georges four, William, Victoria.
> Edward seven, Georgie five,
> Edward, George, and Liz (alive).

If for some reason you had to remember the kings and queens in order—as no doubt many British schoolchildren do—the poem provides a relatively painless way to do it.

People use superimposed meaningful structures in a wide variety of content domains. Here are just a few examples:

Information to Be Learned	Superimposed Meaningful Structure
The shape of Italy	A boot
The five Great Lakes (Huron, Ontario, Michigan, Erie, Superior)	HOMES

Information to Be Learned	Superimposed Meaningful Structure
The spectrum: red, orange, yellow, green, blue, indigo, violet	ROY G. BIV
The correct spelling of *geography*	George Ellen's old grandmother rode a pig home yesterday.
The difference between stalagmites and stalactites	When the "mites" go up, the "tites" come down.
Lines on the treble clef (E G B D F)	Elvis's guitar broke down Friday *or* Every good boy does fine.
Strings on a guitar (E A D G B E)	Edgar ate dynamite; good-bye, Edgar.
The number of days in each month	Thirty days has September, April, June, and November. All the rest have 31, except the second month alone.
Throwing a free throw in basketball	BEEF: Balance the ball, Elbows in, Elevate the arms, Follow through.
Simplifying a complex algebraic expression	Please Excuse My Dear Aunt Sally: First, simplify terms within parentheses, then terms with an exponent, then terms to be multiplied or divided, and finally terms to be added or subtracted
Turning a screw (clockwise to tighten, counterclockwise to loosen)	Righty, tighty. Lefty, loosey.

As you may have figured out on your own, the effectiveness of mnemonics lies in their conformity with some things we've learned about memory. Virtually all of them help us relate new information to something we already have in long-term memory—thereby making meaningful learning possible. Some of them also help us impose a logical organization on a list of items—perhaps in the form of a familiar word (such as *HOMES*) or rhythm. In the next chapter, we'll find that many mnemonics also provide handy *retrieval cues* for assisting our search of long-term memory at a later point in time.

At this point, see if you can recall the meanings of the Chinese words you studied earlier:

fàn   fáng   shū   ké   mén

Did your efforts in the "Five Chinese Words" exercise pay off? I'll tell you one thing: Thanks to the keyword method, I never have any trouble remembering that the capital of Maine is Augusta.

Saving Things for the Long Term

For certain situations, memorizing information word for word is important. For example, this is often the case if we want to remember cherished poems, our lines in a dramatic production, or (for certain religious groups) passages from holy scriptures. Most of the time, however, memorization—especially *meaningless* memorization—is not the way to go. The recommendations I offer here are more consistent with what we know about effective long-term memory storage processes.

THINKING SMART

In one way or another, each of the following strategies can help you make important information more memorable.

▶ *Approach any new learning task with the assumption that you'll be able to make sense of what you're studying.* Effective learners consistently approach new information–specific facts presented in a high school or college class, for instance–with a conscious intention to make some sort of logical "sense" of it.[29] Whether the subject matter is history, biology, math, or law, there usually *is* an underlying logic to it all.

▶ *Talk to yourself about what you're trying to make sense of.* In other words, try to explain to yourself what you're reading or studying–perhaps even doing it out loud. For example, if you're reading a challenging textbook chapter, you might paraphrase the parts you understand, identify parts you're having trouble with ("This is confusing"), draw reasonable inferences, and summarize what you've read. Research is clear on this point: Explicitly explaining new information to yourself can help you better understand and remember it.[30]

▶ ***Organize what you're trying to learn.*** Probably the most effective way to organize a body of information is to identify cause-and-effect relationships and other interconnections among specific facts. Doing so, of course, can enhance your ability to discover the underlying logic to what you're trying to make sense of. Researchers have found that the following organizational strategies can be effective as well:

- Write and circle important concepts on a sheet of paper; leave plenty of room between each of them. Then draw lines between pairs of concepts that are closely related; over each line, explain the nature of the relationship ("this causes that," "this is an example of that," etc.). Such a diagram is known as a *concept map.*

- If the subject matter involves a number of categories and subcategories, create a diagram that shows how various concepts are hierarchically related (for example, in biology, ants and mosquitoes are both insects, crabs and crayfish are both crustaceans, and insects and crustaceans are both arthropods).

- To facilitate comparing and contrasting items that might be alike in some ways but different in others—for instance, various countries or kinds of rocks—create a two-dimensional matrix, listing the items that need to be compared along one dimension (perhaps in the left-most column) and the characteristics on which they need to be compared along the other dimension (perhaps in the top row). Fill in the empty cells as you gather information about each item.[31]

▶ ***Write about what you're learning.*** You're likely to enhance your memory of a topic when you write about it. For instance, you're apt to make better sense of it, better organize it, and encode and elaborate on it in new ways.[32]

▶ ***Create visual representations of new ideas and their interrelationships.*** Sometimes the things you're trying to learn are already in visual form. When they aren't, you can form visual images more easily—and thus remember them more effectively—if you try to capture their meaning in pictures, diagrams, or other graphics.[33]

▶ ***Get emotional about the subject matter, but try to keep your anxiety about learning it in check.*** The more you get emotionally involved with a topic—for instance, the more you find it exciting, depressing, or infuriating—the more likely you are to elaborate on and remember it.

At the same time, you must try to keep a calm head in your efforts to remember something for the long term. One key two-step strategy here is to *plan ahead* about the steps you will take to master a complex topic and then *take those steps in an appropriate timeframe*. Although some chronic procrastinators can actually focus better on a learning task if they wait until the last possible minute, many others become so anxious that they have trouble studying in effective ways.[34] A second important strategy is to approach a new topic with confidence that you can, in fact, master it.[35] By the time you finish this book, I hope that you'll have both the skills and the confidence you need to master any body of information that can reasonably build on what you already know about the world.

▶ ***Use mnemonics for facts that are seemingly arbitrary and defy logic.*** A simple Internet search using a browser such as Google or Yahoo! can turn up a variety of mnemonics for such diverse disciplines as biology, physics, math, geography, medicine, and law. And, of course, the three general mnemonic techniques we've discussed in this chapter—verbal mediation, the keyword, and superimposed meaningful structures—enable you to create a virtually limitless number of your own mnemonics.

HELPING OTHERS THINK SMART

As you work with other human beings—whether as a parent, a teacher, a clinician, a professional colleague, or simply a good citizen—you can do a number of things to help them understand and remember things that in one way or another can enrich their lives.

▶ ***Help people make connections between new ideas and things they already know.*** Children and adults alike don't always make those new-to-old connections that are so essential for meaningful learning. Accordingly, you may sometimes have to explicitly point out how a new idea relates to something your audience already knows.[36] For example, if you're explaining the concept of *inertia*, you might remind your listeners of how their bodies involuntarily jolt to the right when the car they're riding in takes an unexpected left turn. And if you're teaching a class in conversational French, you might encourage students to draw on their knowledge of English vocabulary to help them remember French words with related meanings—the French verb *marcher* ("to walk") is similar to the English word *march,* the French noun *la fenêtre* ("window") sounds a bit like *ventilate,* and so on.

▶ *Provide an overall structure that people can use to organize a complex body of information.* One effective technique is to begin with a general organizational scheme for the information that will follow—perhaps an overview or general outline of the topics you will cover.[37] Another is to distribute a note-taking form that lists key concepts and ideas and leaves room for people to jot down the details in appropriate places.[38] And, of course, you should present the information you want your audience to learn in a logically organized sequence.

▶ *Encourage people to go beyond the specific facts they've learned.* For example, you might ask them to generate their own examples of a new concept, apply a new principle to real-world situations, or debate the pros and cons of various perspectives on a controversial issue.

▶ *Use visual aids to supplement verbal information.* In most situations, visual aids should be simple, concise, clear, and colorful, presenting major ideas without a lot of potentially distracting details.[39] In addition to promoting visual imagery, many visual aids can also show how major ideas relate to and affect one another. Thus they provide one more way of helping people organize information.[40]

▶ *Get people emotionally involved with the topic.* Sometimes topics evoke hot cognition in and of themselves. For example, discussions of the Holocaust typically evoke outrage both about the many merciless ways in which people were killed and about the incredible magnitude of the genocide—about 11 million people in all. But more pleasant "heat" can be effective as well—perhaps curiosity and eagerness to learn more about still-mysterious phenomena in our physical world, such as black holes and dark matter.

You can also promote hot cognition by conveying your own love and enthusiasm for a topic—for instance, by exuding energy and excitement out of every pore as you present new ideas or skills.[41] Of course, it helps if you really *are* excited about your subject matter. In my own experience, almost any topic becomes exciting once you get to know it well.

Teaching Tips

Begin with what students already know. Whenever you introduce a new topic, starting with what students already know will increase the odds that they engage in meaningful rather than meaning*less* learning. For instance, you might begin a first-grade unit about plants by asking students to describe what their parents do to keep flowers or vegetable gardens growing. In a secondary English literature class, you might introduce Sir Walter Scott's *Ivanhoe* (in which Robin Hood is a major character) by asking students to tell the tale of Robin Hood as they know it. It's important to remember, too, that students from diverse economic and cultural backgrounds are apt to have had somewhat different experiences, and so you should modify your starting point accordingly.[42] In general, effective instruction is *differentiated instruction*—it's tailored to each student's current knowledge and skills.

Introduce a new topic with an advance organizer. An *advance organizer* is a general introduction to new material that accomplishes either or both of two purposes. An *expository* organizer provides a rough overview or outline of upcoming material, describing the general topics of a unit and their interrelationships. A *comparative* organizer shows how the new material relates to students' previous experiences, to information they've previously learned in school, or possibly to their own purposes for studying the material. A variety of formats—overviews, outlines, analogies, and thought-provoking questions—all appear to be effective advance organizers.[43] For example, you might introduce a lesson on radar this way:

> Radar means the detection and location of remote objects by reflection of radio waves. The phenomenon of acoustic echoes is familiar. Sound waves reflected

from a building or cliff are received back at the observer after a lapse of a short interval. The effect is similar to you shouting in a canyon and, seconds later, hearing a nearly exact replication of your voice. Radar uses exactly the same principle except that the waves involved are radio waves, not sound waves. These travel very much faster than sound waves, 186,000 miles per second, and can cover much longer distances. Thus, radar involves simply measuring the time between transmission of the waves and their subsequent return or echo, and then converting that to a distance measure.[44]

Communicate the message that students can and should make sense of the things they study. Students learn new information more effectively when they approach it with the attitude that they can understand and make sense of it—in other words, when they have a *meaningful learning set.*[45] Following are examples of what you might do to engender a meaningful learning set:

- Explicitly show how various facts, ideas, and procedures make logical sense within the context of other things students already know.

- Ask students to explain why they think their particular answer to a question makes more sense than other possible answers.

- Create tests and other classroom assessments that require meaningful learning and other effective long-term memory storage processes.[46]

I must especially emphasize the importance of the last of these three strategies: *Assess for meaningful learning.* Unfortunately, many teachers' classroom assessment practices encourage students to learn school subjects in a rote rather than meaningful manner.[47] Think back to your own experiences in school. How many times were you allowed to define a word by repeating a dictionary definition, rather than being expected to explain it in your own words? In fact, how many times were you *required* to learn something word for word? And how many times did an exam assess your knowledge of facts or principles without ever assessing your ability to relate those facts and principles to everyday life or to things you had learned in previous courses? When students discover that assignments and exams focus on recall of unrelated facts—rather than on understanding and application of an integrated body of knowledge—many rely on rehearsal and other meaning-free approaches to learning, believing (incorrectly) that this approach will yield a higher score and that meaningful learning would be counterproductive.[48]

Provide concrete experiences to which students can subsequently connect more abstract ideas. In the early elementary years, students appear to have only a limited ability to think about abstract concepts and ideas.[49] And although abstract thinking ability increases in adolescence, many high school students struggle with abstract concepts in such disciplines as math, science, and history.[50] Even when students are capable of thinking abstractly, sometimes they simply don't have the background knowledge they need to understand a new topic. For such reasons, it's often helpful to provide concrete experiences that provide a foundation on which students can build. For example, students can better understand how large the dinosaurs were if they see a life-size dinosaur skeleton at a museum of natural history. Similarly, they can more easily understand the events of an important battle if they visit the battlefield.

You can provide many concrete, foundational experiences right in the classroom. For example, you might:

■ Create opportunities to work with physical objects and living creatures, such as timing the fall of light versus heavy objects or caring for a class pet.

■ Provide computer software that simulates complex activities, such as running a lemonade stand, designing a new machine to accomplish a particular mechanical task, or dissecting a frog.

■ Conduct in-class activities similar to those in the adult world, such as trying a mock courtroom case or carrying out a political campaign.

Focus on an in-depth understanding of a few key ideas, rather than covering many topics superficially. Effective long-term memory storage processes—meaningful learning, organization, elaboration, visual imagery—often take *time*. Accordingly, many psychologists and educators advocate the principle *Less is more: Less* material studied thoroughly (rather than superficially) is learned *more* completely and with greater understanding.[51]

This strategy can sometimes be a difficult one to implement, especially when school district curricula or government policies require teachers to "cover" a gazillion topics in any single school year.[52] One workable strategy is to organize units around a few core ideas or issues, always relating specific content back to this core.[53] And to the extent that you have input into curriculum planning or assessment practices beyond your own classroom, I urge you *please* to advocate as loudly and vigorously as you can for reasonable expectations about the number of topics students study and learn in any given school year.

Use physical or graphic models to illustrate complex systems and phenomena. By *model,* I mean some sort of concrete representation of a phenomenon that depicts its key components and their interrelationships. Physical models involve tangible objects—parts of an eye, components of a molecule, and so on. For example, in your own schooling you have undoubtedly seen models of our solar system that consist of a sun and eight or nine planets at various distances from it. The models are never to scale—distances between various astronomical entities are, relatively speaking, much smaller than they are in reality—but they can help you conceptualize how the sun and planets are organized and move in space.

Graphic models, such as diagrams and flowcharts, are also useful.[54] Effective teachers and textbooks often use graphic models to show such phenomena as cell mitosis and the water cycle. You've seen two examples of graphic models in earlier chapters of this book: Figure 2.1 (neurons) and Figure 4.1 (the human memory system).

Use analogies to help students make meaningful connections.
Analogies that relate new ideas to familiar concepts and situations can be quite effective.[55] For example, in Chapter 3, I drew an analogy between what you do with your mail and what your memory system needs to do with the almost limitless amount of information your environment sends your way. Here are several other examples of analogies that can help students make sense of what might otherwise be hard-to-comprehend ideas:

- If you think of the earth's history as a *24-hour day,* then human beings have been in existence only for the last minute of the day.

- The growth of a glacier is like *pancake batter being poured into a frying pan.* As more and more substance is added to the middle, the edges spread farther and farther out.

- Peristalsis, a process that moves food through the digestive system, is "like *squeezing ketchup out of a single-serving packet.* You squeeze the packet near one corner and run your fingers along the length of the packet toward an opening at the other corner. When you do this, you push the ketchup through the packet, in one direction, ahead of your fingers, until it comes out of the opening."

- Any horizontal surface, such as a table, exerts force on an object that rests on it. You might think of the table as a *spring* that is compressed when something is put on top of it. The spring pushes up against the object.

- Tying a bowline knot is like *a rabbit guarding the territory around its home.* You hold the rope vertically and make a loop near the middle. The loop is the rabbit hole, the upper end of the rope is the tree, and the lower end is the rabbit. The rabbit goes up and out of the hole, around the tree, and back down the hole.[56]

When you use an analogy to help students understand a new concept or idea, however, you should also point out ways in which the two things being compared are *different*. Otherwise, students may take an analogy too far and make incorrect inferences.[57]

Ask questions that require students to elaborate on what they're learning. For example, you might ask questions such as these:

- "Why does _____ do that?"
- "How is _____ different from _____?"
- "Can you think of another example of _____?"
- "How might you use _____ to _____?"[58]

Alternatively, you might have students *ask one another* questions that require them to expand on what they're learning. Such mutual question asking not only encourages elaboration of the topic at hand but also promotes more effective learning and study strategies over the long run.[59]

Supplement dry, fact-based textbook material with study guides or note-taking structures that can help students effectively read and remember the material. Many textbook authors apparently have little or no knowledge of the basic principles of learning and memory I describe in this book. I've come to this conclusion because a great many school textbooks present seemingly endless lists of facts without pointing out interrelationships among the facts and without regard for what students are likely to know and *not* know before they begin reading.[60] For example, American history textbooks frequently refer to early colonists' distress over Britain's "taxation without representation" policy yet don't always provide an adequate explanation of why the colonists found this policy so upsetting.[61] Most adults can easily relate the idea of taxation without representation to their own frustrations with high taxes. Most fifth graders, however, have little or no experience on which to draw in understanding the colonists' situation.

Unfortunately, teachers often don't have the liberty to choose pedagogically sound textbooks. Instead, they're apt to inherit texts that their school district or department chair has ordered for them. When these texts leave much to be desired in the way of promoting effective learning, teacher-constructed supplementary materials can help students get the most out of what might otherwise be difficult reading. Following are two examples of how you might supplement textbook materials:

■ Give students a list of questions they should try to answer as they read.

■ Give students a general organizational structure (such as an outline or two-dimensional matrix) that they can fill in as they read.[62]

Teach mnemonic strategies for hard-to-remember facts. When meaningful new-to-old connections don't seem possible—and sometimes they really aren't possible—mnemonics for certain facts and lists can often make the difference between learning that is enjoyable and successful, on the one hand, or learning that is tedious and ultimately leads to little knowledge that "sticks," on the other. In some situations you might have ready-made mnemonics for particular sets of facts—for instance, the HOMES mnemonic for the five Great Lakes or "Thirty days has September" for the number of days in each month. But ideally, students should also learn to create their *own* mnemonics for important-but-hard to-remember ideas. And in fact, students *can* learn to create their own mnemonics, often quite effectively.[63]

As noted earlier in the chapter, some mnemonic strategies make use of visual imagery. When encouraging students to use mnemonics based on visual imagery, you should keep a couple of things in mind. First, many young children cannot generate effective images on their own and so probably need to have pictures provided for them. Second, for imagery to be an effective means of remembering a connection between two items—say, between love and *amor*—the two items must be incorporated into the same image in an *interacting* fashion. Thus, while an image of a heart painted on a suit of armor might an effective way of remembering the Spanish word for *love,* an image of a heart placed beside a suit of armor probably is not.[64]

Provide a summary at the end of a unit; alternatively, have students create a summary. On average, students learn more effectively when they hear, read, or create a synopsis of information they've just studied. Summaries probably serve multiple functions for students: They can help students review previously studied material, determine which ideas within that material are most important, and pull key ideas into a cohesive organizational structure.[65]

Many students have difficulty adequately summarizing the things they read and hear, however. If you think about it, you might realize that developing a good summary isn't an easy task: Students must discriminate between important and unimportant information, identify main ideas that may or may not be explicitly stated, and organize critical elements into a unified whole.[66]

Researchers have offered several suggestions for helping students create good summaries of classroom subject matter:

▪ Begin by having students practice developing summaries for short, easy, and well-organized passages (perhaps those only a few paragraphs in length), then gradually introduce longer and more difficult texts to summarize.

▪ When students are writing a summary, suggest that they:

  ● Identify or invent a topic sentence for each paragraph or section.

  ● Identify superordinate concepts or ideas that subsume several more specific points.

  ● Find supporting information for each main idea.

  ● Delete trivial and redundant information.

▪ Have students compare and discuss their summaries, considering what ideas they think are important and why.[67]

Such strategies do seem to help students to write better summaries and, ultimately, to learn and remember classroom material more effectively.

Keep students' anxiety at a productive level. Being a little bit anxious about learning and remembering something can be helpful, but being highly anxious is apt to be counterproductive—students think more about how worried they are than about how they might reasonably make sense of what they're studying. Anxiety (like all emotions) is largely beyond students' immediate control, and so simply telling them to "Relax" or "Calm down" isn't likely to be effective. The following strategies should have more of an impact:

▪ Communicate clear, concrete, and realistic expectations for learning and performance.

▪ Match instruction to students' existing knowledge and ability levels.

▪ Provide supplementary sources of support for learning challenging topics and skills—for instance, provide additional practice, individual tutoring, or a suitable structure for taking notes.

▪ Teach study strategies that can enhance learning and performance.

▪ Assess students' performance independently of how well their classmates are doing, and encourage students to assess their own performance in a similar manner.

▪ Allow students to correct errors, so that no single mistake is ever a "fatal" one.[68]

CHAPTER 6

Not All Roads Lead to Rome: Remembering and Forgetting

Thanks to the limited capacities of attention and working memory, not everything we experience gets into long-term memory. But the things that *do* get in there are apt to stick around for a while. The challenge then becomes one of finding information when we need it—a *retrieval* issue.

Traveling Down Memory Lane: How We Find Things in Long-Term Memory

To understand how long-term memory retrieval works, it will help to recall two points I made in Chapter 4. First, remember that much of the information stored in long-term memory is interconnected, with some pieces of information being closely associated with certain other pieces, which in turn are associated with still other pieces, and so on. In addition, recall the concept of *activation*—the idea that whatever information we're currently thinking about is in an active state, while the rest of our knowledge remains quietly inactive in the background.

When we consider both aspects of long-term memory—its interconnectedness and the varying activation levels of its contents—we can get a good sense of how long-term memory retrieval probably works. In particular, retrieval seems to involve following a pathway of associations. One idea reminds us of another idea—that is, one idea *activates* another—then the second idea reminds us of a third idea, and so on. Almost literally, long-term memory retrieval is a process of going down Memory Lane. If the pathway of associations eventually leads us to what we're trying to remember, we do indeed remember it. If the path takes us in another direction, we're out of luck.

We're more likely to retrieve information we need when we have many possible pathways leading in its direction—in other words, when we have previously connected that information with many other things we also know. For example, consider this fact:

The capital of Italy is Rome.

If you've ever lived in Rome, you have a great deal of knowledge about this city, no doubt including some tidbits related to Italy's federal government. Or possibly you studied the history of ancient Rome in great depth, in which case you know that early Romans' republican government laid the groundwork for many modern-day democracies. In either case, if you're searching for the capital city of Italy, many "roads" lead to *Rome* in your long-term memory. But if, instead, you know almost nothing about Rome, you may have a hard time finding your way there.

Paving Memory Lane: The Value of Automaticity

We retrieve some things from long-term memory very quickly and with little effort. Two and two make four, grass is green, beaches have sand, and so on. Generally speaking, retrieval is easier for things we know *well*—things we think about and use frequently.

In Chapter 5, I stated that rehearsal—repeating something over and over within the course of a few seconds or minutes—is usually *not* a good way to store information in long-term memory. Once information *is* in long-term memory, however, occasional repetition over a period of several weeks, months, or years can help keep it there indefinitely. When we continue to practice recalling or using information we've previously learned, we eventually become able to retrieve it immediately and use it almost without thinking. That is, we acquire *automaticity* for the information.[1]

As an example, think of driving a car, a complicated skill that perhaps you can perform easily. Your first attempts at driving many years ago may have required a great deal of mental effort. But maybe now you can drive without having to pay much attention to what you're doing. Even if your car has a standard transmission that requires frequent gear shifting, driving is, for you, an automatic activity.

In addition to making retrieval quick and easy, learning something to automaticity has a second advantage. Remember that working memory has a limited capacity—the active, "thinking" part of the human memory system can handle only so much at a time. If we have to use much of that capacity for recalling single facts or carrying out simple procedures, we have little "room" left over to think about anything else. One key reason for learning some things to automaticity, then, is to free up working memory capacity for more complex tasks and problems.

Many everyday tasks require performing a number of subtasks at more or less the same time. If we are to perform these tasks successfully, some of the subtasks must be automatic for us. Reading is a good example. To understand what we read, we can't use much working memory for figuring out what the letters *t–h–r–o–u–g–h* spell. In fact, research is clear on this point: The more effort we must devote to identifying the words on the page, the lower our comprehension of what we're reading is likely to be.[2]

Doing several things simultaneously—multitasking—is possible only if we've acquired automaticity for most or all of them.

Writing is another multifaceted process that can easily exceed the limits of working memory unless some processes are automatic for us. To write well, we must devote most of our attention to the communicative aspect of writing—that is, to expressing our thoughts in a clear, logical, and organized fashion—without getting bogged down in concerns about subject–verb agreement or the correct spelling of *psychology*. Thus, we must know the mechanics of writing (grammar, spelling, punctuation, and so on) thoroughly enough to apply them automatically.[3]

Automaticity is achieved in only one way: practice, practice, and more practice. Practice doesn't necessarily make perfect, but it does make knowledge more durable and easily retrievable. When we use information and skills frequently, we essentially "pave" the mental pathways we must travel to find them, in some cases creating superhighways.

Automaticity can have its downsides, however.[4] For one thing, we may perform habitual actions without even thinking about them, to the point that we can't remember whether or not we've done them. For example, occasionally I start to wonder if I've closed the garage door behind me after I've left the house for the day, and I may fret about the issue so much that I return home to make sure that the door is, in fact, closed. And sometimes I need to double-check that I've turned down the thermostat before going to bed at night.

A more serious disadvantage of automaticity is that it increases the likelihood that we'll quickly recall certain ideas or perform certain procedures when other, less automatic ideas or procedures are more useful.[5] We'll be far more flexible—and thus far more likely to identify unique approaches to situations or creative solutions to problems—when we aren't automatically locked in to a particular response. We'll return to this issue in our discussion of *mental set* in Chapter 9.

Finding Old Trails through the Woods: The Tip-of-the-Tongue Phenomenon

In contrast to those well-paved highways and byways, some routes through long-term memory are rarely traveled. When we need to find information at the end of one of them, we may struggle for quite a while: We know that we know it, and we seemingly come closer and closer to it, and eventually—maybe—we track it down. Perhaps the following exercise will elicit this *tip-of-the-tongue* phenomenon for you.

Check It Out: **Four English Words**

Here are definitions of four words in the English language. Can you identify the specific words to which they refer?

- The fluid part of blood

- A picture form of writing used in ancient Egypt

- A small, hard-shelled, ocean-dwelling animal that attaches itself to rocks and ships

- An adjective describing a tree that loses its leaves each year (its opposite is *evergreen*)

Quite possibly you retrieved some of these words with very little effort. But there is a good chance that you couldn't retrieve all four of them instantaneously. For one or more, you may have found yourself looking around in your long-term memory, perhaps for a long time, in "places" where a word might be located. You may even have gotten brief "glimpses" of a word through the trees ("I think it begins with an *h*," "It has at least three syllables, maybe four").[6] In case you couldn't retrieve all four words, they are *plasma, hieroglyphics, barnacle,* and *deciduous.* Of course, some of my readers—especially those for whom English is a second or third language—may never have stored these words in long-term memory in the first place.

It's often difficult to retrieve information that we seldom use. For instance, we may have trouble identifying people whom we haven't seen recently or frequently, even though we *know that we know them.*[7] Place names can be troublesome, too, especially if we've been to those places only once or twice. For example, I have a terrible time remembering Massachusetts's Lake Chargoggagoggmanchauggagoggchaubunagungamaugg, which I've visited only once. Well, okay, it obviously doesn't help that the name is 45 letters long. But my daughter's friend Stacey, who grew up by this lake, can easily tell me its name any time I ask her—she's learned it to automaticity.

Posting Road Signs: The Importance of Retrieval Cues

Retrieval is obviously easier when we have a good idea about where to "look" in long-term memory—that is, when we know which part of long-term memory to activate. To see what I mean, try the next exercise.

Check It Out: **Twenty-Four Words**

Part 1.

Read the following list of 24 words *one time only.* As soon as you have read the list once, cover it with a piece of paper and write down as many of the words as you can remember. After you've finished, *keep the list covered* and proceed to Part 2 of the exercise.

tulip	pencil	spoon	microwave	lawyer	ruby
wrench	mountain	doctor	crayon	daisy	pliers
blender	fork	diamond	canyon	knife	toaster
hill	teacher	rose	pen	hammer	emerald

. . .

Part 2.

If you can't remember all 24 words, see if these words and phrases help you:

flowers	land forms
gemstones	eating utensils
professions	kitchen appliances
carpentry tools	writing implements

I'm guessing that the eight category names helped you remember additional words by steering you in productive directions in your long-term memory. In psychology lingo, I gave you *retrieval cues*—hints about where to "look" in your search efforts.

Occasionally characteristics of our immediate physical environment act as retrieval cues for long-ago memories.[8] For example, certain smells may remind you of, say, a favorite dessert that your mother used to make, a trip you once took, or a visit to the hairdresser that went horribly wrong. Certain songs may remind you of your high school days or an old boyfriend or girlfriend. In an unusual demonstration of how one's physical environment can serve as a retrieval cue, researchers had scuba divers read a list of 36 words in either of two environments: on shore or 20 feet below the water's surface. Later the divers were asked to remember the words in either the same or a different environment. Those who had initially read the words on land remembered more if they again were on land. Those who had read the words 20 feet below remembered more if they were underwater.[9]

Some of the mnemonics described in Chapter 5 provide retrieval cues when we need to remember a list of things. For example, the mnemonic *HOMES* for the five Great Lakes tells us that one lake begins with the letter *H*, prompting us to search among the *H* words in long-term memory until (we hope) we find *Huron*. Then we search our *O* words (leading us to *Ontario*), our *M* words (*Michigan*), our *E* words (*Erie*), and our *S* words (*Superior*). And consider this mnemonic for remembering the hierarchy of categories with which biologists classify living things:

> King Philip comes over for good spaghetti.

The first letters of the words remind us of both the categories and their hierarchical order: *kingdom, phylum, class, order, family, genus,* and *species.*

A potential downside of retrieval cues is that they may occasionally steer us *away* from information in long-term memory that might be helpful in our present circumstances. For example, in an experiment with college students, some participants were given a list of 25 U.S. states to read, whereas others had no such list. All of the students were then asked to name as many of the 50 states as they could. The students who had been given the list of 25 remembered more of the states they had previously read but fewer of the states they *hadn't* read.[10]

Most of the time, however, retrieval cues work to our benefit, providing road signs that indicate which way to travel down Memory Lane.

Revisiting Hot Spots: Flashbulb Memories

In Chapter 5, I introduced you to *hot cognition,* in which thoughts and memories are emotionally charged. Although we may occasionally repress extremely painful memories (more about this point shortly), in general we can more easily retrieve information with high emotional content than we can recall relatively nonemotional information.[11] It's almost as if these memories have gigantic floodlights pointed at them and saying to us, "Here I am—look this way!"

Some memories of significant and emotion-laden events can be very vivid, detailed ones with a seemingly "snapshot" quality to them. Psychologists call them *flashbulb memories.*[12] For example, unless you were very young at the time, you can probably recall in great detail both where you were and what you were doing when you first learned about the attacks on the World Trade

Center and Pentagon on September 11, 2001. Likewise, I can remember November 22, 1963, almost as if it were yesterday. I was at home from school with the flu, and Mom was braiding my hair as I sat on the living room couch watching television. The telephone rang. Mom had a brief conversation with the caller and then returned to the living room white as a sheet. "President Kennedy has just been shot," she said.

Yet we shouldn't let the vividness of such memories lead us to believe that they're accurate, because they *aren't* always accurate.[13] I'm pretty sure I was home sick the day Kennedy was shot, but was my mother really braiding my hair just before she got that phone call? Did she even *get* a phone call telling her about the assassination? And how accurate is your recollection of September 11th? Unless you have a video of yourself when you first learned the news, there's no way to be sure.

Let's consider another well-known disaster, the crash of the space shuttle *Challenger* on January 28, 1986—a horrific event in which seven astronauts perished, including Christa McAuliffe, the first teacher to travel into space. Researchers asked college students to describe the circumstances in which they heard the news both the morning after the incident and then again 2½ years later. Even after all that time, many students were quite confident about their recollections. Yet some of them were way off base. For example, one student gave this (presumably accurate) account the morning after hearing about the disaster:

> I was in my religion class and some people walked in and started talking about [it]. I didn't know any details except that it had exploded and the schoolteacher's students had all been watching, which I thought was so sad. Then after class I went to my room and watched the TV program talking about it and I got all the details from that.[14]

The same student had this recollection 2½ years later:

> When I first heard about the explosion I was sitting in my freshman dorm room with my roommate and we were watching TV. It came on a news flash and we were both totally shocked. I was really upset and I went upstairs to talk to a friend of mine and then I called my parents.[15]

Obviously, then, our long-term memories aren't always accurate records of our experiences. Just as we tend to be constructive, meaning-making individuals as we acquire new knowledge, so, too, can we be constructive at retrieval time, as you'll see in the next section.

Rebuilding Old Memories: Why We Sometimes Misremember

Have you ever remembered an event very differently than a friend did, even though the two of you had been equally active participants in the event? Were you and your friend both certain of the accuracy of your own, individual memories and convinced that the other person remembered the situation incorrectly? Constructive processes in retrieval might explain this difference of opinion.

Retrieving something from long-term memory isn't necessarily an all-or-nothing affair. Often we retrieve only parts of what we've previously learned. In such situations we may construct our "memory" of something by combining the tidbits we can recall with our general knowledge and assumptions about the world. As an example, try the next exercise.

Check It Out: **Missing Letters**

Each of the five words below has one or more letters missing from it. See if you can correctly fill in the missing letter(s) in each one.

1. sep___rate

2. exist___nce

3. adole___nce

4. perc___ve

5. hors d'o___

Were you able to retrieve the missing letters from your long-term memory? If not, you may have found yourself making reasonable guesses using either your knowledge of how the words are pronounced or your knowledge of how words in the English language are typically spelled. For example, perhaps you used the "*i* before *e* except after *c*" rule for Word 4. If so, you reconstructed the correct spelling of *perceive*. Perhaps you used your knowledge that -*ance* is a common word ending. Unfortunately, if you used this knowledge for Word 2, you spelled *existence* incorrectly. Neither pronunciation nor typical English spelling patterns would have helped you with *hors d'oeuvre*, a term borrowed from the French. (The correct spellings for Words 1 and 3 are *separate* and *adolescence*.)

By filling in the gaps in what we can recall based on our general knowledge and assumptions about the world, we get a more complete memory—one that logically hangs together—than we might otherwise. Unfortunately, we can fill in the gaps incorrectly—a phenomenon known as *reconstruction error*. If we're recounting an amusing but otherwise inconsequential event to friends or family members, any inaccuracies in our story may not matter. But in some cases—such as in eyewitness testimony—those incorrect fill-ins can have significant (occasionally life-or-death) consequences. It's important to realize, then, that no matter how confident we are about what we saw or heard, *our recollections are not necessarily accurate ones*.[16]

The Power of Suggestion: Effects of After-the-Fact Information

Sometimes our memories for topics or events are influenced not only by our prior knowledge and beliefs but also by information we receive at some point after we've initially stored whatever we're trying to retrieve. Generally speaking, this is a good thing: We should continually update our knowledge and understanding as new information comes in. However, if the new information is misleading or blatantly incorrect, we may revise our memories inappropriately—a phenomenon known as the *misinformation effect*.[17]

We're often influenced by what other people say they remember about an event. If everyone else in a group recalls an event differently from how we do—or perhaps if just a single, well-respected individual recalls it differently—we may change our minds and memories of what happened.[18] Leading questions, too, can have an impact. In yet another study with college students (the perennial guinea pigs in research on human learning and memory), participants watched a film showing a car accident and then were asked how fast the car was going. The question varied ever so slightly for five different groups of students (I've italicized the differences):

- About how fast were the cars going when they *contacted* each other?

- About how fast were the cars going when they *hit* each other?

- About how fast were the cars going when they *bumped into* each other?

- About how fast were the cars going when they *collided with* each other?

- About how fast were the cars going when they *smashed into* each other?

Students' estimates differed quite a bit, depending on the severity of impact their question implied. For instance, cars that "contacted" each other were, on average, estimated to be going a little less than 32 miles per hour. In contrast, cars that "smashed into" each other were, on average, estimated to be traveling almost 41 miles per hour.[19]

Remembering What but Forgetting When or Where: Problems in Source Monitoring

Another trouble spot in human memory is *source monitoring*—that is, we can't remember when or where we acquired certain information or experienced a particular event.[20] For example, psychologist Donald Thomson was once accused of raping a woman at the exact time he was on television being interviewed about—ironically—memory. The woman who was accusing Dr. Thomson of the assault described him in vivid detail and was certain he had been her attacker. As it turns out, she had watched his interview just before she was raped, and in the process of confusing her sources, his face became an integral part of her recollection of the crime.[21]

Faulty source monitoring can occasionally lead to unintentional plagiarism of another person's ideas. For example, in a U.S. District Court ruling in 1976, a judge found former Beatle George Harrison guilty of copyright infringement after noting striking similarities between Harrison's song "My Sweet Lord" and an earlier piece by the Chiffons called "He's So Fine." Harrison recalled having heard the Chiffons' hit but had no conscious awareness that it might have been the source of his own tune.[22]

Re-Remembering: Effects of Prior Recollections

Certain events in our lives are significant enough that we talk about them over and over again—frequently adding our own embellishments, interpretations, and distortions to the mix. Our memories for these events soon become not what actually happened but what we've previously *recalled* happening.

Essentially we recount these things often enough that our stories about them—rather than the events themselves—become "fact" for us.[23]

As an example, let's return to the research study involving the *Challenger* disaster that I described earlier in the section on flashbulb memories. The researchers interviewed many of the students a third time, 6 months after the second recall session and 3 years after the disaster itself. On the third occasion, most students essentially repeated their recollections of 6 months before. When students who inaccurately remembered the occasion were given hints as to the truth about where they had been and what they had been doing, they stuck with their prior misrecollections. Furthermore, they were quite surprised when they were shown their original, morning-after descriptions. It appeared that these students were remembering not what had actually happened but what they had previously *said* had happened.[24]

"Remembering" What Never Happened: False Memories

The constructive nature of retrieval makes it possible for us to have *false memories*—to "remember" events we've never actually experienced. We're more likely to have false memories when someone we trust suggests that certain events either might have happened or definitely did happen. We're also more likely to remember nonevents that are consistent with other things we know about our lives.[25]

False memories seem to emerge from our own, very constructive imaginations, often in combination with "information"—perhaps true, perhaps not—that someone else gives us. We imagine something happening, conjuring up a plausible scenario complete with vivid images. Then, thanks to a difficulty in source monitoring, we later recall the scenario without its origins—that is, we confuse fiction with fact.[26]

Some false memories are fairly innocuous. What harm is there in, say, recalling an enjoyable trip to a nonexistent amusement park or attending a birthday party that couldn't possibly have taken place? Other false memories are far more troublesome. For instance, false memories of a parent or other family member sexually abusing you as a child can lead to an innocent person being imprisoned and, of course, irreparable damage to your relationship with a loved one. Certainly some memories of childhood sexual abuse are based on horrifying realities, but others are, sadly, figments of people's fertile imaginations.[27]

Huge Attic, Small Flashlight: Why We Sometimes Forget

At the beginning of the chapter, I suggested that long-term memory retrieval involves activating certain memories, which then activate others, which then activate still others, and so on. The Memory Lane metaphor was useful for a while, but to help you further understand activation and its impact on retrieval and forgetting, I now want to switch to a different metaphor: a flashlight in an attic.[28]

Imagine your long-term memory as a very large attic with no windows or overhead lights. You're a bit of a packrat, and so you've put a great many things up there over the years. And now imagine yourself going up to your attic to find something you need. You take a flashlight with you—a flashlight that can illuminate an area roughly the size of your working memory. As you traipse around the attic in search of your desired item, you shine the flashlight on one spot, then on another, continuing to point it in various directions until you locate what you're looking for. If you reflect on your own experiences trying to recall things from your distant past, you may realize that retrieving long-ignored things from long-term memory does seem to have a limited-capacity, "flashlight" quality to it.

Psychologists have offered several possible reasons that we may not always be able to find what we're looking for in that attic we call long-term memory. My attic-and-flashlight analogy will be helpful in making sense of some but not all of them.

Neglecting to Firm Things Up: Consolidation Problems

Researchers have found that the neurological underpinnings of new memories need time to solidify—perhaps a few minutes or a few hours, perhaps even longer. This firming-up process, called *consolidation,* is essential if new information and events are going to "stick" in long-term memory. For example, a person who incurs a serious head injury in an auto accident or other traumatic incident often can't recall things that happened several seconds, minutes, or days prior to the injury, whereas memories of long-ago events remain largely intact. Such amnesia is especially common when the person is unconscious for a short period following the injury and therefore unable to think about events that have recently occurred.[29]

At this point, researchers can only speculate about what the consolidation process entails. Possibly it involves some sort of low-level, unconscious activation or rehearsal. Researchers have discovered, however, that a good night's sleep promotes consolidation, apparently through facilitating certain critical memory processes in the cortex and hippocampus.[30]

One reason why we forget things, then, is that we never firm up the memories we've initially formed of them. It's as if we're trying to save undercooked, wafer-thin crackers that quickly disintegrate.

Misdirecting the Flashlight: Retrieval Problems

Let's return to that hypothetical attic of yours. Imagine that you keep many things up there, including your old books and class notes, out-of-style clothing, extra furniture, seldom-used cooking utensils, holiday decorations, and a good deal of the mail you've accumulated over the years. Perhaps you're a very organized person who has stored all books in one place, all clothes in another, and all holiday decorations somewhere else. But maybe, instead, you've thrown things just any old place in your attic, so that some cooking utensils are with books, others are with clothes, and still others are stuffed in an old dresser or on the bottom shelf of a dilapidated bookcase. How easily you find something in your attic depends on how you've stashed things in there to begin with. If you've been systematic, you should be able to shine your flashlight almost immediately on the spot where a desired item is located. But if you've stored everything in a helter-skelter fashion, you may have to purchase new holiday decorations every year because you can't track down your decorations from any of the previous 13 years.

A second reason that we seemingly forget information, then, is that we never "look" for it in the right location in long-term memory.[31] We later confirm that we haven't lost the information, because we stumble on it days or weeks later when we're looking for something entirely different.

We're more likely to have retrieval problems if we're sloppy about how we initially store information—in particular, if we don't make those crucial connections between the new information and things we already know. This is why rehearsal is such an ineffective strategy for studying new material: It's like throwing things any old place in long-term memory.

Ironically, we're also more likely to have trouble retrieving something when we *really need* to find it—that is, when we're highly anxious. A lot of anxiety prevents us from searching long-term memory in an "open-minded"

An organized long-term memory makes things easier to retrieve.

manner, reducing our chances of locating what we're seeking.[32] Think about what happens when you're late for an important appointment and can't find your car keys. You've looked high and low, yet the keys are nowhere to be found. As you begin to panic, your search strategies become less and less efficient—you look in the same places over and over again. You don't think creatively about the wide variety of places in which the keys might be lurking.

While we're on the subject of anxiety, I should dispel another common myth: that hypnosis helps us remember things we think we've completely forgotten. Hypnosis certainly does help us relax—all traces of anxiety go out the window. It's likely to make us more chatty about an event we've experienced, but it probably *won't* increase our accuracy in recalling it.[33]

Mixing and Matching: Interference Problems

Sometimes we can easily retrieve things we've learned but don't know what goes with what. As an example, try the following exercise.

Check It Out: Six More Chinese Words

Here are six more Mandarin Chinese words and their English meanings (for simplicity's sake, I've omitted the tone marks over the words). Read the words two or three times, and try to store them in your long-term memory. But don't do anything special to learn the words—for instance, don't intentionally develop mnemonics to help you remember them.

Chinese	English
jung	middle
ting	listen
sung	deliver
peng	friend
ching	please
deng	wait

Now cover up the list of words and test yourself. What was the word for *friend? please? listen? wait?*

Did you find yourself getting confused, perhaps forgetting which English meaning went with each Chinese word? If you did, you were the victim of *interference*. The various pieces of information you stored in memory were interfering with one another—they were essentially getting mixed up.

Interference often comes into play when we switch from one language to another, especially if we're not fluent in each of the languages we're using— that is, if we haven't learned each language to automaticity. For instance, I've found interference's effects very annoying when I travel to non-English-speaking countries. I know a modicum of French, Spanish, German, and Chinese—and just the teensiest bit of Italian—but frequently retrieve the wrong words and phrases for my current location. For instance, I might thank a French-speaking merchant with "Grazie" (Italian) or agree with a German acquaintance by saying "Si" (Spanish).

As another example of interference, some students in my college psychology classes continually confuse the concepts *punishment* and *negative reinforcement*, which both refer to consequences that influence people's behavior but in opposite ways. Punishment involves either the presentation of an unpleasant situation or the removal of a pleasant one; behaviors followed by punishment tend to decrease. In contrast, negative reinforcement involves the removal of an unpleasant situation; behaviors followed by negative reinforcement tend to *increase*, not decrease. To some degree, the source of my students' difficulty lies in the common misconception that *negative reinforcement* is nothing more than a politically correct term for *punishment*, but adding to the confusion are the similar terms in the two definitions—*pleasant, unpleasant, removal, decrease,* and *increase.* Trust me, I'm aware that the distinction is often a trouble spot for students and so I regularly stress and illustrate the difference in class, but old, well-engrained habits and misconceptions can be tough nuts to crack.

Interference is especially common when pieces of information are similar to one another and when we try to learn them through rote, meaningless repetition. It's less likely to be a problem if we can make meaningful sense of information or develop mnemonics that help us tell similar items apart.[34] Recall, for example, "When the 'mites' go up, the 'tites' come down." This mnemonic provides an easy way to remember the difference between two very similar-sounding cave formations: stalagmites and stalactites.

Not Going Where It's Too Hot: Repression of Painful Memories

Earlier in the chapter I mentioned that emotionally laden news can result in a flashbulb memory—a vivid, detailed recollection of where we were and what we were doing when experiencing or learning about an especially significant event. But in some situations we may have an experience that is so painful or emotionally distressing that we tend either not to remember it at all or to recall only isolated fragments of it. This phenomenon is known as *repression.*[35]

Let's go back once again to your long-term-memory attic. In one corner of your attic you have stashed away some very unpleasant stuff—stuff you'd rather not look at ever again. Any time you wander toward that section, the heat turns up and you feel increasingly uncomfortable. Eventually you veer in a different direction, toward a cooler part of the attic.

That "heat" to which I'm referring is anxiety, and a lot of it. As you search your long-term memory for prior experiences that might be relevant to an issue or problem you're currently facing, you may wander in the direction of the anxiety-arousing memory. But because anxiety is an unpleasant feeling, you don't want to get too close: The memory may simply be too hot to touch.

As I mentioned before, people sometimes "recall" traumatic events that never happened. Yet research evidence is mounting that we do have some ability to willfully *not* remember things that actually did happen.[36] In general, however, repression appears to be *very rare* as a cause of forgetting. We don't seem to repress painful events as a matter of course.[37]

Using It or Losing It: Possible Decay of Memories

At one time, many psychologists believed that once we learn new information, we keep it permanently in some form.[38] And in fact, it's probably impossible to prove that our memories *don't* last forever. We could never disprove an alternative hypothesis—that certain memories are just exceedingly difficult to find among all of the information "clutter" we've accumulated over the years.

Increasingly, however, most psychologists are beginning to suspect that many memories gradually fade away and eventually disappear—that is, they *decay*—especially if we never use them.[39] To some degree, then, the expression "Use it or lose it" may apply to human memory.

Some kinds of information are apparently more susceptible to decay than others. In particular, the exact details of an event fade more quickly than its underlying meaning, or gist.[40] We find an exception to this rule when certain details capture key features of an event or are in some other way quite distinctive.[41] Meanwhile, less distinctive ones become a blur. As an example, when I think back to my early lessons in U.S. history, I remember the general idea behind the American Revolution: The colonists were fighting for independence from British rule. I also remember certain vivid details. For example, the Battle of Bunker Hill is commemorated by a monument I visited several times as a child, and the Boston Tea Party was a unique and colorful illustration of the colonists' displeasure with British taxation policies. Many other aspects of the revolution escape me now. If I wanted to give you examples, I'd have to Google them, because I have no idea what they might be. See, they really *aren't* in my long-term memory any more, or at least they're not in any form I can easily find my way to.

Forgetting the Long-Ago Past: Infantile Amnesia

You probably remember very little of your infancy and early childhood. I remember a couple of snippets—for instance, I recall waiting patiently in my crib one morning until my parents woke up (we were all sleeping in the same room in Nana and Grampa's house), and I recall being held lovingly by Nana one day in her flower garden—but for all I know, these "memories" never really happened. I certainly don't remember the first birthday party my parents gave me at age 1, even though photographs suggest that it must have been a festive occasion. Generally speaking, people remember little or nothing about specific events in their lives that occurred before age 3—a phenomenon known as *infantile amnesia*.[42]

This is not to say that babies and toddlers don't learn and remember *anything,* of course. In fact, we humans have some ability to learn and remember things even before we're born.[43] In one research study, pregnant women read aloud a passage from a children's book (such as Dr. Seuss's *The Cat and the Hat*) twice a day for the final six weeks of their pregnancies. Later, their newborn babies were given pacifiers, and the babies' sucking rates (either fast or slow) controlled whether they heard a recording of their mother reading the prebirth story or a different one. Even though the infants were only 2 or 3 days old, they began to adjust their sucking rate in order to hear the familiar story—the one they had previously heard while still in the womb.[44]

Much of what very young children learn and remember appears to be in the form of implicit knowledge—knowledge that affects their behavior even though they can't consciously recall it.[45] Researchers have offered at least two plausible explanations for why we recall so little of our early years. First, brain structures that are actively involved in explicit, conscious memories are not fully developed at birth and continue to mature in significant ways for several months or years thereafter.[46] Second, infants and toddlers have only a limited ability to make sense of and *encode* their experiences in ways that they can easily retrieve later on. As young children gain language skills, and especially as people around them begin to engage them in conversations about what they're experiencing, their memories for events significantly improve.[47]

Forgetting to Remember the Future: The Challenge of Prospective Memory

So far we've been talking about forgetting information we've acquired in the past. But sometimes we forget something we need to do in the future—keep an appointment, meet a friend for lunch, fill up an almost-empty gas tank, and so on. Here we're talking about what psychologists call *prospective memory*.[48]

In spite of our best intentions, virtually all of us are apt to have prospective memory problems at one time or another. For example, when I was teaching full time, I would often forget to turn off my car headlights after driving to work on a foggy morning. I occasionally forgot important meetings. Sometimes I forgot to bring crucial materials to class. Yes, yes, I know what you're thinking—that I was suffering from the absentminded professor syndrome.

Certainly all of this information was still in my long-term memory. When I went to the parking lot at the end of the day and discovered my dead car battery, I would quickly recall that I had turned on my headlights before driving to work through the fog. When I was reminded of a meeting I'd missed or got to the point in a class session where I needed the handout I'd forgotten to bring, I would think, "Oh, yes, of course!" My problem was that I *forgot to retrieve* the information at the appropriate time.

In our complex twenty-first–century world, most of us have many obligations—places to go, people to see, promises to keep. And yet the "place" in our memory system where we can consciously think about those obligations—working memory—is quite small. If we want to remember something we need to do in, say, the next two minutes, we can use maintenance rehearsal to keep that memory fresh in our minds. (In Chapter 4, I described how I sing "Ninety-Nine Bottles of Beer in the Mail" to remind myself to mail bills at the post office.) But if we want to remember, say, a dentist appointment that we have three days from now, maintenance rehearsal isn't realistic.

So how do we overcome our absentmindedness about future obligations—absentmindedness that, I should point out, is a *completely normal human memory problem?* Ah, there *is* a solution, which I'll describe in the next section.

Becoming a Good Rememberer

Keep in mind that forgetting isn't necessarily a bad thing. Many of the things we learn on any particular occasion will have little use to us later (especially *much* later), and we rarely need to remember things exactly as we originally experienced them. We really don't need to keep all that environmental "junk mail."

Yet some things are definitely important to remember, perhaps for a few days, a few months, or a lifetime. Simply telling ourselves or others that

"I need to remember this!" isn't going to do the trick. Here I offer several strategies that are more consistent with what research about human memory tells us.

THINKING SMART

To help you with your own forgetfulness, I offer three key strategies. Each of them makes use of one of two important concepts I introduced near the beginning of the chapter: retrieval cues and automaticity.

▶ *Create external retrieval cues to remind yourself about future tasks and obligations.* If I had a nickel for every time I've heard friends fret about imminent senility simply because they've forgotten to do something they were supposed to do . . . well, I could probably retire and buy a nice condo in the Bahamas. These people aren't being realistic about what their memories can reasonably do for them.

Let's return to a point I made in Chapter 1: The human memory system is set up to detect and remember general patterns in our environment. It's *not* set up to remember a lot of nitty-gritty details, and it's certainly not set up to remember something we've scheduled for three o'clock two weeks from next Thursday. For such details we need *external retrieval cues*—things not in our heads but rather in our outside physical environment that remind us of what we need to do.

The classic example of an external retrieval cue is a string around the finger: The string is tied in a spot impossible to overlook and serves as a reminder that something needs to be remembered. Finger strings are terribly unfashionable, but other external retrieval cues can be equally effective. Over the years, I've developed several that have made me one of the *least* absentminded people on the planet. I keep a weekly calendar open by the telephone on my desk, and I write in it not only the meetings and appointments I need to go to but also the things I do regularly every week—playing racquetball Monday and Wednesday evenings, going to yoga class Friday afternoon, and so on. But I must admit that I sometimes forget to look at my calendar, so I do other things as well. I write notes to myself about things I need to do on a particular day or accomplish by the end of the week, and I put them in plain sight on my desk. And if I need to be sure to bring something with me to an appointment or meeting, I put it on the

To-Do List for Today
- Doctor's appt-3pm
- Buy milk and eggs
- Get stamps, mail bills
- Weed rhubarb garden
- Send birthday card to author of memory book

Remembering the things we need to do can be a challenge unless we have appropriate retrieval cues.

floor between my desk and my office door, so that I will definitely see it as I leave. Essentially, what I'm doing is guaranteeing retrieval of the things I need to remember.

As I've grown older, I've gotten increasingly compulsive about creating external retrieval cues for myself, and as a result I've also gotten increasingly dependable. I have notes to myself all over the house, especially in places where I can't overlook them. If I want to remember to hard-boil two eggs in the morning for a salad I'll make later in the day, I put a note that says "Boil eggs" right beside the teakettle I'll use to make a cup of tea—and I *know* I won't forget to make a cup of tea in the morning. If I want to mail some bills on the way to the gym, I put the bills on top of my purse—I can't possibly leave the house without my purse because it holds my car keys. And if I know that I also need to fill up the gas tank before I travel very far, I put a note-to-self on the driver's seat that says "GAS!" in huge letters—and then sing "Ninety-nine bottles of beer on the wall" until I get to the gas station.

▶ *Continually practice things you want to remember quickly and easily.*
Some things you need to know *very, very well,* and for such things repetition and practice are the only ways to achieve the automaticity you'll need to ensure rapid, dependable retrieval. Remember, I'm not talking about short-term rehearsal here. Instead, I'm talking about reviewing and practicing information and procedures at periodic intervals over the course of a few days, weeks, or even longer. To achieve automaticity quickly, you should practice quite frequently at first—ideally every day or so. And if you want to remember something for a very long time—perhaps you want to remember Chinese until you can actually go to China—you should continue your review and practice sessions over the course of several months or years.[49]

▶ *If possible, learn things in the contexts in which you'll need to remember them.* The more retrieval cues you have for something you've learned, the more easily you'll recall it when you need it. And the environment in which you're working can provide a variety of retrieval cues.[50] For instance, if you're studying for an important test on hard-to-remember material, you might study in a classroomlike setting—better still, in the actual room in which you'll be taking the test. If you want to remember the steps you need to take if you're treating an accident victim for possible shock, you might create an accident-like setting, complete with a pseudo-victim and the necessary equipment, such as a blanket and a suitable object to elevate the legs. (I'll say more about the importance of real-world settings in my discussion of *transfer* in Chapter 9.)

HELPING OTHERS THINK SMART

You might have a variety of reasons to help other people remember certain information and events—perhaps as a parent, teacher, clinician, or police detective. Following are several strategies that build on ideas we've pursued in this chapter.

▶ *Talk with young children about recent events.* Young children can make better sense of and remember their experiences if you help them capture those experiences in words.[51] With babies and toddlers, you'll probably need to do much of the talking yourself, but as children gain practice in storytelling, they can gradually take over the process. Such questions as "What did we see when we went to the zoo today?" and "What did we do when your teddy bear fell into the hippo pool?" can often get children mentally revisiting and verbally encoding what they've seen and heard. (In case you're curious, after its swim in the hippo pool at the Tucson zoo, my daughter Tina's teddy bear got a couple of good rounds in the washing machine, followed by a day or so hanging by his ears on the clothesline. Even so, he was never quite the same.)

▶ *Don't put words in people's mouths about what they remember.* Thanks to the constructive and reconstructive nature of long-term memory retrieval, people's memories for events sometimes include distortions and, occasionally, complete fabrications. People are more likely to mentally alter what they have—or perhaps *haven't*—experienced if you present post-event ideas that lead them in certain directions. For instance, if you ask "Where were you when So-And-So attacked you?" you're implying both that an attack occurred and that So-And-So was its perpetrator. Instead, keep your biases and hypotheses to yourself by asking such open-ended questions as "What did you see?" and "What happened next?"[52]

▶ ***Remember that confidence doesn't necessarily mean accuracy.*** Some folks are quite confident—even downright cocky—about what they did and did not see and about what did and did not happen. They're especially likely to be confident about recollections that are especially vivid in their minds—flashbulb memories, for instance—and about recollections that are consistent with things they know or believe to be true about the people and places in their lives.[53] Don't be misled by their confidence. Always double-check—better still, triple-check or quadruple-check—what seem to be the "facts."

I can't say this enough times: Human memory is fallible.

Teaching Tips

▶ **Teach students the importance of self-created retrieval cues.** For example, if you want kindergartners to scour their homes for household objects that begin with the letter T—presumably this assignment would be related to phonics instruction—you might help them create little reminder notes that they pin to their shirts or jackets. Or if you want middle school students to remember to bring in signed permission slips for an upcoming field trip, you might say something like this: "Hmm, if you don't bring in your permission slip tomorrow, you won't be able to go to the natural history museum with the rest of us. What might you do today to make sure you don't forget it?" You could follow up your question with a short brainstorming session about various retrieval-cue strategies.

Self-created retrieval cues become especially important as students gain increasing independence in the secondary school years and higher education. Yet not all students develop such cues on their own, perhaps because they haven't yet learned how difficult prospective memory—"remembering" the future—can be. In such cases, you might describe your own strategies for remembering things you need to do—perhaps using the calendar and alarm functions on your computer or cell phone or (as I do) putting notes-to-self in impossible-to-miss locations at home.

Regularly review material that students should remember for the long run. Ideally, such review is spread out over several weeks or, better still, over several months or years.[54] But students won't necessarily respond favorably to the "same old thing," nor should they. Here are three ways you might encourage review while also asking students to do something new:

- Give frequent quizzes—studying for them requires students to review things they've learned within the past few days or weeks.

- Begin a new unit by asking questions that require students to recall relevant information they've previously learned.

- Assign tasks and projects that require students to combine material they're currently studying with things they've learned in the past.[55]

Promote automaticity for information and skills that students should be able to use quickly and easily. As I mentioned earlier, students can achieve automaticity in only one way: practice, practice, practice. However, I'm *not* suggesting that you continually assign drill-and-practice exercises involving isolated facts and procedures. Such activities promote meaning*less* rather than meaning*ful* learning, are often boring, and are unlikely to convince students of the value of the subject matter.[56] A more effective approach is to routinely incorporate basic knowledge and skills into a variety of meaningful and enjoyable activities— problem-solving tasks, group projects, games, brainteasers, and so on.

Give students time to "look" for what they've learned. Some trips down Memory Lane take time—perhaps a few seconds, perhaps a few minutes, perhaps overnight. It's amazing how much people can recall if they have a bit of time to wander—without undue pressure and anxiety—through their long-term memories.

Research in classrooms provides a simple example of how increasing *wait time* after questions can increase students' performance considerably. After teachers ask a student a question, they typically wait one second or less before saying something—perhaps providing the answer, asking an easier question, or posing the same question to a different student. When teachers instead wait at least *three* seconds after asking a question, more students respond, and students are more likely to answer questions correctly. Furthermore, answers are longer and more sophisticated, and students are more likely to support their responses with evidence or logic.[57]

When appropriate, give hints that help students recall or reconstruct what they've learned. For example, if a student asks what the symbol *Au* stands for, you might respond by saying, "In class we talked about *Au* coming from the Latin word *aurum*. Can you remember what *aurum* means?" Another example comes from one of my former teacher interns, Jess Jensen. A student in her eighth-grade history class had been writing about the Battle of New Orleans, a decisive victory for the United States in the War of 1812. The following exchange took place:

Student: Why was the Battle of New Orleans important?

Jess: Look at the map. Where is New Orleans?

The student locates New Orleans.

Jess: Why is it important?

Student: Oh! It's near the mouth of the Mississippi. It was important for controlling transportation up and down the river.

Help students keep their anxiety in check during important tests and other assessments. As you've learned, a great deal of anxiety tends to interfere with successful retrieval of previously learned information and skills. Some students become extremely anxious in test-taking situations, and these students typically get lower test scores than their less-anxious classmates. Test-anxious students appear to be concerned primarily about the *evaluative* aspect of tests: They're worried that authority figures will make negative judgments about them.[58]

Test anxiety is rare in the early grades but increases throughout the elementary school years. Many upper elementary, secondary, and postsecondary students have test anxiety that interferes with their test performance, especially when taking high-stakes tests whose results influence decisions about promotion, graduation, and other significant consequences. Debilitating test anxiety is particularly common in students from minority groups, students with disabilities, and students with a history of academic failure.[59] In fact, anxiety may be at the root of a phenomenon known as *stereotype threat,* in which students from stereotypically low-achieving groups (for instance, females and members of certain minority groups) perform more poorly on tests in certain content areas than they otherwise would simply because they're aware that their group traditionally *does* do poorly in these areas. When students are aware of the unflattering stereotype—and especially when they know that the task they're performing reflects their ability in an important domain—worrisome thoughts intrude into working memory, heart rate and other physiological correlates of anxiety go up, and performance goes down.[60]

Following are several suggestions for helping students keep their anxiety levels in check during important assessments:

- Create assessments that are closely aligned with central curricular objectives.

- Help students master class material and effective study strategies to the point where successful performance on an assessment is highly likely.

- Portray assessments as means through which you can help students improve, rather than as judgments of students' ability and general worth.

- Give pretests that provide both practice and feedback about how to improve.

- Encourage students to do their best but without creating unnecessary anxiety about the consequences of doing poorly.

- Keep an assessment short enough that students can easily complete it within the allotted time.

- Minimize—ideally, eliminate—opportunities for students to compare their performance with that of classmates.

- Make important decisions about students (such as final grades and decisions about promotion) based on numerous small assessments, rather than on only one or two test scores.[61]

Thinking about Thinking: Metacognition

As a species, we human beings can be a bit vain: We like to look at ourselves in mirrors from time to time. As it turns out, we're not the only creatures that can recognize themselves in mirrors. Gorillas and chimpanzees can do it, too, as can elephants, dolphins, and magpies.[1] But we humans are unsurpassed in our ability to look at ourselves *mentally* as well as physically—for instance, to deliberately reflect on our own thought processes. When we think about our own thinking, we're engaging in *metacognition.*

Metacognition is a key function of that *central executive* I spoke of in Chapter 4. You might think of it as the "manager" or "coach" of thinking and learning: It guides our conscious, intentional efforts to learn and remember new information and skills.[2] But just as the coach of a basketball team can be more or less competent in guiding team players to victory, so, too, can our metacognitive abilities be either a help or a hindrance as we learn.

As you've been reading this book, you've presumably already learned a great deal about how you personally can better learn and remember new things. I'm hoping that you've been applying some of what you've learned in your day-to-day activities. For instance, you may now be trying to pay closer attention to important information, and you may be working harder to make sense of new information rather than just mindlessly repeating it.

In this chapter I describe additional things that truly successful learners think and do as they read, listen, and study. I also explain that what people think knowledge *is* can have a huge impact on learning success.

Being a Good Self-Executive: What Metacognition Involves

At the beginning of Chapter 3, I talked about how I used to "read" and supposedly "study" my high school history textbook—how, in particular, I would diligently move my eyes down each page while my mind was somewhere else altogether. Apparently I was thinking that learning had an osmosis quality to it: In accordance with laws of physics, the words and their meanings would readily transport themselves from a high-density location (the textbook) to a considerably less-dense location (my brain). Metacognitively, then, I was pretty naive—I still had a lot to learn about how human beings think, learn, and remember and about how, as a member of the human species myself, *I* could best learn and remember something.

Effective metacognition encompasses both *knowledge* about thinking and learning and *skills* for controlling thinking and learning. For example, it includes such knowledge and skills as the following:

- Having a reasonable sense of what we can realistically learn within a certain timeframe—for example, realizing that it isn't possible to memorize everything in a 200-page book in a single evening

- Planning an approach to a learning task that is likely to be successful—for example, finding a place to read and study where there will be few distractions

- Knowing which learning strategies are effective and which are not—for example, realizing that we're more likely to remember something if we actively try to make sense of it (meaningful learning) than if we mindlessly repeat it over and over (rehearsal)

- Actually using effective learning strategies—for example, taking detailed notes if we're listening to a lengthy, information-packed lecture about a new topic

- Periodically checking ourselves to see how much we currently understand and can remember—for example, stopping after every two or three pages of a textbook to make sure we can recall what we've just read

- Reflecting on previous learning efforts—for example, accurately assessing whether we have fully mastered a new topic or skill

How, as a metacognitively naive high school student, the author read her history textbook.

Source: Adapted from Ormrod, HUMAN LEARNING, p. 351, © 2008. Reproduced by permission of Pearson Education, Inc.

Such knowledge and skills aren't all that critical when we're learning something under the close tutelage of someone who knows more than we do—perhaps a teacher or a more experienced colleague. Ideally, this person can watch over us to make sure we are "getting" whatever topic we're supposed to be mastering. But metacognitive knowledge and skills are critical if we're trying to learn something with little or no direct assistance from anyone else—for instance, if we're reading a textbook or a how-to manual.

At this point in the book, you are, I hope, more metacognitively sophisticated than you were when you began Chapter 1. The following exercise can give you a rough idea of your current level of metacognitive knowledge and skills.

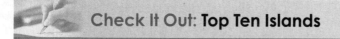

Check It Out: Top Ten Islands

In this exercise, you'll learn the 10 largest islands of the world, listed in order of size from the very largest to the tenth largest. The list doesn't include Australia or Antarctica, both of which are large enough to be categorized as continents rather than islands.[3]

Part 1. Take a quick glance at the list. *Don't try to learn it just yet.*

1. Greenland
2. New Guinea
3. Borneo
4. Madagascar
5. Baffin Island
6. Sumatra
7. Great Britain
8. Honshū
9. Victoria Island
10. Ellesmere Island

Now answer two questions:

1. How quickly and easily do you think you'll be able to learn the list?
2. What approach will you take in learning the list?

. . .

Part 2. Study the list. Take as much time as you need to learn it.

. . .

Part 3. Now answer four more questions:

3. How long did you spend studying the list? A minute? Five minutes? Longer than that?

4. How closely does your answer to Question 3 (how long you spent on the task) match your answer to Question 1 (how quickly you thought you could learn the list)?

5. What strategy or strategies did you use to learn the list? Rehearsal? Elaboration? A mnemonic of some sort?

6. Did you test yourself one or more times to see if your approach was working?

· · ·

Part 4. Cover the list and see if you can remember all 10 islands in the correct order. And answer one final question:

7. Was your approach to learning the list effective? If so, why? If not, why not?

The questions I asked you in the exercise reflect several components of metacognition listed earlier—accurately estimating how much time a learning task will take, planning an approach that's likely to be successful, and so on. But there's another aspect of metacognition I haven't yet mentioned, and this may have influenced what you did or didn't do in the exercise. In particular, metacognition also includes *determining one's purpose(s) and goal(s) for engaging in a learning task*. How much time and effort you put into the exercise no doubt depended on your purposes(s) and goal(s) for reading this book. Possibly you said to yourself, "Hey, I already get her point, and this exercise is going to take a lot more time than I want to spend, so I'm going to skip it." If this was your thinking, I'm guessing that you want to get some useful information from the book without spending all day reading it. For many of my readers, that's quite sensible.

Of course, too, for most of us there's no reason whatsoever to know the 10 largest islands of the world. I confess that I'd be hard pressed to list them all from memory myself. Greenland is the largest, Borneo's somewhere near the top, and Sumatra, Madagascar, and Great Britain are further down the list. Beyond these, I'm pretty clueless unless I look back at the list I just gave you.

Reading for Learning: Being a Metacognitively Astute Reader

When we read a good romance novel or suspense mystery, the plot pulls us in and keeps us reading until we get some kind of resolution—perhaps until Elizabeth Bennet discovers that she really does love Mr. Darcy or until Hercule Poirot finally figures out whodunit on the Orient Express.

Reading textbooks, manuals, and other information-packed nonfiction is, as we might say, an entirely different story. Rarely do we have a spellbinding plot or sympathetic characters to captivate us. Furthermore, we must actually *remember* what we read. In other words, we must *read for learning*.

Reading for learning requires considerable metacognitive skill and often considerable mental effort as well. Good readers—those who understand and effectively remember what they read—tend to engage in certain kinds of metacognitive activities as they read. Here are some common strategies:

- They determine in advance what their purpose is for reading something. For example, depending on the circumstances, they may want to learn the content thoroughly and in great detail or, instead, merely get the general gist and main ideas.

- They read differently depending on what their purpose is. For example, they read something more slowly if they want to learn its contents very, very well than if they need to get only its general gist.

- They identify the points that are most important to learn and remember and focus their time and attention accordingly.

- They draw on their prior knowledge and experiences to help them make sense of what they're reading. For instance, they use things they already know to make logical connections among the various new ideas an author presents.

- They ask themselves questions that they try to answer as they read.

- They envision possible examples and applications in their own lives.

- They critically evaluate what they read.

- They periodically check themselves to make sure they understand and remember what they've read.

- They persist in their efforts to understand when they initially have trouble making sense of something.

- They read with the realization that they may encounter ideas that contradict their current beliefs about a topic and that, accordingly, they may need to modify those beliefs.[4]

In contrast, poor readers—those who have trouble learning and remembering the things they read—do few of these things.

Many of the good-reader characteristics I've just listed involve considerable *self-regulation*, in which readers take charge of their cognitive processes—setting

How the author *should* have read her history textbook.

personal goals for a reading task, monitoring progress toward those goals, working hard to keep themselves on task, and so on. We'll look at various aspects of self-regulation in Chapter 10, but for now I should mention that good readers—and good learners more generally—are typically very much in control of what they're doing both physically and mentally.

Ultimately It's What We Do Inside That Counts: Overt versus Covert Strategies

Some of the learning strategies I describe in this book, such as taking notes, constructing concept maps, and discussing complex topics with peers, are *overt strategies*—strategies that involve observable behaviors. But ultimately the things we do inside our heads—*covert strategies*—are what really count. Only to the extent that we pay attention to and think meaningfully and elaboratively about new information will we be able to effectively remember, apply, and in other ways benefit from our learning experiences.[5]

Nevertheless, going through the motions—engaging in some of the overt behaviors I recommend in this and other chapters—can be good first steps in helping us acquire essential covert strategies. Regularly taking notes can help us focus our attention where it needs to be during lectures and meetings. Creating concept maps can get us in the habit of interrelating and in other ways organizing ideas and concepts related to a new topic. And discussing confusing subject matter with others often helps us clarify and mentally elaborate on it.

Obviously, metacognitive knowledge and skills take time and experience to acquire—typically many years' worth. As children move through the school grades, they gradually get a better handle on what they can reasonably learn within a given time period and how they can most effectively remember it for the long run. As they reach high school and perhaps go on to college, they encounter increasingly challenging subject matter and increasing expectations for do-it-on-your-own learning. Some students acquire enough metacognitive know-how to get good grades in their courses, but others drop by the wayside in part because they *haven't* acquired this know-how. And yet even many college graduates are relatively clueless about their own thinking and learning processes.[6]

As for myself, I don't think I really figured out how I could effectively study and learn until I was in graduate school. This despite the fact that as an undergraduate psychology major, *I had actually taken a course about learning!* Okay, I must admit that at the time (late 1960s), most psychologists' views of learning involved rats, mazes, and pieces of cheese. I don't think the word *metacognition* had even been coined yet.[7] Still, I occasionally wonder how I made it as far as I did in the academic world. Sheer pigheadedness, probably.

What Does It Mean to "Know" Something? Epistemic Beliefs

Please bear with me as I return yet again to my high school days. Not only was I sadly uninformed about how to read my textbooks but I also had some pretty naive notions about what "knowledge" is. I thought that the academic disciplines I was studying—history, science, literature, and so on—were pretty much set in stone, with definite right and wrong ways of looking at things. Experts didn't know everything just yet (they still hadn't figured out how to cure the common cold), but that knowledge was "out there" somewhere just waiting to be found. In the meantime, it was my job as a student to acquire as many facts as I could. I wasn't quite sure what I would do with them all, but I was convinced, deep down, that they would somehow make me a better person.

As people who learn new things every day, we all have ideas about what "knowledge" and "learning" are—ideas that are collectively known as *epistemic beliefs.* Many of these beliefs take the form of implicit rather than explicit knowledge—that is, we aren't consciously aware of them. Nevertheless, these various beliefs we have about knowledge and learning can have significant influences on how we actually *do* learn. Let's look at some examples.

"The Truth Is Out There Somewhere": Beliefs about the Certainty of Knowledge

Some of the knowledge we humans have amassed over the course of civilization is virtually indisputable. As long as we're working in a base-10 number system, two and two will always equal four. And given how human color perception works, grass will, in our eyes, always be green. But many things in our collective knowledge have a *probably* or *maybe* quality to them. For instance, based on the evidence accumulated to date, many cosmologists believe that our universe came into being in an almost instantaneous Big Bang. And archaeological records suggest that Neanderthal man was not our distant ancestor but a separate species that went extinct about 20,000 to 30,000 years ago. We don't know either of these things with 100% certainty. Perhaps we never will, although who can really say with confidence that traveling back in time isn't in the realm of possibility? Thanks to Albert Einstein, we now know—or more accurately, we *think* we know—that even time isn't a sure thing.

In the elementary grades, children tend to think that the absolute truth about virtually any topic is a fixed commodity that is "out there" somewhere, waiting to be discovered. But as they reach adolescence, some (but not all) begin to understand that much of human knowledge is a tentative, dynamic entity that continues to evolve as new discoveries are made. They may also begin to realize that two or more very different perspectives on a topic may each have some merit.[8] For example, as you learned in Chapter 4, psychologists have differing opinions about whether working memory and long-term memory are distinctly different entities or, instead, simply reflect varying activation levels of a single entity. Perhaps some day we'll know what the ultimate "truth" is about human memory, but I personally am not losing sleep over the current lack of closure on this issue.

We adults differ widely in our beliefs about the certainty of knowledge, and these beliefs affect how we study and learn a new topic. If we believe that knowledge about a topic is a fixed, certain entity, we're apt to jump to quick-and-dirty conclusions about it—conclusions that may or may not be accurate. If, on the other hand, we view knowledge as something that continues to evolve and doesn't necessarily involve definitive right and wrong answers, we're more inclined to remain open-minded as we study a topic, to change our minds when the evidence warrants doing so, and to acknowledge that some issues are controversial and not easily resolved.[9]

"Math Is Numbers, History Is Dates": Beliefs about the Simplicity of Knowledge

When we're in elementary school, we learn the basic number facts: $2 + 2 = 4$, $6 \times 7 = 42$, and so on. Later, we learn that the angles in any triangle have a sum of 180 degrees and that for a right triangle, $a^2 + b^2 = c^2$, where a and b are the two sides that meet at the right angle and c is the hypotenuse (you might recognize this as the Pythagorean theorem).

Early on, many of us also learn that "In fourteen hundred and ninety-two, Columbus sailed the ocean blue." Eventually our history instruction includes innumerable other people, places, and dates—who Julius Caesar was, what significant event happened at Waterloo in 1815, and so on.

So is math nothing more than number facts and formulas? Is history nothing more than facts about what happened when and who was on the scene at the time? The answer to both questions is, of course, *no*. Yet the first impressions we get of most academic disciplines would lead us to answer *yes*.

Much of what children learn in elementary school does seem to have a fact-after-fact-after-fact quality to it. Compounding the problem is that many teachers *test* for facts—remembering that Columbus first sailed the ocean in 1492 rather than in, say, 1620 becomes important at quiz time. Not surprisingly, then, most children in the elementary and middle school grades think that knowledge about many topics can be summed up as a collection of discrete, relatively separate facts. Only in the high school grades do some of them begin to realize that truly *knowing* something also involves an understanding of how those various facts might be interconnected—for instance, in the form of cause-and-effect relationships. For many folks, however, the simplistic collection-of-facts view of knowledge persists into adulthood.[10]

If we believe that knowledge about a topic involves nothing more than knowing a bunch of facts, we're likely to focus on memorizing those facts as we study. So, for example, we might worry about memorizing definitions of *biome*, *pulsar*, and *plate tectonics*. Furthermore, we're apt to convince ourselves that we've mastered the topic if we can regurgitate the facts at an appropriate time. In contrast, if we realize that true mastery of a topic includes knowing how everything hangs together to create a logical whole, we're more likely to engage in meaningful learning, organization, and elaboration as we read and study, and we're more likely to evaluate the success of our learning efforts in terms of how well we understand and can apply what we've learned.[11]

"If I Hear It Enough Times, It's Bound to Sink In": Beliefs about the Origins of Knowledge

Where does our knowledge come from? How is it that we know about, say, Julius Caesar's brutal murder or Columbus's first voyage across the Atlantic? Obviously we've depended on certain authority figures—oftentimes school-teachers—to tell us such things.

However, many people—children especially, but also a fair number of adults—take this knowledge-from-authorities perspective too far. In particular, they think of themselves as passive receptacles into which an authority figure "pours" knowledge. Thus all of the work lies in the hands of the authority figure; the person doing the learning can simply sit back and wait for it to sink in.[12]

As an example, a teacher friend of mine once complained about the passive approach many of her students were taking in her eighth-grade math classes. Students frequently insisted that it was *her* job to present new concepts in such a way that they would "get it" immediately and remember it forever. If they didn't catch on right away, it was *her* fault. She described one occasion when she was trying to explain a particular concept to a student named Jason. She asked Mark, the student sitting next to Jason, to watch what she was doing and listen to what she was saying. "I don't need to," Mark responded. "After you're done explaining it to Jason, you can come and explain it to *me*."[13]

As I hope I convinced you in Chapter 3, we human beings are not passive sponges but, instead, active builders of knowledge. Thus, we must ultimately depend on *ourselves* to acquire any meaningful understanding of a topic. Such an active, constructive epistemic belief increases the odds that we'll work hard to make sense of what we're learning—for instance, by deriving our own inferences from new ideas, generating our own examples of new concepts, and revising our current understandings when new and credible information indicates that we should do so.[14]

"Father Knows Best": Criteria for Determining Truth

We don't necessarily want to take everything we hear or read at face value, of course. Some of it might be a bit iffy, and some of it is apt to be downright wrong. So how do we know when we have the real scoop? Here again epistemic beliefs come into the picture. As young children, we relied largely on our parents, teachers, and other adults as infallible fountains of wisdom. And, of course, our dependence on them made sense for those tried-and-true bits of information that our species has known with reasonable certainty for centuries.

As we grew older and delved into more complex and controversial topics, such authority figures couldn't always be relied on to give us accurate information. Neither our parents nor our teachers knew everything there was to know about every conceivable topic. In fact, it would be unreasonable to expect *any* single individual to be a walking encyclopedia. Accordingly, many of us became increasingly judgmental—and I mean that in a good way—about what we were reading and hearing.[15]

Unfortunately, some adults continue to be stuck in the ____-knows-best mode—fill in the blank with "father," "teacher," "textbook," "Internet website," or some other authoritylike source.[16] When we believe that something is probably true if it comes from an apparent expert, we're apt to accept it without question. But in this day and age, people across the world claim to be authorities on topics they know little or nothing about. In my own experience as a long-time teacher of psychology, I could tell you many horror stories about self-proclaimed "experts" spewing misinformation about psychology all over the planet. I'll spare you the details—you probably have enough stories of your own.

As adults, we best serve ourselves if we judge the validity of information based not on where it comes from but on its logical and scientific merit. Here I'm talking about *critical thinking,* a topic we'll look at in depth in Chapter 8.

"Either You Have It or You Don't": Beliefs about the Speed of Learning

I recall a straight-A's college classmate who claimed that she got all of her studying done during a single 2-hour period after dinner every night. I was quite envious, as I usually spent many hours poring over my textbooks and class notes and yet could muster only B's.

I also recall a guy in the graduating class ahead of me who was rumored to have a "photographic memory." Friends said that he could read an entire textbook in a single evening and easily recall every page. Given what I have since learned about human memory, I now find that claim hard to believe. I can't totally discount it, of course—as I've said, we psychologists certainly haven't yet discovered everything there is to know about human memory.

Regardless of whether these stories were accurate or highly exaggerated versions of the truth, we know from our everyday experiences that some people learn faster than others, and probably for a variety of reasons. But we also differ in our beliefs about how fast learning is *in general.* Some of us believe that learning is going to happen quickly or not at all—either we get it or we don't, and we'll know fairly quickly one way or the other. Others of us instead realize that truly mastering a topic can take considerable time and effort.[17]

Given what you've already learned about learning and memory, you can probably predict what I'm going to say next: A belief in learning as a process that takes time and effort is more likely to be productive. If we have the naive notion that learning happens quickly in an all-or-nothing fashion, we're apt to believe that we've learned something before we really have—perhaps after only a single reading of a textbook. We're also apt to give up in the face of initial failure and to express discouragement or dislike regarding whatever topic we're studying. If, instead, we believe that learning is a gradual process that often involves hard work, we're likely to use a wide variety of learning strategies—organization, elaboration, mnemonics, and so on—and to persist until we've made sense of whatever we're studying.[18]

"I Don't Have Any Math Genes": Beliefs about the Nature of Learning Ability

Psychologists have argued long and hard about the nature of intelligence and about the relative roles of heredity and environment in determining its development. With or without a background in psychology, virtually everyone has an opinion on the matter. Some of us think that people are just naturally "gifted" or "slow," perhaps in general or perhaps with respect to a particular subject area—math, say, or music. Others of us are more optimistic, believing that learning ability can and does improve with effort and practice.[19]

Once again, our beliefs influence what we do on the inside and how well we perform on the outside. If we think that intelligence and learning ability are fixed commodities, we quickly give up on challenges we can't immediately surmount. In contrast, if we think that our ability to learn something is under our control, we're apt to pursue a variety of new learning opportunities, and we'll try, try again until we've achieved mastery.[20]

I discuss intelligence in greater detail in Chapter 10. But for now, I must reiterate a point I made in Chapter 5: People who learn and remember effectively are *strategic* learners. If I didn't believe that intelligence and learning ability are *things you can acquire,* I wouldn't be writing this book.

But I Studied So Hard!
The Illusion of Knowing

In the days when I was a full-time college professor, a student would occasionally show up at my office door expressing frustration with a low test score. "I studied so hard!" the student might tell me. "I knew the material *really well*. I think I'm just a bad test taker." I would invite the student to sit down, and we'd go over the troublesome items. But then I'd put the test aside and ask the student to explain what he or she knew about one of the topics covered on the test. Almost invariably the student would hem and haw a bit—"Well, it's like . . . well, I mean . . . I just don't know how to put it in words." After some patient probing on my part, it usually became clear that, in fact, the student had only vague understandings of some ideas and incorrect understandings of others.

Sure, a few of these students might have been trying to con me into giving them a good grade when they hadn't done diddly to prepare for the test. But I'm convinced that most of them had studied long and hard. For them, it was a simple equation: Number of hours studied = amount of knowledge acquired. If for some reason you're underlining or highlighting parts of this book you want to remember, please *don't* mark the preceding equation, because it's wrong. Studying many hours but doing it ineffectively—mindlessly copying textbook material word for word, for instance, or repeating definitions aloud without trying to make sense of them—can lead us to believe we've learned things we really *haven't* learned. In other words, it can lead to an *illusion of knowing*. And when we erroneously believe we've mastered something, naturally we'll stop studying it before we should.[21]

We're more likely to have an illusion of knowing—to think we've mastered something we haven't mastered at all—if the subject matter is especially challenging for us or if we had little or no knowledge about the topic before we started to study it.[22] Our epistemic beliefs come into play as well. If we have an overly simplistic notion of what "knowledge" is—for example, if we believe that mastering a topic involves nothing more than memorizing definitions and other discrete facts—we're almost certain to learn only a small fraction of what we really should be learning. We're also likely to be quite puzzled when, as a result, we do poorly on an exam.[23]

People aren't always accurate judges of what they know and don't know.

Source: Adapted from Ormrod, HUMAN LEARNING, p. 365, © 2008. Reproduced by permission of Pearson Education, Inc.

Becoming a More Metacognitive Learner

In earlier chapters I've offered a variety of recommendations for learning and remembering things more effectively. These recommendations have, I hope, enhanced your own metacognitive knowledge and skills and, if applicable, also enabled you to help other people become more metacognitively astute. In the following sections I offer additional metacognitive strategies.

THINKING SMART

Truly effective learners are *intentional* learners—learners who are consciously and energetically engaged in cognitive and metacognitive activities aimed specifically at thinking about and learning something.[24] Intentional learners identify specific goals they want to accomplish as they learn, develop a plan for achieving those goals, deliberately use effective strategies as they study, and regularly check themselves to be sure they understand and can remember what they've tried to learn.

In addition, effective learners have fairly sophisticated epistemic beliefs. They realize that human beings do not yet know—and may *never* know—certain things about the world and that mastery of many topics involves acquiring a complex body of interrelated concepts and ideas. Thus, gaining true expertise in any subject area is apt to be an ongoing, life-long process.

To supplement my recommendations in previous chapters, then, I offer several suggestions.

► *Identify your purpose(s) and goal(s) for learning something, and adjust your learning and study strategies accordingly.* Sometimes you need to know something "cold." For example, if you were training to be an emergency paramedic, you would need to know how to treat people experiencing a grand mal seizure or diabetic shock *very, very well.* At other times mastery is desirable but not a matter of life and death. This would be the case if, say, you were studying for an exam in a college class. On still other occasions, you might have little or nothing to lose if you don't do well. With this in mind, you might not have spent much time or effort on my "Top Ten Islands" exercise earlier in the chapter.

But it's not just a matter of how much time and effort you expend on a learning task. You must also choose learning strategies appropriate for your goal(s). For instance, if an instructor says that an upcoming quiz will require you to know certain definitions word for word (and for the record, I *don't* recommend this kind of quiz), you had better learn those definitions exactly as they were given to you. If, instead, the instructor says that the quiz will require you to apply what you've learned to new situations, then rote memorization of definitions will do you no good. Instead, you need to gain a genuine understanding of the material, and so you should engage in meaningful learning and elaboration as you study.

► *Regularly monitor your comprehension, both while you're studying and at a later time.* Effective learners regularly engage in *comprehension monitoring*— that is, they periodically check themselves to see if they are understanding and remembering what they've been reading or hearing, and they take steps to remediate any comprehension difficulties.[25] Here are examples of what you might do:

■ Try to recall and explain the things you've read or heard within the past 5 or 10 minutes.

- Try to recall and explain the same things a few days later.

- Reread sections for which you have little or no memory (perhaps your mind was elsewhere when you were supposedly "reading" them).

- Ask yourself and then answer specific questions about the topic; include questions that require you to *elaborate* on what you've learned.

- Try to explain what you've learned to someone else.

- Try to identify your own examples or applications of new concepts and ideas.

- Create a study group in which you and one or more friends can test one another. (However, be careful that you don't take other group members' explanations as "fact"—they might be wrong!)

- Seek clarification of things you don't understand—for instance, ask an instructor or knowledgeable peer, or search for alternative explanations on reputable Internet websites.[26]

It's especially important that you engage in comprehension monitoring not only immediately but also several hours, days, or weeks later. Remember, things stored in long-term memory don't necessarily last forever. Even if they're still in there, they may be hard to retrieve unless you periodically revisit them.[27]

▶ *Recognize that true mastery of a topic often takes time and persistence.* If you think that learning any new topic should be quick and easy, get over it! To truly master a topic, you're probably going to have to work hard, and you must persevere when you come up against the inevitable roadblocks to your understanding. Some people—many East Asians and Asian Americans, for example—seem to know this already, and their dogged persistence in their studies enables them to achieve higher-than-average levels at school and in the workplace. But other people—and I include many North Americans in this category—quickly conclude that they simply "don't have what it takes" to master math, quantum physics, or other notoriously difficult subject areas.[28] Certainly your genetic heritage will have an influence on how quickly you learn something, but rarely will it *prohibit* you from learning something.

The bottom line: No pain, not much gain. But one form of hard work can minimize the pain: *metacognitively smart* hard work.

HELPING OTHERS THINK SMART

Rarely are metacognitive knowledge and skills explicitly taught. But they *can* be taught, and people almost invariably learn more effectively as a result. Many of the recommendations I've offered in previous *Helping Others Think Smart* and *Teaching Tips* sections are effective in part because they enhance people's metacognitive knowledge and skills. Following are two additional recommendations.

▶ *Offer suggestions about how to plan for and carry out independent learning.* For example, you might suggest that people:

- Determine in advance what they want to accomplish in their reading and studying.

- Identify appropriate times and places in which they can read and study effectively—for instance, times of the day in which they are likely to be mentally alert and locations in which they'll have minimal distractions.

- Identify learning strategies that will help them achieve their goal(s).

- Assess the effectiveness of their learning efforts—for instance, by asking themselves questions about what they've just read or studied.[29]

▶ *Communicate that acquiring knowledge is a dynamic, ongoing process— that one never completely "knows" something.* When I teach college courses, sometimes students approach me to say that they've already studied certain topics on my course syllabi. For example, when I list Jean Piaget's theory of cognitive development as a topic we'll address in a unit on child development, a student might complain, "I've already had Piaget." The student's not-so-subtle meaning is "Been there, done that, don't need to do it again." Well, I can tell you (and I usually tell the student) that I've been studying Piaget's work since my undergraduate years in the late 1960s and *still* don't know all there is to know about it. Piaget was a prolific researcher for six decades of the twentieth century. He published dozens of books and articles describing his findings, and each one offers new insights into children's thinking.

Many folks refer to the current era in human history as the Information Age: What we humans collectively know about our physical and social worlds increases exponentially every year, and occasionally we need to revise our understandings of certain phenomena as new evidence comes to light. There's *always* something new to learn about a topic.

It's important, too, that the people with whom you're working understand—as you yourself now understand—that they can learn a great many things if they invest a reasonable amount of effort over a reasonable time period using reasonably effective strategies.[30] Excuses such as "I inherited my mother's lousy math genes" or "I really don't have the mind for auto mechanics" just won't cut it.

Teaching Tips

Actively nurture students' metacognitive awareness and self-reflection. Young children have only a limited ability to think about their own thought processes.[31] Even so, you can do several things to help preschoolers and children in the early elementary grades reflect a bit on how they think and learn:

- Talk often about thinking processes ("I *wonder* if . . ." "Do you *remember* when . . .?").

- Provide opportunities for students to experiment with their memories—for instance, by playing "I'm taking a trip and am going to pack ___," in which each student repeats items previously mentioned and then adds another item to the list.

- Introduce and model simple learning and memory strategies—for instance, oral rehearsal of spelling words, repeated practice of important fine-motor skills, and pinning permission slips on jackets to remind students to get their parents' signatures.[32]

With age and experience, students become increasingly capable of self-reflection. The trick is to get them in the *habit* of thinking metacognitively. For example, you might ask struggling students questions such as "How can you make sure you'll remember what you read in your textbook?" and "What things do you do when you study for a test?" Metacognitively sophisticated students can describe in-the-head strategies—for instance, they might say that they think of new examples of a concept or ask themselves questions about the topic. Less metacognitively astute students are likely to describe only outside behaviors, such as copying class notes or making flashcards. Helping the latter group turn their reflections inward—to their own thought processes—is an essential step in helping them develop their metacognitive knowledge and skills.

Explicitly teach both covert and overt learning strategies throughout the curriculum. The collective results of many, many research studies indicate that learners at all grade and ability levels *can* be taught effective learning and study strategies, with consequent improvements in their memory, classroom performance, and academic achievement. But I'm not talking about a specific "study skills" course offered in, say, ninth grade or the first year of college. Instead, strategy instruction seems to be most effective when it's taught in conjunction with all academic topics—for instance, teaching math-learning strategies in a math class, history-learning strategies in a history class, and so on.[33]

With this point in mind, I offer several, more specific recommendations:

- When teaching specific academic content, simultaneously teach students how to effectively study and remember that content.

- Suggest a wide variety of strategies—taking notes, thinking of new examples, forming mnemonics, summarizing, taking self-check quizzes, and so on—each of which is apt to be useful in different situations and for different purposes.

- Model covert strategies by thinking aloud about topics—for example, by saying things such as "This idea reminds me of something we studied last month" and "What new examples of this concept can we think of?"

- Ask students to share their personal study strategies with their classmates.

- Help students understand why and how new strategies can help them.

- Have students regularly practice new strategies with a variety of learning tasks.

- Guide students' early attempts to use new strategies—for instance, by providing note-taking forms or giving suggestions of mnemonics they might use for hard-to-remember facts.

- Occasionally ask students to study instructional material in pairs or small cooperative learning groups.[34]

Teach and nurture reading comprehension skills in all academic subject areas. As students progress through the grade levels, and especially as they move into the secondary school and college years, their academic success becomes increasingly dependent on their ability to learn from textbooks and other reading materials. Thus teachers of all academic disciplines—science, history, geography, math, and so on—should provide some guidance in how to read school subject matter effectively.

Effective methods for teaching reading comprehension would fill an entire book all by themselves, but here I can at least offer a few general strategies that researchers have found to be effective:

- Consistently communicate the importance of actively thinking about *and making sense of* reading material.

- Encourage students to recall what they already know (or think they know) about a topic before they begin to read.

- Model effective strategies by thinking aloud about particular passages of text ("Hmm, let me see if I can explain what I've just read about metamorphosis in my own words").

- Choose works of fiction and nonfiction that students are likely to find interesting and engaging.

- Conduct group discussions about stories and novels.

- Have students work in pairs to read a passage of text, with the two students taking turns in reading aloud, summarizing what they've read, and predicting what they're likely to learn next.

- Convene students in small groups to read works of nonfiction, and have them take turns serving as "teacher" in which they ask teacherlike questions of other group members ("What does the author mean by _____?" "What do you think will happen next?" "Can someone summarize what we've read so far?").[35]

Notice that the last three of my suggestions involve students talking with one another about what they're reading. Peer-interactive methods have benefits that students might not get from more solitary reading activities. In particular, by tossing around possible interpretations of what they are reading, students often model effective reading comprehension strategies for one another. And as they ask one another teacher-style questions about what they're reading, they begin to direct such questions inward as well. Ultimately they get in the habit of prompting *themselves* to clarify and summarize what they're reading and to make reasonable predictions about what they might read next.[36]

▶ **Especially when working with older children, adolescents, or adults, foster sophisticated beliefs about the nature of knowledge.** Young children undoubtedly gain comfort in knowing that the authority figures in their lives—parents, teachers, book authors, and so on—are reliable sources for many simple facts about their world.[37] But the more the children progress beyond the basic foundations of a particular subject area, the more they benefit from understanding that learning involves actively constructing an integrated, cohesive set of ideas and that even experts sometimes disagree about the "facts."[38] Following are examples of things you might do:

■ Explicitly describe learning as an active, ongoing process of finding interconnections among ideas and constructing an increasingly complex understanding of the world.

■ Have students address complex issues and problems—even in mathematics—that have no clear-cut right or wrong answers.

■ Teach strategies for gathering data and testing competing hypotheses about a particular phenomenon or event.

■ Present puzzling phenomena to demonstrate that students' current understandings—and in some cases even those of experts in the field—don't yet adequately explain all of human experience.[39]

Provide strategies and criteria that students can use to effectively monitor their own learning. The comprehension-monitoring strategies I suggested in the earlier *Thinking Smart* section are certainly applicable in your work with students. Here are four additional possibilities:

■ Have students set specific goals and objectives for a study session and then describe achievements related to each one.

■ Have students formulate questions before a lesson or reading assignment that they then try to answer as they go along.

■ Provide specific criteria that students can use to judge their learning; possibly include students in the development of these criteria.

■ Provide self-test questions that students can use to assess their current understandings of class material.[40]

Common Sense Isn't Always Sensible: Reasoning and Critical Thinking

Let's briefly revisit two long-term memory storage processes I introduced in Chapter 5: elaboration and organization. We better learn and remember new ideas if we embellish on them in some way, perhaps by drawing inferences from them (elaboration). Also, we better learn and remember a body of information about a particular topic if we pull related ideas into an integrated, cohesive whole that includes cause-and-effect relationships and other interconnections among specific facts (organization). We must be careful, however, that our inferences and organizational schemes *make sense*—in other words, that they are logical, valid ones. Deriving appropriate conclusions and interconnections regarding the things we learn involves a number of processes collectively known as *reasoning*.

Not only must we be careful about drawing valid conclusions from the new information we acquire but we must also ascertain whether the information *itself* is valid. Let's face it, the things we read and hear in various media—books, television, the Internet, and so on—aren't always true. Accordingly, we must carefully scrutinize what we read and hear to determine its accuracy, credibility, and general soundness. When we do so, we're engaging in *critical thinking*.

Reasoning and critical thinking are complex, multifaceted mental activities that emerge gradually over the course of childhood, adolescence, and adulthood. Even as adults, the great majority of folks never completely master them.[1] Many adults take the information they acquire from certain acquaintances and media sources at face value, thinking that "If so-and-so said it, it must be true."

To be genuinely intelligent learners in this Information Age, we need to separate the wheat from the chaff—to separate what is accurate and useful from what is not. I don't pretend that, in a single book chapter, I can give you all of the skills you'll need to recognize every misrepresentation, distortion, and other informational garbage for what it is. But I'm hoping that the processes and common pitfalls I describe in this chapter can help you sharpen your existing reasoning and critical thinking skills and also, perhaps, sharpen these skills in other people as well.

Avoiding the Garden Path: Critically Analyzing Arguments

By *argument*, I don't mean a heated debate in which people take opposing positions and scream at one another until someone emerges a winner. Instead, I mean a deliberate attempt to persuade someone to think or behave in a particular way. As an example, try the following exercise.

Check It Out: Eradicold Pills

It's autumn, and the days are becoming increasingly chilly. You see the following advertisement in the newspaper:

> Aren't you tired of sniffles and runny noses all winter? Tired of always feeling less than your best? Get through a whole winter without colds. Take Eradicold Pills as directed.[2]

Should you go out and buy a box of Eradicold Pills?

I hope you weren't tempted to purchase Eradicold Pills, because the ad provides no proof that they reduce cold symptoms. It simply includes the suggestion to "take Eradicold Pills as directed" within the context of a discussion of undesirable symptoms—a frequently used technique in persuasive advertising.

The common expression "being led down the garden path" means being deceived into believing something that isn't true. The path is enticing but leads us in an unproductive direction. Our world is full of people who would like to lead us down various garden paths, and so we must learn to scrutinize their messages carefully.

Sometimes we analyze other people's arguments by using common sense and intuition—that is, by relying on personal insights that almost immediately strike us as being logical and reasonable.[3] Common sense and intuition serve us well on many occasions, but they can sometimes lead us astray. For example, it makes "sense" that the sun revolves around the Earth. After all, we regularly see the sun rise in the east, move slowly across the sky, and eventually set in the west. In the sixteenth and seventeenth centuries, Nicolaus Copernicus and Galileo Galilei had little success in convincing their contemporaries that the sun, rather than the Earth, was the local center of planetary action.

Critical thinkers are much fussier about the criteria they use to evaluate other people's arguments. Common sense simply won't do. Instead, they consider criteria such as these:

- The argument proceeds through a logical train of thought, such that if one thing is true, another thing must definitely be true as well.

- The argument is supported with indisputable evidence.

- The argument presents all relevant facts, including information that might potentially lead to a different conclusion.

- The argument identifies and convincingly rebuts opposing points of view.[4]

In certain situations, of course, we want to be on the giving (rather than receiving) end of persuasive arguments. That is, we want to convince others that a particular point of view or way of doing things is the best one. On such occasions, we'll be more persuasive if we, too, follow a logical train of thought, provide rock-solid evidence to support our position, provide *all* information relevant to the issue, and effectively dismantle opposing viewpoints.

Applying these four criteria to our own and others' arguments takes considerable practice and, ideally, guidance from expert arguers. But in the following section, I give you a general feel for what the first criterion—logical reasoning—entails.

One Thing Leads to Another: Logical Reasoning

Logicians and psychologists distinguish between two systematic forms of logical reasoning. One—deductive reasoning—is quite dependable if certain conditions are met. The other—inductive reasoning—is more chancy but comes in handy when deductive reasoning isn't possible.

If This, Then That: Deductive Reasoning

Deductive reasoning begins with one or more *premises*. These premises are statements or assumptions that the arguer assumes to be true. Reasoning then proceeds logically from these premises to conclusions that must also be true. For example,

> If all tulips are plants, (Premise 1)
>
> And if all plants produce energy through photosynthesis, (Premise 2)
>
> Then all tulips must produce energy through photosynthesis. (Conclusion)

To the extent that the premises are false, the conclusions may also be false. For example,

> If all tulips are platypuses, (Premise 1)
>
> And if all platypuses produce energy through spontaneous combustion, (Premise 2)
>
> Then all tulips must produce energy through spontaneous combustion. (Conclusion)

The if-this-then-that logic is the same in both examples. We reach an erroneous conclusion in the second example (we conclude that tulips are likely to burst into flame at unpredictable times) only because both of our premises are also

Figure 8.1

Why All Tulips Undergo Spontaneous Combustion

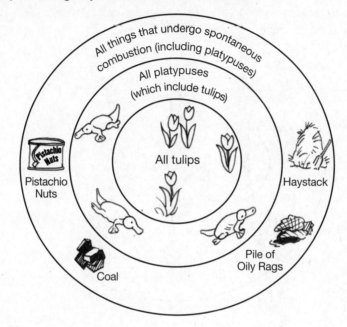

erroneous. The Venn diagram in Figure 8.1 visually illustrates the logic in the tulips–combustion situation.

Sometimes the premises are true but the reasoning is unsound. For example:

If some tulips are red, (Premise 1)

And if some tulips grow in gardens, (Premise 2)

Then some red tulips must grow in gardens. (Conclusion)

There is nothing in the two premises, separately or in combination, to guarantee that some red tulips must inevitably grow in gardens. Perhaps, instead, only nonred tulips grow in gardens (where they might be in the company of other kinds of flowers, possibly including some red nontulips) while all red tulips grow elsewhere—say, in flowerpots or cow pastures (see the Venn diagram in Figure 8.2). I'm not saying that red tulips *can't* grow in gardens, only that the conclusion that they *must* doesn't follow logically from

Figure 8.2
How It Is Possible That We Might Never Find a Red Tulip in a Garden

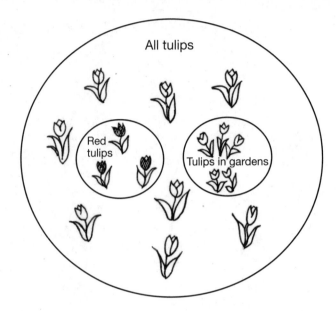

the two premises we're given. The flawed reasoning becomes more obvious in another some-things conclusion following the same logic:

If some flowers are tulips, (Premise 1)

And if some flowers grow on trees, (Premise 2)

Then some tulips must grow on trees. (Conclusion)

As you well know, tulips *don't* grow on trees; they grow from bulbs in the ground.

Not all forms of deductive reasoning involve premises about *all-things-are-this* or *some-things-are-that*. For instance, deductive reasoning might instead involve making comparisons. Here are two examples:

If the Pacific Ocean is larger than the Atlantic Ocean, (Premise 1)

And if the Atlantic Ocean is larger than the Mediterranean Sea, (Premise 2)

Then the Pacific must be larger than the Mediterranean. (Conclusion)

If mongooses are heavier than platypuses, (Premise 1)

And if platypuses are heavier than hippopotamuses, (Premise 2)

Then mongooses must be heavier than hippopotamuses. (Conclusion)

In each example, the two premises—if true—lead logically and indisputably to the conclusion that follows. The premises in the first example are accurate; thus, the conclusion is also accurate. As for the second example, the veracity of the first premise is debatable (different species of mongooses weigh different amounts), and the second premise is definitely incorrect. Thus the conclusion that logically follows (mongooses outweigh hippopotamuses) is absurd.

Our usual downfall in deductive reasoning is that we have trouble separating logic from reality.[5] For instance, we just can't get past the fact that tulips *don't* undergo spontaneous combustion, the fact that many red tulips *do* grow in gardens, or the fact that hippopotamuses are considerably heavier than most other animals.

Generalizing from Few to Many: Inductive Reasoning

Inductive reasoning begins not with a preestablished truth or assumption but instead with an observation. For instance, as a baby in a high chair many years ago, you may have observed that if you held a cracker in front of you and then let go of it, it fell to the floor. "Hmm," you may have thought, "what happens if I do that again?" So you took another cracker from your high chair tray, held it in front of you, and then released it. This cracker, too, fell to the floor. You followed the same procedure with several more crackers, and the result was always the same: The cracker traveled in a downward direction. Eventually you may have performed the same action on other things—blocks, rattles, peas, milk, and so on—and invariably observed the same result. No doubt you eventually drew the conclusion that all things fall when dropped—your first inkling about a force called *gravity*. (You may also have concluded that dropping things from your high chair greatly annoyed your parents, but that's another matter.)

More generally, *inductive reasoning* involves using specific instances or occurrences to draw conclusions about entire classes of objects or events. For instance, if we plant tulip bulbs several years in a row and always see the neighborhood deer chew off the flower buds, we might conclude that deer find tulips quite tasty (see Figure 8.3). And biologists have consistently observed that, despite generally mammal-type characteristics (body hair, warm-bloodedness, mammary glands), female platypuses lay eggs rather than give birth to live young (which other mammals do). Thus biologists have quite reasonably concluded that platypuses are anomalies in the mammalian world.

In our everyday reasoning, we frequently make use of inductive reasoning. In fact, it seems to be human nature to generalize from our experiences. Even babies as young as 3 or 4 months old do it from time to time.[6]

The main weakness of inductive reasoning is that, even if all our specific observations about a particular category are correct, our generalizations about the category as a whole may *not* be correct. For example, if the only tulips we ever see are red ones, we may conclude (incorrectly) that tulips can *only* be red.

Figure 8.3
How Inductive Reasoning Might Lead Us to Conclude That Deer Are Fond of Tulips

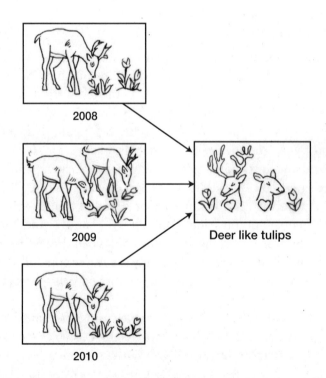

2008

2009

Deer like tulips

2010

And if we have two or three unpleasant experiences with individuals of a particular social or ethnic group—say, members of a certain political party or people from a certain country—we may draw inaccurate conclusions that we unfairly apply to all members of the group. Such inductive inferences provide the basis for racism, homophobia, and other undue, counterproductive prejudices.

Doing the Math: Quantitative Reasoning

For some people, the very thought of working with numbers ratchets up the anxiety level several notches. Many math-anxious folks are convinced that they are mathematical dunces, genetically endowed with the math IQ of, say, a platypus. Anything with numbers turns their thinking into mental mush. Well, okay, maybe I'm exaggerating a bit about their states of mind, but for some of these individuals I'm probably not too far off the mark.[7]

Yet some forms of reasoning and critical thinking do involve numbers. Try to get your own math anxiety under control as you tackle the next exercise.

Check It Out: **Car Repair**

You have a beat-up old car and have invested several thousand dollars to get it in working order. You can sell the car in its present condition for $1,500, or you can invest a couple thousand dollars more on repairs and then sell it for $3,000. What should you do?[8]

You've already invested a considerable amount of money in the car, and probably a considerable amount of blood, sweat, and tears as well. Doesn't it make sense to continue what you've started and get the car in tip-top shape? Many people would think so.[9] But the past is over and done with. If you do the math—simple addition and subtraction—it makes more sense to sell the car now. Making $2,000 worth of repairs and selling the car for $3,000 gets you only $1,000—$500 less than you would otherwise.

Unfortunately, quantitative reasoning isn't always so straightforward. One particular source of difficulty for many people is probabilities, which, by their very nature, are a source of uncertainty and doubt.[10]

What Are the Odds?
Reasoning about Probabilities

When reasoning involves probabilities, we can be not only illogical but also a bit superstitious. In the following exercise, you can check out your own skill at probabilistic thinking.

Check It Out: **Roll of the Die**

You have a few minutes to kill and decide to try your luck at rolling dice. You take a typical six-sided die, one with each of the numbers 1 through 6 represented with the appropriate number of pips (dots) on its six sides. You know for a fact that the die isn't loaded—it's not heavier on one side than another. You start to roll, and in 30 rolls you get the following results:

5 3 3 6 1 2 3 6 5 2 1 1 5 5 3 2 2 6 2 1 5 3 3 3 5 1 2 6 5 1

What are the odds that you'll get a 4 on the next roll?[11]

The probability of rolling a 4 on an evenly balanced die is one in six. The outcomes of previous rolls are irrelevant, because each roll is independent of the others. But when a 4 hasn't shown up even once in 30 rolls, many people believe that a 4 is long overdue and so greatly overestimate its probability—a logical error known as the *gambler's fallacy*.

Even many well-educated adults have trouble thinking logically about probabilities. For example, consider the following problem:

Which one of the following options would you prefer?
a.   A 25% chance of winning $30
b.   A 20% chance of winning $45

Logically, Option b is the smarter choice: With just a small reduction in the odds, you can potentially win 50% more than you would in Option a. Yet in a study with college students, a sizable minority (42%) went for the less profitable option.[12] And a majority of adults will choose a sure thing rather than take any risk at all. For example, consider this problem:

Which one of the following options would you prefer?
a.   A sure win of $30
b.   An 80% chance of winning $45

About three-fourths of college students chose $30, even though the odds of winning 50% more than that sum were quite good.[13]

Yet if a potential outcome is truly fabulous, we can be enticed to go for the long shot. Occasionally I buy a lottery ticket if the PowerBall jackpot reaches $100 million or more. That kind of money would put me, my kids, any future grandkids, and a few of my favorite charities deep in the lap of luxury for a very long time. If I do the math, however, I usually find that, probability-wise, my chances of winning are so slim that I'd be better off investing the one-dollar ticket price in an interest-bearing bank account.

One challenge we face when dealing with probabilities is separating numbers from our feelings about them. As an example, here's another problem for you to ponder:

> Imagine that your country is preparing for an outbreak of a new strain of influenza, which is expected to kill 600 people. Government officials must choose between one of two programs:
>
> If Program A is adopted, exactly 200 people will be saved.
>
> If Program B is adopted, there is a one-third probability that 600 people will be saved but a two-thirds probability that no one will be saved.

In a study with college students, almost three-fourths of the participants opted for Program A—a happy "sure thing" for 200 folks even though 400 others are doomed to certain death.[14] But let's now consider two other program options for the influenza problem:

> If Program C is adopted, exactly 400 people will die.
>
> If Program D is adopted, there is a one-third probability that nobody will die but a two-thirds probability that 600 people will die.

If you look closely, you can see that Program C has the same outcome as Program A, and Program D has the same outcome as Program B. Yet with a simple change in wording, the reworded version of Program B became the overwhelming favorite over the reworded Program A.[15] The odds are the same in all four programs: Each offers a one-third probability of living and two-thirds probability of dying. But in the two choice situations, the options that put a more optimistic spin on things—focusing more on who might live rather than who might die—are the hands-down favorites.

Digging Up the Facts: Scientific Reasoning

At one time or another in our schooling, we all learn about the *scientific method,* a process of acquiring new information that involves an orderly sequence of steps such as these:

1. Identifying a question to be answered

2. Forming a hypothesis regarding the answer to the question

3. Gathering data relevant to the hypothesis

4. Analyzing the data to determine whether they are consistent with the hypothesis

5. Drawing a conclusion

Many people think of the scientific method as a process carried out only by very bright (perhaps somewhat nerdy) individuals who wear white lab coats and work in secluded laboratories. But in fact, we're *all* scientists who continually strive to answer questions in our own lives. Why can't I get any hot water in the shower this morning? Why did Melissa snub me the other day? Who or what has been destroying my tulips? In addressing such questions, we often form hypotheses about potential answers, gather and interpret data, and draw conclusions. Okay, so maybe we don't publish our findings in esoteric scientific journals, but we're scientists just the same.

This is not to say that we're always *good* scientists. In fact, we can be quite sloppy in our data gathering and conclusion drawing.[16] Here I describe four strategies that make for a better scientist—and also for a more critical thinker.

Looking for What You Don't Want to Find: Seeking Contradictory Evidence

Good scientists and critical thinkers don't just look for evidence that confirms what they believe to be true. They also look for evidence that might *disprove* their hypothesis. To see what I mean, try the following exercise.

Check It Out: The Four-Card Problem

Joe Schmoe has an unusual deck of cards: Each card has a letter on one side and a number on the other side. Joe tells you that the cards follow a certain rule:

If a card has a vowel on one side, it must have an even number on the other side.

But when it comes to the truth, Joe hasn't always been a dependable guy. Four of the cards in the deck are shown here. Which card or cards must you turn over to determine whether Joe is telling you the truth about the rule?[17]

$$\boxed{E} \quad \boxed{8} \quad \boxed{M} \quad \boxed{5}$$

You probably picked the E card. Certainly you would want to confirm that this card does, in fact, have an even number on the flip side—if not, Joe's rule isn't correct. Did you also pick the 8 card, looking for a vowel? If so, you wasted your time, because a card with an even number on one side and a consonant on the other doesn't violate the rule. The M card, too, is irrelevant. But here's the clincher: In addition to turning over the E card, you must also turn over the 5 card. If there's a vowel on the other side, Joe's rule is wrong.

We humans seem to be predisposed to look for confirming evidence rather than disconfirming evidence.[18] For many everyday practical matters, this approach serves us well. For example, if we flip a light switch and fail to get any light, we might immediately think, "The light bulb probably burned out." We unscrew the existing light bulb and replace it with a new one—and *voila!* we now have light. Hypothesis confirmed, problem solved, case closed.

But other everyday situations are not so cut and dried. I recall an unsettling conversation I once had in college with my roommate at the time (I'll call her Josephine—Josephine Schmoe). One day midway through the semester, Josephine unexpectedly sprang on me the fact that she wasn't happy with our living arrangement and had managed to secure a single room in the dormitory. She'd be moving her things from our room as quickly as she could.

What??!! Not happy with *moi,* the most affable and accommodating of all people? Why?? It was a most pressing question for me at the time, and one for which I formed an immediate hypothesis: Josephine was a . . . well, a word that rhymes with *witch.* So as to avoid any unpleasantries with Josephine during the moving-out process, I camped out in my best friend's dorm room across campus for a few days. Living in the same dormitory as my best friend were several women who knew Josephine and didn't particularly care for her. Obligingly, they all gathered in my temporary quarters, and we proceeded to swap stories that cast Josephine in an increasingly unfavorable light. By the time I moved back to my own room—now empty of any traces of my ex-roommate—I was basking in the glow of my own high self-esteem.

But what had I really done? I had sought out evidence to confirm my hypothesis about Josephine and, sure enough, I had gotten it. Never did it occur to me to seek out disconfirming evidence—evidence that might suggest that Josephine wasn't really a word that rhymes with *witch* and had legitimate reasons for leaving me behind. I was a happy gal, to be sure, but not a very objective or critical thinker.

When Two Wrongs Can Make a Right: Eliminating Alternative Hypotheses

To conclude unequivocally that a particular hypothesis is correct, we need to show that other, opposing hypotheses are *incorrect.* This isn't always possible in everyday social matters (how could I ever really prove that Josephine Schmoe wasn't really a word that rhymes with *witch?*). But it's very doable in situations where we have only a small number of hypotheses that cover all possibilities.

Let's take an example in education. Let's say that we want to find out which of two reading programs, Reading Is Great (RIG) or Reading and You (RAY), is more effective in improving third graders' reading skills. Our simple question, *Which reading program is better?,* has only three possible answers, which we can treat as hypotheses:

- *Hypothesis 1*: RIG is more effective than RAY.

- *Hypothesis 2*: RAY is more effective than RIG.

- *Hypothesis 3*: RIG and RAY are equally effective.

We take 50 third-grade classrooms and randomly divide them into two groups of 25 classrooms each. We tell the teachers in Group 1 to use the RIG program during the year, and we tell the teachers in Group 2 to use the RAY program. (To keep things simple, let's assume that the teachers and their school districts are willing to do this for us.) Then, at the end of the school year, we give all of the students a reading achievement test. (Let's also assume that the test is a good measure of reading achievement.) We find that the students in the RIG program earn scores that are, on average, 5 points higher than those of the RAY students.

Does this mean that the RIG program is more effective than the RAY program (Hypothesis 1)? Not necessarily. Perhaps such a difference happened by chance—for instance, perhaps in our random selection of classrooms for Group 1 versus Group 2, we just happened to put better readers in the RIG program. Fortunately, a simple statistical analysis can help us out here. In a statistical test known as a *t*-test, we can determine the probability that a 5-point difference between the two groups happened entirely by chance. Imagine that we find that the *t*-test reveals that a 5-point difference between two randomly created groups would occur *by chance* only one time in a thousand. In other words, the probability is 99.9% that the difference in achievement levels *didn't* occur by chance.

What we've done here is eliminate Hypothesis 3: Chances are pretty slim (one in a thousand) that the two programs are equivalent in effectiveness. Given that the 5-point difference favors the RIG group, chances are even slimmer that RAY is the better of the two programs. By ruling out Hypotheses 2 and 3, we have, by process of elimination, found evidence in favor of RIG (Hypothesis 1).

Taking One Thing at a Time: Separating and Controlling Variables

In the RIG-and-RAY experiment just described, we were able to determine that one reading program was better than the other but not *why* it was better. An answer to the latter question would require at least one follow-up experiment, and probably many more. Questions about cause-and-effect require an additional strategy that you may or may not use in the next exercise. The exercise requires some equipment, which I'm hoping you can find close at hand.

Check It Out: **Pendulum Problem**

In the absence of other forces, an object suspended
by a rope or string—a pendulum—swings at a
constant rate. (A yo-yo and a playground swing
are two everyday examples.) Some pendulums swing
back and forth rather slowly, others more quickly.

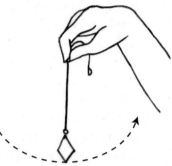

What characteristics of a pendulum determine
how fast it swings? Write down at least three
hypotheses about variables that might affect
a pendulum's oscillation rate.

Now gather several small, heavy objects
(an eraser, a house key, and a metal bolt are three
possibilities) and a piece of string. A variety of items can substitute for the string. Anything
long, thin, and flexible—a shoelace or a cheap necklace chain, for instance—will do.

Tie one or more of the objects to one end of the string—these become the *bob* at
the bottom of your pendulum—and set your pendulum in motion. Then create a different
bob using another object or set of objects and get the pendulum swinging again.
Continue on in this manner, conducting one or more experiments to test each of your
hypotheses.

What can you conclude? What variable(s) affect the rate with which a pendulum
swings?

What hypotheses did you generate? Four common hypotheses are the
weight of the bob, the length of the string, the force with which the pendulum
is pushed, and the height from which the object is first released.

Did you test each of your hypotheses in a systematic fashion? That is, did
you *separate and control variables,* testing one at a time while holding all
others constant? For example, if you were testing the hypothesis that the
weight of the bob makes a difference, you might have tried objects or object-
combinations of different weights while keeping constant the length of the
string, the force with which you pushed the bob, and the height from which
you released or pushed the bob. Similarly, if you hypothesized that the length
of the string was a critical factor, you might have varied the length while
continuing to use the same bob and setting the pendulum in motion in a
consistent manner. If you carefully separated and controlled each variable,

then you would have come to the correct conclusion: Only *length* affects a pendulum's oscillation rate.

If we don't separate and control variables—that is, if we don't test one variable at a time while holding all of the others constant—we have no way of determining what causes a particular outcome. Imagine, for example, that in conducting your pendulum experiments, you consistently changed both the bob weight and the string length for each successive experiment. You might find that a short, heavy pendulum swings faster than a long, lighter one, but what does that tell you? Does the weight make the difference? The length? Both of them? It's impossible to tell.

Separating and controlling variables is relatively easy when experimenting with a pendulum and other simple physical phenomena. However, it can be quite a challenge when studying human behavior, which is often the result of many factors that interact in their effects. To date, then, we humans have identified many more indisputable, no-doubt-about-it cause-and-effect relationships in physics and chemistry than in psychology and sociology.

Did the Butler Really Do It, or Was He Just in the Wrong Place at the Wrong Time? Distinguishing between Causation and Correlation

Knowledge about cause-and-effect relationships is useful for a couple of reasons. First, such knowledge allows us to make predictions about future events and act accordingly. For instance, if a weather forecaster tells us that a frontal system with a lot of moisture and sub-freezing temperatures is moving our way, we should probably get out our woolies and snow boots. If we know that flu shots definitely reduce people's chances of getting sick, we may want to get a shot before flu season comes along. (It may not surprise you to learn that I'm writing this paragraph in November, when winter is imminent.)

In addition, knowing what causes what enables us to change things for the better—perhaps by increasing conditions that bring about favorable outcomes, decreasing conditions that bring about unfavorable ones, or both. For example, if we know that a certain virus causes a certain kind of cancer, then an important strategy for reducing the incidence of that cancer is to figure out how to destroy the virus.

If we're conducting research ourselves, our best approach in identifying cause-and-effect relationships is, if possible, to separate and control variables, pitting one hypothesis against another until eventually we've eliminated all hypotheses except for one. But often, instead, we find ourselves in the position of interpreting what other researchers have found. In such situations we need to think critically about how they have conducted their study and whether their results convincingly lead to conclusions about cause and effect.

As an illustration, let's return to our two reading programs, RIG and RAY. Imagine that two researchers ask certain third-grade teachers to use the RIG program and certain others to use the RAY program. The response of most teachers is essentially, "Who do you think you are, telling me how to teach reading? I'll use the program that *I* think is better!" Fortunately for the researchers, 25 teachers choose to use RIG and 25 teachers choose RAY, so there are still 25 third-grade classrooms in each of the two groups. At the end of the school year, the researchers find that the RIG students earn, on average, 5 more points on a reading achievement test than the RAY students do. As we read their research report, we might quickly jump to the conclusion that RIG promotes better reading skills than RAY—in other words, that a cause-and-effect relationship exists between the reading program and reading achievement. But is this really so?

Not necessarily. In this case, the researchers haven't eliminated all other possible explanations for the difference in students' test scores. Remember, the teachers personally *selected* the instructional program they used. Why did some teachers choose RIG and others choose RAY? Were the teachers who chose RIG different in some way from the teachers who chose RAY? Had RIG teachers taken more graduate courses in reading instruction, were they more open-minded and enthusiastic about using innovative methods, did they have higher expectations for their students, or did they devote more class time to reading instruction? Or, perhaps, did the RIG teachers have students who were, on average, better readers to begin with? If the RIG and RAY classrooms were different from each other in any of these ways—or perhaps different in some other way we haven't thought of—then we cannot conclude that a difference in reading program *per se* was the cause of the students' achievement differences.

As a species, we seem to be eager to identify cause-and-effect relationships in our environment. We're so eager to find them that we often jump to conclusions about causation when all that's really going on is *correlation:* Two things just happen to occur at about the same time. We're not alone here: Even laboratory rats seem to mistake correlation for causation.[19] But if I had a nickel for every time I've seen correlational research findings misinterpreted as evidence for causation, I could afford a far more elaborate Bahamian condo than the one I dreamed about in Chapter 6.

Often the suspected causal culprit is a really obvious characteristic or event—something we can easily see or think about.[20] For instance, it might seem obvious that a certain kind of reading instruction would lead to higher reading achievement than another. But obviousness alone is hardly a reasonable criterion for determining causality. It's like the proverbial butler in classic whodunit mysteries: He was near the scene of the crime and had regular access to the murder victim, but these two facts by themselves don't justify a guilty verdict.

We shouldn't ignore correlational relationships, of course. When two characteristics or events are frequently seen together, maybe one of them does cause or influence the other. But then again, maybe not. And if there *is* a causal relationship, which one causes which? For example, students who have high self-esteem tend to do better in school. Does that mean that high self-esteem leads to higher school achievement or that, instead, higher school achievement brings about higher self-esteem? Alternatively, is a third variable—nurturing adults, say, or physical well-being—the underlying cause of both high self-esteem and high achievement levels? These are intriguing questions to which we might eventually find answers. But a correlational relationship won't, in and of itself, give us the answers.

Jumping to Conclusions or Jumping Off a Cliff? Common Pitfalls in Reasoning

In my earlier discussions of logical reasoning, quantitative reasoning, and scientific reasoning, I've alluded to several potential mental errors we might make:

- Confusing what must logically be true with what seems to be true in the world as we know it (a potential pitfall in deductive reasoning)

- Making generalizations about members of a category after having encountered only a restricted subset of that category (a potential pitfall in inductive reasoning)

■ Making inaccurate predictions about probabilistic events (a potential pitfall in quantitative reasoning)

■ Looking only for evidence that supports our hypotheses, without also looking for evidence that would disconfirm our hypotheses (a potential pitfall in scientific reasoning)

■ Mistaking correlation for causation (another potential pitfall in scientific reasoning)

I now describe several more general pitfalls in reasoning and critical thinking.

"Keep It Simple, Stupid" (KISS): Taking Mental Shortcuts

A common principle in many professions, including my own, is the KISS principle, which boils down to this: Use the simplest possible approach to get the job done effectively. In light of our limited working memory capacity, this principle is often quite sensible.[21] After all, we can think about only so much at once. A great deal of information to consider or a great many steps to execute can overwhelm us, turning our minds into quivering masses of mental jelly.

One common mental shortcut is *representativeness*, in which we jump to conclusions based on currently available data or common stereotypes rather than on overall probabilities.[22] As an example, try the next exercise.

Check It Out: Linda

Linda is in her early thirties. She is single, outspoken, and very bright. As a student she majored in philosophy and was deeply concerned with issues of discrimination and social justice. Which of these possibilities is more likely to be true?

a. Linda is a bank teller.
b. Linda is a bank teller and an active feminist.[23]

Many people are bank tellers, and many people are active feminists—without doing research on the matter, we have no way of knowing the exact probabilities of being either one. But certainly the probability is higher that

Linda is *one* of these things than that she is *both* of them. Thus the correct answer is Option a: Linda is more likely to be a bank teller than to be both a bank teller and an active feminist. But did the "active feminist" lead you to pick Option b? If so, you're not alone. In a study with students at Stanford University (hardly mental slouches), many participants were seduced by the feminist part.[24] Feminists are, by definition, concerned about discrimination and social justice with regard to women. And a widely held stereotype is that, as a group, feminists are quite outspoken.

Another common mental shortcut is *availability,* in which we reason and make decisions using only information that immediately comes to mind— in other words, information that we retrieve quickly and easily.[25] Often that information consists of facts we've acquired recently rather than in the distant past. For example, imagine that you are trying to decide whether to go to California or Florida for a sunny March vacation at the beach. You learned several years ago that, on average, Florida has more rainfall than California. But in February, as you are about to make your choice, you hear on the news that California has just been drenched in a heavy rainstorm. You might easily book a flight to Florida, retrieving the available information about the California rainstorm rather than the overall frequency of rainfall in the two states.

As you can see, then, mental shortcuts don't always work in our favor. In minor decisions—say, where to go on vacation—any errors we make aren't terribly consequential. But in life-and-death matters, of course, we should be much more deliberative.

"I *Knew* This Would Happen!": Confirming Expectations

Consider this hypothetical exchange between you and me:

> **You:** "We're going to have my grandmother for Thanksgiving dinner."
> **Me:** "You are? Well, we're going to have turkey."[26]

Did the conversation startle you a bit? If so, it's probably partly because when I said, "Well, we're going to have . . ." you anticipated that I would complete the sentence with "my cousins" or "a few friends" or something else related to prospective guests for the occasion. (Of course, you may have also been annoyed that I would impose a cannibalistic interpretation on your remark.)

We often form expectations about the things we will see and hear—expectations based on our knowledge, and perhaps also on our misconceptions, about how the world typically operates. Such expectations can influence the ways in which we interpret and reason about our observations.[27] As an example, let's return to Barry, a high school student whom I described in Chapter 3. Barry was participating in an egg drop experiment with some of his classmates. He was convinced that heavier objects fall faster, so he was surprised to see his heavy egg container reach the ground at the same time that his peers' light containers did. Barry interpreted the result not as support for the all-things-fall-at-the-same-rate idea but instead as an indication that "people weren't timing real good."[28]

We've already seen how we're inclined to look primarily for evidence that confirms our hypotheses. But in addition, we tend to ignore or discredit any contradictory evidence that comes our way. Our general tendency to support and not try to refute our existing beliefs is known as *confirmation bias*.[29] For example, a common misconception about pendulums is that the weight of the bob affects oscillation rate—for instance, that heavy pendulums swing faster than light ones. Did you have this misconception when you did the Pendulum Problem exercise earlier in the chapter? If so, perhaps you repeatedly tested your *weight* hypothesis, "seeing" differences in oscillation rates that were actually equivalent. Or, alternatively, perhaps you simultaneously varied both weight and string length (thus not separating and controlling variables) and mistakenly interpreted different rates as being the result of weight rather than length differences.

"I Have It on the Best of Authority": Mistaking Dogma for Fact

Although we might be inclined to view some sources of information with a skeptical, critical eye, we might accept others without question. For example, many of us willingly accept whatever a parent, college professor, favorite politician, or religious leader says to be true. So, too, might we willingly accept what we read in college textbooks, newspaper editorials, political campaign pamphlets, or holy scriptures. In general, we may uncritically accept anything said or written by individuals or groups we hold in high esteem.[30]

Not all authority figures and works of literature are reliable sources of information and guidance, of course, and blind, unquestioning acceptance of them can be worrisome. For example, as a U.S. citizen who has seen and heard countless television ads endorsing various candidates for political office over the years, I've been horrified by the many lies that have been casually cast about. I've been even more horrified by the numbers of voters who have swallowed some of these lies hook, line, and sinker. For example, I recall one rumor that floated about during the 2008 U.S. presidential election: Barack Obama, it was said, was born in Kenya and therefore ineligible to serve as President of the United States. Reputable journalists uncovered not only his Hawaiian birth certificate but also birth announcements in 1961 issues of Hawaiian news-papers, yet to this day some of my compatriots remain convinced that he was born in Africa. We must certainly maintain a healthy skepticism about what politicians and other public figures tell us. But the same goes for the "facts" that other people feed us about these individuals, especially if those "facts" are contradicted by mountains upon mountains of other facts.

"I Know It in My Heart": Letting Emotion Overrule Logic and Objectivity

As you should recall from the discussion of *hot cognition* in Chapter 5, our knowledge and beliefs about a topic are often closely connected to our feelings about it. So, too, do our emotions often infiltrate our efforts to reason and think critically. We're apt to think quite rationally and objectively when we're dealing with topics we don't feel strongly about and yet think in decidedly irrational ways about emotionally charged issues—issues that we find upsetting, infuriating, or personally threatening.[31]

"It's Either Black or White": Thinking Dichotomously

Many species, including our own *homo sapiens,* have a natural tendency to categorize their experiences.[32] Identifying an object or event as a member of a particular category has distinct benefits: It reduces the complexity of our world and enables us to make inferences and predictions about that object or event.[33]

But categorization can have a downside: If we think of something as belonging to one category, we have trouble simultaneously thinking of it as belonging to a distinctly different category. Tulips cannot also be daffodils, platypuses cannot also be hippopotamuses, Catholics cannot also be Muslims, liberals cannot also be conservatives, and so on. Some of these dichotomies are legitimate: Tulips and daffodils really are mutually exclusive categories, as are platypuses and hippopotamuses. But when we get into belief systems, such as certain religions or political persuasions, it's entirely possible to combine elements of seemingly opposite perspectives.

Many people in Western societies—for instance, many in North America and Western Europe—seem to be predisposed to think in either-or terms. People from Asian societies—for instance, those in China and Japan—are less inclined to dichotomize and more willing to accept seemingly opposite perspectives as both having some validity. Sometimes Asians speak of finding the *Middle Way,* one that incorporates disparate views into an integrated, coherent whole.[34] For example, several years ago I was a member of a group touring the People's Republic of China. As my fellow travelers and I became increasingly comfortable with our native tour guide, we began to ask him probing questions about China's politics and about communism as a form of government and way of life. Almost always he gave us both sides of the picture—the pros and the cons—and would ultimately conclude, "It's a little of both."

As we reflect on our own society's ways of doing things, we, too, should resist the urge to see things in strictly black-or-white, good-or-bad, either-it's-this-or-it's-that terms. Truly critical thinkers are also open-minded thinkers who recognize that individuals with diverse perspectives may all have legitimate ideas to contribute to our collective efforts to make sense of our world and ultimately to make it a better place in which to live.

It's Attitude as Much as Aptitude: Essential Qualities of Critical Thinkers

So far we've been talking about the mental skills that reasoning and critical thinking involve. But looking at situations analytically and with a reasonably objective eye requires certain attitudes and beliefs as well. Dispositions come into play, as do certain epistemic beliefs.

Inquiring Minds Want to Know: Dispositions

By *disposition,* I mean a general, relatively stable inclination to approach learning and problem-solving situations in a particular way. Here are several examples of dispositions that researchers have identified:

- *Need for cognition:* Regularly seeking and engaging in challenging cognitive tasks[35]

- *Open-mindedness:* Being willing to consider alternative perspectives and multiple sources of evidence and to suspend judgment rather than leap to immediate conclusions[36]

- *Critical thinking:* Consistently evaluating information or arguments in terms of their accuracy, logic, and credibility, rather than accepting them at face value[37]

- *Consensus seeking:* Striving for a synthesis of diverse perspectives, rather than assuming that perspectives must necessarily be mutually exclusive[38]

Dispositions, then, have a motivational quality to them—it's not just that we have the ability to engage in certain mental activities, but we also *want* to engage in them.[39] You might think of them as general habits of mind.

Only in the past two decades have researchers begun to study dispositions in earnest, but increasingly they are finding that our dispositions can have profound effects on our learning and memory. For example, if we have a high need for cognition, we're apt to learn more from what we read and more likely to base conclusions on sound evidence and logical reasoning.[40] And if we're predisposed to critically evaluate new evidence and are receptive to and open-minded about diverse perspectives, we're likely to have more sophisticated reasoning capabilities, and we're also more likely to revise our understandings of topics when revision is warranted.[41]

Inquiring Minds Also Evaluate the Evidence: Epistemic Beliefs (Again)

In Chapter 7, I introduced you to *epistemic beliefs*—beliefs about the general nature of knowledge and learning. Certain epistemic beliefs enhance our ability and willingness to reason and think critically.[42] First, we must realize that, as a species, our collective knowledge about the world is a dynamic entity that continues to change as new data come in. As individual learners, then, we can never know all there is to know about a topic—there will always be something new to discover about it—and we may sometimes need to *un*learn things that experts have previously thought to be true.

Second, we must acknowledge that we humans may *never* know the ultimate "truth" about certain topics. On some matters, there is no single right answer. Instead, there may be several answers, each of which has strengths and weaknesses.

Finally, we must understand that, even when there is a single right answer, the people we admire and trust don't necessarily have it. Father *doesn't* always know best. Instead, our criteria for separating fact from fiction must rest on sound evidence and logic. This view that acquiring dependable knowledge involves evaluating what we hear and read evolves only slowly as we grow older. Children tend to accept information at face value, especially if it comes from authority figures. Adolescents are more likely to appreciate that different people (even different experts) may have diverse perspectives on complex issues, but they're apt to treat all of them as equally acceptable ("We're all entitled to our own opinions"). With time and experience, some adults begin to realize that certain viewpoints have greater validity than others—for instance, certain viewpoints are more logical and consistent with research evidence—and that effective learners carefully scrutinize and evaluate new ideas and information. This *evaluativist* stance is a key ingredient in our willingness to engage in critical thinking.[43]

I would be remiss here if I didn't also mention epistemic beliefs that stop critical thinking dead in its tracks. In particular, when people believe that knowledge is merely a collection of indisputable facts that can best be acquired from authority figures, they're prone to gullible acceptance of anything that comes out of the mouths of trusted individuals. Such beliefs can lead to a *need for closure,* in which people seek quick and easy answers to what are often complex, difficult questions.[44] In your regular interactions with friends, family members, and professional colleagues, you've undoubtedly encountered many folks with a strong need for closure. Trying to convince them of something other than what they've previously decided must be true is like talking to a brick wall.

Making *Rational* Good Sense

Certainly we don't need to think logically and critically about every aspect of our lives. Some things—for instance, our tastes in food, fashion, and home décor—often don't have any rhyme or reason to them, nor do they need to. But we *must* be logical and critical about topics and issues that can potentially impact the quality of our own and others' lives. In the following sections, I offer a few suggestions for helping yourself and others be more rational and (in a good way) judgmental.

THINKING SMART

I'm hoping that you've already picked up some ideas as you've read this chapter. Here are a few recommendations that might supplement your own inferences.

▶ ***Check your logic.*** This is often easier said than done, of course: It can be quite a challenge to separate what is logically true from what you know in your heart "should" be true. A good first step is to write your assumptions—that is, your *premises*—on a sheet of paper and have a friend or colleague check them for accuracy and reasonableness. If they're accurate and reasonable, does your conclusion follow logically and indisputably from them? Look hard for holes in your thinking—additional assumptions you haven't verbalized, logical steps you've left out, and so on.

Another strategy for certain kinds of logical thinking is to draw or mentally visualize a diagram that illustrates your assumptions and their potential interrelationships. "All X's are Y's" and "Some P's are Q's" problems lend themselves easily to diagrams (look once again at Figures 8.1 and 8.2), as do multiple-comparison problems of an "A is larger than B, and B is larger than C" nature.[45]

▶ ***Remember that what you see and hear in the media is apt to be biased in one way or another.*** Even when we're specifically trained to be objective in our observations—as journalists often are—it's virtually impossible for any of us to keep our personal beliefs, assumptions, and biases from creeping into our explanations of events (see Chapters 3 and 6). Asking yourself questions such as the following can help you separate the credible from the not-so-much in media reports:

- Does the person providing the information have sufficient background and expertise to be reasonably knowledgeable about the topic?

- What is the person's goal here? What is he or she trying to convince me to believe?

- What assumptions is the person making? Are they reasonable?

- What conclusion is the person drawing? What evidence supports this conclusion? What evidence might *not* support it?

- Are there other possible explanations for the evidence the person provides? What additional information might be needed before a definitive conclusion can be reached?[46]

▶ ***Seek out opposing viewpoints on complex issues, and try to integrate them into a sensible resolution.*** You're more likely to get the complete scoop on a situation when you get multiple scoops from different sources. Some of these scoops might be from so-called experts, whereas others might be from thoughtful novices. If some of them come from liberal thinkers, others should come from more conservative ones. And diverse cultural groups almost invariably have productive ideas to add to the mix. Remember the Asian idea of the Middle Way: Seemingly opposite views can often both be partly right.

▶ ***If you get overly emotional about a topic, give yourself time to step back and cool off for a while.*** Hot cognition isn't likely to be helpful if it's a raging inferno. It's extremely difficult to think clearly when you're angry, upset, or feeling personally threatened. In such cases, it's best to defer your reasoning and decision making until the flames die down a bit—perhaps after an hour, a day, or a week has elapsed.

▶ ***Be willing to admit you might be wrong and to change your mind if the facts warrant doing so.*** Personally, I don't know anyone who is right every second of the day. Epistemically sophisticated human beings recognize that understanding of virtually any topic or situation continues to improve—and may sometimes need revision—as new evidence comes in.[47] All human beings are wrong on occasion. Smart ones acknowledge it.

HELPING OTHERS THINK SMART

Certainly you can apply the suggestions I've just offered in your work with other people. Following are several additional ideas.

▶ ***Model curiosity, open-mindedness about diverse viewpoints, and a willingness to suspend judgment until all the facts are in.*** Children, especially, learn by example, but even many adults become more inquisitive and analytical if the people around them show such qualities. Deliberating thoughtfully and open-mindedly about different perspectives communicates the message that reasoning and critical thinking are valued activities.[48]

▶ *Ask questions that encourage critical analysis and evaluation of ideas.*
Here are some examples:

- "The other day I read an editorial saying that [such-and-such]. Would you agree or disagree with that point of view?"

- "Hmm, that's an interesting idea. Can you explain how you came to that conclusion?"

- "Some people think that any kind of income tax deprives people of their hard-earned money. But other people think it's the most equitable way to get funds to support needed public services. Both groups make valid points. Is there a happy medium we might find about this issue?"

▶ *Gently and diplomatically challenge rigid, narrow-minded thinking.* The key words here are *gently* and *diplomatically.* Some people perceive any challenge to their deeply held beliefs as a threat to their personal and emotional well-being. If certain beliefs are highly irrational and can perhaps lead to undesirable outcomes—for instance, if a person advocates violence as a means of addressing a dubious social cause—then some sort of intervention is usually in order. Such questions as these can in some instances lead to critical self-reflection:

- "That's a perspective I haven't heard before. Can you explain why you think as you do?"

- "What if someone were to respond to your statement by saying . . ."

If an antisocial, destructive outcome seems likely and imminent, however, you should contact the appropriate authorities.

▶ *Ask people to play devil's advocate—to argue for a position opposite to what they actually believe.* People are more likely to think open-mindedly and critically about both sides of a controversial coin if they have to make the case for a perspective they didn't previously take seriously.[49]

Teaching Tips

Create an overall classroom environment that welcomes inquiry and critical analysis of ideas. Students must feel free to ask questions, critique ideas, and disagree both with one another and with their teacher.[50] Following are several more specific strategies:

- Communicate the beliefs that asking questions reflects curiosity, that differing perspectives on a controversial topic are both inevitable and healthy, and that changing one's opinion on a topic can be a sign of thoughtful, intelligent reflection.

- Encourage students to try to understand one another's reasoning and explanations.

- Insist that students be respectful in their disagreements: They can challenge other people's ideas, but they must never demean others' intelligence or personal qualities.

- Suggest that students build on one another's ideas whenever possible.

- Ask students to develop compromise solutions that take into account opposing perspectives.[51]

Provide practice in making, defending, and critiquing arguments. Classroom discussions and writing assignments can, of course, be geared to providing such practice. The debating clubs found in many high schools and colleges provide another excellent arena in which to learn how to create persuasive arguments and dissect the arguments of others. Often students can acquire more effective argumentation skills if they work collaboratively in small teams to develop arguments in favor of one point of view and to critique opposing perspectives.[52]

Explicitly teach reasoning and critical thinking skills within the context of real-world, practical issues in various content domains. Students are more likely to think logically and critically when they're explicitly *taught* these reasoning skills.[53] They're also more likely to think logically and critically about concrete topics relevant to their everyday lives than about abstract ones with which they have little experience.[54] Following are examples of what you might do:

- Have students design and conduct experiments to test the effects of sunlight, water, and soil quality on sunflower growth; ask questions that encourage students to separate and control variables ("If you water all the plants by the window three times a week and water the ones in the closet only once a week, how will you know whether it's the sunlight or the water that's making the difference in how tall the sunflowers grow?").

■ Distribute a set of 12 unlabeled horoscope predictions for the previous day (you can find them in many newspapers and a variety of Internet websites). Ask students to choose the prediction that best matches the preceding day's events for them personally, and determine the frequency with which predictions matched reality for the class as a whole. Also, ask students to inspect the 12 horoscopes for strategies that horoscope writers are using to increase readers' perceptions of their "accuracy." Finally, as a class, brainstorm experiments that the class might conduct to test the validity of horoscopes' predictive powers.[55]

■ Have students prepare for and conduct a mock legislative hearing in which they must debate the pros and cons of regulating the use of vitamins and other dietary supplements. Give them age-appropriate readings about research regarding this issue—readings in which they must wrestle with various probabilities and distinguish between correlational and cause-and-effect relationships.[56]

■ When studying a particular historical event, have students read several documents related to the event—perhaps including newspaper reports, entries in personal diaries, and political cartoons—and try to draw conclusions about what probably did and didn't happen. As students scrutinize the documents, ask them to consider questions such as the following:

- Who produced this document?
- What biases or predispositions did the author or authors have?
- How might these biases have affected the content of the document?
- What information in this document is similar to information in other documents?
- What information contradicts information in other documents?
- How might the source or the context explain some of the contradictions?[57]

Provide numerous models of critical thinking. Some students may have encountered few, if any, examples of critical thinking in their own lives. One effective strategy is to think aloud as you yourself reason through complex issues and problems. Another is to show students good and poor examples of critical thinking in newspaper editorials and other printed materials.[58]

Encourage critical analysis of content on Internet websites. It's important that students think critically not only about what they read and hear in the classroom but also about what they see online. People with a wide variety of motives and ideologies post their ideas on websites, and thus students must learn to scrutinize postings with a skeptical eye. All too often, however, students at all levels—even college students—take most information they find on the Internet as "truth."[59]

Once again, teaching students to ask themselves questions about what they're reading can be helpful. Following are examples of such self-questions about an Internet website:

- What individuals or organization created this website? What motives may the individuals or organization have?

- Do the individuals involved have expertise in this topic? If so, are they likely to be objective in discussing it?

- Does the website provide convincing scientific evidence to back up its claims?

- Is the information consistent with information obtained from other sources? If not, why not?[60]

One good resource for teachers is a website maintained by the Center for Media Literacy (www.medialit.org), which provides low-cost software that teaches students to ask themselves a variety of evaluative questions about information they find on the Internet.

Provide frequent opportunities for reflection and critical analysis. For example, such opportunities might take the form of journal entries or other writing assignments in which students either develop a line of reasoning or critique other people's persuasive arguments.[61] It's important, however, to provide standards by which students can appropriately judge the quality of their reflections and critiques. For example, you might ask them to consider questions such as these as they examine their own and others' reasoning:

- What assumptions underlie this argument? Are they reasonable?

- In what ways might someone with a different point of view challenge this argument?

- How strong is the evidence in favor of this argument?

- What evidence exists or might exist that would weaken or contradict the argument?

- Has a correlational relationship been misinterpreted as indicating a causal relationship?

- In what other ways might certain observations or research findings be explained?

Applying the Old to the New: Transfer, Problem Solving, and Creativity

People have long debated the value of acquiring knowledge for knowledge's sake. Personally, I really enjoy learning new information that can titillate my mind—the possibility of multiple universes, say, or the distinct dialects of different dolphin groups. And I must admit that my incessant curiosity about the physical, biological, and social sciences gives me a leg up in Trivial Pursuit, especially when I'm partnered with a son-in-law who can cover the History and Sports categories.

But let's be practical here. Ultimately we should also be able to apply our knowledge to more important matters than a game of Trivial Pursuit. The topics I address in this chapter—transfer, problem solving, and creativity—are all about applying what we've previously learned to new tasks and challenges.

Putting Knowledge to Good Use: The Process of Transfer

Whenever something we've learned in one situation affects how we learn or perform in a subsequent situation, *transfer* is occurring. Transfer is a normal part of everyday life: We continually draw on our existing knowledge and skills to deal with new situations. We'd be in a sorry state if we *didn't* regularly transfer what we've learned. Starting from scratch about how to behave in every new circumstance . . . well, I certainly wouldn't be writing this book, nor would you be reading it. In fact, we wouldn't even be here: Our species would have become extinct ages ago.

Usually It Helps, but Sometimes It Can Hurt: Positive versus Negative Transfer

Put your knowledge of arithmetic to work in the following exercise.

Check It Out: **Another Division Problem**

As quickly as you can, estimate an answer to this division problem:

$$60 \div 0.38$$

Is your answer larger or smaller than 60? If you applied your knowledge of division by whole numbers here, you undoubtedly concluded that the answer is smaller—perhaps somewhere in the neighborhood of 15 to 25. In fact, the answer is approximately 158, a number much *larger* than 60. If you estimated downward rather than upward from 60, you were probably applying a principle you've learned about division: It usually leads to a smaller number than what you started with. This principle will serve you well if you're working only with whole numbers, but it can get you in trouble if you're working with decimals or fractions.

Most of the time, the things we've previously learned are helpful rather than harmful in new situations. Whenever something we've learned at one time facilitates our learning or performance at a later time, *positive transfer* is occurring. Knowing basic arithmetic procedures helps us balance our checkbooks. Knowing how an automobile engine is supposed to work can help us diagnose the problem in a malfunctioning one. Knowing basic procedures in a word-processing program—how to "cut" and "paste," track changes, search for a particular word or word combination, and so on—can often help us master other computer applications, such as a spreadsheet or PowerPoint. And, of course, we transfer our reading and writing skills to a wide variety of literacy tasks.

But when something we've previously learned gets in our way, *negative transfer* is at work. You experienced negative transfer if you erroneously concluded that dividing 60 by 0.38 would give you a number smaller than 60. Many people—even many with college educations—show negative transfer of whole-number principles to situations involving decimals.[1]

Negative transfer rears its ugly head in other situations as well. For example, when people accustomed to driving with a standard transmission must rent a car that has an automatic transmission, they're apt to step on a clutch that isn't there. Adults who learn a second language typically apply patterns of speech production characteristic of their native tongue, giving them a foreign accent.[2] Students in my college classes who've been accustomed to memorizing verbatim facts in other courses usually don't do well on my own application-oriented exams.

How Far Can You Go?
Specific versus General Transfer

In some cases we benefit from *specific transfer*, in which there's considerable overlap between what we've previously learned and what we now need to learn or do. For example, let's say that you already know the numbers 1 to 10 in French and then need to learn them in Spanish:

French	Spanish
un	uno
deux	dos
trois	tres
quatre	cuatro
cinq	cinco
six	seis
sept	siete
huit	ocho
nuef	nueve
dix	diez

Nine of the ten French words should help you count in Spanish. Only *huit* would lead you astray if you tried to remember *ocho*. To remember the Spanish word for "eight," you'd be better off drawing on your knowledge of such English words as *octagon* and *octave*.

In contrast to specific transfer, *general transfer* involves taking knowledge or skills we've acquired in one content area and applying them to a very different content area. As an example, try the next exercise.

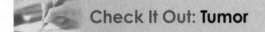 **Check It Out: Tumor**

Imagine that you're an oncologist, a physician who specializes in treating cancer. How might you help Joe Schmoe, one of your patients?

> Joe has a malignant tumor in his stomach. For reasons we don't need to go into here, you can't operate on Joe. However, if you don't remove the tumor somehow, Joe will die. Your best bet is to use radiation to kill the tumor. You'll need to use high-intensity gamma rays to completely remove it, yet in the process you'll also destroy the healthy tissue that the rays must pass through along the way. At lower intensities, the gamma rays are harmless to healthy tissue, but they won't put much of a dent in the tumor either. How might you use gamma rays to destroy the tumor without also affecting the surrounding healthy tissue?[3]

If you're having trouble identifying a solution, consider this situation:

> An army general wants to capture a fort in the middle of a small country. Many roads lead to the fort, but land mines lurk below their surface. Small numbers of soldiers can travel safely on the roads, but a large force will almost inevitably detonate one or more mines, killing many troops. The general solves the problem by dividing his army into small groups, sending each group to a different road, and having them all converge on the fort simultaneously to launch the attack.[4]

Now go back to Joe Schmoe's inoperable stomach tumor. Perhaps the general's strategy in capturing the fort has given you an idea about how to destroy the tumor.

Superficially, there's no overlap between the two situations: One involves medicine and the other involves military science. Yet you (as the oncologist) can attack Joe's tumor in much the same way that the general attacks the fort. In particular, you can shoot a number of low-intensity gamma rays from different directions, such that they all converge on the tumor simultaneously. This is, in fact, a common strategy in radiation therapy.

Historically, many folks have taken a broad view of general transfer, thinking that exercising the mind in one way would help it in other, very different ways. For example, when I was in high school in the mid-1960s, most college-bound students were encouraged to take both French and Latin, the only two languages my school offered. Taking French made a great deal of sense: Living in Massachusetts, we were within a day's drive of French-speaking Quebec. "But why should I take Latin?" I asked my guidance counselor. "I can use it only if I attend Catholic mass or run across phrases like *caveat emptor* or *e pluribus unum*. Hardly anyone speaks the language anymore." The counselor pursed her thin red lips and gave me a look suggesting that she knew best. "Latin will discipline your mind," she told me. "It will help you learn better."

Most research has discredited this mind-as-muscle notion of transfer. For example, practice in memorizing poems doesn't necessarily make us faster poem memorizers. And studying computer programming, though often a worthwhile activity in its own right, doesn't necessarily help us with dissimilar kinds of logical reasoning tasks.[5] When it comes to knowledge of particular academic topics (geometry, physics, history, etc.), specific transfer occurs far more often than general transfer.[6]

Most of the facts we learn in school—say, about World War II battles or the capitals of South American countries—have only limited utility in and of

The mind–as–muscle view of transfer has largely been discredited: Mental exercise simply for its own sake doesn't help us very much with other, very different tasks.

themselves. More helpful are general principles, such as the attack-from-all-sides idea illustrated in the earlier "Tumor" exercise.[7] Likewise, if we're trying to understand recent political upheavals, widespread genocides, and other disheartening current events, general principles of history—for instance, the principle that two groups of people often engage in battle when other attempts to reach a mutually satisfying state of affairs have failed—are more applicable than precise knowledge of World War II battles. And in geography, general map interpretation skills—for instance, determining why various landforms and human settlements are located as they are—are more useful than the names and locations of specific rivers, mountain ranges, and capital cities.

With age and experience, we humans become increasingly capable of deriving general principles that we might apply to a variety of topics. For example, in one research study, fifth graders and college students were asked to develop a plan for increasing the population of bald eagles, an endangered species in their state.[8] None of the students in either age-group had previously studied strategies for eagle preservation, and the plans that both groups developed were largely inadequate. Yet in the process of developing their plans, the college students addressed more sophisticated questions than the fifth graders did. In particular, the fifth graders focused on the eagles themselves ("How big are they?" "What do they eat?"), whereas the college students looked at the larger picture ("What type of ecosystem supports eagles?" "What about predators of eagles and eagle babies?").[9] Thus, the college students were drawing on an important principle they'd acquired in their many years of science study: *Living creatures are more likely to survive and thrive when their habitat supports rather than threatens them.*

"Why Didn't I Think of That?!": The Importance of Retrieval for Transfer

In most cases, we can apply what we know to a new situation only if we retrieve it in the new situation. Accordingly, we increase the chances of making good use of our knowledge and skills if we have previously:

- Connected the knowledge and skills with many other things in long-term memory—that is, if we've learned them meaningfully (rather than in a rote, meaning*less* manner) and perhaps have also organized and elaborated on them[10]

- ■ Studied them thoroughly and perhaps learned them to a level of automaticity[11]

- ■ Used them in a variety of contexts, including real-world situations[12]

In addition to these retrieval-enhancing conditions in our past learning experiences, our present environment makes a difference. We're more likely to apply things we've previously learned if our current surroundings provide one or more retrieval cues that point us in the direction of relevant information in long-term memory. Thus both positive and negative transfer from one situation to another are more common when the two situations are—or at least appear to be—similar.[13]

Unfortunately, in our efforts to deal with challenging tasks and problems, all too often we *don't* retrieve things we've learned at school and elsewhere.[14] And as I've already argued, many of the facts and figures presented in a typical school curriculum aren't terribly transferable anyway. Sure, school teaches us how to read, write, and calculate, and such skills are critical in modern society. And a *good* school teaches us the usefulness of science, history, geography, the fine arts, and other academic disciplines as well.

Ultimately, however, most of us don't ever use much of what we learn in school, and a good deal of it eventually becomes impossible to retrieve—and maybe disappears altogether—from long-term memory. So what's the point of most of that stuff? Hold your horses—the benefits of a formal education go far beyond the specific academic subject matter that may or may not stick with us, as we'll see next.

Applying Yourself as Well as Your Knowledge: Expanding the Notion of Transfer

In truth, we learn a great deal more at school than miscellaneous tidbits about this, that, and something else. For one thing, school is the primary place in which we *learn how to learn*. With age, experience, and increasingly challenging learning tasks—and ideally with explicit instruction and informal guidance as well—we learn how to organize our thoughts, keep our attention where it needs to be, take notes, study both independently and collaboratively, allocate limited study time appropriately, and so on.[15]

Furthermore, if we're diligent students and life-long learners, we're apt to acquire general beliefs, attitudes, and dispositions related to learning and thinking that will serve us in good stead down the road. For example, we may learn that mastering a topic often comes only with hard work and persistence. We may become more open-minded and receptive to hearing diverse viewpoints on controversial topics. And we may acquire a general mindset to think about potential applications of whatever we might read and study on future occasions.[16]

Putting the Pieces Together: Problem Solving

By *problem solving,* I mean using—that is, transferring—existing knowledge and skills to address an unanswered question or troubling situation. The world presents a great many problems that differ widely in content and scope, as illustrated in these three examples:

1. You are building a tree house with the shape and dimensions shown in Figure 9.1. You need to buy planks for a slanted roof. How long must the roof planks be to reach from one side of the tree house to the other?

2. How can a 60-something psychologist and author be helped to control her junk food habit?

3. How can two groups of people of differing political or religious persuasions and a mutual lack of trust be convinced to curtail their proliferation of military weapons and instead work toward cooperation and peaceful coexistence?

Some of the problems we encounter, such as Problem 1, are straightforward: All of the information necessary for a solution is presented, and the solution is definitely right or wrong. Others, such as Problem 2, may require obtaining additional information (does the psychologist keep physically active, or does she spend most of each day writing books, reading research journals, and checking out the latest gossip on Facebook?), and there may be two or more solutions to the problem (perhaps installing an alarm system on the refrigerator door? perhaps spending six months on a small Bahamian island that has no chocolate shops?). Still others, such as Problem 3, may be so complicated that,

Figure 9.1
How Long Do the Roof Planks of This Treehouse Need to Be?

Source: Adapted from Ormrod, EDUCATIONAL PSYCHOLOGY, Fig. 8.4, p. 266, © 2011 by Pearson Education, Inc. Reproduced by permission of Pearson Education, Inc.

even after considerable research and creative thought, no easy solution emerges. Different kinds of problems require different procedures and different solutions.

So What's the Problem Here?
Well-Defined versus Ill-Defined Problems

Problems vary considerably in the extent to which they are clearly specified and structured. At one end of the clarity-and-structure continuum is the *well-defined problem,* in which the goal is clearly stated, all information needed to solve the problem is present, and only one correct answer exists. At the other end of the continuum is the *ill-defined problem,* in which the desired goal is unclear, information needed to solve the problem is missing, and/or several possible solutions exist. Determining the length of a tree house roof (Problem 1) is a well-defined problem, whereas encouraging two contentious groups to move toward military disarmament (Problem 3) is ill defined. Helping the 60-something psychologist improve her eating habits (Problem 2) is somewhere in between.

Unfortunately, researchers have focused more on well-defined problems (often somewhat artificial ones) than on the ill-defined problems that life so often presents. And most of the problems presented in school (such as the math word problems that some students come to dread) are well defined. Yet the real world presents ill-defined problems far more often than well-defined ones, and people of all ages need guidance in how to deal with them.[17]

Working Memory Provides Only a Small Workbench: Recalling Our Limited Capacity

You may recall from an exercise in Chapter 4 just how difficult it can be to solve a long division problem in your head. Remember, working memory has a limited capacity: At any one time it can hold only a few pieces of information and accommodate only so much mental activity. If a problem requires us to deal with a lot of information at once or to manipulate that information in complex ways, our working memory capacity may not be able to handle it all.[18]

When we're tackling difficult problems, we can overcome the limits of our working memory in at least two ways. One obvious way is to create an external record of relevant information—for example, by writing it on a piece of paper (as we often do with long division problems). Another approach is to learn some facts and skills to automaticity—in other words, to learn them so well that we can retrieve them quickly and easily.[19] In the case of automaticity, however, it's possible to have too much of a good thing, as you'll see a bit later.

"As I Was Going to Saint Ives": How Encoding Affects Problem Solving

The first step in solving any problem is to put the problem in working memory to begin with. This step typically involves *encoding* the problem in some way—that is, changing it into a form that will enable us to think effectively about it and perhaps will also suggest possible ways to solve it.[20] As an example of how encoding comes into play—and may sometimes lead us astray—consider this classic children's riddle:

> As I was going to St. Ives,
> I met a man with seven wives.
> Every wife had seven sacks.
> Every sack had seven cats.
> Every cat had seven kits.
> Kits, cats, sacks, wives.
> How many were going to St. Ives?

Many people take this logical approach to the problem: 1 traveler plus 1 man plus 7 wives plus 7^2 sacks (49) plus 7^3 cats (343) plus 7^4 kits (2,401) equal a total of 2,802 going to St. Ives. People who solve the problem in this way have encoded the problem incorrectly. In particular, they've overlooked the first line of the riddle: "As *I* was going to St. Ives." The riddle doesn't tell us where the polygamist was taking his harem and menagerie—perhaps to St. Ives, perhaps not.

Any particular problem might be encoded in working memory in a variety of ways. How we encode it influences our approach in trying to solve it. As an example, see whether you can solve the problem in the following exercise.

Check It Out: Pigs and Chickens

Part 1.
Put your math skills to work in helping a farmer keep track of his livestock:

> Old MacDonald has a barnyard full of pigs and chickens. Altogether there are 21 heads and 60 legs in the barnyard (not counting MacDonald's own head and legs). How many pigs and how many chickens are running around the barnyard?

Limit yourself to a maximum of three minutes in tackling this problem.

· · ·

Part 2.
Were you able to figure out the answer? If you had trouble, think about the problem this way:

> Imagine that the pigs are standing upright on only their two hind legs, with their front two legs raised over their heads. Therefore, both the pigs and the chickens are standing on two legs. Figure out how many legs are on the ground and how many

must be in the air. From this information, can you determine the number of pigs and chickens in the barnyard?

One way to solve Old MacDonald's problem is with algebra. There are two unknowns here, which we might encode as x (number of pigs) and y (number of chickens). We can create two equations, one for the number of heads:

$$x + y = 21$$

and one for the number of legs (the pigs each have four and the chickens each have two):

$$4x + 2y = 60$$

Then, through a series of algebraic steps (for instance, one might begin by changing the first equation to $x = 21 - y$ and then substituting x in the second equation with $21 - y$), you would eventually end up with $x = 9$ and $y = 12$—hence, 9 pigs and 12 chickens.

If, instead, you used the visual image I suggested, you might have taken the following approach:

Because there are 21 heads, the total number of animals must be 21. Thus, there must be 42 legs on the ground (21 x 2), which leaves 18 pigs' legs in the air (60 – 42). There must therefore be 9 pigs (18 ÷ 2) and 12 chickens (21 – 9).

Some ways of encoding a problem lead to more successful problem solving than others.

Source: Adapted from Ormrod, EDUCATIONAL PSYCHOLOGY, pp. 269–270, © 2011 by Pearson Education, Inc. Reproduced by permission of Pearson Education, Inc.

The pigs-and-chickens problem is a well-defined one. But encoding is important in solving ill-defined ones as well. To see what I mean, here's another exercise to tickle your brain.

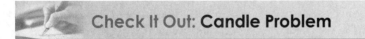

Check It Out: **Increasing Crop Production**

This problem requires a bit of mental time travel:

> Imagine that the year is 1983 and that you are the Minister of Agriculture in the Soviet Union. Crop productivity has been low for the past several years, and people are beginning to go hungry. What would you do to increase crop production?[21]

Take a few minutes to jot down some of your ideas.

How much time did you spend *defining* the problem? Chances are, you didn't spend much time at all; you probably went right to work thinking about possible problem solutions. If you were a political scientist specializing in the Soviet Union, however, you might have spent a fair amount of time identifying various aspects of the problem—perhaps considering Soviet political policies, the amount of land available for farming, and so on—before thinking about how you might solve it. Experts in their fields usually spend a great deal of time pinning down ill-defined problems before attempting to solve them.[22]

Stuck in a Rut: Mental Sets in Problem Solving

I hope you're in a problem-solving mood, because here's another problem for you.

Check It Out: **Candle Problem**

You're in a room in which a bulletin board is firmly attached to the wall. Your task is to stand a thin candle upright beside the bulletin board about 4 feet above the floor. You don't want the candle touching the bulletin board, because the candle's flame must not singe the bulletin board. Instead, you need to place the candle about a centimeter away. How can you accomplish the task using some or all of the materials shown on the next page?[23]

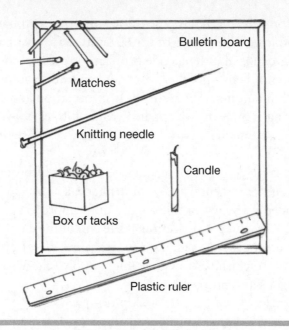

As it turns out, the ruler and knitting needle are useless in solving this problem. Piercing the candle with the knitting needle will probably break the candle, and you're not likely to have much luck balancing the ruler on a few tacks. (I speak from experience here, as my own students have unsuccessfully tried both strategies.) The easiest solution is to turn the thumbtack box upside-down or sideways, attach it to the bulletin board with tacks, and then attach the candle to the top of the box with either a tack or melted wax. Many people don't consider this possibility because they encode the box only as a *container of tacks* and so overlook its potential use as a candle stand.[24] When we encode a problem in a way that excludes potential solutions, we're the victims of a *mental set*.

In most situations, our predisposition to approach similar problems in similar ways enables us to solve routine problems quickly and easily.[25] But a mental set influences how we encode a problem in working memory, and this encoding, in turn, influences the parts of long-term memory that we search for potentially relevant information and procedures. If we encode a problem that steers us in the wrong direction in long-term memory, we're going to have trouble solving the problem.[26]

We sometimes acquire mental sets when we practice solving a particular kind of problem—for instance, doing a series of subtraction problems in math or applying the formula $E = mc^2$ to a sequence of physics problems—without also practicing other kinds of problems at the same time. Such repetitive practice can lead us to encode problems in a certain way without really thinking about them—in other words, it can lead to automaticity in encoding. Although automaticity in the basic information and skills needed for problem solving is often an advantage because it frees up working memory capacity, automaticity in *encoding* problems can lead us to solve them incorrectly.[27]

I don't mean to suggest that all mental sets are counterproductive, however. Certain general mental sets—for instance, a conscious intention to think broad-mindedly about a problem—are quite appropriate and productive. In fact, in the Teaching Tips section at the end of the chapter, I urge teachers to promote a general mental set for transfer—that is, to regularly encourage students to consider how they might apply school subject matter to real-world situations and problems.

There Isn't Always a Prescription for What Ails You: Problem-Solving Strategies

Some problems can be successfully solved with an *algorithm*—a specific sequence of steps that guarantees a correct solution. For example, we can put together an "assembly required" bookshelf if we faithfully follow the instructions that come in the box, and we can make a tasty pumpkin pie if we follow a recipe to the letter in terms of ingredients, measurements, and oven temperature. And we can use the Pythagorean theorem—*in any right triangle, the square of the hypotenuse equals the sum of the squares of the other two sides*—to calculate the length of planks we need for a slanted tree house roof. If we look only at the top part of the tree house I depicted in Figure 9.1—that is, if we ignore the part below the dotted line—we see a right triangle with a horizontal side that's 4 feet long, a vertical side that's 3 feet long (we get this figure by subtracting the shorter side of 2 feet from the longer side of 5 feet), and an unknown hypotenuse. We can then find the length for the roof planks (x) this way:

$$\text{(slanted side)}^2 = \text{(horizontal side)}^2 + \text{(vertical side)}^2$$
$$x^2 = 4^2 + (5 - 2)^2$$

$$x^2 = 16 + 9$$
$$x^2 = 25$$
$$x = 5$$

Thus, we need 5-foot planks to build the roof.

Algorithms are quite dependable. If we apply them to appropriate problems and don't make careless errors, we'll get a correct solution every time. Unfortunately, we don't have algorithms for every conceivable problem that might come our way. For instance, we have no specific algorithms for eliminating a junk food addiction or establishing world peace. And in some situations, algorithms may exist but be too time consuming to be practical. For example, although an algorithm exists for determining the best move in a game of checkers, it doesn't offer a realistic approach to beating an opponent. The algorithm goes like this: Consider every possible move, then consider every possible next move that the opponent could make in response to each of those moves, then consider every follow-up move that could be made in response to each of *those* moves, and so on until you can project a winner for every conceivable series of moves.[28] If you wanted to use this algorithm, you'd better be willing to dedicate the rest of your life to a single game of checkers.

When algorithms for a particular problem are either nonexistent or impractical, we can use *heuristics*—general problem-solving strategies that may or may not yield a correct solution. Following are several heuristics that are potentially applicable to a wide variety of problems:

- *Identify subgoals:* Break a large, complex task into two or more specific subtasks that can be more easily addressed.

- *Use paper and pencil:* Draw a diagram, list a problem's components, or jot down potential solutions or approaches.

- *Draw an analogy:* Identify a situation analogous to the problem situation, and derive potential solutions from the analogy. (This is what you did if you solved the earlier tumor problem by considering the army general's strategy for attacking the fort.)

- *Brainstorm:* Generate a wide variety of possible approaches or solutions without initially evaluating any of them. After a lengthy list has been created, evaluate each item for its potential relevance and usefulness.

■ *"Incubate" the situation:* Let a problem remain unresolved for a few hours or days, allowing time for a broad search of long-term memory for potentially productive approaches.[29]

Whether we use algorithms or heuristics (or perhaps a combination of both) to solve problems, we must be careful that we do so *mindfully and meaningfully.* As an example, here's yet another problem for you to solve.

Check It Out: **Quarters and Dimes**

See if you can solve this problem before you read further:

A man has seven times as many quarters as he has dimes. The value of the dimes exceeds the value of the quarters by $2.50. How many quarters does he have, and how many dimes?[30]

If you found an answer to the problem—any answer at all—then you overlooked an important point: Quarters are worth more than dimes. If there are more quarters than dimes, the value of the dimes can't possibly be greater than the value of the quarters. I asked you a trick question: The problem makes no sense and so cannot be solved in any meaningful fashion. (If you overlooked the problem's nonsensical nature and used algebra to solve it, you were probably quite surprised to find negative values for both the number of quarters and the number of dimes.)

Mathematically disinclined individuals often apply mathematical procedures without thinking them through and can get ridiculous answers as a result. Here are two examples:

■ A student is asked to figure out how many chickens and how many pigs a farmer has if the farmer has 21 animals with 60 legs in all. The student adds 21 and 60, reasoning that, because the problem says "how many in all," addition is the logical operation.[31]

■ Middle school students are asked to calculate how many 40-person buses are needed to transport 540 people to a baseball game. The majority give an answer that includes a fraction—13½ buses—without acknowledging that in the case of buses, only whole numbers are possible.[32]

In general, successful problem solving involves considerable metacognitive involvement: We must identify a reasonable plan of attack and think about what we're doing every step of the way.[33] A key piece of this metacognitive involvement is to make sure that what we're doing *makes sense*.

Thinking Outside the Box: Creativity

In the preceding sections on transfer and problem solving, I've already laid much of the groundwork for my discussion of creativity. Creativity involves applying something we already know to a new situation—that is, it involves transfer. And more often than not, it involves solving a problem of some sort. So, all the things I've already said about transfer and problem solving apply to creativity as well.

Creativity takes things a step further, however, in that it also involves doing things in novel and ingenious ways. Psychologists have offered varying opinions about its nature, but in general *creativity* has two components:

- *New and original behavior:* Behavior not specifically learned from someone else

- *A productive result:* A product appropriate for, and in some way valuable to, one's culture[34]

To illustrate these two components, let's say that I'm giving a lecture on creativity and want a creative way of keeping my listeners' attention. One possible approach would be to come to the lecture hall stark naked. This approach certainly meets the first criterion for creativity (it's new and original), but it doesn't meet the second criterion (it isn't appropriate in our culture). An alternative strategy might be to begin the lecture by giving my listeners several intriguing problems that require creative thinking. This approach is more likely to meet both criteria: Not only is it an unusual way to begin a lecture, but it's also likely to capture people's attention without trespassing beyond acceptable cultural boundaries.

Figure 9.2
Convergent Thinking Involves Pulling Numerous Ideas into a Single, Integrated Whole. Divergent Thinking Involves Taking a Single Idea in Different Directions.

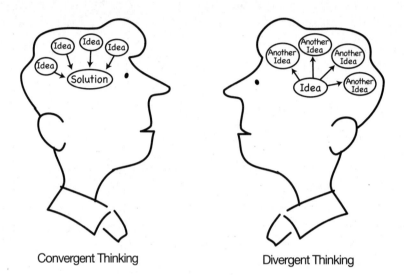

Convergent Thinking   Divergent Thinking

Contrary to popular belief, creativity isn't a single entity that we either have or don't have. Furthermore, creativity is usually somewhat specific to particular situations and content areas. We might show creativity in art, writing, or science, but we won't necessarily be creative in all of these areas.[35]

Great Minds Don't Always Think Alike: Convergent versus Divergent Thinking

When we successfully tackle a problem, we typically do so by pulling together a number of things we know into an integrated whole that resolves the problem. This combining of information into a single idea or product is known as *convergent thinking*. But thinking creatively also involves beginning with a single idea and taking it in a variety of directions, at least one of which leads to something that is new, original, and culturally appropriate. This process of generating many different ideas from a single starting point is known as *divergent thinking*. Figure 9.2 illustrates the difference.

You can engage in divergent thinking yourself in the next exercise.

Check It Out: **Remote Associates**

For each of the following items, identify a single word that is commonly found with all three words in the list. For example, consider the words LIGHT, WHITE, KEEPER. A word found with all three of them is HOUSE (*lighthouse, White House, housekeeper*).

1. CREAM   SKATE   WATER

2. LOSER   THROAT   SPOT

3. CRACKER   FLY   FIGHTER

4. MEASURE   WORM   VIDEO

5. SENSE   COURTESY   PLACE[36]

Did you find yourself going in a variety of mental directions as you thought about each word? For example, with CREAM, did you think about such words as *cow, milk, coffee, cheese,* and *puff?* At some point, you might have stumbled on *ice,* which also goes with SKATE and WATER. Some of the items are more difficult than others. For instance, in several research studies with college students, many participants found Item 5 especially difficult.[37] I've put the answers to Items 2 through 5 in a brief note on page 214.

Origins of Originality: Characteristics of Creative Thinkers

Although divergent thinking is an important component of creativity, other cognitive processes enter into the mix as well. For example, creative individuals tend to:

- Attend to both the broad picture and the nitty-gritty details of a task or problem.

- Think flexibly about how they might interpret a task or problem.

- Broadly search their existing knowledge for potentially helpful information and ideas.

- Recognize the potential relevance of seemingly irrelevant information.

- Identify potentially useful analogies.

- Combine information and ideas in new ways.

- Form visual images related to the situation at hand.

- Closely examine their feelings about a topic (important in artistic creativity).

- Generate many possible approaches to a task or problem, recognizing that only some of them are likely to be successful.

- Metacognitively direct and oversee what they're thinking and doing—for instance, by setting particular goals for their performance and regularly monitoring their progress.[38]

Yet creativity requires certain behaviors, motives, and personality characteristics as well as certain cognitive processes. In particular, creative individuals tend to:

- Seek out and enjoy challenges.

- Have an intense passion for what they're doing.

- Invest a good deal of time and effort in their endeavors.

- Feel comfortable dealing with ambiguous situations.

- Persist in the face of failure.

- Hold high personal standards for evaluating accomplishments.

- Be willing to take risks and make mistakes—that is, to occasionally go out on a limb.

- Have confidence that they can ultimately be successful.[39]

Virtually all of us either have or can acquire the processes, inclinations, and characteristics I've just listed. All of us, then, have the potential to think and act creatively when we put our minds to it.

Maybe You Should Sleep on It: Factors That Facilitate Creative Thinking

Contrary to a popular belief, we're more likely to think creatively about an issue or problem when we know a great deal about the subject matter.[40] The only downside to such a wealth of knowledge is the possibility that we've acquired automaticity for thinking about or doing certain things in certain ways, to the point that we're prone to mental sets that prevent us from thinking outside the box.

Creative thinking also requires time, often a great deal of it.[41] Divergent thinking can be a mental-labor-intensive process that involves traveling down numerous little-used paths in long-term memory, many of which lead to blind alleys or fruitless territory. With perseverance, and perhaps also with a little bit of luck in stumbling into the right (long-term memory) place at the right time, we may eventually come across an idea that's a perfect fit for the task at hand.

In my earlier discussion of problem solving, one of the heuristics I listed was *incubating* a problem—letting it sit unresolved for a lengthy period. Numerous psychologists have vouched for the effectiveness of incubation—including sleeping and dreaming—for enhancing creative thinking and problem solving.[42] They don't completely agree on *why* incubation helps, but presumably it provides time for potentially productive new mental associations to form and also allows factors that might interfere with a broad long-term memory search (fatigue, anxiety, counterproductive mental sets, etc.) to dissipate. And as our minds turn to other tasks and topics, we might unintentionally wander into potentially helpful areas of long-term memory that we haven't previously searched.

In my own experience as a long-time author of books about psychology, I've found incubation to be a highly effective strategy. As I write, I must wrestle with many issues—how best to capture and keep my readers' attention, organize the ever-expanding body of research in my field, explain and illustrate complex concepts, and so on. Sometimes the ideas flow freely, but at other times they don't, and in any case my mind seems to be able to handle only so much strenuous mental exercise in any single day. Oftentimes the best thing I can do is to turn off my computer in midafternoon, take a walk or play a game of racquetball, and essentially let the "mental dust" settle. When I return to my computer the following morning, I often have fresh insights that hadn't occurred to me the day before.

Putting Knowledge to Work

Each of the topics I've addressed in this chapter—transfer, problem solving, and creativity—involves putting previously acquired information and skills to good use in new contexts. The recommendations I offer here can help both you and other people to do exactly that.

THINKING SMART

Many of the strategies I've advocated in previous chapters can enhance your ability to apply what you've learned—making sense of (rather than rote-memorizing) new information, learning essential basic skills to automaticity, studying things in the contexts in which you'll need to remember them, recognizing that true mastery of a topic often takes time and persistence, and so on. Following are some additional suggestions.

 Get into a transfer mindset. You're more likely to apply the things you learn if, from the very beginning, you think about various ways in which you might use them.[43] Underlying this strategy, of course, is the process of *elaboration* I first described in Chapter 5—thinking of new examples, implications, applications, and the like.

Try to pin down and better define ill-defined problems. For example, break a large, complex problem into several subproblems and determine precisely what you need to do to solve each one. Then, identify the additional information you need to solve each of the subproblems and track it down.[44] As you gain expertise in a particular subject area, you'll be able to better define the problems you encounter.[45]

Don't just memorize problem-solving algorithms; make sense of them. You're unlikely to use algorithms appropriately if you're clueless about how and why they work and for what kinds of situations they're appropriate.[46] Mindless use of algorithms is especially common in mathematics, a subject area about which many people are needlessly befuddled. To use math effectively, you *must* make sense of the various techniques you learn. For example, when you divide one fraction by another one, why does it make sense to invert the second fraction and then multiply? And in what contexts might manipulations of equations with unknown quantities—manipulations collectively known as algebra—be the simplest and most dependable course of action?

Brainstorm many possible ways to address complex tasks and problems. Earlier I listed brainstorming among several problem-solving heuristics. Brainstorming is effective not only in increasing problem-solving success but also in enhancing creativity. Although you can certainly brainstorm on your own, doing it with several other people is often better. Individually or as a group, you generate a large number of ideas related to a task or problem, without regard for how realistic or practical any of those ideas might be. Only after you've generated a lengthy set of possibilities—perhaps including some seemingly bizarre, outlandish ones—do you evaluate them to determine each one's likely usefulness and effectiveness. By postponing the evaluation of ideas, you increase the odds that you'll conduct a broad search of long-term memory and, perhaps, stumble on an especially efficacious or creative solution.[47]

▶ *Venture into activities outside of your comfort zone.* You'll become a better, more creative problem solver if you regularly seek out and tackle new challenges and, in so doing, stretch your abilities in new directions.[48] In the process, you'll almost inevitably make mistakes and (gasp!) occasionally embarrass yourself. So what?? Your alternative is to stick only with what you can do well. Personally, I can't think of a better way to mentally stagnate than to continually do what you already know how to do.

Some research even suggests that you might be able to enhance your creative powers by occasionally immersing yourself in diverse cultural environments for lengthy periods.[49] Perhaps exposure to multiple cultures introduces you to ideas and perspectives you wouldn't otherwise have thought of. Perhaps it dislodges you from certain mental ruts you might be in. Who knows? I don't want to draw any definitive conclusions that current research findings don't warrant, but if you want to use this recommendation as a justification to spend a year or two in Ecuador or Thailand . . . well, I say "Go for it."

HELPING OTHERS THINK SMART

The suggestions I've just offered for helping yourself can, of course, also help any people with whom you work, perhaps in the capacity of a teacher, supervisor, or clinician. In your work with others, you might also keep the following strategies in mind.

▶ *Teach new information and skills in the real-world settings in which you want people to apply them.* For example, to teach adolescents how to maintain a balanced diet, you might give them menus from local restaurants and ask them to order a breakfast, lunch, and dinner that, taken together, cover all categories of the food pyramid in appropriate proportions. To show a sales force how to market a new product, you might have them role-play a sales pitch to several colleagues who act as potential buyers.

Real-world practice is especially important for people whose expertise has life-and-death implications. For example, pilots-in-training often spend considerable time practicing basic skills with computer-based flight simulators. And city fire departments occasionally burn down dilapidated old buildings—buildings that were slated to be destroyed anyway—in order to hone their firefighting skills.

▶ ***Explicitly teach and model both algorithmic and heuristic strategies for solving problems.*** Occasionally people develop problem-solving strategies on their own. For instance, many children invent simple addition and subtraction strategies long before they encounter arithmetic at school.[50] But without some systematic instruction in effective strategies, even the most inventive of individuals may sometimes resort to unproductive trial and error to solve problems. Following are several research-based recommendations for teaching problem-solving strategies:

- Describe and demonstrate specific strategies and the situations in which each can be useful.

- Provide worked-out examples of how a particular strategy might be applied, and ask people to explain what is happening at each step.

- Help people understand why particular strategies are relevant and effective in certain situations.

- Initially simplify complex problem-solving situations—for example, by breaking a large problem into two or more smaller ones, giving hints about possible strategies, or providing partial solutions.

- Ask people to explain what they're thinking and doing as they work through a problem.

- Have people solve problems in small groups, sharing ideas about problem-solving strategies, modeling various approaches for one another, and discussing the merits of each approach.[51]

▶ ***Provide practice with a broad range of examples and applications.*** Ideally, practice should encompass the full range of situations in which new knowledge, skills, and problem-solving strategies might be used. It's important to note that people who engage in such diversified practice are apt to perform more poorly in the early stages of instruction than they would otherwise. Over the long run, however, they're usually better able to transfer what they've learned to new situations.[52]

Clearly, then, there's a trade-off between the expediency of instruction and the likelihood of transfer. Personally, I'd opt for maximizing transfer.

▶ ***Also provide practice in identifying problems.*** In traditional elementary, secondary, and college classrooms, teachers usually provide the problems they want their students to solve. But beyond the classroom—for instance, at home, in interpersonal relationships, and in various professional contexts—people must often identify and define for themselves the problems that stand in their way. Giving children and adults alike some guided practice with such *problem finding* is almost certainly a good idea.[53]

▶ ***Communicate that creative thoughts and behaviors are valued.*** One way to do this is to encourage and reward unusual ideas and responses, even those that might fly in the face of conventional ways of thinking. For example, you might express excitement when someone completes a project in a unique and unusual manner. And as you evaluate people's performance in whatever activity you've asked them to do, acknowledge responses that, although not what you were expecting, are quite legitimate. Regularly engaging in creative activities yourself also shows that you value creativity.[54]

Teaching Tips

▶ **Promote mastery of a subject area.** Transfer, effective problem solving, and creative thinking are more likely to occur when students fully understand a topic.[55] For example, if you want students to apply scientific principles in a creative manner—perhaps as they complete a science fair experiment or develop a solution to an environmental problem—they should have those principles down pat.

Encourage a mental set for transfer. Earlier I noted that mental sets in problem solving—predispositions to solve problems in particular ways—sometimes interfere with successful problem solving. Yet a general mental set to apply school subject matter to diverse contexts is clearly beneficial.[56]

What *doesn't* work is to encourage students to learn class material for vague and somewhat mysterious purposes ("You'll need to know this in college," "It will come in handy later in life"). Far more effective is to create a *culture of transfer*—a learning environment in which applying school subject matter to new situations, cross-disciplinary contexts, and real-world problems is both the expectation and the norm.[57] Here are three simple strategies for creating such a culture:

- Regularly tie academic content to a variety of situations both in and out of school.

- Encourage students to be constantly thinking, "How might I use this information?" as they listen, read, and study.

- Provide frequent practice in applying school topics to real-world problems.[58]

To minimize negative transfer, emphasize important differences between two seemingly similar concepts or ideas. Sometimes the differences between two topics are subtle and easy for students to overlook. For example, insects and spiders are in many ways similar critters—they're both small arthropods with exoskeletons and a generally creepy-crawly nature—and so students may inappropriately transfer what they know about one group of creepy-crawlies to the other. And I've already noted the common tendency to inappropriately transfer knowledge of whole-number arithmetic to work with decimals. You can reduce negative transfer from one topic to a seemingly similar one by clearly and emphatically pointing out the differences. Another strategy (although admittedly not always a practical one) is to teach one topic in one setting and the other in a very different environment.[59]

Provide the structure and guidance students may need to be successful in their early problem-solving efforts. Following are several examples of what you might do:

- Present problems in a concrete manner; for example, provide real objects that students can manipulate, or present a graphic illustration of a problem's components.

■   Encourage students to make problems concrete *for themselves;* for instance, encourage them to draw a picture or a diagram.

■   Have students work individually or in small groups to identify several ways of representing a single problem on paper—perhaps as a formula, a table, and a graph.

■   Ask questions that encourage students to think about a problem in productive ways.

■   Help students identify perspectives and strategies that are leading them in counterproductive directions.[60]

   Teach metacognitive strategies that can enhance problem solving and creativity. Especially when complex tasks are involved, successful problem solvers and creative thinkers are not only cognitively but also metacognitively active. For example, they tend to set specific goals for themselves, consciously plan a course of action, identify specific strategies that are likely to be effective, monitor their progress as they go along, and change strategies as necessary.[61]

   Explicitly teaching students to be more metacognitive in their problem-solving and creative endeavors enhances their performance and success rates.[62] Here are several ways in which you might help students become more metacognitively skillful in their efforts to solve problems and think creatively:

■   Ask students to explain what they're doing and why they're doing it as they work on a problem.

■   Give students questions they can ask *themselves* as they work on a task or problem ("What exactly am I doing?" "Why am I doing it?" "Am I getting closer to my goal?" "Why do I think this strategy is the best one?").

■   Teach students to identify common errors in their problem solving and to check regularly for these errors.

■   Ask students to reflect on their problem solutions to determine whether the solutions make sense within the context of the original problems.[63]

   Engage students in authentic activities. An *authentic activity* is one that's similar to a task students might encounter in the outside world. Authentic activities increase the likelihood that students will transfer what they're learning to real-world contexts. Such activities can also be quite motivating: Students readily grasp the point of doing them.[64]

Authentic activities can be developed for virtually any area of the curriculum. For example, you might ask students to engage in one or more of the following activities:

- Write an editorial.
- Conduct an experiment.
- Graph data from a schoolwide survey.
- Create and distribute a class newsletter.
- Tutor a classmate.

- Make a videotape.
- Perform a workplace routine.
- Develop a class website to showcase special projects.

Authentic activities often enhance students' problem-solving skills. For example, preschoolers acquire and use new problem-solving strategies when they actively participate in realistic problem situations while watching the children's television program *Blue's Clues*.[65] And school-age children are more likely to check their solutions to mathematics problems—in particular, to make sure their solutions make logical sense—when they use math for real-life tasks.[66]

In some instances authentic activities take the form of *problem-based* or *project-based learning,* in which students acquire new knowledge and skills as they work on complex problems or projects similar to those they might find in the outside world. To be effective in enhancing students' learning—rather than sources of frustration and failure—most authentic activities of this nature require considerable teacher guidance and support.[67]

Keep in mind that it isn't necessarily desirable to fill the entire school day with complex, authentic tasks. For one thing, students can sometimes achieve automaticity for basic skills more quickly when they practice them in relative isolation from other activities. For example, when learning to play the violin, students need to master their fingering before they join an orchestra, and when learning to play soccer, they need to practice dribbling and passing before they can play effectively in a game. Second, some authentic tasks may be too expensive and time-consuming to warrant regular use in the classroom. It is probably more important that classroom tasks encourage students to engage in learning strategies that promote long-term retention and transfer of classroom subject matter—organization, elaboration, comprehension monitoring, and so on—than that assigned tasks always be authentic.[68]

Present challenging problems and creative tasks within the context of collaborative group activities. Collaborative and cooperative group work can enhance students' problem solving and creative thinking in several ways. For instance, by discussing concepts and principles relevant to a task or problem, students may identify more interrelationships among things they've learned and clarify things about which they're confused. By thinking aloud about how to tackle a problem, they may gain greater metacognitive awareness of what they're doing. By observing the more effective perspectives and strategies that their classmates sometimes demonstrate, they may begin to adopt those perspectives and strategies themselves, leaving their own, less efficient ones behind. And ultimately, students tend to create more sophisticated solutions and products when they work together rather than on their own.[69]

Take advantage of computer technology. For instance, spreadsheet programs can help students organize and analyze large bodies of data, and drawing programs enable them to experiment with a variety of computer tools to create colorful works of art. Many Internet websites also provide problem-solving activities appropriate for children and adolescents. For example, the following websites offer problem-solving activities related to a wide range of topics:

- National Science Foundation (www.nsf.gov)

- Smithsonian Institution (www.smithsonianeducation.org)

- Educator's Reference Desk (www.eduref.org)

- Discovery Education (school.discoveryeducation.com)

Focus students' attention on internal rather than external rewards. Students tend to be more creative when they engage in activities they enjoy and when they can take pride in their accomplishments. To foster creativity, then, you might occasionally give students opportunities to explore their own interests—those they will gladly pursue without having to be prodded. You can also foster creativity by downplaying the importance of grades, focusing students' attention instead on the internal satisfaction that their creative efforts bring.[70]

Give students the freedom, security, and time they need to take risks. To be creative, students must be willing to take risks—something they're unlikely to do if they're afraid of failing. To encourage risk taking, you might allow students to engage in certain activities without evaluating their performance. You can also urge them to think of their mistakes and failures as an inevitable but usually temporary aspect of the creative process. For example, when students are writing a creative short story, you might give them several opportunities to get your feedback—and perhaps the feedback of their peers as well—before they turn in a final product. And ultimately, you must give students the *time* they need to experiment with new materials and ideas, think in divergent directions, and switch gears if their early efforts don't produce desired results.[71]

Answers to the Remote Associates exercise:

> *Item 2*: sore (sore loser, sore throat, sore spot)
> *Item 3*: fire (firecracker, firefly, firefighter)
> *Item 4*: tape (tape measure, tapeworm, videotape)
> *Item 5*: common (common sense, common courtesy, commonplace)

Becoming a More Intelligent Thinker and Learner: Acquiring Productive Perspectives and Habits

In the preceding chapters, I have, I hope, given you a solid understanding of what our brains and minds can reasonably do for us. My intention in this chapter is to convey a sense of optimism about what we human beings can mentally accomplish when we put our minds to it. The fact of the matter is, we can accomplish a great deal under the right conditions, and to a considerable degree those conditions are *under our control*.

You're Probably Smarter Than You Think You Are: The Nature of Intelligence

In your many interactions with your fellow human beings over the years, you've undoubtedly observed that some people pick up new ideas and skills more quickly than others do and that some folks can solve problems more successfully and creatively than others can. We often use the word *intelligence* to refer to such ability differences. But what do we really mean by this term?

Psychologists have been quibbling about the nature of intelligence for almost as long as they've been in business as an academic discipline, and even to this day they don't all agree on the matter. Some suggest that intelligence is a single, general ability—sometimes known as the g *factor* or, more simply, g— that people have to varying degrees and apply in a wide range of activities. Underlying it, these psychologists suspect, may be a general ability to process information quickly and efficiently and, perhaps, a slightly larger working memory capacity as well.[1] But other psychologists strongly disagree, citing evidence that people can be more or less intelligent in different subject areas and on different kinds of tasks.[2] A third group has found a middle ground, suggesting that intelligent thinking and behavior depend both on a general underlying intellectual ability *(g)* and on knowledge and abilities related to specific domains, tasks, and mental processes.[3]

Despite their bickering, most psychologists suggest that intelligence has several distinct qualities:

- It is *adaptive*—it can be used flexibly to respond to a variety of situations and problems.

- It is related to *learning ability*—people who are intelligent in particular domains learn new information and behaviors in those domains more quickly and easily than people who are less intelligent in the domains.

- It involves the *use.of prior knowledge* to analyze and understand new situations effectively.

- It involves the complex interaction and coordination of *many different mental processes.* well-rounded.

- It is *culture specific*—what is intelligent behavior in one culture isn't necessarily intelligent behavior in another culture.[4] being able to go to college / start business.

With these qualities in mind, I offer an intentionally broad definition of *intelligence:* the ability to apply prior knowledge and experiences flexibly to accomplish challenging new tasks.

It's Not All in the Numbers: What IQ Tests Do and Don't Tell Us

Even though psychologists can't agree on what intelligence *is,* they've been trying to measure it for more than a century. Their efforts began in 1904, when school officials in France asked the psychologist Alfred Binet to develop a means of identifying students who would have exceptional difficulty in regular classrooms and might therefore need an alternative educational program. To accomplish the task, Binet devised a test that measured general knowledge, vocabulary, perception, memory, and abstract thought. He found that students who performed poorly on his test tended to perform poorly in school as well. Binet's test was the earliest version of what we now call an *intelligence test*.

Most modern-day intelligence tests include numerous questions and tasks designed to assess various kinds of knowledge and abilities. The following exercise can give you a sense of what intelligence tests are like.

Check It Out: Mock Intelligence Test

Answer each of these questions:

1. What does the word *penitence* mean?

2. How are a goat and a beetle alike?

3. What should you do if you get separated from your family in a large department store?

4. What do people mean when they say, "A rolling stone gathers no moss"?

5. Complete the following analogy: ▲ is to △ as ○● is to:

   a. ●●   b. ●○   c. ◖   d. ▷◀

As you can see, there's nothing especially magical about intelligence tests. The questions and tasks they include are, for the most part, fairly ordinary ones. But in combination they can yield a rough estimate of a person's general level of cognitive functioning. When I was a child, many schools administered intelligence tests to all their students. These days, however, the tests are typically reserved for identifying people who possibly have exceptional

abilities—perhaps quite high or perhaps at the lower end of the continuum—
that require special educational or clinical services.

Scores on intelligence tests were originally calculated using a formula
involving division and so were called intelligence quotient, or *IQ*, scores.
Although we still use the term *IQ*, intelligence test scores are no longer
based on the old formula. Instead, they're determined by comparing a
person's performance on the test with the performance of many other
people in the same age-group. Scores in the range of 100—say, between
85 and 115—indicate average performance. Scores of 130 or higher are
considered quite exceptional: Only about 2½% of people get scores this
high. Scores of 70 or below are also unusual: Only about 2½% of people
get scores this low.

On average, people who get higher scores on intelligence tests tend to
do better in school and achieve at higher levels in the adult workplace.[5]
Notice the first two words in the preceding sentence: *on average*. For a
variety of reasons, some people with high IQ scores don't perform well in
the classroom or on the job, and others achieve at much higher levels than we
would predict from their IQ scores alone. Furthermore, IQ scores seem to
predict performance on traditional academic tasks better than they predict
performance on everyday, real-world tasks or on unusual, multifaceted
problems.[6]

Intelligence tests focus on certain kinds of traits and abilities and largely
ignore others. For example, they don't evaluate the extent to which we're
willing to view a situation from multiple perspectives, examine new information with a critical eye, actively take charge of our own learning, and persist in
our attempts at mastery when the going gets tough. Yet such characteristics are
often just as important as measured intelligence in determining success on
academic and real-world tasks.[7]

It's important to note, too, that *IQ scores can and often do change over
time.* The longer the time interval between two measures of intelligence, the
greater the fluctuation in IQ, especially when initial measures were taken in the
early years.[8] IQ scores and other measures of cognitive ability often increase
over time when people are highly motivated, independent learners and when
they have regular access to stimulating activities and a variety of reading
materials.[9] As a general rule, then, we should *not* use IQ scores to predict
anyone's achievement many years down the road.

Are We Born Smart or Made Smart?
Nature versus Nurture in Intelligence

Both heredity and environment seem to influence intelligence to some degree. For decades the question has been—and continues to be—*How much of each?* Just as psychologists quibble about what intelligence is, so, too, do they quibble about how much our genetic heritage and environmental circumstances each influence its development. This nature–nurture debate *(nature* referring to genetics, *nurture* referring to environment) has spawned more books and research articles than I can begin to count, and some of them reveal a good deal of that hot cognition of which I spoke in Chapter 5. Psychologists get much more emotional about this issue than about, say, the nature of working memory or the usefulness of mnemonics.

Heredity almost certainly plays some role in intelligence. For instance, identical twins (who have the same genetic makeup) tend to have more similar IQ scores than nonidentical (fraternal) twins do, even when the twins are separated at birth and grow up in different homes. Rather than inheriting a single "IQ gene" that determines our intellectual ability, we probably inherit a variety of characteristics that in one way or another affect our particular cognitive abilities and talents.[10]

Nevertheless, it's becoming increasingly evident that environment has a great deal to say about how intelligent we are. A variety of environmental factors influence intelligence, sometimes for the better and sometimes for the worse. Poor nutrition in the early years (including the nine months before birth) leads to lower IQ scores, as does a mother's excessive use of alcohol during pregnancy.[11] Moving a child from a neglectful, impoverished home environment to a more nurturing, stimulating one—for instance, through adoption—can result in IQ gains of 15 points or more.[12] Also effective are long-term intervention programs designed to help children acquire basic cognitive and academic skills.[13] Even simply *going to school* has a positive effect on IQ scores.[14] Since the 1940s, there has been a slow but steady worldwide increase in people's IQ scores—a trend that is probably due to smaller-family sizes, better nutrition, more schooling, increasing cognitive stimulation (through increased access to television, reading materials, etc.), and other long-term changes in people's general environments.[15]

Researchers may never be able to pin down the answer to the *How much of each?* question. Genetic and environmental factors interact in their influences on intelligence in ways that can probably never be disentangled. For one thing, genes require reasonable environmental support to do their work. In an extremely impoverished environment—one with a lack of adequate nutrition and very limited stimulation—heredity may have little influence on our intellectual growth, but under better circumstances it can play a significant role.[16] Second, heredity seems to affect how susceptible or impervious we are to particular environmental conditions: Some people may need considerable guidance and support to do well, but others may thrive even in suboptimal conditions.[17] And third, people who initially have only small genetic advantages in certain domains may venture into activities and learning opportunities that greatly enhance their abilities in those areas.[18] For example, children who inherit genes that give them a slight edge in mathematics are more likely than their less-endowed peers to enroll in advanced math courses and in other ways nurture their inherited talent.

One thing is clear, however: Our environment has a significant impact on our intelligence. This is true not only for our past environment but also for our present one, as you will see now.

Sharing the Mental Load: Distributed Intelligence

When we use the word *intelligence,* we're apt to think of some sort of "thing" that lurks within us—a thing that we carry with us from place to place and apply in various situations. This view of intelligence puts the onus entirely on us as individuals: We either *are* intelligent or we *aren't.*

But now let's change our terminology ever so slightly, from *intelligence* to *intelligent behavior.* With this subtle shift, we can begin to think about ways in which our current environment might support us in our efforts to respond flexibly and adaptively to challenging circumstances. In fact, we're far more likely to think and behave intelligently when we have assistance from our physical, cultural, and/or social environment. Psychologists use the term *distributed intelligence* to refer to this partly-in-the-head-and-partly-in-the-world view of intelligence.

We can "distribute" a challenging task—that is, we can pass some of the cognitive burden onto something or someone else—in at least three ways. First, we can use physical objects, especially technology (calculators, computers, etc.), to handle and manipulate large amounts of information we might be working with. Second, we can encode and think about complex situations and problems using the variety of symbol systems—words, charts, diagrams, mathematical equations, and so on—that our culture has given us. And third, we can work with other people to explore ideas and solve problems—as I mentioned in Chapter 3, two heads are often better than one. Furthermore, when we work with others on complex, challenging tasks and problems, we teach one another strategies and ways of thinking that can help each of us think even *more* intelligently on future occasions.[19]

If we look at intelligence from this distributed perspective, we realize that intelligence isn't entirely a characteristic that resides inside of us, nor is it something that can be easily measured and then summarized as an IQ. Instead, it is a highly variable and context-specific ability that increases when we have appropriate environmental supports to help us on our way.

Giving Credit Where Credit May or May Not Be Due: Attributions

As you now well know, we human beings are predisposed to make sense of our experiences. Such sense making sometimes involves determining why certain things happen to us—in other words, we try to identify cause-and-effect relationships regarding events that affect us personally. Our beliefs about what behaviors and other factors bring about various events in our lives are known as *attributions*.

We form attributions for many aspects of our daily lives—why we do well or poorly on assignments and projects, why we're well liked or unpopular with our peers, why we're skilled athletes or total klutzes, and so on. To gain insight into the kinds of attributions you yourself might form, try the next exercise.

Check It Out: **Carberry and Seville**

Imagine you're a student who is currently taking two college courses, one in psychoceramics and one in sociocosmetology. (So, okay, these two disciplines don't really exist, but go along with me here.) You've recently taken your first exam in each of these courses and today you get your test scores. Let's see how you interpret each score.

1. In Professor Josiah S. Carberry's psychoceramics class, you discover that you've gotten one of the few high test scores in the class, an A–. Why did you do so well when most of your classmates did poorly? Jot down several possible explanations as to why you might have received a high grade in Carberry's class.

2. In Professor Barbara F. Seville's sociocosmetology class, you learn that you *failed* your first test. Why did you get such a low grade? Jot down several possible reasons for your F on Seville's test.

3. You'll be taking a second exam in each of these classes in about three weeks. How much will you study for each exam?

Here are some possible explanations for your A– in Carberry's class:

- You studied hard.

- You're smart.

- You have a natural talent for psychoceramics.

- You were lucky. Carberry asked the right questions; if he'd asked different questions, you might not have done as well.

- Carberry likes you, so he gave you a good grade even though you wrote a bunch of gobbledy-gook on your test paper.

- All those hours you spent brown-nosing Carberry in his office, asking questions about psychoceramics and requesting copies of the research articles he's written (which you never actually read), really paid off.

In contrast, here are some possible reasons that you failed the exam in Seville's class:

- You didn't study enough.

- You studied the wrong things.

- You didn't feel well when you took the test.

- The guy sitting next to you was distracting you with his constant wheezing, coughing, and nose blowing.

- You were unlucky. Seville asked the wrong questions; if she'd asked different questions, you would have done better.

- You're stupid.

- You've never had a knack for sociocosmetology.

- It was a bad test: The questions were ambiguous and tested knowledge of trivial facts.

- Seville hates you and gave you a poor grade out of spite.

We're apt to explain events in our lives in a variety of ways—perhaps attributing them to effort, ability, luck, task difficulty, health, mood, or other people's attitudes and behaviors. Attributions are as much a function of *perception* as of reality, and so they're often distorted in line with our existing beliefs about ourselves and about how the world operates.[20] For example, your poor performance on certain exams in past years may very well have been the result of ineffective study strategies—like many students, you may have tried to learn class material in a rote, meaningless fashion (you obviously hadn't read this book yet!). But because you thought of yourself as a smart person and believed you had studied adequately, you perhaps instead attributed your low scores to the exceptional difficulty or pickiness of the tests or to the fact that your teachers wouldn't recognize true genius if they fell over it.[21]

We haven't yet addressed your answer to Question 3 in the exercise. We'll do so shortly, so don't lose track of how you answered that question.

Where, How Long, and Who's in Control? Three Dimensions of Attributions

Our attributions vary from one another in three major ways.[22] One is the *locus* dimension—that is, whether we attribute an event to something inside or outside of ourselves. Sometimes we attribute events to *internal* things—that is, to factors within ourselves. For example, thinking that winning a prestigious award because you worked hard and believing that you flunked math because you have no "math genes" are both internal attributions. At other times, we attribute events to *external* things—to factors outside of ourselves. Concluding that you won a spelling bee only because you were asked to spell easy words and interpreting a colleague's scowl as a sign of her bad mood (rather than a response to something nasty you might have done to her) are examples of external attributions.

A second dimension of attributions is *stability.* Sometimes we think that events are a result of *stable* factors that probably won't change much in the near future. For example, if you believe that you do well in science because you're just naturally science-minded or that you have trouble making friends because you're overweight, then you're attributing events to stable, relatively long-term causes. But sometimes we instead believe that events are the result of *unstable* factors—to things that can change from one time to the next. Thinking you hit a home run in a softball game because of a lucky break and believing you got a bad test grade because your softball game left you too exhausted to do well on the test are examples of attributions involving unstable factors.

Finally, our attributions vary in *controllability.* On some occasions we attribute events to *controllable* factors—to things we can influence and change. For example, if you believe that an acquaintance invited you to his birthday party because you always smile and say nice things to him and if you think you probably failed a test simply because you didn't study the right things, then you're attributing these events to controllable factors. On other occasions, we attribute events to *uncontrollable* factors—to things over which we have no influence. For example, if you think that you were chosen for a title role in *Romeo and Juliet* because you have the "right face" for the part or that you played a lousy game of basketball because you had a mild case of the flu, then you're attributing these events to uncontrollable factors.

We can analyze virtually any attribution in terms of the three dimensions I've just described. Here are some examples:

Attribution	Locus	Stability	Controllability
Inherited ability	internal	stable	uncontrollable
Personality	internal	stable	uncontrollable
Effort	internal	unstable	controllable
Health	internal	unstable	uncontrollable
Task difficulty	external	stable	uncontrollable
Other people's attitudes	external	stable	uncontrollable
Luck	external	unstable	uncontrollable

As you look at these examples, you might think to yourself that "personality characteristics can change with effort and practice and so are unstable and controllable." Or you might think that "some people are just naturally lucky," in which case luck is an internal rather than external factor. Ultimately our *beliefs* about these various causes of events—rather than the reality of personality, luck, or some other potential cause—have a greater impact on how we feel and behave.[23]

Taking Credit, Placing Blame: Our Self-Protective Bias

As a general rule, we tend to form attributions that maintain or enhance our sense of self-esteem—a tendency known as our *self-protective bias*. In particular, we're apt to attribute our successes to internal causes (such as high ability or hard work) and our failures to external causes (such as bad luck or another person's inconsiderate behaviors). By patting ourselves on the back for the things we do well and putting the blame elsewhere for poor performance, we can take pride in the good things that come our way and have little need to feel ashamed or remorseful when things go poorly.[24]

Although our self-protective bias can do wonders for our egos, it doesn't always work in our best interests. If we inaccurately attribute our failures to factors outside of ourselves—for instance, blaming a low test score on badly written test items—we're unlikely to change our behavior in ways that will lead to greater success.[25]

How We See the Past Affects How We See the Future: Effects of Attributions

Our attributions influence a number of things that, in turn, either directly or indirectly influence our performance in future situations. First, our attributions influence our *emotional reactions to success and failure*. For instance, we're likely to feel proud of our successes and guilty and ashamed about our failures only if we attribute these outcomes to internal causes—for instance, to things we ourselves have done. Unpleasant as guilt and shame might feel, such emotions often spur us to address our shortcomings. If, instead, we think someone else was to blame for an undesirable outcome, we're apt to be angry—an emotion that's unlikely to lead to productive follow-up behaviors.[26]

Second, our attributions have an impact on our *expectations for future successes and failures*. When we attribute previous successes and failures to stable factors—perhaps to innate intelligence or a lack of math genes—we anticipate that our future performance will be similar to our past performance. In contrast, when we attribute successes and failures to *un*stable factors—for instance, to effort or luck—our current success rate has little influence on our future expectations. We're most likely to be optimistic about our chances for future success if we attribute our past successes to stable, dependable (and usually internal) factors, such as innate ability and an enduring work ethic. We can also maintain a reasonably optimistic outlook if we attribute our failures to unstable factors over which we have some control, such as lack of effort or inappropriate strategies.[27]

Third, our attributions affect our *effort and persistence*. If we believe that our failures have been the result of our own lack of effort (a controllable cause), we're apt to try harder and persist in the face of difficulty. If, instead, we attribute failure to a lack of innate ability—we won't be able to do something no matter how hard we try—we're apt to give up easily and might not even take on tasks we've previously done successfully.[28]

Finally, our attributions influence our *learning strategies*. If we believe we can truly master a topic or skill if we work hard to make sense of it, we're apt to engage in meaningful learning, elaboration, and other effective strategies. If, instead, if we have little optimism that we'll understand a topic no matter what we do, we're apt to resort to rehearsal and other relatively "thoughtless" approaches.[29]

With the preceding effects in mind, let's look at how you answered Question 3 in the "Carberry and Seville" exercise: *How much will you study for each exam?* The amount of time you spend studying will depend to some degree on how you've interpreted your earlier test scores. We'll start with your A– on Professor Carberry's exam. If you think you did well because you studied hard, you'll probably spend a lot of time studying for the second test as well. If you think you did well because you're smart or because you're a whiz at psychoceramics, you may not study quite as much. If you believe your success was a matter of luck, you may hardly study at all, but you might wear your lucky sweater when you take the next exam. And if you think the A– reflects how much Carberry likes you, you may decide that time spent flattering him is more important than time spent studying.

As for Seville's second exam, the reasons you identify for your first sociocosmetology grade will, once again, influence how you prepare for her second exam—if, in fact, you prepare at all. If you believe you didn't study enough or didn't study the right things, you may spend more time studying the next time. If you think your poor grade was due to a temporary situation—you were ill, the student sitting next to you distracted you, or Seville asked the wrong questions—then you may study pretty much as you did before, hoping you'll do better the second time around. If you believe your failure was due to your low aptitude for sociocosmetology, Seville's lousy tests, or her inexplicable disdain for you, you may study even less than you did the first time. After all, what good will it do to study when your poor test performance is beyond your control?

Returning to Intelligence: A Permanent Entity or an Incremental Process?

Imagine that you think you did well on Carberry's first psychoceramics test because you're smart—that is, because you have high intelligence. What exactly do you mean by this? Obviously intelligence is an internal factor. But is it stable or unstable? And is it controllable or uncontrollable? How you view intelligence can have a significant influence on your future expectations and behaviors.

Earlier in the chapter I described the nature–nurture debate regarding intelligence. Our personal opinions on this issue have implications for our attributions. If we believe that our intelligence is largely the result of heredity—our genetic luck of the draw—we're likely to have an *entity view* of intelligence. From this perspective, intelligence is a "thing" that is relatively stable and beyond our control. With an entity view, we're apt to see a string of past successes as cause for optimism about future successes. But a consistent record of past failures forecasts a gloomy picture for any future endeavors. "No matter how hard I try, I can't do this," we're apt to think. "Obviously I don't have what it takes."[30]

An alternative view of intelligence, known as an *incremental view,* can help us think optimistically after *either* a success or a failure. From this perspective, intelligence can and often does increase with effort and practice. If we think of intelligence this way, we're apt to work hard to master challenging new tasks, and over the long run we're more likely to be successful.[31]

So how do we acquire one view or the other regarding the nature of intelligence? Our past experiences almost certainly play a key role. If, despite our best efforts, we consistently do poorly in learning activities and other school-like tasks, we're apt to conclude that (1) intelligence is an entity that's relatively stable and out of our control and (2) we don't have very much of it. If, instead, we frequently succeed if we work hard and use effective strategies—and I emphasize the *effective strategies* part here—we're apt to develop an incremental view.[32]

Master of the Universe or Victim of Circumstance: Attributional Style

As we work our way through life, we're constantly forming attributions about this, that, and the other thing. With such "practice" in identifying supposed cause-and-effect relationships, we begin to settle into particular ways of explaining the events and circumstances that come our way. These general tendencies to attribute events to certain kinds of causes—perhaps internal or external, stable or unstable, controllable or uncontrollable—are known as *attributional styles*. Some people develop a general sense of confidence that they can master new tasks and succeed in a variety of endeavors. They attribute their accomplishments to their own ability and effort and have an I-can-do-it attitude known as a *mastery orientation*. But other people, often after a consistent pattern of failures, acquire a growing sense of futility about their ability to control certain aspects of their lives. They have an I-*can't*-do-it attitude known as *learned helplessness*. You might think of this distinction between mastery orientation and learned helplessness—which really reflects a continuum rather than an either-or dichotomy—as a difference between *optimists* and *pessimists*.[33]

Our self-constructed attributions regarding why things are going well or poorly in our lives have a significant impact on our expectations for the future. For example, we're more likely to be optimistic and upbeat if we attribute our failures to things over which we have control.

Even when people with a mastery orientation and people with learned helplessness initially have equal ability, those with a mastery orientation behave in ways that get them further ahead over the long run. In particular, they set ambitious goals for themselves, seek out new challenges, and persist in the face of failure. In academic contexts, they tend to achieve at higher levels than we would expect from their IQ scores and previous grade-point averages. And in athletic contexts, they bounce back from lost games more readily and overcome injuries more quickly than do equally capable but less optimistic athletes.[34]

People with learned helplessness behave quite differently. Because they underestimate their abilities, they set goals they can easily accomplish, avoid the challenging situations that will help them acquire new skills, and respond to failure in counterproductive ways—for instance, by giving up quickly—that almost guarantee future failure. They are also hampered by anxiety-related thoughts, which leave limited working memory capacity for concentrating on what they are doing, and many suffer from chronic depression.[35]

We're most likely to acquire a sense of learned helplessness when unpleasant and seemingly uncontrollable events keep coming our way. Such is often the case for schoolchildren who (perhaps because of an undiagnosed learning disability) consistently have difficulty with reading, math, or some other academic domain.[36] Many victims of long-term physical and psychological abuse by parents or domestic partners also suffer from learned helplessness.[37]

A deeply engrained sense of helplessness acquired after years of failure or abuse isn't likely to be eliminated by a few optimistic words from a teacher, a therapist, or a book such as this one. But it's important to note that learned helplessness is, like any attribution, a *perception* that can, with expert guidance and a sequence of success experiences, change for the better.

Putting Yourself in the Driver's Seat: Self-Regulation

When all is said and done, we are happier and more productive in virtually all aspects of our lives when we have some control—and *know* we have some control—over the things that happen to us. And we can gain some control over our circumstances only when we first take control of our own behaviors and thought processes. Although we can definitely think and act more intelligently when our environment supports us in our efforts, ultimately *we* are the ones who must take charge.

What I'm talking about here is *self-regulation*: consciously and conscientiously deciding how to think and behave and then taking the steps necessary to turn those decisions into reality. The most diligent workers and highest achievers in the classroom, on the athletic field, in the workplace, and elsewhere are likely to be individuals who can effectively self-regulate a number of things, including their behaviors, their learning processes, their feelings, and their motivation.[38] I'll address each of these aspects of self-regulation in turn.

Talking to Yourself Doesn't Mean You're Crazy: Self-Regulated Behavior

As human beings, most of us begin to assume some control of our behavior at a very young age. For instance, by age 2 or 3 we have some knowledge of what behaviors are "good," "bad," "right," and "wrong" and choose our actions accordingly. Increasingly we acquire general standards for behavior that guide us in our daily lives.[39]

One of the first strategies we use to control our own behaviors—often shortly after our second birthday—is *self-talk,* in which we talk our way through new and challenging tasks. As we get a bit older and more skillful, we gradually move our self-talk inward, so that we guide ourselves mentally rather than out loud.[40] Yet even as adults, we occasionally talk our way through difficult tasks and complex maneuvers ("Let's see, first the clutch, then the gas pedal, then the ignition . . ."). For example, my accountant regularly talks to herself as she works her way through complicated tax-preparation software, but then—remembering that she's sitting across the desk from a psychologist (me)—she sheepishly mumbles something about how I must think she's a bit psychotic. I always reassure her that she really *isn't* crazy when she talks to herself—she's quite appropriately being her own boss, giving herself instructions that she can then obediently follow.

Two additional ingredients of self-regulated behavior are *self-monitoring* and *self-evaluation*—that is, keeping tabs on how we're doing, making adjustments as necessary, and passing judgment on the final result.[41] For example, when I return home each morning from my daily walk with my neighborhood walking group, I check my wristwatch to see what time I've arrived. At one point, I was regularly getting to my door at 8:35 a.m, but now I'm more likely to get there at 8:33 a.m. Given that we always begin our 2-mile walk at exactly 8:00 a.m., I consider this progress: My neighbors and I are walking more quickly and aerobically than we used to.

Finally, self-regulated behavior involves *self-imposed consequences* for successes and failures. The following simple exercise can show you what I mean.

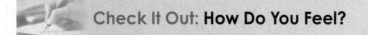

Check It Out: **How Do You Feel?**

How do you feel when you:

1. Get a high grade in a challenging course?

2. Win an athletic competition?

3. Give your time and/or money to a charitable organization?

4. Make careless mistakes on an important project?

5. Thoughtlessly hurt a friend's feelings?

6. Forget an important meeting—one at which your input would have led to a better outcome?

I'm guessing (hoping, really) that you feel some degree of pride regarding Items 1 through 3 and have some sense of regret regarding Items 4 through 6. In general, we're apt to feel proud and give ourselves a mental pat on the back when we've accomplished something we've set out to do, especially if the task was a complex, challenging one. In contrast, when we fail to live up to our own standards for behavior, we're apt to be unhappy, of course, but we may also feel guilty, regretful, or ashamed.[42]

Many self-regulating individuals reward themselves in far more concrete ways when they do something well.[43] For example, writing a book such as this one is a major undertaking. As I sit here in my office tapping on my computer keyboard day after day, I sometimes wonder why in the world I ever committed myself to such a project when I could instead be, say, playing a game of racquetball or joining my walking-group neighbors at their weekly

The author engages in self-regulation.

"Stitch 'n' Bitch" session. Yet each day after my morning walk I go directly to my office to produce a few more pages. How do I do it? I do it by rewarding myself every time I finish a small section of the book. For example, as soon as I finish this section on self-regulated behavior, I'm going to have lunch and watch a little television. But then I'll need to finish the section on self-regulated learning before I can quit for the day and go to the gym to play racquetball.

Mind Control at Its Best: Self-Regulated Learning

When we're young children, our parents and teachers explicitly teach us what they expect us to learn, and they give us ongoing instruction, practice, and feedback until we've mastered it. But as we grow older, our society increasingly expects us to acquire new knowledge and skills on our own, and at this point the most self-regulating learners among us begin to lead the pack in academic and professional endeavors. Meanwhile, non-self-regulating learners start to fall by the wayside.[44]

Self-regulated learning is a complex, multifaceted process that involves the metacognitive skills I described in Chapter 7 and some additional ones as well. People who can effectively learn on their own typically do most or all of the following when they need to tackle a learning task largely on their own:

- *They set one or more goals for their learning.* Self-regulating learners decide in advance what they want to accomplish when they read or study. For example, they may want to learn many specific facts or, instead, simply get the general gist of the material they're studying. Typically they tie their goals for a particular learning activity to their longer-term goals and aspirations.[45]

- *They allocate sufficient time to accomplish their goal(s).* Self-regulating learners determine how much time a particular learning task will require and how best to divvy up that time. Typically they devote more time to more difficult material, but they may sometimes review easy material to make sure they still know it, and they may intentionally ignore material they think is too difficult to master in the time they have. Also, they're apt to set deadlines for themselves as a way of making sure they don't leave important learning tasks until the last minute.[46]

- *They work hard to keep their attention focused on the learning task.* Self-regulating learners try to focus their attention where it needs to be, in part by working in a spot where they're unlikely to be distracted and in part by clearing their minds of potentially distracting thoughts and emotions.[47]

- *They choose and use appropriate learning strategies.* Self-regulating learners have a wide variety of learning strategies at their disposal, and they use different ones depending on the specific goal(s) they want to accomplish. For example, they might read a magazine article differently depending on whether they're reading it for their own pleasure or studying for an exam.[48]

- *They regularly monitor and evaluate their progress.* Self-regulating learners continually check themselves to determine whether they understand and remember what they've just learned, and they either change their learning strategies or modify their goals when necessary.[49]

- *They seek help when they know they need it.* Self-regulated learning doesn't always involve learning independently. Self-regulating learners know when they need an expert's assistance to master certain topics or skills, and on such occasions they actively seek it out.[50]

■ *They reflect on their success or nonsuccess after the fact.* Self-regulating learners continually *learn more about learning* by determining whether their approach to learning has been an effective and expedient one, and if need be, they identify alternative approaches that might be more effective for future learning tasks.[51]

Truly self-regulated learning, then, involves a number of fairly sophisticated skills, many of which we're never explicitly taught. This is not to say that schools *couldn't* teach such skills, only that schools rarely *do* teach them.[52] So, if we don't develop these skills on our own—and some of us don't—we'll have one heckuva time achieving our longer-term educational and professional goals. If we postpone a difficult learning task until the last possible minute, consistently let our minds wander away from the topic at hand, and never check to make sure we remember and understand what we've just read . . . well, we'll go nowhere fast.

Positive Spins and Silver Linings: Self-Regulation of Emotions

We function better in virtually all aspects of our lives when we keep our emotional reactions to events—excitement, anger, anxiety, and so on—within reasonable and culturally appropriate limits.[53] Effective emotional self-regulation often involves a two-pronged approach.[54] First, we learn to control the extent to which we openly *express* our feelings. But in addition, we can better self-regulate our emotions when we *reinterpret events* in order to put a positive spin on what might otherwise be anger- or sadness-provoking circumstances. For instance, if we get an unexpectedly low exam score, we might treat it as a wake-up call to study more diligently in the future. And if we don't get that prestigious job we applied for, we might look on the bright side of things, perhaps thinking, "Maybe this is a blessing in disguise. Now I'll have more time to spend with my family, and I can help out at the local food bank a couple evenings a week."

Try as we might, we can't always control the bad things that happen to us and the good things that don't. But we *can* control how we *think* about what happens to us. Although we certainly don't want our interpretations of events to be too far removed from reality, looking at them through those proverbial rose-colored glasses can often work in our favor over the long run. And many clouds do indeed have silver linings.

Putting Work before Pleasure and Sometimes *Making* Work Pleasure: Self-Regulation of Motivation

On average, truly self-regulating individuals show a great deal of self-discipline. As a group, they can *delay gratification,* putting off activities that might be enjoyable until after they've completed the things that need to be done.[55] Sometimes they do this by giving themselves permission to engage in an enjoyable activity only after they've done the less enjoyable activity first. This is essentially what I do when I make lunch or a racquetball game contingent on completing a section of this book. It's not that I don't enjoy writing—I do, actually—but eating and playing racquetball are a lot more fun. And don't get me started about the chronic muscle aches and carpal tunnel symptoms that a gazillion hours at my computer have given me.

True self-regulators are also skillful at making seemingly unpleasant-but-necessary tasks more enticing in and of themselves. Following are several common strategies:

- They devise ways to make a boring task more interesting—for example, by making it into a game of some sort.

- They try to align a required task with their personal interests—for example, by doing a research paper on a topic they're curious about or signing up for a project that they believe will benefit people they care deeply about.

- They regularly remind themselves about how an activity is a necessary step toward achieving their long-term personal and professional goals.

- They break a lengthy task into several shorter, easier ones, enabling them to gain a sense of accomplishment each time they check an item off their to-do list.

- They engage in self-talk that emphasizes the reasons for completing a task—for example, by saying, "I can help others in my group understand this only if I understand it myself."[56]

In motivation as well as emotion, then, effective self-regulators look for the positive spin, the silver lining.

Taking Charge of Learning and Life

You should now have many reasons to be optimistic about what you and others can learn and accomplish when you put your individual and collective minds to it. Your views about the nature of intelligence, your attributions for various successes and failures, your use of effective self-regulation—all of these in combination with strategies I've described in earlier chapters—can help virtually everyone think and learn more intelligently.

THINKING SMART

Thinking smart requires not only intelligent strategies but also an intelligent mindset and some reality-based optimism about what the future might hold for you. Thus I offer the following suggestions.

▶ *Remember that your intelligence and abilities can improve with practice and environmental support.* After a string of failures in a particular domain or activity—say, in math or basketball—it's all too easy to chalk up the losses to being "hopelessly stupid" or "a total klutz." Such attributions to stable and uncontrollable factors are neither accurate nor productive. Acquiring mastery and expertise in virtually any endeavor requires a great deal of effort, practice, and perseverance. Often, too, it requires learning more effective strategies. Such attributions to unstable and controllable internal factors will serve you in good stead.[57] Sure, you might occasionally have to work a bit harder than some of your peers to get to the same place they are, but so what?

▶ *Seek out activities in which you have some natural talent on which you can build.* All of us have certain things we're especially good at. For some of us, it might be math or science. For others, it might be sports. For still others, it might be interpersonal skills. Whether such seemingly "natural" talents are the result of nature, nurture, or a combination of the two really doesn't matter. What *does* matter is that they can give us an edge up as we venture into new arenas.

When you reach for the sky, then, use any ability "ladders" that can put you a few steps closer to certain parts of the sky. I offer myself as an example here. When

I decided to try my luck at writing a book many years ago, I began by writing, or at least attempting to write, a novel. I quickly discovered that I really wasn't very good at writing fiction—I just didn't seem to have a knack for envisioning characters and plot lines. So I switched gears and steered myself into two things I knew a great deal about: psychology and teaching. The result was a highly enjoyable and rewarding career as a writer of psychology textbooks. I still tinker occasionally with the idea of writing a novel—I envision a pretty seedy one with lots of romance, intrigue, and conniving back-stabbers—but it's a dream that I keep on the back burner while I do things that I know I can do well. Maybe some day. . . .

▶ *Identify both short-term and long-term goals for your learning and performance.* An old saying asks a very good question: "If you don't know where you're going, how will you know when you get there?" Certainly self-chosen long-term goals can help keep you on course. But it often helps to also identify and strive for short-term goals that you can probably achieve in, say, an hour, a day, or a month. By setting, working toward, and accomplishing a series of short-term goals, you'll get regular feedback about the progress you're making, acquire greater self-confidence that you truly have what it takes to be successful in your endeavors, and ultimately achieve at higher levels.[58]

▶ *Reward yourself for your accomplishments.* Feeling proud and gaining a sense of accomplishment are rewards in their own right. But personally, I find it helpful to reward myself in more concrete ways as well. Sometimes my reward is as simple as taking a long walk after completing a challenging section of one of my books. Sometimes it's a small hot fudge sundae after cleaning the house from top to bottom (fortunately for my waistline, I don't clean the house very often). More significant accomplishments—for instance, sending an entire book manuscript to my editor—usually warrant an upscale dinner out with my husband.

The trick is to make your rewards contingent on your accomplishments. That is, treat yourself after—*only* after, never before—you've completed what you need to do. If you have the ice cream sundae before you clean the house, then you have no incentive to clean the house.

I'm giving you an excuse to indulge yourself here—a guilt-free excuse.

▶ *Look for silver linings.* Despite your best efforts, things won't always go as you wish they would. Although you can't control all the unpleasant events that come your way, to some degree you can control how you interpret and feel about them.

You're more likely to remain upbeat and optimistic if you try to find something positive in the negative.[59] For instance, you might see it as a wake-up call to be more diligent and use better strategies or as a "golden opportunity" to try something new and different. Or you might treat it as a "learning experience" that has taught you a valuable lesson or a "challenge" that will ultimately make you stronger and more skillful. I speak from experience here, as my own 60-something years have definitely had their highs and lows, including a couple of pretty devastating lows. I'm much happier—or at least I can better keep my misery within manageable bounds—when I think about how the unexpected dips in life's road are ultimately making me a stronger, more resilient traveler.

HELPING OTHERS THINK SMART

My discussions of intelligence, attributions, and self-regulation in this chapter have implications for your work with other people as well. Here I list several recommendations, with additional ones to follow in the *Teaching Tips* section.

▶ *Provide the support that others need to think and act intelligently.* Such support can take a variety of forms. For example, it might involve:

- Showing people how to use computer software that makes certain tasks easier

- Teaching concepts and mental procedures that enable people to look at certain issues and problems in potentially more insightful ways

- Conducting brainstorming sessions that help people generate ideas for tackling especially challenging problems

- Having people work in small teams to complete a project that none of them would be able to do on their own

An especially intensive form of support is an *apprenticeship,* in which a novice works with an expert for a lengthy period to learn how to perform complex tasks within a particular domain. Ideally, an apprenticeship shows a novice not only what an expert does but also how the expert typically *thinks* about a task or activity. The expert provides considerable structure and guidance throughout the process, gradually removing the support as the novice's competence increases.[60]

An example of an apprenticeship is the relationship between a university professor and a graduate student.[61] For instance, I used to teach a graduate-student seminar called Cognition and Instruction, in which I assigned a gigantic collection of outside readings (the required articles and book chapters stacked up to a pile about 2 feet high). As a class we spent two or three hours over the course of the semester talking about how to read such a large amount of material productively. I shared such strategies as skimming, reading with particular goals in mind, and relating one theorist's perspectives to another's, and I provided a list of questions that students should try to answer as they read. Students were also required to complete a major research project by the end of the semester; I met with each of them periodically to help them narrow down their topic, identify fruitful directions to pursue, organize their thoughts, and consider possible conclusions.

▶ *Give feedback that communicates productive attributions.* In our efforts to make sense of our world, we tend to form attributions not only about our own successes and failures but also about *other people's* successes and failures.[62] For example, imagine that your friend Joe Schmoe has just passed the bar exam, which is an essential step on the road to his hoped-for future career as an attorney. Here are several things you might say to Joe:

- "You did it! You're so smart!"

- "That's wonderful. Your hard work certainly paid off, didn't it?"

- "Wow! It's clear that you really know how to study."

- "Terrific! This is definitely your lucky day!"

But now imagine, instead, that Joe failed the bar exam. Here are several things you might say in your efforts to console him:

- "Maybe law just isn't something you're good at. I bet you'd be a really good engineer, though."

- "Surely if you study more, you'll pass it next time."

- "Hmm, maybe it would help to talk with a few people who passed the exam. They could give you some suggestions about how you might better study for it."

- "You probably just had a bad day."

All of these comments are presumably intended to make Joe feel good. But notice the different attributions they imply—in some cases to uncontrollable abilities (being smart or not "good at" something), in other cases to controllable and therefore changeable behaviors (hard work, lack of practice, effective or ineffective study strategies), and in still other cases to external, uncontrollable causes (a lucky break, a bad day).

To help other people be realistically optimistic about their future performance, it's best to attribute their past successes partly to stable, dependable factors such as natural talent and a consistently supportive environment (thus communicating that success wasn't a fluke) and partly to unstable but controllable factors such as effort and strategies (thus encouraging them to continue to work hard). When things haven't gone so well, however, you can usually best help them by attributing their failures to unstable factors they can control and change, such as insufficient effort and specific strategies they've used or not used.[63]

▶ *Attribute people's successes and failures to effort only if amount of effort really had an impact.* If you're not careful, attributing events to effort can backfire on you. To see what I mean, try my final exercise.

Check It Out: Revisiting Carberry and Seville

Imagine that you're still enrolled in Josiah S. Carberry's psychoceramics course and Barbara F. Seville's sociocosmetology course. On one particular day you find both of their office doors open, and so you drop in for brief conferences with them.

1. As you chat with Professor Carberry, he suggests that you could almost certainly ace his class if you learn to spell the word *psychoceramics*. He gives you 10 minutes of intensive training in the spelling of the word. He then praises you profusely when you're able to spell it correctly. In which of the following ways would you be most likely to respond?
    a. You are delighted that he approves of your performance.
    b. You proudly show him that you've also learned how to spell *sociocosmetology*.
    c. You wonder, "Hey, is this all he thinks I can do?"

2. When you meet with Professor Seville, you express your dismay about doing poorly on her sociocosmetology exam. She is warm and supportive and suggests that you simply try harder next time. But the fact is, you tried as hard as you could the *first* time. Which one of the following conclusions would you be most likely to draw?

a. You need to try even harder next time.

b. You need to exert the same amount of effort the next time and just keep your fingers crossed that you'll make some lucky guesses.

c. Perhaps you just weren't meant to be a sociocosmetologist.

Chances are good that you answered *c* to both questions. Let's first consider the situation in which Carberry spent 10 minutes teaching you how to spell *psychoceramics.* When people succeed at a very easy task and are then praised for their effort, they may get the unintended message that the person lavishing the praise doesn't have much confidence in their ability. Attributing someone's successes to effort is apt to be helpful only when the person has, in fact, exerted a great deal of effort.[64]

Now consider the second scenario, in which Seville encouraged you to try harder even though you had previously studied very hard indeed. When people fail at a task on which they've expended a great deal of effort and are then told that they didn't try hard enough, they're likely to conclude that they simply don't have the ability to perform the task successfully.[65] In such circumstances, it's usually better to attribute their failure to ineffective strategies. As I hope I've convinced you in this book, most people can become considerably more strategic over time, especially if they're specifically *taught* effective strategies. By teaching good strategies, not only do you help other people be more successful, but you can also help them acquire the belief that they can *control* their successes—an important step on the road to developing a mastery-oriented attributional style.[66]

► ***Provide guidance in self-regulation strategies.*** Thanks, in part, to brain maturation over the course of childhood and adolescence, most people become increasingly self-regulating as they grow older.[67] But even many adolescents and adults have few self-regulation skills, often because they've never been taught such skills.[68] Simply setting them loose to sink or swim on their own usually doesn't work: They sink. A better approach is *coregulation,* in which you turn the regulation reins over to them very gradually as they gain increasing competence in controlling their own behaviors, learning, emotions, and motivation.[69] For example, you might:

- Have people set specific goals for themselves, and then ask them to describe their achievements in relation to these goals.

- Provide specific criteria that people can use to judge their own performance.

- Ask them to keep ongoing records of their performance and to reflect on their achievements in journals or portfolios.

- Teach strategies for controlling inappropriate emotional outbursts—for instance, by counting to 10 or by temporarily standing still and taking a few deep breaths.

- Suggest a particular way that they might make an unenjoyable but necessary task into some sort of game.

- Suggest a way that they might reward themselves for completing a task.[70]

Without doubt, the smartest and most successful individuals are those who can strategically take charge of themselves both in the short term and over the long run.[71]

Teaching Tips

Take an incremental view of intelligence. Many teachers have an entity view of intelligence—rather than the more optimistic incremental view—and so perceive students' ability levels to be relatively fixed and stable.[72] Their attributions regarding these "stable" abilities affect their expectations for students' performance, which in turn lead them to treat various students in distinctly different ways. When teachers have high expectations for students, they present more challenging topics and tasks, interact with students frequently, persist in their efforts to help students understand, and give a lot of positive feedback. In contrast, when teachers have low expectations for certain students, they present few if any challenging assignments, ask easy questions, offer few opportunities for speaking in class, and provide little feedback in response to students' efforts.[73]

Remember, intelligence can and does change over time, and with ongoing guidance and support it will almost invariably change in the upward direction. Here are several suggestions that can help you maintain an incremental view of students' intelligence and other abilities:

- Keep in mind that good teachers and good schools can have a significant impact on students' ability levels.

■ Look for every student's particular strengths and talents.

■ Objectively assess students' progress, and be open to evidence that contradicts your initial assessments of students' abilities.

■ Consider multiple possible explanations for students' low achievement—perhaps including lack of relevant prior knowledge on which to build, poor strategies, and missing self-regulation skills.

■ Think of any available IQ scores as rough and in some cases inaccurate assessments of students' current cognitive functioning, *not* as dead-on measures of long-term genetic potential. Be especially skeptical of IQs obtained for students who come from diverse cultural backgrounds, know little English, or were quite young when they were tested.[74]

Scaffold students' early attempts at challenging new tasks.
Psychologists and educators often use the term *scaffolding* in reference to the various kinds of structure and guidance that teachers might provide to help students with initially difficult tasks. You may recognize some of the following examples as recommendations I've made earlier in the book, but all of them help students to "distribute" part of their cognitive burden onto something or somebody else and, as a result, to perform more intelligently:

■ Help students develop a plan for dealing with a new task.

■ Give students specific suggestions about how they might effectively complete the task.

■ Provide a calculator, computer software (word-processing program, spreadsheet, etc.), or other technology that makes some aspects of the task easier.

■ Have students meet in small groups to tackle a task; give each student a specific role to play in the overall group effort.

■ Ask questions that help students think about the task in productive ways.

As students become more adept at performing a task, you can modify the scaffolding to nurture newly emerging skills.[75] And over time, you should gradually phase out the scaffolding, eventually letting students complete the task entirely on their own.

Communicate optimistic attributions and expectations. Assigning challenging tasks and giving students the scaffolding they need to accomplish those tasks successfully is one way of telling students that you have great faith in their abilities. Here are other things you can do:

■ Communicate that new abilities and skills come with effort and practice—in other words, convey an incremental view of intelligence.

■ Attribute students' successes to a combination of high ability and such controllable factors as effort and effective strategies, with a particular focus on strategies.

■ When students fail despite obvious effort, attribute their failures to a lack of effective strategies and help them acquire such strategies.

■ Explicitly teach students to regularly tell themselves that their successes and failures are due to the strategies they're using or not using.

■ Accompany any feedback about errors and weaknesses with concrete suggestions about how students can improve.

■ Provide the extra support and assistance that some students may need to master the skills that most of their classmates have already mastered.[76]

Be careful with the last of these suggestions: providing help. Teacher assistance can be counterproductive if students don't really need it. When students struggle temporarily with a task, unsolicited help from their teacher may communicate the message that they have low ability and little control over their own successes and failures. In contrast, allowing students to struggle on their own for a reasonable amount of time—not to the point of counterproductive frustration, of course— conveys the belief that students do have the ability to succeed on their own.[77]

■ **Teach strategies for self-regulating behavior.** In the preceding "Helping Others Think Smart" section, I offered several recommendations for helping other people more effectively self-regulate their learning, and those recommendations are certainly applicable to classroom situations. But to be successful over the long run, students must actively regulate their behavior as well as their learning. Here are some examples of teaching strategies that researchers have found to be effective:

■ Have students observe and record their own behavior—for instance, by giving them a specially designed recording sheet on which they can keep track of how often they're on and off task over the course of the school day.

- Teach students instructions they can give themselves to help them remember what they're supposed to do.

- Provide specific criteria students can use to evaluate their own behaviors.

- Teach students how to reinforce themselves for appropriate behaviors or academic accomplishments.[78]

Teach strategies for self-regulating emotions and motivation. To some extent, students' ability to control their emotions depends on neurological changes that are driven largely by heredity and emerge only slowly over childhood and adolescence.[79] Even so, you can teach strategies that help students control any feelings that might lead them to behave in ways they will later regret. For instance, you might suggest that students count to 10 in order to calm down before responding to provocations on the playground. And you can help them brainstorm possible silver linings in disappointing circumstances.

You can teach self-motivational strategies as well—self-reinforcement, of course, but also aligning assigned tasks with personal interests and inserting an element of fun and merriment into what might otherwise be tedious tasks. Perhaps most important, however, is to encourage students to identify short-term and long-term goals toward which they want to work. For example, you might ask them to decide how many addition facts they think they can learn by Friday or choose particular skills they would like to master during a gymnastics unit.

Students are typically more motivated to work toward goals—and thus more likely to accomplish those goals—when they have set the goals for themselves instead of having goals imposed on them. Self-chosen goals are especially motivating when they are specific ("I want to learn how to do a cartwheel"), challenging ("Writing a limerick looks difficult, but I'm sure I can do it"), and short-term ("I'm going to learn to count to 100 in French by the end of the month"). By setting and working for a series of short-term, concrete goals, students get regular feedback about the progress they're making, develop self-confidence that they can master school subject matter, and achieve at higher levels.[80]

Ideally, you should encourage students to establish goals that are challenging but also realistic. One thing that *isn't* realistic is continual perfection: Occasional errors are inevitable when tackling new and difficult tasks. When students are satisfied only if every assignment is flawless and every grade is 100%, they are inevitably doomed to occasional failure and may become excessively anxious or depressed about their inability to live up to such an impossible standard.[81]

Being genuinely intelligent doesn't mean consistently exhibiting flawless performance. Instead, it means continually stretching one's abilities by tackling new tasks and challenges and being open and eager to learn from mistakes.

Enhancing Minds and Memories: The Big Picture

My purpose in writing this book has been to spread the word about how human beings really think and learn. I hope that I've dispelled misconceptions you may have had about what we humans can reasonably do—mentally—with new information and experiences. I hope, too, that I've given you some ideas about how to think and learn more effectively and how to help others do likewise.

In this final, short chapter, I offer four key recommendations for thinking smart and helping others think smart. You've seen them all before in one form or another in earlier chapters. But as you learned in Chapter 6, a little review is almost always a good idea.

▶ *Remember that, for better or worse, human minds and memories are invariably constructive and fallible.* Our brains are mind-bogglingly complex organs that are constantly deluged with many, many bits of information from a wide variety of environmental sources. Mother Nature has designed us to focus on the seemingly most important bits and to combine them into general, overall impressions of what is happening around us. The result is that our learning and memories involve constructed interpretations—*not* exact reproductions—of our experiences.

In building our understandings of new situations and events, we use not only new information—which, in any case, is often incomplete and ambiguous—but also our existing knowledge and beliefs. Thanks, in part, to differing personal histories that result in differing bodies of knowledge and beliefs from which to draw, we all construct our own, idiosyncratic interpretations of what we see and hear. Occasionally two or more of us perceive or remember the same situation or event so differently that we have to wonder if we're all on the same planet.

Fortunately, most of us are usually on the same page—or at least in the same book—about everyday matters. When we do have opposing perspectives, it's important that we all keep open minds in an effort to determine what the facts may be. And, of course, truly objective facts aren't always there to be had. Sometimes the truth is really out there somewhere, but sometimes it isn't.

▶ **Be optimistic that you and others can learn to think and behave in increasingly intelligent ways.** We construct beliefs not only about the world around us but also about ourselves as human beings. Some of our self-beliefs—such as the realization that mastering a topic or skill often takes considerable time and effort—work to our benefit. Others—such as the mistaken beliefs that our minds can passively absorb anything we look at and that we've inherited bad "math genes"—aren't terribly productive.

A concept I've alluded to in previous chapters but haven't specifically named is *self-efficacy*—a self-constructed judgment about one's own ability to execute certain behaviors or reach certain goals.[1] We're more likely to engage in tasks and activities we think we can accomplish successfully than those at which we think we'll fail. Our egos can be a bit fragile, after all. I mean, who wants to encounter failure time after time after time after time?

But let's be realistic. As human beings who have unique sets of strengths and weaknesses, we can't possibly have immediate success in tackling all of the many new tasks and activities that come our way. What we *can* have, however, is high *self-efficacy for learning*—a belief that, with reasonable effort and effective strategies, we can continually improve on, and perhaps eventually master, topics and skills that are near and dear to us.[2]

Those of us who teach others must also have high *teacher efficacy*—that is, we must be confident that we can help our students learn and achieve at high levels. And in fact, high-quality instruction can have a significant impact on students' short- and long-term achievements.[3]

▶ **Acquire and teach effective learning strategies—especially cognitive strategies but also behavioral ones.** Once again I need to repeat a point I first made in Chapter 5: People who effectively learn and remember new things are *strategic* learners. In this book I've described a wide variety of learning strategies: taking notes, elaborating on new information, forming visual images, constructing concept maps, monitoring comprehension, using mnemonics, creating study groups . . . the list goes on and on. The covert, inside-the-head strategies, such as elaboration and comprehension monitoring, are ultimately the most important ones. But the overt, behavioral ones, such as taking notes and constructing concept maps, can help foster the covert ones.

▶ ***Identify environmental supports that can help make strategic, intelligent thinking and behavior possible.*** Remember the concept of *distributed intelligence:* We can often think more intelligently when we have physical tools and/or social support systems to help us in our efforts. Some of these, such as structured note-taking forms and teacher guidance, can be gradually left behind as we gain competence. But others, such as laptop computers and brainstorming sessions with peers, can serve us in good stead throughout our lifetimes.

No man or woman is—or should be—an island. We all function more effectively when we work in close conjunction and collaboration with our physical and social worlds.

Suggested Readings

The Human Brain

Bruer, J. T. (1999). *The myth of the first three years: A new understanding of early brain development and lifelong learning*. New York: Free Press.

Byrnes, J. P. (2001). *Minds, brains, and learning: Understanding the psychological and educational relevance of neuroscientific research*. New York: Guilford Press.

Koob, A. (2009). *The root of thought*. Upper Saddle River, NJ: Pearson.

Marcus, G. (2008). *Kluge: The haphazard construction of the human mind*. Boston: Houghton Mifflin.

Ornstein, R. (1997). *The right mind: Making sense of the hemispheres*. San Diego, CA: Harcourt Brace.

Steinberg, L. (2009). Should the science of adolescent brain development inform public policy? *American Psychologist, 64,* 739–750.

Human Memory and Its Idiosyncrasies

Brainerd, C. J., & Reyna, V. F. (2005). *The science of false memory*. Oxford, England: Oxford University Press.

Forgas, J. P. (2001) (Ed.). *Handbook of affect and social cognition*. Mahwah, NJ: Erlbaum.

Langer, E. J. (1997). *The power of mindful learning*. Reading, MA: Addison-Wesley.

Schacter, D. L. (1999). The seven sins of memory: Insights from psychology and neuroscience. *American Psychologist, 54,* 182–203.

Sinatra, G. M., & Pintrich, P. R. (Eds.) (2003). *Intentional conceptual change*. Mahwah, NJ: Erlbaum.

Metacognition and Epistemic Beliefs

Hacker, D. J., Dunlosky, J., & Graesser, A. C. (Eds.) (1998). *Metacognition in educational theory and practice*. Mahwah, NJ: Erlbaum.

Hofer, B. K., & Pintrich, P. R. (Eds.) (2002). *Personal epistemology: The psychology of beliefs about knowledge and knowing*. Mahwah, NJ: Erlbaum.

Waters, H. S., & Schneider, W. (Eds.) (2010). *Metacognition, strategy use, and instruction*. New York: Guilford.

Reasoning and Critical Thinking

Damasio, A. R. (1994). *Descartes' error: Emotion, reason, and the human brain*. New York: Avon Books.

Halpern, D. F. (1997). *Critical thinking across the curriculum: A brief edition of thought and knowledge*. Mahwah, NJ: Erlbaum.

Marcus, G. (2008). *Kluge: The haphazard construction of the human mind*. Boston: Houghton Mifflin.

Moon, J. (2008). *Critical thinking: An exploration of theory and practice*. London: Routledge.

Transfer, Problem Solving, and Creativity

Csikszentmihalyi, M. (1996). *Creativity: Flow and the psychology of discovery and invention*. New York: HarperCollins.

Davidson, J. E., & Sternberg, R. J. (Eds.) (2003). *The psychology of problem solving*. Cambridge, England: Cambridge University Press.

Haskell, R. E. (2001). *Transfer of learning: Cognition, instruction, and reasoning*. San Diego, CA: Academic Press.

Simonton, D. K. (2000). Creativity: Cognitive, personal, developmental, and social aspects. *American Psychologist, 55,* 151–158.

Intelligence, Attributions, and Self-Regulation

Bronson, M. B. (2000). *Self-regulation in early childhood: Nature and nurture*. New York: Guilford Press.

Graham, S., & Folkes, V. S. (Eds.) (1990). *Attribution theory: Applications to achievement, mental health, and interpersonal conflict*. Hillsdale, NJ: Erlbaum.

Meltzer, L. (Ed.) (2007). *Executive function in education: From theory to practice*. New York: Guilford Press.

Nisbett, R. E. (2009). *Intelligence and how to get it*. New York: W. W. Norton.

Perkins, D. (1995). *Outsmarting IQ: The emerging science of learnable intelligence*. New York: Free Press.

Schunk, D. H., & Zimmerman, B. J. (Eds.) (1998). *Self-regulated learning: From teaching to self-reflective practice*. New York: Guilford Press.

Weiner, B. (1986). *An attributional theory of motivation and emotion*. New York: Springer-Verlag.

Reader's Guide: Questions for Discussion

1. What misconceptions did you have about thinking, learning, memory, or the brain before you read this book?

2. Why might the human brain have evolved to be a general pattern detector and summarizer rather than a detailed repository of specific information and events?

3. In what ways do adolescents behave differently from adults? Which differences might be the result of developmental differences in brain maturation?

4. What specific techniques do you personally use to keep yourself mentally alert and attentive?

5. What common misconceptions about the world have you observed in children? in teenagers? in adults?

6. What challenges are there in conducting group discussions about controversial issues?

7. On what kinds of occasions have you found rehearsal to be effective?

8. What strategies do you use to help you mentally organize the things you're learning?

9. What specific mnemonics have you found especially helpful in your own life?

10. The author suggests that writing about something is one good way to better understand and remember it. Have you personally found writing to be helpful as an aid to your learning and memory?

11. What are your earliest memories? Do you know whether they're accurate representations of actual events?

12. Has the author adequately explained why you occasionally have lapses of memory? If not, which incidents of forgetting in your own life still puzzle you?

13. What strategies do you use to help you with prospective memory tasks—that is, with tasks involving remembering the future?

14. In your own schooling, what kinds of instruction did you have that you might reasonably classify as "metacognitive" instruction? For example, did your teachers ever talk about how you could best learn and remember something?

15. How have your own epistemic beliefs changed as you've grown older? What kinds of experiences led you to acquire more sophisticated epistemic beliefs?

16. What strategies do you use to monitor your comprehension when you need to understand and remember something you're reading?

17. Why do you think most people intentionally seek evidence that confirms rather than disconfirms what they already believe to be true?

18. What common pitfalls in reasoning do you often observe in people you know? Which pitfalls seem to be especially prevalent during contentious political campaigns?

19. What behaviors might lead you to believe that a person has a strong need for cognition?

20. What examples of negative transfer have you experienced in your own life?

21. What problem-solving heuristics have you found to be especially helpful?

22. In what ways might immersing yourself in a diverse culture for an extended period enhance your creative thinking abilities?

23. Are there certain domains in which you have a sense of learned helplessness? If so, why?

24. Has your own view of intelligence become more "incremental" as a result of reading this book? If so, why? If not, why not?

25. What self-regulation strategies do you use? In what aspects of self-regulation might you need to improve?

Endnotes

Note: Consistent with the American Psychological Association's *Style Manual,* initials are provided for first authors only when two or more first authors in the reference list have the same surname.

Chapter 1
1. Bransford & Franks, 1971.

Chapter 2
1. Barch, 2003; Clarke, Dalley, Crofts, Robbins, & Roberts, 2004.
2. C. S. Goodman & Tessier-Lavigne, 1997; Lichtman, 2001.
3. Bruer & Greenough, 2001; Byrnes, 2001; Lichtman, 2001; Merzenich, 2001; C. A. Nelson, Thomas, & de Haan, 2006; Trachtenberg et al., 2002.
4. Koob, 2009; Oberheim et al., 2009; Verkhratsky & Butt, 2007.
5. Byrnes, 2001; R. Ornstein, 1997; Siegel, 1999.
6. R. Ornstein, 1997; Siegel, 1999.
7. Bressler, 2002; Huey, Krueger, & Grafman, 2006; Lashley, 1929; Posner & Rothbart, 2007; Rayner, Foorman, Perfetti, Pesetsky, & Seidenberg, 2001.
8. When children lose most of one hemisphere, their remaining hemisphere can often take over many of its functions; for example, see Immordino-Yang & Fischer, 2007.
9. Diamond & Hopson, 1998; Koob, 2009.
10. Diamond & Hopson, 1998; Goldman-Rakic, 1986; Huttenlocher, 1993; Koob, 2009.
11. M. H. Johnson & de Haan, 2001; Kolb & Whishaw, 1990.
12. Koob, 2009.
13 Bruer, 1999; Huttenlocher, 1979, 1990.
14. Huttenlocher & Dabholkar, 1997; C. A. Nelson et al., 2006; Steinberg, 2009.
15. Dempster, 1992; Lichtman, 2001; Merzenich, 2001.
16. Diamond & Hopson, 1998; Gogtay et al., 2004; Lenroot & Giedd, 2007.
17. Koob, 2009; Merzenich, 2001; C. A. Nelson et al., 2006; Paus et al., 1999; Steinberg, 2009.
18. Giedd, Blumenthal, et al., 1999; Sowell & Jernigan, 1998; E. F. Walker, 2002.
19. Luna & Sweeney, 2004; Pribram, 1997; Sowell, Thompson, Holmes, Jernigan, & Toga, 1999; Spear, 2007; Steinberg, 2009.
20. Kolb, Gibb, & Robinson, 2003; Steinberg, 2009; E. F. Walker, 2002.
21. N. R. Carlson, 1999; Giedd, Jeffries, et al., 1999; Huang et al., 2007; L. K. Jacobsen, Giedd, Berquin, et al., 1997; L. K. Jacobsen, Giedd, Castellanos, et al., 1997.
22. Gould, Beylin, Tanapat, Reeves, & Shors, 1999; Leuner et al., 2004; C. A. Nelson et al., 2006; Pereira et al., 2007; Sapolsky, 1999.
23. Koob, 2009.
24. Draganski et al., 2004; Maguire et al., 2000.
25. Gorus, De Raedt, Lambert, Lemper, & Mets, 2008; Hertzog, Kramer, Wilson, & Linderberger, 2009; Lenroot & Giedd, 2007; Poston, Van Gemmert, Barduson, & Stelmach, 2009.
26. Basak, Boot, Voss, & Kramer, 2008; Dye, Green, & Bavelier, 2009; Hertzog et al., 2009; Koob, 2009; C. A. Nelson et al., 2006.
27. Verghese et al., 2007; Wang, Karp, Winbald, & Fratiglioni, 2002; R. S. Wilson, Scherr, Schneider, Li, & Bennett, 2007.
28. Colcombe & Kramer, 2003; Colcombe et al., 2004; Pereira et al., 2007; Yaffe et al., 2009.
29. Dinges & Rogers, 2008; Dumay & Gaskell, 2007; Hahn, Sakmann, & Mehta, 2007; Rasch & Born, 2008.
30. Bruer, 1999.
31. Curtiss, 1977; M. Harris, 1992; Newport, 1990; Pettito, 1997.
32. Hattie, 2009; Ludwig & Phillips, 2007; NICHD Early Child Care Research Network, 2002; Nisbett, 2009; Zigler, 2003.
33. L. B. Cohen & Cashon, 2006; Elkind, 1987.
34. Bronfenbrenner, 1999; R. D. Brown & Bjorklund, 1998; Campbell & Ramey, 1995; Gustafsson & Undheim, 1996; McCall & Plemons, 2001.
35. Bialystok, 1994; Bortfeld & Whitehurst, 2001; Doupe & Kuhl, 1999; Flege, Munro, & MacKay, 1995; J. S. Johnson & Newport, 1989; M. S. C. Thomas & Johnson, 2008.

36. Mechelli et al., 2004.
37. Cleveland, Gibbons, Gerrard, Pomery, & Brody, 2005; V. F. Reyna & Farley, 2006; Steinberg, 2007, 2009.
38. Meltzer, Pollica, & Barzillai, 2007.

Chapter 3

1. Bachevalier, Malkova, & Beauregard, 1996; Bargh & Chartrand, 1999; Frensch & Rünger, 2003.
2. Maus & Nijhawan, 2008; Myin & O'Regan, 2009.
3. Passage from R. C. Anderson, Reynolds, Schallert, & Goetz, 1977, p. 372.
4. R. C. Anderson et al., 1977.
5. Frazier, Gelman, & Wellman, 2009; Gelman, 2003; Kemler Nelson, Egan, & Holt, 2004; Stanovich, 1999; Taleb, 2007; Tulving, 1962.
6. Hong, Morris, Chiu, & Benet-Martínez, 2000; O. Lee, 1999; Tomasello, 2000.
7. Kelemen, 2004; Koltko-Rivera, 2004; Losh, 2003; Medin, 2005.
8. Atran, Medin, & Ross, 2005; O. Lee, 1999; Medin, 2005; Mosborg, 2002.
9. diSessa, 1996; Harvard University, 1988; Haskell, 2001; C. Shanahan, 2004; Winer & Cottrell, 1996.
10. Begg, Anas, & Farinacci, 1992; Brophy, Alleman, & Knighton, 2009; Duit, 1991; Marcus, 2008.
11. Kuhn, 2001b; Marcus, 2008; Porat, 2004; Reiner, Slotta, Chi, & Resnick, 2000.
12. Hynd, 1998, p. 34.
13. Elkind, 1987; Frazier, Gelman, & Wellman, 2009; Kemler Nelson et al., 2004.
14. Hacker, 1998b; Schank & Abelson, 1995; Tessler & Nelson, 1994.
15. Andriessen, 2006; Chinn, 2006; Murphy & Mason, 2006; Nussbaum, 2008.
16. E. M. Evans, 2008; Marcus, 2008; Mosborg, 2002; Porat, 2004; Sherman & Cohen, 2002; Sinatra & Pintrich, 2003; C. L. Smith, Maclin, Grosslight, & Davis, 1997.
17. M. C. Brown, McNeil, & Glenberg, 2009; Hardy, Jonen, Möller, & Stern, 2006; Moreno, 2006; Patrick, Mantzicopoulos, & Samarapungavan, 2009; Vygotsky, 1934/1986.
18. Driver, 1995; Karpov & Haywood, 1998; Sweller, Kirschner, & Clark, 2007; Vygotsky, 1934/1986.
19. Patrick et al., 2009; J. M. Zaragoza & Fraser, 2008.

20. Maria, 1998, p. 13.
21. Murphy & Alexander, 2004, 2008; Putnam, 1992.
22. Chinn & Malhotra, 2002; D. B. Clark, 2006; diSessa, 1996, 2006; diSessa & Minstrell, 1998; Hatano & Inagaki, 2003; Murphy & Alexander, 2008; Murphy & Mason, 2006; Pine & Messer, 2000; Posner, Strike, Hewson, & Gertzog, 1982; K. Roth, 1990, 2002; Sherman & Cohen, 2002; Sinatra & Pintrich, 2003; C. L. Smith, 2007; Vosniadou, 2008.
23. Andre & Windschitl, 2003; Derry, DuRussel, & O'Donnell, 1998; Do & Schallert, 2004; S. Ellis & Rogoff, 1986; D. M. Hogan & Tudge, 1999; K. Hogan et al., 2000; I. Levy, Kaplan, & Patrick, 2000; Stacey, 1992; Wiley & Bailey, 2006; Wittenbaum & Park, 2001.
24. A.-M. Clark et al., 2003; Deutsch, 1993; Hatano & Inagaki, 2003; Lampert, Rittenhouse, & Crumbaugh, 1996; Onosko, 1996; Ormrod, 2008.

Chapter 4

1. Coltheart, Lea, & Thompson, 1974; Cowan, 1995.
2. Cowan, 1995; Wingfield & Byrnes, 1981.
3. R. C. Atkinson & Shiffrin, 1968; Cowan, 1995; Kulhavy, Peterson, & Schwartz, 1986.
4. Cowan, 1995; Horstmann, 2002; Hunt & Worthen, 2006; Rakison, 2003; Sergeant, 1996.
5. Csikszentmihalyi, 1993; Urdan & Turner, 2005; T. D. Wilson & Gilbert, 2008.
6. G. H. Bower, 1994; Edwards & Bryan, 1997; Phelps, Ling, & Carrasco, 2006.
7. J. R. Anderson, 2005; Cherry, 1953; Cowan, 2007.
8. Strayer & Drews, 2007; Strayer & Johnston, 2001.
9. Cowan, Wood, Nugent, & Treisman, 1997; Gold, Murray, Sekuler, Bennett, & Sekuler, 2005; J. S. Reitman, 1974.
10. Aron, 2008; Banich, 2009; S. M. Carlson, Davis, & Leach, 2005; Dehaene, 2007; Kuhn, 2006; Zelazo, Müller, Frye, & Marcovitch, 2003.
11. J. R. Anderson, 2005; Cowan, 2007; R. W. Engle, 2002; Nee, Berman, Moore, & Jonides, 2008; Posner & Rothbart, 2007.
12. G. A. Miller, 1956.
13. Alvarez & Cavanagh, 2004; Baddeley, 2001; Cowan, Chen, & Rouder, 2004.

14. Hills, Maouene, Maouene, Sheya, & Smith, 2009.
15. Heil, Rösler, & Hennighausen, 1994; Reisberg, 1997; Sadoski & Paivio, 2001; Sporer, 1991.
16. N. C. Ellis, 1994; Reber, 1993.
17. Newcombe & Fox, 1994.
18. Kelly, Burton, Kato, & Akamatsu, 2001.
19. J. R. Anderson, 2005; Baddeley, 2001; Cowan, 1995; Nee et al., 2008; Sadoski & Paivio, 2001.
20. Kane et al., 2007; Marcus, 2008.
21. Kliegl & Philipp, 2008.
22. Di Vesta & Gray, 1972; Kiewra, 1989.
23. Grabe, 1986; Krapp, Hidi, & Renninger, 1992; Marmolejo, Wilder, & Bradley, 2004.
24. Alexander & Jetton, 1996; Dole, Duffy, Roehler, & Pearson, 1991; Reynolds & Shirey, 1988.
25. J. Hartley, Bartlett, & Branthwaite, 1980; McAndrew, 1983; McCrudden, Schraw, & Hartley, 2006; McCrudden, Schraw, & Kambe, 2005; Reynolds & Shirey, 1988.
26. Alexander & Jetton, 1996; Broekkamp, Van Hout-Wolters, Rijlaarsdam, & van den Bergh, 2002; Dee-Lucas & Larkin, 1991; Dole et al., 1991; Garner, Alexander, Gillingham, Kulikowich, & Brown, 1991; Reynolds & Shirey, 1988; Schellings, Van Hout-Wolters, & Vermunt, 1996.
27. Gronlund & Brookhart, 2009; McAshan, 1979.
28. Gronlund & Brookhart, 2009; R. L. Linn & Miller, 2005; McCrudden et al., 2005; Popham, 1995.
29. Andre & Windschitl, 2003; Blumenfeld, Kempler, & Krajcik, 2006; Brophy, 1987, 2004, 2008; Brophy & Alleman, 1991; Certo, Cauley, & Chafin, 2002; Chinn, 2006; L. L. Davis & O'Neill, 2004; Doyle, 1986; Flum & Kaplan, 2006; Good & Brophy, 1994; Grabe, 1986; Hidi & Harackiewicz, 2000; Hidi & Renninger, 2006; Krapp et al., 1992; Lambert, Cartledge, Heward, & Lo, 2006; Lepper & Hodell, 1989; Levstik, 1993; Marmolejo et al., 2004; Pellegrini & Bjorklund, 1997; Zahorik, 1994.
30. Fry & Hale, 1996; Kail, 2007; L. M. Oakes & Bauer, 2007.
31. Butcher, 2006; R. Carlson, Chandler, & Sweller, 2003; P. Shah & Hoeffner, 2002; Vekiri, 2002.
32. Benton, Kiewra, Whitfill, & Dennison, 1993; Di Vesta & Gray, 1972; S. W. Evans, Pelham, & Grudberg, 1995; Kiewra, 1989; Peverly,

Brobst, Graham, & Shaw, 2003; Shrager & Mayer, 1989.
33. Benton et al., 1993; Cohn, Hult, & Engle, 1990; Jackson, Ormrod, & Salih, 1999; Kiewra, 1989.
34. Benton et al., 1993; Kiewra, 1989; Meltzer et al., 2007; Pressley et al., 1997; Van Meter, Yokoi, & Pressley, 1994; Yokoi, 1997.

Chapter 5
1. Cowan, Saults, & Morey, 2006; Gathercole & Hitch, 1993; Lehmann & Hasselhorn, 2007; P. A. Ornstein, Grammer, & Coffman, 2010; Pressley & Hilden, 2006.
2. T. O. Nelson, 1977; Rundus, 1971.
3. J. R. Anderson, 2005; Craik & Watkins, 1973; Nickerson & Adams, 1979.
4. Passage from Bransford and Johnson, 1972, p. 722.
5. Bransford & Johnson, 1972.
6. G. H. Bower, Karlin, & Dueck, 1975.
7. Heatherton, Macrae, & Kelley, 2004.
8. Rogers, Kuiper, & Kirker, 1977.
9. Bousfield, 1953; Bransford & Franks, 1971; Buschke, 1977; Jenkins & Russell, 1952; P. A. Ornstein et al., 2010; Tulving, 1962.
10. Nesbit & Adesope, 2006; Novak, 1998; D. H. Robinson & Kiewra, 1995.
11. Passage from G. H. Bower, Black, & Turner, 1979, p. 190.
12. J. R. Anderson, 2005; N. C. Hall, Hladkyj, Perry, & Ruthig, 2004; McDaniel & Einstein, 1989; Muis & Franco, 2009; Myers & Duffy, 1990.
13. Graesser & Bower, 1990; E. F. Loftus, 2003; Reder & Ross, 1983.
14. Marcus, 2008.
15. Behrmann, 2000; J. M. Clark & Paivio, 1991; Kosslyn, 1985.
16. J. M. Clark & Paivio, 1991; Dewhurst & Conway, 1994; Edens & McCormick, 2000; R. Shepard, 1967.
17. Mayer, 2003; Moreno, 2006; Sadoski & Paivio, 2001; Winn, 1991.
18. Cooper, Tindall-Ford, Chandler, & Sweller, 2001; Gambrell & Bales, 1986; Sadoski & Quast, 1990; Speer, Reynolds, Swallow, & Zacks, 2009; Thrailkill, 1996.
19. Carmichael, Hogan, & Walters, 1932; Chambers & Reisberg, 1985; G. R. Loftus & Bell, 1975; Reed, 1974.
20. Benes, 2007; G. H. Bower & Forgas, 2001; Damasio, 1994; Ochsner & Lieberman, 2001; Phelps & Sharot, 2008.

21. P. J. Bauer, 2006; G. H. Bower, 1994; Heuer & Reisberg, 1992; Hu, Stylos-Allan, & Walker, 2006; Talarico, LaBar, & Rubin, 2004; Zeelenberg, Wagenmakers, & Rotteveel, 2006.

22. Buehl & Alexander, 2001; Harmon-Jones, 2001; Marcus, 2008; Zohar & Aharon-Kraversky, 2005.

23. Ashcraft, 2002; Beilock, 2008; Cassady, 2004; Zeidner & Matthews, 2005.

24. V. C. Hall & Edmondson, 1992; Kuhara-Kojima & Hatano, 1991; Schneider, Körkel, & Weinert, 1990; Spilich, Vesonder, Chiesi, & Voss, 1979; C. H. Walker, 1987.

25. Chase & Simon, 1973; Chi, 1978; deGroot, 1965.

26. P. A. Alexander, 2003, 2004; Chi, Glaser, & Rees, 1982; Hatano & Oura, 2003; Rabinowitz & Glaser, 1985; Voss, Greene, Post, & Penner, 1983.

27. Bellezza, 1986; Glanzer & Nolan, 1986.

28. R. K. Atkinson et al., 1999; Jones, Levin, Levin, & Beitzel, 2000; Pressley, Levin, & Delaney, 1982.

29. Ausubel, Novak, & Hanesian, 1978; Church, Elliot, & Gable, 2001.

30. R. K. Atkinson, Derry, Renkl, & Wortham, 2000; de Bruin, Whittingham, Hillebrand, & Rikers, 2003; deLeeuw & Chi, 2003.

31. R. K. Atkinson et al., 1999; G. H. Bower, Clark, Lesgold, & Winzenz, 1969; Nesbit & Adesope, 2006; Novak, 1998; O'Donnell, Dansereau, & Hall, 2002; D. H. Robinson & Kiewra, 1995.

32. Bangert-Drowns, Hurley, & Wilkinson, 2004; Benton, 1997; Klein, 1999; T. Shanahan, 2004.

33. Edens & Potter, 2001; Van Meter, 2001; Van Meter & Garner, 2005.

34. Schraw, Wadkins, & Olafson, 2007; Tice & Baumeister, 1997; Wolters, 2003b.

35. Such confidence is sometimes called *self-efficacy*, or, more specifically, *self-efficacy for learning* (Bandura, 1997; Lodewyk & Winne, 2005; Schunk & Pajares, 2004).

36. Paris & Lindauer, 1976; Spires & Donley, 1998; Stodolsky, Salk, & Glaessner, 1991.

37. Ausubel et al., 1978; Corkill, 1992; Zook, 1991.

38. Meltzer et al., 2007; Pressley, Yokoi, van Meter, Van Etten, & Freebern, 1997.

39. Butcher, 2006; P. Shah & Hoeffner, 2002; Spence, Wong, Rusan, & Rastegar, 2006; Vekiri, 2002.

40. Levin & Mayer, 1993; Mayer, 1989; Winn, 1991.

41. Brophy, 2004.

42. Garcia, 1992; Machiels-Bongaerts, Schmidt, & Boshuizen, 1993; Nelson-Barber & Estrin, 1995; Resnick, 1989; Spires & Donley, 1998.

43. Ausubel et al., 1978; Corkill, 1992; Frase, 1975; Glynn & Di Vesta, 1977; Mayer, 1984; Zook, 1991.

44. Mayer, 1984, p. 30.

45. Ausubel et al., 1978; Ausubel & Robinson, 1969; Church et al., 2001.

46. Ausubel et al., 1978; Lundeberg & Fox, 1991; Middleton & Midgley, 2002; Rittle-Johnson, Siegler, & Alibali, 2001; L. Shepard, Hammerness, Darling-Hammond, & Rust, 2005.

47. Doyle, 1983; Fennema, Carpenter, & Peterson, 1989; Mac Iver, Reuman, & Main, 1995; Schoenfeld, 1985.

48. Crooks, 1988; Ormrod, 2011; L. Shepard et al., 2005.

49. S. R. Beck, Robinson, Carroll, & Apperly, 2006; S. Carey, 1985; McNeil & Uttal, 2009; Metz, 1995.

50. Kuhn & Franklin, 2006; Lovell, 1979; Tamburrini, 1982.

51. Brophy et al., 2009; Perkins & Ritchhart, 2004; Prawat, 1993; Sizer, 1992, 2004.

52. Au, 2007; R. M. Thomas, 2005; Valli & Buese, 2007.

53. Brophy et al., 2009; Brophy & VanSledright, 1997; Perkins & Ritchhart, 2004.

54. Glynn, Yeany, & Britton, 1991; Schwarz & White, 2005.

55. Bulgren, Deshler, Schumaker, & Lenz, 2000; Donnelly & McDaniel, 1993; English, 1997; Zook, 1991.

56. D. E. Brown, 1992; Hartmann, Miller, & Lee, 1984; Hayes & Henk, 1986; Newby, Ertmer, & Stepich, 1994, p. 4 (peristalsis analogy); glacier example courtesy of my husband, a former geography teacher.

57. Duit, 1990; Glynn, 1991; Morra, Gobbo, Marini, & Sheese, 2008; Sfard, 1997; Zook & Di Vesta, 1991.

58. A. King, 1992; McCrudden & Schraw, 2007.

59. O'Donnell & King, 1999; Rosenshine, Meister, & Chapman, 1996; E. Wood et al., 1999.

60. Alleman & Brophy, 1992; I. L. Beck & McKeown, 1994, 2001; Berti, 1994; Brophy et al., 2009; Calfee & Chambliss, 1988; Chambliss, Calfee, & Wong, 1990.

61. I. L. Beck & McKeown, 1994.
62. R. K. Atkinson et al., 1999; Callender & McDaniel, 2007; Kiewra, DuBois, Christian, & McShane, 1988; Ku, Chan, Wu, & Chen, 2008; D. H. Robinson & Kiewra, 1995.
63. Barton, Tan, & Rivet, 2008; Carney & Levin, 1994, 2000; Carney, Levin, & Stackhouse, 1997; Mastropieri & Scruggs, 1992.
64. G. H. Bower, 1972; Dempster & Rohwer, 1974.
65. J. Hartley & Trueman, 1982; Jonassen, Hartley, & Trueman, 1986; A. King, 1992; Lorch, Lorch, & Inman, 1993; Rinehart, Stahl, & Erickson, 1986; Wade-Stein & Kintsch, 2004; Wittrock & Alesandrini, 1990.
66. V. Anderson & Hidi, 1988/1989; Byrnes, 1996; S. Greene & Ackerman, 1995; Jonassen et al., 1986; Spivey, 1997.
67. V. Anderson & Hidi, 1988/1989; A. L. Brown & Day, 1983; Rinehart et al., 1986; Rosenshine & Meister, 1992.
68. Brophy, 1986; Hattie & Timperley, 2007; Hill & Wigfield, 1984; McCoy, 1990; I. G. Sarason, 1980; Stipek, 1993; Tryon, 1980; Zeidner, 1998.

Chapter 6

1. J. R. Anderson, 2005; Pashler, Rohrer, Cepeda, & Carpenter, 2007; Proctor & Dutta, 1995.
2. B. A. Greene & Royer, 1994; LaBerge & Samuels, 1974; Perfetti & Lesgold, 1979.
3. Berninger, Fuller, & Whitaker, 1996; Birnbaum, 1982; Flower & Hayes, 1981; McCutchen, 1996; Pianko, 1979.
4. Reason & Mycielska, 1982.
5. Killeen, 2001; Langer, 2000; LeFevre, Bisanz, & Mrkonjic, 1988.
6. A. Brown, 1991; R. Brown & McNeill, 1966; R. Thompson, Emmorey, & Gollan, 2005.
7. Yarmey, 1973.
8. Balch, Bowman, & Mohler, 1992; Cann & Ross, 1989; Holland, Hendriks, & Aarts, 2005; Rubin, 2006; Schab, 1990.
9. Godden & Baddeley, 1975.
10. J. Brown, 1968.
11. P. J. Bauer, 2006; G. H. Bower, 1994; Heuer & Reisberg, 1992; Talarico et al., 2004; Zeelenberg et al., 2006.
12. Bohannon & Symons, 1992; Brewer, 1992; R. Brown & Kulik, 1977.
13. Brewer, 1992; Rubin, 1992; Schmolck, Buffalo, & Squire, 2000; Talarico & Rubin, 2003.
14. Neisser & Harsch, 1992, p. 9.
15. Neisser & Harsch, 1992, p. 9.
16. Brainerd & Reyna, 2005; E. F. Loftus, Wolchover, & Page, 2006; Perfect, 2002; Wells, Olson, & Charman, 2002.
17. Brainerd & Reyna, 2005; Lindsay, 1993; E. F. Loftus, 1992; MacLeod & Saunders, 2008; M. S. Zaragoza & Mitchell, 1996.
18. Sutton, 2009; Wells et al., 2002; Wright, Memon, Skagerberg, & Gabbert, 2009.
19. E. F. Loftus & Palmer, 1974.
20. M. Carroll & Perfect, 2002; Payne, Neuschatz, Lampinen, & Lynn, 1997; Odegard, Cooper, Lampinen, Reyna, & Brainerd, 2009; E. J. Robinson & Whitcombe, 2003; Schacter, 1999.
21. Schacter, 1999; Thomson, 1988.
22. M. Carroll & Perfect, 2002.
23. J. C. K. Chan, Thomas, & Bulevich, 2009; Coman, Manier, & Hirst, 2009; Jacoby, 2008; E. J. Marsh, 2007; Mazzoni & Kirsch, 2002; Paller, 2004; Winograd & Neisser, 1992.
24. Neisser & Harsch, 1992.
25. Geraerts et al., 2009; Ghetti & Alexander, 2004; E. F. Loftus, 2003, 2004; Pezdek, Finger, & Hodge, 1997.
26. M. Carroll & Perfect, 2002; Giles, Gopnik, & Heyman, 2002; M. K. Johnson, 2006.
27. D. Davis & Loftus, 2009; McNally & Geraerts, 2009.
28. Lindsay & Norman, 1977.
29. J. L. C. Lee, Everitt, & Thomas, 2004; Wixted, 2005; Woodman & Vogel, 2005.
30. Dumay & Gaskell, 2007; Hahn et al., 2007; Massimini et al., 2005; Rasch & Born, 2008; Stickgold, 2005; Woodman & Vogel, 2005.
31. J. R. Anderson, 2005; E. F. Loftus & Loftus, 1980
32. Ashcraft, 2002; Kirkland, 1971; Marcus, 2008; Tobias, 1980.
33. Brainerd & Reyna, 2005; Dinges et al., 1992; Lynn, Lock, Myers, & Payne, 1997.
34. Dempster, 1985; Lustig & Hasher, 2001; Lustig, Konkel, & Jacoby, 2004.
35. Arrigo & Pezdek, 1997; B. P. Jones, 1993; E. F. Loftus & Kaufman, 1992; Nadel & Jacobs, 1998; Ray et al., 2006; Wegman, 1985.
36. M. C. Anderson & Levy, 2009; M. C. Anderson & Green, 2001; B. J. Levy & Anderson, 2002; McNally & Geraerts, 2009.
37. Erdelyi, 1985; G. S. Goodman et al., 2003; B. P. Jones, 1993; McNally & Geraerts, 2009; S. Porter & Peace, 2007.
38. E. F. Loftus & Loftus, 1980.

39. Altmann & Gray, 2002; Brainerd & Reyna, 2005; Schacter, 1999.
40. Brainerd & Reyna, 2005; G. Cohen, 2000.
41. D. Davidson, 2006; Hunt & Worthen, 2006; Pansky & Koriat, 2004; Reisberg, 1997.
42. Newcombe, Drummey, Fox, Lie, & Ottinger-Albergs, 2000; Pillemer & White, 1989.
43. DeCasper & Spence, 1986; Dirix, Nijhuis, Jongsma, & Hornstra, 2009.
44. DeCasper & Spence, 1986.
45. Nadel, 2005; C. A. Nelson, 1995; Newcombe et al., 2000.
46. P. J. Bauer, DeBoer, & Lukowski, 2007; LeDoux, 1998; Nell, 2002; C. A. Nelson et al., 2006; Newcombe et al., 2000.
47. Eacott, 1999; Haden, Ornstein, Eckerman, & Didow, 2001; K. Nelson, 1996; Simcock & Hayne, 2002.
48. Einstein & McDaniel, 2005; Stokes, Pierroutsakos, & Einstein, 2007.
49. J. R. Anderson, 1983; Bahrick, Bahrick, Bahrick, & Bahrick, 1993; Cepeda, Vul, Rohrer, Wixted, & Pashler, 2008; Péladeau, Forget, & Gagné, 2003; Proctor & Dutta, 1995.
50. J. S. Brown, Collins, & Duguid, 1989; Greeno, Collins, & Resnick, 1996; Lave & Wenger, 1991; M. C. Linn, 2008.
51. P. J. Bauer, 2006; Fivush, Haden, & Reese, 2006; Fivush & Nelson, 2004; Leichtman, Pillemer, Wang, Koreishi, & Han, 2000; McGuigan & Salmon, 2004.
52. Giles et al., 2002; Gilstrap & Ceci, 2005; G. S. Goodman & Quas, 2008; Hirstein, 2005; Holliday, 2003; Wells & Bradfield, 1999; Wells, Olson, & Charman, 2002; M. S. Zaragoza, Payment, Ackil, Drivdahl, & Beck, 2001.
53. Brainerd & Reyna, 2005; Ghetti & Alexander, 2004; M. K. Johnson, 2006; Mazzoni & Kirsch, 2002; Perfect, 2002; Wells et al., 2002.
54. Bahrick et al., 1993; Cepeda et al., 2008; Péladeau et al., 2003; Proctor & Dutta, 1995.
55. Dempster, 1991; Frederiksen, 1984b; Halpin & Halpin, 1982; C. I. Johnson & Mayer, 2009; Roediger & Karpicke, 2006; L. Shepard, 2000; Wixson, 1984.
56. Mac Iver et al., 1995.
57. Jegede & Olajide, 1995; M. B. Rowe, 1974; Tharp, 1989; Tobin, 1987.
58. Cassady & Johnson, 2002; Chapell et al., 2005; Harter, Whitesell, & Kowalski, 1992; Hembree, 1988; Phillips, Pitcher, Worsham, & Miller, 1980.

59. Chabrán, 2003; Kirkland, 1971; Phillips et al., 1980; S. B. Sarason, 1972.
60. Aronson et al., 1999; Cadinu, Maass, Rosabianca, & Kiesner, 2005; Inzlicht & Ben-Zeev, 2003; McKown & Weinstein, 2003; Osborne & Simmons, 2002; Steele, 1997.
61. Brophy, 1986, 2004; Covington, 1992; Dweck, Mangels, & Good, 2004; Gaudry & Spielberger, 1971; Gaynor & Millham, 1976; Hill, 1984; Hill & Wigfield, 1984; Josephs, Newman, Brown, & Beer, 2003; Kirkland, 1971; McKown & Weinstein, 2003; Paris & Turner, 1994; I. G. Sarason, 1980; S. B. Sarason, 1972; Stipek, 1993.

Chapter 7
1. S. T. Parker, Mitchell, & Boccia, 1994; Plotnik, de Waal, & Reiss, 2006; Prior, Schwarz, & Güntürkün, 2008.
2. Schoenfeld, 1985.
3. I thank Russell Carney for suggesting this learning task (Carney, Levin, & Webb, 2009). Internet websites disagree regarding the relative sizes of Great Britain, Honshu, and Victoria, so don't think of me as the ultimate authority on this topic.
4. Afflerbach & Cho, 2010; Baker, 1989; J. E. Barnett, 1999; A. L. Brown & Palincsar, 1987; C. Chan, Burtis, & Bereiter, 1997; Dole et al., 1991; Hacker, 1998b; Myers & Duffy, 1990; Oakhill, 1993; Palincsar & Brown, 1989; K. Roth & Anderson, 1988; Schraw & Bruning, 1995; van der Broek, 1990.
5. J. A. Greene & Azevedo, 2009; Kardash & Amlund, 1991.
6. Dunning, Heath, & Suls, 2004; Hacker, Bol, Horgan, & Rakow, 2000; Kuhn, Garcia-Mila, Zohar, & Andersen, 1995; Schneider, 2010; Schneider & Lockl, 2002; Sinkavich, 1995; J. W. Thomas, 1993.
7. The origin of the term is generally credited to John Flavell (1976, 1979).
8. Baxter Magolda, 2002; Belenky, Clinchy, Goldberger, & Tarule, 1986/1997; Bendixen & Rule, 2004; Hofer, 2004; Kuhn & Weinstock, 2002; Schommer, Calvert, Gariglietti, & Bajaj, 1997.
9. Kardash & Howell, 2000; Kardash & Scholes, 1996; Mason, 2003; Patrick & Pintrich, 2001; Schommer, 1994a.
10. Hofer & Pintrich, 1997; Muis, 2004; Schommer et al., 1997; Schommer-Aikins, Hopkins, Anderson, & Drouhard, 2005; P. Wood & Kardash, 2002.

11. Hammer, 1994; Hofer & Pintrich, 1997; Mason, 2003; Purdie & Hattie, 1996; Schommer, 1994a; Schommer-Aikins, 2002.
12. Bendixen & Rule, 2004; Hofer & Pintrich, 1997; Schommer-Aikins et al., 2005.
13. Ormrod, 2009, p. 99.
14. Mason, Gava, & Boldrin, 2008; Muis, 2007; Schommer-Aikins, 2002; Sinatra & Pintrich, 2003.
15. Belenky et al., 1986/1997; Hofer & Pintrich, 1997; P. M. King & Kitchener, 2002; Kuhn & Weinstock, 2002; Moon, 2008.
16. Marcus, 2008; Wiley et al., 2009.
17. Schommer, 1994a; Schommer-Aikins et al., 2005; P. Wood & Kardash, 2002.
18. Kardash & Howell, 2000; Schommer, 1994a, 1994b.
19. Dweck, 2000; Dweck & Molden, 2005; P. Wood & Kardash, 2002.
20. Blackwell, Trzesniewski, & Dweck, 2007; Dweck & Molden, 2005; K. Hartley & Bendixen, 2001; Schommer, 1994a, 1994b.
21. Dunlosky & Lipko, 2007; Hacker et al., 2000; Metcalfe, 2009; Schneider, 2010.
22. Hacker, 1998a; Stone, 2000; Winne & Jamieson-Noel, 2001.
23. Dunning et al., 2004; Hacker et al., 2000; Hofer & Pintrich, 1997; Voss & Schauble, 1992.
24. Bereiter & Scardamalia, 1989; Langer, 1997, 2000; Sinatra & Pintrich, 2003.
25. Baker, 1989; Dunlosky, Rawson, & McDonald, 2002; Hacke et al., 2000; Stone, 2000; Weaver & Kelemen, 1997.
26. deLeeuw & Chi, 2003; Dunlosky & Lipko, 2007; Dunning et al., 2004; Hacker, 1998b; Martínez, Bannan-Ritland, Kitsantas, & Baek, 2008.
27. Cepeda et al., 2008; Dunlosky et al., 2002.
28. Nisbett, 2009.
29. Meltzer, 2007; Morgan, 1985; Rosenshine et al., 1996.
30. Blackwell et al., 2007; Dweck, 2009; Nisbett, 2009.
31. Flavell, Green, & Flavell, 2000.
32. Lovett & Flavell, 1990; T. M. McDevitt & Ormrod, 2010; Wellman & Hickling, 1994.
33. Hattie, Biggs, & Purdie, 1996; Paris & Paris, 2001; Pressley, El-Dinary, Marks, Brown, & Stein, 1992; Pressley, Harris, & Marks, 1992.
34. Meltzer et al., 2007; Ormrod, 2008, 2011; Pressley, El-Dinary, et al., 1992; Pressley, Harris, & Marks, 1992; Pressley & Hilden, 2006; Volet, Vaura, & Salonen, 2009.
35. Alfassi, 2004; R. C. Anderson et al., 2001; A. L. Brown & Palincsar, 1987; D. Fuchs, Fuchs, Mathes, & Simmons, 1997; Gaskins, Satlow, & Pressley, 2007; Guthrie et al., 1998, 2004; McGee, Knight, & Boudah, 2001; P. A. Ornstein et al., 2010; Palincsar & Brown, 1984; Palincsar & Herrenkohl, 1999; Pressley, El-Dinary, et al., 1992; Spires & Donley, 1998; H. Thompson & Carr, 1995.
36. R. C. Anderson et al., 2001; Palincsar & Brown, 1989.
37. T. M. McDevitt & Ormrod, 2010.
38. Buehl & Alexander, 2005; Kardash & Sinatra, 2003; P. M. King & Kitchener, 2002; Moon, 2008; Muis, Bendixen, & Haerle, 2006; Murphy & Mason, 2006.
39. Andre & Windschitl, 2003; C. Chan et al., 1997; De Corte, Op't Eynde, & Verschaffel, 2002; Gaskins & Pressley, 2007; Kardash & Scholes, 1996; P. M. King & Kitchener, 2002; Muis et al., 2006; Schommer, 1994b; C. L. Smith, Maclin, Houghton, & Hennessey, 2000; Vosniadou, 1991.
40. Bragstad & Stumpf, 1982; Dunlosky et al., 2002; Eilam, 2001; A. King, 1992; Mithaug & Mithaug, 2003; Morgan, 1985; Nietfeld & Cao, 2004; Paris & Ayres, 1994; Rosenshine et al., 1996; Windschitl, 2002; Winne, 1995b.

Chapter 8

1. Amsterlaw, 2006; Heyman, 2008; Kuhn & Franklin, 2006; Metz, 2004; Morra et al., 2008; Pillow, 2002.
2. R. J. Harris, 1977, p. 605.
3. Frank, Cohen, & Sanfey, 2009; Klaczynski, 2001; Minsky, 2006; Sadoski & Paivio, 2001.
4. Halpern, 1997; Kuhn & Franklin, 2006; Kuhn & Udell, 2003; Spoehr & Spoehr, 1994.
5. J. Evans, Over, & Manktelow, 1993; Kuhn & Franklin, 2006; Newstead, Pollard, & Evans, 1992.
6. Quinn, 2002; Rakison & Oakes, 2003.
7. Ashcraft, 2002; Zeidner & Matthews, 2005.
8. Problem modeled after Halpern, 1998.
9. Halpern, 1998.
10. Morsanyi, Primi, Chiesi, & Handley, 2009.
11. Problem modeled after Halpern, 1998.
12. Kahneman & Tversky, 1984, p. 345.
13. Kahneman & Tversky, 1984, p. 345.
14. Kahneman & Tversky, 1984, p. 343.
15. Kahneman & Tversky, 1984, p. 343.
16. Kuhn & Franklin, 2006; Schauble, 1996.
17. Problem modeled after Wason, 1968.

18. Marcus, 2008; E. R. Smith & Conrey, 2009; Wason, 1968.
19. L. B. Cohen & Cashon, 2006; Kuhn, Black, Keselman, & Kaplan, 2000; Taleb, 2007; Waldmann, Hagmayer, & Blaisdell, 2006.
20. Lassiter, 2002.
21. Brighton & Todd, 2009.
22. Kahneman & Tversky, 1996; Klaczynski, 2001; E. R. Smith & Conrey, 2009.
23. Problem based on Kahneman & Tversky, 1996.
24. Kahneman & Tversky, 1996.
25. Halpern, 1997; Kahneman & Tversky, 1996; Marcus, 2008; A. K. Shah & Oppenheimer, 2009.
26. Gleitman, 1985, p. 432.
27. Kaiser, McCloskey, & Proffitt, 1986; Schacter, 1999.
28. Hynd, 1998, p. 34.
29. De Lisi & Golbeck, 1999; Kunda, 1990; Murphy & Mason, 2006; E. R. Smith & Conrey, 2009.
30. Marcus, 2008; Morris, Carranza, & Fox, 2008; Mosborg, 2002; Porat, 2004; Southerland & Sinatra, 2003.
31. Blanchette & Richards, 2004; Damasio, 1994; Moon, 2008; Sherman & Cohen, 2002; Winkielman & Berridge, 2004.
32. Behl-Chadha, 1996; Killeen, 1991; Pfeifer, Brown, & Juvonen, 2007; Quinn, 2003; Wasserman, 1993; Wasserman, DeVolder, Coppage, 1992.
33. Bruner, 1957; Halford & Andrews, 2006; Mandler, 2000; Ormrod, 2008.
34. Kağıtçıbaşi, 2007; Moon, 2008; Norenzayan, Choi, & Peng, 2007; Sinha & Tripathi, 1994.
35. Cacioppo, Petty, Feinstein, & Jarvis, 1996; P. M. King & Kitchener, 2002; West, Toplak, & Stanovich, 2008.
36. Halpern, 2008; Kardash & Scholes, 1996; Moon, 2008; Perkins, Tishman, Ritchhart, Donis, & Andrade, 2000; Southerland & Sinatra, 2003; West et al., 2008.
37. Halpern, 2008; Perkins et al., 2000; Toplak & Stanovich, 2002.
38. Halpern, 1997.
39. Kuhn, 2001a; Perkins & Ritchhart, 2004; Stanovich, 1999.
40. Cacioppo et al., 1996; Dai, 2002; Murphy & Mason, 2006.
41. Matthews, Zeidner, & Roberts, 2006; Southerland & Sinatra, 2003; Stanovich, 1999.
42. Kardash & Scholes, 1996; P. M. King & Kitchener, 2002; Kuhn, 2001b; Moon, 2008; Sinatra & Mason, 2008; Schommer-Aikins, 2002; vanSledright & Limón, 2006.
43. Kuhn & Park, 2005; Kuhn & Weinstock, 2002; Hofer & Pintrich, 1997.
44. DeBacker & Crowson, 2006, 2008; Jost, Glaser, Kruglanski, & Sulloway, 2003; Kruglanski & Webster, 1996.
45. M. I. Bauer & Johnson-Laird, 1993; Johnson-Laird, 1989; Ormrod, 1979.
46. Questions based on Halpern, 1998, p. 454; Stahl & Shanahan, 2004, pp. 110–111; Wiley et al., 2009, pp. 1098–1099.
47. Bendixen & Rule, 2004; Halpern, 1997; Sinatra & Pintrich, 2003.
48. Kuhn, Daniels, & Krishnan, 2003; Kuhn & Weinstock, 2002; M. McDevitt, 2005; Moon, 2008; Perkins & Ritchhart, 2004.
49. D. W. Johnson & Johnson, 2009; Reiter, 1994.
50. Flum & Kaplan, 2006; Kuhn, 2001b, 2006; Lampert et al., 1996; Moon, 2008; Muis et al., 2006.
51. Ormrod, 2008.
52. D. W. Johnson & Johnson, 2009; Kuhn & Udell, 2003; Murphy, 2007; Nussbaum, 2008.
53. Abrami et al., 2008; Marcus, 2008; Wiley et al., 2009.
54. Derry, Levin, Osana, & Jones, 1998; Girotto & Light, 1993; M. C. Linn, Clement, Pulos, & Sullivan, 1989; Schliemann & Carraher, 1993.
55. Ward & Grasha, 1986.
56. Derry et al., 1998.
57. Stahl & Shanahan, 2004, pp. 110–111.
58. Brophy et al., 2009; Moon, 2008.
59. Metzger, Flanagin, & Zwarun 2003; Wiley et al., 2009.
60. Questions based on Afflerbach & Cho, 2010; Wiley et al., 2009.
61. Monte-Sano, 2008; Moon, 2008.

Chapter 9

1. Behr & Harel, 1988; Ni & Zhou, 2005; Tirosh & Graeber, 1990.
2. Schmidt & Young, 1987.
3. Problem based on Gick & Holyoak, 1980, pp. 307–308.
4. Analogous problem based on Gick & Holyoak, 1980, p. 309.
5. Haskell, 2001; James, 1890; Mayer & Wittrock, 1996; Perkins & Salomon, 1989; Thorndike, 1924.

6. S. M. Barnett & Ceci, 2002; Gray & Orasanu, 1987.

7. J. R. Anderson, Reder, & Simon, 1996; Fong, Krantz, & Nisbett, 1986; Gick & Holyoak, 1987; Judd, 1932; Perkins, 1995; Perkins & Salomon, 1989; M. Perry, 1991; Singley & Anderson, 1989.

8. Bransford & Schwartz, 1999.

9. Bransford & Schwartz, 1999, p. 67.

10. Brooks & Dansereau, 1987; Mayer & Wittrock, 1996; Prawat, 1989.

11. Brophy, 1992b; Cormier & Hagman, 1987; Haskell, 2001; Voss, 1987.

12. Chen, 1999; Cox, 1997; Schmidt & Bjork, 1992.

13. Bassok, 2003; Di Vesta & Peverly, 1984; Haskell, 2001.

14. Haskell, 2001; Light & Butterworth,1993; Perkins & Salomon, 1989; Renkl, Mandl, & Gruber, 1996.

15. J. R. Anderson, Greeno, Reder, & Simon, 2000; S. M. Barnett & Ceci, 2002; Bransford et al., 2006; Perkins, 1995; Posner & Rothbart, 2007.

16. Bransford & Schwartz, 1999; De Corte, 2003; Pugh & Bergin, 2006; Pugh, Linnenbrink, Kelly, Manzey, & Stewart, 2006.

17. J. E. Davidson & Sternberg, 2003; M. W. Eysenck & Keane, 1990; Mayer & Wittrock, 2006; Sternberg et al., 2000; Zimmerman & Campillo, 2003.

18. Hambrick & Engle, 2003; Johnstone & El-Banna, 1986; Perkins, 1995; H. L. Swanson, Jerman, & Zheng, 2008.

19. Frederiksen, 1984a; Mayer & Wittrock, 1996.

20. Mayer, 1986; Ormrod, 1979; Prawat, 1989; Whitten & Graesser, 2003.

21. Problem based on Voss, Greene, Post, & Penner, 1983; Voss, Tyler, & Yengo, 1983.

22. Mitchell, 1989; Swanson, O'Connor, & Cooney, 1990; Voss, Tyler, et al., 1983; Voss, Wolfe, Lawrence, & Engle, 1991.

23. Modeled after Duncker, 1945.

24. Duncker, 1945; Glucksberg & Weisberg, 1966.

25. Maier, 1945.

26. Alexander & Judy, 1988; Mayer, 1992; Stein, 1989.

27. Langer, 2000; Luchins, 1942.

28. Samuel, 1963.

29. J. R. Anderson, 2005; J. E. Davidson & Sternberg, 1998, 2003; Halpern, 1997; Minsky, 2006; Zhong, Dijksterhuis, & Galinsky, 2008.

30. Problem based on Paige & Simon, 1966, p. 79.

31. Lester, 1985.

32. Silver, Shapiro, & Deutsch, 1993.

33. Carr & Biddlecomb, 1998; J. E. Davidson & Sternberg, 1998, 2003; Dominowski, 1998.

34. Plucker, Beghetto, & Dow, 2004; Ripple, 1989; Runco & Chand, 1995; Sawyer, 2003.

35. Glover et al., 1989; Ripple, 1989; Runco, 2005.

36. Items from Bowden & Jung-Beeman, 2003.

37. Bowden & Jung-Beeman, 2003.

38. H.J. Eysenck, 1997; Glover, Ronning, & Reynolds, 1989; Halpern, 1997; Haskell, 2001; Leung, Maddux, Galinsky, & Chiu, 2008; Lubart & Mouchiroud, 2003; Runco, 2004; Russ, 1993; Simonton, 2000, 2004; Zhong et al., 2008.

39. Csikszentmihalyi, 1996; Glover et al., 1989; Halpern, 1997; Leung et al., 2008; Russ, 1993; Simonton, 2000, 2004; Sternberg, 2003; Weisberg, 1993.

40. Amabile & Hennessey, 1992; Haskell, 2001; Simonton, 2000; Sternberg, 2003.

41. Feldhusen & Treffinger, 1980; Pruitt, 1989; Sternberg, 2003.

42. Cai, Mednick, Harrison, Kanady, & Mednick, 2009; J. E. Davidson, 2003; Dijksterhuis & Nordgren, 2006; H. C. Ellis & Hunt, 1983; Pretz, Naples, & Sternberg, 2003; Wallas, 1926; Zhong et al., 2008.

43. Haskell, 2001; Perkins, 1992; Stein, 1989; Sternberg & Frensch, 1993.

44. Chi & Glaser, 1985; W. R. Reitman, 1964; Simon, 1973, 1978.

45. Bédard & Chi, 1992; Frederiksen, 1984a.

46. Carr, 2010; Geary, 1994; Greeno, 1991; Hiebert & Wearne, 1993; Perkins & Simmons, 1988; Rittle-Johnson et al., 2001.

47. Halpern, 1997; Osborn, 1963; Runco & Chand, 1995.

48. Bransford et al., 2006; Vygotsky, 1987.

49. Leung et al., 2008.

50. Bermejo, 1996; Ginsburg, Cannon, Eisenband, & Pappas, 2006; Siegler & Jenkins, 1989.

51. R. K. Atkinson et al., 2000; R. K. Atkinson, Renkl, & Merrill, 2003; Calin-Jageman & Ratner, 2005; Chinn, 2006; Gauvain, 2001; Kirschner, Sweller, & Clark, 2006; Mayer, 1985; Reimann & Schult, 1996; Renkl & Atkinson, 2003; Rittle-Johnson, 2006.

52. Carr & Biddlecomb, 1998; Chen, 1999; Collins, Brown, & Newman, 1989; De Corte

et al., 1996; Lave, 1988, 1993; Schmidt &
Bjork, 1992.

53. S. I. Brown & Walter, 1990; Eisner, 1994;
Hiebert et al., 1996; A. Porter, 1989; Resnick,
Bill, Lesgold, & Leer, 1991.

54. Hennessey & Amabile, 1987; Lubart &
Mouchiroud, 2003; Runco, 2004; Sternberg,
Grigorenko, & Zhang, 2008.

55. Amabile & Hennessey, 1992; Frederiksen,
1984a; Haskell, 2001; Hiebert & Lefevre,
1986; Simonton, 2000.

56. Stein, 1989; Sternberg & Frensch, 1993.

57. R. A. Engle, 2006; Haskell, 2001; Pea, 1987.

58. R. E. Clark & Blake, 1997; Cox, 1997;
Haskell, 2001; Perkins & Salomon, 1989;
Rogoff, 2003; Sternberg & Frensch, 1993.

59. Bilodeau & Schlosberg, 1951; Greenspoon
& Ranyard, 1957; Sternberg & Frensch,
1993.

60. Anzai, 1991; Brenner et al., 1997; Mayer,
1992; Mayer & Wittrock, 2006; N. E. Perry
& Winne, 2004; Rittle-Johnson & Koedinger,
2005; Turner et al., 1998; Webb et al., 2008.

61. Carr & Biddlecomb, 1998; J. E. Davidson &
Sternberg, 1998, 2003; Dominowski, 1998.

62. L. S. Fuchs et al., 2003; Hattie, 2009; Rittle-
Johnson, 2006.

63. Berthold & Renkl, 2009; Carr, 2010;
Dominowski, 1998; Hoffman & Spatariu,
2008; Johanning, D'Agostino, Steele, &
Shumow, 1999; A. King, 1999; Kramarski &
Mevarech, 2003; Rittle-Johnson, 2006; Roditi
& Steinberg, 2007; Schoenfeld, 1992.

64. S. M. Barnett & Ceci, 2002; Collins et al.,
1989; Rogoff, 2003; Wasley, Hampel, &
Clark, 1997.

65. Crawley, Anderson, Wilder, Williams, &
Santomero, 1999.

66. Cognition and Technology Group at
Vanderbilt, 1993; Rogoff, 2003.

67. Hmelo-Silver, 2004, 2006; Hmelo-Silver,
Duncan, & Chinn, 2007; Krajcik &
Blumenfeld, 2006; Mergendoller, Markham,
Ravitz, & Larmer, 2006; Polman, 2004.

68. J. R. Anderson et al., 1996; Bransford et al.,
2006; Griffin & Griffin, 1994.

69. Brenner et al., 1997; Carr & Biddlecomb,
1998; Chiu, 2008; R. A. Engle, 2006; Good,
McCaslin, & Reys, 1992; Hiebert et al., 1997;
Kilpatrick, 1985; Palincsar & Herrenkohl,
1999; Qin, Johnson, & Johnson, 1995;
Schoenfeld, 1985.

70. Hennessey, 1995; Lubart & Mouchiroud,
2003; Perkins, 1990.

71. Hennessey & Amabile, 1987; Houtz, 1990:
Pruitt, 1989; Sternberg, 2003.

Chapter 10

1. Bornstein et al., 2006; Brody, 1999; Cornoldi,
2010; Demetriou, Christou, Spanoudis, &
Platsidou, 2002; Haier, 2003; Spearman,
1904, 1927; Swanson, 2008.

2. Gardner, 1983, 1999, 2003; Gardner &
Hatch, 1990; Sternberg, 1998, 2004;
Sternberg et al., 2000.

3. Ackerman & Lohman, 2006; J. B. Carroll,
1993, 2003; Flanagan & Ortiz, 2001; Horn,
2008.

4. Greenfield, 1998; Laboratory of Comparative
Human Cognition, 1982; Neisser et al., 1996;
Sternberg, 1997, 2004, 2007; Sternberg &
Detterman, 1986.

5. Brody, 1997; Gustafsson & Undheim, 1996;
Sattler, 2001.

6. J. E. Davidson, 2003; Sternberg, Grigorenko,
& Kidd, 2005; Wenke & Frensch, 2003

7. Duckworth & Seligman, 2005; Kuhn, 2001a;
Nisbett, 2009; Perkins et al., 2000.

8. Bracken & Walker, 1997; Hayslip, 1994;
Sattler, 2001.

9. Echols, West, Stanovich, & Kehr, 1996;
Kyllonen, Stankov, & Roberts, 2008;
Sameroff, Seifer, Baldwin, & Baldwin, 1993;
Stanovich, West, & Harrison, 1995.

10. Horn, 2008; Bouchard, 1997; Kovas &
Plomin, 2007; Plomin, 1994; Simonton, 2001.

11. D'Amato, Chitooran, & Whitten, 1992;
Neisser et al., 1996; Ricciuti, 1993.

12. Beckett et al., 2006; Capron & Duyme, 1989;
Nisbett, 2009; van IJzendoorn & Juffer,
2005.

13. Campbell & Burchinal, 2008; Kağitçibaşi,
2007.

14. Ceci, 2003; Ramey, 1992.

15. Flynn, 2007; E. Hunt, 2008; Neisser, 1998;
Nisbett, 2009.

16. Ceci, 2003; D. C. Rowe, Jacobson, & Van
den Oord, 1999; Turkheimer, Haley,
Waldron, D'Onofrio, & Gottesman, 2003.

17. Kim-Cohen, Moffitt, Caspi, & Taylor, 2004;
Rutter, 1997.

18. Flynn, 2003; Halpern & LaMay, 2000;
Nisbett, 2009; Scarr & McCartney, 1983.

19. Barab & Plucker, 2002; Pea, 1993; Perkins,
1992, 1995; Salomon, 1993.

20. Dweck, 1978; Dweck & Elliott, 1983;
Paris & Byrnes, 1989.

21. Horgan, 1990.

22. Weiner, 1986, 2000, 2004.

23. Dweck & Leggett, 1988; Weiner, 1994.

24. H. W. Marsh, 1990; Paris & Byrnes, 1989; Rhodewalt & Vohs, 2005; Weiner, 1992; Whitley & Frieze, 1985.

25. Seligman, 1991; Zimmerman, 2004.

26. Hareli & Weiner, 2002; Pekrun, 2006.

27. Dweck, 2000; Pomerantz & Saxon, 2001; Weiner, 1984, 1986.

28. Blackwell et al., 2007; Dweck, 2000; Hong, Chiu, & Dweck, 1995; Feather, 1982; Weiner, 1984.

29. Dweck et al., 2004; Mangels, 2004; Palmer & Goetz, 1988; Pressley, Borkowski, & Schneider, 1987; Zimmerman, 1998.

30. Dweck, 2000; Dweck & Leggett, 1988; Hong et al., 1995; Weiner, 1984, 1994.

31. Blackwell et al., 2007; Dweck, 2000; Dweck & Leggett, 1988; Ericsson, 2003; Weiner, 1994.

32. Paris & Byrnes, 1989; Pressley et al., 1987; Schunk, 1990; Stipek, 1993.

33. Dweck, 2000; Peterson, 1990, 2006; Seligman, 1991.

34. Daniels et al., 2009; Dweck, 2000; Graham, 1989; Peterson, 1990, 2006; Seligman, 1991.

35. Dweck, 2000; Graham, 1989; Mikulincer, 1994; Peterson, 1990, 2006; Seligman, 1975, 1991.

36. Dweck, 1986; B. Jacobsen, Lowery, & DuCette, 1986; Stipek & Kowalski, 1989.

37. Bargai, Ben-Shakhar, & Shalev, 2007; van der Kolk, 2007.

38. Bandura, 2008; Duckworth & Seligman, 2005; Pintrich, 2000; Schraw, 2006; Trautwein, Lüdtke, Kastens, & Köller, 2006; Zimmerman & Kitsantas, 2005.

39. Bandura, 1986, 1989; Dunn, 1988; Kochanska, Casey, & Fukumoto, 1995; Lamb, 1991.

40. Berk, 1994; Schimmoeller, 1998; Vygotsky, 1934/1986; Winsler & Naglieri, 2003.

41. Dunning et al., 2004; K. R. Harris, Santangelo, & Graham, 2010; Mace, Belfiore, & Hutchinson, 2001; Vye et al., 1998; Zimmerman & Schunk, 2004.

42. Bandura, 1986; Harter, 1999; Krebs, 2008.

43. Bandura, 1977; K. R. Harris et al., 2010; Wolters, 2003a; Wolters & Rosenthal, 2000.

44. Bandura, 1997; Bronson, 2000; Zimmerman & Bandura, 1994; Zimmerman & Risemberg, 1997.

45. Muis, 2007; Nolen, 1996; Winne & Hadwin, 1998; Wolters, 1998; Zimmerman, 2004.

46. Ariely & Wertenbroch, 2002; Metcalfe, 2002; Son & Metcalfe, 2000; Son & Schwartz, 2002; Zimmerman & Schunk, 2004.

47. Harnishfeger, 1995; Kuhl, 1985; Winne, 1995a; Wolters, 2003a; Zimmerman, 2008.

48. Linderholm, Gustafson, van den Broek, & Lorch, 1997; Schunk & Zimmerman, 1997; Winne, 1995a; Wolters, 2003a.

49. Butler & Winne, 1995; Muis, 2007; Thiede, Anderson, & Therriault, 2003; Zimmerman & Schunk, 2004.

50. Aleven, Stahl, Schworm, Fischer, & Wallace, 2003; Karabenick & Sharma, 1994; Newman, 2008; Ryan, Pintrich, & Midgley, 2001.

51. Kuhn, 2001b; Winne & Stockley, 1998; Zimmerman, 1998, 2004.

52. Hamman, Berthelot, Saia, & Crowley, 2000; Paris & Ayres, 1994; Pressley & Hilden, 2006; Zimmerman & Bandura, 1994.

53. Bronson, 2000; Labouvie-Vief & González, 2004; Peterson, 2006; Wisner Fries & Pollak, 2007.

54. J. E. Bower, Moskowitz, & Epel, 2009; Pekrun, 2006; Richards, 2004; Silk, Steinberg, & Morris, 2003.

55. Bembenutty & Karabenick, 2004; Duckworth & Seligman, 2005; Fries, Dietz, & Schmid, 2008; Trautwein & Köller, 2004.

56. Covington, 2000; R. B. Miller & Brickman, 2004; Sansone, Weir, Harpster, & Morgan, 1992; Wolters, 2003a; Wolters & Rosenthal, 2000.

57. Dweck, 2000; Pomerantz & Saxon, 2001; Weiner, 1984, 1986.

58. Bandura, 1997; Kluger & DeNisi, 1998; Page-Voth & Graham, 1999; Wolters, 2003a.

59. J. E. Bower et al., 2009; N. C. Hall, Goetz, Haynes, Stupnisky, & Chipperfield, 2006; Peterson, 2006.

60. J. S. Brown et al., 1989; Collins, 2006; Elliott, 1995; Lave & Wenger, 1991; Rogoff, 1990, 1991.

61. W. Roth & Bowen, 1995.

62. Weiner, 2000.

63. Curtis & Graham, 1991; Dweck, 2000; Pomerantz & Saxon, 2001; Weiner, 1984.

64. Graham, 1991; Schunk & Pajares, 2004.

65. Curtis & Graham, 1991; Robertson, 2000; Stipek, 1996.

66. Pressley et al., 1987; Weinstein, Hagen, & Meyer, 1991.

67. K. R. Harris et al., 2010; Rothbart, Sheese, & Posner, 2007; Steinberg, 2007.

68. Meltzer, 2007; Paris & Ayres, 1994; Roderick & Camburn, 1999; Zimmerman & Risemberg, 1997.

69. Azevedo, 2005; McCaslin & Good, 1996; N. E. Perry, 1998; Quintana, Zhang, & Krajcik, 2005.

70. Allen, 1998; Belfiore & Hornyak, 1998; Eilam, 2001; Meltzer, 2007; Paris & Ayres, 1994; Paris & Paris, 2001; N. E. Perry, 1998; Winne, 1995b; Wolters, 2003a.

71. Butler & Winne, 1995; Corno et al., 2002; Duckworth & Seligman, 2005; Zimmerman & Risemberg, 1997.

72. J. Oakes & Guiton, 1995; C. Reyna, 2000.

73. Babad, 1993; Brophy, 2006; Good & Brophy, 1994; Graham, 1990; Rosenthal, 1994.

74. Ashton, 1985; Carrasco, 1981; Ceci, 2003; Goldenberg, 1992; Ormrod, 2011; Weinstein, Madison, & Kuklinski, 1995.

75. Puntambekar & Hübscher, 2005.

76. Brophy, 2004; Dweck, 2000; Robertson, 2000; Weinstein et al., 1995.

77. Graham, 1990; Stipek, 1996; Weiner, 1984.

78. Belfiore & Hornyak, 1998; Mace et al., 2001; Meichenbaum, 1985; Meltzer et al., 2007; Reid, Trout, & Schartz, 2005; Webber & Plotts, 2008; Webber, Scheuermann, McCall, & Coleman, 1993.

79. Lewis & Stieben, 2004; Steinberg, 2007, 2009; Wisner Fries & Pollak, 2007.

80. Bandura, 1997; Brophy, 2004; Locke & Latham, 2002, 2006; Page-Voth & Graham, 1999; Schunk, 1996; Wentzel, 1999.

81. Bandura, 1986; Covington, 1992; W. D. Parker, 1997.

Chapter 11

1. Bandura, 1982, 1989, 2006; Schunk & Pajares, 2004.

2. Cornoldi, 2010; Lodewyk & Winne, 2005; Schunk & Pajares, 2004.

3. Brophy, 2006; Hattie, 2009; Skaalvik & Skaalvik, 2008; Tschannen-Moran, Woolfolk Hoy, & Hoy, 1998.

References

Abrami, P. C., Bernard, R. M., Borokhovski, E., Wade, A., Surkes, M. A., Tamim, R., et al. (2008). Instructional interventions affecting critical thinking skills and dispositions: A stage 1 meta-analysis. *Review of Educational Research, 78,* 1102–1134.

Ackerman, P. L., & Lohman, D. F. (2006). Individual differences in cognitive functions. In P. A. Alexander & P. H. Winne (Eds.), *Handbook of educational psychology* (2nd ed., pp. 139–161). Mahwah, NJ: Erlbaum.

Afflerbach, P., & Cho, B.-Y. (2010). Determining and describing reading strategies: Internet and traditional forms of reading. In H. S. Waters & W. Schneider (Eds.), *Metacognition, strategy use, and instruction* (pp. 201–225). New York: Guilford.

Aleven, V., Stahl, E., Schworm, S., Fischer, F., & Wallace, R. (2003). Help seeking and help design in interactive learning environments. *Review of Educational Research, 73,* 277–320.

Alexander, P. A. (2003). The development of expertise: The journey from acclimation to proficiency. *Educational Researcher, 32*(8), 10–14.

Alexander, P. A. (2004). A model of domain learning: Reinterpreting expertise as a multidimensional, multistage process. In D. Y. Dai & R. J. Sternberg (Eds.), *Motivation, emotion, and cognition: Integrative perspectives on intellectual functioning and development* (pp. 273–298). Mahwah, NJ: Erlbaum.

Alexander, P. A., & Jetton, T. L. (1996). The role of importance and interest in the processing of text. *Educational Psychology Review, 8,* 89–121.

Alexander, P. A., & Judy, J. E. (1988). The interaction of domain-specific and strategic knowledge in academic performance. *Review of Educational Research, 58,* 375–404.

Alfassi, M. (1998). Reading for meaning: The efficacy of reciprocal teaching in fostering reading comprehension in high school students in remedial reading classes. *American Educational Research Journal, 35,* 309–332.

Alleman, J., & Brophy, J. (1992). Analysis of the activities in a social studies curriculum. In J. Brophy (Ed.), *Advances in research on teaching: Vol. 3. Planning and managing learning tasks and activities* (pp. 47–80). Greenwich, CT: JAI Press.

Allen, K. D. (1998). The use of an enhanced simplified habit-reversal procedure to reduce disruptive outbursts during athletic performance. *Journal of Applied Behavior Analysis, 31,* 489–492.

Altmann, E. M., & Gray, W. D. (2002). Forgetting to remember: The functional relationship of decay and interference. *Psychological Science, 13,* 27–33.

Alvarez, G. A., & Cavanagh, P. (2004). The capacity of visual short-term memory is set both by visual information load and by number of objects. *Psychological Science, 15,* 106–111.

Amabile, T. M., & Hennessey, B. A. (1992). The motivation for creativity in children. In A. K. Boggiano & T. S. Pittman (Eds.), *Achievement and motivation: A social-developmental perspective* (pp. 54–74). Cambridge, England: Cambridge University Press.

American Psychological Association (2010). *Publication manual* (6th ed.). Washington, DC: Author.

Amsterlaw, J. (2006). Children's beliefs about everyday reasoning. *Child Development, 77,* 443–464.

Anderson, J. R. (1983). *The architecture of cognition.* Cambridge, MA: Harvard University Press.

Anderson, J. R. (2005). *Cognitive psychology and its implications* (6th ed.). New York: Worth.

Anderson, J. R., Greeno, J. G., Reder, L. M., & Simon, H. A. (2000). Perspectives on learning, thinking, and activity. *Educational Researcher, 29*(4), 11–13.

Anderson, J. R., Reder, L. M., & Simon, H. A. (1996). Situated learning and education. *Educational Researcher, 25*(4), 5–11.

Anderson, M. C., & Green, C. (2001). Suppressing unwanted memories by executive control. *Nature, 410,* 366–369.

Anderson, M. C., & Levy, B. J. (2009). Suppressing unwanted memories. *Current Directions in Psychological Science, 18,* 189–194.

Anderson, R. C., Nguyen-Jahiel, K., McNurlen, B., Archodidou, A., Kim, S.-Y., Reznitskaya, A., Tillmanns, M., & Gilbert, L. (2001). The snowball phenomenon: Spread of ways of talking and ways of thinking across groups of children. *Cognition and Instruction, 19,* 1–46.

Anderson, R. C., Reynolds, R. E., Schallert, D. L., & Goetz, E. T. (1977). Frameworks for comprehending discourse. *American Educational Research Journal, 14,* 367–381.

Anderson, V., & Hidi, S. (1988/1989). Teaching students to summarize. *Educational Leadership, 46*(4), 26–28.

Andre, T., & Windschitl, M. (2003). Interest, epistemological belief, and intentional conceptual change. In G. M. Sinatra & P. R. Pintrich (Eds.), *Intentional conceptual change* (pp. 173–197). Mahwah, NJ: Erlbaum.

Andriessen, J. (2006). Arguing to learn. In R. K. Sawyer (Ed.), *The Cambridge handbook of the learning sciences* (pp. 443–459). Cambridge, England: Cambridge University Press.

Anzai, Y. (1991). Learning and use of representations for physics expertise. In K. A. Ericsson & J. Smith (Eds.), *Toward a general theory of expertise: Prospects and limits* (pp. 64–92). Cambridge, England: Cambridge University Press.

Ariely, D., & Wertenbroch, K. (2002). Procrastination, deadlines, and performance: Self-control by precommitment. *Psychological Science, 13,* 219–224.

Aron, A. R. (2008). Progress in executive-function research: From tasks to functions to regions to networks. *Current Directions in Psychological Science, 17,* 124–129.

Aronson, J., Lustina, M. J., Good, C., Keough, K., Steele, C. M., & Brown, J. (1999). When white men can't do math: Necessary and sufficient factors in stereotype threat. *Journal of Experimental Social Psychology, 35,* 29–46.

Arrigo, J. M., & Pezdek, K. (1997). Lessons from the study of psychogenic amnesia. *Current Directions in Psychological Science, 6,* 148–152.

Ashcraft, M. H. (2002). Math anxiety: Personal, educational, and cognitive consequences. *Current Directions in Psychological Science, 11,* 181–184.

Ashton, P. (1985). Motivation and the teacher's sense of efficacy. In C. Ames & R. Ames (Eds.), *Research on motivation in education: Vol. 2. The classroom milieu* (pp. 141–174). San Diego, CA: Academic Press.

Atkinson, R. C., & Shiffrin, R. M. (1968). Human memory: A proposed system and its control processes. In K. W. Spence & J. T. Spence (Eds.), *The psychology of learning and motivation: Advances in research and theory* (Vol. 2). San Diego, CA: Academic Press.

Atkinson, R. K., Derry, S. J., Renkl, A., & Wortham, D. (2000). Learning from examples: Instructional principles from the worked examples research. *Review of Educational Research, 70,* 181–214.

Atkinson, R. K., Levin, J. R., Kiewra, K. A., Meyers, T., Kim, S., Atkinson, L. A., Renandya, W. A., & Hwang, Y. (1999). Matrix and mnemonic text-processing adjuncts: Comparing and combining their components. *Journal of Educational Psychology, 91,* 342–357.

Atkinson, R. K., Renkl, A., & Merrill, M. M. (2003). Transitioning from studying examples to solving problems: Effects of self-explanation prompts and fading worked-out steps. *Journal of Educational Psychology, 95,* 774–783.

Atran, S., Medin, D. L., & Ross, N. O. (2005). The cultural mind: Environmental decision making and cultural modeling within and across populations. *Psychological Review, 112,* 744–776.

Au, W. (2007). High-stakes testing and curricular control: A qualitative metasynthesis. *Educational Researcher, 36,* 258–267.

Ausubel, D. P., Novak, J. D., & Hanesian, H. (1978). *Educational psychology: A cognitive view* (2nd ed.). New York: Holt, Rinehart & Winston.

Ausubel, D. P., & Robinson, F. G. (1969). *School learning: An introduction to educational psychology.* New York: Holt, Rinehart & Winston.

Azevedo, R. (2005). Computer environments as metacognitive tools for enhancing learning. *Educational Psychologist, 40,* 193–197.

Babad, E. (1993). Teachers' differential behavior. *Educational Psychology Review, 5,* 347–376.

Bachevalier, J., Malkova, L., & Beauregard, M. (1996). Multiple memory systems: A neuropsychological and developmental perspective. In G. R. Lyon & N. A. Krasnegor (Eds.), *Attention, memory, and executive function.* Baltimore: Brookes.

Baddeley, A. D. (2001). Is working memory still working? *American Psychologist, 56,* 851–864.

Bahrick, H. P., Bahrick, L. E., Bahrick, A. S., & Bahrick, P. E. (1993). Maintenance of foreign language vocabulary and the spacing effect. *Psychological Science, 4,* 316–321.

Baker, L. (1989). Metacognition, comprehension monitoring, and the adult reader. *Educational Psychology Review, 1,* 3–38.

Balch, W., Bowman, K., & Mohler, L. (1992). Music-dependent memory in immediate and delayed word recall. *Memory and Cognition, 20,* 21–28.

Bandura, A. (1977). *Social learning theory.* Englewood Cliffs, NJ: Prentice Hall.

Bandura, A. (1982). Self-efficacy mechanism in human agency. *American Psychologist, 37,* 122–147.

Bandura, A. (1986). *Social foundations of thought and action: A social cognitive theory.* Englewood Cliffs, NJ: Prentice Hall.

Bandura, A. (1989). Human agency in social cognitive theory. *American Psychologist, 44,* 1175–1184.

Bandura, A. (1997). *Self-efficacy: The exercise of control.* New York: Freeman.

Bandura, A. (2006). Toward a psychology of human agency. *Perspectives on Psychological Science, 1,* 164–180.

Bandura, A. (2008). Toward an agentic theory of the self. In H. W. Marsh, R. G. Craven, & D. M. McInerney (Eds.), *Self-processes, learning, and enabling human potential* (pp. 15–49). Charlotte, NC: Information Age.

Bangert-Drowns, R. L., Hurley, M. M., & Wilkinson, B. (2004). The effects of school-based writing-to-learn interventions on academic achievement: A meta-analysis. *Review of Educational Research, 74,* 29–58.

Banich, M. T. (2009). Executive function: The search for an integrated account. *Current Directions in Psychological Science, 18,* 89–94.

Barab, S. A., & Plucker, J. A. (2002). Smart people or smart contexts? Cognition, ability, and talent development in an age of situated approaches to knowing and learning. *Educational Psychologist, 37,* 165–182.

Barch, D. M. (2003). Cognition in schizophrenia: Does working memory work? *Current Directions in Psychological Science, 12,* 146–150.

Bargai, N., Ben-Shakhar, G., & Shalev, A. Y. (2007). Posttraumatic stress disorder and depression in battered women: The mediating role of learned helplessness. *Journal of Family Violence, 22,* 267–275.

Bargh, J. A., & Chartrand, T. L. (1999). The unbearable automaticity of being. *American Psychologist, 54,* 462–479.

Barnett, J. E. (1999, April). *Adaptive studying across disciplines: A think-aloud study.* Paper presented at the annual meeting of the American Educational Research Association, Montreal.

Barnett, S. M., & Ceci, S. J. (2002). When and where do we apply what we learn? A taxonomy of far transfer. *Psychological Bulletin, 128,* 612–637.

Barton, A. C., Tan, E., & Rivet, A. (2008). Creating hybrid spaces for engaging school science among urban middle school girls. *American Educational Research Journal, 45,* 68–103.

Basak, C., Boot, W. R., Voss, M. W., & Kramer, A. F. (2008). Can training in a real-time strategy videogame attenuate cognitive decline in older adults? *Psychology and Aging, 23,* 765–777.

Bassok, M. (2003). Analogical transfer in problem solving. In J. E. Davidson & R. J. Sternberg (Eds.), *The psychology of problem solving* (pp. 343–369). Cambridge, England: Cambridge University Press.

Bauer, M. I., & Johnson-Laird, P. N. (1993). How diagrams can improve reasoning. *Psychological Science, 4,* 372–378.

Bauer, P. J. (2006). Event memory. In W. Damon & R. M. Lerner (Series Eds.), D. Kuhn, & R. Siegler (Vol. Eds.), *Handbook of child psychology: Vol. 2. Cognition, perception, and language* (6th ed., pp. 373–425). New York: Wiley.

Bauer, P. J., DeBoer, T., & Lukowski, A. F. (2007). In the language of multiple memory systems: Defining and describing developments in long-term declarative memory. In L. M. Oakes & P. J. Bauer (Eds.), *Short- and long-term memory in infancy and early childhood: Taking the first steps toward remembering* (pp. 240–270). New York: Oxford University Press.

Baxter Magolda, M. B. (2002). Epistemological reflection: The evolution of epistemological assumptions from age 18 to 30. In B. K. Hofer & P. R. Pintrich (Eds.), *Personal epistemology: The psychology of beliefs about knowledge and knowing* (pp. 89–102). Mahwah, NJ: Erlbaum.

Beck, I. L., & McKeown, M. G. (1994). Outcomes of history instruction: Paste-up accounts. In M. Carretero & J. F. Voss (Eds.), *Cognitive and instructional processes in history and the social sciences* (pp. 237–256). Mahwah, NJ: Erlbaum.

Beck, I. L., & McKeown, M. G. (2001). Inviting students into the pursuit of meaning. *Educational Psychology Review, 13,* 225–241.

Beck, S. R., Robinson, E. J., Carroll, D. J., & Apperly, I. A. (2006). Children's thinking about counterfactuals and future hypotheticals as possibilities. *Child Development, 77,* 413–426.

Beckett, C., Maughan, B., Rutter, M., Castle, J., Colvert, E., Groothues, C., Kreppner, J., Stevens, S., O'Connor, T. G., & Sonuga-Barke, E. J. S. (2006). Do the effects of early severe deprivation on cognition persist into early adolescence? Findings from the English and Romanian adoptees study. *Child Development, 77,* 696–711.

Bédard, J., & Chi, M. T. H. (1992). Expertise. *Current Directions in Psychological Science, 1,* 135–139.

Begg, I., Anas, A., & Farinacci, S. (1992). Dissociation of processes in belief: Source recollection, statement familiarity, and the illusion of truth. *Journal of Experimental Psychology: General, 121,* 446–458.

Behl-Chadha, G. (1996). Basic-level and superordinate-like categorical representations in early infancy. *Cognition, 60,* 105–141.

Behr, M., & Harel, G. (1988, April). Cognitive conflict in procedure applications. In D. Tirosh (Chair), *The role of inconsistent ideas in learning mathematics.* Symposium conducted at the annual meeting of the American Educational Research Association, New Orleans, LA.

Behrmann, M. (2000). The mind's eye mapped onto the brain's matter. *Current Directions in Psychological Science, 9,* 50–54.

Beilock, S. L. (2008). Math performance in stressful situations. *Current Directions in Psychological Science, 17,* 339–343.

Belenky, M., Clinchy, B., Goldberger, N. R., & Tarule, J. (1997). *Women's ways of knowing: The development of self, mind, and voice.* New York: Basic Books. (Originally published 1986)

Belfiore, P. J., & Hornyak, R. S. (1998). Operant theory and application to self-monitoring in adolescents. In D. H. Schunk & B. J. Zimmerman (Eds.), *Self-regulated learning: From teaching to self-reflective practice* (pp. 184–202). New York: Guilford.

Bellezza, F. S. (1986). Mental cues and verbal reports in learning. In G. H. Bower (Ed.), *The psychology of learning and motivation: Advances in research and theory* (Vol. 20). Orlando, FL: Academic Press.

Bembenutty, H., & Karabenick, S. A. (2004). Inherent association between academic delay of gratification, future time perspective, and self-regulated learning. *Educational Psychology Review, 16,* 35–57.

Bendixen, L. D., & Rule, D. C. (2004). An integrative approach to personal epistemology: A guiding model. *Educational Psychologist, 39,* 69–80.

Benes, F. M. (2007). Corticolimbic circuitry and psychopathology: Development of the corticolimbic system. In D. Coch, G. Dawson, & K. W. Fischer (Eds.), *Human behavior, learning, and the developing brain: Atypical development* (pp. 331–361). New York: Guilford.

Benton, S. L. (1997). Psychological foundations of elementary writing instruction. In G. D. Phye (Ed.), *Handbook of academic learning: Construction of knowledge* (pp. 235–264). San Diego, CA: Academic Press.

Benton, S. L., Kiewra, K. A., Whitfill, J. M., & Dennison, R. (1993). Encoding and external-storage effects on writing processes. *Journal of Educational Psychology, 85,* 267–280.

Bereiter, C., & Scardamalia, M. (1989). Intentional learning as a goal of instruction. In L. B. Resnick (Ed.), *Knowing, learning and instruction: Essays in honour of Robert Glaser* (pp. 361–392). Mahwah, NJ: Erlbaum.

Berk, L. E. (1994). Why children talk to themselves. *Scientific American, 271,* 78–83.

Bermejo, V. (1996). Cardinality development and counting. *Developmental Psychology, 32,* 263–268.

Berninger, V. W., Fuller, F., & Whitaker, D. (1996). A process model of writing development across the life span. *Educational Psychology Review, 8,* 193–218.

Berthold, K., & Renkl, A. (2009). Instructional aids to support a conceptual understanding of multiple representations. *Journal of Educational Psychology, 101,* 70–87.

Berti, A. E. (1994). Children's understanding of the concept of the state. In M. Carretero & J. F. Voss (Eds.), *Cognitive and instructional processes in history and the social sciences* (pp. 49–75). Mahwah, NJ: Erlbaum.

Bialystok, E. (1994). Representation and ways of knowing: Three issues in second language acquisition. In N. C. Ellis (Ed.), *Implicit and explicit learning of languages.* London: Academic Press.

Bilodeau, I. M., & Schlosberg, H. (1951). Similarity in stimulating conditions as a variable in retroactive inhibition. *Journal of Experimental Psychology, 41,* 199–204.

Birnbaum, J. C. (1982). The reading and composing behaviors of selected fourth- and seventh-grade students. *Research in the Teaching of English, 16,* 241–260.

Blackwell, L. S., Trzesniewski, K. H., & Dweck, C. S. (2007). Implicit theories of intelligence predict achievement across an adolescent transition: A longitudinal study and an intervention. *Child Development, 78,* 246–263.

Blanchette, I., & Richards, A. (2004). Reasoning about emotional and neutral materials: Is logic affected by emotion? *Psychological Science, 15,* 745–752.

Blumenfeld, P. C., Kempler, T. M., & Krajcik, J. S. (2006). Motivation and cognitive engagement in learning environments. In R. K. Sawyer (Ed.), *The Cambridge handbook of the learning sciences* (pp. 475–488). Cambridge, England: Cambridge University Press.

Bohannon, J. N., III, & Symons, V. L. (1992). Flashbulb memories: Confidence, consistency, and quantity. In E. Winograd & U. Neisser (Eds.), *Affect and accuracy in recall: Studies of "flashbulb" memories* (pp. 65–90). Cambridge, England: Cambridge University Press.

Bornstein, M. H., Hahn, C.-S., Bell, C., Haynes, O. M., Slater, A., Golding, J., Wolke, D., & the ALSPAC Study Team. (2006). Stability in cognition across early childhood: A developmental cascade. *Psychological Science, 17,* 151–158.

Bortfeld, H., & Whitehurst, G. J. (2001). Sensitive periods in first language acquisition. In D. B. Bailey, Jr., J. T. Bruer, F. J. Symons, & J. W. Lichtman (Eds.), *Critical thinking about critical periods* (pp. 173–192). Baltimore: Brookes.

Bouchard, T. J., Jr. (1997). IQ similarity in twins reared apart: Findings and responses to critics. In R. J. Sternberg & E. L. Grigorenko (Eds.), *Intelligence, heredity, and environment* (pp. 126–160). Cambridge, England: Cambridge University Press.

Bousfield, W. A. (1953). The occurrence of clustering in the recall of randomly arranged associates. *Journal of General Psychology, 49,* 229–240.

Bowden, E. M., & Jung-Beeman, M. (2003). Normative data for 144 compound remote associates problems. *Behavior Research Methods, Instruments, & Computers, 35,* 634–639.

Bower, G. H. (1972). Mental imagery and associative learning. In L. W. Gregg (Ed.), *Cognition in learning and memory* (pp. 51–88). New York: Wiley.

Bower, G. H. (1994). Some relations between emotions and memory. In P. Ekman & R. J. Davidson (Eds.), *The nature of emotion: Fundamental questions.* New York: Oxford University Press.

Bower, G. H., Black, J. B., & Turner, T. J. (1979). Scripts in memory for text. *Cognitive Psychology, 11,* 177–220.

Bower, G. H., Clark, M. C., Lesgold, A. M., & Winzenz, D. (1969). Hierarchical retrieval schemes in recall of categorized word lists. *Journal of Verbal Learning and Verbal Behavior, 8,* 323–343.

Bower, G. H., & Forgas, J. P. (2001). Mood and social memory. In J. P. Forgas (Ed.), *Handbook of affect and social cognition* (pp. 95–120). Mahwah, NJ: Erlbaum.

Bower, G. H., Karlin, M. B., & Dueck, A. (1975). Comprehension and memory for pictures. *Memory and Cognition, 3,* 216–220.

Bower, J. E., Moskowitz, J. T., & Epel, E. (2009). Is benefit finding good for your health? Pathways linking positive life changes after stress and physical health outcomes. *Current Directions in Psychological Science, 18,* 337–341.

Bracken, B. A., & Walker, K. C. (1997). The utility of intelligence tests for preschool children. In D. P. Flanagan, J. L. Genshaft, & P. L. Harrison (Eds.), *Contemporary intellectual assessment: Theories, tests, and issues* (pp. 484-502). New York: Guilford.

Bragstad, B. J., & Stumpf, S. M. (1982). *A guidebook for teaching study skills and motivation.* Boston: Allyn & Bacon.

Brainerd, C. J., & Reyna, V. F. (2005). *The science of false memory.* Oxford, England: Oxford University Press.

Bransford, J. D., & Franks, J. J. (1971). The abstraction of linguistic ideas. *Cognitive Psychology, 2,* 331–350.

Bransford, J. D., & Johnson, M. K. (1972). Contextual prerequisites for understanding: Some investigations of comprehension and recall. *Journal of Verbal Learning and Verbal Behavior, 11,* 717–726.

Bransford, J. D., & Schwartz, D. L. (1999). Rethinking transfer: A simple proposal with multiple implications. *Review of Research in Education* (Vol. 24, pp. 61–100). Washington,

DC: American Educational Research Association.

Bransford, J. D., Stevens, R., Schwartz, D., Meltzoff, A., Pea, R., Reschelle, J., Vye, N., Kuhl, P., Bell, P., Barron, B., Reeves, B., & Sabelli, N. (2006). Learning theories and education: Toward a decade of synergy. In P. A. Alexander & P. H. Winne (Eds.), *Handbook of educational psychology* (2nd ed., pp. 209–244). Mahwah, NJ: Erlbaum.

Brenner, M. E., Mayer, R. E., Moseley, B., Brar, T., Durán, R., Reed, B. S., & Webb, D. (1997). Learning by understanding: The role of multiple representations in learning algebra. *American Educational Research Journal, 34*, 663–689.

Bressler, S. L. (2002). Understanding cognition through large-scale cortical networks. *Current Directions in Psychological Science, 11*, 58–61.

Brewer, W. F. (1992). The theoretical and empirical status of the flashbulb memory hypothesis. In E. Winograd & U. Neisser (Eds.), *Affect and accuracy in recall: Studies of "flashbulb" memories* (pp. 274–305). Cambridge, England: Cambridge University Press.

Brighton, H., & Todd, P. M. (2009). Situating rationality: Ecologically rational decision making with simple heuristics. In P. Robbins & M. Aydede (Eds.), *The Cambridge handbook of situated cognition* (pp. 322–346). Cambridge, England: Cambridge University Press.

Brody, N. (1997). Intelligence, schooling, and society. *American Psychologist, 52*, 1046–1050.

Brody, N. (1999). What is intelligence? *International Review of Psychiatry, 11*, 19–25.

Broekkamp, H., Van Hout-Wolters, B. H. A. M., Rijlaarsdam, G., & van den Bergh, H. (2002). Importance in instructional text: Teachers' and students' perceptions of task demands. *Journal of Educational Psychology, 94*, 260–271.

Bronfenbrenner, U. (1999). Is early intervention effective? Some studies of early education in familial and extra-familial settings. In A. Montagu (Ed.), *Race and IQ* (expanded ed., pp. 343–378). New York: Oxford University Press.

Bronson, M. B. (2000). *Self-regulation in early childhood: Nature and nurture.* New York: Guilford.

Brooks, L. W., & Dansereau, D. F. (1987). Transfer of information: An instructional perspective. In S. M. Cormier & J. D. Hagman (Eds.), *Transfer of learning: Contemporary research and applications* (pp. 121–150). San Diego, CA: Academic Press.

Brophy, J. E. (1986). *On motivating students.* Occasional Paper No. 101, Institute for Research on Teaching, Michigan State University, East Lansing.

Brophy, J. E. (1987). Synthesis of research on strategies for motivating students to learn. *Educational Leadership, 45*(2), 40–48.

Brophy, J. (2004). *Motivating students to learn* (2nd ed.). Mahwah, NJ: Erlbaum.

Brophy, J. E. (2006). Observational research on generic aspects of classroom teaching. In P. A. Alexander & P. H. Winne (Eds.), *Handbook of educational psychology* (2nd ed., pp. 755–780). Mahwah, NJ: Erlbaum.

Brophy, J. (2008). Developing students' appreciation for what is taught in school. *Educational Psychologist, 43*, 132–141.

Brophy, J. E., & Alleman, J. (1991). Activities as instructional tools: A framework for analysis and evaluation. *Educational Researcher, 20*(4), 9–23.

Brophy, J., Alleman, J., & Knighton, B. (2009). *Inside the social studies classroom.* New York: Routledge.

Brophy, J. E., & VanSledright, B. (1997). *Teaching and learning history in elementary schools.* New York: Teachers College Press.

Brown, A. (1991). A review of the tip-of-the-tongue experience. *Psychological Bulletin, 109*, 204–223.

Brown, A. L., & Day, J. D. (1983). Macrorules for summarizing texts: The development of expertise. *Journal of Verbal Learning and Verbal Behavior, 22*, 1–14.

Brown, A. L., & Palincsar, A. S. (1987). Reciprocal teaching of comprehension strategies: A natural history of one program for enhancing learning. In J. Borkowski & J. D. Day (Eds.), *Cognition in special education: Comparative approaches to retardation, learning disabilities, and giftedness.* Norwood, NJ: Ablex.

Brown, D. E. (1992). Using examples and analogies to remediate misconceptions in physics: Factors influencing conceptual change. *Journal of Research in Science Teaching, 29*, 17–34.

Brown, J. (1968). Reciprocal facilitation and impairment of free recall. *Psychonomic Science, 10*, 41–42.

Brown, J. S., Collins, A., & Duguid, P. (1989). Situated cognition and the culture of learning. *Educational Researcher, 18*(1), 32–42.

Brown, M. C., McNeil, N. M., & Glenberg, A. M. (2009). Using concreteness in education: Real problems, potential solutions. *Child Development Perspectives, 3,* 160–164.

Brown, R., & Kulik, J. (1977). Flashbulb memories. *Cognition, 5,* 73–99.

Brown, R., & McNeill, D. (1966). The "tip of the tongue" phenomenon. *Journal of Verbal Learning and Verbal Behavior, 5,* 325–337.

Brown, R. D., & Bjorklund, D. F. (1998). The biologizing of cognition, development, and education: Approach with cautious enthusiasm. *Educational Psychology Review, 10,* 355–373.

Brown, S. I., & Walter, M. I. (1990). *The art of problem posing* (2nd ed.). Hillsdale, NJ: Erlbaum.

Bruer, J. T. (1999). *The myth of the first three years: A new understanding of early brain development and lifelong learning.* New York: Free Press.

Bruer, J. T., & Greenough, W. T. (2001). The subtle science of how experience affects the brain. In D. B. Bailey, Jr., J. T. Bruer, F. J. Symons, & J. W. Lichtman (Eds.), *Critical thinking about critical periods* (pp. 209–232). Baltimore: Brookes.

Bruner, J. S. (1957). On going beyond the information given. In *Contemporary approaches to cognition: A symposium held at the University of Colorado.* Cambridge, MA: Harvard University Press.

Buehl, M. M., & Alexander, P. A. (2001). Beliefs about academic knowledge. *Educational Psychology Review, 13,* 385–418.

Buehl, M. M., & Alexander, P. A. (2005). Motivation and performance differences in students' domain-specific epistemological belief profiles. *American Educational Research Journal, 42,* 697–726.

Bulgren, J. A., Deshler, D. D., Schumaker, J. B., & Lenz, B. K. (2000). The use and effectiveness of analogical instruction in diverse secondary content classrooms. *Journal of Educational Psychology, 92,* 426–441.

Buschke, H. (1977). Two-dimensional recall: Immediate identification of clusters in episodic and semantic memory. *Journal of Verbal Learning and Verbal Behavior, 16,* 201–215.

Butcher, K. R. (2006). Learning from text with diagrams: Promoting mental model development and inference generation. *Journal of Educational Psychology, 98,* 182–197.

Butler, D. L., & Winne, P. H. (1995). Feedback and self-regulated learning: A theoretical synthesis. *Review of Educational Research, 65,* 245–281.

Byrnes, J. P. (1996). *Cognitive development and learning in instructional contexts.* Boston: Allyn & Bacon.

Byrnes, J. P. (2001). *Minds, brains, and learning: Understanding the psychological and educational relevance of neuroscientific research.* New York: Guilford.

Cacioppo, J. T., Petty, R. E., Feinstein, J. A., & Jarvis, W. B. G. (1996). Dispositional differences in cognitive motivation: The life and times of individuals varying in need for cognition. *Psychological Bulletin, 119,* 197–253.

Cadinu, M., Maass, A., Rosabianca, A., & Kiesner, J. (2005). Why do women underperform under stereotype threat? Evidence for the role of negative thinking. *Psychological Science, 16,* 572–578.

Cai, D. J., Mednick, S. A., Harrison, E. M., Kanady, J. C., & Mednick, S. C. (2009). REM, not incubation, improves creativity by priming associative networks. *Proceedings of the National Academy of Sciences, 106,* 10130–10134.

Calfee, R., & Chambliss, M. J. (1988, April). *The structure of social studies textbooks: Where is the design?* Paper presented at the annual meeting of the American Educational Research Association, New Orleans.

Calin-Jageman, R. J., & Ratner, H. H. (2005). The role of encoding in the self-explanation effect. *Cognition and Instruction, 23,* 523–543.

Callender, A. A., & McDaniel, M. A. (2009). The limited benefits of rereading educational texts. *Contemporary Educational Psychology, 34,* 30–41.

Campbell, F. A., & Burchinal, M. R. (2008). Early childhood interventions: The Abecedarian Project. In P. C. Kyllonen, R. D. Roberts, & L. Stankov (Eds.), *Extending intelligence: Enhancement and new constructs* (pp. 61–84). New York: Erlbaum/Taylor & Francis.

Campbell, F. A., & Ramey, C. T. (1995). Cognitive and school outcomes for high-risk African-American students at middle adolescence: Positive effects of early intervention. *American Educational Research Journal, 32,* 742–772.

Cann, A., & Ross, D. (1989). Olfactory stimuli as context cues in human memory. *American Journal of Psychology, 102,* 91–102.

Capron, C., & Duyme, M. (1989). Assessment of effects of socio-economic status on IQ in a full cross-fostering study. *Nature, 340,* 552–554.

Carey, S. (1985). *Conceptual change in childhood.* Cambridge, MA: MIT Press.

Carlson, N. R. (1999). *Foundations of physiological psychology*. Boston: Allyn & Bacon.

Carlson, R., Chandler, P., & Sweller, J. (2003). Learning and understanding science instructional material. *Journal of Educational Psychology, 95,* 629–640.

Carlson, S. M., Davis, A. C., & Leach, J. C. (2005). Less is more: Executive function and symbolic representation in preschool children. *Psychological Science, 16,* 609–616.

Carmichael, L., Hogan, H. P., & Walters, A. A. (1932). An experimental study of the effect of language on the reproduction of visually perceived form. *Journal of Experimental Psychology, 15,* 73–86.

Carney, R. N., & Levin, J. R. (1994). Combining mnemonic strategies to remember who painted what when. *Contemporary Educational Psychology, 19,* 323–339.

Carney, R. N., & Levin, J. R. (2000). Mnemonic instruction, with a focus on transfer. *Journal of Educational Psychology, 92,* 783–790.

Carney, R. N., Levin, J. R., & Stackhouse, T. L. (1997). The face-name mnemonic strategy from a different perspective. *Contemporary Educational Psychology, 22,* 399–412.

Carney, R. N., Levin, J. R., & Webb, A. M. (2009, April). *Can mnemonic strategies help students combat forgetting caused by interference?* Paper presented at the annual meeting of the American Educational Research Association, San Diego, CA.

Carr, M. (2010). The importance of metacognition for conceptual change and strategy use in mathematics. In H. S. Waters & W. Schneider (Eds.), *Metacognition, strategy use, and instruction* (pp. 176–197). New York: Guilford.

Carr, M., & Biddlecomb, B. (1998). Metacognition in mathematics from a constructivist perspective. In D. J. Hacker, J. Dunlosky, & A. C. Graesser (Eds.), *Metacognition in educational theory and practice* (pp. 69–91). Mahwah, NJ: Erlbaum.

Carrasco, R. L. (1981). Expanded awareness of student performance: A case study in applied ethnographic monitoring in a bilingual classroom. In H. T. Trueba, G. P. Guthrie, & K. H. Au (Eds.), *Culture and the bilingual classroom: Studies in classroom ethnography* (pp. 153–177). Rowley, MA: Newbury House.

Carroll, J. B. (1993) *Human cognitive abilities: A survey of factor-analytic studies*. New York: Cambridge University Press.

Carroll, J. B. (2003). The higher stratum structure of cognitive abilities: Current evidence supports *g* and about ten broad factors. In H. Nyborg (Ed.), *The scientific study of general intelligence* (pp. 5–21). New York: Pergamon.

Carroll, M., & Perfect, T. J. (2002). Students' experiences of unconscious plagiarism: Did I beget or forget? In T. J. Perfect & B. L. Schwartz (Eds.), *Applied metacognition* (pp. 146–166). Cambridge, England: Cambridge University Press.

Cassady, J. C. (2004). The influence of cognitive test anxiety across the learning-testing cycle. *Learning and Instruction, 14,* 569–592.

Cassady, J. C., & Johnson, R. E. (2002). Cognitive test anxiety and academic performance. *Contemporary Educational Psychology, 27,* 270–295.

Ceci, S. J. (2003). Cast in six ponds and you'll reel in something: Looking back on 25 years of research. *American Psychologist, 58,* 855–864.

Center for Media Literacy. (n.d.). CML's five key questions. In *Five key questions that can change the world: Deconstruction*. Retrieved January 27, 2009, from www.medialit.org/reading_room/article661.html.

Cepeda, N. J., Vul, E., Rohrer, D., Wixted, J. T., & Pashler, H. (2008). Spacing effects in learning: A temporal ridgeline of optimal retention. *Psychological Science, 19,* 1095–1102.

Certo, J., Cauley, K. M., & Chafin, C. (2002, April). *Students' perspectives on their high school experience*. Paper presented at the annual meeting of the American Educational Research Association, New Orleans, LA.

Chabrán, M. (2003). Listening to talk from and about students on accountability. In M. Carnoy, R. Elmore, & L. S. Siskin (Eds.), *The new accountability: High schools and high-stakes testing* (pp. 129–145). New York: Routledge Falmer.

Chambers, D., & Reisberg, D. (1985). Can mental images be ambiguous? *Journal of Experimental Psychology: Human Perception and Performance, 11,* 317–328.

Chambliss, M. J., Calfee, R. C., & Wong, I. (1990, April). *Structure and content in science textbooks: Where is the design?* Paper presented at the annual meeting of the American Educational Research Association, Boston.

Chan, C., Burtis, J., & Bereiter, C. (1997). Knowledge building as a mediator of conflict in conceptual change. *Cognition and Instruction, 15,* 1–40.

Chan, J. C. K., Thomas, A. K., & Bulevich, J. B. (2009). Recalling a witnessed event increases eyewitness suggestibility: The reversed testing effect. *Psychological Science, 20,* 66–73.

Chapell, M. S., Blanding, Z. B., Silverstein, M. F., Takahashi, M., Newman, B., Gubi, A., & McCann, N. (2005). Test anxiety and academic performance in undergraduate and graduate students. *Journal of Educational Psychology, 97,* 268–274.

Chase, W. G., & Simon, H. A. (1973). Perception in chess. *Cognitive Psychology, 4,* 55–81.

Chen, Z. (1999). Schema induction in children's analogical problem solving. *Journal of Educational Psychology, 91,* 703–715.

Cherry, E. C. (1953). Some experiments on the recognition of speech, with one and with two ears. *Journal of the Acoustical Society of America, 25,* 975–979.

Chi, M. T. H. (1978). Knowledge structures and memory development. In R. S. Siegler (Ed.), *Children's thinking: What develops?* (pp. 73–96). Hillsdale, NJ: Erlbaum.

Chi, M. T. H., & Glaser, R. (1985). Problem-solving ability. In R. J. Sternberg (Ed.), *Human abilities: An information-processing approach* (pp. 227–257). New York: W. H. Freeman.

Chi, M. T. H., Glaser, R., & Rees, E. (1982). Expertise in problem solving. In R. J. Sternberg (Ed.), *Advances in the psychology of human intelligence.* Hillsdale, NJ: Erlbaum.

Chinn, C. A. (2006). Learning to argue. In A. M. O'Donnell, C. E. Hmelo-SIlver, & G. Erkens (Eds.), *Collaborative learning, reasoning, and technology* (pp. 355–383). Mahwah, NJ: Erlbaum.

Chinn, C. A., & Malhotra, B. A. (2002). Children's responses to anomalous scientific data: How is conceptual change impeded? *Journal of Educational Psychology, 94,* 327–343.

Chiu, M. M. (2008). Effects of argumentation on group micro-creativity: Statistical discourse analyses of algebra students' collaborative problem solving. *Contemporary Educational Psychology, 33,* 382–402.

Church, M. A., Elliot, A. J., & Gable, S. L. (2001). Perceptions of classroom environment, achievement goals, and achievement outcomes. *Journal of Educational Psychology, 93,* 43–54.

Clark, A.-M., Anderson, R. C., Kuo, L., Kim, I., Archodidou, A., & Nguyen-Jahiel, K. (2003). Collaborative reasoning: Expanding ways for children to talk and think in school. *Educational Psychology Review, 15,* 181–198.

Clark, D. B. (2006). Longitudinal conceptual change in students' understanding of thermal equilibrium: An examination of the process of conceptual restructuring. *Cognition and Instruction, 24,* 467–563.

Clark, J. M., & Paivio, A. (1991). Dual coding theory and education. *Educational Psychology Review, 3,* 149–210.

Clark, R. E., & Blake, S. B. (1997). Designing training for novel problem-solving transfer. In R. D. Tennyson, F. Schott, N. M. Seel, & S. Dijkstra (Eds.), *Instructional design: International perspectives. Vol. 1: Theory, research, and models* (pp. 183–214). Mahwah, NJ: Erlbaum.

Clarke, H. F., Dalley, J. W., Crofts, H. S., Robbins, T. W., & Roberts, A. C. (2004). Cognitive inflexibility after prefrontal serotonin depletion. *Science, 304,* 878–880.

Cleveland, M. J., Gibbons, F. X., Gerrard, M., Pomery, E. A., & Brody, G. H. (2005). The impact of parenting on risk cognitions and risk behavior: A study of mediation and moderation in a panel of African American adolescents. *Child Development, 76,* 900–916.

Cognition and Technology Group at Vanderbilt. (1993). Anchored instruction and situated cognition revisited. *Educational Technology, 33*(3), 52–70.

Cohen, G. (2000). Hierarchical models in cognition: Do they have psychological reality? *European Journal of Cognitive Psychology, 12*(1), 1–36.

Cohen, L. B., & Cashon, C. H. (2006). Infant cognition. In W. Damon & R. M. Lerner (Series Eds.), D. Kuhn, & R. Siegler (Vol. Eds.), *Handbook of child psychology: Vol. 2. Cognition, perception, and language* (6th ed., pp. 214–251). New York: Wiley.

Cohn, S., Hult, R. E., & Engle, R. W. (1990, April). *Working memory, notetaking, and learning from a lecture.* Paper presented at the annual meeting of the American Educational Research Association, Boston.

Colcombe, S., & Kramer, A. F. (2003). Fitness effects on the cognitive function of older adults: A meta-analytic study. *Psychological Science, 14,* 125–130.

Colcombe, S. J., Kramer, A. F., Erickson, K. I., Scalf, P., McAuley, E., Cohen, N. J., et al. (2004). Cardiovascular fitness, cortical plasticity, and aging. *Proceedings of the National Academy of Sciences, USA, 101,* 3316–3321.

Collins, A. (2006). Cognitive apprenticeship. In R. K. Sawyer (Ed.), *The Cambridge handbook of the learning sciences* (pp. 47–60). Cambridge, England: Cambridge University Press.

Collins, A., Brown, J. S., & Newman, S. E. (1989). Cognitive apprenticeship: Teaching the crafts of reading, writing, and mathematics. In L. B. Resnick (Ed.), *Knowing, learning, and instruction: Essays in honor of Robert Glaser* (pp. 453–494). Hillsdale, NJ: Erlbaum.

Coltheart, M., Lea, C. D., & Thompson, K. (1974). In defense of iconic memory. *Quarterly Journal of Experimental Psychology, 26,* 633–641.

Coman, A., Manier, D., & Hirst, W. (2009). Forgetting the unforgettable through conversation: Socially shared retrieval-induced forgetting of September 11 memories. *Psychological Science, 20,* 627–633.

Cooper, G., Tindall-Ford, S., Chandler, P., & Sweller, J. (2001). Learning by imagining procedures and concepts. *Journal of Experimental Psychology: Applied, 7,* 68–82.

Corkill, A. J. (1992). Advance organizers: Facilitators of recall. *Educational Psychology Review, 4,* 33–67.

Cormier, S. M., & Hagman, J. D. (1987). Introduction. In S. M. Cormier & J. D. Hagman (Eds.), *Transfer of learning: Contemporary research and applications* (pp. 1–8). San Diego, CA: Academic Press.

Corno, L., Cronbach, L. J., Kupermintz, H., Lohman, D. F., Mandinach, E. B., Porteu, A. W., & Talbert, J. E. (2002). *Remaking the concept of aptitude: Extending the legacy of Richard E. Snow.* Mahwah, NJ: Erlbaum.

Cornoldi, C. (2010). Metacognition, intelligence, and academic performance. In H. S. Waters & W. Schneider (Eds.), *Metacognition, strategy use, and instruction* (pp. 257–277). New York: Guilford.

Covington, M. V. (1992). *Making the grade: A self-worth perspective on motivation and school reform.* Cambridge, England: Cambridge University Press.

Covington, M. V. (2000). Intrinsic versus extrinsic motivation in schools: A reconciliation. *Current Directions in Psychological Science, 9,* 22–25.

Cowan, N. (1995). *Attention and memory: An integrated framework.* New York: Oxford University Press.

Cowan, N. (2007). What infants can tell us about working memory development. In L. M. Oakes & P. J. Bauer (Eds.), *Short- and long-term memory in infancy and early childhood: Taking the first steps toward remembering* (pp. 126–150). New York: Oxford University Press.

Cowan, N., Chen, Z., & Rouder, J. N. (2004). Constant capacity in an immediate serial-recall task: A logical sequel to Miller (1956). *Psychological Science, 15,* 634–640.

Cowan, N., Saults, J. S., & Morey, C. C. (2006). Development of working memory for verbal-spatial associations. *Journal of Memory and Language, 55,* 274–289.

Cowan, N., Wood, N. L., Nugent, L. D., & Treisman, M. (1997). There are two word-length effects in verbal short-term memory: Opposed effects of duration and complexity. *Psychological Science, 8,* 290–295.

Cox, B. D. (1997). The rediscovery of the active learner in adaptive contexts: A developmental-historical analysis of transfer of training. *Educational Psychologist, 32,* 41–55.

Craik, F. I. M., & Watkins, M. J. (1973). The role of rehearsal in short-term memory. *Journal of Verbal Learning and Verbal Behavior, 12,* 598–607.

Crawley, A. M., Anderson, D. R., Wilder, A., Williams, M., & Santomero, A. (1999). Effects of repeated exposures to a single episode of the television program *Blue's Clues* on the viewing behaviors and comprehension of preschool children. *Journal of Educational Psychology 91,* 630–637.

Crooks, T. J. (1988). The impact of classroom evaluation practices on students. *Review of Educational Research, 58,* 438–481.

Csikszentmihalyi, M. (1993). *The evolving self: A psychology for the third millennium.* New York: HarperCollins.

Csikszentmihalyi, M. (1996). *Creativity: Flow and the psychology of discovery and invention.* New York: HarperCollins.

Curtis, K. A., & Graham, S. (1991, April). *Altering beliefs about the importance of strategy: An attributional intervention.* Paper presented at the annual meeting of the American Educational Research Association, Chicago.

Curtiss, S. (1977). *Genie: A psycholinguistic study of a modern-day "wild child."* New York: Academic Press.

Dai, D. Y. (2005, April). Introductory remarks. In D. Y. Dai (Chair), *Beyond cognitivism: Where are we now?* Symposium presented at the annual meeting of the American Educational Research Association, Montreal.

Damasio, A. R. (1994). *Descartes' error: Emotion, reason, and the human brain.* New York: Avon Books.

D'Amato, R. C., Chitooran, M. M., & Whitten, J. D. (1992). Neuropsychological consequences of malnutrition. In D. I. Templer, L. C. Hartlage, & W. G. Cannon (Eds.), *Preventable brain damage: Brain vulnerability and brain health.* New York: Springer.

Daniels, L. M., Stupnisky, R. H., Pekrun, R., Haynes, T. L., Perry, R. P., & Newall, N. E. (2009). A longitudinal analysis of achievement goals: From affective antecedents to emotional effects and achievement outcomes. *Journal of Educational Psychology, 101,* 948–963.

Davidson, D. (2006). Memory for bizarre and other unusual events: Evidence from script research. In R. R. Hunt & J. B. Worthen (Eds.), *Distinctiveness and memory* (pp. 157–179). Oxford, England: Oxford University Press.

Davidson, J. E. (2003). Insights about insightful problem solving. In J. E. Davidson & R. J. Sternberg (Eds.), *The psychology of problem solving* (pp. 149–175). Cambridge, England: Cambridge University Press.

Davidson, J. E., & Sternberg, R. J. (1998). Smart problem solving: How metacognition helps. In D. J. Hacker, J. Dunlosky, & A. C. Graesser (Eds.), *Metacognition in educational theory and practice* (pp. 47–68). Mahwah, NJ: Erlbaum.

Davidson, J. E., & Sternberg, R. J. (Eds.) (2003). *The psychology of problem solving.* Cambridge, England: Cambridge University Press.

Davis, D., & Loftus, E. F. (2009). The scientific status of "repressed" and "recovered" memories of sexual abuse. In K. S. Douglas, J. L. Skeem, & S. O. Lilienfeld (Eds.), *Psychological science in the courtroom: Consensus and controversy* (pp. 55–79). New York: Guilford.

Davis, L. L., & O'Neill, R. E. (2004). Use of response cards with a group of students with learning disabilities including those for whom English is a second language. *Journal of Applied Behavior Analysis, 37,* 219–222.

DeBacker, T. K., & Crowson, H. M. (2006). Influences on cognitive engagement and achievement: Personal epistemology and achievement motives. *British Journal of Educational Psychology, 76,* 535–551.

DeBacker, T. K., & Crowson, H. M. (2008). Measuring need for closure in classroom learners. *Contemporary Educational Psychology, 33,* 711–732.

de Bruin, A., Whittingham, J., Hillebrand, C., & Rikers, R. (2003, April). *The effect of self-explanations and anticipations on acquiring chess skill in novices.* Paper presented at the annual meeting of the American Educational Research Association, Chicago.

DeCasper, A. J., & Spence, M. J. (1986). Prenatal maternal speech influences newborns' perception of speech sounds. *Infant Behavior and Development, 9,* 133–150.

De Corte, E. (2003). Transfer as the productive use of acquired knowledge, skills, and motivations. *Current Directions in Psychological Science, 12,* 142–146.

De Corte, E., Op't Eynde, P., & Verschaffel, L. (2002). "Knowing what to believe": The relevance of students' mathematical beliefs for mathematics education. In B. K. Hofer & P. R. Pintrich (Eds.), *Personal epistemology: The psychology of beliefs about knowledge and knowing* (pp. 297–320). Mahwah, NJ: Erlbaum.

Dee-Lucas, D., & Larkin, J. H. (1991). Equations in scientific proofs: Effects on comprehension. *American Educational Research Journal, 28,* 661–682.

deGroot, A. D. (1965). *Thought and choice in chess.* The Hague: Mouton.

Dehaene, S. (2007). A few steps toward a science of mental life. *Mind, Brain, and Education, 1*(1), 28–47.

deLeeuw, N., & Chi, M. T. H. (2003). Self-explanation: Enriching a situation model or repairing a domain model? In G. M. Sinatra & P. R. Pintrich (Eds.), *Intentional conceptual change* (pp. 55–78). Mahwah, NJ: Erlbaum.

De Lisi, R., & Golbeck, S. L. (1999). Implications of Piagetian theory for peer learning. In A. M. O'Donnell & A. King (Eds.), *Cognitive perspectives on peer learning* (pp. 3–37). Mahwah, NJ: Erlbaum.

Demetriou, A., Christou, C., Spanoudis, G., & Platsidou, M. (2002). The development of mental processing: Efficiency, working memory, and thinking. *Monographs of the Society for Research in Child Development, 67* (1, Serial No. 268).

Dempster, F. N. (1985). Proactive interference in sentence recall: Topic-similarity effects and individual differences. *Memory and Cognition, 13,* 81–89.

Dempster, F. N. (1991). Synthesis of research on reviews and tests. *Educational Leadership, 48*(7), 71–76.

Dempster, F. N. (1992). The rise and fall of the inhibitory mechanism: Toward a unified theory of cognitive development and aging. *Developmental Review, 12,* 45–75.

Dempster, F. N., & Rohwer, W. D. (1974). Component analysis of the elaborative encoding effect in paired-associate learning. *Journal of Experimental Psychology, 103,* 400–408.

Derry, S. J., DuRussel, L. A., & O'Donnell, A. M. (1998). Individual and distributed cognitions in interdisciplinary teamwork: A developing case study and emerging theory. *Educational Psychology Review, 10,* 25–56.

Derry, S. J., Levin, J. R., Osana, H. P., & Jones, M. S. (1998). Developing middle school students' statistical reasoning abilities through simulation gaming. In S. P. Lajoie (Ed.), *Reflections on statistics: Learning, teaching, and assessment in grades K–12* (pp. 175–195). Mahwah, NJ: Erlbaum.

Deutsch, M. (1993). Educating for a peaceful world. *American Psychologist, 48,* 510–517.

Dewhurst, S. A., & Conway, M. A. (1994). Pictures, images, and recollective experience. *Journal of Experimental Psychology: Learning, Memory, and Cognition, 20,* 1088–1098.

Diamond, M., & Hopson, J. (1998). *Magic trees of the mind.* New York: Dutton.

Dijksterhuis, A., & Nordgren, L. F. (2006). A theory of unconscious thought. *Perspectives on Psychological Science, 1,* 95–109.

Dinges, D. F., & Rogers, N. L. (2008). The future of human intelligence: Enhancing cognitive capability in a 24/7 world. In P. C. Kyllonen, R. D. Roberts, & L. Stankov (Eds.), *Extending intelligence: Enhancement and new constructs* (pp. 407–430). New York: Erlbaum/Taylor & Francis.

Dinges, D. F., Whitehouse, W. G., Orne, E. C., Powell, J. W., Orne, M. T., & Erdelyi, M. H. (1992). Evaluating hypnotic memory enhancement (hypermnesia and reminiscence) using multitrial forced recall. *Journal of Experimental Psychology: Learning, Memory, and Cognition, 18,* 1139–1147.

Dirix, C. E. H., Nijhuis, J. G., Jongsma, H. W., & Hornstra, G. (2009). Aspects of fetal learning and memory. *Child Development, 80,* 1251–1258.

diSessa, A. A. (1996). What do "just plain folk" know about physics? In D. R. Olson &

N. Torrance (Eds.), *The handbook of education and human development: New models of learning, teaching, and schooling.* Cambridge, MA: Blackwell.

diSessa, A. A. (2006). A history of conceptual change research. In R. K. Sawyer (Ed.), *The Cambridge handbook of the learning sciences* (pp. 265–281). Cambridge, England: Cambridge University Press.

diSessa, A. A., & Minstrell, J. (1998). Cultivating conceptual change with benchmark lessons. In J. G. Greeno & S. V. Goldman (Eds.), *Thinking practices in mathematics and science learning* (pp. 155–187). Hillsdale, NJ: Erlbaum.

Di Vesta, F. J., & Gray, S. G. (1972). Listening and notetaking. *Journal of Educational Psychology, 63,* 8–14.

Di Vesta, F. J., & Peverly, S. T. (1984). The effects of encoding variability, processing activity and rule example sequences on the transfer of conceptual rules. *Journal of Educational Psychology, 76,* 108–119.

Do, S. L., & Schallert, D. L. (2004). Emotions and classroom talk: Toward a model of the role of affect in students' experiences of classroom discussions. *Journal of Educational Psychology, 96,* 619–634.

Dole, J. A., Duffy, G. G., Roehler, L. R., & Pearson, P. D. (1991). Moving from the old to the new: Research on reading comprehension instruction. *Review of Educational Research, 61,* 239–264.

Dominowski, R. L. (1998). Verbalization and problem solving. In D. J. Hacker, J. Dunlosky, & A. C. Graesser (Eds.), *Metacognition in educational theory and practice* (pp. 25–45). Mahwah, NJ: Erlbaum.

Donnelly, C. M., & McDaniel, M. A. (1993). Use of analogy in learning scientific concepts. *Journal of Experimental Psychology: Learning, Memory, and Cognition, 19,* 975–987.

Doupe, A., & Kuhl, P. (1999). Birdsong and human speech: Common themes and mechanisms. *Annual Review of Neuroscience, 22,* 567–631.

Doyle, W. (1983). Academic work. *Review of Educational Research. 53,* 159–199.

Doyle, W. (1986). Classroom organization and management. In M. C. Wittrock (Ed.), *Handbook of research on teaching* (3rd ed., pp. 392–431). New York: Macmillan.

Draganski, B., Gaser, C., Busch, V., Schuierer, G., Bogdahn, U., & May, A. (2004). Changes in grey matter induced by training. *Nature, 427,* 311–312.

Driver, R. (1995). Constructivist approaches to science teaching. In L. P. Steffe & J. Gale (Eds.), *Constructivism in education* (pp. 385–400). Mahwah, NJ: Erlbaum.

Duckworth, A. L., & Seligman, M. E. P. (2005). Self-discipline outdoes IQ in predicting academic performance of adolescents. *Psychological Science, 16,* 939–944.

Duit, R. (1991). Students' conceptual frameworks: Consequences for learning science. In S. M. Glynn, R. H. Yeany, & B. K. Britton (Eds.), *The psychology of learning science.* Mahwah, NJ: Erlbaum.

Dumay, N., & Gaskell, M. G. (2007). Sleep-associated changes in the mental representation of spoken words. *Psychological Science, 18,* 35–39.

Duncker, K. (1945). On problem solving. *Psychological Monographs, 58* (Whole No. 270).

Dunlosky, J., & Lipko, A. R. (2007). Metacomprehension: A brief history and how to improve its accuracy. *Current Directions in Psychological Science, 16,* 228–232.

Dunlosky, J., Rawson, K. A., & McDonald, S. L. (2002). Influence of practice tests on the accuracy of predicting memory performance for paired associates, sentences, and text material. In T. J. Perfect & B. L. Schwartz (Eds.), *Applied metacognition* (pp. 68–92). Cambridge, England: Cambridge University Press.

Dunn, J. (1988). *The beginnings of social understanding.* Cambridge, MA: Harvard University Press.

Dunning, D., Heath, C., & Suls, J. M. (2004). Flawed self-assessment: Implications for health, education, and the workplace. *Psychological Science in the Public Interest, 5,* 69–106.

Dweck, C. S. (1978). Achievement. In M. E. Lamb (Ed.), *Social and personality development* (pp. 114–130). New York: Holt, Rinehart & Winston.

Dweck, C. S. (1986). Motivational processes affecting learning. *American Psychologist, 41,* 1040–1048.

Dweck, C. S. (2000). *Self-theories: Their role in motivation, personality, and development.* Philadelphia: Psychology Press.

Dweck, C. S. (2009). Foreword. In F. D. Horowitz, R. F. Subotnik, & D. J. Matthews (Eds.), *The development of giftedness and talent across the life span* (pp. xi–xiv). Washington, DC: American Psychological Association.

Dweck, C. S., & Elliott, E. S. (1983). Achievement motivation. In E. M. Hetherington (Ed.), *Handbook of child psychology: Vol. 4. Socialization, personality, and social development* (4th ed., pp. 643–691). New York: Wiley.

Dweck, C. S., & Leggett, E. L. (1988). A social-cognitive approach to motivation and personality. *Psychological Review, 95,* 256–273.

Dweck, C. S., Mangels, J. A., & Good, C. (2004). Motivational effects on attention, cognition, and performance. In D. Y. Dai & R. J. Sternberg (Eds.), *Motivation, emotion, and cognition: Integrative perspectives on intellectual functioning and development* (pp. 41–55). Mahwah, NJ: Erlbaum.

Dweck, C. S., & Molden, D. C. (2005). Self-theories: Their impact on competence motivation and acquisition. In A. J. Elliot & C. S. Dweck (Eds.), *Handbook of competence and motivation* (pp. 122–140). New York: Guilford.

Dye, M. W. G., Green, C. S., & Bavelier, D. (2009). Increasing speed of processing with action video games. *Current Directions in Psychological Science, 18,* 321–326.

Eacott, M. J. (1999). Memory for the events of early childhood. *Current Directions in Psychological Science, 8,* 46–49.

Echols, L. D., West, R. F., Stanovich, K. E., & Kehr, K. S. (1996). Using children's literacy activities to predict growth in verbal cognitive skills: A longitudinal investigation. *Journal of Educational Psychology, 88,* 296–304.

Edens, K. M., & McCormick, C. B. (2000). How do adolescents process advertisements? The influence of ad characteristics, processing objective, and gender. *Contemporary Educational Psychology, 25,* 450–463.

Edens, K. M., & Potter, E. F. (2001). Promoting conceptual understanding through pictorial representation. *Studies in Art Education, 42,* 214–233.

Edwards, K., & Bryan, T. S. (1997). Judgmental biases produced by instructions to disregard: The (paradoxical) case of emotional information. *Personality and Social Psychology Bulletin, 23,* 849–864.

Eilam, B. (2001). Primary strategies for promoting homework performance. *American Educational Research Journal, 38,* 691–725.

Einstein, G. O., & McDaniel, M. A. (2005). Prospective memory: Multiple retrieval processes. *Current Directions in Psychological Science, 14*, 286–290.

Eisner, E. W. (1994). *Cognition and curriculum reconsidered*. New York: Teachers College Press.

Elkind, D. (1987). *Miseducation: Preschoolers at risk*. New York: Alfred A Knopf.

Elliott, D. J. (1995). *Music matters: A new philosophy of music education*. New York: Oxford University Press.

Ellis, H. C., & Hunt, R. R. (1983). *Fundamentals of human memory and cognition* (3rd ed.). Dubuque, IA: Wm. C. Brown.

Ellis, N. C. (Ed.) (1994). *Implicit and explicit learning of languages*. London: Academic Press.

Ellis, S., & Rogoff, B. (1986). Problem solving in children's management of instruction. In E. C. Mueller & C. R. Cooper (Eds.), *Process and outcome in peer relationships* (pp. 301–325). Orlando, FL: Academic Press.

Engle, R. A. (2006). Framing interactions to foster generative learning: A situative explanation of transfer in a community of learners. *Journal of the Learning Sciences, 15*, 451–498.

Engle, R. W. (2002). Working memory capacity as executive attention. *Current Directions in Psychological Science, 11*, 19–23.

English, L. D. (Ed.) (1997). *Mathematical reasoning: Analogies, metaphors, and images*. Mahwah, NJ: Erlbaum.

Erdelyi, M. H. (1985). *Psychoanalysis: Freud's cognitive psychology*. New York: W. H. Freeman.

Ericsson, K. A. (2003). The acquisition of expert performance as problem solving. In J. E. Davidson & R. J. Sternberg (Eds.), *The psychology of problem solving* (pp. 31–83). Cambridge, England: Cambridge University Press.

Evans, E. M. (2008). Conceptual change and evolutionary biology: A developmental analysis. In S. Vosniadou (Ed.), *International handbook on conceptual change* (pp. 263–294). New York: Routledge.

Evans, J., Over, D., & Manktelow, K. (1993). Reasoning, decision making, and rationality. *Cognition, 49*, 165–187.

Evans, S. W., Pelham, W., & Grudberg, M. V. (1995). The efficacy of notetaking to improve behavior and comprehension of adolescents with attention deficit hyperactivity disorder. *Exceptionality, 5*, 1–17.

Eysenck, H. J. (1997). Creativity and personality. In M. A. Runco (Ed.), *The creativity research handbook* (pp. 41–66). Cresskill, NJ: Hampton.

Eysenck, M. W., & Keane, M. T. (1990). *Cognitive psychology: A student's handbook*. Hove, England: Erlbaum.

Feather, N. T. (1982). *Expectations and actions: Expectancy-value models in psychology*. Hillsdale, NJ: Erlbaum.

Feldhusen, J. F., & Treffinger, D. J. (1980). *Creative thinking and problem solving in gifted education*. Dubuque, IA: Kendall/Hunt.

Fennema, E., Carpenter, T. P., & Peterson, P. L. (1989). Learning mathematics with understanding: Cognitively guided instruction. In J. Brophy (Ed.), *Advances in research on teaching* (Vol. 1, pp. 195–222). Greenwich, CT: JAI Press.

Fivush, R., Haden, C., & Reese, E. (1996). Remembering, recounting, and reminiscing: The development of autobiographical memory in social context. In D. C. Rubin (Ed.), *Remembering our past: Studies in autobiographical memory* (pp. 341–359). Cambridge, England: Cambridge University Press.

Fivush, R., & Nelson, K. (2004). Culture and language in the emergence of autobiographical memory. *Psychological Science, 15*, 573–577.

Flanagan, D. P., & Ortiz, S. O. (2001). *Essentials of cross-battery assessment*. New York: Wiley.

Flavell, J. H. (1976). Metacognitive aspects of problem solving. In L. B. Resnick (Ed.), *The nature of intelligence* (pp. 231–236). Hillsdale, NJ: Erlbaum.

Flavell, J. H. (1979). Metacognition and cognitive monitoring: A new area of cognitive-developmental inquiry. *American Psychologist, 34*, 906–911.

Flavell, J. H., Green, F. L., & Flavell, E. R. (2000). Development of children's awareness of their own thoughts. *Journal of Cognitive Development, 1*, 97–112.

Flege, J. E., Munro, M. J., & MacKay, I. R. A. (1995). Effects of age of second-language learning on the production of English consonants. *Speech Communication, 16*(1), 1–26.

Flower, L. S., & Hayes, J. R. (1981). A cognitive process theory of writing. *College Composition and Communication, 32*, 365–387.

Flum, H., & Kaplan, A. (2006). Exploratory orientation as an educational goal. *Educational Psychologist, 41*, 99–110.

Flynn, J. R. (2003). Movies about intelligence: The limitations of *g*. *Current Directions in Psychological Science, 12,* 95–99.

Flynn, J. R. (2007). *What is intelligence? Beyond the Flynn effect.* New York: Cambridge University Press.

Fong, G. T., Krantz, D. H., & Nisbett, R. E. (1986). The effects of statistical training on thinking about everyday problems. *Cognitive Psychology, 18,* 253–292.

Frank, M. J., Cohen, M. X., & Sanfey, A. G. (2009). Multiple systems in decision making: A neurocomputational perspective. *Current Directions in Psychological Science, 18,* 73–77.

Frase, L. T. (1975). Prose processing. In G. H. Bower (Ed.), *The psychology of learning and motivation* (Vol. 9, pp. 1–47). New York: Academic Press.

Frazier, B. N., Gelman, S. A., & Wellman, H. M. (2009). Preschoolers' search for explanatory information within adult–child conversation. *Child Development, 80,* 1592–1611.

Frederiksen, N. (1984a). Implications of cognitive theory for instruction in problem-solving. *Review of Educational Research, 54,* 363–407.

Frederiksen, N. (1984b). The real test bias: Influences of testing on teaching and learning. *American Psychologist, 39,* 193–202.

Frensch, P. A., & Rünger, D. (2003). Implicit learning. *Current Directions in Psychological Science, 12,* 13–18.

Fries, S., Dietz, F., & Schmid, S. (2008). Motivational interference in learning: The impact of leisure alternatives on subsequent self-regulation. *Contemporary Educational Psychology, 33,* 119–133.

Fry, A. F., & Hale, S. (1996). Processing speed, working memory, and fluid intelligence. *Psychological Science, 7,* 237–241.

Fuchs, D., Fuchs, L. S., Mathes, P. G., & Simmons, D. C. (1997). Peer-assisted learning strategies: Making classrooms more responsive to diversity. *American Educational Research Journal, 34,* 174–206.

Fuchs, L. S., Fuchs, D., Prentice, K., Burch, M., Hamlett, C. L., Owen, R., & Schroeter, K. (2003). Enhancing third-grade students' mathematical problem solving with self-regulated learning strategies. *Journal of Educational Psychology, 95,* 306–315.

Gambrell, L. B., & Bales, R. J. (1986). Mental imagery and the comprehension-monitoring performance of fourth- and fifth-grade poor readers. *Reading Research Quarterly, 21,* 454–464.

Garcia, E. E. (1992). "Hispanic" children: Theoretical, empirical, and related policy issues. *Educational Psychology Review, 4,* 69–93.

Gardner, H. (1983). *Frames of mind: The theory of multiple intelligences.* New York: Basic Books.

Gardner, H. (1999). *Intelligence reframed: Multiple intelligences for the 21st century.* New York: Basic Books.

Gardner, H. (2003, April). *Multiple intelligences after twenty years.* Paper presented at the annual meeting of the American Educational Research Association, Chicago.

Gardner, H., & Hatch, T. (1990). Multiple intelligences go to school: Educational implications of the theory of multiple intelligences. *Educational Researcher, 18*(8), 4–10.

Garner, R., Alexander, P. A., Gillingham, M. G., Kulikowich, J. M., & Brown, R. (1991). Interest and learning from text. *American Educational Research Journal, 28,* 643–659.

Gaskins, I. W., & Pressley, M. (2007). Teaching metacognitive strategies that address executive function processes within a schoolwide curriculum. In L. Meltzer (Ed.), *Executive function in education: From theory to practice* (pp. 261–286). New York: Guilford.

Gaskins, I. W., Satlow, E., & Pressley, M. (2007). Executive control of reading comprehension in the elementary school. In L. Meltzer (Ed.), *Executive function in education: From theory to practice* (pp. 194–215). New York: Guilford.

Gathercole, S. E., & Hitch, G. J. (1993). Developmental changes in short-term memory: A revised working memory perspective. In A. F. Collins, S. E. Gathercole, M. A. Conway, & P. E. Morris (Eds.), *Theories of memory* (pp. 189–210). Hove, England: Erlbaum.

Gaudry, E., & Spielberger, C. D. (Eds.) (1971). *Anxiety and educational achievement.* Sydney, Australia: Wiley.

Gauvain, M. (2001). *The social context of cognitive development.* New York: Guilford.

Gaynor, J., & Millham, J. (1976). Student performance and evaluation under variant teaching and testing methods in a large college course. *Journal of Educational Psychology, 68,* 312–317.

Geary, D. C. (1994). *Children's mathematical development: Research and practical applications.* Washington, DC: American Psychological Association.

Gelman, S. A. (2003). *The essential child: Origins of essentialism in everyday thought.* New York: Oxford University Press.

Geraerts, E., Lindsay, D. S., Merckelbach, H., Jelicic, M., Raymaekers, L., Arnold, M. M., et al. (2009). Cognitive mechanisms underlying recovered-memory experiences of childhood sexual abuse. *Psychological Science, 20,* 92–98.

Ghetti, S., & Alexander, K. W. (2004). "If it happened, I would remember it": Strategic use of event memorability in the rejection of false autobiographical events. *Child Development, 75,* 542–561.

Gick, M. L., & Holyoak, K. J. (1980). Analogical problem solving. *Cognitive Psychology, 12,* 306–355.

Gick, M. L., & Holyoak, K. J. (1987). The cognitive basis of knowledge transfer. In S. M. Cormier & J. D. Hagman (Eds.), *Transfer of learning: Contemporary research and applications* (pp. 9–46). San Diego, CA: Academic Press.

Giedd, J. N., Blumenthal, J., Jeffries, N. O., Rajapakse, J. C., Vaituzis, A. C., Liu, H., et al. (1999). Development of the human corpus callosum during childhood and adolescence: A longitudinal MRI study. *Progress in Neuro-Psychopharmacology and Biological Psychiatry, 23,* 571–588.

Giedd, J. N., Jeffries, N. O., Blumenthal, J., Castellanos, F. X., Vaituzis, A. C., Fernandez, T., et al. (1999). Childhood-onset schizophrenia: Progressive brain changes during adolescence. *Biological Psychiatry, 46,* 892–898.

Giles, J. W., Gopnik, A., & Heyman, G. D. (2002). Source monitoring reduces the suggestibility of preschool children. *Psychological Science, 13,* 288–291.

Gilstrap, L. L., & Ceci, S. J. (2005). Reconceptualizing children's suggestibility: Bidirectional and temporal properties. *Child Development, 76,* 40–53.

Ginsburg, H. P., Cannon, J., Eisenband, J., & Pappas, S. (2006). Mathematical thinking and learning. In K. McCartney & D. Phillips (Eds.), *Blackwell handbook of early childhood development* (pp. 208–229). Malden, MA: Blackwell.

Girotto, V., & Light, P. (1993). The pragmatic bases of children's reasoning. In P. Light &

G. Butterworth (Eds.), *Context and cognition: Ways of learning and knowing* (pp. 134–156). Hillsdale, NJ: Erlbaum.

Glanzer, M., & Nolan, S. D. (1986). Memory mechanisms in text comprehension. In G. H. Bower (Ed.), *The psychology of learning and motivation: Advances in research and theory* (Vol. 20, pp. 275–317). San Diego, CA: Academic Press.

Gleitman, H. (1985). Some trends in the study of cognition. In S. Koch & D. E. Leary (Eds.), *A century of psychology as science* (pp. 420–436). New York: McGraw-Hill.

Glover, J. A., Ronning, R. R., & Reynolds, C. R. (Eds.) (1989). *Handbook of creativity.* New York: Plenum Press.

Glucksberg, S., & Weisberg, R. W. (1966). Verbal behavior and problem solving: Some effects of labeling in a functional fixedness problem. *Journal of Experimental Psychology, 71,* 659–664.

Glynn, S. M. (1991). Explaining science concepts: A teaching-with-analogies model. In S. M. Glynn, R. H. Yeany, & B. K. Britton (Eds.), *The psychology of learning science* (pp. 219–240). Hillsdale, NJ: Erlbaum.

Glynn, S. M., & Di Vesta, F. J. (1977). Outline and hierarchical organization as aids for study and retrieval. *Journal of Educational Psychology, 69,* 89–95.

Glynn, S. M., Yeany, R. H., & Britton, B. K. (1991). A constructive view of learning science. In S. M. Glynn, R. H. Yeany, & B. K. Britton (Eds.), *The psychology of learning science* (pp. 3–20). Hillsdale, NJ: Erlbaum.

Godden, D. R., & Baddeley, A. D. (1975). Context-dependent memory in two natural environments: On land and underwater. *British Journal of Psychology, 66,* 325–332.

Gogtay, N., Giedd, J. N., Lusk, L., Hayashi, K. M., Greenstein, D., Vaituzis, A. C., et al. (2004). Dynamic mapping of human cortical development during childhood through early adulthood. *Proceedings of the National Academy of Sciences, USA, 101,* 8174–8179.

Gold, J. M., Murray, R. F., Sekuler, A. B., Bennett, P. J., & Sekuler, R. (2005). Visual memory decay is deterministic. *Psychological Science, 16,* 769–774.

Goldenberg, C. (1992). The limits of expectations: A case for case knowledge about teacher expectancy effects. *American Educational Research Journal, 29,* 517–544.

Goldman-Rakic, P. S. (1986). Setting the stage: Neural development before birth. In S. L. Friedman, K. A. Klivington, & R. W. Peterson (Eds.), *The brain, cognition, and education*. Orlando, FL: Academic Press.

Good, T. L., & Brophy, J. E. (1994). *Looking in classrooms* (6th ed.). New York: HarperCollins.

Good, T. L., McCaslin, M. M., & Reys, B. J. (1992). Investigating work groups to promote problem solving in mathematics. In J. Brophy (Ed.), *Advances in research on teaching: Vol. 3. Planning and managing learning tasks and activities* (pp. 115–160). Greenwich, CT: JAI Press.

Goodman, C. S., & Tessier-Lavigne, M. (1997). Molecular mechanisms of axon guidance and target recognition. In W. M. Cowan, T. M. Jessell, & S. L. Zipursky (Eds.), *Molecular and cellular approaches to neural development* (pp. 108–137). New York: Oxford University Press.

Goodman, G. S., Ghetti, S., Quas, J. A., Edelstein, R. S., Alexander, K. W., Redlich, A. D., Cordon, I. M., & Jones, D. P. H. (2003). A prospective study of memory for child sexual abuse: New findings relevant to the repressed-memory controversy. *Psychological Science, 14*, 113–118.

Goodman, G. S., & Quas, J. A. (2008). Repeated interviews and children's memory: It's more than just how many. *Current Directions in Psychological Science, 17*, 386–390.

Gorus, E., De Raedt, R., Lambert, M., Lemper, J.-C., & Mets, T. (2008). Reaction times and performance variability in normal aging, mild cognitive impairment, and Alzheimer's disease. *Journal of Geriatric Psychiatry and Neurology, 21*, 204–218.

Gould, E., Beylin, A., Tanapat, P., Reeves, A., & Shors, T. J. (1999). Learning enhances adult neurogenesis in the hippocampal formation. *Nature Neuroscience, 2*, 260–265.

Grabe, M. (1986). Attentional processes in education. In G. D. Phye & T. Andre (Eds.), *Cognitive classroom learning: Understanding, thinking, and problem solving*. San Diego, CA: Academic Press.

Graesser, A. C., & Bower, G. H. (Eds.) (1990). *Inferences and text comprehension. The psychology of learning and motivation: Advances in research and theory* (Vol. 25). Orlando: Academic Press.

Graham, S. (1989). Motivation in Afro-Americans. In G. L. Berry & J. K. Asamen (Eds.), *Black students: Psychosocial issues and academic achievement* (pp. 40–68). Newbury Park, CA: Sage.

Graham, S. (1990). Communicating low ability in the classroom: Bad things good teachers sometimes do. In S. Graham & V. S. Folkes (Eds.), *Attribution theory: Applications to achievement, mental health, and interpersonal conflict* (pp. 17–36). Hillsdale, NJ: Erlbaum.

Graham, S. (1991). A review of attribution theory in achievement contexts. *Educational Psychology Review, 3*, 5–39.

Gray, W. D., & Orasanu, J. M. (1987). Transfer of cognitive skills. In S. M. Cormier & J. D. Hagman (Eds.), *Transfer of learning: Contemporary research and applications* (pp. 183–215). San Diego, CA: Academic Press.

Greene, B. A., & Royer, J. M. (1994). A developmental review of response time data that support a cognitive components model of reading. *Educational Psychology Review, 6*, 141–172.

Greene, J. A., & Azevedo, R. (2009). A macro-level analysis of SRL processes and their relations to the acquisition of a sophisticated mental model of a complex system. *Contemporary Educational Psychology, 34*, 18–29.

Greene, S., & Ackerman, J. M. (1995). Expanding the constructivist metaphor: A rhetorical perspective on literacy research and practice. *Review of Educational Research, 65*, 383–420.

Greenfield, P. M. (1998). The cultural evolution of IQ. In U. Neisser (Ed.), *The rising curve: Long-term gains in IQ and related measures* (pp. 81–123). Washington, DC: American Psychological Association.

Greeno, J. G. (1991). A view of mathematical problem solving in school. In M. U. Smith (Ed.), *Toward a unified theory of problem solving: Views from the content domains* (pp. 69–98). Hillsdale, NJ: Erlbaum.

Greeno, J. G., Collins, A. M., & Resnick, L. B. (1996). Cognition and learning. In D. C. Berliner & R. C. Calfee (Eds.), *Handbook of educational psychology* (pp. 15–46). New York: Macmillan.

Greenspoon, J., & Ranyard, R. (1957). Stimulus conditions and retroactive inhibition. *Journal of Experimental Psychology, 53*, 55–59.

Griffin, M. M., & Griffin, B. W. (1994, April). *Some can get there from here: Situated learning, cognitive style, and map skills*. Paper presented at the annual meeting of the

American Educational Research Association, New Orleans, LA.

Gronlund, N. E., & Brookhart, S. M. (2009). *Writing instructional objectives* (8th ed.). Upper Saddle River, NJ: Merrill/Pearson.

Gustafsson, J., & Undheim, J. O. (1996). Individual differences in cognitive functions. In D. C. Berliner & R. C. Calfee (Eds.), *Handbook of educational psychology* (pp. 186–242). New York: Macmillan.

Guthrie, J. T., Cox, K. E., Anderson, E., Harris, K., Mazzoni, S., & Rach, L. (1998). Principles of integrated instruction for engagement in reading. *Educational Psychology Review, 10,* 177–199.

Guthrie, J. T., Wigfield, A., Barbosa, P., Perencevich, K. C., Taboada, A., Davis, M. H., et al. (2004). Increasing reading comprehension and engagement through concept-oriented reading instruction. *Journal of Educational Psychology, 96,* 403–423.

Hacker, D. J. (1998a). Definitions and empirical foundations. In D. J. Hacker, J. Dunlosky, & A. C. Graesser (Eds.), *Metacognition in educational theory and practice* (pp. 1–23). Mahwah, NJ: Erlbaum.

Hacker, D. J. (1998b). Self-regulated comprehension during normal reading. In D. J. Hacker, J. Dunlosky, & A. C. Graesser (Eds.), *Metacognition in educational theory and practice* (pp. 165–191). Mahwah, NJ: Erlbaum.

Hacker, D. J., Bol, L., Horgan, D. D., & Rakow, E. A. (2000). Test prediction and performance in a classroom context. *Journal of Educational Psychology, 92,* 160–170.

Haden, C. A., Ornstein, P. A., Eckerman, C. O., & Didow, S. M. (2001). Mother-child conversational interactions as events unfold: Linkages to subsequent remembering. *Child Development, 72,* 1016–1031.

Hahn, T. T. G., Sakmann, B., & Mehta, M. R. (2007). Differential responses of hippocampal subfields to cortical up-down states. *Proceedings of the National Academy of Sciences, 104,* 5169–5174.

Haier, R. J. (2001). PET studies of learning and individual differences. In J. L. McClelland & R. S. Siegler (Eds.), *Mechanisms of cognitive development: Behavioral and neural perspectives* (pp. 123–145). Mahwah, NJ: Erlbaum.

Halford, G. S., & Andrews, G. (2006). Reasoning and problem solving. In W. Damon & R. M. Lerner (Series Eds.), D. Kuhn, & R. Siegler (Vol. Eds.), *Handbook of child psychology: Vol. 2. Cognition, perception, and language* (6th ed., pp. 557–608). New York: Wiley.

Hall, N. C., Goetz, T., Haynes, T. L., Stupnisky, R. H., & Chipperfield, J. G. (2006, April). *Self-regulation of primary and secondary control: Optimizing control striving in an academic achievement setting.* Paper presented at the annual meeting of the American Educational Research Association, San Francisco.

Hall, N. C., Hladkyj, S., Perry, R. P., & Ruthig, J. C. (2004). The role of attributional retraining and elaborative learning in college students' academic development. *Journal of Social Psychology, 144,* 591–612.

Hall, V. C., & Edmondson, B. (1992). Relative importance of aptitude and prior domain knowledge on immediate and delayed posttests. *Journal of Educational Psychology, 84,* 219–223.

Halpern, D. F. (1997). *Critical thinking across the curriculum: A brief edition of thought and knowledge.* Mahwah, NJ: Erlbaum.

Halpern, D. F. (1998). Teaching critical thinking for transfer across domains: Dispositions, skills, structure, training, and metacognitive monitoring. *American Psychologist, 53,* 449–455.

Halpern, D. F. (2008). Is intelligence critical thinking? Why we need a new definition of intelligence. In P. C. Kyllonen, R. D. Roberts, & L. Stankov (Eds.), *Extending intelligence: Enhancement and new constructs* (pp. 349–370). New York: Erlbaum/Taylor & Francis.

Halpern, D. F., & LaMay, M. L. (2000). The smarter sex: A critical review of sex differences in intelligence. *Educational Psychology Review, 12,* 229–246.

Halpin, G., & Halpin, G. (1982). Experimental investigations of the effects of study and testing on student learning, retention, and ratings of instruction. *Journal of Educational Psychology, 74,* 32–38.

Hambrick, D. Z., & Engle, R. W. (2003). The role of working memory in problem solving. In J. E. Davidson & R. J. Sternberg (Eds.), *The psychology of problem solving* (pp. 176–206). Cambridge, England: Cambridge University Press.

Hamman, D., Berthelot, J., Saia, J., & Crowley, E. (2000). Teachers' coaching of learning and its relation to students' strategic learning. *Journal of Educational Psychology, 92,* 342–348.

Hammer, D. (1994). Epistemological beliefs in introductory physics. *Cognition and Instruction, 12*, 151–183.

Hardy, I., Jonen, A., Möller, K., & Stern, E. (2006). Effects of instructional support within constructivist learning environments for elementary school students' understanding of "floating and sinking." *Journal of Educational Psychology, 98*, 307–326.

Hareli, S., & Weiner, B. (2002). Social emotions and personality inferences: A scaffold for a new direction in the study of achievement motivation. *Educational Psychologist, 37*, 183–193.

Harmon-Jones, E. (2001). The role of affect in cognitive-dissonance processes. In J. P. Forgas (Ed.), *Handbook of affect and social cognition* (pp. 237–255). Mahwah, NJ: Erlbaum.

Harnishfeger, K. K. (1995). The development of cognitive inhibition: Theories, definitions, and research evidence. In F. N. Dempster & C. J. Brainerd (Eds.), *Interference and inhibition in cognition* (pp. 175–204). San Diego, CA: Academic Press.

Harris, K. R., Santangelo, T., & Graham, S. (2010). Metacognition and strategies instruction in writing. In H. S. Waters & W. Schneider (Eds.), *Metacognition, strategy use, and instruction* (pp. 226–256). New York: Guilford.

Harris, M. (1992). *Language experience and early language development: From input to uptake.* Hove, England: Erlbaum.

Harris, R. J. (1977). Comprehension of pragmatic implications in advertising. *Journal of Applied Psychology, 62*, 603–608.

Harter, S. (1999). *The construction of the self: A developmental perspective.* New York: Guilford.

Harter, S., Whitesell, N. R., & Kowalski, P. (1992). Individual differences in the effects of educational transitions on young adolescents' perceptions of competence and motivational orientation. *American Educational Research Journal, 29*, 777–807.

Hartley, J., Bartlett, S., & Branthwaite, A. (1980). Underlining can make a difference—sometimes. *Journal of Educational Research, 73*, 218–224.

Hartley, J., & Trueman, M. (1982). The effects of summaries on the recall of information from prose: Five experimental studies. *Human Learning, 1*, 63–82.

Hartley, K., & Bendixen, L. D. (2001). Educational research in the Internet age: Examining the role of individual characteristics. *Educational Researcher, 30*(9), 22–26.

Hartmann, W. K., Miller, R., & Lee, P. (1984). *Out of the cradle: Exploring the frontiers beyond earth.* New York: Workman.

Harvard University (Producer) (1988). *A private universe* (DVD). Available from www.pyramidmedia.com/.

Haskell, R. E. (2001). *Transfer of learning: Cognition, instruction, and reasoning.* San Diego, CA: Academic Press.

Hatano, G., & Inagaki, K. (2003). When is conceptual change intended? A cognitive-sociocultural view. In G. M. Sinatra & P. R. Pintrich (Eds.), *Intentional conceptual change* (pp. 407–427). Mahwah, NJ: Erlbaum.

Hatano, G., & Oura, Y. (2003). Commentary: Reconceptualizing school learning using insight from expertise research. *Educational Researcher, 32*(8), 26–29.

Hattie, J. A. C. (2009). *Visible learning: A synthesis of over 800 meta-analyses relating to achievement.* London: Routledge.

Hattie, J., Biggs, J., & Purdie, N. (1996). Effects of learning skills interventions on student learning: A meta-analysis. *Review of Educational Research, 66*, 99–136.

Hattie, J., & Timperley, H. (2007). The power of feedback. *Review of Educational Research, 77*, 81–112.

Hayes, D. A., & Henk, W. A. (1986). Understanding and remembering complex prose augmented by analogic and pictorial illustration. *Journal of Reading Behavior, 18*, 63–78.

Hayslip, B., Jr. (1994). Stability of intelligence. In R. J. Sternberg (Ed.), *Encyclopedia of human intelligence* (Vol. 2). New York: Macmillan.

Heatherton, T. F., Macrae, C. N., & Kelley, W. M. (2004). What the social brain sciences can tell us about the self. *Current Directions in Psychological Science, 13*, 190–193.

Heil, M., Rösler, F., & Hennighausen, E. (1994). Dynamics of activation in long-term memory: The retrieval of verbal, pictorial, spatial, and color information. *Journal of Experimental Psychology: Learning, Memory, and Cognition, 20*, 169–184.

Hembree, R. (1988). Correlates, causes, effects, and treatment of test anxiety. *Review of Educational Research, 58*, 47–77.

Hennessey, B. A. (1995). Social, environmental, and developmental issues and creativity. *Educational Psychology Review, 7*, 163–183.

Hennessey, B. A., & Amabile, T. M. (1987). *Creativity and learning.* Washington, DC: National Education Association.

Hertzog, C., Kramer, A. F., Wilson, R. S., & Lindenberger, U. (2009). Enrichment effects on adult cognitive development: Can the functional capacity of older adults be preserved and enhanced? *Psychological Science in the Public Interest, 9,* 1–65.

Heuer, F., & Reisberg, D. (1992). Emotion, arousal, and memory for detail. In S. Christianson (Ed.), *Handbook of emotion and memory* (pp. 151–180). Hillsdale, NJ: Erlbaum.

Heyman, G. D. (2008). Children's critical thinking when learning from others. *Current Directions in Psychological Science, 17,* 344–347.

Hidi, S., & Harackiewicz, J. M. (2000). Motivating the academically unmotivated: A critical issue for the 21st century. *Review of Educational Research, 70,* 151–179.

Hidi, S., & Renninger, K. A. (2006). The four-phase model of interest development. *Educational Psychologist, 41,* 111–127.

Hiebert, J., Carpenter, T. P., Fennema, E., Fuson, K., Human, P., Murray, H., Olivier, A., & Wearne, D. (1996). Problem solving as a basis for reform in curriculum and instruction: The case of mathematics. *Educational Researcher, 25*(4), 12–21.

Hiebert, J., Carpenter, T. P., Fennema, E., Fuson, K. C., Wearne, D., Murray, H., et al. (1997). *Making sense: Teaching and learning mathematics with understanding.* Portsmouth, NH: Heinemann.

Hiebert, J., & Lefevre, P. (1986). Conceptual and procedural knowledge in mathematics: An introductory analysis. In J. Hiebert (Ed.), *Conceptual and procedural knowledge: The case of mathematics* (pp. 1–27). Hillsdale, NJ: Erlbaum.

Hiebert, J., & Wearne, D. (1993). Instructional tasks, classroom discourse, and students' learning in second-grade arithmetic. *American Educational Research Journal, 30,* 393–425.

Hill, K. T. (1984). Debilitating motivation and testing: A major educational problem, possible solutions, and policy applications. In R. Ames & C. Ames (Eds.), *Research on motivation in education: Vol. 1. Student motivation* (pp. 245–274). New York: Academic Press.

Hill, K. T., & Wigfield, A. (1984). Test anxiety: A major educational problem and what can be done about it. *Elementary School Journal, 85,* 105–126.

Hills, T. T., Maouene, M., Maouene, J., Sheya, A., & Smith, L. (2009). Longitudinal analysis of early semantic networks: Preferential attachment or preferential acquisition? *Psychological Science, 20,* 729–739.

Hirstein, W. (2005). *Brain fiction: Self-deception and the riddle of confabulation.* Cambridge, MA: MIT Press/Bradford.

Hmelo-Silver, C. E. (2004). Problem-based learning: What and how do students learn? *Educational Psychology Review, 16,* 235–266.

Hmelo-Silver, C. E. (2006). Design principles for scaffolding technology-based inquiry. In A. M. O'Donnell, C. E. Hmelo-Silver, & G. Erkens (Eds.), *Collaborative learning, reasoning, and technology* (pp. 147–170). Mahwah, NJ: Erlbaum.

Hmelo-Silver, C. E., Duncan, R. G., & Chinn, C. A. (2007). Scaffolding and achievement in problem-based and inquiry learning: A response to Kirschner, Sweller, and Clark (2006). *Educational Psychologist, 42,* 99–107.

Hofer, B. K. (2004). Epistemological understanding as a metacognitive process: Thinking aloud during online searching. *Educational Psychologist, 39,* 43–55.

Hofer, B. K., & Pintrich, P. R. (1997). The development of epistemological theories: Beliefs about knowledge and knowing and their relation to learning. *Review of Educational Research, 67,* 88–140.

Hoffman, B., & Spatariu, A. (2008). The influence of self-efficacy and metacognitive prompting on math problem-solving efficiency. *Contemporary Educational Psychology, 33,* 875–893.

Hogan, D. M., & Tudge, J. R. H. (1999). Implications of Vygotsky's theory for peer learning. In A. M. O'Donnell & A. King (Eds.), *Cognitive perspectives on peer learning* (pp. 39–65). Mahwah, NJ: Erlbaum.

Hogan, K., Nastasi, B. K., & Pressley, M. (2000). Discourse patterns and collaborative scientific reasoning in peer and teacher-guided discussions. *Cognition and Instruction, 17,* 379–432.

Holland, R. W., Hendriks, M., & Aarts, H. (2005). Smells like clean spirit: Nonconscious effects of scent on cognition and behavior. *Psychological Science, 16,* 689–693.

Holliday, R. E. (2003). Reducing misinformation effects in children with cognitive interviews: Dissociating recollection and familiarity. *Child Development, 74,* 728–751.

Hong, Y., Chiu, C., & Dweck, C. S. (1995). Implicit theories of intelligence: Reconsidering the role of confidence in achievement motivation. In M. H. Kernis (Ed.), *Efficacy, agency, and self-esteem* (pp. 197–216). New York: Plenum Press.

Hong, Y., Morris, M. W., Chiu, C., & Benet-Martínez, V. (2000). Multicultural minds: A dynamic constructivist approach to culture and cognition. *American Psychologist, 55,* 709–720.

Horgan, D. (1990, April). *Students' predictions of test grades: Calibration and metacognition.* Paper presented at the annual meeting of the American Educational Research Association, Boston.

Horn, J. L. (2008). Spearman, g, expertise, and the nature of human cognitive capability. In P. C. Kyllonen, R. D. Roberts, & L. Stankov (Eds.), *Extending intelligence: Enhancement and new constructs* (pp. 185–230). New York: Erlbaum/Taylor & Francis.

Horstmann, G. (2002). Evidence for attentional capture by a surprising color singleton in visual search. *Psychological Science, 13,* 499–505.

Houtz, J. C. (1990). Environments that support creative thinking. In C. Hedley, J. Houtz, & A. Baratta (Eds.), *Cognition, curriculum, and literacy* (pp. 61–76) Norwood, NJ: Ablex.

Hu, P., Stylos-Allan, M., & Walker, M. P. (2006). Sleep facilitates consolidation of emotional declarative memory. *Psychological Science, 17,* 891–898.

Huang, H.-S., Matevossian, A., Whittle, C., Kim, S. Y., Schumacher, A., Baker, S. P., et al. (2007). Prefrontal dysfunction in schizophrenia involves mixed-lineage leukemia 1-regulated histone methylation at GABAergic gene promoters. *Journal of Neuroscience, 27,* 11254–11262.

Huey, E. D., Krueger, F., & Grafman, J. (2006). Representations in the human prefrontal cortex. *Current Directions in Psychological Science, 15,* 167–171.

Hunt, E. (2008). Improving intelligence: What's the difference from education? In P. C. Kyllonen, R. D. Roberts, & L. Stankov (Eds.), *Extending intelligence: Enhancement and new constructs* (pp. 15–35). New York: Erlbaum/Taylor & Francis.

Hunt, R. R., & Worthen, J. B. (Eds.) (2006). *Distinctiveness and memory.* Oxford, England: Oxford University Press.

Huttenlocher, P. R. (1979). Synaptic density in human frontal cortex—developmental changes and effects of aging. *Brain Research, 163,* 195–205.

Huttenlocher, P. R. (1990). Morphometric study of human cerebral cortex development. *Neuropsychologia, 28,* 517–527.

Huttenlocher, P. R. (1993). Morphometric study of human cerebral cortex development. In M. H. Johnson (Ed.), *Brain development and cognition: A reader.* Cambridge, MA: Blackwell.

Huttenlocher, P. R., & Dabholkar, A. S. (1997). Regional differences in synaptogenesis in human cerebral cortex. *Journal of Comparative Neurology, 387,* 167–178.

Hynd, C. (1998). Conceptual change in a high school physics class. In B. Guzzetti & C. Hynd (Eds.), *Perspectives on conceptual change: Multiple ways to understand knowing and learning in a complex world* (pp. 27–36). Mahwah, NJ: Erlbaum.

Immordino-Yang, M. H., & Fischer, K. W. (2007). Dynamic development of hemispheric biases in three cases: Cognitive/hemispheric cycles, music, and hemispherectomy. In D. Coch, K. W. Fischer, & G. Dawson (Eds.), *Human behavior, learning, and the developing brain: Typical development* (pp. 74–111). New York: Guilford.

Inzlicht, M., & Ben-Zeev, T. (2003). Do high-achieving female students underperform in private? The implications of threatening environments on intellectual processing. *Journal of Educational Psychology, 95,* 796–805.

Jackson, D. L., Ormrod, J. E., & Salih, D. J. (1999, April). *Promoting students' achievement by teaching them to generate higher-order self-questions.* Paper presented at the annual meeting of the American Educational Research Association, Montreal.

Jacobsen, B., Lowery, B., & DuCette, J. (1986). Attributions of learning disabled children. *Journal of Educational Psychology, 78,* 59–64.

Jacobsen, L. K., Giedd, J. N., Berquin, P. C., Krain, A. L., Hamburger, S. D., Kumra, S., et al. (1997). Quantitative morphology of the cerebellum and fourth ventricle in childhood-onset schizophrenia. *American Journal of Psychiatry, 154,* 1663–1669.

Jacobsen, L. K., Giedd, J. N., Castellanos, F. X., Vaituzis, A. C., Hamburger, S. D., Kumra, S., et al. (1997). Progressive reduction of temporal lobe structures in childhood-onset schizophrenia. *American Journal of Psychiatry, 155,* 678–685.

Jacoby, K. (2008). *Shadows at dawn: A borderlands massacre and the violence of history.* New York: Penguin Press.

James, W. (1890). *Principles of psychology.* New York: Holt.

Jegede, O. J., & Olajide, J. O. (1995). Wait-time, classroom discourse, and the influence of sociocultural factors in science teaching. *Science Education, 79,* 233–249.

Jenkins, J. J., & Russell, W. A. (1952). Associative clustering during recall. *Journal of Abnormal and Social Psychology, 47,* 818–821.

Johanning, D. I., D'Agostino, J. V., Steele, D. F., & Shumow, L. (1999, April). *Student writing, post-writing group collaboration, and learning in pre-algebra.* Paper presented at the annual meeting of the American Educational Research Association, Montreal, Canada.

Johnson, C. I., & Mayer, R. E. (2009). A testing effect with multimedia learning. *Journal of Educational Psychology, 101,* 621–629.

Johnson, D. W., & Johnson, R. T. (2009). Energizing learning: The instructional power of conflict. *Educational Researcher, 38,* 37–51.

Johnson, J. S., & Newport, E. L. (1989). Critical period effects in second language learning: The influence of maturational state on acquisition of English as a second language. *Cognitive Psychology, 21,* 60–99.

Johnson, M. H., & de Haan, M. (2001). Developing cortical specialization for visual-cognitive function: The case of face recognition. In J. L. McClelland & R. S. Siegler (Eds.), *Mechanisms of cognitive development: Behavioral and neural perspectives* (pp. 253–270). Mahwah, NJ: Erlbaum.

Johnson, M. K. (2006). Memory and reality. *American Psychologist, 61,* 760–771.

Johnson-Laird, P. N. (1989). Mental models. In M. I. Posner (Ed.), *Foundations of cognitive science* (pp. 469–499). Cambridge, MA: MIT Press.

Johnstone, A. H., & El-Banna, H. (1986). Capacities, demands, and processes—a predictive model for science education. *Education in Chemistry, 23,* 80–84.

Jonassen, D. H., Hartley, J., & Trueman, M. (1986). The effects of learner-generated versus text-provided headings on immediate and delayed recall and comprehension: An exploratory study. *Human Learning, 5,* 139–150.

Jones, M. S., Levin, M. E., Levin, J. R., & Beitzel, B. D. (2000). Can vocabulary-learning strategies and pair-learning formats be profitably combined? *Journal of Educational Psychology, 92,* 256–262.

Josephs, R. A., Newman, M. L., Brown, R. P., & Beer, J. M. (2003). Status, testosterone, and human intellectual performance: Stereotype threat as status concern. *Psychological Science, 14,* 158–163.

Jost, J. T., Glaser, J., Kruglanski, A. W., & Sulloway, F. J. (2003). Exceptions that prove the rule: Using a theory of motivated social cognition to account for ideological incongruities and political anomalies. *European Journal of Social Psychology, 33,* 13–36.

Judd, C. H. (1932). Autobiography. In C. Murchison (Ed.), *History of psychology in autobiography* (Vol. 2). Worcester, MA: Clark University Press.

Kağitçibaşi, Ç. (2007). *Family, self, and human development across cultures: Theory and applications* (2nd ed.). Mahwah, NJ: Erlbaum.

Kahneman, D., & Tversky, A. (1984). Choices, values, and frames. *American Psychologist, 39,* 341–350.

Kahneman, D., & Tversky, A. (1996). On the reality of cognitive illusions. *Psychological Review, 103,* 582–591.

Kail, R. V. (2007). Longitudinal evidence that increases in processing speed and working memory enhance children's reasoning. *Psychological Science, 18,* 312–313.

Kaiser, M. K., McCloskey, M., & Proffitt, D. R. (1986). Development of intuitive theories of motion: Curvilinear motion in the absence of external forces. *Developmental Psychology, 22,* 67–71.

Kane, M. J., Brown, L. H., McVay, J. C., Silvia, P. J., Myin-Germeys, I., & Kwapil, T. R. (2007). For whom the mind wanders, and when: An experience-sampling study of working memory and executive control in daily life. *Psychological Science, 18,* 614–621.

Karabenick, S. A., & Sharma, R. (1994). Seeking academic assistance as a strategic learning resource. In P. R. Pintrich, D. R. Brown, & C. E. Weinstein (Eds.), *Student motivation, cognition, and learning: Essays in honor of Wilbert J. McKeachie* (pp. 189–211). Hillsdale, NJ: Erlbaum.

Kardash, C. A. M., & Amlund, J. T. (1991). Self-reported learning strategies and learning from expository text. *Contemporary Educational Psychology, 16,* 117–138.

Kardash, C. A. M., & Howell, K. L. (2000). Effects of epistemological beliefs and topic-specific beliefs on undergraduates' cognitive and strategic processing of dual-positional text. *Journal of Educational Psychology, 92,* 524–535.

Kardash, C. A. M., & Scholes, R. J. (1996). Effects of pre-existing beliefs, epistemological beliefs, and need for cognition on interpretation of controversial issues. *Journal of Educational Psychology, 88,* 260–271.

Kardash, C. A. M., & Sinatra, G. M. (2003, April). *Epistemological beliefs and dispositions: Are we measuring the same construct?* Paper presented at the annual meeting of the American Educational Research Association, Chicago.

Karpov, Y. V., & Haywood, H. C. (1998). Two ways to elaborate Vygotsky's concept of mediation: Implications for instruction. *American Psychologist, 53,* 27–36.

Kelemen, D. (2004). Are children "intuitive theists"?: Reasoning about purpose and design in nature. *Psychological Science, 15,* 295–301.

Kelly, S. W., Burton, A. M., Kato, T., & Akamatsu, S. (2001). Incidental learning of real-world regularities. *Psychological Science, 12,* 86–89.

Kemler Nelson, D. G., Egan, L. C., & Holt, M. B. (2004). When children ask, "What is it?" what do they want to know about artifacts? *Psychological Science, 15,* 384–389.

Kiewra, K. A. (1989). A review of note-taking: The encoding-storage paradigm and beyond. *Educational Psychology Review, 1,* 147–172.

Kiewra, K. A., DuBois, N. F., Christian, D., & McShane, A. (1988). Providing study notes: Comparison of three types of notes for review. *Journal of Educational Psychology, 80,* 595–597.

Killeen, P. R. (1991). Behavior's time. In G. H. Bower (Ed.), *The psychology of learning and motivation: Advances in research and theory* (Vol. 27, pp. 294–334). San Diego, CA: Academic Press.

Killeen, P. R. (2001). The four causes of behavior. *Current Directions in Psychological Science, 10,* 136–140.

Kilpatrick, J. (1985). A retrospective account of the past 25 years of research on teaching mathematical problem solving. In E. A. Silver (Ed.), *Teaching and learning mathematical problem solving: Multiple research perspectives* (pp. 1–15). Hillsdale, NJ: Erlbaum.

Kim-Cohen, J., Moffitt, T. E., Caspi, A., & Taylor A. (2004). Genetic and environmental processes in young children's resilience and vulnerability to socioeconomic deprivation. *Child Development, 75,* 651–668.

King, A. (1992). Comparison of self-questioning, summarizing, and notetaking-review as strategies for learning from lectures. *American Educational Research Journal, 29,* 303–323.

King, A. (1999). Discourse patterns for mediating peer learning. In A. M. O'Donnell & A. King (Eds.), *Cognitive perspectives on peer learning* (pp. 87–115). Mahwah, NJ: Erlbaum.

King, P. M., & Kitchener, K. S. (2002). The reflective judgment model: Twenty years of research on epistemic cognition. In B. K. Hofer & P. R. Pintrich (Eds.), *Personal epistemology: The psychology of beliefs about knowledge and knowing* (pp. 37–61). Mahwah, NJ: Erlbaum.

Kirkland, M. C. (1971). The effect of tests on students and schools. *Review of Educational Research, 41,* 303–350.

Kirschner, P. A., Sweller, J., & Clark, R. E. (2006). Why minimal guidance during instruction does not work: An analysis of the failure of constructivist, discovery, problem-based, experiential, and inquiry-based teaching. *Educational Psychologist, 41,* 75–86.

Klaczynski, P. A. (2001). Analytic and heuristic processing influences on adolescent reasoning and decision-making. *Child Development, 72,* 844–861.

Klein, P. D. (1999). Reopening inquiry into cognitive processes in writing-to-learn. *Educational Psychology Review, 11,* 203–270.

Kliegl, R., & Philipp, D. (2008). Become a Demosthenes! Compensating age-related memory deficits with expert strategies. In P. C. Kyllonen, R. D. Roberts, & L. Stankov (Eds.), *Extending intelligence: Enhancement and new constructs* (pp. 231–244). New York: Erlbaum/Taylor & Francis.

Kluger, A. N., & DeNisi, A. (1998). Feedback interventions: Toward the understanding of a double-edged sword. *Current Directions in Psychological Science, 7,* 67–72.

Kochanska, G., Casey, R. J., & Fukumoto, A. (1995). Toddlers' sensitivity to standard violations. *Child Development, 66,* 643–656.

Kolb, B., Gibb, R., & Robinson, T. E. (2003). Brain plasticity and behavior. *Current Directions in Psychological Science, 12,* 1–5.

Kolb, B., & Whishaw, I. Q. (1990). *Fundamentals of human neuropsychology* (3rd ed.). New York: Freeman.

Koltko-Rivera, M. E. (2004). The psychology of worldviews. *Review of General Psychology, 8,* 3–58.

Koob, A. (2009). *The root of thought.* Upper Saddle River, NJ: Pearson.

Kosslyn, S. M. (1985). Mental imagery ability. In R. J. Sternberg (Ed.), *Human abilities: An information-processing approach.* New York: W. H. Freeman.

Kovas, Y., & Plomin, R. (2007). Learning abilities and disabilities: Generalist genes, specialist environments. *Current Directions in Psychological Science, 16,* 284–288.

Krajcik, J. S., & Blumenfeld, P. C. (2006). In R. Sawyer (Ed.), *The Cambridge handbook of the learning sciences* (pp. 317–333). New York: Cambridge University Press.

Kramarski, B., & Mevarech, Z. R. (2003). Enhancing mathematical reasoning in the classroom: The effects of cooperative learning and metacognitive training. *American Educational Research Journal, 40,* 281–310.

Krapp, A., Hidi, S., & Renninger, K. A. (1992). Interest, learning, and development. In K. A. Renninger, S. Hidi, & A. Krapp (Eds.), *The role of interest in learning and development.* Hillsdale, NJ: Erlbaum.

Krebs, D. L. (2008). Morality: An evolutionary account. *Perspectives on Psychological Science, 3,* 149–172.

Kruglanski, A. W., & Webster, D. M. (1996). Motivated closing of the mind: "Seizing" and "freezing." *Psychological Review, 103,* 263–283.

Ku, Y.-M., Chan, W.-C., Wu, Y.-C., & Chen, Y.-H. (2008, March). *Improving children's comprehension of science text: Effects of adjunct questions and notetaking.* Paper presented at the annual meeting of the American Educational Research Association, New York.

Kuhara-Kojima, K., & Hatano, G. (1991). Contribution of content knowledge and learning ability to the learning of facts. *Journal of Educational Psychology, 83,* 253–263.

Kuhl, J. (1985). Volitional mediators of cognition–behavior consistency: Self-regulatory processes and actions versus state orientation. In J. Kuhl & J. Beckmann (Eds.), *Action control: From cognition to behavior* (pp. 101–128). Berlin, Germany: Springer-Verlag.

Kuhn, D. (2001a). How do people know? *Psychological Science, 12,* 1–8.

Kuhn, D. (2001b). Why development does (and does not) occur: Evidence from the domain of inductive reasoning. In J. L. McClelland & R. S. Siegler (Eds.), *Mechanisms of cognitive development: Behavioral and neural perspectives* (pp. 221–249). Mahwah, NJ: Erlbaum.

Kuhn, D. (2006). Do cognitive changes accompany developments in the adolescent brain? *Perspectives on Psychological Science, 1,* 59–67.

Kuhn, D., Black, J., Keselman, A., & Kaplan, D. (2000). The development of cognitive skills to support inquiry learning. *Cognition and Instruction, 18,* 495–523.

Kuhn, D., Daniels, S., & Krishnan, A. (2003, April). *Epistemology and intellectual values as core metacognitive constructs.* Paper presented at the annual meeting of the American Educational Research Association, Chicago.

Kuhn, D., & Franklin, S. (2006). The second decade: What develops (and how)? In W. Damon & R. M. Lerner (Series Eds.), D. Kuhn, & R. Siegler (Vol. Eds.), *Handbook of child psychology: Vol. 2. Cognition, perception, and language* (6th ed., pp. 953–993). New York: Wiley.

Kuhn, D., Garcia-Mila, M., Zohar, A., & Andersen, C. (1995). Strategies of knowledge acquisition. *Monographs of the Society for Research in Child Development, 60* (Whole No. 245).

Kuhn, D., & Park, S.-H. (2005). Epistemological understanding and the development of intellectual values. *International Journal of Educational Research, 43,* 111–124.

Kuhn, D., & Udell, W. (2003). The development of argument skills. *Child Development, 74,* 1245–1260.

Kuhn, D., & Weinstock, M. (2002). What is epistemological thinking and why does it matter? In B. K. Hofer & P. R. Pintrich (Eds.), *Personal epistemology: The psychology of beliefs about knowledge and knowing* (pp. 121–144). Mahwah, NJ: Erlbaum.

Kulhavy, R. W., Peterson, S., & Schwartz, N. H. (1986). Working memory: The encoding process. In G. D. Phye & T. Andre (Eds.), *Cognitive classroom learning: Understanding, thinking, and problem solving.* Orlando, FL: Academic Press.

Kunda, Z. (1990). The case for motivated reasoning. *Psychological Bulletin, 18,* 480–498.

Kyllonen, P. C., Stankov, L., & Roberts, R. D. (2008). Enhancement and new constructs: Overview and rationale. In P. C. Kyllonen, R. D. Roberts, & L. Stankov (Eds.), *Extending intelligence: Enhancement and new constructs* (pp. 3–11). New York: Erlbaum/Taylor & Francis.

LaBerge, D., & Samuels, S. J. (1974). Toward a theory of automatic information processing in reading. *Cognitive Psychology, 6*, 293–323.

Laboratory of Comparative Human Cognition. (1982). Culture and intelligence. In R. J. Sternberg (Ed.), *Handbook of human intelligence* (pp. 642–722). Cambridge, England: Cambridge University Press.

Labouvie-Vief, G., & González, M. M. (2004). Dynamic integration: Affect optimization and differentiation in development. In D. Y. Dai & R. J. Sternberg (Eds.), *Motivation, emotion, and cognition: Integrative perspectives on intellectual functioning and development* (pp. 237–272). Mahwah, NJ: Erlbaum.

Lamb, S. (1991). First moral sense: Aspects of and contributions to a beginning morality in the second year of life. In W. M. Kurtines & J. L. Gewirtz (Eds.), *Handbook of moral behavior and development: Vol. 2. Research* (pp. 171–189). Hillsdale, NJ: Erlbaum.

Lambert, M. C., Cartledge, G., Heward, W. L., & Lo, Y.-Y. (2006). Effects of response cards on disruptive behavior and academic responding during math lessons by fourth-grade urban students. *Journal of Positive Behavioral Interventions, 8*, 88–99.

Lampert, M., Rittenhouse, P., & Crumbaugh, C. (1996). Agreeing to disagree: Developing sociable mathematical discourse. In D. R. Olson & N. Torrance (Eds.), *The handbook of education and human development: New models of learning, teaching, and schooling* (pp. 731–764). Cambridge, MA: Blackwell.

Langer, E. J. (1997). *The power of mindful learning.* Reading, MA: Addison-Wesley.

Langer, E. J. (2000). Mindful learning. *Current Directions in Psychological Science, 9*, 220–223.

Lashley, K. S. (1929). *Brain mechanisms and intelligence.* Chicago: University of Chicago Press.

Lassiter, G. D. (2002). Illusory causation in the courtroom. *Current Directions in Psychological Science, 11*, 204–208.

Lave, J. (1988). *Cognition in practice: Mind, mathematics, and culture in everyday life.* Cambridge, England: Cambridge University Press.

Lave, J. (1993). Word problems: A microcosm of theories of learning. In P. Light & G. Butterworth (Eds.), *Context and cognition: Ways of learning and knowing* (pp. 74–92). Hillsdale, NJ: Erlbaum.

Lave, J., & Wenger, E. (1991). *Situated learning: Legitimate peripheral participation.* Cambridge, England: Cambridge University Press.

LeDoux, J. (1998). *The emotional brain.* London: Weidenfeld and Nicholson.

Lee, J. L. C., Everitt, B. J., & Thomas, K. L. (2004). Independent cellular processes for hippocampal memory consolidation and reconsolidation. *Science, 304*, 839–843.

Lee, O. (1999). Science knowledge, world views, and information sources in social and cultural contexts: Making sense after a natural disaster. *American Educational Research Journal, 36*, 187–219.

LeFevre, J., Bisanz, J., & Mrkonjic, J. (1988). Cognitive arithmetic: Evidence for obligatory activation of arithmetic facts. *Memory and Cognition, 16*, 45–53.

Lehmann, M., & Hasselhorn, M. (2007). Variable memory strategy use in children's adaptive intratask learning behavior: Developmental changes and working memory influences in free recall. *Child Development, 78*, 1068–1082.

Leichtman, M. D., Pillemer, D. B., Wang, Q., Koreishi, A., & Han, J. J. (2000). When Baby Maisy came to school: Mothers' interview styles and preschoolers' event memories. *Cognitive Development, 15*, 99–114.

Lenroot, R. K., & Giedd, J. N. (2007). The structural development of the human brain as measured longitudinally with magnetic resonance imaging. In D. Coch, K. W. Fischer, & G. Dawson (Eds.), *Human behavior, learning, and the developing brain: Typical development* (pp. 50–73). New York: Guilford.

Lepper, M. R., & Hodell, M. (1989). Intrinsic motivation in the classroom. In C. Ames & R. Ames (Eds.), *Research on motivation in education: Vol. 3. Goals and cognitions* (pp. 73–105). San Diego, CA: Academic Press.

Lester, F. K., Jr. (1985). Methodological considerations in research on mathematical problem-solving instruction. In E. A. Silver (Ed.), *Teaching and learning mathematical problem solving: Multiple research perspectives* (pp. 41–70). Hillsdale, NJ: Erlbaum.

Leuner, B., Mendolia-Loffredo, S., Kozorovitskiy, Y., Samburg, D., Gould, E., & Shors, T. J. (2004). Learning enhances the survival of new neurons beyond the time when the hippocampus is required for memory. *Journal of Neuroscience, 24,* 7477–7481.

Leung, A. K., Maddux, W. W., Galinsky, A. D., & Chiu, C. (2008). Multicultural experience enhances creativity: The when and how. *American Psychologist, 63,* 169–181.

Levin, J. R., & Mayer, R. E. (1993). Understanding illustrations in text. In B. K. Britton, A. Woodward, & M. Binkley (Eds.), *Learning from textbooks: Theory and practice* (pp. 95–113). Hillsdale, NJ: Erlbaum.

Levstik, L. S. (1993). Building a sense of history in a first-grade classroom. In J. Brophy (Ed.), *Advances in research on teaching: Vol. 4. Case studies of teaching and learning in social studies* (pp. 1–31). Greenwich, CT: JAI Press.

Levy, B. J., & Anderson, M. C. (2002). Inhibitory processes and the control of memory retrieval. *Trends in Cognitive Sciences, 6,* 299–305.

Levy, I., Kaplan, A., & Patrick, H. (2000, April). *Early adolescents' achievement goals, intergroup processes, and attitudes towards collaboration.* Paper presented at the annual meeting of the American Educational Research Association, New Orleans, LA.

Lewis, M. D., & Stieben, J. (2004). Emotion regulation in the brain: Conceptual issues and directions for developmental research. *Child Development, 75,* 371–376.

Lichtman, J. W. (2001). Developmental neurobiology overview: Synapses, circuits, and plasticity. In D. B. Bailey, Jr., J. T. Bruer, F. J. Symons, & J. W. Lichtman (Eds.), *Critical thinking about critical periods* (pp. 27–42). Baltimore: Brookes.

Light, P., & Butterworth, G. (Eds.) (1993). *Context and cognition: Ways of learning and knowing.* Hillsdale, NJ: Erlbaum.

Linderholm, T., Gustafson, M., van den Broek, P., & Lorch, R. F., Jr. (1997, March). *Effects of reading goals on inference generation.* Paper presented at the annual meeting of the American Educational Research Association, Chicago.

Lindsay, D. S. (1993). Eyewitness suggestibility. *Current Directions in Psychological Science, 2,* 86–89.

Lindsay, P. H., & Norman, D. A. (1977). *Human information processing.* New York: Academic Press.

Linn, M. C. (2008). Teaching for conceptual change: Distinguish or extinguish ideas. In S. Vosniadou (Ed.), *International handbook on conceptual change* (pp. 694–722). New York: Routledge.

Linn, M. C., Clement, C., Pulos, S., & Sullivan, P. (1989). Scientific reasoning during adolescence: The influence of instruction in science knowledge and reasoning strategies. *Journal of Research in Science Teaching, 26,* 171–187.

Linn, R. L., & Miller, M. D. (2005). *Measurement and assessment in teaching* (9th ed.). Upper Saddle River, NJ: Merrill/Prentice Hall.

Locke, E. A., & Latham, G. P. (2002). Building a practically useful theory of goal setting and task motivation: A 35-year odyssey. *American Psychologist, 57,* 705–717.

Locke, E. A., & Latham, G. P. (2006). New directions in goal-setting theory. *Current Directions in Psychological Science, 15,* 265–268.

Lodewyk, K. R., & Winne, P. H. (2005). Relations among the structure of learning tasks, achievement, and changes in self-efficacy in secondary students. *Journal of Educational Psychology, 97,* 3–12.

Loftus, E. F. (1992). When a lie becomes memory's truth: Memory distortion after exposure to misinformation. *Current Directions in Psychological Science, 1,* 121–123.

Loftus, E. F. (2003). Make-believe memories. *American Psychologist, 58,* 867–873.

Loftus, E. F. (2004). Memories of things unseen. *Current Directions in Psychological Science, 13,* 145–147.

Loftus, E. F., & Kaufman, L. (1992). Why do traumatic experiences sometimes produce good memory (flashbulbs) and sometimes no memory (repression)? In E. Winograd & U. Neisser (Eds.), *Affect and accuracy in recall: Studies of "flashbulb" memories* (pp. 212–223). Cambridge, England: Cambridge University Press.

Loftus, E. F., & Palmer, J. C. (1974). Reconstruction of automobile destruction: An example of the interaction between language and memory. *Journal of Verbal Learning and Verbal Behavior, 13,* 585–589.

Loftus, E. F., Wolchover, D., & Page, D. (2006). General review of the psychology of eyewitness testimony. In A. Heaton-Armstrong, E. Shepherd, G. Gudjonsson, & D. Wolchover (Eds.), *Witness testimony: Psychological, investigative, and evidential perspectives* (pp. 7–22). New York: Oxford University Press.

Loftus. G. R., & Bell, S. M. (1975). Two types of information in picture memory. *Journal of Experimental Psychology: Human Learning and Perception, 104,* 103–113.

Lorch, R. F., Jr., Lorch, E. P., & Inman, W. E. (1993). Effects of signaling topic structure on text recall. *Journal of Educational Psychology, 85,* 281–290.

Losh, S. C. (2003). On the application of social cognition and social location to creating causal explanatory structures. *Educational Research Quarterly, 26*(3), 17–33.

Lovell, K. (1979). Intellectual growth and the school curriculum. In F. B. Murray (Ed.), *The impact of Piagetian theory: On education, philosophy, psychiatry, and psychology.* Baltimore: University Park Press.

Lovett, S. B., & Flavell, J. H. (1990). Understanding and remembering: Children's knowledge about the differential effects of strategy and task variables on comprehension and memorization. *Child Development, 61,* 1842–1858.

Lubart, T. I., & Mouchiroud, C. (2003). Creativity: A source of difficulty in problem solving. In J. E. Davidson & R. J. Sternberg (Eds.), *The psychology of problem solving* (pp. 127–148). Cambridge, England: Cambridge University Press.

Luchins, A. S. (1942). Mechanization in problem solving: The effect of Einstellung. *Psychological Monographs, 54* (Whole No. 248).

Ludwig, J., & Phillips, D. (2007). The benefits and costs of Head Start. *Social Policy Report, 21*(3).

Luna, B., & Sweeney, J. A. (2004). The emergence of collaborative brain function: fMRI studies of the development of response inhibition. *Annals of the New York Academy of Sciences, 1021,* 296–309.

Lundeberg, M. A., & Fox, P. W. (1991). Do laboratory findings on test expectancy generalize to classroom outcomes? *Review of Educational Research, 61,* 94–106.

Lustig, C., & Hasher, L. (2001). Implicit memory is vulnerable to proactive interference. *Psychological Science, 12,* 408–412.

Lustig, C., Konkel, A., & Jacoby, L. L. (2004). Which route to recovery? Controlled retrieval and accessibility bias in retroactive interference. *Psychological Science, 15,* 729–735.

Lynn, S. J., Lock, T. G., Myers, B., & Payne, D. G. (1997). Recalling the unrecallable: Should hypnosis be used to recover memories in psychotherapy? *Current Directions in Psychological Science, 6,* 79–83.

Mace, F. C., Belfiore, P. J., & Hutchinson, J. M. (2001). Operant theory and research on self-regulation. In B. Zimmerman & D. Schunk (Eds.), *Learning and academic achievement: Theoretical perspectives* (pp. 39–65). Mahwah, NJ: Erlbaum.

Machiels-Bongaerts, M., Schmidt, H. G., & Boshuizen, H. P. A. (1991, April). *The effects of prior knowledge activation on free recall and study time allocation.* Paper presented at the annual meeting of the American Educational Research Association, Chicago.

Mac Iver, D. J., Reuman, D. A., & Main, S. R. (1995). Social structuring of the school: Studying what is, illuminating what could be. In J. T. Spence, J. M. Darley, & D. J. Foss (Eds.), *Annual review of psychology* (Vol. 46, pp. 375–400). Palo Alto, CA: Annual Review, Inc.

MacLeod, M. D., & Saunders, J. (2008). Retrieval inhibition and memory distortion: Negative consequences of an adaptive process. *Current Directions in Psychological Science, 17,* 26–30.

Maguire, E. A., Gadian, D. G., Johnsrude, I. S., Good, C. D., Ashburnre, J., Frackowiak, R., et al. (2000). Navigation-related structural change in the hippocampi of taxi drivers. *Proceedings of the National Academy of Sciences, USA, 97,* 4398–4403.

Maier, N. R. F. (1945). Reasoning in humans III: The mechanisms of equivalent stimuli and of reasoning. *Journal of Experimental Psychology, 35,* 349–360.

Mandler, J. M. (2000). Perceptual and conceptual processes in infancy. *Journal of Cognition and Development, 1,* 3–36.

Mangels, J. (2004, May). *The influence of intelligence beliefs on attention and learning: A neurophysiological approach.* Invited address presented at the annual meeting of the American Psychological Society, Chicago.

Marcus, G. (2008). *Kluge: The haphazard construction of the human mind.* Boston: Houghton Mifflin.

Maria, K. (1998). Self-confidence and the process of conceptual change. In B. Guzzetti & C. Hynd (Eds.), *Perspectives on conceptual change: Multiple ways to understand knowing and learning in a complex world* (pp. 7–16). Mahwah, NJ: Erlbaum.

Marmolejo, E. K., Wilder, D. A., & Bradley, L. (2004). A preliminary analysis of the effects of response cards on student performance and participation in an upper division university course. *Journal of Applied Behavior Analysis, 37,* 405–410.

Marsh, E. J. (2007). Retelling is not the same as recalling: Implications for memory. *Current Directions in Psychological Science, 16,* 16–20.

Marsh, H. W. (1990). Causal ordering of academic self-concept and academic achievement: A multiwave, longitudinal panel analysis. *Journal of Educational Psychology, 82,* 646–656.

Martínez, P., Bannan-Ritland, B., Kitsantas, A., & Baek, J. Y. (2008, March). *The impact of an integrated science reading intervention on elementary children's misconceptions regarding slow geomorphological changes caused by water.* Paper presented at the annual meeting of the American Educational Research Association, New York.

Mason, L. (2003). Personal epistemologies and intentional conceptual change. In G. M. Sinatra & P. R. Pintrich (Eds.), *Intentional conceptual change* (pp. 199–236). Mahwah, NJ: Erlbaum.

Mason, L., Gava, M., & Boldrin, A. (2008). On warm conceptual change: The interplay of text, epistemological beliefs, and topic interest. *Journal of Educational Psychology, 100,* 291–309.

Massimini, M., Ferrarelli, F., Huber, R., Esser, S. K., & Tononi, G. (2005). Breakdown of cortical effective connectivity during sleep. *Science, 310,* 1768–1769.

Mastropieri, M. A., & Scruggs, T. E. (1992). Science for students with disabilities. *Review of Educational Research, 62,* 377–411.

Matthews, G., Zeidner, M., & Roberts, R. D. (2006). Models of personality and affect for education: A review and synthesis. In P. A. Alexander & P. H. Winne (Eds.), *Handbook of educational psychology* (2nd ed., pp. 163–186). Mahwah, NJ: Erlbaum.

Maus, G. W., & Nijhawan, R. (2008). Motion extrapolation into the blind spot. *Psychological Science, 19,* 1087–1091.

Mayer, R. E. (1984). Aids to text comprehension. *Educational Psychologist, 19,* 30–42.

Mayer, R. E. (1985). Implications of cognitive psychology for instruction in mathematical problem solving. In E. A. Silver (Ed.), *Teaching and learning mathematical problem solving: Multiple research perspectives* (pp. 123–138). Hillsdale, NJ: Erlbaum.

Mayer, R. E. (1986). Mathematics. In R. F. Dillon & R. J. Sternberg (Eds.), *Cognition and instruction* (pp. 127–154). San Diego, CA: Academic Press.

Mayer, R. E. (1989). Models for understanding. *Review of Educational Research, 59,* 43–64.

Mayer, R. E. (1992). *Thinking, problem solving, cognition* (2nd ed.). New York: W. H. Freeman.

Mayer, R. E. (2003). The promise of multimedia learning: Using the same instructional design methods across different media. *Learning and Instruction, 13,* 125–139.

Mayer, R. E., & Wittrock, M. C. (1996). Problem-solving transfer. In D. C. Berliner & R. C. Calfee (Eds.), *Handbook of educational psychology* (pp. 47–62). New York: Macmillan.

Mayer, R. E., & Wittrock, M. C. (2006). Problem solving. In P. A. Alexander & P. H. Winne (Eds.), *Handbook of educational psychology* (2nd ed., pp. 287–303). Mahwah, NJ: Erlbaum.

Mazzoni, G., & Kirsch, I. (2002). Autobiographical memories and beliefs: A preliminary metacognitive model. In T. J. Perfect & B. L. Schwartz (Eds.), *Applied metacognition* (pp. 121–145). Cambridge, England: Cambridge University Press.

McAndrew, D. A. (1983). Underlining and notetaking: Some suggestions from research. *Journal of Reading, 27,* 103–108.

McAshan, H. H. (1979). *Competency-based education and behavioral objectives.* Englewood Cliffs, NJ: Educational Technology.

McCall, R. B., & Plemons, B. W. (2001). The concept of critical periods and their implications for early childhood services. In D. B. Bailey, Jr., J. T. Bruer, F. J. Symons, & J. W. Lichtman (Eds.), *Critical thinking about critical periods* (pp. 267–287). Baltimore: Brookes.

McCaslin, M., & Good, T. L. (1996). The informal curriculum. In D. C. Berliner & R. C. Calfee (Eds.), *Handbook of educational psychology* (pp. 622–670). New York: Macmillan.

McCoy, L. P. (1990, April). *Correlates of mathematics anxiety.* Paper presented at the annual meeting of the American Educational Research Association, Boston.

McCrudden, M. T., & Schraw, G. (2007). Relevance and goal-focusing in text processing. *Educational Psychology Review, 19,* 113–139.

McCrudden, M. T., Schraw, G., & Hartley, K. (2006). The effect of general relevance instructions on shallow and deeper learning and reading time. *Journal of Experimental Education, 74,* 293–310.

McCrudden, M. T., Schraw, G., & Kambe, G. (2005). The effect of relevance instructions on reading time and learning. *Journal of Educational Psychology, 97,* 88–102.

McCutchen, D. (1996). A capacity theory of writing: Working memory in composition. *Educational Psychology Review, 8,* 299–325.

McDaniel, M. A., & Einstein, G. O. (1989). Material-appropriate processing: A contextualist approach to reading and studying strategies. *Educational Psychology Review, 1,* 113–145.

McDevitt, M. (2005). The partisan child: Developmental provocation as a model of political socialization. *International Journal of Public Opinion, 18*(1), 67–88.

McDevitt, T. M., & Ormrod, J. E. (2010). *Child development and education* (4th ed.). Upper Saddle River, NJ: Merrill.

McGee, K. D., Knight, S. L., & Boudah, D. J. (2001, April). *Using reciprocal teaching in secondary inclusive English classroom instruction.* Paper presented at the annual meeting of the American Educational Research Association, Seattle, WA.

McGuigan, F., & Salmon, K. (2004). The time to talk: The influence of the timing of adult-child talk on children's event memory. *Child Development, 75,* 669–686.

McKown, C., & Weinstein, R. S. (2003). The development and consequences of stereotype consciousness in middle childhood. *Child Development, 74,* 498–515.

McNally, R. J., & Geraerts, E. (2009). A new solution to the recovered memory debate. *Perspectives on Psychological Science, 4,* 126–134.

McNeil, N. M., & Uttal, D. H. (2009). Rethinking the use of concrete materials in learning: Perspectives from development and education. *Child Development Perspectives, 3,* 137–139.

Mechelli, A., Crinion, J. T., Noppeney, U., O'Doherty, J., Ashburner, J., Frackowiak, R., & Price, C. J. (2004). Structural plasticity in the bilingual brain. *Nature, 431,* 757.

Medin, D. L. (2005, August). *Role of culture and expertise in cognition.* Invited address presented at the annual meeting of the American Psychological Association, Washington, DC.

Meichenbaum, D. (1985). Teaching thinking: A cognitive-behavioral perspective. In S. F. Chipman, J. W. Segal, & R. Glaser (Eds.), *Thinking and learning skills: Vol. 2. Research and open questions* (pp. 407–426). Hillsdale, NJ: Erlbaum.

Meltzer, L. (Ed.) (2007). *Executive function in education: From theory to practice.* New York: Guilford.

Meltzer, L., Pollica, L. S., & Barzillai, M. (2007). Executive function in the classroom: Embedding strategy instruction into daily teaching practices. In L. Meltzer (Ed.), *Executive function in education: From theory to practice* (pp. 165–193). New York: Guilford.

Mergendoller, J. R., Markham, T., Ravitz, J., & Larmer, J. (2006). Pervasive management of project based learning: Teachers as guides and facilitators. In C. M. Evertson & C. S. Weinstein (Eds.), *Handbook of classroom management: Research, practice, and contemporary issues* (pp. 583–615). Mahwah, NJ: Erlbaum.

Merzenich, M. M. (2001). Cortical plasticity contributing to child development. In J. L. McClelland & R. S. Siegler (Eds.), *Mechanisms of cognitive development: Behavioral and neural perspectives* (pp. 67–95). Mahwah, NJ: Erlbaum.

Metcalfe, J. (2002). Is study time allocated selectively to a region of proximal learning? *Journal of Experimental Psychology: General, 131,* 349–363.

Metcalfe, J. (2009). Metacognitive judgments and control of study. *Current Directions in Psychological Science, 18,* 159–163.

Metz, K. E. (1995). Reassessment of developmental constraints on children's science instruction. *Review of Educational Research, 65,* 93–127.

Metz, K. E. (2004). Children's understanding of scientific inquiry: Their conceptualizations of uncertainty in investigations of their own design. *Cognition and Instruction, 22,* 219–290.

Metzger, M. J., Flanagin, A. J., & Zwarun, L. (2003). College student Web use, perceptions of information credibility, and verification behavior. *Computers and Education, 41,* 271–290.

Middleton, M. J., & Midgley, C. (2002). Beyond motivation: Middle school students' perceptions of press for understanding in math. *Contemporary Educational Psychology, 27,* 373–391.

Mikulincer, M. (1994). *Human learned helplessness: A coping perspective.* New York: Plenum Press.

Miller, G. A. (1956). The magical number seven, plus or minus two: Some limits on our capacity for processing information. *Psychological Review, 63,* 81–97.

Miller, R. B., & Brickman, S. J. (2004). A model of future-oriented motivation and self-regulation. *Educational Psychology Review, 16,* 9–33.

Minsky, M. (2006). *The emotion machine: Commonsense thinking, artificial intelligence, and the future of the human mind.* New York: Simon & Schuster.

Mitchell, J. B. (1989). Current theories on expert and novice thinking: A full faculty considers the implications for legal education. *Journal of Legal Education, 39,* 275–297.

Mithaug, D. K., & Mithaug, D. E. (2003). Effects of teacher-directed versus student-directed instruction on self-management of young children with disabilities. *Journal of Applied Behavior Analysis, 36,* 133–136.

Monte-Sano, C. (2008). Qualities of historical writing instruction: A comparative case study of two teachers' practices. *American Educational Research Journal, 45,* 1045–1079.

Moon, J. (2008). *Critical thinking: An exploration of theory and practice.* London: Routledge.

Moreno, R. (2006). Learning in high-tech and multimedia environments. *Current Directions in Psychological Science, 15,* 63–67.

Morgan, M. (1985). Self-monitoring of attained subgoals in private study. *Journal of Educational Psychology, 77,* 623–630.

Morra, S., Gobbo, C., Marini, Z., & Sheese, R. (2008). *Cognitive development: Neo-Piagetian perspectives.* New York: Erlbaum.

Morris, M. W., Carranza, E., & Fox, C. R. (2008). Mistaken identity: Activating conservative political identities induces "conservative" financial decisions. *Psychological Science, 19,* 1154–1160.

Morsanyi, K., Primi, C., Chiesi, F., & Handley, S. (2009). The effects and side-effects of statistics education: Psychology students' (mis-)conceptions of probability. *Contemporary Educational Psychology, 34,* 210–220.

Mosborg, S. (2002). Speaking of history: How adolescents use their knowledge of history in reading the daily news. *Cognition and Instruction, 20,* 323–358.

Muis, K. R. (2004). Personal epistemology and mathematics: A critical review and synthesis of research. *Review of Educational Research, 74,* 317–377.

Muis, K. R. (2007). The role of epistemic beliefs in self-regulated learning. *Educational Psychologist, 42,* 173–190.

Muis, K. R., Bendixen, L. D., & Haerle, F. C. (2006). Domain-generality and domain-specificity in personal epistemology research: Philosophical and empirical reflections in the development of a theoretical framework. *Educational Psychology Review, 18,* 3–54.

Muis, K. R., & Franco, G. M. (2009). Epistemic beliefs: Setting the standards for self-regulated learning. *Contemporary Educational Psychology, 34,* 306–318.

Murphy, P. K. (2007). The eye of the beholder: The interplay of social and cognitive components in change. *Educational Psychologist, 42,* 41–53.

Murphy, P. K., & Alexander, P. A. (2004). Persuasion as a dynamic, multidimensional process: An investigation of individual and intraindividual differences. *American Educational Research Journal, 41,* 337–363.

Murphy, P. K., & Alexander, P. A. (2008). Examining the influence of knowledge, beliefs, and motivation in conceptual change. In S. Vosniadou (Ed.), *Handbook of research on conceptual change* (pp. 583–616). New York: Taylor and Francis.

Murphy, P. K., & Mason, L. (2006). Changing knowledge and beliefs. In P. A. Alexander & P. H. Winne (Eds.), *Handbook of educational psychology* (2nd ed., pp. 305–324). Mahwah, NJ: Erlbaum.

Myers, J. L., & Duffy, S. A. (1990). Causal inferences and text memory. In A. C. Graessner & G. H. Bower (Eds.), *Inferences and text comprehension. The psychology of learning and motivation: Advances in research and theory* (Vol. 25, pp. 159–173). Orlando: Academic Press.

Myin, E., & O'Regan, J. K. (2009). Situated perception and sensation in vision and other modalities. In P. Robbins & M. Aydede (Eds.), *The Cambridge handbook of situated cognition* (pp. 185–200). Cambridge, England: Cambridge University Press.

Nadel, L. (2005, August). *Memory, stress, and the brain: In Miller's footsteps.* Invited address presented at the annual meeting of the American Psychological Association, Washington, DC.

Nadel, L., & Jacobs, W. J. (1998). Traumatic memory is special. *Current Directions in Psychological Science, 7,* 154–157.

Nee, D. E., Berman, M. G., Moore, K. S., & Jonides, J. (2008). Neuroscientific evidence about the distinction between short- and long-term memory. *Current Directions in Psychological Science, 17,* 102–106.

Neisser, U. (Ed.) (1998). *The rising curve: Long-term gains in IQ and related measures.* Washington, DC: American Psychological Association.

Neisser, U., Boodoo, G., Bouchard, T. J., Boykin, A. W., Brody, N., Ceci, S. J., Halpern, D. F., Loehlen, J. C., Perloff, R., Sternberg, R. J., & Urbina, S. (1996). Intelligence: Knowns and unknowns. *American Psychologist, 51,* 77–101.

Neisser, U., & Harsch, N. (1992). Phantom flashbulbs: False recollections of hearing the news about *Challenger.* In E. Winograd & U. Neisser (Eds.), *Affect and accuracy in recall: Studies of "flashbulb" memories* (pp. 9–31). Cambridge, England: Cambridge University Press.

Nell, V. (2002). Why young men drive dangerously: Implications for injury prevention. *Current Directions in Psychological Science, 11,* 75–79.

Nelson, C. A. (1995). The ontogeny of human memory: A cognitive neuroscience perspective. *Developmental Psychology, 31,* 723–738.

Nelson, C. A., III, Thomas, K. M., & de Haan, M. (2006). Neural bases of cognitive development. In D. Kuhn, R. Siegler (Vol. Eds.), W. Damon, & R. M. Lerner (Series Eds.), *Handbook of child psychology. Vol. 2: Cognition, perception, and language* (6th ed., pp. 3–57). New York: Wiley.

Nelson, K. (1996). *Language in cognitive development: The emergence of the mediated mind.* Cambridge, England: Cambridge University Press.

Nelson, T. O. (1977). Repetition and depth of processing. *Journal of Verbal Learning and Verbal Behavior, 16,* 151–171.

Nelson-Barber, S., & Estrin, E. T. (1995). Bringing Native American perspectives to mathematics and science teaching. *Theory into Practice, 34,* 174–185.

Nesbit, J. C., & Adesope, O. O. (2006). Learning with concept and knowledge maps: A meta-analysis. *Review of Educational Research, 76,* 413–448.

Newby, T. J., Ertmer, P. A., & Stepich, D. A. (1994, April). *Instructional analogies and the learning of concepts.* Paper presented at the annual meeting of the American Educational Research Association, New Orleans, LA.

Newcombe, N. S., Drummey, A. B., Fox, N. A., Lie, E., & Ottinger-Albergs, W. (2000). Remembering early childhood: How much, how, and why (or why not). *Current Directions in Psychological Science, 9,* 55–58.

Newcombe, N. S., & Fox, N. A. (1994). Infantile amnesia: Through a glass darkly. *Child Development, 65,* 31–40.

Newman, R. S. (2008). Adaptive and nonadaptive help seeking with peer harassment: An integrative perspective of coping and self-regulation. *Educational Psychologist, 43,* 1–15.

Newport, E. L. (1990). Maturational constraints on language learning. *Cognitive Science, 14,* 11–28.

Newstead, S. E., Pollard, P., & Evans, J. S. (1992). The source of belief bias effects in syllogistic reasoning. *Cognition, 45,* 257–284.

Ni, Y., & Zhou, Y.-D. (2005). Teaching and learning fraction and rational numbers: The origins and implications of whole number bias. *Educational Psychologist, 40,* 27–52.

NICHD Early Child Care Research Network. (2002). Early child care and children's development prior to school entry: Results from the NICHD study of early child care. *American Educational Research Journal, 39*(1), 133–164.

Nickerson, R. S., & Adams, M. J. (1979). Long-term memory for a common object. *Cognitive Psychology, 1,* 287–307.

Nietfeld, J. L., & Cao, L. (2004, April). *The effect of distributed monitoring exercises and feedback on performance and monitoring accuracy.* Paper presented at the American Educational Research Association, San Diego, CA.

Nisbett, R. E. (2009). *Intelligence and how to get it.* New York: W. W. Norton.

Nolen, S. B. (1996). Why study? How reasons for learning influence strategy selection. *Educational Psychology Review, 8,* 335–355.

Norenzayan, A., Choi, I., & Peng, K. (2007). Perception and cognition. In S. Kitayama & D. Cohen (Eds.), *Handbook of cultural psychology* (pp. 569–594). New York: Guilford.

Novak, J. D. (1998). *Learning, creating, and using knowledge: Concept maps as facilitative tools in schools and corporations*. Mahwah, NJ: Erlbaum.

Nussbaum, E. M. (2008). Collaborative discourse, argumentation, and learning: Preface and literature review. *Contemporary Educational Psychology, 33,* 345–359.

Oakes, J., & Guiton, G. (1995). Matchmaking: The dynamics of high school tracking decisions. *American Educational Research Journal, 32,* 3–33.

Oakes, L. M., & Bauer, P. J. (Eds.) (2007). *Short- and long-term memory in infancy and early childhood: Taking the first steps toward remembering*. New York: Oxford University Press.

Oakhill, J. (1993). Children's difficulties in reading comprehension. *Educational Psychology Review, 5,* 223–237.

Oberheim, N. A., Takano, T., Han, X., He, W., Lin, J. H. C., Wang, F., et al. (2009). Uniquely hominid features of adult human astrocytes. *Journal of Neuroscience, 29,* 3276–3287.

Ochsner, K. N., & Lieberman, M. D. (2001). The emergence of social cognitive neuroscience. *American Psychologist, 56,* 717–734.

Odegard, T. N., Cooper, C. M., Lampinen, J. M., Reyna, V. F., & Brainerd, C. J. (2009). Children's eyewitness memory for multiple real-life events. *Child Development, 80,* 1877–1890.

O'Donnell, A. M., Dansereau, D. F., & Hall, R. H. (2002). Knowledge maps as scaffolds for cognitive processing. *Educational Psychology Review, 14,* 71–86.

O'Donnell, A. M., & King, A. (Eds.) (1999). *Cognitive perspectives on peer learning*. Mahwah, NJ: Erlbaum.

Onosko, J. J. (1996). Exploring issues with students despite the barriers. *Social Education, 60*(1), 22–27.

Ormrod, J. E. (1979). Cognitive processes in the solution of three-term series problems. *American Journal of Psychology, 92,* 235–255.

Ormrod, J. E. (2008). *Human learning* (5th ed.). Upper Saddle River, NJ: Merrill/Prentice Hall/Pearson.

Ormrod, J. E. (2009). *Essentials of educational psychology* (2nd ed.). Upper Saddle River, NJ: Merrill/Prentice Hall/Pearson.

Ormrod, J. E. (2011). *Educational psychology: Developing learners* (7th ed.). Upper Saddle River, NJ: Allyn & Bacon/Pearson Education.

Ornstein, P. A., Grammer, J. K., & Coffman, J. L. (2010). Teachers' "mnemonic style" and the development of skilled memory. In H. S. Waters & W. Schneider (Eds.), *Metacognition, strategy use, and instruction* (pp. 23–53). New York: Guilford.

Ornstein, R. (1997). *The right mind: Making sense of the hemispheres*. San Diego, CA: Harcourt Brace.

Osborn, A. F. (1963). *Applied imagination* (3rd ed.). New York: Scribner.

Osborne, J. W., & Simmons, C. M. (2002, April). *Girls, math, stereotype threat, and anxiety: Physiological evidence*. Paper presented at the annual meeting of the American Educational Research Association, New Orleans, LA.

Page-Voth, V., & Graham, S. (1999). Effects of goal setting and strategy use on the writing performance and self-efficacy of students with writing and learning problems. *Journal of Educational Psychology, 91,* 230–240.

Paige, J. M., & Simon, H. A. (1966). Cognitive processes in solving algebra word problems. In B. Kleinmuntz (Ed.), *Problem solving* (pp. 51–119). New York: Wiley.

Palincsar, A. S., & Brown, A. L. (1984). Reciprocal teaching of comprehension-fostering and comprehension-monitoring activities. *Cognition and Instruction, 1,* 117–175.

Palincsar, A. S., & Brown, A. L. (1989). Classroom dialogues to promote self-regulated comprehension. In J. Brophy (Ed.), *Advances in research on teaching* (Vol. 1, pp. 35–71). Greenwich, CT: JAI Press.

Palincsar, A. S., & Herrenkohl, L. R. (1999). Designing collaborative contexts: Lessons from three research programs. In A. M. O'Donnell & A. King (Eds.), *Cognitive perspectives on peer learning* (pp. 151–177). Mahwah, NJ: Erlbaum.

Paller, K. A. (2004). Electrical signals of memory and of the awareness of remembering. *Current Directions in Psychological Science, 13,* 49–55.

Palmer, D. J., & Goetz, E. T. (1988). Selection and use of study strategies: The role of the studier's beliefs about self and strategies. In C. E. Weinstein, E. T. Goetz, & P. A. Alexander (Eds.), *Learning and study strategies: Issues in assessment, instruction, and evaluation* (pp. 41–62). San Diego, CA: Academic Press.

Pansky, A., & Koriat, A. (2004). The basic-level convergence effect in memory distortions. *Psychological Science, 15,* 52–59.

Paris, S. G., & Ayres, L. R. (1994). *Becoming reflective students and teachers with portfolios and authentic assessment.* Washington, DC: American Psychological Association.

Paris, S. G., & Byrnes, J. P. (1989). The constructivist approach to self-regulation and learning in the classroom. In B. J. Zimmerman & D. H. Schunk (Eds.), *Self-regulated learning and academic achievement: Theory, research, and practice* (pp. 169–200). New York: Springer-Verlag.

Paris, S. G., & Lindauer, B. K. (1976). The role of inference in children's comprehension and memory. *Cognitive Psychology, 8,* 217–227.

Paris, S. G., & Paris, A. H. (2001). Classroom applications of research on self-regulated learning. *Educational Psychologist, 36,* 89–101.

Paris, S. G., & Turner, J. C. (1994). Situated motivation. In P. R. Pintrich, D. R. Brown, & C. E. Weinstein (Eds.), *Student motivation, cognition, and learning: Essays in honor of Wilbert J. McKeachie* (pp. 213–237). Hillsdale, NJ: Erlbaum.

Parker, S. T., Mitchell, R. W., & Boccia, M. L. (Eds.) (1994). *Self-awareness in animals and humans: Developmental perspectives.* Cambridge, England: Cambridge University Press.

Parker, W. D. (1997). An empirical typology of perfectionism in academically talented children. *American Educational Research Journal, 34,* 545–562.

Pashler, H., Rohrer, D., Cepeda, N. J., & Carpenter, S. K. (2007). Enhancing learning and retarding forgetting: Choices and consequences. *Psychonomic Bulletin & Review, 14,* 187–193.

Patrick, H., Mantzicopoulos, Y., & Samarapungavan, A. (2009). Motivation for learning science in kindergarten: Is there a gender gap and does integrated inquiry and literacy instruction make a difference? *Journal of Research in Science Teaching, 46,* 166–191.

Patrick, H., & Pintrich, P. R. (2001). Conceptual change in teachers' intuitive conceptions of learning, motivation, and instruction: The role of motivational and epistemological beliefs. In B. Torff & R. J. Sternberg (Eds.), *Understanding and teaching the intuitive mind: Student and teacher learning* (pp. 117–143). Mahwah, NJ: Erlbaum.

Paus, T., Zijdenbos, A., Worsley, K., Collins, D. L., Blumenthal, J., Giedd, J. N., et al. (1999). Structural maturation of neural pathways in children and adolescents: In vivo study. *Science, 283,* 1908–1911.

Payne, D. G., Neuschatz, J. S., Lampinen, J. M., & Lynn, S. J. (1997). Compelling memory illusions: The qualitative characteristics of false memories. *Current Directions in Psychological Science, 6,* 56–60.

Pea, R. D. (1987). Socializing the knowledge transfer problem. *International Journal of Educational Research, 11,* 639–663.

Pea, R. D. (1993). Practices of distributed intelligence and designs for education. In G. Salomon (Ed.), *Distributed cognitions: Psychological and educational considerations* (pp. 47–87). Cambridge, England: Cambridge University Press.

Pekrun, R. (2006). The control-value theory of achievement emotions: Assumptions, corollaries, and implications for educational research and practice. *Educational Psychology Review, 18,* 315–341.

Péladeau, N., Forget, J., & Gagné, F. (2003). Effect of paced and unpaced practice on skill application and retention: How much is enough? *American Educational Research Journal, 40,* 769–801.

Pellegrini, A. D., & Bjorklund, D. F. (1997). The role of recess in children's cognitive performance. *Educational Psychologist, 32,* 35–40.

Pereira, A. C., Huddleston, D. E., Brickman, A. M., Sosunov, A. A., Hen, R., McKhann, G. M., et al. (2007). An in vivo correlate of exercise-induced neurogenesis in the adult dentate gyrus. *Proceedings of the National Academy of Sciences, USA, 104,* 5638–5643.

Perfect, T. J. (2002). When does eyewitness confidence predict performance? In T, J. Perfect & B. L. Schwartz (Eds.), *Applied metacognition* (pp. 95–120). Cambridge, England: Cambridge University Press.

Perfetti, C. A., & Lesgold, A. M. (1979). Coding and comprehension in skilled reading and implications for reading instruction. In L. B. Resnick & P. Weaver (Eds.), *Theory and practice of early reading* (Vol. 1, pp. 57–84). Hillsdale, NJ: Erlbaum.

Perkins, D. (1990). The nature and nurture of creativity. In B. F. Jones & L. Idol (Eds.), *Dimensions of thinking and cognitive instruction* (pp. 415–444). Mahwah, NJ: Erlbaum.

Perkins, D. (1992). *Smart schools: From training memories to educating minds.* New York: Free Press/Macmillan.

Perkins, D. (1995). *Outsmarting IQ: The emerging science of learnable intelligence.* New York: Free Press.

Perkins, D., & Ritchhart, R. (2004). When is good thinking? In D. Y. Dai & R. J. Sternberg (Eds.), *Motivation, emotion, and cognition: Integrative perspectives on intellectual functioning and development* (pp. 351–384). Mahwah, NJ: Erlbaum.

Perkins, D. N., & Salomon, G. (1989). Are cognitive skills context-bound? *Educational Researcher, 18*(1), 16–25.

Perkins, D. N., & Simmons, R. (1988). Patterns of misunderstanding: An integrative model for science, math, and programming. *Review of Educational Research, 58,* 303–326.

Perkins, D. N., Tishman, S., Ritchhart, R., Donis, K., & Andrade, A. (2000). Intelligence in the wild: A dispositional view of intellectual traits. *Educational Psychology Review, 12,* 269–293.

Perry, M. (1991). Learning and transfer: Instructional conditions and conceptual change. *Cognitive Development, 6,* 449–468.

Perry, N. E. (1998). Young children's self-regulated learning and contexts that support it. *Journal of Educational Psychology, 90,* 715–729.

Perry, N. E., & Winne, P. H. (2004). Motivational messages from home and school: How do they influence young children's engagement in learning? In D. M. McNerney & S. Van Etten (Eds.), *Big theories revisited* (pp. 199–222). Greenwich, CT: Information Age.

Peterson, C. (1990). Explanatory style in the classroom and on the playing field. In S. Graham & V. S. Folkes (Eds.), *Attribution theory: Applications to achievement, mental health, and interpersonal conflict* (pp. 53–75). Hillsdale, NJ: Erlbaum.

Peterson, C. (2006). *A primer in positive psychology.* New York: Oxford University Press.

Pettito, L. A. (1997). In the beginning: On the genetic and environmental factors that make early language acquisition possible. In M. Gopnik (Ed.), *The inheritance and innateness of grammars.* New York: Oxford University Press.

Peverly, S. T., Brobst, K. E., Graham, M., & Shaw, R. (2003). College adults are not good at self-regulation: A study on the relationship of self-regulation, note taking, and test taking. *Journal of Educational Psychology, 95,* 335–346.

Pezdek, K., Finger, K., & Hodge, D. (1997). Planting false childhood memories: The role of event plausibility. *Psychological Science, 8,* 437–441.

Pfeifer, J. H., Brown, C. S., & Juvonen, J. (2007). Teaching tolerance in schools: Lessons learned since *Brown v. Board of Education* about the development and reduction of children's prejudice. *Social Policy Report, 21*(2), 3–13, 16–17, 20–23.

Phelps, E. A., Ling, S., & Carrasco, M. (2006). Emotion facilitates perception and potentiates the perceptual benefits of attention. *Psychological Science, 17,* 292–299.

Phelps, E. A., & Sharot, T. (2008). How (and why) emotion enhances the subjective sense of recollection. *Current Directions in Psychological Science, 17,* 147–152.

Phillips, B. N., Pitcher, G. D., Worsham, M. E., & Miller, S. C. (1980). Test anxiety and the school environment. In I. G. Sarason (Ed.), *Test anxiety: Theory, research, and applications* (pp. 327–346). Hillsdale, NJ: Erlbaum.

Pianko, S. (1979). A description of the composing processes of college freshmen writers. *Research in the Teaching of English, 13,* 5–22.

Pillemer, D. B., & White, S. H. (1989). Childhood events recalled by children and adults. In H. W. Reese (Ed.), *Advances in child development and behavior* (Vol. 21, pp. 297–340). New York: Academic Press.

Pillow, B. H. (2002). Children's and adults' evaluation of the certainty of deductive inferences, inductive inferences, and guesses. *Child Development, 73,* 779–792.

Pine, K. J., & Messer, D. J. (2000). The effect of explaining another's actions on children's implicit theories of balance. *Cognition and Instruction, 18,* 35–51.

Pintrich, P. R. (2000). The role of goal orientation in self-regulated learning. In M. Boekaerts, P. R. Pintrich, & M. Zeidner (Eds.), *Handbook of self-regulation* (pp. 451–502). San Diego, CA: Academic Press.

Plomin, R. (1994). *Genetics and experience: The interplay between nature and nurture.* Thousand Oaks, CA: Sage.

Plotnik, J. M., de Waal, F. B. M., & Reiss, D. (2006). Self-recognition in an Asian elephant.

Proceedings of the National Academy of Sciences, USA, 103, 17053–17057.

Plucker, J. A., Beghetto, R. A., & Dow, G. T. (2004). Why isn't creativity more important to educational psychologists? Potentials, pitfalls, and future directions in creativity research. *Educational Psychologist, 39,* 83–96.

Polman, J. L. (2004). Dialogic activity structures for project-based learning environments. *Cognition and Instruction, 22,* 431–466.

Pomerantz, E. M., & Saxon, J. L. (2001). Conceptions of ability as stable and self-evaluative processes: A longitudinal examination. *Child Development, 72,* 152–173.

Popham, W. J. (1995). *Classroom assessment.* Boston: Allyn & Bacon.

Porat, D. A. (2004). *It's not written here, but this is what happened:* Students' cultural comprehension of textbook narratives on the Israeli-Arab conflict. *American Educational Research Journal, 41,* 963–996.

Porter, A. (1989). A curriculum out of balance: The case of elementary school mathematics. *Educational Researcher, 18*(5), 9–15.

Porter, S., & Peace, K. A. (2007). The scars of memory: A prospective, longitudinal investigation of the consistency of traumatic and positive emotional memories in adulthood. *Psychological Science, 18,* 435–441.

Posner, G. J., Strike, K. A., Hewson, P. W., & Gertzog, W. A. (1982). Accommodation of a scientific conception: Toward a theory of conceptual change. *Science Education, 66,* 211–227.

Posner, M. I., & Rothbart, M. K. (2007). *Educating the human brain.* Washington, DC: American Psychological Association.

Poston, B., Van Gemmert, A. W. A., Barduson, B., & Stelmach, G. E. (2009). Movement structure in young and elderly adults during goal-directed movements of the left and right arm. *Brain and Cognition, 69,* 30–38.

Prawat, R. S. (1989). Promoting access to knowledge, strategy, and disposition in students: A research synthesis. *Review of Educational Research, 59,* 1–41.

Prawat, R. S. (1993). The value of ideas: Problems versus possibilities in learning. *Educational Researcher, 22*(6), 5–16.

Pressley, M., Borkowski, J. G., & Schneider, W. (1987). Cognitive strategies: Good strategy users coordinate metacognition and knowledge. In R. Vasta & G. Whitehurst (Eds.), *Annals of child development* (Vol. 5, pp. 89–129). Greenwich, CT: JAI Press.

Pressley, M., El-Dinary, P. B., Marks, M. B., Brown, R., & Stein, S. (1992). Good strategy instruction is motivating and interesting. In K. A. Renninger, S. Hidi, & A. Krapp (Eds.), *The role of interest in learning and development* (pp. 333–358). Mahwah, NJ: Erlbaum.

Pressley, M., Harris, K. R., & Marks, M. B. (1992). But good strategy instructors are constructivists! *Educational Psychology Review, 4,* 3–31.

Pressley, M., & Hilden, K. (2006). Cognitive strategies: Production deficiencies and successful strategy instruction everywhere. In W. Damon & R. M. Lerner (Series Eds.), D. Kuhn, & R. Siegler (Vol. Eds.), *Handbook of child psychology: Vol. 2. Cognition, perception, and language* (6th ed., pp. 511–556). New York: Wiley.

Pressley, M., Levin, J. R., & Delaney, H. D. (1982). The mnemonic keyword method. *Review of Educational Research, 52,* 61–91.

Pressley, M., Yokoi, L., Van Meter, P., Van Etten, S., & Freebern, G. (1997). Some of the reasons why preparing for exams is so hard: What can be done to make it easier? *Educational Psychology Review, 9,* 1–38.

Pretz, J. E., Naples, A. J., & Sternberg, R. J. (2003). Recognizing, defining, and representing problems. In J. E. Davidson & R. J. Sternberg (Eds.), *The psychology of problem solving* (pp. 3–30). Cambridge, England: Cambridge University Press.

Pribram, K. H. (1997). The work in working memory: Implications for development. In N. A. Krasnegor, G. R. Lyon, & P. S. Goldman-Rakic (Eds.), *Development of the prefrontal cortex: Evolution, neurobiology, and behavior* (pp. 359–378). Baltimore: Brookes.

Prior, H., Schwarz, A., & Güntürkün, O. (2008). Mirror-induced behavior in the magpie (*Pica pica*): Evidence of self-recognition. *PLoS Biology* (Public Library of Science), 6(8), e202. Retrieved from www.plosbiology.org/article/info:doi/10.1371/journal.pbio.0060202.

Proctor, R. W., & Dutta, A. (1995). *Skill acquisition and human performance.* Thousand Oaks, CA: Sage.

Pruitt, R. P. (1989). Fostering creativity: The innovative classroom environment. *Educational Horizons, 68*(1), 51–54.

Pugh, K. J., & Bergin, D. A. (2006). Motivational influences on transfer. *Educational Psychologist, 41,* 147–160.

Pugh, K. J., Linnenbrink, E. A., Kelly, K. L., Manzey, C., & Stewart, V. C. (2006, April). *Motivation, learning, and transformative experience: A study of deep engagement in science.* Paper presented at the annual meeting of the American Educational Research Association, San Francisco.

Puntambekar, S., & Hübscher, R. (2005). Tools for scaffolding students in a complex learning environment: What have we gained and what have we missed? *Educational Psychologist, 40,* 1–12.

Purdie, N., & Hattie, J. (1996). Cultural differences in the use of strategies for self-regulated learning. *American Educational Research Journal, 33,* 845–871.

Putnam, R. T. (1992). Thinking and authority in elementary-school mathematics tasks. In J. Brophy (Ed.), *Advances in research on teaching: Vol. 3. Planning and managing learning tasks and activities* (pp. 167–189). Greenwich, CT: JAI Press.

Qin, Z., Johnson, D. W., & Johnson, R. T. (1995). Cooperative versus competitive efforts and problem solving. *Review of Educational Research, 65,* 129–143.

Quinn, P. C. (2002). Category representation in young infants. *Current Directions in Psychological Science, 11,* 66–70.

Quinn, P. C. (2003). Concepts are not just for objects: Categorization of spatial relation information by young infants. In D. H. Rakison & L. M. Oakes (Eds.), *Early category and concept development: Making sense of the blooming, buzzing confusion* (pp. 50–76). Oxford, England: Oxford University Press.

Quintana, C., Zhang, M., & Krajcik, J. (2005). A framework for supporting metacognitive aspects of online inquiry through software-based scaffolding. *Educational Psychologist, 40,* 235–244.

Rabinowitz, M., & Glaser, R. (1985). Cognitive structure and process in highly competent performance. In F. D. Horowitz & M. O'Brien (Eds.), *The gifted and the talented: Developmental perspectives.* Washington, DC: American Psychological Association.

Rakison, D. H. (2003). Parts, motion, and the development of the animate-inanimate distinction in infancy. In D. H. Rakison & L. M. Oakes (Eds.), *Early category and concept development: Making sense of the blooming, buzzing confusion* (pp. 159–192). Oxford, England: Oxford University Press.

Rakison, D. H., & Oakes, L. M. (2003). *Early category and concept development: Making sense of the blooming, buzzing confusion.* Oxford, England: Oxford University Press.

Ramey, C. T. (1992). High-risk children and IQ: Altering intergenerational patterns. *Intelligence, 16,* 239–256.

Rasch, B., & Born, J. (2008). Reactivation and consolidation of memory during sleep. *Current Directions in Psychological Science, 17,* 188–192.

Ray, W. J., Odenwald, M., Neuner, F., Schauer, M., Ruf, M., Wienbruch, C., Rockstroh, B., & Elbert, T. (2006). Decoupling neural networks from reality: Dissociative experiences in torture victims are reflected in abnormal brain waves in left frontal cortex. *Psychological Science, 17,* 825–829.

Rayner, K., Foorman, B. R., Perfetti, C. A., Pesetsky, D., & Seidenberg, M. S. (2001). How psychological science informs the teaching of reading. *Psychological Science in the Public Interest, 2,* 31–74.

Reason, J., & Mycielska, K. (1982). *Absent-minded? The psychology of mental lapses and everyday errors.* Upper Saddle River, NJ: Prentice Hall.

Reber, A. S. (1993). *Implicit learning and tacit knowledge: An essay on the cognitive unconscious.* New York: Oxford University Press.

Reder, L. M., & Ross, B. H. (1983). Integrated knowledge in different tasks: Positive and negative fan effects. *Journal of Experimental Psychology: Human Learning and Memory, 8,* 55–72.

Reed, S. (1974). Structural descriptions and the limitations of visual images. *Memory and Cognition, 2,* 329–336.

Reid, R., Trout, A. L., & Schartz, M. (2005). Self-regulation interventions for children with attention deficit/hyperactivity disorder. *Exceptional Children, 71,* 361–377.

Reimann, P., & Schult, T. J. (1996). Turning examples into cases: Acquiring knowledge structures for analogical problem solving. *Educational Psychologist, 31,* 123–132.

Reiner, M., Slotta, J. D., Chi, M. T. H., & Resnick, L. B. (2000). Naive physics reasoning: A commitment to substance-based conceptions. *Cognition and Instruction, 18,* 1–34.

Reisberg, D. (1997). *Cognition: Exploring the science of the mind.* New York: W. W. Norton.

Reiter, S. N. (1994). Teaching dialogically: Its relationship to critical thinking in college students. In P. R. Pintrich, D. R. Brown, & C. E. Weinstein (Eds.), *Student motivation, cognition, and learning: Essays in honor of Wilbert J. McKeachie* (pp. 275–310). Hillsdale, NJ: Erlbaum.

Reitman, J. S. (1974). Without surreptitious rehearsal, information in short-term memory decays. *Journal of Verbal Learning and Verbal Behavior, 13,* 365–377.

Reitman, W. R. (1964). Heuristic decision procedures, open constraints, and the structure of ill-defined problems. In M. W. Shelley & G. L. Bryan (Eds.), *Human judgments and optimality* (pp. 282–315). New York: Wiley.

Renkl, A., & Atkinson, R. K. (2003). Structuring the transition from example study to problem solving in cognitive skill acquisition: A cognitive load perspective. *Educational Psychologist, 38,* 15–22.

Renkl, A., Mandl, H., & Gruber, H. (1996). Inert knowledge: Analyses and remedies. *Educational Psychologist, 31,* 115–121.

Resnick, L. B. (1989). Developing mathematical knowledge. *American Psychologist, 44,* 162–169.

Resnick, L. B., Bill, V. L., Lesgold, S. B., & Leer, M. N. (1991). Thinking in arithmetic class. In B. Means, C. Chelemer, & M. S. Knapp (Eds.), *Teaching advanced skills to at-risk students* (pp. 27–53). San Francisco: Jossey-Bass.

Reyna, C. (2000). Lazy, dumb, or industrious: When stereotypes convey attribution information in the classroom. *Educational Psychology Review, 12,* 85–110.

Reyna, V. F., & Farley, F. (2006). Risk and rationality in adolescent decision making: Implications for theory, practice, and public policy. *Psychological Science in the Public Interest, 7*(1), 1–44.

Reynolds, R. E., & Shirey, L. L. (1988). The role of attention in studying and learning. In C. E. Weinstein, E. T. Goetz, & P. A. Alexander (Eds.), *Learning and study strategies: Issues in assessment, instruction, and evaluation.* San Diego, CA: Academic Press.

Rhodewalt, F., & Vohs, K. D. (2005). Defensive strategies, motivation, and the self: A self-regulatory process view. In A. J. Elliot & C. S. Dweck (Eds.), *Handbook of competence and motivation* (pp. 548–565). New York: Guilford.

Ricciuti, H. N. (1993). Nutrition and mental development. *Current Directions in Psychological Science, 2,* 43–46.

Richards, J. M. (2004). The cognitive consequences of concealing feelings. *Current Directions in Psychological Science, 13,* 131–134.

Rinehart, S. D., Stahl, S. A., & Erickson, L. G. (1986). Some effects of summarization training on reading and studying. *Reading Research Quarterly, 21,* 422–438.

Ripple, R. E. (1989). Ordinary creativity. *Contemporary Educational Psychology, 14,* 189–202.

Rittle-Johnson, B. (2006). Promoting transfer: Effects of self-explanation and direct instruction. *Child Development, 77,* 1–15.

Rittle-Johnson, B., & Koedinger, K. R. (2005). Designing knowledge scaffolds to support mathematical problem solving. *Cognition and Instruction, 23,* 313–349.

Rittle-Johnson, B., Siegler, R. S., & Alibali, M. W. (2001). Developing conceptual understanding and procedural skill in mathematics: An iterative process. *Journal of Educational Psychology, 93,* 346–362.

Robertson, J. S. (2000). Is attribution training a worthwhile classroom intervention for K–12 students with learning difficulties? *Educational Psychology Review, 12,* 111–134.

Robinson, D. H., & Kiewra, K. A. (1995). Visual argument: Graphic organizers are superior to outlines in improving learning from text. *Journal of Educational Psychology, 87,* 455–467.

Robinson, E. J., & Whitcombe, E. L. (2003). Children's suggestibility in relation to their understanding about sources of knowledge. *Child Development, 74,* 48–62.

Roderick, M., & Camburn, E. (1999). Risk and recovery from course failure in the early years of high school. *American Educational Research Journal, 36,* 303–343.

Roditi, B. N., & Steinberg, J. (2007). The strategy math classroom: Executive function processes and mathematics learning. In L. Meltzer (Ed.), *Executive function in education: From theory to practice* (pp. 237–260). New York: Guilford.

Roediger, H. L., III, & Karpicke, J. D. (2006). Test-enhanced learning: Taking memory tests improves long-term retention. *Psychological Science, 17,* 249–255.

Rogers, T. B., Kuiper, N. A., & Kirker, W. S. (1977). Self-reference and the encoding of personal information. *Journal of Personality and Social Psychology, 35,* 677–688.

Rogoff, B. (1990). *Apprenticeship in thinking: Cognitive development in social context.* New York: Oxford University Press.

Rogoff, B. (1991). Social interaction as apprenticeship in thinking: Guidance and participation in spatial planning. In L. B. Resnick, J. M. Levine, & S. D. Teasley (Eds.), *Perspectives on socially shared cognition* (pp. 349–364). Washington, DC: American Psychological Association.

Rogoff, B. (2003). *The cultural nature of human development.* Oxford, England: Oxford University Press.

Rosenshine, B., & Meister, C. (1992). The use of scaffolds for teaching higher-level cognitive strategies. *Educational Leadership, 49*(7), 26–33.

Rosenshine, B., Meister, C., & Chapman, S. (1996). Teaching students to generate questions: A review of the intervention studies. *Review of Educational Research, 66,* 181–221.

Rosenthal, R. (1994). Interpersonal expectancy effects: A 30–year perspective. *Current Directions in Psychological Science, 3,* 176–179.

Roth, K. (1990). Developing meaningful conceptual understanding in science. In B. F. Jones & L. Idol (Eds.), *Dimensions of thinking and cognitive instruction* (pp. 139–175). Hillsdale, NJ: Erlbaum.

Roth, K. (2002). Talking to understand science. In J. Brophy (Ed.), *Social constructivist teaching: Affordances and constraints* (pp. 197–262). New York: Elsevier.

Roth, K., & Anderson, C. (1988). Promoting conceptual change learning from science textbooks. In P. Ramsden (Ed.), *Improving learning: New perspectives* (pp. 109–141). London: Kogan Page.

Roth, W., & Bowen, G. M. (1995). Knowing and interacting: A study of culture, practices, and resources in a grade 8 open-inquiry science classroom guided by a cognitive apprenticeship metaphor. *Cognition and Instruction, 13,* 73–128.

Rothbart, M. K., Sheese, B. E., & Posner, M. I. (2007). Executive attention and effortful control: Linking temperament, brain networks, and genes. *Child Development Perspectives, 1,* 2–7.

Rowe, D. C., Jacobson, K. C., & Van den Oord, E. J. C. G. (1999). Genetic and environmental influences on Vocabulary IQ: Parental education level as moderator. *Child Development, 70,* 1151–1162.

Rowe, M. B. (1974). Wait-time and rewards as instructional variables, their influence on language, logic, and fate control: Part I. Wait time. *Journal of Research in Science Teaching, 11,* 81–94.

Rubin, D. C. (1992). Constraints on memory. In E. Winograd & U. Neisser (Eds.), *Affect and accuracy in recall: Studies of "flashbulb" memories* (pp. 265–273). Cambridge, England: Cambridge University Press.

Rubin, D. C. (2006). The basic-systems model of episodic memory. *Perspectives on Psychological Science, 1,* 277–311.

Runco, M. A. (2004). Creativity as an extracognitive phenomenon. In L. V. Shavinina & M. Ferrari (Eds.), *Beyond knowledge: Extracognitive aspects of developing high ability* (pp. 17–25). Mahwah, NJ: Erlbaum.

Runco, M. A. (2005). Motivation, competence, and creativity. In A. J. Elliot & C. S. Dweck (Eds.), *Handbook of competence and motivation* (pp. 609–623). New York: Guilford.

Runco, M. A., & Chand, I. (1995). Cognition and creativity. *Educational Psychology Review, 7,* 243–267.

Rundus, D. (1971). Analysis of rehearsal processes in free recall. *Journal of Experimental Psychology, 89,* 63–77.

Russ, S. W. (1993). *Affect and creativity: The role of affect and play in the creative process.* Hillsdale, NJ: Erlbaum.

Rutter, M. L. (1997). Nature-nurture integration: The example of antisocial behavior. *American Psychologist, 52,* 390–398.

Ryan, A. M., Pintrich, P. R., & Midgley, C. (2001). Avoiding seeking help in the classroom: Who and why? *Educational Psychology Review, 13,* 93–114.

Sadoski, M., & Paivio, A. (2001). *Imagery and text: A dual coding theory of reading and writing.* Mahwah, NJ: Erlbaum.

Sadoski, M., & Quast, Z. (1990). Reader response and long-term recall for journalistic text: The roles of imagery, affect, and importance. *Reading Research Quarterly, 25,* 256–272.

Salomon, G. (1993). No distribution without individuals' cognition: A dynamic interactional view. In G. Salomon (Ed.), *Distributed cognitions: Psychological and educational considerations* (pp. 111–138). Cambridge, England: Cambridge University Press.

Sameroff, A. J., Seifer, R., Baldwin, A., & Baldwin, C. (1993). Stability of intelligence from preschool to adolescence: The influence of social and family risk factors. *Child Development, 64,* 80–97.

Samuel, A. L. (1963). Some studies in machine learning using the game of checkers. In E. A. Feigenbaum & J. Feldman (Eds.), *Computers and thought* (pp. 39–70). New York: McGraw-Hill.

Sansone, C., Weir, C., Harpster, L., & Morgan, C. (1992). Once a boring task always a boring task? Interest as a self-regulatory mechanism. *Journal of Personality and Social Psychology, 63,* 379–390.

Sapolsky, R. M. (1999). Glucocorticoids, stress, and their adverse neurological effects: Relevance to aging. *Experimental Gerontology, 34,* 721–732.

Sarason, I. G. (Ed.) (1980). *Test anxiety: Theory, research, and applications.* Hillsdale, NJ: Erlbaum.

Sarason, S. B. (1972). What research says about test anxiety in elementary school children. In A. R. Binter & S. H. Frey (Eds.), *The psychology of the elementary school child.* Chicago: Rand McNally.

Sattler, J. M. (2001). *Assessment of children: Cognitive applications* (4th ed.). San Diego, CA: Author.

Sawyer, R. K. (2003). Emergence in creativity and development. In R. K. Sawyer, V. John-Steiner, S. Moran, R. J. Sternberg, D. H. Feldman, J. Nakamura, & M. Csikszentmihalyi, *Creativity and development* (pp. 12–60). Oxford, England: Oxford University Press.

Scarr, S., & McCartney, K. (1983). How people make their own environments: A theory of genotype environment effects. *Child Development, 54,* 424–435.

Schab, F. (1990). Odors and the remembrance of things past. *Journal of Experimental Psychology: Learning, Memory, and Cognition, 16,* 648–655.

Schacter, D. L. (1999). The seven sins of memory: Insights from psychology and neuroscience. *American Psychologist, 54,* 182–203.

Schank, R. C., & Abelson, R. P. (1995). Knowledge and memory: The real story. In R. S. Wyer, Jr. (Ed.), *Advances in social cognition: Vol. 8. Knowledge and memory: The real story.* Mahwah, NJ: Erlbaum.

Schauble, L. (1996). The development of scientific reasoning in knowledge-rich contexts. *Developmental Psychology, 32,* 102–119.

Schellings, G. L. M., Van Hout-Wolters, B., & Vermunt, J. D. (1996). Individual differences in adapting to three different tasks of selecting information from texts. *Contemporary Educational Psychology, 21,* 423–446.

Schimmoeller, M. A. (1998, April). *Influence of private speech on the writing behaviors of young children: Four case studies.* Paper presented at the annual meeting of the American Educational Research Association, San Diego, CA.

Schliemann, A. D., & Carraher, D. W. (1993). Proportional reasoning in and out of school. In P. Light & G. Butterworth (Eds.), *Context and cognition: Ways of learning and knowing* (pp. 47–73). Hillsdale, NJ: Erlbaum.

Schmidt, R. A., & Bjork, R. A. (1992). New conceptualizations of practice: Common principles in three paradigms suggest new concepts for training. *Psychological Science, 3,* 207–217.

Schmidt, R. A., & Young, D. E. (1987). Transfer of movement control in motor skill learning. In S. M. Cormier & J. D. Hagman (Eds.), *Transfer of learning: Contemporary research and applications* (pp. 47–79). San Diego, CA: Academic Press.

Schmolck, H., Buffalo, E. A., & Squire, L. R. (2000). Memory distortions develop over time: Recollections of the O. J. Simpson trial verdict after 15 and 32 months. *Psychological Science, 11,* 39–45.

Schneider, W. (2010). Metacognition and memory development in childhood and adolescence. In H. S. Waters & W. Schneider (Eds.), *Metacognition, strategy use, and instruction* (pp. 54–81). New York: Guilford.

Schneider, W., Körkel, J., & Weinert, F. E. (1990). Expert knowledge, general abilities, and text processing. In W. Schneider & F. E. Weinert (Eds.), *Interactions among aptitudes, strategies, and knowledge in cognitive performance* (pp. 235–251). New York: Springer-Verlag.

Schneider, W., & Lockl, K. (2002). The development of metacognitive knowledge in children and adolescents. In T. J. Perfect & B. L. Schwartz (Eds.), *Applied metacognition* (pp. 224–257). Cambridge, England: Cambridge University Press.

Schoenfeld, A. H. (1985). Metacognitive and epistemological issues in mathematical understanding. In E. A. Silver (Ed.), *Teaching and learning mathematical problem solving: Multiple research perspectives* (361–379). Hillsdale, NJ: Erlbaum.

Schoenfeld, A. H. (1992). Learning to think mathematically: Problem solving, metacognition, and sense-making in mathematics. In D. A. Grouws (Ed.), *Handbook of research on mathematics teaching and learning* (pp. 334–370). New York: Macmillan.

Schommer, M. (1994a). An emerging conceptualization of epistemological beliefs and their role in learning. In R. Garner & P. A. Alexander (Eds.), *Beliefs about text and instruction with text* (pp. 25–40). Hillsdale, NJ: Erlbaum.

Schommer, M. (1994b). Synthesizing epistemological belief research: Tentative understandings and provocative confusions. *Educational Psychology Review, 6,* 293–319.

Schommer, M., Calvert, C., Gariglietti, G., & Bajaj, A. (1997). The development of epistemological beliefs among secondary students: A longitudinal study. *Journal of Educational Psychology, 89,* 37–40.

Schommer-Aikins, M. (2002). An evolving theoretical framework for an epistemological belief system. In B. K. Hofer & P. R. Pintrich (Eds.), *Personal epistemology: The psychology of beliefs about knowledge and knowing* (pp. 103–118). Mahwah, NJ: Erlbaum.

Schommer-Aikins, M., Hopkins, L., Anderson, C., & Drouhard, B. (2005, April). *Epistemological beliefs and need for cognition of traditional and non-traditional students.* Paper presented at the annual meeting of the American Educational Research Association, Montreal.

Schraw, G. (2006). Knowledge: Structures and processes. In P. A. Alexander & P. H. Winne (Eds.), *Handbook of educational psychology* (2nd ed., pp. 245–263). Mahwah, NJ: Erlbaum.

Schraw, G., & Bruning, R. (1995, April). *Reader beliefs and reading comprehension.* Paper presented at the annual meeting of the American Educational Research Association, San Francisco.

Schraw, G., Wadkins, T., & Olafson, L. (2007). Doing the things we do: A grounded theory of academic procrastination. *Journal of Educational Psychology, 99,* 12–25.

Schunk, D. H. (1990, April). *Socialization and the development of self-regulated learning: The role of attributions.* Paper presented at the

annual meeting of the American Educational Research Association, Boston.

Schunk, D. H. (1996). Goal and self-evaluative influences during children's cognitive skill learning. *American Educational Research Journal, 33,* 359–382.

Schunk, D. H., & Pajares, F. (2004). Self-efficacy in education revisited: Empirical and applied evidence. In D. M. McNerney & S. Van Etten (Eds.), *Big theories revisited* (pp. 115–138). Greenwich, CT: Information Age.

Schunk, D. H., & Zimmerman, B. J. (1997). Social origins of self-regulatory competence. *Educational Psychologist, 32,* 195–208.

Schwarz, C. V., & White, B. Y. (2005). Metamodeling knowledge: Developing students' understanding of scientific modeling. *Cognition and Instruction, 23,* 165–205.

Seligman, M. E. P. (1975). *Helplessness.* San Francisco: W. H. Freeman.

Seligman, M. E. P. (1991). *Learned optimism.* New York: Alfred Knopf.

Sergeant, J. (1996). A theory of attention: An information processing perspective. In G. R. Lyon & N. A. Krasnegor (Eds.), *Attention, memory, and executive function* (pp. 57–69). Baltimore: Brookes.

Sfard, A. (1997). Commentary: On metaphorical roots of conceptual growth. In L. D. English (Ed.), *Mathematical reasoning: Analogies, metaphors, and images* (pp. 339–371). Mahwah, NJ: Erlbaum.

Shah, A. K., & Oppenheimer, D. M. (2009). The path of least resistance: Using easy-to-access information. *Current Directions in Psychological Science, 18,* 232–236.

Shah, P., & Hoeffner, J. (2002). Review of graph comprehension research: Implications for instruction. *Educational Psychology Review, 14,* 47–69.

Shanahan, C. (2004). Teaching science through literacy. In T. L. Jetton & J. A. Dole (Eds.), *Adolescent literacy research and practice* (pp. 75–93). New York: Guilford.

Shanahan, T. (2004). Overcoming the dominance of communication: Writing to think and to learn. In T. L. Jetton & J. A. Dole (Eds.), *Adolescent literacy research and practice* (pp. 59–74). New York: Guilford.

Shepard, L. (2000). The role of assessment in a learning culture. *Educational Researcher, 29*(7), 4–14.

Shepard, L., Hammerness, K., Darling-Hammond, L., & Rust, F. (with Snowden, J. B., Gordon,

E., Gutierrez, C., & Pacheco, A.) (2005). Assessment. In L. Darling-Hammond & J. Bransford (Eds.), *Preparing teachers for a changing world: What teachers should learn and be able to do* (pp. 275–326). San Francisco: Jossey-Bass/Wiley.

Shepard, R. N. (1967). Recognition memory for words, sentences, and pictures. *Journal of Verbal Learning and Verbal Behavior, 6,* 156–163.

Sherman, D. K., & Cohen, G. L. (2002). Accepting threatening information: Self-affirmation and the reduction of defensive biases. *Current Directions in Psychological Science, 11,* 119–123.

Shrager, L., & Mayer, R. E. (1989). Note-taking fosters generative learning strategies in novices. *Journal of Educational Psychology, 81,* 263–264.

Siegel, D. J. (1999). *The developing mind: How relationships and the brain interact to shape who we are.* New York: Guilford.

Siegler, R. S., & Jenkins, E. (1989). *How children discover new strategies.* Hillsdale, NJ: Erlbaum.

Silk, J. S., Steinberg, L., & Morris, A. S. (2003). Adolescents' emotion regulation in daily life: Links to depressive symptoms and problem behavior. *Child Development, 74,* 1869–1880.

Silver, E. A., Shapiro, L. J., & Deutsch, A. (1993). Sense making and the solution of division problems involving remainders: An examination of middle school students' solution processes and their interpretations of solutions. *Journal of Research in Mathematics Education, 24,* 117–135.

Simcock, G., & Hayne, H. (2002). Breaking the barrier? Children fail to translate their preverbal memories into language. *Psychological Science, 13,* 225–231.

Simon, H. A. (1973). The structure of ill-structured problems. *Artificial Intelligence, 4,* 181–201.

Simon, H. A. (1978). Information-processing theory of human problem solving. In W. K. Estes (Ed.), *Handbook of learning and cognitive processes: Vol. 5. Human information processing* (pp. 271–295). Hillsdale, NJ: Erlbaum.

Simonton, D. K. (2000). Creativity: Cognitive, personal, developmental, and social aspects. *American Psychologist, 55,* 151–158.

Simonton, D. K. (2001). Talent development as a multidimensional, multiplicative, and dynamic process. *Current Directions in Psychological Science, 10,* 39–42.

Simonton, D. K. (2004). Exceptional creativity and chance: Creative thought as a stochastic combinatorial process. In L. V. Shavinina & M. Ferrari (Eds.), *Beyond knowledge: Extracognitive aspects of developing high ability* (pp. 39–72). Mahwah, NJ: Erlbaum.

Sinatra, G. M., & Mason, L. (2008). Beyond knowledge: Learner characteristics influencing conceptual change. In S. Vosniadou (Ed.), *International handbook on conceptual change* (pp. 560–582). New York: Routledge.

Sinatra, G. M., & Pintrich, P. R. (Eds.) (2003). *Intentional conceptual change.* Mahwah, NJ: Erlbaum.

Singley, M. K., & Anderson, J. R. (1989). *The transfer of cognitive skill.* Cambridge, MA: Harvard University Press.

Sinha, D., & Tripathi, R. C. (1994). Individualism in a collectivist culture: A case of coexistence of opposites. In U. Kim, H. C. Triandis, Ç. Kağitçibaşi, S.-C. Choi, & G. Yoon (Eds.), *Individualism and collectivism: Theory, method, and applications* (pp. 123–138). Newbury Park, CA: Sage.

Sinkavich, F. J. (1995). Performance and metamemory: Do students know what they don't know? *Instructional Psychology, 22,* 77–87.

Sizer, T. R. (1992). *Horace's school: Redesigning the American high school.* Boston: Houghton Mifflin.

Sizer, T. R. (2004). *Horace's compromise: The dilemma of the American high school.* Boston: Houghton Mifflin.

Skaalvik, E. M., & Skaalvik, S. (2008). Teacher self-efficacy: Conceptual analysis and relations with teacher burnout and perceived school context. In H. W. Marsh, R. G. Craven, & D. M. McInerney (Eds.), *Self-processes, learning, and enabling human potential* (pp. 223–247). Charlotte, NC: Information Age.

Smith, C. L. (2007). Bootstrapping processes in the development of students' commonsense matter theories: Using analogical mappings, thought experiments, and learning to measure to promote conceptual restructuring. *Cognition and Instruction, 25,* 337–398.

Smith, C. L., Maclin, D., Grosslight, L., & Davis, H. (1997). Teaching for understanding: A study of students' preinstruction theories of matter and a comparison of the effectiveness of two approaches to teaching about matter and density. *Cognition and Instruction, 15,* 317–393.

Smith, C. L., Maclin, D., Houghton, C., & Hennessey, M. G. (2000). Sixth-grade students' epistemologies of science: The impact of school science experiences on epistemological development. *Cognition and Instruction, 18,* 349–422.

Smith, E. R., & Conrey, F. R. (2009). The social context of cognition. In P. Robbins & M. Aydede (Eds.), *The Cambridge handbook of situated cognition* (pp. 454–466). Cambridge, England: Cambridge University Press.

Son, L. K., & Metcalfe, J. (2000). Metacognitive and control strategies in study-time allocation. *Journal of Experimental Psychology: Learning, Memory, and Cognition, 26,* 204–221.

Son, L. K., & Schwartz, B. L. (2002). The relation between metacognitive monitoring and control. In T. J. Perfect & B. L. Schwartz (Eds.), *Applied metacognition* (pp. 15–38). Cambridge, England: Cambridge University Press.

Southerland, S. A., & Sinatra, G. M. (2003). Learning about biological evolution: A special case of intentional conceptual change. In G. M. Sinatra & P. R. Pintrich (Eds.), *Intentional conceptual change* (pp. 317–345). Mahwah, NJ: Erlbaum.

Sowell, E. R., & Jernigan, T. L. (1998). Further MRI evidence of late brain maturation: Limbic volume increases and changing asymmetries during childhood and adolescence. *Developmental Neuropsychology, 14,* 599–617.

Sowell, E. R., Thompson, P. M., Holmes, C. J., Jernigan, T. L., & Toga, A. W. (1999). *In vivo* evidence for post-adolescent brain maturation in frontal and striatal regions. *Nature Neuroscience, 2,* 859–861.

Spear, L. P. (2007). Brain development and adolescent behavior. In D. Coch, K. W. Fischer, & G. Dawson (Eds.), *Human behavior, learning, and the developing brain: Typical development* (pp. 362–396). New York: Guilford.

Spearman, C. (1904). General intelligence, objectively determined and measured. *American Journal of Psychology, 15,* 201–293.

Spearman, C. (1927). *The abilities of man: Their nature and measurement.* New York: Macmillan.

Speer, N. K., Reynolds, J. R., Swallow, K. M., & Zacks, J. M. (2009). Reading stories activates neural representations of visual and motor experiences. *Psychological Science, 20,* 989–999.

Spence, I., Wong, P., Rusan, M., & Rastegar, N. (2006). How color enhances visual memory for natural scenes. *Psychological Science, 17,* 1–6.

Spilich, G. J., Vesonder, G. T., Chiesi, H. L., & Voss, J. F. (1979). Text processing of domain-related information for individuals with high and low domain knowledge. *Journal of Verbal Learning and Verbal Behavior, 18,* 275–290.

Spires, H. A., & Donley, J. (1998). Prior knowledge activation: Inducing engagement with informational texts. *Journal of Educational Psychology, 90,* 249–260.

Spivey, N. N. (1997). *The constructivist metaphor: Reading, writing, and the making of meaning.* San Diego, CA: Academic Press.

Spoehr, K. T., & Spoehr, L. W. (1994). Learning to think historically. *Educational Psychologist, 29,* 71–77.

Sporer, S. (1991). Deep-deeper-deepest? Encoding strategies and the recognition of human faces. *Journal of Experimental Psychology: Learning, Memory, and Cognition, 17,* 323–333.

Stacey, K. (1992). Mathematical problem solving in groups: Are two heads better than one? *Journal of Mathematical Behavior, 11,* 261–275.

Stahl, S. A., & Shanahan, C. (2004). Learning to think like a historian: Disciplinary knowledge through critical analysis of multiple documents. In T. L. Jetton & J. A. Dole (Eds.), *Adolescent literacy research and practice* (pp. 94–115). New York: Guilford.

Stanovich, K. E. (1999). *Who is rational? Studies of individual differences in reasoning.* Mahwah, NJ: Erlbaum.

Stanovich, K. E., West, R. F., & Harrison, M. R. (1995). Knowledge growth and maintenance across the life span: The role of print exposure. *Developmental Psychology, 31,* 811–826.

Steele, C. (1997). A threat in the air: How stereotypes shape intellectual identity and performance. *American Psychologist, 52,* 613–629.

Stein, B. S. (1989). Memory and creativity. In J. A. Glover, R. R. Ronning, & C. R. Reynolds (Eds.), *Handbook of creativity* (pp. 163–176) New York: Plenum Press.

Steinberg, L. (2007). Risk taking in adolescence. *Current Directions in Psychological Science, 16,* 55–59.

Steinberg, L. (2009). Should the science of adolescent brain development inform public policy? *American Psychologist, 64,* 739–750.

Sternberg, R. J. (1997). The concept of intelligence and its role in lifelong learning and success. *American Psychologist, 52,* 1030–1037.

Sternberg, R. J. (1998). Teaching triarchically improves school achievement. *Journal of Educational Psychology, 90,* 374–384.

Sternberg, R. J. (2003). *Wisdom, intelligence, and creativity synthesized.* Cambridge, England: Cambridge University Press.

Sternberg, R. J. (2004). Culture and intelligence. *American Psychologist, 59,* 325–338.

Sternberg, R. J. (2007). Intelligence and culture. In S. Kitayama & D. Cohen (Eds.), *Handbook of cultural psychology* (pp. 547–568). New York: Guilford.

Sternberg, R. J., & Detterman, D. K. (Eds.) (1986). *What is intelligence? Contemporary views on its nature and definition.* Norwood, NJ: Ablex.

Sternberg, R. J., Forsythe, G. B., Hedlund, J., Horvath, J. A., Wagner, R. K., Williams, W. M., Snook, S. A., & Grigorenko, E. L. (2000). *Practical intelligence in everyday life.* Cambridge, England: Cambridge University Press.

Sternberg, R. J., & Frensch, P. A. (1993). Mechanisms of transfer. In D. K. Detterman & R. J. Sternberg (Eds.), *Transfer on trial: Intelligence, cognition, and instruction* (pp. 25–38). Norwood, NJ: Ablex.

Sternberg, R. J., Grigorenko, E. L., & Kidd, K. K. (2005). Intelligence, race, and genetics. *American Psychologist, 60,* 46–59.

Sternberg, R. J., Grigorenko, E. L., & Zhang, L.-F. (2008). Styles of learning and thinking matter in instruction and assessment. *Perspective on Psychological Science, 3,* 486–506.

Stickgold, R. (2005). Sleep-dependent memory consolidation. *Nature, 437,* 1272–1278.

Stipek, D. J. (1993). *Motivation to learn: From theory to practice* (2nd ed.). Boston: Allyn & Bacon.

Stipek, D. J. (1996). Motivation and instruction. In D. C. Berliner & R. C. Calfee (Eds.), *Handbook of educational psychology* (pp. 85–113). New York: Macmillan.

Stipek, D. J., & Kowalski, P. S. (1989). Learned helplessness in task-orienting versus performance-orienting testing conditions. *Journal of Educational Psychology, 81,* 384–391.

Stodolsky, S. S., Salk, S., & Glaessner, B. (1991). Student views about learning math and social studies. *American Educational Research Journal, 28,* 89–116.

Stokes, S. A., Pierroutsakos, S. L., & Einstein, G. (2007, March). *Remembering to remember: Strategic and spontaneous processes in children's prospective memory.* Paper presented at the biennial meeting of the Society for Research in Child Development, Boston.

Stone, N. J. (2000). Exploring the relationship between calibration and self-regulated learning. *Educational Psychology Review, 12,* 437–475.

Strayer, D. L., & Drews, F. A. (2007). Cell-phone-induced driver distraction. *Current Directions in Psychological Science, 16,* 128–131.

Strayer, D. L., & Johnston, W. A. (2001). Driven to distraction: Dual-task studies of simulated driving and conversing on a cellular telephone. *Psychological Science, 12,* 462–466.

Sutton, J. (2009). Remembering. In P. Robbins & M. Aydede (Eds.), *The Cambridge handbook of situated cognition* (pp. 217–235). Cambridge, England: Cambridge University Press.

Swanson, H. L. (2008). Working memory and intelligence in children: What develops? *Journal of Educational Psychology, 100,* 581–602.

Swanson, H. L., Jerman, O., & Zheng, X. (2008). Growth in working memory and mathematical problem solving in children at risk and not at risk for serious math difficulties. *Journal of Educational Psychology, 100,* 343–379.

Swanson, H. L., O'Connor, J. E., & Cooney, J. B. (1990). An information processing analysis of expert and novice teachers' problem solving. *American Educational Research Journal, 27,* 533–556.

Sweller, J., Kirschner, P. A., & Clark, R. E. (2007). Why minimally guided teaching techniques do not work: A reply to commentaries. *Educational Psychologist, 42,* 115–121.

Talarico, J. M., LaBar, K. S., & Rubin, D. C. (2004). Emotional intensity predicts autobiographical memory experience. *Memory & Cognition, 32,* 1118–1132.

Talarico, J. M., & Rubin, D. C. (2003). Confidence, not consistency, characterizes flashbulb memories. *Psychological Science, 14,* 455–461.

Taleb, N. N. (2007). *The black swan: The impact of the highly improbable.* New York: Random House.

Tamburrini, J. (1982). Some educational implications of Piaget's theory. In S. Modgil &

C. Modgil (Eds.), *Jean Piaget: Consensus and controversy*. New York: Praeger.

Tessler, M., & Nelson, K. (1994). Making memories: The influence of joint encoding on later recall by young children. *Consciousness and Cognition, 3,* 307–326.

Tharp, R. G. (1989). Psychocultural variables and constants: Effects on teaching and learning in schools. *American Psychologist, 44,* 349–359.

Thiede, K. W., Anderson, M. C. M., & Therriault, D. (2003). Accuracy of metacognitive monitoring affects learning of texts. *Journal of Educational Psychology, 95,* 66–73.

Thomas, J. W. (1993). Expectations and effort: Course demands, students' study practices, and academic achievement. In T. M. Tomlinson (Ed.), *Motivating students to learn: Overcoming barriers to high achievement.* Berkeley, CA: McCutchan.

Thomas, M. S. C., & Johnson, M. H. (2008). New advances in understanding sensitive periods in brain development. *Current Directions in Psychological Science, 17,* 1–5.

Thomas, R. M. (2005). *High-stakes testing: Coping with collateral damage.* Mahwah, NJ: Erlbaum.

Thompson, H., & Carr, M. (1995, April). *Brief metacognitive intervention and interest as predictors of memory for text.* Paper presented at the annual meeting of the American Educational Research Association, San Francisco.

Thompson, R., Emmorey, K., & Gollan, T. H. (2005). "Tip of the fingers" experience by deaf signers: Insights into the organization of a sign-based lexicon. *Psychological Science, 16,* 856–860.

Thomson, D. M. (1988). Context and false recognition. In G. M. Davies & D. M. Thomson (Eds.), *Memory in context: Context in memory* (pp. 285–304). Chichester, England: Wiley.

Thorndike, E. L. (1924). Mental discipline in high school studies. *Journal of Educational Psychology, 15,* 1–22, 83–98.

Thrailkill, N. (1996). *Effects of visual images on recall of verbal prose* (unpublished doctoral dissertation). Greeley: University of Northern Colorado.

Tice, D. M., & Baumeister, R. F. (1997). Longitudinal study of procrastination, performance, stress, and health: The costs and benefits of dawdling. *Psychological Science, 8,* 454–458.

Tirosh, D., & Graeber, A. O. (1990). Evoking cognitive conflict to explore preservice teachers' thinking about division. *Journal for Research in Mathematics Education, 21,* 98–108.

Tobias, S. (1980). Anxiety and instruction. In I. G. Sarason (Ed.), *Test anxiety: Theory, research, and applications* (pp. 289–309). Hillsdale, NJ: Erlbaum.

Tobin, K. (1987). The role of wait time in higher cognitive level learning. *Review of Educational Research, 57,* 69–95.

Tomasello, M. (2000). Culture and cognitive development. *Current Directions in Psychological Science, 9,* 37–40.

Toplak, M. E., & Stanovich, K. E. (2002). The domain specificity and generality of disjunctive searching for a generalizable critical thinking skill. *Journal of Educational Psychology, 94,* 197–209.

Trachtenberg, J. T., Chen, B. E., Knott, G. W., Feng, G., Sanes, J. R., Welker, E., et al. (2002). Long-term *in vivo* imaging of experience-dependent synaptic plasticity in adult cortex. *Nature, 420,* 788–794.

Trautwein, U., & Köller, O. (2004, April). *Time investment doesn't always pay off: The role of self-regulatory strategies in homework execution.* Paper presented at the American Educational Research Association, San Diego, CA.

Trautwein, U., Lüdtke, O., Kastens, C., & Köller, O. (2006). Effort on homework in grades 5–9: Development, motivational antecedents, and the association with effort on classwork. *Child Development, 77,* 1094–1111.

Tryon, G. S. (1980). The measurement and treatment of test anxiety. *Review of Educational Research, 50,* 343–372.

Tschannen-Moran, M., Woolfolk Hoy, A., & Hoy, W. K. (1998). Teacher efficacy: Its meaning and measure. *Review of Educational Research, 68,* 202–248.

Tulving, E. (1962). Subjective organization in free recall of "unrelated" words. *Psychological Review, 69,* 344–354.

Turkheimer, E., Haley, A., Waldron, M., D'Onofrio, B., & Gottesman, I. I. (2003). Socioeconomic status modifies heritability of IQ in young children. *Psychological Science, 14,* 623–628.

Turner, J. C., Meyer, D. K., Cox, K. E., Logan, C., DiCintio, M., & Thomas, C. T. (1998). Creating contexts for involvement in mathematics. *Journal of Educational Psychology, 90*, 730–745.

Urdan, T., & Turner, J. C. (2005). Competence motivation in the classroom. In A. J. Elliot & C. S. Dweck (Eds.), *Handbook of competence and motivation* (pp. 297–317). New York: Guilford.

Valli, L., & Buese, D. (2007). The changing roles of teachers in an era of high-stakes accountability. *American Educational Research Journal, 44*, 519–558.

van der Broek, P. (1990). Causal inferences and the comprehension of narrative text. In A. C. Graessner & G. H. Bower (Eds.), *Inferences and text comprehension. The psychology of learning and motivation: Advances in research and theory* (Vol. 25, pp. 175–196). Orlando, FL: Academic Press.

van der Kolk, B. A. (2007). The developmental impact of childhood trauma. In L. J. Kirmayer, R. Lemelson, & M. Barad (Eds.), *Understanding trauma: Integrating biological, clinical, and cultural perspectives* (pp. 224–241). New York: Cambridge University Press.

van IJzendoorn, M. H., & Juffer, F. (2005). Adoption is a successful natural intervention enhancing adopted children's IQ and school performance. *Current Directions in Psychological Science, 14*, 326–330.

Van Meter, P. (2001). Drawing construction as a strategy for learning from text. *Journal of Educational Psychology, 93*, 129–140.

Van Meter, P., & Garner, J. (2005). The promise and practice of learner-generated drawing: Literature review and synthesis. *Educational Psychology Review, 17*, 285–325.

Van Meter, P., Yokoi, L., & Pressley, M. (1994). College students' theory of notetaking derived from their perceptions of notetaking. *Journal of Educational Psychology, 86*, 323–338.

vanSledright, B., & Limón, M. (2006). Learning and teaching social studies: A review of cognitive research in history and geography. In P. A. Alexander & P. H. Winne (Eds.), *Handbook of educational psychology* (2nd ed., pp. 545–570). Mahwah, NJ: Erlbaum.

Vekiri, I. (2002). What is the value of graphical displays in learning? *Educational Psychology Review, 14*, 261–312.

Verghese, J., Lipton, R. B., Katz, M. J., Hall, C. B., Derby, C. A., Kuslansky, G., et al. (2007). Leisure activities and the risk of dementia in the elderly. *New England Journal of Medicine, 348*, 2508–2516.

Verkhratsky, A., & Butt, A. (2007). *Glial neurobiology.* Chichester, England: Wiley.

Volet, S., Vaura, M., & Salonen, P. (2009). Self- and social regulation in learning contexts: An integrative perspective. *Educational Psychologist, 44*, 215–226.

Vosniadou, S. (1991). Conceptual development in astronomy. In S. M. Glynn, R. H. Yeany, & B. K. Britton (Eds.), *The psychology of learning science* (pp. 149–177). Hillsdale, NJ: Erlbaum.

Vosniadou, S. (Ed.) (2008). *International handbook on conceptual change.* New York: Routledge.

Voss, J. F. (1987). Learning and transfer in subject-matter learning: A problem-solving model. *International Journal of Educational Research, 11*, 607–622.

Voss, J. F., Greene, T. R., Post, T. A., & Penner, B. D. (1983). Problem-solving skill in the social sciences. In G. H. Bower (Ed.), *The psychology of learning and motivation* (Vol. 17, pp. 165–213). New York: Academic Press.

Voss, J. F., & Schauble, L. (1992). Is interest educationally interesting? An interest-related model of learning. In K. A. Renninger, S. Hidi, & A. Krapp (Eds.), *The role of interest in learning and development* (pp. 101–120). Hillsdale, NJ: Erlbaum.

Voss, J. F., Tyler, S. W., & Yengo, L. A. (1983). Individual differences in the solving of social science problems. In R. F. Dillon & R. R. Schmeck (Eds.), *Individual differences in cognition* (pp. 205–232). New York: Academic Press.

Voss, J. F., Wolfe, C. R., Lawrence, J. A., & Engle, R. A. (1991). From representation to decision: An analysis of problem solving in international relations. In R. J. Sternberg & P. A. Frensch (Eds.), *Complex problem solving: Principles and mechanisms* (pp. 119–158). Hillsdale, NJ: Erlbaum.

Vye, N. J., Schwartz, D. L., Bransford, J. D., Barron, B. J., Zech, L., & The Cognition and Technology Group at Vanderbilt (1998). SMART environments that support monitoring, reflection, and revision. In D. J. Hacker, J. Dunlosky, & A. C. Graesser (Eds.), *Metacognition in educational theory and practice* (pp. 305–346). Mahwah, NJ: Erlbaum.

Vygotsky, L. S. (1986). *Thought and language* (rev. ed; A. Kozulin, Ed. and Trans.). Cambridge, MA: MIT Press. (Original work published 1934)

Vygotsky, L. S. (1987). *The collected works of L. S. Vygotsky* (Vol. 3; R. W. Rieber & A. S. Carton, Eds.). New York: Plenum Press.

Wade-Stein, D., & Kintsch, E. (2004). Summary Street: Interactive computer support for writing. *Cognition and Instruction, 22,* 333–362.

Waldmann, M. R., Hagmayer, Y., & Blaisdell, A. P. (2006). Beyond the information given: Causal models in learning and reasoning. *Current Directions in Psychological Science, 15,* 307–311.

Walker, C. H. (1987). Relative importance of domain knowledge and overall aptitude on acquisition of domain-related information. *Cognition and Instruction, 4,* 25–42.

Walker, E. F. (2002). Adolescent neurodevelopment and psychopathology. *Current Directions in Psychological Science, 11,* 24–28.

Wallas, G. (1926). *The art of thought.* New York: Harcourt Brace Jovanovich.

Wang, H. X., Karp, A., Winbald, B., & Fratiglioni, L. (2002). Late-life engagement in social and leisure activities is associated with a decreased risk of dementia: A longitudinal study from the Kungsholmen Project. *American Journal of Epidemiology, 155,* 1081–1087.

Ward, R. A., & Grasha, A. F. (1986). Using astrology to teach research methods to introductory psychology students. *Teaching of Psychology, 13,* 143–145.

Wasley, P. A., Hampel, R. L., & Clark, R. W. (1997). *Kids and school reform.* San Francisco: Jossey-Bass.

Wason, P. (1968). Reasoning about a rule. *Quarterly Journal of Experimental Psychology, 20,* 273–281.

Wasserman, E. A. (1993). Comparative cognition: Toward a general understanding of cognition in behavior. *Psychological Science, 4,* 156–161.

Wasserman, E. A., DeVolder, C. L., & Coppage, D. J. (1992). Non-similarity-based conceptualization in pigeons via secondary or mediated generalization. *Psychological Science, 3,* 374–379.

Weaver, C. A., III, & Kelemen, W. L. (1997). Judgments of learning at delays: Shifts in response patterns or increased metamemory accuracy? *Psychological Science, 8,* 318–321.

Webb, N. M., Franke, M. L., Ing, M., Chan, A., De, T., Freund, D., et al. (2008). The role of teacher instructional practices in student collaboration. *Contemporary Educational Psychology, 33,* 360–381.

Webber, J., & Plotts, C. A. (2008). *Emotional and behavioral disorders: Theory and practice* (5th ed.). Boston: Allyn & Bacon.

Webber, J., Scheuermann, B., McCall, C., & Coleman, M. (1993). Research on self-monitoring as a behavior management technique in special education classrooms: A descriptive review. *Remedial and Special Education, 14*(2), 38–56.

Wegman, C. (1985). *Psychoanalysis and cognitive psychology.* London: Academic Press.

Weiner, B. (1984). Principles for a theory of student motivation and their application within an attributional framework. In R. Ames & C. Ames (Eds.), *Research on motivation in education: Vol. 1. Student motivation* (pp. 15–38). Orlando, FL: Academic Press.

Weiner, B. (1986). *An attributional theory of motivation and emotion.* New York: Springer-Verlag.

Weiner, B. (1992). *Human motivation: Metaphors, theories, and research.* Newbury Park, CA: Sage.

Weiner, B. (1994). Ability versus effort revisited: The moral determinants of achievement evaluation and achievement as a moral system. *Educational Psychologist, 29,* 163–172.

Weiner, B. (2000). Intrapersonal and interpersonal theories of motivation from an attributional perspective. *Educational Psychology Review, 12,* 1–14.

Weiner, B. (2004). Attribution theory revisited: Transforming cultural plurality into theoretical unity. In D. M. McNerney & S. Van Etten (Eds.), *Big theories revisited* (pp. 13–29). Greenwich, CT: Information Age.

Weinstein, C. E., Hagen, A. S., & Meyer, D. K. (1991, April). *Work smart ... not hard: The effects of combining instruction in using strategies, goal using, and executive control on attributions and academic performance.* Paper presented at the annual meeting of the American Educational Research Association, Chicago.

Weinstein, R. S., Madison, S. M., & Kuklinski, M. R. (1995). Raising expectations in schooling: Obstacles and opportunities for change. *American Educational Research Journal, 32,* 121–159.

Weisberg R. W. (1993). *Creativity: Beyond the myth of genius.* New York: Freeman.

Wellman, H. M., & Hickling, A. K. (1994). The mind's "I": Chldren's conception of the mind as an active agent. *Child Development, 65,* 1564–1580.

Wells, G. L., & Bradfield, A. L. (1999). Distortions in eyewitnesses recollections: Can the postidentification-feedback effect be moderated? *Psychological Science, 10,* 138–144.

Wells, G. L., Olson, E. A., & Charman, S. D. (2002). The confidence of eyewitnesses in their identifications from lineups. *Current Directions in Psychological Science, 11,* 151–154.

Wenke, D., & Frensch, P. A. (2003). Is success or failure at solving complex problems related to intellectual ability? In J. E. Davidson & R. J. Sternberg (Eds.), *The psychology of problem solving* (pp. 87–126). Cambridge, England: Cambridge University Press.

Wentzel, K. R. (1999). Social-motivational processes and interpersonal relationships: Implications for understanding motivation at school. *Journal of Educational Psychology, 91,* 76–97.

West, R. F., Toplak, M. E., & Stanovich, K. E. (2008). Heuristics and biases as measures of critical thinking: Associations with cognitive ability and thinking dispositions. *Journal of Educational Psychology, 100,* 930–941.

Whitley, B. E., Jr., & Frieze, I. H. (1985). Children's causal attributions for success and failure in achievement settings: A meta-analysis. *Journal of Educational Psychology, 77,* 608–616.

Whitten, S., & Graesser, A. C. (2003). Comprehension of text in problem solving. In J. E. Davidson & R. J. Sternberg (Eds.), *The psychology of problem solving* (pp. 207–229). Cambridge, England: Cambridge University Press.

Wiley, J., & Bailey, J. (2006). Effects of collaboration and argumentation on learning from Web pages. In A. M. O'Donnell, C. E. Hmelo-Silver, & G. Erkens (Eds.), *Collaborative learning, reasoning, and technology* (pp. 297–321). Mahwah, NJ: Erlbaum.

Wiley, J., Goldman, S. R., Graesser, A. C., Sanchez, C. A., Ash, I. K., & Hemmerich, J. A. (2009). Source evaluation, comprehension, and learning in Internet science inquiry tasks. *American Educational Research Journal, 46,* 1060–1106.

Wilson, R. S., Scherr, P. A., Schneider, J. A., Li, Y., & Bennett, D. A. (2007). The relation of cognitive activity to risk of developing Alzheimer's disease. *Neurology, 69,* 1911–1920.

Wilson, T. D., & Gilbert, D. T. (2008). Explaining away: A model of affective adaptation. *Perspectives on Psychological Science, 3,* 370–386.

Windschitl, M. (2002). Framing constructivism in practice as the negotiation of dilemmas: An analysis of the conceptual, pedagogical, cultural, and political challenges facing teachers. *Review of Educational Research, 72,* 131–175.

Winer, G. A., & Cottrell, J. E. (1996). Does anything leave the eye when we see? Extramission beliefs of children and adults. *Current Directions in Psychological Science, 5,* 137–142.

Wingfield, A., & Byrnes, D. L. (1981). *The psychology of human memory.* San Diego, CA: Academic Press.

Winkielman, P., & Berridge, K. C. (2004). Unconscious emotion. *Current Directions in Psychological Science, 13,* 120–123.

Winn, W. (1991). Learning from maps and diagrams. *Educational Psychology Review, 3,* 211–247.

Winne, P. H. (1995a). Inherent details in self-regulated learning. *Educational Psychologist, 30,* 173–187.

Winne, P. H. (1995b). Self-regulation is ubiquitous but its forms vary with knowledge. *Educational Psychologist, 30,* 223–228.

Winne, P. H., & Hadwin, A. F. (1998). Studying as self-regulated learning. In D. J. Hacker, J. Dunlosky, & A. C. Graesser (Eds.), *Metacognition in educational theory and practice* (pp. 277–304). Mahwah, NJ: Erlbaum.

Winne, P. H., & Jamieson-Noel, D. (2001, April). *How self perceptions of prior knowledge and self-regulated learning interact to affect learning.* Paper presented at the annual meeting of the American Educational Research Association, Seattle, WA.

Winne, P. H., & Stockley, D. B. (1998). Computing technologies as sites for developing self-regulated learning. In D. H. Schunk & B. J. Zimmerman (Eds.), *Self-regulated learning: From teaching to self-reflective practice* (pp. 106–136). New York: Guilford.

Winograd, E., & Neisser, U. (1992). *Affect and accuracy in recall: Studies of "flashbulb" memories.* Cambridge, England: Cambridge University Press.

Winsler, A., & Naglieri, J. (2003). Overt and covert verbal problem-solving strategies:

Developmental trends in use, awareness, and relations with task performance in children aged 5 to 17. *Child Development, 74,* 659–678.

Wisner Fries, A. B., & Pollak, S. D. (2007). Emotion processing and the developing brain. In D. Coch, K. W. Fischer, & G. Dawson (Eds.), *Human behavior, learning, and the developing brain: Typical development* (pp. 329–361). New York: Guilford.

Wittenbaum, G. M., & Park, E. S. (2001). The collective preference for shared information. *Current Directions in Psychological Science, 10,* 70–73.

Wittrock, M. C., & Alesandrini, K. (1990). Generation of summaries and analogies and analytic and holistic abilities. *American Educational Research Journal, 27,* 489–502.

Wixson, K. K. (1984). Level of importance of post-questions and children's learning from text. *American Educational Research Journal, 21,* 419–433.

Wixted, J. T. (2005). A theory about why we forget what we once knew. *Current Directions in Psychological Science, 14,* 6–9.

Wolters, C. A. (1998). Self-regulated learning and college students' regulation of motivation. *Journal of Educational Psychology, 90,* 224–235.

Wolters, C. A. (2003a). Regulation of motivation: Evaluating an underemphasized aspect of self-regulated learning. *Educational Psychologist, 38,* 189–205.

Wolters, C. A. (2003b). Understanding procrastination from a self-regulated learning perspective. *Journal of Educational Psychology, 95,* 179–187.

Wolters, C. A., & Rosenthal, H. (2000). The relation between students' motivational beliefs and their use of motivational regulation strategies. *International Journal of Educational Research, 33,* 801–820.

Wood, E., Willoughby, T., McDermott, C., Motz, M., Kaspar, V., & Ducharme, M. J. (1999). Developmental differences in study behavior. *Journal of Educational Psychology, 91,* 527–536.

Wood, P., & Kardash, C. A. M. (2002). Critical elements in the design and analysis of studies of epistemology. In B. K. Hofer & P. R. Pintrich (Eds.), *Personal epistemology: The psychology of beliefs about knowledge and knowing* (pp. 231–260). Mahwah, NJ: Erlbaum.

Woodman, G. F., & Vogel, E. K. (2005). Fractionating working memory: Consolidation and maintenance are independent processes. *Psychological Science, 16,* 106–113.

Wright, D. B., Memon, A., Skagerberg, E. M., & Gabbert, F. (2009). When eyewitnesses talk. *Current Directions in Psychological Science, 18,* 174–178.

Yaffe, K., Fiocco, A., Lindquist, K., Vittinghoff, E., Simonsick, E. Newman, A., et al. (2009). Predictors of maintaining cognitive function in older adults: The Health ABC Study. *Neurology, 72,* 2029–2035.

Yarmey, A. D. (1973). I recognize your face but I can't remember your name: Further evidence on the tip-of-the-tongue phenomenon. *Memory and Cognition, 1,* 287–290.

Yokoi, L. (1997, March). *The developmental context of notetaking: A qualitative examination of notetaking at the secondary level.* Paper presented at the annual meeting of the American Educational Research Association, Chicago.

Zahorik, J. A. (1994, April). *Making things interesting.* Paper presented at the annual meeting of the American Educational Research Association, New Orleans, LA.

Zaragoza, J. M., & Fraser, B. J. (2008, March). *Learning environments and attitudes among elementary-school students in traditional environmental science and field-study classrooms.* Paper presented at the annual meeting of the American Educational Research Association, New York.

Zaragoza, M. S., & Mitchell, K. J. (1996). Repeated exposure to suggestion and the creation of false memories. *Psychological Science, 7,* 294–300.

Zaragoza, M. S., Payment, K. E., Ackil, J. K., Drivdahl, S. B., & Beck, M. (2001). Interviewing witnesses: Forced confabulation and confirmatory feedback increase false memories. *Psychological Science, 12,* 473–477.

Zeelenberg, R., Wagenmakers, E.-J., & Rotteveel, M. (2006). The impact of emotion on perception: Bias or enhanced processing? *Psychological Science, 17,* 287–291.

Zeidner, M. (1998). *Test anxiety: The state of the art.* New York: Plenum Press.

Zeidner, M., & Matthews, G. (2005). Evaluation anxiety: Current theory and research. In A. J. Elliot & C. S. Dweck (Eds.), *Handbook of competence and motivation* (pp. 141–163). New York: Guilford.

Zelazo, P. D., Müller, U., Frye, D., & Marcovitch, S. (2003). The development of executive function in early childhood. *Monographs of the Society for Research in Child Development, 68*(3), Serial No. 274.

Zhong, C.-B., Dijksterhuis, A., & Galinsky, A. D. (2008). The merits of unconscious thought in creativity. *Psychological Science, 19,* 912–918.

Zigler, E. (2003). Forty years of believing in magic is enough. *Social Policy Report, 17*(1), 10.

Zimmerman, B. J. (1998). Developing self-fulfilling cycles of academic regulation: An analysis of exemplary instructional models. In D. H. Schunk & B. J. Zimmerman (Eds.), *Self-regulated learning: From teaching to self-reflective practice* (pp. 1–19). New York: Guilford.

Zimmerman, B. J. (2004). Sociocultural influence and students' development of academic self-regulation: A social-cognitive perspective. In D. M. McNerney & S. Van Etten (Eds.), *Big theories revisited* (pp. 139–164). Greenwich, CT: Information Age.

Zimmerman, B. J. (2008). In search of self-regulated learning: A personal quest. In H. W. Marsh, R. G. Craven, & D. M. McInerney (Eds.), *Self-processes, learning, and enabling human potential* (pp. 171–191). Charlotte, NC: Information Age.

Zimmerman, B. J., & Bandura, A. (1994). Impact of self-regulatory influences on writing course attainment. *American Educational Research Journal, 31,* 845–862.

Zimmerman, B. J., & Campillo, M. (2003). Motivating self-regulated problem solvers. In J. E. Davidson & R. J. Sternberg (Eds.), *The psychology of problem solving* (pp. 233–262). Cambridge, England: Cambridge University Press.

Zimmerman, B. J., & Kitsantas, A. (2005). The hidden dimension of personal competence: Self-regulated learning and practice. In A. J. Elliot & C. S. Dweck (Eds.), *Handbook of competence and motivation* (pp. 509–526). New York: Guilford.

Zimmerman, B. J., & Risemberg, R. (1997). Self-regulatory dimensions of academic learning and motivation. In G. D. Phye (Ed.), *Handbook of academic learning: Construction of knowledge* (pp. 105–125). San Diego, CA: Academic Press.

Zimmerman, B. J., & Schunk, D. H. (2004). Self-regulating intellectual processes and outcomes: A social cognitive perspective. In D. Y. Dai & R. J. Sternberg (Eds.), *Motivation, emotion, and cognition: Integrative perspectives on intellectual functioning and development* (pp. 323–349). Mahwah, NJ: Erlbaum.

Zohar, A., & Aharon-Kraversky, S. (2005). Exploring the effects of cognitive conflict and direct teaching for students of different academic levels. *Journal of Research in Science Teaching, 42,* 829–855.

Zook, K. B. (1991). Effects of analogical processes on learning and misrepresentation. *Educational Psychology Review, 3,* 41–72.

Zook, K. B., & Di Vesta, F. J. (1991). Instructional analogies and conceptual misrepresentations. *Journal of Educational Psychology, 83,* 246–252.

Index

© Copyright 2011
SitePoint Pty. Ltd.

All Rights Reserved.

Unauthorized copying,
sale, or distribution of
these files is prohibited.

HTML5 & CSS3
FOR THE REAL WORLD

CD-ROM

The CD-ROM is not missing.
Download all the code in this book from:
http://www.sitepoint.com/books/htmlcss1/code.php

Summary of Contents

HTML5 & CSS3 FOR THE REAL WORLD

BY ALEXIS GOLDSTEIN
LOUIS LAZARIS
ESTELLE WEYL

HTML5 & CSS3 for the Real World

by Alexis Goldstein, Louis Lazaris, and Estelle Weyl

Copyright © 2011 SitePoint Pty. Ltd.

Program Director: Lisa Lang   **Indexer**: Michele Combs
Technical Editor: Louis Simoneau   **Editor**: Kelly Steele
Expert Reviewer: Russ Weakley   **Cover Design**: Alex Walker
Printing History:

   First Edition: May 2011

Notice of Rights

Notice of Liability

Trademark Notice

Published by SitePoint Pty. Ltd.

48 Cambridge Street, Collingwood
VIC 3066 Australia
Web: www.sitepoint.com
Email: business@sitepoint.com

ISBN 978-0-9808469-0-4
Printed and bound in the United States of America

About Alexis Goldstein

Alexis Goldstein first taught herself HTML while a high school student in the mid-1990s, and went on to get her degree in Computer Science from Columbia University. She runs her own software development and training company, aut faciam LLC. Before striking out on her own, Alexis spent seven years in technology on Wall Street, where she worked in both the cash equity and equity derivative spaces at three major firms, and learned to love daily code reviews. She is a teacher and co-organizer of Girl Develop It, a group that conducts low-cost programming classes for women, and a very proud member of the NYC Resistor hackerspace in Brooklyn, NY. You can find Alexis at her website, http://alexisgo.com/.

About Louis Lazaris

Louis Lazaris is a freelance web designer and front-end developer based in Toronto, Canada who has been involved in the web design industry since 2000. Louis has been working on websites ever since the days when table layouts and one-pixel GIFs dominated the industry. Over the past five years he has transitioned to embrace web standards while endeavoring to promote best practices that help both developers and their clients reach practical goals for their projects. Louis writes regularly for a number of top web design blogs including his own site, Impressive Webs (http://www.impressivewebs.com/.

About Estelle Weyl

Estelle Weyl is a front-end engineer from San Francisco who has been developing standards-based accessible websites since 1999. Estelle began playing with CSS3 when the iPhone was released in 2007, and after four years of web application development for mobile WebKit, she knows (almost) every CSS3 quirk on WebKit, and has vast experience implementing components of HTML5. She writes two popular technical blogs with tutorials and detailed grids of CSS3 and HTML5 browser support (http://www.standardista.com/). Estelle's passion is teaching web development, where you'll find her speaking on CSS3, HTML5, JavaScript, and mobile web development at conferences around the USA (and, she hopes, the world).

About the Expert Reviewer

Russ Weakley has worked in the design field for over 18 years, primarily in web design and development, and web training. Russ co-chairs the Web Standards Group and is a founding committee member of the Web Industry Professionals Association of Australia (WIPA). Russ has produced a series of widely acclaimed CSS tutorials, and is internationally recognized for his presentations and workshops. He manages Max Design (http://maxdesign.com.au/).

About SitePoint

SitePoint specializes in publishing fun, practical, and easy-to-understand content for web professionals. Visit http://www.sitepoint.com/ to access our blogs, books, newsletters, articles, and community forums.

To my parents, who always encourage and believe in me.

And to my talented, prolific, and loving Grandma Joan. You always keep me painting, no matter what else I may be doing.

—Alexis

To Melanie, the best cook in the world.

And to my parents, for funding the original course that got me into this unique industry.

—Louis

To Amie, for putting up with me, and to Spazzo and Puppers, for snuggling with me as I worked away.

—Estelle

Table of Contents

Chapter 7   CSS3 Gradients and Multiple Backgrounds

Chapter 10   Geolocation, Offline Web Apps, and Web Storage 225

Foreword

Heard of Sjoerd Visscher? I'd venture to guess you haven't, but what he considered a minor discovery is at the foundation of our ability to use HTML5 today.

Back in 2002, in The Hague, Netherlands, Mr. Visscher was attempting to improve the performance of his XSL output. He switched from `createElement` calls to setting the `innerHTML` property, and then realized that all the unknown, non-HTML elements were no longer able to be styled by CSS.

Fast forward to 2008, and HTML5 is gaining momentum. New elements have been specified, but in practice Internet Explorer versions 6-8 pose a problem, as they fail to recognize unknown elements; the new elements are unable to hold children and CSS has no effect on them. This depressing fact was posing quite a hindrance to HTML5 adoption.

Now, half a decade after his discovery, Sjoerd innocently mentions this trick in a comment on the blog of the W3C HTML Working Group co-chair, Sam Ruby: "BTW, if you want CSS rules to apply to unknown elements in IE, you just have to do `document.createElement(elementName)`. This somehow lets the CSS engine know that elements with that name exist."

Ian Hickson, lead editor of the HTML5 spec, was as surprised as the rest of the Web. Having never heard of this trick before, he was happy to report: "This piece of information makes building an HTML5 compatibility shim for IE7 far easier than had previously been assumed."

A day later, John Resig wrote the post that coined the term "HTML5 shiv." Here's a quick timeline of what followed:

- January 2009: Remy Sharp creates the first distributable script for enabling HTML5 element use in IE.

- June 2009: Faruk Ateş includes the HTML5 shiv in Modernizr's initial release.

- February 2010: A ragtag team of superstar JavaScript developers including Remy, Kangax, John-David Dalton, and PorneL collaborate and drop the file size of the script.

- March 2010: Mathias Bynens and others notice that the shiv doesn't affect pages printed from IE. It was a sad day. I issue an informal challenge to developers to find a solution.

- April 2010: Jonathan Neal answers that challenge with the IE Print Protector (IEPP), which captured the scope of the HTML5 shiv but added in support for printing the elements as well.

- April 2010: Remy replaces the legacy HTML5 shiv solution with the new IEPP.

- February 2011: Alexander Farkas carries the torch, moving the IEPP project to GitHub, adding a test suite, fixing bugs, and improving performance.

- April 2011: IEPP v2 comes out. Modernizr and the HTML5 shiv inherit the latest code while developers everywhere continue to use HTML5 elements in a cross-browser fashion without worry.

The tale of the HTML5 shiv is just one example of community contribution that helps to progress the open web movement. It's not just the W3C or the browsers who directly affect how we work on the Web, but people like you and me. I hope this book encourages you to contribute in a similar manner; the best way to further your craft is to actively share what you learn.

Adopting HTML5 and CSS3 today is easier than ever, and seriously fun. This book presents a wealth of practical information that gives you what you need to know to take advantage of HTML5 now. The authors—Alexis, Louis, and Estelle—are well-respected web developers who present a realistic learning curve for you to absorb the best practices of HTML5 development easily.

I trust this book is able to serve you well, and that you'll be as excited about the next generation of the Web as I am.

—

Paul Irish
jQuery Dev Relations,
Lead Developer of Modernizr and HTML5 Boilerplate
April 2011

Preface

Welcome to *HTML5 & CSS3 for the Real World*. We're glad you've decided to join us on this journey of discovering some of the latest and the greatest in front-end website building technology.

If you've picked up a copy of this book, it's likely that you've dabbled to some degree in HTML and CSS. You might even be a bit of a seasoned pro in certain areas of markup, styling, or scripting, and now want to extend those skills further by dipping into the new features and technologies associated with HTML5 and CSS3.

Learning a new task can be difficult. You may have limited time to invest in poring over the official documentation and specifications for these web-based languages. You also might be turned off by some of the overly technical books that work well as references but provide little in the way of real-world, practical examples.

To that end, our goal with this book is to help you learn through hands-on, practical instruction that will assist you to tackle the real-world problems you face in building websites today—with a specific focus on HTML5 and CSS3.

But this is more than just a step-by-step tutorial. Along the way, we'll provide plenty of theory and technical information to help fill in any gaps in your understanding—the whys and hows of these new technologies—while doing our best not to overwhelm you with the sheer volume of cool new stuff. So let's get started!

Who Should Read This Book

This book is aimed at web designers and front-end developers who want to learn about the latest generation of browser-based technologies. You should already have at least intermediate knowledge of HTML and CSS, as we won't be spending any time covering the basics of markup and styles. Instead, we'll focus on teaching you what new powers are available to you in the form of HTML5 and CSS3.

The final two chapters of this book cover some of the new JavaScript APIs that have come to be associated with HTML5. These chapters, of course, require some basic familiarity with JavaScript—but they're not critical to the rest of the book. If you're

unfamiliar with JavaScript, there's no harm in skipping over them for now, returning later when you're better acquainted with it.

What's in This Book

This book comprises eleven chapters and three appendices. Most chapters follow on from each other, so you'll probably get the most benefit reading them in sequence, but you can certainly skip around if you only need a refresher on a particular topic.

Chapter 1: *Introducing HTML5 and CSS3*

Before we tackle the hands-on stuff, we'll present you with a little bit of history, along with some compelling reasons to start using HTML5 and CSS3 today. We'll also look at the current state of affairs in terms of browser support, and argue that a great deal of these new technologies are ready to be used today—so long as they're used wisely.

Chapter 2: *Markup, HTML5 Style*

In this chapter, we'll show you some of the new structural and semantic elements that are new in HTML5. We'll also be introducing *The HTML5 Herald*, a demo site we'll be working on throughout the rest of the book. Think divs are boring? So do we. Good thing HTML5 now provides an assortment of options: article, section, nav, footer, aside, and header!

Chapter 3: *More HTML5 Semantics*

Continuing on from the previous chapter, we turn our attention to the new way in which HTML5 constructs document outlines. Then we look at a plethora of other semantic elements that let you be a little more expressive with your markup.

Chapter 4: *HTML5 Forms*

Some of the most useful and currently applicable features in HTML5 pertain to forms. A number of browsers now support native validation on email types like emails and URLs, and some browsers even support native date pickers, sliders, and spinner boxes. It's almost enough to make you enjoy coding forms! This chapter covers everything you need to know to be up to speed writing HTML5 forms, and provides scripted fallbacks for older browsers.

Chapter 5: *HTML5 Audio and Video*

HTML5 is often touted as a contender for the online multimedia content crown, long held by Flash. The new `audio` and `video` elements are the reason—they provide native, scriptable containers for your media without relying on a third-party plugin like Flash. In this chapter, you'll learn all the ins and outs of putting these new elements to work.

Chapter 6: *Introducing CSS3*

Now that we've covered just about all of HTML5, it's time to move onto its close relative CSS3. We'll start our tour of CSS3 by looking at some of the new selectors that let you target elements on the page with unprecedented flexibility. Then we'll follow up with a look at some new ways of specifying color in CSS3, including transparency. We'll close the chapter with a few quick wins—cool CSS3 features that can be added to your site with a minimum of work: text shadows, drop shadows, and rounded corners.

Chapter 7: *CSS3 Gradients and Multiple Backgrounds*

When was the last time you worked on a site that didn't have a gradient or a background image on it? CSS3 provides some overdue support to developers spending far too much time wrangling with Photoshop, trying to create the perfect background gradients and images without breaking the bandwidth bank. Now you can specify linear or radial gradients right in your CSS without images, and you can give an element any number of background images. Time to ditch all those spare `div`s you've been lugging around.

Chapter 8: *CSS3 Transforms and Transitions*

Animation has long been seen as the purview of JavaScript, but CSS3 lets you offload some of the heavy lifting to the browser. Transforms let you rotate, flip, skew, and otherwise throw your elements around. Transitions can add some subtlety to the otherwise jarring all-on or all-off state changes we see on our sites. We wrap up this chapter with a glimpse of the future; while CSS keyframe animations still lack widespread support, we think you'll agree they're pretty sweet.

Chapter 9: *Embedded Fonts and Multicolumn Layouts*

Do you prefer Arial or Verdana? Georgia or Times? How about none of those? In this chapter, we'll look at how we can move past the "web-safe" fonts of yesteryear and embed any fonts right into our pages for visitors to download

along with our stylesheets and images. We'll also look at a promising new CSS feature that allows us to lay out content across multiple columns without using extra markup or the dreaded `float`.

Chapter 10: *Geolocation, Offline Web Apps, and Web Storage*

The latest generation of browsers come equipped with a wide selection of new standard JavaScript APIs. Many of these are specifically geared towards mobile browsers, but still carry benefits for desktop users. In this chapter, we'll look at three of the most exciting: Geolocation, Offline Web Apps, and Web Storage. We'll also touch briefly on some of the APIs that we won't be covering in detail—either because they're poorly supported, or have limited use cases—and give you some pointers should you want to investigate further.

Chapter 11: *Canvas, SVG, and Drag and Drop*

We devote the book's final chapter to, first of all, covering two somewhat competing technologies for drawing and displaying graphics. Canvas is new to HTML5, and provides a pixel surface and a JavaScript API for drawing shapes to it. SVG, on the other hand, has been around for years, but is now achieving very good levels of browser support, so it's an increasingly viable alternative. Finally, we'll cover one more new JavaScript API—Drag and Drop—which provides native handling of drag-and-drop interfaces.

Appendix A: *Modernizr*

A key tool in any HTML5 superhero's utility belt, Modernizr is a nifty little JavaScript library that detects support for just about every HTML5 and CSS3 feature, allowing you to selectively style your site or apply fallback strategies. We've included a quick primer on how to use Modernizr in this appendix, even though Modernizr is used throughout the book. This way, you have a ready reference available in one place, while the other chapters focus on the meat of HTML5 and CSS3.

Appendix B: *WAI-ARIA*

A separate specification that's often mentioned in the same breath as HTML5, WAI-ARIA is the latest set of tools to help make sophisticated web applications accessible to users of assistive technology. While a whole book could be devoted to WAI-ARIA, we thought it beneficial to include a quick summary of what it is, as well as some pointers to places where you can learn more.

Appendix C: *Microdata*

Microdata is part of the HTML5 specification that deals with annotating markup with machine-readable labels. It's still somewhat in flux, but we thought it was worthwhile to get you up to speed with a few examples.

Where to Find Help

SitePoint has a thriving community of web designers and developers ready and waiting to help you out if you run into trouble. We also maintain a list of known errata for the book, which you can consult for the latest updates.

The SitePoint Forums

The SitePoint Forums[1] are discussion forums where you can ask questions about anything related to web development. You may, of course, answer questions too. That's how a forum site works—some people ask, some people answer, and most people do a bit of both. Sharing your knowledge benefits others and strengthens the community. A lot of interesting and experienced web designers and developers hang out there. It's a good way to learn new stuff, have questions answered in a hurry, and generally have a blast.

The Book's Website

Located at http://sitepoint.com/books/rw1/, the website that supports this book will give you access to the following facilities:

The Code Archive

As you progress through this book, you'll note a number of references to the code archive. This is a downloadable ZIP archive that contains every line of example source code printed in this book. If you want to cheat (or save yourself from carpal tunnel syndrome), go ahead and download the archive.[2]

Updates and Errata

No book is perfect, and we expect that watchful readers will be able to spot at least one or two mistakes before the end of this one. The Errata page[3] on the book's

---

[1] http://www.sitepoint.com/forums/
[2] http://www.sitepoint.com/books/rw1/code.php
[3] http://www.sitepoint.com/books/rw1/errata.php

website will always have the latest information about known typographical and code errors.

The SitePoint Newsletters

In addition to books like this one, SitePoint publishes free email newsletters, such as the *SitePoint Tech Times*, *SitePoint Tribune*, and *SitePoint Design View*, to name a few. In them, you'll read about the latest news, product releases, trends, tips, and techniques for all aspects of web development. Sign up to one or more SitePoint newsletters at http://www.sitepoint.com/newsletter/.

The SitePoint Podcast

Join the SitePoint Podcast team for news, interviews, opinion, and fresh thinking for web developers and designers. We discuss the latest web industry topics, present guest speakers, and interview some of the best minds in the industry. You can catch up on the latest and previous podcasts at http://www.sitepoint.com/podcast/, or subscribe via iTunes.

Your Feedback

If you're unable to find an answer through the forums, or if you wish to contact us for any other reason, the best place to write is `books@sitepoint.com`. We have a well-staffed email support system set up to track your inquiries, and if our support team members can't answer your question, they'll send it straight to us. Suggestions for improvements, as well as notices of any mistakes you may find, are especially welcome.

Acknowledgments

Alexis Goldstein

Thank you to Lisa Lang, Russ Weakley, and Louis Simoneau. Your attention to detail, responsiveness, and impressive technical expertise made this book an absolute joy to work on. Thank you to my co-authors, Louis and Estelle, who never failed to impress me with their deep knowledge, vast experience, and uncanny ability to find bugs in the latest browsers. A special thank you to Estelle for the encouragement, for which I am deeply grateful. Finally, thank you to my girlfriend Tabatha, who now knows more about HTML5's JavaScript APIs than most of my nerdy friends. Thank you for your patience, your feedback, and all your support. You help me take things less seriously, which, as anyone who knows me knows, is a monumental task. Thank you for always making me laugh.

Louis Lazaris

Thank you to my wife for putting up with my odd work hours while I took part in this great project. Thanks to my talented co-authors, Estelle and Alexis, for gracing me with the privilege of having my name alongside theirs, and, of course, to our expert reviewer Russ for his great technical insight during the writing process. And special thanks to the talented staff at SitePoint for their super-professional handling of this project and everything that goes along with such an endeavor.

Estelle Weyl

Thank you to the entire open source community. With the option to "view source," I have learned from every developer who opted for markup rather than plugins. I would especially like to thank Jen Mei Wu and Sandi Watkins, who helped point me in the right direction when I began my career. Thank you to Dave Gregory and Laurie Voss who have always been there to help me find the words when they escaped me. Thank you to Stephanie Sullivan for brainstorming over code into the wee hours of the morning. And thank you to my developer friends at Opera, Mozilla, and Google for creating awesome browsers, providing us with the opportunity to not just play with HTML5 and CSS, but also to write this book.

Conventions Used in This Book

You'll notice that we've used certain typographic and layout styles throughout the book to signify different types of information. Look out for the following items:

Code Samples

Code in this book will be displayed using a fixed-width font, like so:

```
<h1>A Perfect Summer's Day</h1>
<p>It was a lovely day for a walk in the park. The birds
were singing and the kids were all back at school.</p>
```

If the code is to be found in the book's code archive, the name of the file will appear at the top of the program listing, like this:

example.css

```
.footer {
  background-color: #CCC;
  border-top: 1px solid #333;
}
```

If only part of the file is displayed, this is indicated by the word *excerpt*:

example.css *(excerpt)*

```
  border-top: 1px solid #333;
```

If additional code is to be inserted into an existing example, the new code will be displayed in bold:

```
function animate() {
  new_variable = "Hello";
}
```

Where existing code is required for context, rather than repeat all the code, a vertical ellipsis will be displayed:

```
function animate() {
  ⋮
  return new_variable;
}
```

Some lines of code are intended to be entered on one line, but we've had to wrap them because of page constraints. A ➡ indicates a line break that exists for formatting purposes only, and should be ignored:

```
URL.open("http://www.sitepoint.com/blogs/2007/05/28/user-style-she
➡ets-come-of-age/");
```

Tips, Notes, and Warnings

Hey, You!

Tips will give you helpful little pointers.

Ahem, Excuse Me ...

Notes are useful asides that are related—but not critical—to the topic at hand. Think of them as extra tidbits of information.

Make Sure You Always ...

... pay attention to these important points.

Watch Out!

Warnings will highlight any gotchas that are likely to trip you up along the way.

Chapter

Introducing HTML5 and CSS3

This chapter gives a basic overview of how we arrived where we are today, why HTML5 and CSS3 are so important to modern websites and web apps, and how using these technologies will be invaluable to your future as a web professional.

Of course, if you'd prefer to just get into the meat of the project that we'll be building, and start learning how to use all the new bells and whistles that HTML5 and CSS3 bring to the table, you can always skip ahead to Chapter 2 and come back later.

What is HTML5?

What we understand today as HTML5 has had a relatively turbulent history. You probably already know that HTML is the predominant markup language used to describe content, or data, on the World Wide Web. HTML5 is the latest iteration of that markup language, and includes new features, improvements to existing features, and scripting-based APIs.

That said, HTML5 is not a reformulation of previous versions of the language—it includes all valid elements from both HTML4 and XHTML 1.0. Furthermore, it's been designed with some primary principles in mind to ensure it works on just

about every platform, is compatible with older browsers, and handles errors gracefully. A summary of the design principles that guided the creation of HTML5 can be found on the W3C's HTML Design Principles page[1].

First and foremost, HTML5 includes redefinitions of existing markup elements, and new elements that allow web designers to be more expressive in the semantics of their markup. Why litter your page with `div`s when you can have `article`s, `section`s, `header`s, `footer`s, and more?

The term "HTML5" has additionally been used to refer to a number of other new technologies and APIs. Some of these include drawing with the `<canvas>` element, offline storage, the new `<video>` and `<audio>` elements, drag-and-drop functionality, Microdata, embedded fonts, and others. In this book, we'll be covering a number of those technologies, and more.

What's an API?

API stands for Application Programming Interface. Think of an API the same way you think of a graphical user interface—except that instead of being an interface for humans, it's an interface for your code. An API provides your code with a set of "buttons" (predefined methods) that it can press to elicit the desired behavior from the system, software library, or browser.

API-based commands are a way of abstracting the more complex stuff that's done in the background (or sometimes by third-party software). Some of the HTML5-related APIs will be introduced and discussed in later sections of this book.

Overall, you shouldn't be intimidated if you've had little experience with JavaScript or any scripting-related APIs. While it would certainly be beneficial to have some experience with JavaScript, it isn't mandatory.

Whatever the case, we'll walk you through the scripting parts of our book gradually, to ensure you're not left scratching your head!

It should also be noted that some of the technologies that were once part of HTML5 have been separated from the specification, so technically, they no longer fall under the "HTML5" umbrella. Certain other technologies were *never* part of HTML5, yet have at times been lumped in under the same label. This has instigated the use of

---

[1] http://www.w3.org/TR/html-design-principles/

broad, all-encompassing expressions such as "HTML5 and related technologies." Bruce Lawson even half-jokingly proposed the term "NEWT" (New Exciting Web Technologies)[2] as an alternative.

However, in the interest of brevity—and also at the risk of inciting heated arguments—we'll generally refer to these technologies collectively as "HTML5."

How did we get here?

The web design industry has evolved in a relatively short time period. Twelve years ago, a website that included images and an eye-catching design was considered "top of the line" in terms of web content.

Now, the landscape is quite different. Simple, performance-driven, Ajax-based web apps that rely on client-side scripting for critical functionality are becoming more and more common. Websites today often resemble standalone software applications, and an increasing number of developers are viewing them as such.

Along the way, web markup evolved. HTML4 eventually gave way to XHTML, which is really just HTML 4 with strict XML-style syntax. Currently, both HTML 4 and XHTML are in general use, but HTML5 is gaining headway.

HTML5 originally began as two different specifications: Web Forms 2.0 and Web Apps 1.0. Both were a result of the changed web landscape, and the need for faster, more efficient, maintainable web applications. Forms and app-like functionality are at the heart of web apps, so this was the natural direction for the HTML5 spec to take. Eventually, the two specs were merged to form what we now call HTML5.

During the time that HTML5 was in development, so was XHTML 2.0. That project has since been abandoned to allow focus on HTML5.

Would the real HTML5 spec please stand up?

Because the HTML5 specification is being developed by two different bodies (the WHATWG and the W3C), there are two different versions of the spec. The W3C (or World Wide Web Consortium) you're probably familiar with: it's the organization that maintains the original HTML and CSS specifications, as well as a host of other

---

[2] http://www.brucelawson.co.uk/2010/meet-newt-new-exciting-web-technologies/

web-related standards, such as SVG (scalable vector graphics) and WCAG (web content accessibility guidelines.)

The WHATWG (aka the Web Hypertext Application Technology Working Group), on the other hand, might be new to you. It was formed by a group of people from Apple, Mozilla, and Opera after a 2004 W3C meeting left them disheartened. They felt that the W3C was ignoring the needs of browser makers and users by focusing on XHTML 2.0, instead of working on a backwards-compatible HTML standard. So they went off on their own and developed the Web Apps and Web Forms specifications discussed above, which were then merged into a spec they called HTML5. On seeing this, the W3C eventually gave in and created its own HTML5 specification based on the WHATWG's spec.

This can seem a little confusing. Yes, there are some politics behind the scenes that we, as designers and developers, have no control over. But should it worry us that there are two versions of the spec? In short, no.

The WHATWG's version of the specification can be found at http://www.whatwg.org/html/, and has recently been renamed "HTML" (dropping the "5"). It's now called a "living standard," meaning that it will be in constant development and will no longer be referred to using incrementing version numbers.[3]

The WHATWG version contains information covering HTML-only features, including what's new in HTML5. Additionally, there are separate specifications being developed by the WHATWG that cover the related technologies. These specifications include Microdata, Canvas 2D Context, Web Workers, Web Storage, and others.[4]

The W3C's version of the spec can be found at http://dev.w3.org/html5/spec/, and the separate specifications for the other technologies can be accessed through http://dev.w3.org/html5/.

So what's the difference between the W3C spec and that of WHATWG? Briefly, the WHATWG version is a little more informal and experimental (and, some might argue, more forward-thinking). But overall, they're very similar, so either one can be used as a basis for studying new HTML5 elements and related technologies.

---

[3] See http://blog.whatwg.org/html-is-the-new-html5/ for an explanation of this change.

[4] For details, see http://wiki.whatwg.org/wiki/FAQ#What_are_the_various_versions_of_the_spec.3F.

Why should I care about HTML5?

As mentioned, at the core of HTML5 are a number of new semantic elements, as well as several related technologies and APIs. These additions and changes to the language have been introduced with the goal of web pages being easier to code, use, and access.

These new semantic elements, along with other standards like WAI-ARIA and Microdata (which we cover in Appendix B and Appendix C respectively), help make our documents more accessible to both humans and machines—resulting in benefits for both accessibility and search engine optimization.

The semantic elements, in particular, have been designed with the dynamic web in mind, with a particular focus on making pages more modular and portable. We'll go into more detail on this in later chapters.

Finally, the APIs associated with HTML5 help improve on a number of techniques that web developers have been using for years. Many common tasks are now simplified, putting more power in developers' hands. Furthermore, the introduction of HTML5-based audio and video means there will be less dependence on third-party software and plugins when publishing rich media content on the Web.

Overall, there is good reason to start looking into HTML5's new features and APIs, and we'll discuss more of those reasons as we go through this book.

What is CSS3?

Another separate—but no less important—part of creating web pages is Cascading Style Sheets (CSS). As you probably know, CSS is a style language that describes how HTML markup is presented or styled. CSS3 is the latest version of the CSS specification. The term "CSS3" is not just a reference to the new features in CSS, but the third level in the progress of the CSS specification.[5]

CSS3 contains just about everything that's included in CSS2.1 (the previous version of the spec). It also adds new features to help developers solve a number of problems without the need for non-semantic markup, complex scripting, or extra images.

---

[5] http://www.w3.org/Style/CSS/current-work.en.html

New features in CSS3 include support for additional selectors, drop shadows, rounded corners, multiple backgrounds, animation, transparency, and much more.

CSS3 is distinct from HTML5. In this publication, we'll be using the term CSS3 to refer to the third level of the CSS specification, with a particular focus on what's new in CSS3. Thus, CSS3 is separate from HTML5 and its related APIs.

Why should I care about CSS3?

Later in this book, we'll look in greater detail at what's new in CSS3. In the mean-time, we'll give you a taste of why CSS3's new techniques are so exciting to web designers.

Some design techniques find their way into almost every project. Drop shadows, gradients, and rounded corners are three good examples. We see them everywhere. When used appropriately, and in harmony with a site's overall theme and purpose, these enhancements can make a design flourish.

Perhaps you're thinking: we've been creating these design elements using CSS for years now. But have we?

In the past, in order to create gradients, shadows, and rounded corners, web designers have had to resort to a number of tricky techniques. Sometimes extra HTML elements were required. In cases where the HTML is kept fairly clean, scripting hacks were required. In the case of gradients, the use of extra images was inevitable. We put up with these workarounds, because there was no other way of accomplishing those designs.

CSS3 allows you to include these and other design elements in a forward-thinking manner that leads to so many benefits: clean markup that is accessible to humans and machines, maintainable code, fewer extraneous images, and faster loading pages.

A Note on Vendor Prefixes

In order to use many of the new CSS3 features today, you'll be required to include quite a few extra lines of code. This is because browser vendors have implemented many of the new features in CSS3 using their own "prefixed" versions of a property. For example, to transform an element in Firefox, you need to use the `-moz-transform` property; to do the same in WebKit-based browsers such as Safari and Google Chrome, you have to use `-webkit-transform`. In some cases, you'll need up to four lines of code for a single CSS property. This can seem to nullify some of the benefits gained from avoiding hacks, images, and nonsemantic markup.

But browser vendors have implemented features this way for a good reason: the specifications are yet to be final, and early implementations tend to be buggy. So, for the moment, you provide values to current implementations using the vendor prefixes, and *also* provide a perennial version of each property using an unprefixed declaration. As the specs become finalized and the implementations refined, browser prefixes will eventually be dropped.

Even though it may seem like a lot of work to maintain code with all these prefixes, the benefits of using CSS3 today still outweigh the drawbacks. Despite having to change a number of prefixed properties just to alter one design element, maintaining a CSS3-based design is still easier than, say, making changes to background images through a graphics program, or dealing with the drawbacks of extra markup and hacky scripts. And, as we have mentioned, your code is much less likely to become outdated or obsolete.

What do we mean by the "real world"?

In the real world, we don't create a website and then move on to the next project while leaving previous work behind. We create web applications and we update them, fine-tune them, test them for potential performance problems, and continually tweak their design, layout, and content.

In other words, in the real world, we don't write code that we have no intention of revisiting. We write code using the most reliable, maintainable, and effective methods available, with every intention of returning to work on that code again to make any necessary improvements or alterations. This is evident not only in websites and web apps that we build and maintain on our own, but also in those we create and maintain for our clients.

We need to continually search out new and better ways to write our code. HTML5 and CSS3 are a big step in that direction.

The Varied Browser Market

Although HTML5 is still in development, and does present significant changes in the way content is marked up, it's worth noting that those changes won't cause older browsers to choke, or result in layout problems or page errors.

What this means is that you could take any of your current projects containing valid HTML4 or XHTML markup, change the doctype to HTML5 (which we'll cover in Chapter 2), and the page will still validate and appear the same as it did before. The changes and additions in HTML5 have been implemented into the language in such a way so as to ensure backwards compatibility with older browsers—even IE6!

But that's just the markup. What about all the other features of HTML5, CSS3, and related technologies? According to one set of statistics,[6] about 47% of users are on a version of Internet Explorer that has no support for most of these new features.

As a result, developers have come up with various solutions to provide the equivalent experience to those users, all while embracing the exciting new possibilities offered by HTML5 and CSS3. Sometimes this is as simple as providing fallback content, like a Flash video player to browsers without native video support. At other times, though, it's been necessary to use scripting to mimic support for new features. These "gap-filling" techniques are referred to as **polyfills**. Relying on scripts to emulate native features isn't always the best approach when building high-performance web apps, but it's a necessary growing pain as we evolve to include new enhancements and features, such as the ones we'll be discussing in this book.

So, while we'll be recommending fallback options and polyfills to plug the gaps in browser incompatibilities, we'll also try to do our best in warning you of potential drawbacks and pitfalls associated with using these options.

Of course, it's worth noting that sometimes no fallbacks or polyfills are required at all: for example, when using CSS3 to create rounded corners on boxes in your design, there's often no harm in users of older browsers seeing square boxes instead. The

---

[6] http://gs.statcounter.com/#browser_version-ww-monthly-201011-201101-bar

functionality of the site isn't degraded, and those users will be none the wiser about what they're missing.

With all this talk of limited browser support, you might be feeling discouraged. Don't be! The good news is that more than 40% of worldwide users are on a browser that *does* offer support for a lot of the new stuff we'll discuss in this book. And this support is growing all the time, with new browser versions (such as Internet Explorer 9) continuing to add support for many of these new features and technologies.

As we progress through the lessons, we'll be sure to inform you where support is lacking, so you'll know how much of what you create will be visible to your audience in all its HTML5 and CSS3 glory. We'll also discuss ways you can ensure that nonsupporting browsers have an acceptable experience, even without all the bells and whistles that come with HTML5 and CSS3.

The Growing Mobile Market

Another compelling reason to start learning and using HTML5 and CSS3 today is the exploding mobile market.

According to StatCounter, in 2009, just over 1% of all web usage was mobile.[7] In less than two years, that number has quadrupled to over 4%.[8] Some reports have those numbers even higher, depending on the kind of analysis being done. Whatever the case, it's clear that the mobile market is growing at an amazing rate.

4% of total usage may seem small, and in all fairness, it is. But it's the growth rate that makes that number so significant—400% in two years! So what does this mean for those learning HTML5 and CSS3?

HTML5, CSS3, and related cutting-edge technologies are very well supported in many mobile web browsers. For example, mobile Safari on iOS devices like the iPhone and iPad, Opera Mini and Opera Mobile, as well as the Android operating system's web browser all provide strong levels of HTML5 and CSS3 support. New features and technologies supported by some of those browsers include CSS3 colors and opacity, the Canvas API, Web Storage, SVG, CSS3 rounded corners, Offline Web Apps, and more.

---

[7] http://gs.statcounter.com/#mobile_vs_desktop-ww-monthly-200901-200912-bar

[8] http://gs.statcounter.com/#mobile_vs_desktop-ww-monthly-201011-201101-bar

In fact, some of the new technologies we'll be introducing in this book have been specifically designed with mobile devices in mind. Technologies like Offline Web Apps and Web Storage have been designed, in part, because of the growing number of people accessing web pages with mobile devices. Such devices can often have limitations with online data usage, and thus benefit greatly from the ability to access web applications offline.

We'll be touching on those subjects in Chapter 10, as well as others throughout the course of the book that will provide the tools you need to create web pages for a variety of devices and platforms.

On to the Real Stuff

It's unrealistic to push ahead into new technologies and expect to author pages and apps for only one level of browser. In the real world, and in a world where we desire HTML5 and CSS3 to make further inroads, we need to be prepared to develop pages that work across a varied landscape. That landscape includes modern browsers, older versions of Internet Explorer, and an exploding market of mobile devices.

Yes, in some ways, supplying a different set of instructions for different user agents resembles the early days of the Web with its messy browser sniffing and code forking. But this time around, the new code is future-proof, so that when the older browsers fall out of general use, all you need to do is remove the fallbacks and polyfills, leaving only the code base that's aimed at modern browsers.

HTML5 and CSS3 are the leading technologies ushering in a much more exciting world of web page authoring. Because all modern browsers (including IE9) provide significant levels of support for a number of HTML5 and CSS3 features, creating powerful, easy-to-maintain, future-proof web pages is more accessible to web developers than ever before.

As the market share of older browsers declines, the skills you gain today in understanding HTML5 and CSS3 will become that much more valuable. By learning these technologies today, you're preparing for a bright future in web design. So, enough about the "why," let's start digging into the "how"!

Markup, HTML5 Style

Now that we've given you a bit of a history primer, along with some compelling reasons to learn HTML5 and start using it in your projects today, it's time to introduce you to the sample site that we'll be progressively building in this book.

After we briefly cover what we'll be building, we'll discuss some HTML5 syntax basics, along with some suggestions for best practice coding. We'll follow that with some important info on cross-browser compatibility, and the basics of page structure in HTML5. Lastly, we'll introduce some specific HTML5 elements and see how they'll fit into our layout.

So let's get into it!

Introducing *The HTML5 Herald*

For the purpose of this book, we've put together a sample website project that we'll be building from scratch.

The website is already built—check it out now at http://thehtml5herald.com/. It's an old-time newspaper-style website called *The HTML5 Herald*. The home page of

the site contains some media in the form of video, images, articles, and advertisements. There's also another page comprising a registration form.

Go ahead and view the source, and try some of the functionality if you like. As we proceed through the book, we'll be working through the code that went into making the site. We'll avoid discussing every detail of the CSS involved, as most of it should already be familiar to you: float layouts, absolute and relative positioning, basic font styling, and the like. We'll primarily focus on the new HTML5 elements, along with the APIs, plus all the new CSS3 techniques being used to add styles and interactivity to the various elements.

Figure 2.1 shows a bit of what the finished product looks like.

Figure 2.1. The front page of *The HTML5 Herald*

While we build the site, we'll do our best to explain the new HTML5 elements, APIs, and CSS3 features, and we'll try to recommend some best practices. Of course, many of these technologies are still new and in development, so we'll try not to be too dogmatic about what you can and can't do.

A Basic HTML5 Template

As you learn HTML5 and add new techniques to your toolbox, you're likely going to want to build yourself a blueprint, or boilerplate, from which you can begin all your HTML5-based projects. In fact, you've probably already done something similar for your existing XHTML or HTML 4.0 projects. We encourage this, and you may also consider using one of the many online sources that provide a basic HTML5 starting point for you.[1]

In this project, however, we want to build our code from scratch and explain each piece as we go along. Of course, it would be impossible for even the most fantastical and unwieldy sample site we could dream up to include *every* new element or technique, so we'll also explain some new features that don't fit into the project. This way, you'll be familiar with a wide set of options when deciding how to build your HTML5 and CSS3 websites and web apps, so you'll be able to use this book as a quick reference for a number of techniques.

Let's start simple, with a bare-bones HTML5 page:

index.html *(excerpt)*

```
<!doctype html>
<html lang="en">
<head>
  <meta charset="utf-8">

  <title>The HTML5 Herald</title>
  <meta name="description" content="The HTML5 Herald">
  <meta name="author" content="SitePoint">

  <link rel="stylesheet" href="css/styles.css?v=1.0">

  <!--[if lt IE 9]>
  <script src="http://html5shiv.googlecode.com/svn/trunk/html5.js">
➥</script>
  <![endif]-->
</head>
<body>
```

---

[1] A few you might want to look into can be found at http://www.html5boilerplate.com/ and http://html5reset.org/.

```
    <script src="js/scripts.js"></script>
</body>
</html>
```

Look closely at the above markup. If you're making the transition to HTML5 from XHTML or HTML 4, then you'll immediately notice quite a few areas in which HTML5 differs.

The Doctype

First, we have the Document Type Declaration, or **doctype**. This is simply a way to tell the browser—or any other parsers—what type of document they're looking at. In the case of HTML files, it means the specific version and flavor of HTML. The doctype should always be the first item at the top of all your HTML files. In the past, the doctype declaration was an ugly and hard-to-remember mess. For XHTML 1.0 Strict:

```
<!DOCTYPE html PUBLIC "-//W3C//DTD XHTML 1.0 Strict//EN"
   "http://www.w3.org/TR/xhtml1/DTD/xhtml1-strict.dtd">
```

And for HTML4 Transitional:

```
<!DOCTYPE HTML PUBLIC "-//W3C//DTD HTML 4.01 Transitional//EN"
   "http://www.w3.org/TR/html4/loose.dtd">
```

Over the years, code editing software began to provide HTML templates with the doctype already included, or else they offered a way to automatically insert one. And naturally, a quick web search will easily bring up the code to insert whatever doctype you require.

Although having that long string of text at the top of our documents hasn't really hurt us (other than forcing our sites' viewers to download a few extra bytes), HTML5 has done away with that indecipherable eyesore. Now all you need is this:

```
<!doctype html>
```

Simple, and to the point. You'll notice that the "5" is conspicuously missing from the declaration. Although the current iteration of web markup is known as "HTML5," it really is just an evolution of previous HTML standards—and future specifications

will simply be a development of what we have today. Because browsers have to support all existing content on the Web, there's no reliance on the doctype to tell them which features should be supported in a given document.

The `html` Element

Next up in any HTML document is the `html` element, which has not changed significantly with HTML5. In our example, we've included the `lang` attribute with a value of `en`, which specifies that the document is in English. In XHTML-based syntax, you'd be required to include an `xmlns` attribute. In HTML5, this is no longer needed, and even the `lang` attribute is unnecessary for the document to validate or function correctly.

So here's what we have so far, including the closing `</html>` tag:

```
<!doctype html>
<html lang="en">

</html>
```

The `head` Element

The next part of our page is the `<head>` section. The first line inside the `head` is the one that defines the character encoding for the document. This is another element that's been simplified. Here's how you used to do this:

```
<meta http-equiv="Content-Type" content="text/html; charset=utf-8">
```

HTML5 improves on this by reducing the character encoding `<meta>` tag to the bare minimum:

```
<meta charset="utf-8">
```

In nearly all cases, `utf-8` is the value you'll be using in your documents. A full explanation of character encoding is beyond the scope of this chapter, and it probably won't be that interesting to you, either. Nonetheless, if you want to delve a little deeper, you can read up on the topic on the W3C's site.[2]

---

[2] http://www.w3.org/TR/html-markup/syntax.html#character-encoding

Get In Early

To ensure that all browsers read the character encoding correctly, the entire character encoding declaration must be included somewhere within the first 512 characters of your document. It should also appear before any content-based elements (like the `<title>` element that follows it in our example site).

There's much more we could write about this subject, but we want to keep you awake—so we'll spare you those details! For now, we're content to accept this simplified declaration and move on to the next part of our document:

```html
<title>The HTML5 Herald</title>
<meta name="description" content="The HTML5 Herald">
<meta name="author" content="SitePoint">

<link rel="stylesheet" href="css/styles.css?v=1.0">
```

In these lines, HTML5 barely differs from previous syntaxes. The page title is declared the same as it always was, and the `<meta>` tags we've included are merely optional examples to indicate where these would be placed; you could put as many `meta` elements here as you like.

The key part of this chunk of markup is the stylesheet, which is included using the customary `link` element. At first glance, you probably didn't notice anything different. But customarily, `link` elements would include a `type` attribute with a value of `text/css`. Interestingly, this was never required in XHTML or HTML 4—even when using the Strict doctypes. HTML5-based syntax encourages you to drop the `type` attribute completely, since all browsers recognize the content type of linked stylesheets without requiring the extra attribute.

Leveling the Playing Field

The next element in our markup requires a bit of background information before it can be introduced.

HTML5 includes a number of new elements, such as `article` and `section`, which we'll be covering later on. You might think this would be a major problem for older browsers, but you'd be wrong. This is because the majority of browsers don't actually care what tags you use. If you had an HTML document with a `<recipe>` tag (or even

a `<ziggy>` tag) in it, and your CSS attached some styles to that element, nearly every browser would proceed as if this were totally normal, applying your styling without complaint.

Of course, this hypothetical document would fail to validate, but it *would* render correctly in *almost* all browsers—the exception being Internet Explorer. Prior to version 9, IE prevented unrecognized elements from receiving styling. These mystery elements were seen by the rendering engine as "unknown elements," so you were unable to change the way they looked or behaved. This includes not only our imagined elements, but also any elements which had yet to be defined at the time those browser versions were developed. That means (you guessed it) the new HTML5 elements.

At the time of writing, Internet Explorer 9 has only just been released (and adoption will be slow), so this is a bit of a problem. We want to start using the shiny new tags, but if we're unable to attach any CSS rules to them, our designs will fall apart.

Fortunately, there's a solution: a very simple piece of JavaScript, originally developed by John Resig, can magically make the new HTML5 elements visible to older versions of IE.

We've included this so-called "HTML5 shiv"[3] in our markup as a `<script>` tag surrounded by **conditional comments**. Conditional comments are a proprietary feature implemented by Microsoft in Internet Explorer. They provide you with the ability to target specific versions of that browser with scripts or styles.[4] This conditional comment is telling the browser that the enclosed markup should only appear to users viewing the page with Internet Explorer prior to version 9:

```
<!--[if lt IE 9]>
<script src="http://html5shiv.googlecode.com/svn/trunk/html5.js">
➥</script>
<![endif]-->
```

It should be noted that if you're using a JavaScript library that deals with HTML5 features or the new APIs, it's possible that it will already have the HTML5 enabling

---

[3] You might be more familiar with its alternative name: the HTML5 shim. Whilst there are identical code snippets out there that go by both names, we'll be referring to all instances as the HTML5 shiv, its original name.

[4] For more information see http://reference.sitepoint.com/css/conditionalcomments

script present; in this case, you could remove reference to Remy Sharp's script. One example of this would be Modernizr,[5] a JavaScript library that detects modern HTML and CSS features—and which we cover in Appendix A. Modernizr includes code that enables the HTML5 elements in older versions of IE, so Remy's script would be redundant.

What about users on IE 6-8 who have JavaScript disabled?

Of course, there's still a group of users who won't benefit from Remy's HTML5 shiv: those who have, for one reason or another, disabled JavaScript. As web designers, we're constantly told that the content of our sites should be fully accessible to all users, even those without JavaScript. When between 40% and 75% of your audience uses Internet Explorer, this can seem like a serious concern.

But it's not as bad as it seems. A number of studies have shown that the number of users that have JavaScript disabled is low enough to be of little concern.

In one study[6] conducted on the Yahoo network, published in October 2010, users with JavaScript disabled amounted to around 1% of total traffic worldwide. Another study[7] indicated a similar number across a billion visitors. In both studies, the US had the highest number of visitors with JavaScript disabled in comparison to other parts of the world.

There *are* ways to use HTML5's new elements without requiring JavaScript for the elements to appear styled in nonsupporting browsers. Unfortunately, those methods are rather impractical and have other drawbacks.

If you're still concerned about these users, it might be worth considering a hybrid approach; for example, use the new HTML5 elements where the lack of styles won't be overly problematic, while relying on traditional elements like `div`s for key layout containers.

The Rest is History

Looking at the rest of our starting template, we have the usual body element along with its closing tag and the closing `</html>` tag. We also have a reference to a JavaScript file inside a `script` element.

---

[5] http://www.modernizr.com/

[6] http://developer.yahoo.com/blogs/ydn/posts/2010/10/how-many-users-have-javascript-disabled/

[7] http://visualrevenue.com/blog/2007/08/eu-and-us-javascript-disabled-index.html

Much like the `link` element discussed earlier, the `<script>` tag does not require that you declare a `type` attribute. In XHTML, to validate a page that contains external scripts, your `<script>` tag should look like this:

```
<script src="js/scripts.js" type="text/javascript"></script>
```

Since JavaScript is, for all practical purposes, the only real scripting language used on the Web, and since all browsers will assume that you're using JavaScript even when you don't explicitly declare that fact, the `type` attribute is unnecessary in HTML5 documents:

```
<script src="js/scripts.js"></script>
```

We've put the `script` element at the bottom of our page to conform to best practices for embedding JavaScript. This has to do with the page loading speed; when a browser encounters a script, it will pause downloading and rendering the rest of the page while it parses the script. This results in the page appearing to load much more slowly when large scripts are included at the top of the page before any content. This is why most scripts should be placed at the very bottom of the page, so that they'll only be parsed after the rest of the page has loaded.

In some cases (like the HTML5 shiv) the script may *need* to be placed in the `head` of your document, because you want it to take effect before the browser starts rendering the page.

HTML5 FAQ

After this quick introduction to HTML5 markup, you probably have a bunch of questions swirling inside your head. Here are some answers to a few of the likely ones.

Why do these changes still work in older browsers?

This is what a lot of developers seem to have trouble accepting. To understand why this isn't a problem, we can compare HTML5 to some of the new features added in CSS3, which we'll be discussing in later chapters.

In CSS, when a new feature is added (for example, the `border-radius` property that adds rounded corners to elements), it also has to be added to browsers' rendering

engines, so older browsers won't recognize it. So if a user is viewing the page on a browser with no support for border-radius, the rounded corners will appear square. Other CSS3 features behave similarly, causing the experience to be degraded to some degree.

Many developers expect that HTML5 will work in a similar way. While this might be true for some of the advanced features and APIs we'll be considering later in the book, it's not the case with the changes we've covered so far; that is, the simpler syntax, the reduced redundancies, and the new doctype.

HTML5's syntax was defined after a careful study of what older browsers can and can't handle. For example, the 15 characters that comprise the doctype declaration in HTML5 are the minimum characters required to get every browser to display a page in standards mode.

Likewise, while XHTML required a lengthier character-encoding declaration and an extra attribute on the html element for the purpose of validation, browsers never required them in order to display a page correctly. Again, the behavior of older browsers was carefully examined, and it was determined that the character encoding could be simplified and the xmlns attribute be removed—and browsers would still see the page the same way.

The simplified script and link elements also fall into this category of "simplifying without breaking older pages." The same goes for the Boolean attributes we saw above; browsers have always ignored the values of attributes like checked and disabled, so why insist on providing them?

Thus, as mentioned in Chapter 1, you shouldn't be afraid to use HTML5 today. The language was designed with backwards compatibility in mind, with the goal of trying to support as much existing content as possible.

Unlike changes to CSS3 and JavaScript, where additions are only supported when browser makers actually implement them, there's no need to wait for new browser versions to be released before using HTML5's syntax. And when it comes to using the new semantic elements, a small snippet of JavaScript is all that's required to bring older browsers into line.

What is standards mode?

When standards-based web design was in its infancy, browser makers were faced with a problem: supporting emerging standards would, in many cases, break backwards compatibility with existing web pages that were designed to older, nonstandard browser implementations. Browser makers needed a signal indicating that a given page was meant to be rendered according to the standards. They found such a signal in the doctype: new, standards-compliant pages included a correctly formatted doctype, while older, nonstandard pages generally didn't.

Using the doctype as a signal, browsers could switch between **standards mode** (in which they try to follow standards to the letter in the way they render elements) and **quirks mode** (where they attempt to mimic the "quirky" rendering capabilities of older browsers to ensure that the page renders how it was intended).

It's safe to say that in the current development landscape, nearly every web page has a proper doctype, and thus will render in standards mode; it's therefore unlikely that you'll ever have to deal with a page being rendered in quirks mode. Of course, if a user is viewing a web page using a very old browser (like IE4), the page will be rendered using that browser's rendering mode. This is what quirks mode mimics, and it will do so regardless of the doctype being used.

Although the XHTML and older HTML doctypes include information about the exact version of the specification they refer to, browsers have never actually made use of that information. As long as a seemingly correct doctype is present, they'll render the page in standards mode. Consequently, HTML5's doctype has been stripped down to the bare minimum required to trigger standards mode in any browser.

Further information, along with a chart that outlines what will cause different browsers to render in quirks mode, can be found on Wikipedia.[8] You can also read a good overview of standards and quirks mode on SitePoint's CSS reference.[9]

Shouldn't all tags be closed?

In XHTML-based syntax, all elements need to be closed—either with a corresponding closing tag (like `</html>`) or in the case of **void** elements, a forward slash at the end

---

[8] http://en.wikipedia.org/wiki/Quirks_mode/
[9] http://reference.sitepoint.com/css/doctypesniffing/

of the tag. The latter are elements that *can't* contain child elements (such as `input`, `img`, or `link`).

You can still use that style of syntax in HTML5—and you might prefer it for consistency and maintainability reasons—but it's no longer required to add a trailing slash to void elements for validation. Continuing with the theme of "cutting the fat," HTML5 allows you to omit the trailing slash from such elements, arguably leaving your markup cleaner and less cluttered.

It's worth noting that in HTML5, most elements that *can* contain nested elements —but simply happen to be empty—still need to be paired with a corresponding closing tag. There are exceptions to this rule, but it's simpler to assume that it's universal.

What about other XHTML-based syntax customs?

While we're on the subject, omitting closing slashes is just one aspect of HTML5-based syntax that differs from XHTML. In fact, syntax style issues are completely ignored by the HTML5 validator, which will only throw errors for code mistakes that threaten to disrupt your document in some way.

What this means is that through the eyes of the validator, the following five lines of markup are identical:

```
<link rel="stylesheet" href="css/styles.css" />
<link rel="stylesheet" href="css/styles.css">
<LINK REL="stylesheet" HREF="css/styles.css">
<Link Rel="stylesheet" Href="css/styles.css">
<link rel=stylesheet href=css/styles.css>
```

In HTML5, you can use lowercase, uppercase, or mixed-case tag names or attributes, as well as quoted or unquoted attribute values (as long as those values don't contain spaces or other reserved characters)—and it will all validate just fine.

In XHTML, all attributes have to have values, even if those values are redundant. For example, you'd often see markup like this:

```
<input type="text" disabled="disabled" />
```

In HTML5, attributes that are either "on" or "off" (called **Boolean attributes**) can simply be specified with no value. So, the above input element could now be written as follows:

```
<input type="text" disabled>
```

Hence, HTML5 has much looser requirements for validation, at least as far as syntax is concerned. Does this mean you should just go nuts and use whatever syntax you want on any given element? No, we certainly don't recommend that.

We encourage developers to choose a syntax style and stick to it—especially if you are working in a team, where code maintenance and readability are crucial. We also recommend (though this is certainly not required) that you choose a minimalist coding style while staying consistent.

Here are some guidelines that you can consider using:

- Use lowercase for all elements and attributes, as you would in XHTML.

- Despite some elements not requiring closing tags, we recommend that all elements that contain content be closed (as in `<p>Text</p>`).

- Although you can leave attribute values unquoted, it's highly likely that you'll have attributes that require quotes (for example, when declaring multiple classes separated by spaces, or when appending a query string value to a URL). As a result, we suggest that you always use quotes for the sake of consistency.

- Omit the trailing slash from elements that have no content (like `meta` or `input`).

- Avoid providing redundant values for Boolean attributes (for instance, use `<input type="checkbox" checked>` rather than `<input type="checkbox" checked="checked">`).

Again, the recommendations above are by no means universally accepted. But we believe they're reasonable syntax suggestions for achieving clean, easy-to-read maintainable markup.

If you run amok with your code style, including too much that's unnecessary, you run the risk of negating the strides taken by the creators of HTML5 in trying to simplify the language.

Defining the Page's Structure

Now that we've broken down the basics of our template, let's start adding some meat to the bones, and give our page some basic structure.

Later in the book, we're going to specifically deal with adding CSS3 features and other HTML5 goodness; for now, we'll consider what elements we want to use in building our site's overall layout. We'll be covering a lot in this section, and throughout the coming chapters, about **semantics**. When we use this term, we're referring to the way a given HTML element describes the meaning of its content. Because HTML5 includes a wider array of semantic elements, you might find yourself spending a bit more time thinking about your content's structure and meaning than you've done in the past with HTML 4 or XHTML. That's great! Understanding what your content *means* is what writing good markup is all about.

If you look back at the screenshot of *The HTML5 Herald* (or view the site online), you'll see that it's divided up as follows:

- header section with a logo and title
- navigation bar
- body content divided into three columns
- articles and ad blocks within the columns
- footer containing some author and copyright information

Before we decide which elements are appropriate for these different parts of our page, let's consider some of our options. First of all, we'll introduce you to some of the new HTML5 semantic elements that could be used to help divide our page up and add more meaning to our document's structure.

The header Element

Naturally, the first element we'll look at is the header element. The WHATWG spec describes it succinctly as "a group of introductory or navigational aids."[10] Essentially, this means that whatever content you were accustomed to including inside of <div id="header">, you would now include in the header.

---

[10] http://www.whatwg.org/specs/web-apps/current-work/multipage/sections.html#the-header-element

But there's a catch that differentiates `header` from the customary `div` element that's often used for a site's header: there's no restriction to using it just once per page. Instead, you can include a new `header` element to introduce each section of your content. When we use the word "section" here, we're not limiting ourselves to the actual `section` element described below; technically, we're referring to what HTML5 calls "sectioning content." This will be covered in greater detail in the next chapter; for now, you can safely understand it to mean any chunk of content that might need its own header.

A `header` element can be used to include introductory content or navigational aids that are specific to any single section of a page, or that apply to the entire page—or both.

While a `header` element will frequently be placed at the top of a page or section, its definition is independent from its position. Your site's layout might call for the title of an article or blog post to be off to the left, right, or even below the content; regardless, you can still use `header` to describe this content.

The `section` Element

The next element you should become familiar with is HTML5's `section` element. The WHATWG spec defines `section` as follows:[11]

> The `section` element represents a generic section of a document or application. A section, in this context, is a thematic grouping of content, typically with a heading.

It further explains that a `section` shouldn't be used as a generic container that exists for styling or scripting purposes only. If you're unable to use `section` as a generic container—for example, in order to achieve your desired CSS layout—then what *should* you use? Our old friend, the `div`—which is semantically meaningless.

Going back to the definition from the spec, the `section` element's content should be "thematic," so it would be incorrect to use it in a generic way to wrap unrelated pieces of content.

---

[11] http://www.whatwg.org/specs/web-apps/current-work/multipage/sections.html#the-section-element

Some examples of acceptable uses for `section` elements include:

- individual sections of a tabbed interface

- segments of an "About" page; for example, a company's "About" page might include sections on the company's history, its mission statement, and its team

- different parts of a lengthy "terms of service" page

- various sections of an online news site; for example, articles could be grouped into `sections` covering sports, world affairs, and economic news

 Semantics!

Every time new semantic markup is made available to web designers, there will be debate over what constitutes correct use of these elements, what the spec's intention was, and so on. You may remember discussions about the appropriate use of the `dl` element in previous HTML specifications. Unsurprisingly, therefore, HTML5 has not been immune to this phenomenon—particularly when it comes to the `section` element.

Even Bruce Lawson, a well-respected authority on HTML5, has admitted to using `section` incorrectly in the past. For a bit of clarity, Bruce's post[12] explaining his error is well worth the read. In short:

- `section` is *generic*, so if a more specific semantic element is appropriate (like `article`, `aside`, or `nav`), use that instead.

- `section` *has semantic meaning*; it implies that the content it contains is related in some way. If you're unable to succinctly describe all the content you're trying to put in a `section` using just a few words, it's likely you need a semantically neutral container instead: the humble `div`.

That said, as is always the case with semantics, it's open to interpretation in some instances. If you feel you can make a case for why you're using a given element rather than another, go for it. In the unlikely event that anyone ever calls you on it, the resulting discussion can be both entertaining and enriching for everyone involved, and might even contribute to the wider community's understanding of the specification.

---

[12] http://html5doctor.com/the-section-element/

Keep in mind, also, that you're permitted to nest `section` elements inside existing `section` elements, if it's appropriate. For example, for an online news website, the world news `section` might be further subdivided into a `section` for each major global region.

The `article` Element

The `article` element is similar to the `section` element, but there are some notable differences. Here's the definition according to WHATWG:[13]

> The article element represents a self-contained composition in a document, page, application, or site and that is, in principle, independently distributable or reusable, e.g. in syndication.

The key terms in that definition are *self-contained composition* and *independently distributable*. Whereas a `section` can contain any content that can be grouped thematically, an `article` must be a single piece of content that can stand on its own. This distinction can be hard to wrap your head around—so when in doubt, try the test of syndication: if a piece of content can be republished on another site without being modified, or pushed out as an update via RSS, or on social media sites like Twitter or Facebook, it has the makings of an `article`.

Ultimately, it's up to you to decide what constitutes an `article`, but here are some suggestions:

- forum posts
- magazine or newspaper articles
- blog entries
- user-submitted comments

Finally, just like `section` elements, `article` elements can be nested inside other `article` elements. You can also nest a `section` inside an `article`, and vice versa.

The `nav` Element

It's safe to assume that this element will appear in virtually every project. `nav` represents exactly what it implies: a group of navigation links. Although the most common use for `nav` will be for wrapping an unordered list of links, there are other

---

[13] http://www.whatwg.org/specs/web-apps/current-work/multipage/sections.html#the-article-element

options. You could also wrap the nav element around a paragraph of text that contained the major navigation links for a page or section of a page.

In either case, the nav element should be reserved for navigation that is of primary importance. So, it's recommended that you avoid using nav for a brief list of links in a footer, for example.

nav and Accessibility

A design pattern you may have seen implemented on many sites is the "skip navigation" link. The idea is to allow users of screen readers to quickly skip past your site's main navigation if they've already heard it—after all, there's no point listening to a large site's entire navigation menu every time you click through to a new page!

The nav element has the potential to eliminate this need; if a screen reader sees a nav element, it could allow its users to skip over the navigation without requiring an additional link. The specification states:

> User agents (such as screen readers) that are targeted at users who can benefit from navigation information being omitted in the initial rendering, or who can benefit from navigation information being immediately available, can use this element as a way to determine what content on the page to initially skip and/or provide on request.

Current screen readers fail to recognize nav, but this doesn't mean you shouldn't use it. Assistive technology will continue to evolve, and it's likely your page will be on the Web well into the future. By building to the standards now, you ensure that as screen readers improve, your page will become more accessible over time.

What's a user agent?

You'll encounter the term **user agent** a lot when browsing through specifications. Really, it's just a fancy term for a browser—a software "agent" that a user employs to access the content of a page. The reason the specs don't simply say "browser" is that user agents can include screen readers, or any other technological means to read a web page.

You can use nav more than once on a given page. If you have a primary navigation bar for the site, this would call for a nav element.

Additionally, if you had a secondary set of links pointing to different parts of the current page (using in-page anchors), this too could be wrapped in a nav element.

As with section, there's been some debate over what constitutes acceptable use of nav and why it isn't recommended in some circumstances (such as inside a footer). Some developers believe this element is appropriate for pagination or breadcrumb links, or for a search form that constitutes a primary means of navigating a site (as is the case on Google).

This decision will ultimately be up to you, the developer. Ian Hickson, the primary editor of WHATWG's HTML5 specification, responded to the question directly: "use [it] whenever you would have used class=nav".[14]

The aside Element

This element represents a part of the page that's "tangentially related to the content around the aside element, and which could be considered separate from that content."[15]

The aside element could be used to wrap a portion of content that is tangential to:

- a specific standalone piece of content (such as an article or section)

- an entire page or document, as is customarily done when adding a "sidebar" to a page or website

The aside element should never be used to wrap sections of the page that are part of the primary content; in other words, it's not meant to be parenthetical. The aside content could stand on its own, but it should still be part of a larger whole.

Some possible uses for aside include a sidebar, a secondary lists of links, or a block of advertising. It should also be noted that the aside element (as in the case of header) is not defined by its position on the page. It could be on the "side," or it could be elsewhere. It's the content itself, and its relation to other elements, that defines it.

---

[14] See http://html5doctor.com/nav-element/#comment-213

[15] http://dcv.w3.org/html5/opoo/Ovorviow.html#the-aside-element

The `footer` Element

The final element we'll discuss in this chapter is the `footer` element. As with `header`, you can have multiple `footers` on a single page, and you should use `footer` to wrap the section of your page that you would normally wrap inside of `<div id="footer">`.

A `footer` element, according to the spec, represents a footer for the section of content that is its nearest ancestor. The "section" of content could be the entire document, or it could be a `section`, `article`, or `aside` element.

Often a footer will contain copyright information, lists of related links, author information, and similar content that you normally think of as coming at the end of a block of content. However, much like `aside` and `header`, a `footer` element is not defined in terms of its position on the page; hence, it does not have to appear at the end of a section, or at the bottom of a page. Most likely it will, but this is not required. For example, information about the author of a blog post might be displayed above the post instead of below it, and still be considered `footer` information.

How did HTML5's creators decide which new elements to include?

You might wonder how the creators of the language came up with new semantic elements. After all, you could feasibly have dozens more semantic elements—why not have a `comment` element for user-submitted comments, or an `ad` element specifically for advertisements?

The creators of HTML5 ran tests to search through millions of web pages to see what kinds of elements were most commonly being used. The elements were decided based on the `id` and `class` attributes of the elements being examined. The results helped guide the introduction of a number of new HTML semantic elements.

Thus, instead of introducing new techniques that might be rejected or go unused, the editors of HTML5 are endeavoring to include elements that work in harmony with what web page authors are already doing. In other words, if it's common for most web pages to include a `div` element with an `id` of `header`, it makes sense to include a new element called `header`.

Structuring *The HTML5 Herald*

Now that we've covered the basics of page structure and the elements in HTML5 that will assist in this area, it's time to start building the parts of our page that will hold the content.

Let's start from the top, with a `header` element. It makes sense to include the logo and title of the paper in here, as well as the tagline. We can also add a `nav` element for the site navigation.

After the `header`, the main content of our site is divided into three columns. While you might be tempted to use `section` elements for these, stop and think about the content. If each column contained a separate "section" of information (like a sports section and an entertainment section), that would make sense. As it is, though, the separation into columns is really only a visual arrangement—so we'll use a plain old `div` for each column.

Inside those `div`s, we have newspaper articles; these, of course, are perfect candidates for the `article` element.

The column on the far right, though, contains three ads in addition to an article. We'll use an `aside` element to wrap the ads, with each ad placed inside an `article` element. This may seem odd, but look back at the description of `article`: "a self-contained composition [...] that is, in principle, independently distributable or re-usable." An ad fits the bill almost perfectly, as it's usually intended to be reproduced across a number of websites without modification.

Next up, we'll add another `article` element for the final article that appears below the ads. That final article will *not* be included in the `aside` element that holds the three ads. To belong in the `aside`, the `article` would need to be tangentially related to the page's content. This isn't the case: the `article` is part of the page's main content, so it would be wrong to include it in the `aside`.

Now the third column consists of two elements: an `aside` and an `article`, stacked one on top of the other. To help hold them together and make them easier to style, we'll wrap them in a `div`. We're not using a `section`, or any other semantic markup, because that would imply that the `article` and the `aside` were somehow topically related. They're not—it's just a feature of our design that they happen to be in the same column together.

We'll also have the entire upper section below the header wrapped in a generic `div` for styling purposes.

Finally, we have a `footer` in its traditional location, at the bottom of the page. Because it contains a few different chunks of content, each of which forms a self-contained and topically related unit, we've split them out into `section` elements. The author information will form one `section`, with each author sitting in their own nested `section`. Then there's another `section` for the copyright and additional information.

Let's add the new elements to our page, so that we can see where our document stands:

```
index.html (excerpt)

<body>

<header>
  <nav></nav>
</header>

<div id="main">
  <div id="primary">
    <article></article>
      ⋮
  </div>
  <div id="secondary">
    <article></article>
      ⋮
  </div>
  <div id="tertiary">
    <aside>
      <article></article>
        ⋮
    </aside>
    <article></article>
  </div>
</div><!-- #main -->

<footer>
  <section id="authors">
    <section></section>
  </section>
```

```
    <section id="copyright"></section>
</footer>

<script src="js/scripts.js"></script>
</body>
```

Figure 2.2 shows a screenshot that displays our page with some labels indicating the major structural elements we've used.

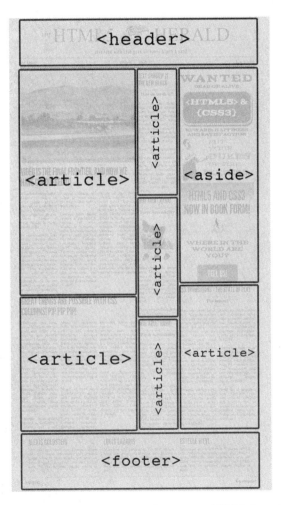

Figure 2.2. *The HTML5 Herald*, broken into structural HTML5 elements

We now have a structure that can serve as a solid basis for the content.

Wrapping Things Up

That's it for this chapter. We've learned some of the basics of content structure in HTML5, and we've started to build our sample project using the knowledge we've gained.

In the next chapter, we'll have a more in-depth look at how HTML5 deals with different types of content. Then, we'll continue to add semantics to our page when we deal with more new HTML elements.

More HTML5 Semantics

Our sample site is coming along nicely. We've given it some basic structure, along the way learning more about marking up content using HTML5's new elements.

In this chapter, we'll discuss even more new elements, along with some changes and improvements to familiar elements. We'll also add some headings and basic text to our project, and we'll discuss the potential impact of HTML5 on SEO and accessibility.

Before we dive into that, though, let's take a step back and examine a few new—and a little tricky—concepts that HTML5 brings to the table.

A New Perspective on Types of Content

For layout and styling purposes, developers have become accustomed to thinking of elements in an HTML page as belonging to one of two categories: block and inline. Although elements are still rendered as either block or inline by browsers, the HTML5 spec takes the categorization of content a step further. The specification now defines a set of more granular **content models**. These are broad definitions about the kind of content that should be found inside a given element. Most of the

time they'll have little impact on the way you write your markup, but it's worth having a passing familiarity with them, so let's have a quick look.

Metadata content

This category is what it sounds like: data that's not present on the page itself, but affects the page's presentation or includes other information *about* the page. This includes elements like `title`, `link`, `meta`, and `style`.

Flow content

Flow content includes just about every element that's used in the body of an HTML document, including elements like `header`, `footer`, and even `p`. The only elements *excluded* are those that have no effect on the document's flow: `script`, `link`, and `meta` elements in the page's head, for example.

Sectioning content

This is the most interesting—and for our purposes, most relevant—type of content in HTML5. In the last chapter, we often found ourselves using the generic term "section" to refer to a block of content that could contain a heading, footer, or aside. In fact, what we were actually referring to was **sectioning content**. In HTML5, this includes `article`, `aside`, `nav`, and `section`. We'll talk about sectioning content and how it can affect the way you write your markup in more detail very shortly.

Heading content

This type of content defines the header of a given section, and includes the various levels of heading (`h1`, `h2`, and so on), as well as the new `hgroup` element, which we'll cover a bit later.

Phrasing content

This category is roughly the equivalent to what you're used to thinking of as *inline* content, it includes elements like `em`, `strong`, `cite`, and the like.

Embedded content

This one's fairly straightforward, and includes elements that are, well, *embedded* into a page, such as `img`, `object`, `embed`, `video`, `canvas`, and others.

Interactive content

This category includes any content with which users can interact. It consists mainly of form elements, as well as links and other elements that are interactive only when certain attributes are present.

As you might gather from reading the list above, some elements can belong to more than one category. There are also some elements that fail to fit into *any* category. Don't worry if this seems confusing: just remember that these distinctions exist—that should be more than enough.

The Document Outline

In previous versions of HTML, you could draw up an outline of any given document by looking at the various levels of headings (h1 through to h6) contained in the page. Each time a new level of heading was added, you'd go one step deeper into the hierarchy of your outline. For example, take this markup:

```
<h1>Title</h1>
    ⋮
<h2>Subtitle</h2>
    ⋮
<h3>Another level</h3>
    ⋮
<h2>Another subtitle</h2>
```

This would produce the document outline shown in Figure 3.1.

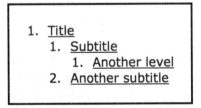

Figure 3.1. A simple document outline

It was preferred that each page have a single h1 element, with other headings following sequentially.

In order to make content easier to syndicate and more portable, the HTML5 specification provides a clear algorithm for constructing the outline of an HTML document. Each element that falls under the category of "sectioning content" creates a new node in the document outline. Heading (h1–h6) elements within a block of sectioning content also create "implied" sections—this is actually what was happening in our simple outline above.

This all sounds more complicated than it is. To start to gain an understanding of it, let's look at how the above example could be rewritten using some additional HTML5 elements:

```
<section>
  <h1>Title</h1>
  ⋮
  <article>
    <h1>Article Title</h1>
    ⋮
    <h2>Article Subtitle</h2>
    ⋮
  </article>
  <article>
    <h1>Another subtitle</h1>
    ⋮
  </article>
</section>
```

This results in exactly the same document outline as above: each piece of sectioning content (the article elements in this example) creates a new branch in the document tree, and so can have its own h1. This way, each section has its own mini document outline.

The advantage of the new outlining algorithm is that it allows us to move an entire section to a completely different document while preserving the same markup. Beforehand, a post's title on that post's page might have been an h1, but the same post's title on the home page or a category page listing might have been an h2 or h3. Now, you can just keep the same markup, as long as the headings are grouped together in a sectioning content element.

Testing Document Outlines

Getting a document's outline right in HTML5 can be tricky at first. If you're having trouble, you can use a handy JavaScript bookmarklet called h5o[1] to show the outline of any document you're viewing with the HTML5 outline algorithm. The resulting display will reveal your document's hierarchy in accordance with the HTML5 standard, so you can make corrections as needed.

To install it in your browser, download the HTML file from the site and open it in your browser; then drag the link to your favorites or bookmarks bar. Now you can use the h5o link to display a document outline for any page you're viewing.

It's important to note that the old way of coding and structuring content, with a single h1 on each page, is still valid HTML5. Your pages will still be valid, even though you'll miss out on the portability and syndication benefits.

Understanding Sectioning Roots

Distinct from—but similar to—sectioning content, HTML5 also defines a type of element called a **sectioning root**. These include blockquote, body, details, fieldset, figure, and td. What makes the sectioning root elements distinct is that, although they may individually have their own outlines, the sectioning content and headings inside these elements do *not* contribute to the overall document outline (with the exception of body, the outline of which *is* the document's outline).

Breaking News

Now that we've got a solid handle on HTML5's content types and document outlines, it's time to dive back into *The HTML5 Herald* and add some headings for our articles.

For brevity, we'll deal with each section individually. Let's add a title and subtitle to our header, just above the navigation:

```
<header>

  <hgroup>
    <h1>The HTML5 Herald</h1>
```

---

[1] http://code.google.com/p/h5o/

```
        <h2>Produced With That Good Ol' Timey HTML5 &amp; CSS3</h2>
    </hgroup>
    <nav>
        ⋮
    </nav>

</header>
```

The hgroup Element

You'll notice we have introduced three elements into our markup: the title of the website, which is marked up with the customary h1 element; a tagline immediately below the primary page title, marked up with an h2; and a new HTML5 element that wraps our title and tagline, the hgroup element.

To understand the purpose of the hgroup element, consider again how a page's outline is built. Let's take our heading markup without the hgroup element:

```
<h1>The HTML5 Herald</h1>
<h2>Produced With That Good Ol' Timey HTML5 &amp; CSS3</h2>
```

This would produce the document outline shown in Figure 3.2.

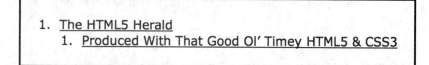

Figure 3.2. A subtitle generates an unwanted node in the document outline

The h2 element creates a new, implicit section: all content that follows is logically grouped under a subsection created by that tagline—and that's not what we want at all. Furthermore, if we have additional headings (for example, for article titles) that use h2, those new headings will be hierarchically on the same level as our tagline; this is also incorrect, as shown in Figure 3.3.

1. The HTML5 Herald
   1. Produced With That Good Ol' Timey HTML5 & CSS3
   2. An Article Title

Figure 3.3. Other headlines in the content wrongly appear grouped with the tagline

Well, we could mark up subsequent headings starting with h3, right? But again, this causes problems in our document's outline. Now, the headings beginning with h3 will become subsidiary to our tagline, as Figure 3.4 shows.

1. The HTML5 Herald
   1. Produced With That Good Ol' Timey HTML5 & CSS3
      1. An Article Title

Figure 3.4. Using further nested heading levels fails to solve the problem

That's also undesirable; we want the new headings to be subsections of our primary heading, the h1 element.

What if, instead, we opted to mark up our tagline using a generic element like a p or span:

```
<h1>HTML5 Herald</h1>
<p id="tagline">Produced With That Good Ol' Timey HTML5 &amp; CSS3
➥</p>
```

While this does avoid cluttering up the document outline with a superfluous branch, it's a little lacking in terms of semantics. You might be thinking that the id attribute helps define the element's meaning by using a value of tagline. But the id attribute cannot be used by the browser to infer meaning for the element in question—it adds nothing to the document's semantics.

This is where the hgroup element comes in. The hgroup element tells the user agent that the headings nested within it form a composite heading (a heading group, as it were), with the h1 being the primary parent element. This prevents our document

outline from becoming jumbled, and it helps us avoid using nonsemantic elements in our page.

So any time you want to include a subheading without affecting the document's outline, just wrap the headings in an `hgroup` element; this will resolve the problem without resorting to undesirable methods. Figure 3.5 shows the outline produced for the header, with the `hgroup` wrapping the two headings.

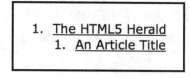

Figure 3.5. hgroup to the rescue

Much better!

More New Elements

In addition to the structural elements we saw in Chapter 2 and the `hgroup` element we've just covered, HTML5 introduces a number of new semantic elements. Let's examine some of the more useful ones.

The `figure` and `figcaption` Elements

The `figure` and `figcaption` elements are another pair of new HTML5 elements that contribute to the improved semantics in HTML5. The `figure` element is explained in the spec as follows:

> The element can [...] be used to annotate illustrations, diagrams, photos, code listings, etc, that are referred to from the main content of the document, but that could, without affecting the flow of the document, be moved away from that primary content, e.g. to the side of the page, to dedicated pages, or to an appendix.

Think of charts, graphs, images to accompany text, or example code. All those types of content might be good places to use `figure` and potentially `figcaption`.

The `figcaption` element is simply a way to mark up a caption for a piece of content that appears inside of a `figure`.

In order to use the `figure` element, the content being placed inside it must have some relation to the main content in which the `figure` appears. If you can completely remove it from a document, and the document's content can still be fully understood, you probably shouldn't be using `figure`; you might, however, need to use `aside` or another alternative. Likewise, if the image or listing forms part of the flow of the document, and the text would need rewording if you moved it, it's probably best to use another option.

Let's look at how we'd mark up a `figure` inside an `article`:

```
<article>
  <hgroup>
    <h1>WAI-ARIA</h1>
    <h2>Web App Accessibility</h2>
  </hgroup>

  <p>Lorem ipsum dolor … </p>

  <p>As you can see in <a href="#fig1">Figure 1</a>,

  <figure id="fig1">
    <figcaption>Screen Reader Support for WAI-ARIA</figcaption>
    <img src="figure1.png" alt="JAWS: Landmarks 1/1, Forms 4/5 … ">
  </figure>

  <p>Lorem ipsum dolor … </p>
</article>
```

The mark Element

The `mark` element "indicates a part of the document that has been highlighted due to its likely relevance to the user's current activity." Admittedly, there are very few uses we can think of for the `mark` element. The most common is in the context of a search, where the keywords that were searched for are highlighted in the results.

Avoid confusing `mark` with `em` or `strong`; those elements add contextual importance, whereas `mark` separates the targeted content based on a user's current browsing or search activity.

For example, if a user has arrived at an article on your site from a Google search for the word "HTML5," you might highlight words in the article using the mark element, like this:

```
<h1>Yes, You Can Use <mark>HTML5</mark> Today!</h1>
```

The mark element can be added to the document either using server-side code, or JavaScript once the page has loaded.

The progress and meter Elements

Two new elements added in HTML5 allow for marking up of data that's being measured or gauged in some way. The difference between them is fairly subtle: progress is used to describe the current status of a changing process that's headed for completion, regardless of whether the completion state is defined. The traditional download progress bar is a perfect example of progress.

The meter element, meanwhile, represents an element whose range is known, meaning it has definite minimum and maximum values. The spec gives the examples of disk usage, or a fraction of a voting population—both of which have a definite maximum value. Therefore, it's likely you wouldn't use meter to indicate an age, height, or weight—all of which normally have unknown maximum values.

Let's first look at progress. The progress element can have a max attribute to indicate the point at which the task will be complete, and a value attribute to indicate the task's status. Both of these attributes are optional. Here's an example:

```
<h1>Your Task is in Progress</h1>
<p>Status: <progress min="0" max="100" value="0"><span>0</span>%
➥</progress></p>
```

This element would best be used (along with some JavaScript) to dynamically change the value of the percentage as the task progresses. You'll notice that the code includes <span> tags, isolating the number value; this facilitates targeting the number directly from your script when you need to update it.

The meter element has six associated attributes. In addition to max and value, it also allows use of min, high, low, and optimum.

The `min` and `max` attributes reference the lower and upper boundaries of the range, while `value` indicates the current specified measurement. The `high` and `low` attributes indicate thresholds for what is considered "high" or "low" in the context. For example, your grade on a test can range from 0% to 100% (`max`), but anything below 60% is considered low and anything above 85% is considered high. `optimum` refers to the ideal value. In the case of a test score, the value of `optimum` would be 100.

Here's an example of `meter`, using the premise of disk usage:

```
<p>Total current disk usage: <meter value="63" min="0" max="320"
➡low="10" high="300" title="gigabytes">63 GB</meter>
```

The `time` Element

Dates and times are invaluable components of web pages. Search engines are able to filter results based on time, and in some cases, a specific search result can receive more or less weight by a search algorithm depending on when it was first published.

The `time` element has been specifically designed to deal with the problem of humans reading dates and times differently from machines. Take the following example:

```
<p>We'll be getting together for our next developer conference on
➡12 October of this year.</p>
```

While humans reading this paragraph will understand when the event will take place, it would be less clear to a machine attempting to parse the information.

Here's the same paragraph with the `time` element introduced:

```
<p>We'll be getting together for our next developer conference on
➡<time datetime="2011-10-12">12 October of this year</time>.</p>
```

The `time` element also allows you to express dates and times in whichever format you like while retaining an unambiguous representation of the date and time behind the scenes, in the `datetime` attribute. This value could then be converted into a localized or preferred form using JavaScript, or by the browser itself, though currently no browsers implement any special handling of the `time` element.

If you want to include a time along with the date, you would do it like this:

```
<time datetime="2011-10-12T16:24:34.014Z">12 October of this year.
➥</time>
```

In the above example, the T character is used to indicate the start of the time. The format is HH:MM:SS with milliseconds after the decimal point. The Z character is optional and indicates that the time zone is Coordinated Universal Time (UTC). To indicate a time zone offset (instead of UTC), you would append it with a plus or minus, like this:

```
<time datetime="2011-10-12T16:24:34.014-04:00">12 October of
this year</time>
```

In addition to the datetime attribute shown in the above examples, the time element allows use of the pubdate attribute. This is a Boolean attribute, and its existence indicates that the content within the closest ancestor article element was published on the specified date. If there's no article element, the pubdate attribute would apply to the entire document.

For example, in the header of *The HTML5 Herald*, the issue's publication date is a perfect candidate for the time element with a pubdate attribute:

index.html *(excerpt)*

```
<p id="issue"><time datetime="1904-06-04" pubdate>June 4, 1904
➥</time></p>
```

Because this element indicates the publication date of our newspaper, we've added the pubdate attribute. Any other dates referred to on the page—in the text of articles, for example—would omit this attribute.

The time element has some associated rules and guidelines:

- You should not use time to encode unspecified dates or times (for example, "during the ice age" or "last winter").

- The date represented cannot be "BC" or "BCE" (before the common era); it must be a date on the Gregorian Calendar.

- The datetime attribute has to be a valid date string.

■ If the `time` element lacks a `datetime` attribute, the element's text content (whatever appears between the opening and closing tags) needs to be a valid date string.

The uses for the `time` element are endless: calendar events, publication dates (for blog posts, videos, press releases, and so forth), historic dates, transaction records, article or content updates, and much more.

Changes to Existing Features

While new elements and APIs have been the primary focus of HTML5, this latest iteration of web markup has also brought with it changes to existing elements. For the most part, any changes that have been made have been done with backwards compatibility in mind, to ensure that the markup of existing content is still usable.

We've already considered some of the changes (the doctype declaration, character encoding, content types, and the document outline, for example). Let's look at other significant changes introduced in the HTML5 spec.

The Word "Deprecated" is Deprecated

In previous versions of HTML and XHTML, elements that were no longer recommended for use (and so removed from the spec), were considered "deprecated." In HTML5, there is no longer any such thing as a deprecated element; the term now used is "obsolete."

This may seem like an insignificant change, but the difference is important: while a deprecated element would be removed from the specification, an obsolete element will remain there. This is so that browser makers still have a standard way of rendering these elements consistently, even if their use is no longer recommended. For example, you can view information in the W3C's specification on frames (an obsolete feature) at http://dev.w3.org/html5/spec/Overview.html#frames.

Block Elements Inside Links

Although most browsers handled this situation just fine in the past, it was never actually valid to place a block-level element inside an `a` element. Instead, to produce valid HTML, you'd have to use multiple `a` elements and style the group to appear as a single block.

In HTML5, you're now permitted to wrap almost anything—other than form elements or other links—in an a element without having to worry about validation errors.

Bold Text

A few changes have been made in the way that bold text is semantically defined in HTML5. There are essentially two ways to make text bold in most browsers: using the b element, or using the strong element.

Although the b element was never deprecated, before HTML5 it was discouraged in favor of strong. The b element previously was a way of saying "make this text appear in boldface." Since HTML markup is supposed to be all about the meaning of the content, leaving the presentation to CSS, this was unsatisfactory.

In HTML5, the b element has been redefined to represent a section of text that is "stylistically offset from the normal prose without conveying any extra importance."

The strong element, meanwhile, still conveys more or less the same meaning. In HTML5, it represents "strong importance for its contents." Interestingly, the HTML5 spec allows for nesting of strong elements. So, if an entire sentence consisted of an important warning, but certain words were of even greater importance, the sentence could be wrapped in one strong element, and each important word could be wrapped in its own nested strong.

Italicized Text

Along with the modifications to the b and strong elements, changes have been made in the way the i element is defined in HTML5.

Previously, the i element was used to simply render italicized text. As with b, this definition was unsatisfactory. In HTML5, the definition has been updated to "a span of text in an alternate voice or mood, or otherwise offset from the normal prose." So the appearance of the text has nothing to do with the semantic meaning, although it may very well still be italic—that's up to you.

An example of content that can be offset using i tags might be an idiomatic phrase from another language, such as *reductio ad absurdum*, a latin phrase meaning "reduction to the point of absurdity." Other examples could be text representing a dream sequence in a piece of fiction, or the scientific name of a species in a journal article.

The em element is unchanged, but its definition has been expanded to clarify its use. It still refers to text that's emphasized, as would be the case colloquially. For example, the following two phrases have the exact same wording, but their meanings change because of the different use of em:

```
<p>Harry's Grill is the best <em>burger</em> joint in town.</p>
<p>Harry's Grill <em>is</em> the best burger joint in town.</p>
```

In the first sentence, because the word "burger" is emphasized, the meaning of the sentence focuses on the type of "joint" being discussed. In the second sentence, the emphasis is on the word "is," thus moving the sentence focus to the question of whether Harry's Grill really is the best of all burger joints in town.

Neither i nor em should be used to mark up a publication title; instead, use cite (see the section called "A cite for Sore Eyes").

Of all the four elements discussed here (b, i, em, and strong), the only one that gives contextual importance to its content is the strong element.

Big and Small Text

The big element was previously used to represent text displayed in a large font. The big element is now obsolete and should not be used. The small element, however, is still valid, but has a different meaning.

Previously, small was intended to describe "text in a small font." In HTML5, it represents "side comments such as small print." Some examples where small might be used include information in footer text, fine print, and terms and conditions. The small element should only be used for short runs of text.

Although the presentational implications of small have been removed from the definition, text inside small tags will more than likely still appear in a smaller font than the rest of the document.

For example, the footer of *The HTML5 Herald* includes a copyright notice. Since this is essentially legal fine print, it's perfect for the small element:

```
<small>&copy; SitePoint Pty. Ltd.</small>
```

A `cite` for Sore Eyes

The `cite` element is another one that's been redefined in HTML5, accompanied by a fair bit of controversy. In HTML4, the `cite` element represented "a citation or a reference to other sources." Within the scope of that definition, the spec permitted a person's name to be marked up with `cite` (in the case of a quotation attributed to an individual, for example).

HTML5 expressly forbids the use of `cite` for a person's name, seemingly going against the principle of backwards compatibility. Now the spec describes `cite` as "the title of a work," and gives a whole slew of examples, including a book, a song, a TV show, and a theatre production.

Some notable web standards advocates (including Jeremy Keith and Bruce Lawson) have opposed this new definition forbidding people's names within `cite`. For more information on the ongoing debate, see the page on this topic on the WHATWG Wiki.[2]

Description (not Definition) Lists

The existing `dl` (definition list) element, along with its associated `dt` (term) and `dd` (description) children, has been redefined in the HTML5 spec. Previously, in addition to terms and definitions, the spec allowed the `dl` element to mark up dialogue, but the spec now prohibits this.

In HTML5, these lists are no longer called "definition lists"; they're now the more generic-sounding "description lists." They should be used to mark up any kind of name-value pairs, including terms and definitions, metadata topics and values, and questions and answers.

Other New Elements and Features

We've introduced you to and expounded upon some of the more practical new elements and features. Now, in this section, we'll touch on lesser-known elements, attributes, and features that have been added to the HTML5 spec.

---

[2] http://wiki.whatwg.org/wiki/Cite_element

The `details` Element

This new element helps mark up a section of the document that's hidden, but can be expanded to reveal additional information. The aim of the element is to provide native support for a feature common on the Web—a collapsible box that has a title, and more info or functionality hidden away.

Normally this kind of widget is created using a combination of markup and scripting. The inclusion of it in HTML5 intends to remove the scripting requirements and simplify its implementation for web authors.

Here's how it might look:

```
<details>
  <summary>Some Magazines of Note</summary>
  <ul>
    <li><cite>Bird Watchers Digest</cite></li>
    <li><cite>Rowers Weekly</cite></li>
    <li><cite>Fishing Monthly</cite></li>
  </ul>
</details>
```

The example above would cause the contents of the `summary` element to appear to the user, with the rest of the content hidden. Upon clicking `summary`, the hidden content appears.

If `details` lacks a defined `summary`, the user agent will define a default summary (for example, "Details"). If you want the hidden content to be visible by default, you can use the Boolean `open` attribute.

The `summary` element can only be used as a child of `details`, and it must be the first child, if used.

So far, `details` has little to no support in browsers. A couple of JavaScript-based polyfills are available, including one by Mathias Bynens.[3]

---

[3] http://mathiasbynens.be/notes/html5-details-jquery

Customized Ordered Lists

Ordered lists, using the `ol` element, are quite common in web pages. HTML5 introduces a new Boolean attribute called `reversed` that, when present, reverses the order of the list items.

While we're on the topic of ordered lists, HTML5 has brought back the `start` attribute, deprecated in HTML4. The `start` attribute lets you specify with which number your list should begin.

Support is good for `start`, but `reversed` has yet to be implemented in most browsers.

Scoped Styles

The `style` element, used for embedding styles directly in your pages, now allows use of a Boolean attribute called `scoped`. Take the following code example:

```
<h1>Page Title</h1>
<article>
  <style scoped>
    h1 { color: blue; }
  </style>
  <h1>Article Title</h1>
  <p>Article content.</p>
</article>
```

Because the `scoped` attribute is present, the styles declared inside the `style` element will only apply to the parent element and its children (if cascading rules permit), instead of the entire document. This allows specific sections inside documents (like the `article` in the above example) to be easily portable along with their associated styles.

This is certainly a handy new feature, but as of this writing, no browser supports the `scoped` attribute. As a temporary solution, a jQuery-based polyfill is available at https://github.com/thingsinjars/jQuery-Scoped-CSS-plugin.

The `async` Attribute for Scripts

The `script` element now allows the use of the `async` attribute, which is similar to the existing `defer` attribute. Using `defer` specifies that the browser should wait until the page's markup is parsed before loading the script. The new `async` attribute

allows you to specify that a script should load asynchronously (meaning it should load as soon as it's available), without causing other elements on the page to delay while it loads. Both `defer` and `async` are Boolean attributes.

These attributes must only be used when the `script` element defines an external file. For legacy browsers, you can include both `async` and `defer` to ensure that one or the other is used, if necessary. In practice, both attributes will have the effect of not pausing the browser's rendering of the page while scripts are downloaded; however, `async` can often be more advantageous, as it will load the script "in the background" while other rendering tasks are taking place, and execute the script as soon as it's available.

The `async` attribute is particularly useful if the script you're loading has no other dependencies, and it would benefit the user experience if the script is loaded as soon as possible, rather than after the page loads.

Validating HTML5 Documents

In chapter two, we introduced you to a number of syntax changes in HTML5, and touched on some issues related to validation. Let's expand upon those concepts a little more so that you can better understand how validating pages has changed.

The HTML5 validator is no longer concerned with code style. You can use uppercase, lowercase, omit quotes from attributes, leave tags open, and be as inconsistent as you like, and your page will often still be valid.

So, you ask, what *does* count as an error for the HTML5 validator? It will alert you to incorrect use of elements, elements included where they shouldn't be, missing required attributes, incorrect attribute values, and the like. In short, the validator will let you know if your markup conflicts with the specification, so it's still an extremely valuable tool when developing your pages.

However, since many of us are accustomed to the stricter validation rules imposed on XHTML documents, let's go through some specifics. This way, you can understand what is considered valid in HTML5 that was invalid when checking XHTML-based pages:

- Some elements that were required in XHTML-based syntax are no longer required for a document to pass HTML5 validation; examples include the html and body elements.

- Void elements, or elements that stand alone and don't contain any content, are not required to be closed using a closing slash; examples include <meta> and <br>.

- Elements and attributes can be in uppercase, lowercase, or mixed case.

- Quotes are unnecessary around attribute values, unless multiple space-delimited values are used, or a URL appears as a value and contains a query string with an equals (=) character in it.

- Some attributes that were required in XHTML-based syntax are no longer required in HTML5; examples include the type attribute for the script element, and the xmlns attribute for the html element.

- Some elements that were deprecated and thus invalid in XHTML are now valid; one example is the embed element.

- Stray text that doesn't appear inside any element would invalidate an XHTML document; this is not the case in HTML5.

- Some elements that needed to be closed in XHTML can be left open without causing validation errors in HTML5; examples include p, li, and dt.

- The form element isn't required to have an action attribute.

- Form elements, such as input , can be placed as direct children of the form element; in XHTML, another element (such as fieldset or div) was required to wrap form elements.

- The textarea element is not required to have rows and cols attributes.

- The target attribute, deprecated and thus invalid in XHTML, is now valid in HTML5.

- Block elements can be placed inside a elements.

- The ampersand character (&) doesn't need to be encoded as & if it appears as text on the page.

That's a fairly comprehensive, though hardly exhaustive, list of differences between XHTML and HTML5 validation. Some are style choices, so you're encouraged to choose a style and be consistent. We outlined some preferred style choices in the previous chapter, and you're welcome to incorporate some if not all of those suggestions in your own HTML5 projects.

Lint Tools

If you want to validate your markup's syntax style using stricter guidelines, you can use an HTML5 **lint tool**, such as http://lint.brihten.com/html/. At the time of writing, it's still in development, but it works well. You can use it to check that your attributes and tags are lowercase, that void tags are self-closed, that Boolean attributes omit their value, that closing tags are never omitted—or any combination of these style rules. It can even ensure that your markup is indented consistently!

Summary

By now, we've gotten our heads around just about all the new semantic and syntactic changes in HTML5. Some of this information may be a little hard to digest straight away, but don't worry! The best way to become familiar with HTML5 is to use it—you can start with your next project. Try using some of the structural elements we covered in the last chapter, or some of the text-level semantics we saw in this chapter. If you're unsure about how exactly an element is meant to be used, go back and read the section about it, or better yet, read the specification itself. While the language is certainly drier than the text in this book (at least, we hope it is!), the specifications can give you a more complete picture of how a given element is intended to be used. Remember that the HTML5 specification is still in development, so some of what we've covered is still subject to change. The specifications will always contain the most up-to-date information.

In the next chapter, we'll look at a crucial segment of new functionality introduced in HTML5: forms and form-related features.

HTML5 Forms

We've coded most of the page, and you now know most of what there is to know about new HTML5 elements and their semantics. But before we start work on the *look* of the site—which we do in Chapter 6—we'll take a quick detour away from *The HTML5 Herald*'s front page to have a look at the sign-up page. This will illustrate what HTML5 has to offer in terms of web forms.

HTML5 web forms have introduced new form elements, input types, attributes, and other features. Many of these features we've been using in our interfaces for years: form validation, combo boxes, placeholder text, and the like. The difference is that where before we had to resort to JavaScript to create these behaviors, they're now available directly in the browser; all you need to do is set an attribute in your markup to make them available.

HTML5 not only makes marking up forms easier on the developer, it's also better for the user. With client-side validation being handled natively by the browser, there will be greater consistency across different sites, and many pages will load faster without all that redundant JavaScript.

Let's dive in!

Dependable Tools in Our Toolbox

Forms are often the last thing developers include in their pages—many developers find forms just plain boring. The good news is that HTML5 injects a little bit more joy into coding forms. By the end of this chapter, we hope you'll look forward to employing form elements, as appropriate, in your markup.

Let's start off our sign-up form with plain, old-fashioned HTML:

register.html *(excerpt)*

```
<form id="register" method="post">
  <hgroup>
    <h1>Sign Me Up!</h1>
    <h2>I would like to receive your fine publication.</h2>
  </hgroup>

  <ul>
    <li>
      <label for="register-name">My name is:</label>
      <input type="text" id="register-name" name="name">
    </li>
    <li>
      <label for="address">My email address is:</label>
      <input type="text" id="address" name="address">
    </li>
    <li>
      <label for="url">My website is located at:</label>
      <input type="text" id="url" name="url">
    </li>
    <li>
      <label for="password">I would like my password to be:</label>
      <p>(at least 6 characters, no spaces)</p>
      <input type="password" id="password" name="password">
    </li>
    <li>
      <label for="rating">On a scale of 1 to 10, my knowledge of
➥HTML5 is:</label>
      <input type="text" name="rating" id=rating">
    </li>
    <li>
      <label for="startdate">Please start my subscription on:
➥</label>
      <input type="text" id="startdate" name="startdate">
```

```
    </li>
    <li>
      <label for="quantity">I would like to receive <input
➡type="text" name="quantity" id="quantity"> copies of <cite>
➡The HTML5 Herald</cite>.</label>
    </li>
    <li>
      <label for="upsell">Also sign me up for <cite>The CSS3
➡Chronicle</cite></label>
      <input type="checkbox" id="upsell" name="upsell">
    </li>
    <li>
      <input type="submit" id="register-submit" value="Send Post
➡Haste">
    </li>
  </ul>
</form>
```

This sample registration form uses form elements that have been available since the earliest versions of HTML. This form provides clues to users about what type of data is expected in each field via the label and p elements, so even your users on Netscape 4.7 and IE5 (kidding!) can understand the form. It works, but it can certainly be improved upon.

In this chapter we're going to enhance this form to include HTML5's features. HTML5 provides new input types specific to email addresses, URLs, numbers, dates, and more. In addition to those new input types, HTML5 also introduces attributes that can be used with both new and existent input types. These allow you to provide placeholder text, mark fields as required, and declare what type of data is acceptable—all without JavaScript.

We'll cover all the newly added input types later in the chapter. Before we do that, let's take a look at the new form attributes HTML5 provides.

HTML5 Form Attributes

For years, developers have written (or copied and pasted) snippets of JavaScript to validate the information users entered into form fields: what elements are required, what type of data is accepted, and so on. HTML5 provides us with several attributes that allow us to dictate what is an acceptable value, and inform the user of errors, all without the use of any JavaScript.

Browsers that support these HTML5 attributes will compare data entered by the user against regular expression patterns provided by the developer (you). Then they check to see if all required fields are indeed filled out, enable multiple values if allowed, and so on. Even better, including these attributes won't harm older browsers; they'll simply ignore the attributes they don't understand. In fact, you can use these attributes and their values to power your scripting fallbacks, instead of hardcoding validation patterns into your JavaScript code, or adding superfluous classes to your markup. We'll look at how this is done a bit later; for now, let's go through each of the new attributes.

The `required` Attribute

The Boolean `required` attribute tells the browser to only submit the form if the field in question is filled out correctly. Obviously, this means that the field can't be left empty, but it also means that, depending on other attributes or the field's type, only certain types of values will be accepted. Later in the chapter, we'll be covering different ways of letting browsers know what kind of data is expected in a form.

If a required field is empty or invalid, the form will fail to submit, and focus will move to the first invalid form element. Opera, Firefox, and Chrome provide the user with error messages; for example, "Please fill out this field" or "You have to specify a value" if left empty, and "Please enter an email address" or "xyz is not in the format this page requires" when the data type or pattern is wrong.

 Out of focus?

Time for a quick refresher: a form element is **focused** either when a user clicks on the field with their mouse, or tabs to it with their keyboard. For `input` elements, typing with the keyboard will enter data into that element.

In JavaScript terminology, the `focus` event will fire on a form element when it receives focus, and the `blur` event will fire when it *loses* focus.

In CSS, the `:focus` pseudo-class can be used to style elements that currently have focus.

The `required` attribute can be set on any input type except `button`, `range`, `color`, and `hidden`, all of which generally have a default value. As with other Boolean at-

tributes we've seen so far, the syntax is either simply `required`, or `required="re-quired"` if you're using XHTML syntax.

Let's add the `required` attribute to our sign-up form. We'll make the name, email address, password, and subscription start date fields required:

```
                                                register.html (excerpt)
<ul>
  <li>
    <label for="register-name">My name is:</label>
    <input type="text" id="register-name" name="name"
➥required aria-required="true">
  </li>
  <li>
    <label for="email">My email address is:</label>
    <input type="text" id="email" name="email"
➥required aria-required="true">
  </li>
  <li>
    <label for="url">My website is located at:</label>
    <input type="text" id="url" name="url">
  </li>
  <li>
    <label for="password">I would like my password to be:</label>
    <p>(at least 6 characters, no spaces)</p>
    <input type="password" id="password" name="password"
➥required aria-required="true">
  </li>
  <li>
    <label for="rating">On a scale of 1 to 10, my knowledge of
➥HTML5 is:</label>
    <input type="text" name="rating" type="range">
  </li>
  <li>
    <label for="startdate">Please start my subscription on:
➥</label>
    <input type="text" id="startdate" name="startdate"
➥required aria-required="true">
  </li>
  <li>
    <label for="quantity">I would like to receive <input
➥type="text" name="quantity" id="quantity"> copies of <cite>
➥The HTML5 Herald</cite></label>
  </li>
```

```
<li>
  <label for="upsell">Also sign me up for <cite>The CSS3
➥Chronicle</cite></label>
  <input type="checkbox" id="upsell" name="upsell">
</li>
<li>
  <input type="submit" id="register-submit" value="Send Post
➥Haste">
</li>
</ul>
```

For improved accessibility, whenever the `required` attribute is included, add the ARIA attribute `aria-required="true"`. Many screen readers lack support for the new HTML5 attributes, but many *do* have support for WAI-ARIA roles, so there's a chance that adding this role could let a user know that the field is required—see Appendix B for a brief introduction to WAI-ARIA.

Figure 4.1, Figure 4.2, and Figure 4.3 show the behavior of the required attribute when you attempt to submit the form.

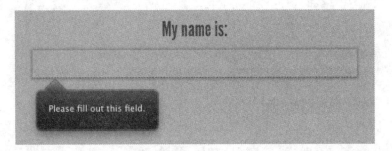

Figure 4.1. The required field validation message in Firefox 4

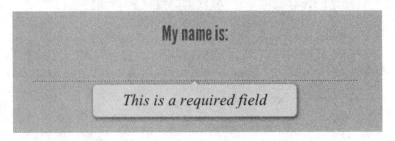

Figure 4.2. How it looks in Opera ...

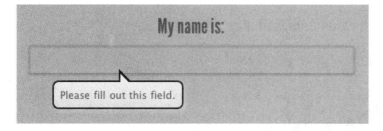

Figure 4.3. ... and in Google Chrome

Styling Required Form Fields

You can style required form elements with the :required pseudo-class. You can also style valid or invalid fields with the :valid and :invalid pseudo-classes. With these pseudo-classes and a little CSS magic, you can provide visual cues to sighted users indicating which fields are required, and also give feedback for successful data entry:

```
input:required {
  background-image: url('../images/required.png');
}
input:focus:invalid {
  background-image: url('../images/invalid.png');
}
input:focus:valid {
  background-image: url('../images/valid.png');
}
```

We're adding a background image (an asterisk) to required form fields. We've also added separate background images to valid and invalid fields. The change is only apparent when the form element has focus, to keep the form from looking too cluttered.

Beware Default Styles

Note that Firefox 4 applies its own styles to invalid elements (a red shadow), as shown in Figure 4.1 earlier. You may want to remove the native drop shadow with the following CSS:

```
:invalid { box-shadow: none; }
```

> ### 💡 Backwards Compatibility
>
> Older browsers mightn't support the `:required` pseudo-class, but you can still provide targeted styles using the attribute selector:
>
> ```css
> input:required,
> input[required] {
>    background-image: url('../images/required.png');
> }
> ```
>
> You can also use this attribute as a hook for form validation in browsers without support for HTML5. Your JavaScript code can check for the presence of the `required` attribute on empty elements, and fail to submit the form if any are found.

The `placeholder` Attribute

The `placeholder` attribute allows a short hint to be displayed inside the form element, space permitting, telling the user what data should be entered in that field. The placeholder text disappears when the field gains focus, and reappears on blur if no data was entered. Developers have provided this functionality with JavaScript for years, but in HTML5 the placeholder attribute allows it to happen natively, with no JavaScript required.

For *The HTML5 Herald*'s sign-up form, we'll put a placeholder on the website URL and start date fields:

register.html (excerpt)

```html
<li>
  <label for="url">My website is located at:</label>
  <input type="text" id="url" name="url"
➥placeholder="http://example.com">
</li>
⋮
<li>
  <label for="startdate">Please start my subscription on:</label>
  <input type="text" id="startdate" name="startdate" required
➥aria-required="true" placeholder="1911-03-17">
</li>
```

Because support for the `placeholder` attribute is still restricted to the latest crop of browsers, you shouldn't rely on it as the only way to inform users of requirements. If your hint exceeds the size of the field, describe the requirements in the input's `title` attribute or in text next to the `input` element.

Currently, Safari, Chrome, Opera, and Firefox 4 support the `placeholder` attribute.

Polyfilling Support with JavaScript

Like everything else in this chapter, it won't hurt nonsupporting browsers to include the `placeholder` attribute.

As with the `required` attribute, you can make use of the `placeholder` attribute and its value to make older browsers behave as if they supported it—all by using a little JavaScript magic.

Here's how you'd go about it: first, use JavaScript to determine which browsers lack support. Then, in those browsers, use a function that creates a "faux" placeholder. The function needs to determine which form fields contain the `placeholder` attribute, then temporarily grab that attribute's content and put it in the `value` attribute.

Then you need to set up two event handlers: one to clear the field's value on focus, and another to replace the placeholder value on blur if the form control's value is still `null` or an empty string. If you do use this trick, make sure that the value of your `placeholder` attribute isn't one that users might actually enter, and remember to clear the faux placeholder when the form is submitted. Otherwise, you'll have lots of "(XXX) XXX-XXXX" submissions!

Let's look at a sample JavaScript snippet (using the jQuery JavaScript library for brevity) to progressively enhance our form elements using the `placeholder` attribute.

jQuery

In the code examples that follow, and throughout the rest of the book, we'll be using the jQuery[1] JavaScript library. While all the effects we'll be adding could be accomplished with plain JavaScript, we find that jQuery code is generally more readable; thus, it helps to illustrate what we want to focus on—the HTML5 APIs—rather than spending time explaining a lot of hairy JavaScript.

[1] http://jquery.com/

Here's our placeholder polyfill:

register.html *(excerpt)*

```
<script>
if(!Modernizr.input.placeholder) {

  $("input[placeholder], textarea[placeholder]").each(function() {
    if($(this).val()==""){
      $(this).val($(this).attr("placeholder"));
      $(this).focus(function(){
        if($(this).val()==$(this).attr("placeholder")) {
          $(this).val("");
          $(this).removeClass('placeholder');
        }
      });
      $(this).blur(function(){
        if($(this).val()==""){
          $(this).val($(this).attr("placeholder"));
          $(this).addClass('placeholder');
        }
      });
    }
  });

  $('form').submit(function(){
    // first do all the checking for required
    // element and form validation.
    // Only remove placeholders before final submission
    var placeheld = $(this).find('[placeholder]');
    for(var i=0; i<placeheld.length; i++){
      if($(placeheld[i]).val() ==
➥$(placeheld[i]).attr('placeholder')) {
        // if not required, set value to empty before submitting
        $(placeheld[i]).attr('value','');
      }
    }
  });
}
</script>
```

The first point to note about this script is that we're using the Modernizr[2] JavaScript library to detect support for the `placeholder` attribute. There's more information

[2] http://www.modernizr.com/

about Modernizr in Appendix A, but for now it's enough to understand that it provides you with a whole raft of `true` or `false` properties for the presence of given HTML5 and CSS3 features in the browser. In this case, the property we're using is fairly self-explanatory. `Modernizr.input.placeholder` will be `true` if the browser supports `placeholder`, and `false` if it doesn't.

If we've determined that placeholder support is absent, we grab all the `input` and `textarea` elements on the page with a `placeholder` attribute. For each of them, we check that the value isn't empty, then replace that value with the value of the `placeholder` attribute. In the process, we add the `placeholder` class to the element, so you can lighten the color of the font in your CSS, or otherwise make it look more like a native placeholder. When the user focuses on the input with the faux placeholder, the script clears the value and removes the `class`. When the user removes focus, the script checks to see if there is a value. If not, we add the placeholder text and `class` back in.

This is a great example of an HTML5 polyfill: we use JavaScript to provide support *only for those browsers that lack native support*, and we do it by *leveraging the HTML5 elements and attributes already in place*, rather than resorting to additional classes or hardcoded values in our JavaScript.

The `pattern` Attribute

The `pattern` attribute enables you to provide a regular expression that the user's input must match in order to be considered valid. For any `input` where the user can enter free-form text, you can limit what syntax is acceptable with the `pattern` attribute.

The regular expression language used in patterns is the same Perl-based regular expression syntax as JavaScript, except that the `pattern` attribute must match the entire value, not just a subset. When including a `pattern`, you should always indicate to users what is the expected (and required) pattern. Since browsers currently show the value of the `title` attribute on hover like a tooltip, include pattern instructions that are more detailed than placeholder text, and which form a coherent statement.

The Skinny on Regular Expressions

Regular expressions are a feature of most programming languages that allow developers to specify patterns of characters and check to see if a given string matches the pattern. Regular expressions are famously indecipherable to the uninitiated. For instance, one possible regular expression to check if a string is formatted as an email address looks like this: [A-Z0-9._%+-]+@[A-Z0-9.-]+\.[A-Z]{2,4}.

A full tutorial on the syntax of regular expressions is beyond the scope of this book, but there are plenty of great resources and tutorials available online if you'd like to learn. Alternately, you can search the Web or ask around on forums for a pattern that will serve your purposes.

For a simple example, let's add a `pattern` attribute to the password field in our form. We want to enforce the requirement that the password be at least six characters long, with no spaces:

register.html *(excerpt)*

```
<li>
  <label for="password">I would like my password to be:</label>
  <p>(at least 6 characters, no spaces)</p>
  <input type="password" id="password" name="password" required
➥pattern="\S{6,}">
</li>
```

\S refers to "any nonwhitespace character," and {6,} means "at least six times." If you wanted to stipulate the maximum amount of characters, the syntax would be, for example, \S{6,10} for between six and ten characters.

As with the `required` attribute, the `pattern` attribute will prevent the form being submitted if the pattern isn't matched, and will provide an error message.

If your pattern is not a valid regular expression, it will be ignored for the purposes of validation. Note also that similar to the `placeholder` and `required` attributes, you can use the value of this attribute to provide the basis for your JavaScript validation code for nonsupporting browsers.

The `disabled` Attribute

The Boolean `disabled` attribute has been around longer than HTML5, but it has been expanded on, to a degree. It can be used with any form control except the new `output` element—and unlike previous versions of HTML, HTML5 allows you to set the `disabled` attribute on a `fieldset` and have it apply to all the form elements contained in that `fieldset`.

Generally, form elements with the `disabled` attribute have the content grayed out in the browser—the text is lighter than the color of values in enabled form controls. Browsers will prohibit the user from focusing on a form control that has the `disabled` attribute set. This attribute is often used to disable the submit button until all fields are correctly filled out, for example.

You can employ the `:disabled` pseudo-class in your CSS to style disabled form controls.

Form controls with the `disabled` attribute aren't submitted along with the form; so their values will be inaccessible to your form processing code on the server side. If you want a value that users are unable to edit, but can still see and submit, use the `readonly` attribute.

The `readonly` Attribute

The `readonly` attribute is similar to the `disabled` attribute: it makes it impossible for the user to edit the form field. Unlike `disabled`, however, the field *can* receive focus, and its value is submitted with the form.

In a comments form, we may want to include the URL of the current page or the title of the article that is being commented on, letting the user know that we are collecting this data without allowing them to change it:

```
<label for="about">Article Title</label>
<input type="text" name="about" id="about" readonly>
```

The `multiple` Attribute

The `multiple` attribute, if present, indicates that multiple values can be entered in a form control. While it has been available in previous versions of HTML, it only applied to the `select` element. In HTML5, it can be added to `email` and `file` input

types as well. If present, the user can select more than one file, or include several comma-separated email addresses.

At the time of writing, multiple file input is only supported in Chrome, Opera, and Firefox.

Spaces or Commas?

You may notice that the iOS touch keyboard for email inputs includes a space. Of course, spaces aren't permitted in email addresses, but some browsers allow you to separate multiple emails with spaces. Firefox 4 and Opera both support multiple emails separated with either commas or spaces. WebKit has no support for the space separator, even though the space is included in the touch keyboard.

Soon, all browsers will allow extra whitespace. This is how most users will likely enter the data; plus, this allowance has recently been added to the specification.

The `form` Attribute

Not to be confused with the `form` element, the `form` *attribute* in HTML5 allows you to associate form elements with forms in which they're not nested. This means you can now associate a fieldset or form control with any other form in the document. The `form` attribute takes as its value the `id` of the `form` element with which the fieldset or control should be associated.

If the attribute is omitted, the control will only be submitted with the `form` in which it's nested.

The `autocomplete` Attribute

The `autocomplete` attribute specifies whether the form, or a form control, should have autocomplete functionality. For most form fields, this will be a drop-down that appears when the user begins typing. For password fields, it's the ability to save the password in the browser. Support for this attribute has been present in browsers for years, though it was never in the specification until HTML5.

By default, autocomplete is on. You may have noticed this the last time you filled out a form. In order to disable it, use `autocomplete="off"`. This is a good idea for sensitive information, such as a credit card number, or information that will never need to be reused, like a CAPTCHA.

Autocompletion is also controlled by the browser. The user will have to turn on the autocomplete functionality in their browser for it to work at all; however, setting the `autocomplete` attribute to `off` overrides this preference.

The `datalist` Element and the `list` Attribute

Datalists are currently only supported in Firefox and Opera, but they are very cool. They fulfill a common requirement: a text field with a set of predefined autocomplete options. Unlike the `select` element, the user can enter whatever data they like, but they'll be presented with a set of suggested options in a drop-down as they type.

The `datalist` element, much like `select`, is a list of options, with each one placed in an `option` element. You then associate the `datalist` with an input using the `list` attribute on the input. The `list` attribute takes as its value the `id` attribute of the `datalist` you want to associate with the input. One `datalist` can be associated with several input fields.

Here's what this would look like in practice:

```
<label for="favcolor">Favorite Color</label>
<input type="text" list="colors" id="favcolor" name="favcolor">

<datalist id="colors">
  <option value="Blue">
  <option value="Green">
  <option value="Pink">
  <option value="Purple">
</datalist>
```

In supporting browsers, this will display a simple text field that drops down a list of suggested answers when focused. Figure 4.4 shows what this looks like.

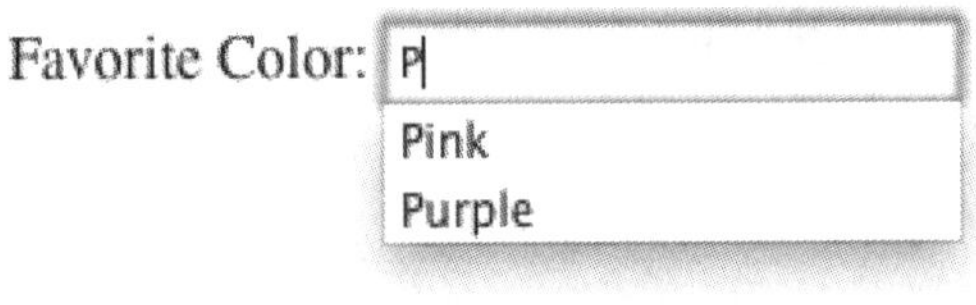

Favorite Color: P|
Pink
Purple

Figure 4.4. The `datalist` element in action in Firefox

The `autofocus` Attribute

The Boolean `autofocus` attribute specifies that a form control should be focused as soon as the page loads. Only one form element can have `autofocus` in a given page.

HTML5 New Form Input Types

You're probably already familiar with the `input` element's `type` attribute. This is the attribute that determines what kind of form input will be presented to the user. If it is omitted—or, in the case of new input types and older browsers, not understood—it still works: the `input` will default to `type="text"`. This is the key that makes HTML5 forms usable today. If you use a new input type, like `email` or `search`, older browsers will simply present users with a standard text field.

Our sign-up form currently uses four of the ten input types you're familiar with: `checkbox`, `text`, `password`, and `submit`. Here's the full list of types that were available before HTML5:

- button
- checkbox
- file
- hidden
- image
- password
- radio
- reset
- submit
- text

HTML5 gives us input types that provide for more data-specific UI elements and native data validation. HTML5 has a total of 13 new input types:

- search
- email
- url
- tel
- datetime
- date

- month
- week
- time
- datetime-local
- number
- range
- color

Let's look at each of these new types in detail, and see how we can put them to use.

Search

The search input type (type="search") provides a search field—a one-line text input control for entering one or more search terms. The spec states:

> The difference between the text state and the search state is primarily stylistic: on platforms where search fields are distinguished from regular text fields, the search state might result in an appearance consistent with the platform's search fields rather than appearing like a regular text field.

Many browsers style search inputs in a manner consistent with the browser or the operating system's search boxes. Some browsers have added the ability to clear the input with the click of a mouse, by providing an x icon once text is entered into the field. You can see this behavior in Chrome on Mac OS X in Figure 4.5.

Figure 4.5. The search input type is styled to resemble the operating system's search fields

Currently, only Chrome and Safari provide a button to clear the field. Opera 11 displays a rounded corner box without a control to clear the field, but switches to display a normal text field if any styling, such as a background color, is applied.

While you can still use type="text" for search fields, the new search type is a visual cue as to where the user needs to go to search the site, and provides an interface the user is accustomed to. *The HTML5 Herald* has no search field, but here's an example of how you'd use it:

```
<form id="search" method="get">
  <input type="search" id="s" name="s">
  <input type="submit" value="Search">
</form>
```

Since search, like all the new input types, appears as a regular text box in nonsupporting browsers, there's no reason not to use it when appropriate.

Email Addresses

The email type (type="email") is, unsurprisingly, used for specifying one or more email addresses. It supports the Boolean multiple attribute, allowing for multiple, comma-separated email addresses.

Let's change our form to use type="email" for the registrant's email address:

register.html *(excerpt)*

```
<label for="email">My email address is</label>
<input type="email"  id="email" name="email">
```

If you change the input type from text to email, as we've done here, you'll notice no visible change in the user interface; the input still looks like a plain text field. However, there are differences behind the scenes.

The change becomes apparent if you're using an iOS device. When you focus on the email field, the iPhone, iPad, and iPod will all display a keyboard optimized for email entry (with a shortcut key for the @ symbol), as shown in Figure 4.6.

Figure 4.6. The email input type provides a specialized keyboard on iOS devices

Firefox, Chrome, and Opera also provide error messaging for `email` inputs: if you try to submit a form with content unrecognizable as one or more email addresses, the browser will tell you what is wrong. The default error messages are shown in Figure 4.7.

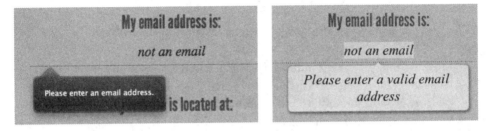

Figure 4.7. Error messages for incorrectly formatted email addresses on Firefox 4 (left) and Opera 11 (right)

Custom Validation Messages

Don't like the error messages provided? In some browsers, you can set your own with `.setCustomValidity(errorMsg)`. `setCustomValidity` takes as its only parameter the error message you want to provide. You can pass an empty string to `setCustomValidity` if you want to remove the error message entirely.

Unfortunately, while you can change the *content* of the message, you're stuck with its appearance, at least for now.

URLs

The `url` input (`type="url"`) is used for specifying a web address. Much like `email`, it will display as a normal text field. On many touch screens, the on-screen keyboard displayed will be optimized for web address entry, with a forward slash (/) and a ".com" shortcut key.

Let's update our registration form to use the `url` input type:

```
                                              register.html (excerpt)

<label for="url">My website is located at:</label>
<input type="url" id="url" name="url">
```

Opera, Firefox, and WebKit support the `url` input type, reporting the input as invalid if the URL is incorrectly formatted. Only the general format of a URL is validated,

so, for example, q://example.xyz will be considered valid, even though `q://` isn't a real protocol and `.xyz` isn't a real top-level domain. As such, if you want the value entered to conform to a more specific format, provide information in your label (or in a placeholder) to let your users know, and use the `pattern` attribute to ensure that it's correct—we'll cover `pattern` in detail later in this chapter.

> ### 📝 WebKit
>
> When we refer to WebKit in this book, we're referring to browsers that use the WebKit rendering engine. This includes Safari (both on the desktop and on iOS), Google Chrome, the Android browser, and a number of other mobile browsers. You can find more information about the WebKit open source project at http://www.webkit.org/.

Telephone Numbers

For telephone numbers, use the `tel` input type (`type="tel"`). Unlike the `url` and `email` types, the `tel` type doesn't enforce a particular syntax or pattern. Letters and numbers—indeed, any characters other than new lines or carriage returns—are valid. There's a good reason for this: all over the world countries have different types of valid phone numbers, with various lengths and punctuation, so it would be impossible to specify a single format as standard. For example, in the USA, +1(415)555-1212 is just as well understood as 415.555.1212.

You can encourage a particular format by including a placeholder with the correct syntax, or a comment after the input with an example. Additionally, you can stipulate a format by using the `pattern` attribute or the `setCustomValidity` method to provide for client-side validation.

Numbers

The `number` type (`type="number"`) provides an input for entering a number. Usually, this is a "spinner" box, where you can either enter a number or click on the up or down arrows to select a number.

Let's change our quantity field to use the `number` input type:

register.html *(excerpt)*

```
<label for="quantity">I would like to receive <input type="number"
➥name="quantity" id="quantity"> copies of <cite>The HTML5 Herald
➥</cite></label>
```

Figure 4.8 shows what this looks like in Opera.

Figure 4.8. The number input seen in Opera

The number input has `min` and `max` attributes to specify the minimum and maximum values allowed. We highly recommend that you use these, otherwise the up and down arrows might lead to different (and very odd) values depending on the browser.

When is a number not a number?

There will be times when you may think you want to use `number`, when in reality another input type is more appropriate. For example, it might seem to make sense that a street address should be a number. But think about it: would you want to click the spinner box all the way up to 34154? More importantly, many street numbers have non-numeric portions: think 24½ or 36B, neither of which work with the `number` input type.

Additionally, account numbers may be a mixture of letters and numbers, or have dashes. If you know the pattern of your number, use the `pattern` attribute. Just remember not to use `number` if the range is extensive or the number could contain non-numeric characters and the field is required. If the field is optional, you might want to use `number` anyway, in order to prompt the number keyboard as the default on touchscreen devices.

If you do decide that `number` is the way to go, remember also that the `pattern` attribute is unsupported in the `number` type. In other words, if the browser supports the `number` type, that supersedes any `pattern`. That said, feel free to include a `pattern`, in case the browser supports `pattern` but not the `number` input type.

You can also provide a `step` attribute, which determines the increment by which the number steps up or down when clicking the up and down arrows. The `min`, `max`, and `step` attributes are supported in Opera and WebKit.

On many touchscreen devices, focusing on a number input type will bring up a number touch pad (rather than a full keyboard).

Ranges

The range input type (type="range") displays a slider control in browsers that support it (currently Opera and WebKit). As with the number type, it allows the min, max, and step attributes. The difference between number and range, according to the spec, is that the exact value of the number is unimportant with range. It's ideal for inputs where you want an imprecise number; for example, a customer satisfaction survey asking clients to rate aspects of the service they received.

Let's change our registration form to use the range input type. The field asking users to rate their knowledge of HTML5 on a scale of 1 to 10 is perfect:

register.html (excerpt)

```
<label for="rating">On a scale of 1 to 10, my knowledge of HTML5
➥is:</label>
<input type="range" min="1" max="10" name="rating" type="range">
```

The step attribute defaults to 1, so it's not required. Figure 4.9 shows what this input type looks like in Safari.

Figure 4.9. The range input type in Chrome

The default value of a range is the midpoint of the slider—in other words, halfway between the minimum and the maximum.

The spec allows for a reversed slider (with values from right to left instead of from left to right) if the maximum specified is less than the minimum; however, currently no browsers support this.

Colors

The `color` input type (`type="color"`) provides the user with a color picker—or at least it does in Opera (and, surprisingly, in the built-in browser on newer BlackBerry smartphones). The color picker should return a hexadecimal RGB color value, such as #FF3300.

Until this input type is fully supported, if you want to use a color input, provide placeholder text indicating that a hexadecimal RGB color format is required, and use the `pattern` attribute to restrict the entry to only valid hexadecimal color values.

We don't use color in our form, but, if we did, it would look a little like this:

```
<label for="clr">Color: </label>
<input id="clr" name="clr" type="text" placeholder="#FFFFFF"
➥pattern="#(?:[0-9A-Fa-f]{6}|[0-9A-Fa-f]{3})" required>
```

The resulting color picker is shown in Figure 4.10. Clicking the **Other…** button brings up a full color wheel, allowing the user to select any hexadecimal color value.

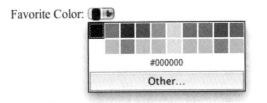

Figure 4.10. Opera's color picker control for the `color` input type

WebKit browsers support the color input type as well, and can indicate whether the color is valid, but don't provide a color picker … yet.

Dates and Times

There are several new date and time input types, including `date`, `datetime`, `date-time-local`, `month`, `time`, and `week`. All date and time inputs accept data formatted according to the ISO 8601 standard.[3]

---

[3] http://en.wikipedia.org/wiki/ISO_8601

date

> This comprises the date (year, month, and day), but no time; for example, 2004-06-24.

month

> Only includes the year and month; for example, 2012-12.

week

> This covers the year and week number (from 1 to 52); for example, 2011-W01 or 2012-W52.

time

> A time of day, using the military format (24-hour clock); for example, 22:00 instead of 10.00 p.m.

datetime

> This includes both the date and time, separated by a "T", and followed by either a "Z" to represent UTC (Coordinated Universal Time), or by a time zone specified with a + or - character. For example, "2011-03-17T10:45-5:00" represents 10:45am on the 17th of March, 2011, in the UTC minus 5 hours time zone (Eastern Standard Time).

datetime-local

> Identical to datetime, except that it omits the time zone.

The most commonly used of these types is date. The specifications call for the browser to display a date control, yet at the time of writing, only Opera does this by providing a calendar control.

Let's change our subscription start date field to use the date input type:

register.html *(excerpt)*

```
<label for="startdate">Please start my subscription on:</label>
<input type="date" min="1904-03-17" max="1904-05-17"
➥id="startdate" name="startdate" required aria-required="true"
➥placeholder="1911-03-17">
```

Now, we'll have a calendar control when we view our form in Opera, as shown in Figure 4.11. Unfortunately, it's unable to be styled with CSS at present.

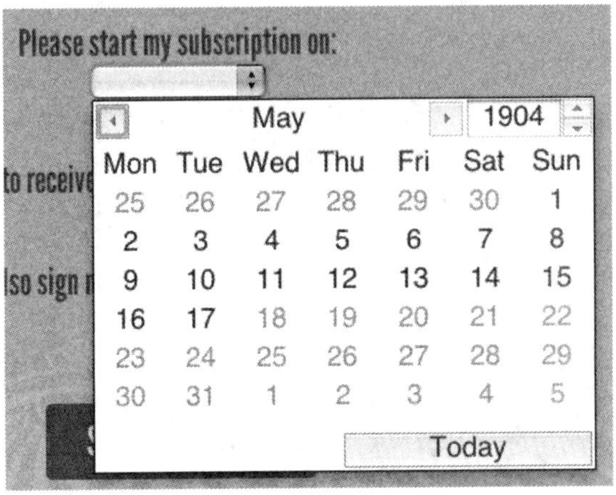

Figure 4.11. Opera's date picker for `date`, `datetime`, `datetime-local`, week, and month input types

For the `month` and `week` types, Opera displays the same date picker, but only allows the user to select full months or weeks. In those cases, individual days are unable to be selected; instead, clicking on a day selects the whole month or week.

Currently, WebKit provides *some* support for the `date` input type, providing a user interface similar to the `number` type, with up and down arrows. Safari behaves a little oddly when it comes to this control; the default value is the very first day of the Gregorian calendar: 1582-10-15. The default in Chrome is 0001-01-01, and the maximum is 275760-09-13. Opera functions more predictably, with the default value being the current date. Because of these oddities, we highly recommend including a minimum and maximum when using any of the date-based input types (all those listed above, except `time`). As with `number`, this is done with the `min` and `max` attributes.

The `placeholder` attribute we added to our start date field earlier is made redundant in Opera by the date picker interface, but it makes sense to leave it in place to guide users of other browsers.

Eventually, when all browsers support the UI of all the new input types, the `placeholder` attribute will only be relevant on `text`, `search`, URL, `telephone`, `email`, and `password` types. Until then, placeholders are a good way to hint to your users what kind of data is expected in those fields—remember that they'll just look like regular text fields in nonsupporting browsers.

💡 Dynamic Dates

In our example above, we hardcoded the `min` and `max` values into our HTML. If, for example, you wanted the minimum to be the day after the current date (this makes sense for a newspaper subscription start date), this would require updating the HTML every day. The best thing to do is dynamically generate the minimum and maximum allowed dates on the server side. A little PHP can go a long way:

```php
<?php
function daysFromNow($days){
  $added = ($days * 24 * 3600) + time();
  echo(date("Y-m-d", $added));
}
?>
```

In our markup where we had static dates, we now dynamically create them with the above function:

```html
<li>
  <label for="startdate">Please start my subscription on:
➥</label>
  <input type="date" min="<?php daysFromNow(1); ?>"
➥max="<?php daysFromNow(60); ?>" id="startdate"
➥name="startdate" required aria-required="true"
➥placeholder="1911-03-17">
</li>
```

This way, the user is limited to entering dates that make sense in the context of the form.

You can also include the `step` attribute with the `date` and `time` input types. For example, `step="6"` on month will limit the user to selecting either January or July. On `time` and `datetime` inputs, the `step` attribute must be expressed in seconds, so `step="900"` on the time input type will cause the input to step in increments of 15 minutes.

Other New Form Controls in HTML5

We've covered the new values for the input element's type attribute, along with some attributes that are valid on most form elements. But HTML5 web forms still have more to offer us! There are four new form elements in HTML5: output, keygen, progress, and meter. We covered progress and meter in the last chapter, since they're often useful outside of forms, so let's take a look at the other two elements.

The output Element

The purpose of the output element is to accept and display the result of a calculation. The output element should be used when the user can see the value, but not directly manipulate it, and when the value can be derived from other values entered in the form. An example use might be the total cost calculated after shipping and taxes in a shopping cart.

The output element's value is contained between the opening and closing tags. Generally, it will make sense to use JavaScript in the browser to update this value. The output element has a for attribute, which is used to reference the ids of form fields whose values went into the calculation of the output element's value.

It's worth noting that the output element's name and value are submitted along with the form.

The keygen Element

The keygen element is a control for generating a public-private keypair[4] and for submitting the public key from that key pair. Opera, WebKit, and Firefox all support this element, rendering it as a drop-down menu with options for the length of the generated keys; all provide different options, though.

The keygen element introduces two new attributes: the challenge attribute specifies a string that is submitted along with the public key, and the keytype attribute specifies the type of key generated. At the time of writing, the only supported keytype value is rsa, a common algorithm used in public-key cryptography.

---

[4] http://en.wikipedia.org/wiki/Public-key_cryptography

Changes to Existing Form Controls and Attributes

There have been a few other changes to form controls in HTML5.

The `form` Element

Throughout this chapter, we've been talking about attributes that apply to various form field elements; however, there are also some new attributes specific to the `form` element itself.

First, as we've seen, HTML5 provides a number of ways to natively validate form fields; certain input types such as `email` and `url`, for example, as well as the `required` and `pattern` attributes. You may, however, want to use these input types and attributes for styling or semantic reasons without preventing the form being submitted. The new Boolean `novalidate` attribute allows a form to be submitted without native validation of its fields.

Next, forms no longer need to have the `action` attribute defined. If omitted, the form will behave as though the `action` were set to the current page.

Lastly, the `autocomplete` attribute we introduced earlier can also be added directly to the `form` element; in this case, it will apply to all fields in that form unless those fields override it with their own `autocomplete` attribute.

The `optgroup` Element

In HTML5, you can have an `optgroup` as a child of another `optgroup`, which is useful for multilevel select menus.

The `textarea` Element

In HTML 4, we were required to specify a `textarea` element's size by specifying values for the `rows` and `cols` attributes. In HTML5, these attributes are no longer required; you should use CSS to define a `textarea`'s width and height.

New in HTML5 is the `wrap` attribute. This attribute applies to the `textarea` element, and can have the values `soft` (the default) or `hard`. With `soft`, the text is submitted without line breaks other than those actually entered by the user, whereas `hard` will

submit any line breaks introduced by the browser due to the size of the field. If you set the `wrap` to `hard`, you need to specify a `cols` attribute.

In Conclusion

As support for HTML5 input elements and attributes grows, sites will require less and less JavaScript for client-side validation and user interface enhancements, while browsers handle most of the heavy lifting. Legacy user agents are likely to stick around for the foreseeable future, but there is no reason to avoid moving forward and using HTML5 web forms, with appropriate polyfills and fallbacks filling the gaps where required.

In the next chapter, we'll continue fleshing out *The HTML5 Herald* by adding what many consider to be HTML5's killer feature: native video and audio.

HTML5 Audio and Video

No book on HTML5 would be complete without an examination of the new video and audio elements. These ground-breaking new elements have already been utilized on the Web, albeit in a limited capacity, but more and more developers and content creators are starting to incorporate them into their projects.

For *The HTML5 Herald*, we're going to be placing a video element in the first column of our three-column layout. But before we explore the details of the video element and its various attributes and associated elements, let's take a brief look at the state of video on the Web today.

For the most part, this chapter will focus on the video element, since that's what we're using in our sample project. However, the audio element behaves relatively identically: almost all the attributes and properties that we'll be using for video also apply to audio. Where there are exceptions, we'll be sure to point them out.

A Bit of History

Up until now, multimedia content on the Web has, for the most part, been placed in web pages by means of third-party plugins or applications that integrate with the

web browser. Some examples of such software include QuickTime, RealPlayer, and Silverlight.

By far the most popular way to embed video and audio on web pages is by means of Adobe's Flash Player plugin. The Flash Player plugin was originally developed by Macromedia and is now maintained by Adobe as a result of their 2005 buy-out of the company. The plugin has been available since the mid-90s, but did not really take off as a way to serve video content until well into the 2000s.

Before HTML5, there was no standard way to embed video into web pages. A plugin like Adobe's Flash Player is controlled solely by Adobe, and is not open to community development.

The introduction of the `video` and `audio` elements in HTML5 resolves this problem and makes multimedia a seamless part of a web page, the same as the `img` element. With HTML5, there's no need for the user to download third-party software to view your content, and the video or audio player is easily accessible via scripting.

The Current State of Play

Unfortunately, as sublime as HTML5 video and audio sounds in theory, it's less simple in practice. A number of factors need to be considered before you decide to include HTML5's new multimedia elements on your pages.

First, you'll need to understand the state of browser support. At the time of writing, the only browsers with a significant market share that don't support native HTML5 video and audio are Internet Explorer 8 and earlier. Unfortunately, this is still a sizable slice of most sites' audiences.

The other major browser makers offer HTML5 video support in versions now in wide use (Chrome 3+, Safari 4+, and Firefox 3.5+). The last version of Chrome without HTML5 video support (version 2) has a nonexistent market share, and the same is true for the nonsupporting versions of Safari and Opera.

Although IE's market share is significant, you can still use HTML5 video on your pages today. Later on, we'll show you how the new `video` element has been designed with backwards compatibility in mind, so that users of nonsupporting browsers will still have access to your multimedia content.

Video Container Formats

Video on the Web is based on container formats and codecs. A **container** is a wrapper that stores all the necessary data that comprises the video file being accessed, much like a ZIP file wraps or contains files. Some examples of well-known video containers include Flash Video (**.flv**), MPEG-4 (**.mp4** or **.m4v**), and AVI (**.avi**).

The video container houses data, including a video track, an audio track with markers that help synchronize the audio and video, language information, and other bits of metadata that describe the content.

The video container formats relevant to HTML5 are MPEG-4, Ogg, and WebM.

Video Codecs

A video **codec** defines an algorithm for encoding and decoding a multimedia data stream. A codec can encode a data stream for transmission, storage, or encryption, or it can decode it for playback or editing. For the purpose of HTML5 video, we're concerned with the decoding and playback of a video stream. The video codecs that are most pertinent to HTML5 video are H.264, Theora, and VP8.

Audio Codecs

An audio codec in theory works the same as a video codec, except it's concerned with the streaming of sound, rather than video frames. The audio codecs that are most pertinent to HTML5 video are AAC and Vorbis.

What combinations work in current browsers?

It would be nice if browser support allowed us to choose a single container, video codec, and audio codec to create a standard way of embedding video using the new `video` element in HTML5. Unfortunately, it's not quite that simple—although things are improving.

In Table 5.1, we've outlined video container and codec support in the most popular browser versions. This chart only includes browser versions that offer support for the HTML5 `video` element.

Table 5.1. Browser support for HTML5 video

Container/Video Codec/Audio Codec	Firefox	Chrome	IE	Opera	Safari	iOS Safari	Android
Ogg/Theora/Vorbis	3.5+	3+	–	10.5+	–	–	–
MP4/H.264/AAC	–	3–11	9+	–	4+	4+	2.1+[a]
WebM/VP8/Vorbis	4+	6+	9+[b]	10.6+	–	–	2.3+

[a] Versions of Android prior to 2.3 require JavaScript to play the video.

[b] IE9 supports playback of WebM video with a VP8 codec when the user has installed a VP8 codec on Windows.

Opera Mini and Opera Mobile currently offer no support for HTML5 video, but Opera has announced there are plans to include support in upcoming releases.[1]

Licensing Issues

While the new `video` element itself is free to use in any context, the containers and codecs are not always as simple. For example, while the Theora and VP8 (WebM) codecs are not patent-encumbered, the H.264 codec is patent-encumbered and licensing for it is provided by the MPEG-LA group.

Currently, for H.264, if your video is provided to your users for free, there's no requirement for you to pay royalties. However, detailed licensing issues are far beyond the scope and intent of this book, so just be aware that you may need to do some research before using any particular video format when including HTML5 video in your pages.

The Markup

After all that necessary business surrounding containers, codecs, browser support, and licensing issues, it's time to examine the markup of the `video` element and its associated attributes.

The simplest way to include HTML5 video in a web page is as follows: <video src="example.webm"></video>

---

[1] http://my.opera.com/operamobile/blog/2010/12/04/developing-opera-mobile-for-android/

But, as you've probably figured out from the preceding sections, this will only work in a limited number of browsers. It is, however, the minimum code required to have HTML5 video working to some extent. In a perfect world, it would work everywhere—the same way the img element works everywhere—but that's a little way off just yet.

Similar to the img element, the video element should also include width and height attributes:

```
<video src="example.webm" width="375" height="280"></video>
```

Even though the dimensions can be set in the markup, they'll have no effect on the aspect ratio of the video. For example, if the video in the above example was actually 375×240 and the markup was as shown above, the video would be centered vertically inside the 280-pixel space specified in the HTML. This stops the video from stretching unnecessarily and looking distorted.

The width and height attributes accept integers only, and their values are always in pixels. Naturally, these values can be overridden via scripting or CSS.

Enabling Native Controls

No embedded video would be complete without giving the user the ability to play, pause, stop, seek through the video, or adjust the volume. HTML5's video element includes a controls attribute that does just that:

```
<video src="example.webm" width="375" height="280" controls></video>
```

controls is a Boolean attribute, so no value is required. Its inclusion in the markup tells the browser to make the controls visible and accessible to the user.

Each browser is responsible for the look of the built-in video controls. Figure 5.1 to Figure 5.4 show how these controls differ in appearance from browser to browser.

Figure 5.1. The native video controls in Firefox 4

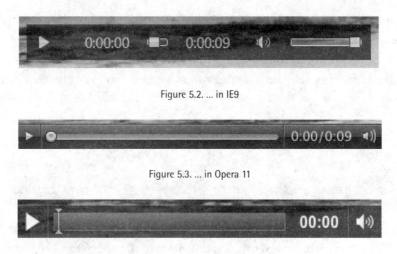

Figure 5.2. ... in IE9

Figure 5.3. ... in Opera 11

Figure 5.4. ... and in Chrome

The `autoplay` Attribute

We'd love to omit reference to this particular attribute, since its use will be undesirable for the most part. However, there are cases where it can be appropriate. The Boolean `autoplay` attribute does exactly what it says: it tells the web page to play the video as soon as possible.

Normally, this is a bad practice; most of us know too well how jarring it can be if a website starts playing video or audio as soon as it loads—especially if our speakers are turned up. Usability best practices dictate that sounds and movement on web pages should only be triggered when requested by the user. But this doesn't mean that the `autoplay` attribute can never be used.

For example, if the page in question contains nothing but a video—that is, the user clicked on a link to a page for the sole purpose of viewing a specific video—it may be acceptable to allow it to play automatically, depending on the video's size, any surrounding content, and the audience.

Here's how you'd do that:

```
<video src="example.webm" width="375" height="280" controls
➥autoplay></video>
```

Autoplaying on the iPhone

Safari on the iPhone will ignore the `autoplay` attribute; all video will wait for the user to press the play button before starting. This is sensible, given that mobile bandwidth is often limited.

The `loop` Attribute

Another attribute that you should think twice about before using is the Boolean `loop` attribute. Again, it's fairly self-explanatory: according to the spec, this attribute, when present, will tell the browser to "seek back to the start of the media resource upon reaching the end."

So if you created a web page whose sole intention was to annoy its visitors, it might contain code like this:

```
<video src="example.webm" width="375" height="280" controls
➥autoplay loop></video>
```

Autoplay and an infinite loop! We just need to remove the native controls and we'd have a trifecta of worst practices.

Of course, there are some situations where `loop` can be useful: imagine a browser-based game, in which ambient sounds and music should play continuously as long as the page is open.

The `preload` Attribute

In contrast to the two previous attributes, `preload` could definitely come in handy in a number of cases. The `preload` attribute accepts one of three values:

auto

A value of `auto` indicates that the video and its associated metadata will start loading before the video is played. This way, the browser can start playing the video more quickly when the user requests it.

none

A value of `none` indicates that the video shouldn't load in the background before the user presses play.

metadata

This works like none, except that any metadata associated with the video (for example, its dimensions, duration, and the like) can be preloaded, even though the video itself won't be.

This particular attribute does not have a spec-defined default in cases where it's omitted; each browser decides which of those three values should be the default state, which makes sense. It allows desktop browsers to preload the video and/or metadata automatically (having no real adverse effect) while permitting mobile browsers to default to either metadata or none, as many mobile users have restricted bandwidth and will prefer to have the choice of downloading the video or not.

The poster Attribute

When you go to view a video on the Web, normally a single frame of the video will display in order to provide a teaser of its content. The poster attribute makes it easy to choose such a teaser. This attribute, similar to src, will point to an image file on the server by means of a URL.

Here's how our video element would look with a poster attribute defined:

```
<video src="example.webm" width="375" height="280"
➥poster="teaser.jpg" controls></video>
```

Although the poster attribute is useful, there's a bug in iOS3 (corrected in iOS4) that prevents playback of the video if this attribute is present. If you know that many of your visitors use iOS 3.x, you should either avoid using the poster attribute, or remove it for those devices specifically.

The audio Attribute

The audio attribute attribute controls the default state of the audio track for the video element, and currently accepts only a single possible value: muted. The spec states that other values are likely to be added in the future, for specifying the default audio track or volume, for example.

A value of muted will cause the video's audio track to default to muted, potentially overriding any user preferences. This will only control the default state of the element—the user interacting with the controls, or JavaScript can change this.

Here it is added to our `video` element:

```
<video src="example.webm" width="375" height="280"
➥poster="teaser.jpg" audio="muted"></video>
```

Adding Support for Multiple Video Formats

As we discussed earlier, using a single container format to serve your video is not currently an option, even though that's really the ultimate idea behind having the `video` element, and one which we hope will be realized in the future. To allow inclusion of multiple video formats, the `video` element allows `source` elements to be defined so that you can allow every user agent to display the video using the format of its choice. These elements serve the same function as the `src` attribute on the `video` element; so if you're providing `source` elements, there's no need to specify a `src` for your video.

Taking current browser support into consideration, here's how we might declare our `source` elements:

```
<source src="example.mp4" type="video/mp4">
<source src="example.webm" type="video/webm">
<source src="example.ogv" type="video/ogg">
```

The `source` element (oddly enough) takes a `src` attribute that specifies the location of the video file. It also accepts a `type` attribute that specifies the container format for the resource being requested. This latter attribute allows the browser to determine if it can play the file in question, thus preventing the browser from unnecessarily downloading an unsupported format.

The `type` attribute also allows a codec parameter to be specified, which defines the video and audio codecs for the requested file. Here's how our `source` elements will look with the codecs specified:

```
<source src="example.mp4"
➥type='video/mp4; codecs="avc1.42E01E, mp4a.40.2"'>
<source src="example.webm" type='video/webm; codecs="vp8, vorbis"'>
<source src="example.ogv" type='video/ogg; codecs="theora, vorbis"'>
```

You'll notice that the syntax for the `type` attribute has been slightly modified to accommodate the container and codec values. The double quotes surrounding the values have been changed to single quotes, and another set of nested double quotes is included specifically for the codecs.

This can be a tad confusing at first glance, but in most cases you'll just be copying and pasting those values once you have a set method for encoding the videos (which we'll touch on later in this chapter). The important point is that you define the correct values for the specified file to ensure that the browser can determine which (if any) file it will be able to play.

source Order

In our example above, the MP4/H.264/AAC container/codec combination is included first. This is to ensure that the video will play on the iPad. On that device, a bug causes only the first `source` element to be recognized. It's safe to assume that this bug is fixed in subsequent versions of the iPad, but for now it's necessary to include the MP4/H.264 file first to ensure compatibility.

The first `source` element will be recognized by IE9, Safari, and older versions of Chrome, so that covers quite a large chunk of our HTML5-ready audience.

The next element in the list defines the WebM/VP8/Vorbis container/codec combination. This is supported by later versions of Chrome that will eventually drop support for H.264. In addition to Chrome, WebM video will also play in Firefox 4 and Opera 10.6.

Finally, the third `source` element declares the Ogg/Theora/Vorbis container/codec combination, which is supported by Firefox 3.5 and Opera 10.5. Although other browsers also support this combination, they'll be using the other formats since they appear ahead of this one in the source order. The browsers that support only this combination are older versions of browsers whose current versions support other formats, so it will be possible to drop this format once those versions become sufficiently rare.

These three `source` elements are placed as children of the `video` element, so with our three file formats declared, our code will now look like this:

```
<video width="375" height="280" poster="teaser.jpg" audio="muted">
  <source src="example.mp4" type='video/mp4;
➥codecs="avc1.42E01E, mp4a.40.2"'>
  <source src="example.webm" type='video/webm;
➥codecs="vp8, vorbis"'>
  <source src="example.ogv" type='video/ogg;
➥codecs="theora, vorbis"'>
</video>
```

You'll notice that our code above is now without the `src` attribute on the `video` element. As well as being redundant, it would also override any video files defined in the `source` elements.

What about Internet Explorer 6–8?

The three `source` elements that we included inside our `video` element will cover all modern browsers. But we're yet to ensure that our video will play for a potentially large portion of our audience. As mentioned earlier, a significant percentage of users are still using browsers without native support for HTML5 video. Most of those users are on some version of Internet Explorer prior to version 9.

In keeping with the principle of graceful degradation, the HTML5 `video` element has been designed so that older browsers can access the video by some alternate means. Older browsers that fail to recognize the `video` element will simply ignore it, along with its `source` children. But if the `video` element contains content that the browser recognizes as valid HTML, it will read and display that content instead.

What kind of content can we serve to those nonsupporting browsers? According to Adobe,[2] 99% of users have the Flash plugin installed on their systems. Additionally, most of those instances of the Flash plugin are version 9 or later, which offer support for the MPEG-4 video container format. To allow Internet Explorer 6 to 8 (and other older browsers lacking support for HTML5 video) to play the video, we declare an embedded Flash video to use as a fallback. Here's the completed code for the video on *The HTML5 Herald*, with the Flash fallback code included:

---

[2] http://www.adobe.com/products/player_census/flashplayer/version_penetration.html

```
                                        index.html (excerpt)
<video width="375" height="280" poster="teaser.jpg" audio="muted">
  <source src="example.mp4" type='video/mp4;
➥codecs="avc1.42E01E, mp4a.40.2"'>
  <source src="example.webm" type='video/webm;
➥codecs="vp8, vorbis"'>
  <source src="example.ogv" type='video/ogg;
➥codecs="theora, vorbis"'>
  <!-- fallback to Flash: -->
  <object width="375" height="280" type="application/x-shockwave-
➥flash" data="mediaplayer-5.5/player.swf">
    <param name="movie" value="mediaplayer-5.5/player.swf">
    <param name="allowFullScreen" value="true">
    <param name="wmode" value="transparent">
    <param name="flashvars" value="controlbar=over&amp;image=
➥images/teaser.jpg&amp;file=example.mp4">
    <!-- fallback image -->
    <img src="teaser.jpg" width="375" height="280" alt=""
➥title="No video playback capabilities">
  </object>
</video>
```

We'll avoid going into a detailed discussion of how this newly added code works
(this isn't a Flash book, after all!), but here are a few points to note about this addition
to our markup:

■ The width and height attributes on the object element should be the same as
those on the video element.

■ We're using the open source JW Player by LongTail Video[3] to play the file; you
can use whichever video player you prefer.

■ The Flash video code has a fallback of its own—an image file that displays if
the code for the Flash video fails to work.

■ The fourth param element defines the file to be used (**example.mp4**); as mentioned,
most instances of the Flash player now support video playback using the MPEG-
4 container format, so there's no need to encode another video format.

---

[3] http://www.longtailvideo.com/players/jw-flv-player/

■ HTML5-enabled browsers that support HTML5 video are instructed by the spec to ignore any content inside the `video` element that's not a `source` tag, so the fallback is safe in all browsers.

The last thing we'll mention here is that, in addition to the Flash fallback content, you could also provide an optional "download video" link that allows the user to get a local copy of the video and view it at their leisure. This would ensure that nobody is left without a means to view the video.

MIME Types

If you find that you've followed our instructions closely and your videos still won't play from your server, the issue could be related to the content-type information being sent.

Content-type, also known as the MIME type, tells the browser what kind of content they're looking at. Is this a text file? If so, what kind? HTML? JavaScript? Is this a video file? The content-type answers these questions for the browser. Every time your browser requests a page, the server sends "headers" to your browser before sending any files. These headers tell your browser how to interpret the file that follows. Content-type is an example of one of the headers the server sends to the browser.

The MIME type for each video file that you include via the `source` element is the same as the value of the `type` attribute (minus any codec information). For the purpose of HTML5 video, we're concerned with three MIME types. To ensure that your server is able to play all three types of video file, place the following lines of code in your **.htaccess** file (or the equivalent if you're using a web server other than Apache):

```
AddType video/ogg  .ogv
AddType video/mp4  .mp4
AddType video/webm .webm
```

If this fails to fix your problem, you may have to talk to your host or server administrator to find out if your server is using the correct MIME types. To learn more

about configuring other types of web servers, read the excellent article "Properly Configuring Server MIME Types" from the Mozilla Developer Network.[4]

What's an .htaccess file?

An **.htaccess** file provides a way to make configuration changes on a per-directory basis when using the Apache web server. The directives in an **.htaccess** file apply to the directory it lives in and all subdirectories. For more on **.htaccess** files, see the Apache documentation.[5]

Encoding Video Files for Use on the Web

The code we've presented for *The HTML5 Herald* is virtually bullet-proof, and will enable the video to be viewable by nearly everyone that sees the page. Because we need to encode our video in at least two formats (possibly three, if we want to), we need an easy way to encode our original video file into these HTML5-ready formats. Fortunately, there are some online resources and desktop applications that allow you to do exactly that.

Miro Video Converter[6] is free software with a super-simple interface that offers the ability to encode your video into all the necessary formats for HTML5 video. It's available for Mac and Windows.[7]

Simply drag a file to the window, or browse for a file in the customary way. A drop-down box offers options for encoding your video in Theora, WebM, or MPEG-4 format. There's also an option for MP3 and a number of presets for device-specific video output.

There are a number of other options for encoding HTML5 video, but this should suffice to help you create the two (or three) files necessary for embedding video that 99% of users can view.

---

[4] https://developer.mozilla.org/en/properly_configuring_server_mime_types

[5] http://httpd.apache.org/docs/1.3/howto/htaccess.html

[6] http://www.mirovideoconverter.com/

[7] Linux users can use FFmpeg, [http://ffmpeg.org/] the command-line utility on which Miro Video Converter is based.

Creating Custom Controls

There's another huge benefit to using HTML5 video compared to the customary method of embedding video with a third-party technology. With HTML5 video, the video element becomes a real part of the web page, rather than an inaccessible plugin. It's as much a part of the web page as an img element or any other native HTML element would be. This means we can target the video element and its various components using JavaScript—and we can even style the video element with CSS.

As previously mentioned, each browser that supports HTML5 video embeds a native set of controls to help the user access the video content. These controls have a different appearance in each browser, which may vex those concerned with a site's branding. No problem: by using the JavaScript API provided by the video element, we can create our own custom controls and link them up to the video's behavior.

Custom controls are created using whichever elements you want—images, plain HTML and CSS, or even elements drawn using the Canvas API—the choice is yours. To harness this API, create your own custom controls, insert them into the page, and then use JavaScript to convert those otherwise static graphic elements into dynamic, fully functioning video controls.

Some Markup and Styling to Get Us Started

For our sample site, we're going to build a very simple set of video controls to demonstrate the power of the new HTML5 video API. To start off, Figure 5.5 shows a screenshot of the set of controls we'll be using to manipulate the video.

Figure 5.5. The simple set of video controls we'll be building

Both of those buttons have alternate states: Figure 5.6 shows how the controls will look if the video is playing and the sound has been muted.

Figure 5.6. Our controls again, this time with the sound muted and the video playing

Our controls have three components:

- play/pause button
- timer that counts forward from zero
- mute/unmute button

In most cases, your custom video controls should have all the features of the default controls that various browsers natively provide. If your set of controls introduces fewer or inferior features, it's likely you'll end up frustrating your users.

For the purpose of introducing the API, rather than trying to mimic what the browsers natively do, we want to introduce the important parts of the video API gradually; this will allow you to get your feet wet while establishing a foundation from which to work.

We'll be creating a very simple, yet usable, set of controls for our video. The main feature missing from our set of controls is the seek bar that lets the user "scrub" through the video to find a specific part. This means there will be no way to go back to the start of the video aside from refreshing the page. Other than that, the controls will function adequately—they'll allow the user to play, pause, mute, or unmute the video.

Here's the HTML we'll be using to represent the different parts of the video controls:

index.html *(excerpt)*

```
<div id="controls" class="hidden">
  <a id="playPause">Play/Pause</a>
  <span id="timer">00:00</span>
  <a id="muteUnmute">Mute/Unmute</a>
</div>
```

We'll avoid going into the CSS in great detail, but here's a summary of what we've done (you can view the demo page's source in the code archive if you want to see how it's all put together):

- The text in the play/pause and mute/unmute buttons is removed from view using the text-indent property.

- A single CSS sprite image is used as a background image to represent the different button states (play, pause, mute, unmute).

- CSS classes are being used to represent the different states; those classes will be added and removed using JavaScript.

- The controls wrapper element is absolutely positioned and placed to overlay the bottom of the video.

- We've given the controls a default opacity level of 50%, but on hover the opacity increases to 100% (we'll be talking more about opacity in Chapter 6).

- By default, the controls wrapper element is set to `display: none` using a `class` of `hidden`, which we'll remove with JavaScript.

If you're following along building the example, go ahead and style the three elements however you like. The appearance of the controls is really secondary to what we're accomplishing here, so feel free to fiddle until you have a look you're happy with.

Introducing the Media Elements API

Let's go through the steps needed to create our custom controls, and in the process we'll introduce you to some aspects of the video API. Afterwards, we'll summarize some other methods and attributes from the API that we won't be using in our controls, so you can have a good overview of what the API includes.

In order to work with our new custom controls, we'll first cache them by placing them into JavaScript variables. Here are the first few lines of our code:

js/videoControls.js *(excerpt)*

```
var videoEl = $('video')[0],
  playPauseBtn = $('#playPause'),
  vidControls = $('#controls'),
  muteBtn = $('#muteUnmute'),
  timeHolder = $('#timer');
```

Of course, caching our selections isn't necessary, but it's always best practice (for maintainability and performance) to work with cached objects, rather than needlessly repeating the same code to target various elements on the page.

The first line is targeting the `video` element itself. We'll be using this `videoEl` variable quite a bit when using the API—since most API methods need to be called from the media element. The next four lines of code should be fairly familiar to you

if you took note of the HTML that comprises our controls. Those are the four elements on the page that we'll be manipulating based on user interaction.

Our first task is make sure the native controls are hidden. We could do this easily by simply removing the `controls` attribute from the HTML. But since our custom controls are dependent on JavaScript, visitors with JavaScript disabled would be deprived of any way of controlling the video. So we're going to remove the `controls` attribute in our JavaScript, like this:

js/videoControls.js (excerpt)

```
videoEl.removeAttribute("controls");
```

The next step is to make our own custom controls visible. As mentioned earlier, we've used CSS to remove our controls from view by default. By using JavaScript to enable the visibility of the custom controls, we ensure that the user will never see two sets of controls.

So our next chunk of code will look like this:

js/videoControls.js (excerpt)

```
videoEl.addEventListener('canplaythrough', function () {
  vidControls.removeClass("hidden");
}, false);
```

This is the first place we've used a feature from the HTML5 video API. First, take note of the `addEventListener` method. This method does exactly what its name implies: it listens for the specified event occurring on the targeted element.

But `addEventListener` isn't cross-browser!

If you're familiar with cross-browser JavaScript techniques, you probably know that the `addEventListener` method isn't cross-browser. In this case, it poses no problem. The only browsers in use that lack support for `addEventListener` are versions of Internet Explorer prior to version 9—and those browsers have no support for HTML5 video anyway.

All we have to do is use Modernizr (or some equivalent JavaScript) to detect support for the HTML5 video API, and then only run the code for supporting browsers—all of which will support `addEventListener`.

In this case, we're targeting the video element itself. The event we're registering to be listened for is the canplaythrough event from the video API. According to the definition of this event in the spec:[8]

> The user agent estimates that if playback were to be started now,
> the media resource could be rendered at the current playback rate
> all the way to its end without having to stop for further buffering.

There are other events we can use to check if the video is ready, each of which has its own specific purpose. We'll touch on some of those other events later in this chapter. This particular one ensures continuous playback, so it's a good fit for us as we'd like to avoid choppy playback.

Playing and Pausing the Video

When the canplaythrough event fires, a callback function is run. In that function, we've put a single line of code that removes the hidden class from the controls wrapper, so now our controls are visible. Now we want to add some functionality to our controls. Let's bind a click event handler to our play/pause button:

js/videoControls.js (excerpt)

```
playPauseBtn.bind('click', function () {
  if (videoEl.paused) {
    videoEl.play();
  } else {
    videoEl.pause();
  }
});
```

When the button is clicked, we run an if/else block that's using three additional features from the video API. Here's a description of all three:

The paused attribute is being accessed to see if the video is currently in the "paused" state. This doesn't necessarily mean the video has been paused by the user; it could equally just represent the start of the video, before it's been played. So this attribute will return true if the video isn't currently playing.

---

[8] http://www.whatwg.org/specs/web-apps/current-work/multipage/video.html#event-media-canplay-through

Since we've now determined that the play/pause button has been clicked, and the video is not currently playing, we can safely call the play() method on the video element. This will play the video from its last paused location.

Finally, if the paused attribute doesn't return true, the else portion of our code will fire, and this will trigger the pause() method on the video element, stopping the video.

You may have noticed that our custom controls have no "stop" button (customarily represented by a square icon). You could add such a button if you feel it's necessary, but many video players don't use it since the seek bar can be used to move to the beginning of the video. The only catch is that the video API has no "stop" method; to counter this, you can cause the video to mimic the traditional "stop" behavior by pausing it and then sending it to the beginning (more on this later).

You'll notice that something's missing from our if/else construct. Earlier, we showed you a couple of screenshots displaying the controls in their two states. We need to use JavaScript to alter the background position of our sprite image; we want to change the button from "play me" to "pause me."

Here's how we'll do that:

js/videoControls.js *(excerpt)*

```
videoEl.addEventListener('play', function () {
  playPauseBtn.addClass("playing");
}, false);
videoEl.addEventListener('pause', function () {
  playPauseBtn.removeClass("playing");
}, false);
```

Here we have two more uses of the addEventListener method (you'll need to get used to it if you're going to use the video and audio APIs!). The first block is listening for play events. So if the click handler we wrote triggers the play() method (or if something else causes the video to play, such as some other code on the page), the play event will be detected by the listener and the callback function will run.

The same thing is happening in the second block of code, except that it's listening for the pause event (not to be confused with the paused attribute).

If the element has been played, the first block will add the class `playing` to our play/pause button. This `class` will change the background position of the sprite on the play/pause button to make the "pause me" icon appear. Similarly, the second block of code will remove the `playing` `class`, causing the state of the button to go back to the default (the "play me" state).

You're probably thinking, "why not just add or remove the `playing` `class` in the code handling the button click?" While this would work just fine for when the button is clicked (or accessed via the keyboard), there's another behavior we need to consider here, demonstrated in Figure 5.7.

Figure 5.7. Some video controls are accessible via the context menu

The menu above appears when you bring up the `video` element's context menu. As you can see, clicking the controls on the `video` element isn't the only way to play/pause or mute/unmute the video.

To ensure that the button states are changed no matter how the `video` element's features are accessed, we instead listen for `play` and `pause` events (and, as you'll see in a moment, sound-related events) to change the states of the buttons.

Disabling the Context Menu

You may also be concerned that the `video` element's context menu has an option for **Save video as...**. There's been discussion online about how easy it is to save HTML5 video, and this could affect how copyrighted videos will be distributed. Some content producers might feel like avoiding HTML5 video for this reason alone.

Whatever you choose to do, just recognize the realities associated with web video. Most users who are intent on copying and distributing copyrighted video will find ways to do it, regardless of any protection put in place. There are many web apps and software tools that can easily rip even Flash-based video. You should also be aware that even if you do disable the context menu on the `video` element, the user can still view the source of the page and find the location of the video file(s).

Some sites, like YouTube, have already implemented features to combat this when using HTML5 video. YouTube has a page that allows you to opt in to their HTML5 video trial.[9] After opting in, when you view a video and open the `video` element's context menu, there's a custom context menu. The "**Save Video As...**" option is still present. But not so fast! If you choose this option, (as of this writing) you'll be "rickrolled."[10] Sneaky!

YouTube also dynamically adds the `video` element to the page, so that you're unable to find the URL to the video file by poking around in the source.

So, realize that you do have options, and that it's possible to make it more difficult (but not impossible) for users to rip your copyrighted videos. But also recognize there are drawbacks to changing user expectations, in addition to the performance and maintainability issues associated with convoluting your scripts and markup for what could be little, if any, gain.

Muting and Unmuting the Video's Audio Track

The next bit of functionality we want to add to our script is the mute/unmute button. This piece of code is virtually the same as what was used for the play/pause button. This time, we've bound the `click` event to the mute/unmute button, following with a similar if/else construct:

---

[9] http://www.youtube.com/html5
[10] http://en.wikipedia.org/wiki/Rickrolling

js/videoControls.js *(excerpt)*

```
muteBtn.bind('click', function () {
  if (videoEl.muted) {
    videoEl.muted = false;
  } else {
    videoEl.muted = true;
  }
});
```

This block of code introduces a new part of the API: the `muted` attribute. After the mute button is clicked, we check to see the status of this attribute. If it's `true` (meaning the sound is muted), we set it to `false` (which unmutes the sound); if it's `false`, we set its status to `true`.

Again, we haven't done any button state handling here, for the same reasons mentioned earlier when discussing the play/pause buttons; the context menu allows for muting and unmuting, so we want to change the mute button's state depending on the actual muting or unmuting of the video, rather than the clicking of the button.

But unlike the play/pause button, we don't have the ability to listen for `mute` and `unmute` events. Instead, the API offers the `volumechange` event:

js/videoControls.js *(excerpt)*

```
videoEl.addEventListener('volumechange', function () {
  if (videoEl.muted) {
    muteBtn.addClass("muted");
  } else {
    muteBtn.removeClass("muted");
  }
}, false);
```

Again, we're using an event listener to run some code each time the specified event (in this case a change in volume) takes place. As you can probably infer from the name of this event, the `volumechange` event isn't limited to detecting muting and unmuting; it can detect volume changes.

Once we have detected the change in volume, we check the status of the `video` element's `muted` attribute, and we change the `class` on the mute/unmute button accordingly.

Responding When the Video Ends Playback

The code we've written so far will allow the user to play and pause the video, as well as mute and unmute the sound. All of this is done using our custom controls.

At this point, if you let the video play to the end, it will stop on the last frame. We think it's best to send the video back to the first frame, ready to be played again. This gives us the opportunity to introduce two new features of the API:

js/videoControls.js (excerpt)

```
videoEl.addEventListener('ended', function () {
  videoEl.currentTime = 0;
  videoEl.pause();
}, false);
```

This block of code listens for the `ended` event, which tells us that the video has reached its end and stopped. Once we detect this event, we set the video's `currentTime` property to zero. This property represents the current playback position, expressed in seconds (with decimal fractions).

Which brings us to the next step in our code.

Updating the Time as the Video Plays

Now for the last step: we want our timer to update the current playback time as the video plays. We've already introduced the `currentTime` property; we can use it to update the content of our `#timeHolder` element. Here's how we do it:

js/videoControls.js (excerpt)

```
videoEl.addEventListener('timeupdate', function () {
  timeHolder[0].innerHTML = secondsToTime(videoEl.currentTime);
}, false);
```

In this case, we're listening for `timeupdate` events. The `timeupdate` event fires each time the video's time changes, which means even a fraction of a second's change will fire this event.

This alone would suffice to create a bare-bones timer. Unfortunately, the time would be unhelpful, and ugly on the eye because you'd see the time changing every milli-second to numerous decimal places, as shown in Figure 5.8.

Figure 5.8. Using the `currentTime` property directly in our HTML is less than ideal

In addition, the timer in this state will not display minutes or hours, just seconds—which could end up being in the hundreds or thousands, depending on the length of the video. That's impractical, to say the least.

To format the seconds into a more user-friendly time, we've written a function called `secondsToTime()`, and called it from our `timeupdate` handler above. We don't want to show the milliseconds in this case, so our function rounds the timer to the nearest second. Here's the start of our function:

js/videoControls.js *(excerpt)*

```
var h = Math.floor(s / (60 * 60)),
  dm = s % (60 * 60),
  m = Math.floor(dm / 60),
  ds = dm % 60,
  secs = Math.ceil(ds);
```

After those five lines of code, the final variable `secs` will hold a rounded number of seconds, calculated from the number of seconds passed into the function.

Next, we need to ensure that a single digit amount of seconds or minutes is expressed using 05 instead of just 5. The next code block will take care of this:

js/videoControls.js *(excerpt)*

```
if (secs === 60) {
  secs = 0;
  m = m + 1;
}

if (secs < 10) {
  secs = "0" + secs;
}
```

```
if (m === 60) {
  m = 0;
  h = h + 1;
}

if (m < 10) {
  m = "0" + m;
}
```

Finally, we return a string that represents the current time of the video in its correct format:

js/videoControls.js *(excerpt)*

```
if (h === 0) {
  fulltime = m + ":" + secs;
} else {
  fulltime = h + ":" + m + ":" + secs;
}

return fulltime;
```

The if/else construct is included to check if the video is one hour or longer; if so, we'll format the time with two colons. Otherwise, the formatted time will use a single colon that divides minutes from seconds, which will be the case in most circumstances.

Remember where we're running this function. We've included this inside our timeupdate event handler. The function's returned result will become the content of the timeHolder element (which is the cached element with an id of timer):

js/videoControls.js *(excerpt)*

```
timeHolder[0].innerHTML = secondsToTime(videoEl.currentTime);
```

Because the timeupdate event is triggered with every fraction of a second's change, the content of the timeHolder element will change rapidly. But because we're rounding the value to the nearest second, the *visible* changes will be limited to a time update every second, even though technically the content of the timer element is changing more rapidly.

And that's it, our custom controls are done. The buttons work as expected and the timer runs smoothly. As we mentioned at the top, this isn't quite a fully functional set of controls. But you should at least have a good handle on the basics of interacting with HTML5 video from JavaScript, so have a tinker and see what else you can add.

Further Features of the Media Elements API

The API has much more to it than what we've covered here. Here's a summary of some events and attributes that you might want to use when building your own custom controls, or when working with `video` and `audio` elements.

One point to remember is that these API methods and properties can be used anywhere in your JavaScript—they don't need to be linked to custom controls. If you'd like to play a video when the mouse hovers over it, or use `audio` elements to play various sounds associated with your web application or game, all you need to do is call the appropriate methods.

Events

We've already seen the `canplaythrough`, `play`, `pause`, `volumechange`, `ended`, and `timeupdate` events. Here are some of the other events available to you when working with HTML5 video and audio:

`canplay`

This is similar to `canplaythrough`, but will fire as soon as the video is playable, even if it's just a few frames. (This contrasts with `canplaythrough`, as you'll remember, which only fires if the browser thinks it can play the video all the way to the end without rebuffering.)

`error`

This event is sent when an error has occurred; there's also an `error` attribute.

`loadeddata`

The first frame of the media has loaded.

`loadedmetadata`

This event is sent when the media's metadata has finished loading. This would include dimensions, duration, and any text tracks (for captions).

playing

> This indicates that the media has begun to play. The difference between `playing` and `play` is that `play` will not be sent if the video loops and begins playing again, whereas `playing` will.

seeking

> This is sent when a seek operation begins. It might occur when a user starts to move the seek bar to choose a new part of the video or audio.

seeked

> This event fires when a seek operation is completed.

Attributes

In addition to the attributes we've already seen, here's a number of useful ones available to you:

playbackRate

> The default playback rate is 1. This can be changed to speed up or slow down playback. This is naturally of practical use if you're creating a fast-forward or rewind button, or a slow-motion or slow-rewind button.

src

> As its name implies, this attribute returns the URL that points to the video being played. This only works if you're using the `src` attribute on the `video` element.

currentSrc

> This will return the value of the URL pointing to the video file being played, whether it's from the `video` element's `src` attribute or one of the `source` elements.

readyState

> This attribute returns a numeric value from 0 to 4, with each state representing the readiness level of the media element. For example, a value of "1" indicates that the media's metadata is available. A value of "4" is virtually the same as the condition for firing the `canplaythrough` event, meaning the video is ready to play, and won't be interrupted by buffering or loading.

duration

> This returns the length of the video in seconds.

buffered

This represents the time ranges of the video that have buffered and are available for the browser to play.

videoWidth, videoHeight

These values return the intrinsic dimensions of the video, the actual width and height as the video was encoded—not what's declared in the HTML or CSS. Those values can be accessed through the customary width and height attributes.

You can also access attributes that are able to be declared directly in the HTML, such as preload, controls, autoplay, loop, and poster.

What about audio?

Much of what we've discussed in relation to HTML5 video and its API also apply to the audio element, with the obvious exceptions being those related to visuals.

Similar to the video element, the preload, autoplay, loop, and controls attributes can be used (or not used!) on the audio element.

The audio element won't display anything unless controls are present, but even if the element's controls are absent, the element is still accessible via scripting. This is useful if you want your site to use sounds that aren't tied to controls presented to the user. The audio element nests source tags, similar to video, and it will also treat any child element that's not a source tag as fallback content for nonsupporting browsers.

As for codec/format support, Firefox, Opera, and Chrome all support Ogg/Vorbis; Safari, Chrome, and IE9 support MP3; and every supporting browser supports WAV. Safari also supports AIFF. At present, MP3 and Ogg/Vorbis will be enough to cover you for all supporting browsers.

Accessible Media

In addition to their status as first-class citizens of the page, making them intrinsically more keyboard accessible (using `tabindex`, for example), the HTML5 media elements also give you access to the `track` element to display captions or a transcript of the media file being played. Like `source` elements, `track` elements should be placed as children of the `video` or `audio` element.

The `track` element is still in flux, but if included as a child of the `video` element, it would look like the example shown here (similar to an example given in the spec):

```
<video src="brave.webm">
  <track kind="subtitles" src="brave.en.vtt" srclang="en"
➥label="English">
  <track kind="captions" src="brave.en.vtt" srclang="en"
➥label="English for the Hard of Hearing">
  <track kind="subtitles" src="brave.fr.vtt" srclang="fr"
➥label="Français">
  <track kind="subtitles" src="brave.de.vtt" srclang="de"
➥label="Deutsch">
</video>
```

The code here has four `track` elements, each referencing a text track for captions in a different language (or, in the case of the second one, alternate content in the same language).

The `kind` attribute can take one of five values: `subtitles`, `captions`, `descriptions`, `chapters`, and `metadata`. The `src` attribute is required, and points to an external file that holds the track information. The `srclang` attribute specifies the language. Finally, the `label` attribute gives a user-readable title for the track.

As of this writing, the `track` element is yet to be supported by any browser. For more info on this new element, see the W3C spec.[11]

---

[11] http://dev.w3.org/html5/spec/Overview.html#the-track-element

It's Showtime

Video and audio on the Web have long been the stronghold of Flash, but, as we've seen, HTML5 is set to change that. While the codec and format landscape is presently fragmented, the promises of fully scriptable multimedia content, along with the performance benefits of running audio and video natively in the browser instead of in a plugin wrapper, are hugely appealing to web designers, developers, and content providers.

Because we have access to nearly foolproof fallback techniques, there's no reason not to start experimenting with these elements now. At the very least, we'll be better prepared when support is more universal.

We've now covered just about everything on HTML5 "proper" (that is, the bits that are in the HTML5 spec). In the next few chapters, we'll turn our attention to CSS3, and start to make *The HTML5 Herald* look downright *fancy*. After that, we'll finish by looking at the new JavaScript APIs that are frequently bundled with the term "HTML5."

Introducing CSS3

The content layer is done! Now it's time to make it pretty. The next four chapters focus on presentation. In this one, we'll start by covering some basics: we'll first do a quick overview of CSS selectors, and see what's been added to our arsenal in CSS3. Then, we'll take a look at a few new ways of specifying colors. We'll then dive into rounded corners, drop shadows, and text shadows—tips and tricks enabling us to style pages without having to make dozens of rounded-corner and text images to match our designs.

But first, we need to make sure older browsers recognize the new elements on our page, so that we can style them.

Getting Older Browsers on Board

As we mentioned back in Chapter 1, styling the new HTML5 elements in older versions of Internet Explorer requires a snippet of JavaScript called an HTML5 shiv. If you're using the Modernizr library detailed in Appendix A (which includes a similar piece of code), you'll be fine.

Even with this JavaScript in place, though, you're not quite ready to roll. IE6 through 8 will now be aware of these new elements, but they'll still lack any default styles. In fact, this will be the case for previous versions of other browsers as well; while they may allow arbitrary elements, they've no way of knowing, for example, that `article` should be block-level and `mark` should be inline. Because elements render as inline by default, it makes sense to tell these browsers which elements should be block-level.

This can be done with the following simple CSS rule:

css/styles.css (excerpt)

```
article, aside, figure, footer, header, hgroup, nav, section {
    display:block;
}
```

With this CSS and the required JavaScript in place, all browsers will start off on an even footing when it comes to styling HTML5 elements.

CSS3 Selectors

Selectors are at the heart of CSS. Without selectors to target elements on the page, the only way to modify the CSS properties of an element would be to use the element's `style` attribute and declare the styles inline. This, of course, is ugly, awkward, and unmaintainable. So we use selectors. Originally, CSS allowed the matching of elements by type, class, and/or id. This required adding `class` and `id` attributes to our markup to create hooks and differentiate between elements of the same type. CSS2.1 added pseudo-elements, pseudo-classes, and combinators. With CSS3, we can target almost any element on the page with a wide range of selectors.

In the descriptions that follow, we'll be including the selectors provided to us in earlier versions of CSS. They are included because, while we can now start using CSS3 selectors, all the selectors from previous versions of CSS are still supported. Even for those selectors that have been around for quite some time, it's worth going over them here, as browser support for many of them has only just reached the point of making them usable.

Relational Selectors

Relational selectors target elements based on their relationship to another element within the markup. All of these are supported in IE7+, Firefox, Opera, and WebKit:

Descendant (E F)

You should definitely be familiar with this one. The descendant selector targets any element F that is a descendant (child, grandchild, great grandchild, and so on) of an element E. For example, `ol li` targets `li` elements that are inside ordered lists. This would include `li` elements in a `ul` that's nested in an `ol`—which might not be what you want.

Child (E > F)

This selector matches any element F that is a *direct child* of element E—any further nested elements will be ignored. Continuing the above example, `ol > li` would only target `li` elements directly inside the `ol`, and would omit those nested inside a `ul`.

Adjacent Sibling (E + F)

This will match any element F that shares the same parent as E, and comes *directly after* E in the markup. For example, `li + li` will target all `li` elements except the first `li` in a given container.

General Sibling (E ~ F)

This one's a little trickier. It will match any element F that shares the same parent as any E and comes after it in the markup. So, `h1~h2` will match any `h2` that follows an `h1`, as long as they both share the same direct parent—that is, as long as the `h2` is not nested in any other element.

Let's look at a quick example:

```
<article>
  <header>
    <h1>Main title</h1>
    <h2>This subtitle is matched </h2>
  </header>
 <p> blah, blah, blah …</p>
  <h2>This is not matched by h1~h2, but is by header~h2</h2>
   <p> blah, blah, blah …</p>
</article>
```

The selector string h1~h2 will match the first h2, because they're both children, or direct descendants, of the header. The second h2 doesn't match, since its parent is article, not header. It would, however, match header~h2. Similarly, h2~p only matches the last paragraph, since the first paragraph precedes the h2 with which it shares the parent article.

There Are No Backwards Selectors

You'll notice that there's no "parent" or "ancestor" selector, and there's also no "preceding sibling" selector. This can be annoying sometimes, but there's a reason for it: if the browser had to go backwards up the DOM tree, or recurse into sets of nested elements before deciding whether or not to apply a style, rendering would be exponentially slower and more demanding in terms of processing. See http://snook.ca/archives/html_and_css/css-parent-selectors for a more in-depth explanation of this issue.

Looking through the stylesheet for *The HTML5 Herald*, you'll see a number of places where we've used these selectors. For example, when determining the overall layout of the site, we want the three-column divs to be floated left. To avoid this style being applied to any other divs nested inside them, we use the child selector:

css/styles.css *(excerpt)*

```
#main > div {
  float: left;
  overflow:hidden;
}
```

As we add new styles to the site over the course of the next few chapters, you'll be seeing a lot of these selector types.

Attribute Selectors

CSS2 introduced several attribute selectors. These allow for matching elements based on their attributes. CSS3 expands upon those attribute selectors, allowing for some targeting based on pattern matching.

E[attr]

Matches any element E that has the attribute attr with any value. We made use of this back in Chapter 4 to style required inputs—input:required works in

the latest browsers, but `input[required]` has the same effect and works in some slightly older ones.

E[attr=val]

Matches any element E that has the attribute `attr` with the exact, case-insensitive value `val`. While not new, it's helpful in targeting form input types—for instance, target checkboxes with `input[type=checkbox]`.

E[attr|=val]

Matches any element E whose attribute `attr` either has the value `val` or begins with `val-`. This is most commonly used for the `lang` attribute (as in `lang="en-us"`). For example, `p[lang|="en"]` would match any paragraph that has been defined as being in English, whether it be UK or US English.

E[attr~=val]

Matches any element E whose attribute `attr` has within its value the full word `val`, surrounded by whitespace. For example, `.info[title~=more]` would match any element with the class `info` that had a `title` attribute containing the word "more," such as "Click here for more information."

E[attr^=val] (IE8+, WebKit, Opera, Mozilla)

Matches any element E whose attribute `attr` starts with the value `val`. In other words, the `val` matches the beginning of the attribute value.

E[attr$=val] (IE8+, WebKit, Opera, Mozilla)

Matches any element E whose attribute `attr` *ends* in `val`. In other words, the `val` matches the end of the attribute value.

E[attr*=val] (IE8+, WebKit, Opera, Mozilla)

Matches any element E whose attribute `attr` matches `val` anywhere within the attribute. In other words, the string `val` is matched anywhere in the attribute value. It is similar to `E[attr~=val]` above, except the `val` can be part of a word. Using the same example as above, `.fakelink[title~=info] {}` would match any element with the class `fakelink` that has a `title` attribute containing the string `info`, such as "Click here for more information."

Pseudo-classes

It's likely that you're already familiar with some of the user interaction pseudo-classes, namely `:link`, `:visited`, `:hover`, `:active`, and `:focus`.

Key Points to Remember

1. The `:visited` pseudo-class may pose a security risk, and may not be fully supported in the future. In short, malicious sites can apply a style to a `visited` link, then use JavaScript to check the styles of links to popular sites. This allows the attacker to glimpse the user's browsing history without their permission. As a result, several browsers have begun limiting the styles that can be applied with `:visited`, and some others (notably Safari 5) have disabled it entirely.

   The spec explicitly condones these changes, saying: "UAs [User Agents] may therefore treat all links as unvisited links, or implement other measures to preserve the user's privacy while rendering visited and unvisited links differently."

2. For better accessibility, add `:focus` wherever you include `:hover`, as not all visitors will use a mouse to navigate your site.

3. `:hover` can apply to any element on the page—not just links and form controls.

4. `:focus` and `:active` are relevant to links, form controls, and any element with a `tabindex` attribute.

While it's likely you've been using these basic pseudo-classes for some time, there are many other pseudo-classes available. Several of these have been in the specification for years, but weren't supported (or commonly known) until browsers started supporting the new HTML5 form attributes that made them more relevant.

The following pseudo-classes match elements based on attributes, user interaction, and form control state:

`:enabled`
> A user interface element that's enabled.

`:disabled`
> Conversely, a user interface element that's disabled.

:checked

> Radio buttons or checkboxes that are selected or ticked.

:indeterminate

> Form elements that are neither checked nor unchecked. This pseudo-class is still being considered, and may be included in the specification in the future.

:target

> This selector singles out the element that is the target of the currently active intrapage anchor. That sounds more complicated than it is: you already know you can have links to anchors within a page by using the # character with the id of the target. For example, you may have `<a href="#content">Skip to content</a>` link in your page that, when clicked, will jump to the element with an id of `content`.
>
> This changes the URL in the address bar to `thispage.html#content`—and the `:target` selector now matches the #content element, as if you had included, temporarily, the selector #content. We say "temporarily" because as soon as the user clicks on a different anchor, `:target` will match the new target.

:default

> Applies to one or more UI elements that are the default among a set of similar elements.

:valid

> Applies to elements that are valid, based on the `type` or `pattern` attributes (as we discussed in Chapter 4).

:invalid

> Applies to empty required elements, and elements failing to match the requirements defined by the `type` or `pattern` attributes.

:in-range

> Applies to elements with range limitations, where the value is within those limitations. This applies, for example, to `number` and `range` input types with `min` and `max` attributes.

:out-of-range

> The opposite of :in-range: elements whose value is *outside* the limitations of their range.

:required

> Applies to form controls that have the required attribute set.

:optional

> Applies to all form controls that *do not* have the required attribute.

:read-only

> Applies to elements whose contents are unable to be altered by the user. This is usually most elements other than form fields.

:read-write

> Applies to elements whose contents are user-alterable, such as text input fields.

Browser support for these pseudo-classes is uneven, but improving fairly rapidly. Browsers that support form control attributes like required and pattern also support the associated :valid and :invalid pseudo-classes.

IE6 fails to understand :hover on elements other than links, and neither IE6 nor IE7 understand :focus. IE8 and earlier lack support for :checked, :enabled, :disabled, and :target. The good news is that IE9 *does* support these selectors.

While support is still lacking, JavaScript libraries such as jQuery can help in targeting these pseudo-classes in nonsupporting browsers.

Structural Pseudo-classes

So far, we've seen how we can target elements based on their attributes and states. CSS3 also enables us to target elements based simply on their location in the markup. These selectors are grouped under the heading structural pseudo-classes.[1]

These might seem complicated right now, but they'll make more sense as we look at ways to apply them later on. These selectors are supported in IE9, as well as current and older versions of all the other browsers—but not in IE8 and below.

---

[1] http://www.w3.org/TR/css3-selectors/#structural-pseudos

:root

The root element, which is always the `html` element.

E F:nth-child(n)

The element F that is the nth child of its parent E.

E F:nth-last-child(n)

The element F that is the nth child of its parent E, counting backwards from the last one. `li:nth-last-child(1)` would match the last item in any list—this is the same as `li:last-child` (see below).

E:nth-of-type(n)

The element that is the nth element of its type in a given parent element.

E:nth-last-of-type(n)

Like `nth-of-type(n)`, except counting backwards from the last element in a parent.

E:first-child

The element E that is the first child E of its parent. This is the same as `:nth-child(1)`.

E:last-child

The element E that is the last child E of its parent, same as `:nth-last-child(1)`.

E:first-of-type

Same as `:nth-of-type(1)`.

E:last-of-type

Same as `:nth-last-of-type(1)`.

E:only-child

An element that's the only child of its parent.

E:only-of-type

An element that's the only one of its type inside its parent element.

E:empty

An element that has no children; this includes text nodes, so `<p>hello</p>` will not be matched.

E:lang(en)

An element in the language denoted by the two-letter abbreviation (en).

E:not(exception)

This is a particularly useful one: it will select elements that *don't* match the selector in the parentheses.

Selectors with the :not pseudo-class match everything to the left of the colon, and then exclude from that matched group the elements that also match what's to the right of the colon. The left-hand side matching goes first. For example, p:not(.copyright) will match all the paragraphs in a document first, and then exclude all the paragraphs from the set that also have the class of copyright. You can string several :not pseudo-classes together. h2:not(header > h2):not(.logo) will match all h2s on a page except those that are in a header and those that have a class of logo.

What is n?

There are four pseudo-classes that take an *n* parameter in parentheses: :nth-child(n), :nth-last-child(n), :nth-of-type(n), and :nth-last-of-type(n).

In the simplest case, *n* can be an integer. For example, :nth-of-type(1) will target the first element in a series. You can also pass one of the two keywords odd or even, targeting every other element. You can also, more powerfully, pass a number expression such as :nth-of-type(3n+1). 3n means every third element, defining the frequency, and +1 is the offset. The default offset is zero, so where :nth-of-type(3n) would match the 3rd, 6th, and 9th elements in a series, :nth-of-type(3n+1) would match the 1st, 4th, 7th, and so on. Negative offsets are also allowed.

With these numeric pseudo-classes, you can pinpoint which elements you want to target without adding classes to the markup. The most common example is a table where every other row should be a slightly darker color to make it easier to read. We used to have to add odd or even classes to every tr to accomplish this. Now, we can simply declare tr:nth-of-type(odd) to target every odd line without touching the markup. You can even take it a step further with three-colored striped tables: target :nth-of-type(3n), :nth-of-type(3n+1), and :nth-of-type(3n+2) and apply a different color to each.

Pseudo-elements and Generated Content

In addition to pseudo-classes, CSS gives us access to **pseudo-elements**. Pseudo-elements allow you to target text that's part of the document, but not otherwise targetable in the document tree. Pseudo-classes generally reflect some attribute or state of the element that is not otherwise easily or reliably detectable in CSS. Pseudo-elements, on the other hand, represent some structure of the document that's outside of the DOM.

For example, all text nodes have a first letter and a first line, but how can you target them without wrapping them in a span? CSS provides the `::first-letter` and `::first-line` pseudo-elements that match the first letter and first line of a text node, respectively. These can alternatively be written with just a single colon: `:first-line` and `:first-letter`.

Why bother with the double colon?

The double colon is the correct syntax, but the single colon is better supported. IE6, IE7, and IE8 only understand the single-colon notation. All other browsers support both. Even though `:first-letter`, `:first-line`, `:first-child`, `:before`, and `:after` have been around since CSS2, these pseudo-elements in CSS3 have been redefined using double colons to differentiate them from pseudo-classes.

Generated Content

The `::before` and `::after` pseudo-elements don't refer to content that exists in the markup, but rather to a location where you can insert additional content, generated right there in your CSS. While this generated content doesn't become part of the DOM, it can be styled.

To generate content for a pseudo-element, use the `content` property. For example, let's say you wanted all external links on your page to be followed by the URL they point to in parentheses, to make it clear to your users that they'll be leaving your page. Rather than hardcoding the URLs into your markup, you can use the combination of an attribute selector and the `::after` pseudo-element:

```
a[href^=http]:after {
  content: " (" attr(href) ")";
}
```

attr() allows you to access any attributes of the selected element, coming in handy here for displaying the link's target. And you'll remember from the attribute selectors section that a[href^=http] means "any a element whose href attribute begins with http"; in other words, external links.

Here's another example:

```
a[href$=pdf] {
  background: transparent url(pdficon.gif) 0 50% no-repeat;
  padding-left: 20px;
}
a[href$=pdf]:after {
  content: " (PDF)";
}
```

Those styles will add a PDF icon and the text "(PDF)" after links to PDFs. Remember that the [attr$=val] selector matches the *end* of an attribute—so document.pdf will match but page.html won't.

::selection

The ::selection pseudo-element matches text that is highlighted.

This is supported in WebKit, and with the -moz vendor prefix in Firefox. Let's use it on *The HTML5 Herald*, to bring the selection background and text color in line with the monochrome style of the rest of the site:

```
                                                    css/styles.css (excerpt)
::-moz-selection{
  background: #484848;
  color:#fff;
}
::selection {
  background:#484848;
  color:#fff;
}
```

CSS3 Colors

We know you're probably chomping at the bit to put the *really* cool stuff from CSS3 into practice, but before we do there's one more detour we need to take. CSS3 brings with it support for some new ways of describing colors on the page. Since we'll be using these in examples over the next few chapters, it's important we cover them now.

Prior to CSS3, we almost always declared colors using the hexadecimal format (#FFF, or #FFFFFF for white). It was also possible to declare colors using the rgb() notation, providing either integers (0–255) or percentages. For example, white is rgb(255,255,255) or rgb(100%,100%,100%). In addition, we had access to a few named colors, like purple, lime, aqua, red, and the like. While the color keyword list has been extended in the CSS3 color module[2] to include 147 additional keyword colors (that are generally well supported), CSS3 also provides us with a number of other options: HSL, HSLA, and RGBA. The most notable change with these new color types is the ability to declare semitransparent colors.

RGBA

RGBA works just like RGB, except that it adds a fourth value: **alpha**, the opacity level. The first three values still represent red, green, and blue. For the alpha value, 1 means fully opaque, 0 is fully transparent, and 0.5 is 50% opaque. You can use any number between 0 and 1, inclusively.

Unlike RGB, which can also be represented with hexadecimal notation as #RRGGBB, there is no hexadecimal notation for RGBA. There's been some discussion of including an eight-character hexadecimal value for RGBA as #RRGGBBAA, but this has yet to be added to the draft specification.

For an example, let's look at our registration form. We want the form to be a darker color, while still preserving the grainy texture of the site's background. To accomplish this, we'll use an RGBA color of 0,0,0,0.2—in other words, solid black that's 80% transparent:

---

[2] http://www.w3.org/TR/css3-color/

```
                                                    css/styles.css (excerpt)
form {
    ⋮
    background: rgba(0,0,0,0.2) url(../images/bg-form.png) no-repeat
➥bottom center;
}
```

Since Internet Explorer 8 and below lack support for RGBA, if you declare an RGBA color, make sure you *precede* it with a color IE can understand. IE will render the last color it can make sense of, so it will just skip the RGBA color. Other browsers will understand both colors, but thanks to the CSS cascade, they'll overwrite the IE color with the RGBA color as it comes later.

In the above example, we're actually fine with older versions of IE having no background color, because the color we're using is mostly transparent anyway.

HSL and HSLA

HSL stands for hue, saturation, and lightness. Unlike RGB, where you need to manipulate the saturation or brightness of a color by changing all three color values in concert, with HSL you can tweak either just the saturation, or the lightness, while keeping the same base hue. The syntax for HSL comprises integer for hue, and percentage values for saturation and lightness.[3]

Although monitors display colors as RGB, the browser simply converts the HSL value you give it into one the monitor can display.

The hsl() declaration accepts three values:

- The hue, in degrees from 0 to 359. Some examples: 0 = red, 60 = yellow, 120 = green, 180 = cyan, 240 = blue, and 300 = magenta. Of course, feel free to use everything in between.

---

[3] A full exploration of color theory—along with what is meant by the terms saturation and lightness—is beyond the scope of this book. If you want to read more, Jason Beaird's *The Principles of Beautiful Web Design* (SitePoint: Melbourne, 2010) [http://www.sitepoint.com/books/design2/] includes a great primer on color.

- The saturation, as a percentage. 100% is the norm for saturation. Saturation of 100% will be the full hue, and saturation of 0 will give you a shade of gray—essentially causing the hue value to be ignored.

- A percentage for lightness, with 50% being the norm. Lightness of 100% will be white, 50% will be the actual hue, and 0% will be black.

HSL also allows for an opacity value. For example, `hsla(300, 100%, 50%, 0.5)` is magenta with full saturation and normal lightness, which is 50% opaque.

HSL mimics the way the human eye perceives color, so it can be more intuitive for designers to understand —and, as mentioned above, it can make adjustments a bit quicker and easier. Feel free to use whatever syntax you're most comfortable with—but remember that if you need to support IE8 or below, you'll generally want to limit yourself to hexadecimal notation.

Let's sum up with a review of all the ways to write colors in CSS. A shade of dark red can be written as:

- `#800000`
- `maroon`
- `rgb(128,0,0)`
- `rgba(128,0,0,1.0)`
- `hsl(0,100%,13%)`
- `hsla(0,100%,13%,1.0)`

Opacity

In addition to specifying transparency with HSLA and RGBA colors, CSS3 also provides us with the `opacity` property. `opacity` sets the opaqueness of the element on which it's declared. Similar to alpha transparency, the opacity value is a floating point number between (and including) 0 and 1. An opacity value of 0 defines the element as fully transparent, whereas an opacity value of 1 means the element is fully opaque.

Let's look at an example:

```
div.halfopaque {
  background-color: rgb(0, 0, 0);
  opacity: 0.5;
  color: #000000;
}

div.halfalpha{
  background-color: rgba(0, 0, 0, 0.5);
  color: #000000;
}
```

While the two declaration blocks above may seem to be identical at first glance, there's actually a key difference. While `opacity` sets the opacity value for an element *and all of its children*, a semitransparent RGBA or HSLA color has no impact on elements other than the one it's declared on.

Looking at the example above, any text in the `halfopaque` div will also be 50% opaque (most likely making it difficult to read!); the text on the `halfalpha` div, though, will still be 100% opaque.

So, while the `opacity` property is a quick and easy solution for creating semitransparent elements, you should be aware of this consequence.

Putting It into Practice

Now that we've been through all the available CSS selectors and new color types, we're ready to really start styling.

For the rest of the chapter, we'll style a small section of *The HTML5 Herald* front page; this will demonstrate how to add rounded corners, text shadow, and box shadow.

In the right-hand sidebar of *The HTML5 Herald*'s front page are a series of whimsical advertisements—we marked them up as `article` elements within an `aside` way back in Chapter 2. The first of these is an old "Wanted" poster-style ad, advising readers to be on the look out for the armed and dangerous HTML5 and CSS3. The ad's final appearance is depicted in Figure 6.1.

Figure 6.1. Our "Wanted" ad

You'll notice that the dark gray box in the center of the ad has a double border with rounded corners, as well as a three-dimensional "pop" to it. The text that reads "<HTML5> & {CSS3}" also has a shadow that offsets it from the background. Thanks to CSS3, all these effects can be achieved with some simple code, and with no reliance on images or JavaScript. Let's learn how it's done.

The markup for the box is simply `<a href="…">&lt;HTML5&gt; &amp; {CSS3}</a>`. Other than the HTML entities, it's as straightforward as it gets!

Before we can apply any styles to it, we need to select it. Of course, we could just add a `class` attribute to the markup, but where's the fun in that? We're here to learn CSS3, so we should try and use some fancy new selectors instead.

Our box isn't the only a element on the page, but it might be the only a immediately following a paragraph in the sidebar. In this case, that's good enough to single out the box. We also know how to add some pre-CSS3 styling for the basics, so let's do that:

css/styles.css *(excerpt)*

```
aside p + a {
  display: block;
  text-decoration: none;
  border: 5px double;
  color: #ffffff;
  background-color: #484848;
  text-align: center;
```

```
    font-size: 28px;
    margin: 5px 5px 9px 5px;
    padding: 15px 0;
    position: relative;
}
```

Not bad! As Figure 6.2 shows, we're well on our way to the desired appearance. This will also be the appearance shown to IE8 and below except for the font styling, which we'll be adding in Chapter 9.

Figure 6.2. The basic appearance of our ad link, which will be seen by older browsers

Remember that IE6 lacks support for the adjacent sibling selector—so if you need to provide support to that browser, you can use a more common `id` or `class` selector.

This presentation is fine, and should be acceptable—no need for web pages to look identical in all browsers. Users with older versions of Internet Explorer will be unaware that they're missing anything. But we can still provide treats to better browsers. Let's go ahead and add a bit of polish.

Rounded Corners: `border-radius`

The `border-radius` property lets you create rounded corners without the need for images or additional markup. To add rounded corners to our box, we simply add:

```
-moz-border-radius: 25px;
border-radius: 25px;
```

Safari, Chrome, Opera, IE9, and Firefox 4 support rounded corners without a vendor prefix (just `border-radius`). We still need to include the vendor-prefixed `-moz-border-radius` for Firefox 3.6 and earlier, though by the time you read this those versions may have dwindled enough for it to be no longer necessary.

Figure 6.3 shows what our link looks like with the addition of these properties.

Figure 6.3. Adding rounded corners to our link

The border-radius property is actually a shorthand. For our a element, the corners are all the same size and symmetrical. If we had wanted different-sized corners, we could declare up to four unique values—border-radius: 5px 10px 15px 20px;, for example. Just like padding, margin, and border, you can adjust each value individually:

```
border-top-left-radius: 5px;
border-top-right-radius: 10px;
border-bottom-right-radius: 15px;
border-bottom-left-radius: 40px;
```

The -moz- prefixed form for older versions of Firefox uses a slightly different syntax:

```
-moz-border-radius-topleft: 5px;
-moz-border-radius-topright: 10px;
-moz-border-radius-bottomright: 15px;
-moz-border-radius-bottomleft: 40px;
```

The resulting off-kilter box is shown in Figure 6.4.

Figure 6.4. It's possible to set the radius of each corner independently

When using the shorthand border-radius, the order of the corners is top-left, top-right, bottom-right, and bottom-left. You can also declare only two values, in which case the first is for top-left and bottom-right, and the second is for top-right and bottom-left. If you declare three values, the first refers to top-left, the second sets both the top-right and bottom-left, and the third is bottom-right.

We recommend using the shorthand—because it's much shorter, and because until old versions of Firefox no longer require support, it avoids the need to use two different syntaxes.

You can also create asymmetrical corners with a different radius on each side. Rather than being circular, these will appear elliptical. If two values are supplied to any of the four longhand values, you'll be defining the horizontal and vertical radii of a quarter ellipse respectively. For example, border-bottom-left-radius: 20px 10px; will create an elliptical bottom-left corner.

When using the shorthand for elliptical corners, separate the value of the horizontal and vertical radii with a slash. border-radius: 20px / 10px; will create four equal, elliptical corners, and border-radius: 5px 10px 15px 20px / 10px 20px 30px 40px; will create four unequal, elliptical corners. That last example will create corners seen in Figure 6.5. Interesting? Yes. Aesthetically pleasing? Not so much.

Figure 6.5. Four interesting, unequal, elliptical corners

With an Eye to the Future

When including prefixed properties, always follow with the correctly written, nonprefixed, standards-compliant syntax. This will ensure that your site is forward compatible!

There's only one other element on *The HTML5 Herald* that uses rounded corners: the registration form's submit button. Let's round those corners now:

```
                                                    css/styles.ss (excerpt)

input[type=submit] {
  -moz-border-radius: 10%;
  border-radius: 10%;
}
```

You'll note two things about the above CSS: we've used an attribute selector to target the submit input type, and we've used percentages instead of pixel values for the rounded corners. This will come in handy if we need to add more forms to the site later; other submit buttons might be smaller than the one on the registration page, and by using percentages, rounded corners will scale in proportion to the size of the button.

The border-radius property can be applied to all elements, except the table element when the border-collapse property is set to collapse.

What about older browsers?

Generally speaking, there's no need to provide an identical look in older browsers, but sometimes a client may insist on it. In the case of rounded corners, one common method is to dynamically generate four additional elements—one for each corner. You'd then use JavaScript to add four spans to all the elements you want rounded and, in your CSS, provide background images to each span corresponding to the relevant corner.

While methods like this one provide the desired look, they require JavaScript, additional markup, CSS, and/or images. Additionally, if there's a design change —for example, the color, radius, or border—the background images will need to be recreated. Fortunately, there are some JavaScript solutions that provide CSS3 decorations to older versions of IE without requiring additional images or markup; CSS3 PIE[4] is one that's worth looking into.

---

[4] http://css3pie.com/

Drop Shadows

CSS3 provides the ability to add drop shadows to elements using the box-shadow property. This property lets you specify the color, height, width, blur, and offset of one or multiple inner and/or outer drop shadows on your elements.

We usually think of drop shadows as an effect that makes an element look like it's "hovering" over the page and leaving a shadow; however, with such fine-grained control over all those variables, you can be quite creative. For our advertisement link, we can use a box-shadow with no blur to create the appearance of a 3D box.

The box-shadow property takes a comma-separated list of shadows as its value. Each shadow is defined by two to four size values, a color, and the key term inset for inset—or internal—shadows. If you fail to specify inset, the default is for the shadow to be drawn outside of the element:

Let's look at the shadow we're using on our element, so that we can break down what each value is doing:

css/styles.css *(excerpt)*

```
-webkit-box-shadow: 2px 5px 0 0 rgba(72,72,72,1);
-moz-box-shadow: 2px 5px 0 0 rgba(72,72,72,1);
box-shadow: 2px 5px 0 0 rgba(72,72,72,1);
```

The first value is the horizontal offset. A positive value will create a shadow to the right of the element, a negative value to the left. In our case, our shadow is two pixels to the right of the a.

The second value is the vertical offset. A positive value pushes the shadow down, creating a shadow on the bottom of the element. A negative value pushes the shadow up. In our case, the shadow is five pixels below the a.

The third value, if included, is the blur distance of the shadow. The greater the value, the more the shadow is blurred. Only positive values are allowed. Our shadow is not blurred, so we can either include a value of zero (0), or omit the value altogether.

The fourth value determines the spread distance of the shadow. A positive value will cause the shadow shape to expand in all directions. A negative value contracts

the shadow. Our shadow has no spread, so again we can either include a value of zero (0), or omit the value altogether.

The fifth value above is the color. You will generally want to declare the color of the shadow. If it's omitted, the spec states that it should default to the same as the `color` property of the element. Opera and Firefox support this default behavior, but WebKit doesn't, so be sure to include the color. In the example above, we used an RGBA color. In this particular design, the shadow is a solid color, so we could just have used the hex value. Most of the time, though, shadows will be partially transparent, so you'll be using RGBA or HSLA, usually.

The drop shadow created by these declarations is shown in Figure 6.6.

Figure 6.6. Adding a drop shadow to our box gives it the illusion of depth

By default, the shadow is a drop shadow—occurring on the outside of the box. You can create an inset shadow by adding the word `inset` to the start of your shadow declaration.

Opera, Firefox 4, and IE9 support the nonprefixed syntax. We're still including the `-moz-` prefix for Firefox 3.6 and earlier, and the `-webkit-` prefix for Safari and Chrome. However, current development versions of WebKit support the unprefixed version, and Firefox 4 will soon supplant the older versions, so the need for prefixing should wane.

Drop Shadows on IE6+

To include box shadows in IE6 through IE8, you have to use a proprietary filter like the one shown below. Be warned, though, that it's almost impossible to make it look the same as a CSS3 shadow. You should also be aware that filters have a significant impact on performance, so you should only use them if it's *absolutely* necessary for those older browsers to see your shadows. Moreover, these styles should be in a separate stylesheet targeted to earlier versions of IE with the help of conditional comments—otherwise they'll mess with your standard CSS3 shadows on IE9:

```
filter: shadow(color=#484848, direction=220, Strength=8);
filter:progid:DXImageTransform.Microsoft.dropshadow(OffX=2,
➥OffY=5, Color='#484848', Positive='true');
```

Nonrectangular shadows?

Drop shadows look good on rectangular elements, including those with rounded corners like ours. We're using the `border-radius` property on our element, so the shadow will follow the curve of the corners, which looks good.

Keep in mind, though, that the shadow follows the *edges* of your element, rather than the pixels of your content. So, if you try to use drop shadows on semitransparent images, you'll receive an ugly surprise: the shadow follows the rectangular borders of the image instead of the contour of the image's content.

To include more than one box shadow on an element, define a comma-separated list of shadows. When more than one shadow is specified, the shadows are layered front to back, as if the browser drew the last shadow first, and the previous shadow on top of that.

Like an element's outline, box shadows are *supposed* to be invisible in terms of the box model. In other words, they should have no impact on the layout of a page —they'll overlap other boxes and their shadows if necessary. We say "supposed to," because there are bugs in some browsers, though these are few, and will likely be fixed fairly quickly.

Inset and Multiple Shadows

The registration form for *The HTML5 Herald* has what looks like a gradient background around the edges, but it's actually a few inset box shadows.

To create an inset box shadow, add the `inset` key term to your declaration. In our
case, we have to include two shadows so that we cover all four sides: one shadow
for the top left, and one for the bottom right:

```
                                                        css/styles.css (excerpt)

form {
  -webkit-box-shadow:
    inset 1px 1px 84px rgba(0,0,0,0.24),
    inset -1px -1px 84px rgba(0,0,0,0.24);
  -moz-box-shadow:
    inset 1px 1px 84px rgba(0,0,0,0.24),
    inset -1px -1px 84px rgba(0,0,0,0.24);
  box-shadow:
    inset 1px 1px 84px rgba(0,0,0,0.24),
    inset -1px -1px 84px rgba(0,0,0,0.24);
}
```

As you can see, to add multiple shadows to an element, you simply need to repeat
the same syntax again, separated with a comma.

WebKit and Inset Shadows

Current versions of WebKit-based browsers suffer from *very* slow performance
when rendering inset box shadows with a large `blur` value, like the one we're
using on *The HTML5 Herald*'s registration form.

Because WebKit supports both the `-webkit-` prefixed and unprefixed forms of
the `box-shadow` property, we've had to omit both of these from the finished CSS.
We could only include the `-moz-` prefixed property, so, unfortunately, Firefox is
the sole beneficiary of our nice big inset shadow.

This bug has been fixed in the current development version of the WebKit engine,
but it might be some time before the fix makes its way into releases of every
WebKit-based browser. Therefore, if you're using inset shadows, be sure to do
plenty of browser testing.

Text Shadow

Where `box-shadow` lets us add shadows to boxes, `text-shadow` adds shadows to individual characters in text nodes. Added in CSS2, `text-shadow` has been supported in Safari since version 1, and is now supported in all current browser releases except IE9.

The syntax of the `text-shadow` property is very similar to `box-shadow`, including prefixes, offsets, and the ability to add multiple shadows; the exceptions are that there's no spread, and inset shadows aren't permitted:

```css
/* single shadow */
text-shadow: topOffset leftOffset blurRadius color;

/* multiple shadows */
text-shadow: topOffset1 leftOffset1 blurRadius1 color1,
             topOffset2 leftOffset2 blurRadius2 color2,
             topOffset3 leftOffset3 blurRadius3 color3;
```

Like `box-shadow`, when multiple shadows are declared, they're painted from front to back with the first shadow being the topmost. Text shadows appear behind the text itself. If a shadow is so large that it touches another letter, it will continue behind that character.

Our text has a semi-opaque shadow to the bottom right:

css/styles.css *(excerpt)*

```css
text-shadow: 3px 3px 1px rgba(0, 0, 0, 0.5);
```

This states that the shadow extends three pixels below the text, three pixels to the right of the text, is slightly blurred (one pixel), and has a base color of black at 50% opacity.

With that style in place, our ad link is nearly complete, as Figure 6.7 shows. The finishing touch—a custom font—will be added in Chapter 9.

Figure 6.7. Our ad link is looking quite snazzy!

More Shadows

We now know how to create drop shadows on both block-level elements and text nodes. But so far, we've only styled a fraction of our page: only one link in one advertisement, in fact. Let's do the rest of the shadows before moving on.

Looking back at the site design, we can see that all the h1 elements on the page are uppercase and have drop shadows. The text is dark gray with a very subtle, solid-white drop shadow on the bottom right, providing a bit of depth.[5] The tagline in the site header also has a drop shadow, but is all lowercase. The taglines for the articles, meanwhile, have no drop shadow.

We know from the section called "CSS3 Selectors" that we can target all these elements without using classes. Let's target these elements without any additional markup:

```
                                                  css/styles.css (excerpt)

h1, h2 {
  text-transform: uppercase;
  text-shadow: 1px 1px #FFFFFF;
}
:not(article) > header h2 {
  text-transform: lowercase;
  text-shadow: 1px 1px #FFFFFF;
}
```

The first declaration targets all the h1 elements and h2 elements on the page. The second targets all the h2 elements that are in a header, but only if that header is not nested in an article element.

---

[5] See http://twitter.com/#!/themaninblue/status/27210719975964673.

Our text shadows are a solid white, so there's no need to use alpha transparent colors, or a blur radius.

Up Next

Now that we have shadows and rounded corners under our belt, it's time to have some more fun with CSS3. In the next chapter, we'll be looking at CSS3 gradients and multiple background images.

Chapter 7

CSS3 Gradients and Multiple Backgrounds

In Chapter 6, we learned a few ways to add decorative styling features—like shadows and rounded corners—to our pages without the use of additional markup or images. The next most common feature frequently added to websites that used to require images is gradients. CSS3 provides us with the ability to create native radial and linear gradients, as well as include multiple background images on any element. With CSS3, there's no need to create the multitudes of JPEGs of years past, or add nonsemantic hooks to our markup.

Browser support for gradients and multiple backgrounds is still evolving, but as you'll see in this chapter, it's possible to develop in a way that supports the latest versions of all major browsers—including IE9.

We'll start by looking at CSS3 gradients—but first, what *are* gradients? **Gradients** are smooth transitions between two or more specified colors. In creating gradients, you can specify multiple in-between color values, called **color stops**. Each color stop is made up of a color and a position; the browser fades the color from each stop to the next to create a smooth gradient. Gradients can be utilized anywhere a

background image can be used. This means that in your CSS, a gradient can be theoretically employed anywhere a url() value can be used, such as background-image, border-image, and even list-style-type, though for now the most consistent support is for background images.

By using CSS gradients to replace images, you avoid forcing your users to download extra images, support for flexible layouts is improved, and zooming is no longer pixelated the way it can be with images.

There are two types of gradients currently available in CSS3: linear and radial. Let's go over them in turn.

Linear Gradients

Linear gradients are those where colors transition across a straight line: from top to bottom, left to right, or along any arbitrary axis. If you've spent any time with image-editing tools like Photoshop and Fireworks, you should be familiar with linear gradients—but as a refresher, Figure 7.1 shows some examples.

Figure 7.1. Linear gradient examples

Similar to image-editing programs, to create a linear gradient you specify a direction, the starting color, the end color, and any color stops you want to add along that line. The browser takes care of the rest, filling the entire element by painting lines of color perpendicular to the line of the gradient. It produces a smooth fade from one color to the next, progressing in the direction you specify.

When it comes to browsers and linear gradients, things get a little messy. WebKit first introduced gradients several years ago using a particular and, many argued, convoluted syntax. After that, Mozilla implemented gradients using a simpler and

more straightforward syntax. Then, in January of 2011, the W3C included a proposed syntax in CSS3. The new syntax is very similar to Firefox's existing implementation—in fact, it's close enough that any gradient written with the new syntax will work just fine in Firefox. The W3C syntax has also been adopted by WebKit, though, at the time of writing it's only in the nightly builds, and yet to make its way into Chrome and Safari; they are still using the old-style syntax. For backwards compatibility reasons, those browsers will continue to support the old syntax even once the standard form is implemented. And Opera, with the release of version 11.10, supports the new W3C standard for linear gradients. All the current implementations use vendor prefixes (`-webkit-`, `-moz-`, and `-o-`).

WebKit Nightly Builds

The WebKit engine that sits at the heart of Chrome and Safari exists independently as an open source project at http://www.webkit.org/. However, new features implemented in WebKit take some time to be released in Chrome or Safari. In the meantime, it's still possible to test these features by installing one of the **nightly builds**, so-called because they're built and released on a daily basis, incorporating new features or code changes from a day's work by the community. Because they're frequently released while in development, they can contain incomplete features or bugs, and will often be unstable. Still, they're great if you want to test new features (like the W3C gradient syntax) that are yet to make it into Chrome or Safari. Visit http://nightly.webkit.org/ to obtain nightly builds of WebKit for Mac or Windows.

That still leaves us with the question of how to handle gradients in IE and older versions of Opera. Fortunately, IE9 and Opera 11.01 and earlier support SVG backgrounds—and it's fairly simple to create gradients in SVG. (We'll be covering SVG in more detail in Chapter 11.) And finally, all versions of IE support a proprietary filter that enables the creation of basic linear gradients.

Confused? Don't be. While gradients are important to understand, it's unnecessary to memorize all the browser syntaxes. We'll cover the new syntax, as well as the soon-to-be-forgotten old-style WebKit syntax, and then we'll let you in on a little secret: there are tools that will create all the required styles for you, so there's no need to remember all the specifics of each syntax. Let's get started.

There's one linear gradient in *The HTML5 Herald*, in the second advertisement block shown in Figure 7.2 (which happens to be advertising this very book!). You'll

note that the gradient starts off dark at the top, lightens, then darkens again as if to create a road under the cyclist, before lightening again.

Figure 7.2. A linear gradient in *The HTML5 Herald*

To create a cross-browser gradient for our ad, we'll start with the new standard syntax. It's the simplest and easiest to understand, and likely to be the only one you'll need to use in a few years' time. After that, we'll look at how the older WebKit and Firefox syntaxes differ from it.

The W3C Syntax

Here's the basic syntax for linear gradients:

```
background-image: linear-gradient( … );
```

Inside those parentheses, you specify the direction of the gradient, and then provide some color stops. For the direction, you can provide either the angle along which the gradient should proceed, or the side or corner from which it should start—in which case it will proceed towards the opposite side or corner. For angles, you use values in degrees (deg). 0deg points to the right, 90deg is up, and so on counterclockwise. For a side or corner, use the top, bottom, left, and right keywords. After specifying the direction, provide your color stops; these are made up of a color and a percentage or length specifying how far along the gradient that stop is located.

That's a lot to take in, so let's look at some gradient examples. For the sake of illustration we'll use a gradient with just two color stops: #FFF (white) to #000 (black).

To have the gradient go from top to bottom of an element, as shown in Figure 7.3, you could specify any of the following (our examples are using the `-moz-` prefix, but remember that `-webkit-` and `-o-` support the same syntax):

```
background-image: -moz-linear-gradient(270deg, #FFF 0%, #000 100%);
background-image: -moz-linear-gradient(top, #FFF 0%, #000 100%);
background-image: -moz-linear-gradient(#FFF 0%, #000 100%);
```

Figure 7.3. A white-to-black gradient from the top center to the bottom center of an element

The last declaration works because `top` is the default in the absence of a specified direction.

Because the first color stop is assumed to be at 0%, and the last color stop is assumed to be at 100%, you could also omit the percentages from that example and achieve the same result:

```
background-image: -moz-linear-gradient(#FFF, #000);
```

Now, let's put our gradient on an angle, and place an additional color stop. Let's say we want to go from black to white, and then back to black again:

```
background-image: -moz-linear-gradient(30deg, #000, #FFF 75%, #000);
```

We've placed the color stop 75% along the way, so the white band is closer to the gradient's end point than its starting point, as shown in Figure 7.4.

Figure 7.4. A gradient with three color stops

You can place your first color stop somewhere other than 0%, and your last color stop at a place other than 100%. All the space between 0% and the first stop will be the same color as the first stop, and all the space between the last stop and 100% will be the color of the last stop. Here's an example:

```
background-image: -moz-linear-gradient(30deg, #000 50%, #FFF 75%,
➥#000 90%);
```

The resulting gradient is shown in Figure 7.5.

Figure 7.5. A gradient confined to a narrow band by offsetting the start and end color stops

You don't actually need to specify positions for any of the color stops. If you omit them, the stops will be evenly distributed. Here's an example:

```
background-image:
  -moz-linear-gradient(45deg,
    #FF0000 0%,
    #FF6633 20%,
    #FFFF00 40%,
    #00FF00 60%,
    #0000FF 80%,
    #AA00AA 100%);

background-image:
  -moz-linear-gradient(45deg,
    #FF0000,
    #FF6633,
    #FFFF00,
    #00FF00,
    #0000FF,
    #AA00AA);
```

Either of the previous declarations makes for a fairly unattractive angled rainbow. Note that we've added line breaks and indenting for ease of legibility—they are not essential.

Colors transition smoothly from one color stop to the next. However, if two color stops are placed at the same position along the gradient, the colors won't fade, but will stop and start on a hard line. This is a way to create a striped background effect, like the one shown in Figure 7.6.

Figure 7.6. Careful placement of color stops can create striped backgrounds

Here are the styles used to construct that example:

```
background-image:
  -moz-linear-gradient(45deg,
    #000000 30%,
    #666666 30%,
    #666666 60%,
    #CCCCCC 60%,
    #CCCCCC 90%);
```

At some point in the reasonably near future, you can expect this updated version of the syntax to be the only one you'll need to write—but we're not quite there yet.

The Old WebKit Syntax

As we've mentioned, the latest development version of WebKit has adopted the W3C syntax; however, most current releases of WebKit-based browsers still use an older syntax, which is a little more complicated. Because those browsers still need to be supported, let's quickly take a look at the old syntax, using our first white-to-black gradient example again:

```
background-image:
  -webkit-gradient(linear, 0% 0%, 0% 100%, from(#FFFFFF),
➡to(#000000));
```

Rather than use a specific linear-gradient property, there's a general-purpose -webkit-gradient property, where you specify the type of gradient (linear in this case) as the first parameter. The linear gradient then needs both a start and end point to determine the direction of the gradient. The start and end points can be specified using percentages, numeric values, or the keywords top, bottom, left, right, or center.

The next step is to declare color stops of the gradients. You can include the originating color with the from keyword, and the end color with the to keyword. Then, you can include any number of intermediate colors using the color-stop() function to create a color stop. The first parameter of the color-stop() function is the position of the stop, expressed as a percentage, and the second parameter is the color at that location.

Here's an example:

```
background-image:
  -webkit-gradient(linear, left top, right bottom,
    from(red),
    to(purple),
    color-stop(20%, orange),
    color-stop(40%, yellow),
    color-stop(60%, green),
    color-stop(80%, blue));
```

With that, we've recreated our angled rainbow, reminiscent of GeoCities circa 1996.

It's actually unnecessary to specify the start and end colors using from and to. As from(red) is the equivalent to color-stop(0, red), we could also have written:

```
background-image:
  -webkit-gradient(linear, left top, right bottom,
    color-stop(0, red),
    color-stop(20%, orange),
    color-stop(40%, yellow),
    color-stop(60%, green),
    color-stop(80%, blue),
    color-stop(100%, purple));
```

If you don't declare a from or a 0% color stop, the color of the first color stop is used for all the area up to that first stop. The element will have a solid area of the color declared from the edge of the container to the first specified color stop, at which point it becomes a gradient morphing into the color of the next color stop. At and after the last stop, the color of the last color stop is used. In other words, if the first color stop is at 40% and the last color stop is at 60%, the first color will be used from 0% to 40%, and the last color will be displayed from 60% to 100%, with the area from 40% to 60% a gradient morphing between the two colors.

As you can see, this is more complicated than the Mozilla syntax. Fortunately, tools exist to generate all the required code for a given gradient automatically. We'll be looking at some of them at the end of this section, but first, we'll see how to use both syntaxes to create a cross-browser gradient for *The HTML5 Herald*. The good news is that since the old WebKit syntax uses a different property name (-webkit-gradient instead of -webkit-linear-gradient), you can use both syntaxes side-by-side without conflict. In fact, the old syntax is still supported in the newer WebKit, so the browser will just use whichever one was declared last.

Putting It All Together

Now that we have a fairly good understanding of how to declare linear gradients, let's declare ours.

If your designer included a gradient in the design, it's likely to have been created in Photoshop or another image-editing program. You can use this to your advantage; if you have the original files, it's fairly easy to replicate exactly what your designer intended.

If we pop open Photoshop and inspect the gradient we want to use for the ad (shown in Figure 7.7), our gradient is linear, with five color stops that simply change the opacity of a single color (black).

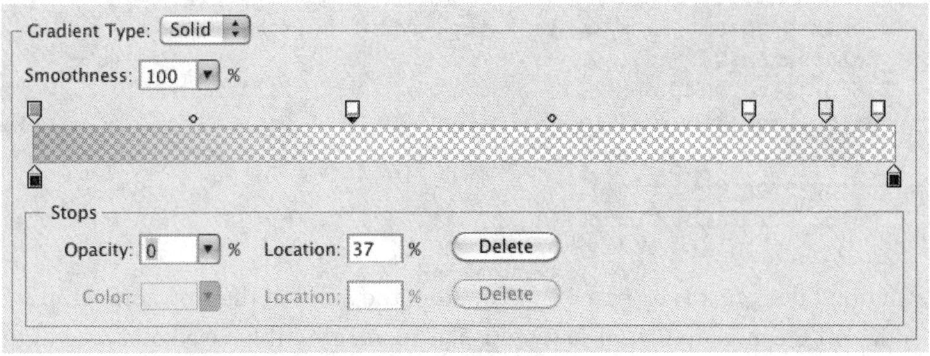

Figure 7.7. An example linear gradient in Photoshop

You'll note via the Photoshop screengrab that the color starts from 40% opacity, and that the first color stop's location is at 37%, with an opacity of 0%. We can use this tool to grab the data for our CSS declaration, beginning with the W3C syntax declaration for Firefox, Opera 11.10, and newer WebKit browsers:

css/styles.css *(excerpt)*

```
#ad2 {
  ⋮
  background-image:
    -moz-linear-gradient(
      270deg,
      rgba(0,0,0,0.4) 0,
      rgba(0,0,0,0) 37%,
      rgba(0,0,0,0) 83%,
```

```
        rgba(0,0,0,0.06) 92%,
        rgba(0,0,0,0) 98%
      );
    background-image:
      -webkit-linear-gradient(
        270deg,
        rgba(0,0,0,0.4) 0,
        rgba(0,0,0,0) 37%,
        rgba(0,0,0,0) 83%,
        rgba(0,0,0,0.06) 92%,
        rgba(0,0,0,0) 98%
      );
    background-image:
      -o-linear-gradient(
        270deg,
        rgba(0,0,0,0.4) 0,
        rgba(0,0,0,0) 37%,
        rgba(0,0,0,0) 83%,
        rgba(0,0,0,0.06) 92%,
        rgba(0,0,0,0) 98%
      );
  }
```

We want the gradient to run from the very top of the ad to the bottom, so we set the angle to 270deg (towards the bottom). We've then added all the color stops from the Photoshop gradient. Note that we've omitted the end point of the gradient, because the last color stop is at 98%—everything after that stop will be the same color as the stop in question (in this case, black at 0% opacity, or full transparency).

Now let's add in the old WebKit syntax, with the unprefixed version last to future-proof the declaration:

css/styles.css (excerpt)

```
#ad2 {
  ⋮
  background-image:
    -webkit-gradient(linear,
      from(rgba(0,0,0,0.4)),
      color-stop(37%, rgba(0,0,0,0)),
      color-stop(83%, rgba(0,0,0,0)),
      color-stop(92%, rgba(0,0,0,0.16)),
      color-stop(98%, rgba(0,0,0,0)));
```

```
background-image:
  -webkit-linear-gradient(
    270deg,
    rgba(0,0,0,0.4) 0,
    rgba(0,0,0,0) 37%,
    rgba(0,0,0,0) 83%,
    rgba(0,0,0,0.06) 92%,
    rgba(0,0,0,0) 98%
  );
background-image:
  linear-gradient(
    270deg,
    rgba(0,0,0,0.4) 0,
    rgba(0,0,0,0) 37%,
    rgba(0,0,0,0) 83%,
    rgba(0,0,0,0.06) 92%,
    rgba(0,0,0,0) 98%
  );
}
```

We now have our gradient looking just right in Mozilla, Opera, and WebKit-based browsers.

Linear Gradients with SVG

We still have a few more browsers to add our linear gradient to. In Opera 11.01 and earlier—and more importantly, IE9—we can declare SVG files as background images. By creating a gradient in an SVG file, and declaring that SVG as the background image of an element, we can recreate the same effect we achieved with CSS3 gradients.

SV what?

SVG stands for Scalable Vector Graphics. It's an XML-based language for defining vector graphics using a set of elements—like what you use in HTML to define the structure of a document. We'll be covering SVG in much more depth in Chapter 11, but for now we'll just skim over the basics, since all we're creating is a simple gradient.

An SVG file sounds scary, but for creating gradients it's quite straightforward. Here's our gradient again, in SVG form:

images/gradient.svg *(excerpt)*

```
<?xml version="1.0" standalone="no"?>
<!DOCTYPE svg PUBLIC "-//W3C//DTD SVG 1.0//EN"
  "http://www.w3.org/TR/2001/REC-SVG-20050904/DTD/svg10.dtd">
<svg xmlns="http://www.w3.org/2000/svg"
    xmlns:xlink="http://www.w3.org/1999/xlink" version="1.1">
<title>Module Gradient</title>
 <defs>
  <linearGradient id="grad"  x1="0" y1="0" x2="0" y2="100%">
    <stop offset="0" stop-opacity="0.3" color-stop="#000000" />
    <stop offset="0.37" stop-opacity="0" stop-color="#000000" />
    <stop offset="0.83" stop-opacity="0" stop-color="#000000" />
    <stop offset="0.92" stop-opacity="0.06" stop-color="#000000" />
    <stop offset="0.98" stop-opacity="0" stop-color="#000000" />
  </linearGradient>
</defs>
<rect x="0" y="0" width="100%" height="100%"
➥style="fill:url(#grad)" />
</svg>
```

Looking at the SVG file, you should notice that it's quite similar to the syntax for linear gradients in CSS3. We declare the gradient type and the orientation in the `linearGradient` element; then add color stops. The orientation is set with start and end coordinates, from `x1`, `y1` to `x2`, `y2`. The color stops are fairly self-explanatory, having an offset between 0 and 1 determining their position and a stop-color for their color. After declaring the gradient, we then have to create a rectangle (the `rect` element) and fill it with our gradient using the `style` attribute.

So, we've created a nifty little gradient, but how do we use it on our site? Save the SVG file with the *.svg* extension. Then, in your CSS, simply declare the SVG as your background image with the same syntax, as if it were a JPEG, GIF, or PNG:

css/styles.css *(excerpt)*

```
#ad2 {
  ⋮
  background-image: url(../images/gradient.svg);
  ⋮
}
```

The SVG background should be declared before the CSS3 gradients, so browsers that understand both will use the latter. Many browsers are even smart enough not

to download the SVG if it's overwritten by another `background-image` property later on in your CSS.

The major difference between our CSS linear gradients and the SVG version is that the SVG background image won't default to 100% of the height and width of the container the way that CSS gradients do. To make the SVG fill the container, declare the `height` and `width` of your SVG rectangle as 100%.

Linear Gradients with IE Filters

For Internet Explorer prior to version 9, we can use the proprietary IE filter syntax to create simple gradients. The IE gradient filter doesn't support color stops, gradient angle, or, as we'll see later, radial gradients. All you have is the ability to specify whether the gradient is horizontal or vertical, as well as the "to" and "from" colors. It's fairly basic, but if you need a gradient on these older browsers, it can provide the solution.

The filter syntax for IE is:

```
filter:progid:DXImageTransform.Microsoft.gradient(GradientType=0,
➥startColorstr='#COLOR', endColorstr='#COLOR); /* IE6 & IE7 */
-ms-filter:"progid:DXImageTransform.Microsoft.gradient(GradientType=
➥0,startColorstr='#COLOR', endColorstr='#COLOR')"; /* IE8 */
```

The *GradientType* parameter should be set to 1 for a horizontal gradient, or 0 for a vertical gradient.

Since the gradient we're using for our ad block requires color stops, we'll skip using the IE filters. The ad still looks fine without the gradient, so it's all good.

 Filters Kinda Suck

As we've mentioned before, IE's filters can have a significant impact on performance, so use them sparingly, if at all. Calculating the display of filter effects takes processing time, with some effects being slower than others. SVGs can have a similar—albeit lesser—effect, so be sure to test your site in a number of browsers if you're using these fallbacks.

Tools of the Trade

Now that you understand how to create linear gradients and have mastered the intricacies of their convoluted syntax, you can forget almost everything you've learned. There are some very cool tools to help you create linear gradients without having to recreate your code four times for each different browser syntax.

John Allsop's http://www.westciv.com/tools/gradients/ is a tool that enables you to create gradients with color stops for both Firefox and WebKit. Note that there are separate tabs for Firefox and WebKit, and for radial and linear gradients. The tool only creates gradients with hexadecimal color notation, but it does provide you with copy-and-paste code, so you can copy it, and then switch the hexadecimal color values to RGBA or HSLA if you prefer.

Damian Galarza's http://gradients.glrzad.com/ provides for both color stops and RGB. It even lets you set colors with an HSL color picker, but converts it to RGB in the code. It does not provide for alpha transparency, but since the code generated is in RGB, it's easy to update. This gradient generator is more powerful than the Westciv one, but may be a bit overwhelming for a newbie.

Finally, Paul Irish's http://css3please.com/ allows you to create linear gradients, though it has no support for color stops. You may wonder why it's even worth mentioning—but it is, because it's the only one of the tools mentioned that provides the filter syntax for IE alongside the other gradient syntaxes. Plus, as well as gradients, it can give you cross-browser syntax for lots of other features as well, like shadows and rounded corners.

Radial Gradients

Radial gradients are circular or elliptical gradients. Rather than proceeding along a straight axis, colors blend out from a starting point in all directions. Radial gradients are supported in WebKit and Mozilla (beginning with Firefox 3.6). While Opera 11.10 has begun supporting linear gradients, it does not provide support for radial gradients; however, as with linear gradients, radial gradients can be created in SVG, so support can be provided to Opera and IE9. Radial gradients are entirely unsupported in IE8 and earlier—not even with filters.

The W3C Syntax

Let's start with a simple circular gradient to illustrate the standard syntax:

```
background-image: -moz-radial-gradient(#FFF, #000);
background-image: -moz-radial-gradient(center, #FFF, #000);
background-image: -moz-radial-gradient(center, ellipse cover,
➥#FFF, #000);
```

The above three declarations are functionally identical, and will all result in the gradient shown in Figure 7.8. At the minimum, you need to provide a start color and an end color. Alternatively, you can also provide a position for the center of the gradient as the first parameter, and a shape and size as the second parameter.

Figure 7.8. A simple, centered radial gradient

Let's start by playing with the position:

```
background-image: -moz-radial-gradient(30px 30px, #FFF, #000);
```

This will place the center of the gradient 30 pixels from the top and 30 pixels from the left of the element, as you can see in Figure 7.9. As with background-position, you can use values, percentages, or keywords to set the gradient's position.

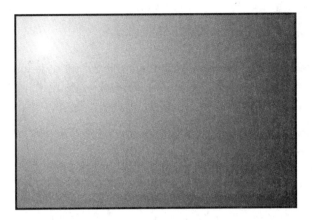

Figure 7.9. A gradient positioned off center

Now let's look at the shape and size parameter. The shape can take one of two values, `circle` or `ellipse`, with the latter being the default.

For the size, you can use one of the following values:

closest-side

The gradient's shape meets the side of the box closest to its center (for circles), or meets both the vertical and horizontal sides closest to the center (for ellipses).

closest-corner

The gradient's shape is sized so it meets exactly the closest corner of the box from its center.

farthest-side

Similar to `closest-side`, except that the shape is sized to meet the side of the box farthest from its center (or the farthest vertical and horizontal sides in the case of ellipses).

farthest-corner

The gradient's shape is sized so that it meets exactly the farthest corner of the box from its center.

contain

A synonym for `closest-side`.

cover

A synonym for `farthest-corner`.

According to the spec, you can also provide a second set of values to explicitly define the horizontal and vertical size of the radial gradient. This is currently only supported in WebKit, though support should be added to Firefox in the near future. For now, though, you should probably stick to the above constraints if you want to create the same gradient in all supporting browsers.

The color stop syntax is the same as for linear gradients: a color value followed by an optional stop position. Let's look at one last example:

```
background-image: -moz-radial-gradient(30px 30px, circle
➥farthest-side, #FFF, #000 30%, #FFF);
```

This will create a gradient like the one in Figure 7.10.

Figure 7.10. A radial gradient with a modified size and shape, and an extra color stop

The Old WebKit Syntax

To create the example in Figure 7.10 using the old-style WebKit syntax currently supported in Safari and Chrome, you'd need to write it as follows:

```
background-image: -webkit-gradient(radial, 30 30, 0, 30 30, 100%,
➥from(#FFFFFF), to(#FFFFFF), color-stop(.3,#000000))
```

The same -webkit-gradient property used earlier for linear gradients is used for radial gradients; the difference is that we pass radial as the first parameter. The next four parameters are the respective position and radius of two circles, with the gradient proceeding from the inner circle to the outer circle. Just to make it more confusing, these values are defined in pixels, but without the px unit. You can also specify the values as percentages, in which case you *do* need to include the % symbol. You should be starting to see why the W3C opted for a version of the Mozilla syntax rather than this one.

Furthermore, your inner circle doesn't need to be centered in your outer circle. If the first point is equal to the second point, the gradient will be symmetrical like the one in Figure 7.10. If they differ, however, your inner circle will be off-center, so the gradient will be asymmetrical. If your inner circle's center is outside the boundary of your outer circle, instead of having a circle off-center inside another circle, you'll have a very odd triangle gradient effect, as Figure 7.11 illustrates.

Figure 7.11. The older WebKit radial gradient syntax allowed for some interesting effects

Here's the code used to create that gradient:

```
background-image:-webkit-gradient(radial, 200 200, 100, 100 100, 40,
from(#FFFFFF), to(#000000));
```

As with the linear gradients, you can insert more colors with the color-stop function. The syntax for color stops is the same for both linear and radial gradients.

You'll generally want to create gradients that look the same in older versions of Chrome and Safari as they do in newer versions of those browsers and Firefox, so

you should limit yourself to the kinds of gradients that can be replicated using the W3C syntax. However, if you do find yourself building specifically for WebKit browsers (for mobile platforms, for example), it can be useful to know that these additional options exist. As mentioned earlier, the old syntax will continue to be supported in WebKit browsers for the foreseeable future.

Putting it All Together

Let's take all we've learned and implement a radial gradient for *The HTML5 Herald*. You may yet to have noticed, but the form submit button has a radial gradient in the background. The center of the radial gradient is outside the button area, towards the left and a little below the bottom, as Figure 7.12 shows.

Figure 7.12. A radial gradient on a button in *The HTML5 Herald*'s sign-up form

We'll want to declare at least three background images: an SVG file for Opera and IE9, the older WebKit syntax for Chrome and Safari, and the -moz- vendor prefixed version for Firefox. You can also declare the newer WebKit vendor prefixed version (currently only in the WebKit nightly builds), as well as the non-prefixed version:

css/styles.css (excerpt)

```
input[type=submit] {
    ⋮
  background-color: #333;
  /* SVG for IE9 and Opera */
  background-image: url(../images/button-gradient.svg);
  /* Old WebKit */
  background-image: -webkit-gradient(radial,
    30% 120%, 0, 30% 120%, 100,
    color-stop(0,rgba(144,144,144,1)),
    color-stop(1,rgba(72,72,72,1)));
  /* W3C for Mozilla */
  background-image: -moz-radial-gradient(30% 120%, circle,
    rgba(144,144,144,1) 0%,
    rgba(72,72,72,1) 50%);
  /* W3C for new WebKit */
```

```
    background-image: -webkit-radial-gradient(30% 120%, circle,
      rgba(144,144,144,1) 0%,
      rgba(72,72,72,1) 50%);
    /* W3C unprefixed */
    background-image: radial-gradient(30% 120%, circle,
      rgba(144,144,144,1) 0%,
      rgba(72,72,72,1) 50%);
}
```

The center of the circle is 30% from the left, and 120% from the top, so it's actually *below* the bottom edge of the container. We've included two color stops for the color #484848 (or rgb(72,72,72)) and #909090 (or rbg(144,144,144)).

And here's the SVG file used as a fallback, though we'll stop short of explaining it here, as the syntax is fairly explanatory and we'll be covering SVG in Chapter 11:

button-gradient.svg *(excerpt)*

```
<?xml version="1.0" standalone="no"?>
<!DOCTYPE svg PUBLIC "-//W3C//DTD SVG 1.0//EN"
➥"http://www.w3.org/TR/2001/REC-SVG-20050904/DTD/svg10.dtd">
<svg xmlns="http://www.w3.org/2000/svg" xmlns:xlink="
➥http://www.w3.org/1999/xlink" version="1.1">
<title>Button Gradient</title>
 <defs>
   <radialGradient id="grad"  cx="30%" cy="120%" fx="30%" fy="120%"
➥r="50%" gradientUnits="userSpaceOnUse">
     <stop offset="0" stop-color="#909090" />
     <stop offset="1" stop-color="#484848" />
   </radialGradient>
 </defs>
<rect x="0" y="0" width="100%" height="100%"
➥style="fill:url(#grad)" />
</svg>
```

Repeating Gradients

Sometimes you'll find yourself wanting to create a gradient "pattern" that repeats over the background of an element. While linear-repeating gradients can be created by repeating the background image (with `background-repeat`), there's no equivalent way to easily create repeating radial gradients. Fortunately, CSS3 comes to the rescue with both a `repeating-linear-gradient` and a `repeating-radial-gradient` syntax. The vendor-prefixed `repeating-linear-gradient` syntax is supported in Firefox 3.6+, Safari 5.0.3+, Chrome 10+, and Opera 11.10+.

Gradients with `repeating-linear-gradient` and `repeating-radial-gradient` have the same syntax as the nonrepeating versions.

Supported in Firefox 3.6, Chrome 10, and the WebKit nightly build (hence, Safari 6), here are examples of what can be created with just a few lines of CSS (again using only the `-webkit-` prefixed syntax for brevity):

```
.repeat_linear_1 {
  background-image:
    -webkit-repeating-linear-gradient(left,
      rgba(0,0,0,0.5) 10%,
      rgba(0,0,0,0.1) 30%);
}
.repeat_radial_2 {
  background-image:
    -webkit-repeating-radial-gradient(top left, circle,
      rgba(0,0,0,0.9),
      rgba(0,0,0,0.1) 10%,
      rgba(0,0,0,0.5) 20%);
}
.multiple_gradients_3 {
  background-image:
    -webkit-repeating-linear-gradient(left,
      rgba(0,0,0,0.5) 10%,
      rgba(0,0,0,0.1) 30%),
    -webkit-repeating-radial-gradient(top left, circle,
      rgba(0,0,0,0.9),
      rgba(0,0,0,0.1) 10%,
      rgba(0,0,0,0.5) 20%);
}
```

The resulting gradients are shown in Figure 7.13.

Figure 7.13. A few examples of repeating gradients

Multiple Background Images

You probably noticed that our advertisement with the linear gradient is incomplete: we're missing the bicycle. Prior to CSS3, adding the bicycle would have required placing an additional element in the markup to contain the new background image. In CSS3, there's no need to include an element for every background image; it provides us with the ability to add more than one background image to any element, even to pseudo-elements.

To understand multiple background images, you need to understand the syntax and values of the various background properties. The syntax for the values of all the background properties, including background-image and the shorthand background property, are the same whether you have one background image or many. To make a declaration for multiple background images, simply separate the values for each individual image with a comma. For example:

```
background-image:
  url(firstImage.jpg),
  url(secondImage.gif),
  url(thirdImage.png);
```

This works just as well if you're using the shorthand background property:

```
background:
  url(firstImage.jpg) no-repeat 0 0,
  url(secondImage.gif) no-repeat 100% 0,
  url(thirdImage.png) no-repeat 50% 0;
```

The background images are layered one on top of the other with the first declaration on top, as if it had a high z-index. The final image is drawn under all the images preceding it in the declaration, as if it had a low z-index. Basically, think of the images as being stacked in reverse order: first on top, last on the bottom.

If you want to declare a background color—which you should, especially if it's light-colored text on a dark-colored background image—declare it last. It's often simpler and more readable to declare it separately using the background-color property.

As a reminder, the shorthand background property is short for eight longhand background properties. If you use the shorthand, any longhand background property value that's omitted from the declaration will default to the longhand property's default (or initial) value. The default values for the various background properties are listed below:

- background-color: transparent;
- background-image: none;
- background-position: 0 0;
- background-size: auto;
- background-repeat: repeat;
- background-clip: border-box;
- background-origin: padding-box;
- background-attachment: scroll;

Just like for a declaration of a single background image, you can include a gradient as one of several background images. Here's how we do it for our advertisement. For brevity, only the unprefixed version is shown. The bicycle image would be included similarly in each background-image declaration:

css/styles.css (excerpt)

```
#ad2 {
  ⋮
  background-image:
    url(../images/bg-bike.png),
    linear-gradient(top,
    rgba(0,0,0,0.4) 0,
    rgba(0,0,0,0) 37%,
    rgba(0,0,0,0) 83%,
```

```
    rgba(0,0,0,0.06) 92%,
    rgba(0,0,0,0) 98%);
  background-position: 50% 88%, 0 0;
}
```

Note that we've put the bicycle picture first in the series of background images, since we want the bicycle to sit on top of the gradient, instead of the other way around. We've also declared the background position for each image by putting them in the same order as the images were declared in the background-image property. If only one set of values was declared—for example, background-position: 50% 88%;—all images would have the same background position as if you'd declared background-position: 50% 88%, 50% 88%;. In this case, the 50% 80% positions the bicycle, which was declared first, and the 0 0 (or left top) positions the gradient.

Because a browser will only respect one background-image property declaration (whether it has one or many images declared), the bicycle image must be included in each background-image declaration, since they're all targeting different browsers. Remember, browsers ignore CSS that they fail to understand. So if Safari doesn't understand -moz-linear-gradient (which it doesn't), it will ignore the entire property/value pair.

The heading on our sign-up form also has two background images. While we could attach a single extra-wide image in this case, spanning across the entire form, there's no need! With multiple background images, CSS3 allows us to attach two separate small images, or a single image sprite twice with different background positions. This saves on bandwidth, of course, but it could also be beneficial if the heading needed to stretch; a single image would be unable to accommodate differently sized elements. This time, we'll use the background shorthand:

```
background:
  url(../images/bg-formtitle-left.png) left 13px no-repeat,
  url(../images/bg-formtitle-right.png) right 13px no-repeat;
```

The background Shorthand

When all the available background properties are fully supported, the following two statements will be equivalent:

```css
div {
  background: url("tile.png") no-repeat scroll center
➥bottom / cover rgba(0, 0, 0, 0.2);
}

div {
  background-color: rgba(0,0,0,0.2);
  background-position: 50% 100%;
  background-size: cover;
  background-repeat: no-repeat;
  background-clip: border-box;
  background-origin: padding-box;
  background-attachment: scroll;
  background-image: url(form.png);
}
```

Currently, though, since only some browsers support all the values available, we recommend including color, position, repeat, attachment, and image in your shorthand declaration, with clip, origin, and size following, or avoiding the shorthand altogether. You must declare the shorthand *before* the longhand properties, as any value not explicitly declared in the shorthand will be treated as though you'd declared the default value.

Background Size

The background-size property allows you to specify the size you want your background images to have. In theory, you can include background-size within the shorthand background declaration by adding it after the background's position, separated with a slash (/). As it stands, no browser understands this shorthand; in fact, it will cause them to ignore the entire background declaration, since they see it as incorrectly formatted. As a result, you'll want to use the background-size property as a separate declaration instead.

Support for background-size is as follows:

▪ Opera 11.01+: background-size (unprefixed)

■ Safari and Chrome: current versions support unprefixed, but older versions require `-webkit-background-size`

■ Firefox: `-moz-background-size` for 3.6, `background-size` for 4+

■ IE9: `background-size`

As you can see, adoption of the unprefixed version of this syntax was very quick; it's a simple property with a straightforward implementation that was unlikely to change. This is a great example of why you should always include the unprefixed version in your CSS.

If declaring the background image size in pixels, be careful to avoid the image distorting; define either the width or the height, not both, and set the other value to `auto`. This will preserve the aspect ratio of your image. If you only include one value, the second value is assumed to be `auto`. In other words, both these lines have the same meaning:

```
background-size: 100px auto, auto auto;
background-size: 100px, auto auto;
```

As with all background properties, use commas to separate values for each image declared. If we wanted our bicycle to be really big, we could declare:

```
-webkit-background-size: 100px, cover;
-moz-background-size: 100px, cover;
-o-background-size: 100px, cover;
background-size: 100px auto, cover;
```

By declaring just the width of the image, the second value will default to `auto`, and the browser will determine the correct height of the image based on the aspect ratio.

The default size of a background image is the actual size of the image. Sometimes the image is just a bit smaller or larger than its container. You can define the size of your background image in pixels (as shown above) or percentages, or you can use the `contain` or `cover` key terms.

The `contain` value scales the image while preserving its aspect ratio; this may leave uncovered space. The `cover` value scales the image so that it completely covers the

element. This can result in clipping the image if the element and its background image have different aspect ratios.

> ### 💡 Screen Pixel Density, or DPI
>
> The `background-size` property comes in handy for devices that have different pixel densities, such as the newest generation of smartphones. For example, the iPhone 4 has a pixel density four times higher than previous iPhones; however, to prevent pages designed for older phones from looking tiny, the browser on the iPhone 4 *behaves* as though it only has a 320×480px display. In essence, every pixel in your CSS corresponds to four screen pixels. Images are scaled up to compensate, but this means they can sometimes look a little rough compared to the smoothness of the text displayed.
>
> To deal with this, you can provide higher-resolution images to the iPhone 4. For example, if we were providing a high-resolution image of a bicycle for the iPhone, it would measure 74×90px instead of 37×45px. However, we don't actually want it to be twice as big! We only want it to take up 37×45px worth of space. We can use `background-size` to ensure that our high-resolution image still takes up the right amount of space:
>
> ```
> -webkit-background-size: 37px 45px, cover;
> -moz-background-size: 37px 45px, cover;
> -o-background-size: 37px 45px, cover;
> background-size: 37px 45px, cover;
> ```

In the Background

That's all for CSS3 backgrounds and gradients. In the next chapter, we'll be looking at transforms, animations, and transitions. These allow you to add dynamic effects and movement to your pages without relying on bandwidth- and processor-heavy JavaScript.

CSS3 Transforms and Transitions

Our page is fairly static. Actually, it's completely static. In Chapter 4 we learned a little about how to alter a form's appearance based on its state with the `:invalid` and `:valid` pseudo-classes. But what about really moving things around? What about changing the appearance of elements—rotating or skewing them?

For years, web designers have relied on JavaScript for in-page animations, and the only way to display text on an angle was to use an image. This is far from ideal. Enter CSS3: without a line of JavaScript or a single JPEG, you can tilt, scale, move, and even flip your elements with ease.

Let's see how it's done.

Transforms

Supported in Firefox 3.5+, Opera 10.5, WebKit since 3.2 (Chrome 1), and even Internet Explorer 9, the CSS3 `transform` property lets you translate, rotate, scale, or skew any element on the page. While some of these effects were possible using previously existing CSS features (like relative and absolute positioning), CSS3 gives you unprecedented control over many more aspects of an element's appearance.

We manipulate an element's appearance using **transform functions**. The value of the transform property is one or more transform functions, separated by spaces, which will be applied in the order they're provided. In this book, we'll cover all the two-dimensional transform functions. WebKit also supports the transformation of elements in 3D space—3D transforms—but that's beyond the scope of this book.

To illustrate how transforms work, we'll be working on another advertisement block from *The HTML5 Herald*, shown in Figure 8.1.

Figure 8.1. This block will serve to illustrate CSS3 transforms

Translation

Translation functions allow you to move elements left, right, up, or down. These functions are similar to the behavior of position: relative; where you declare top and left. When you employ a translation function, you're moving elements without impacting the flow of the document.

Unlike position: relative, which allows you to position an element either against its current position or against a parent or other ancestor, a translated element can only be moved relative to its current position.

The translate(x,y) function moves an element by x from the left, and y from the top:

```
-webkit-transform: translate(45px,-45px);
-moz-transform: translate(45px,-45px);
-ms-transform: translate(45px,-45px);
-o-transform: translate(45px,-45px);
transform: translate(45px,-45px);
```

If you only want to move an element vertically or horizontally, you can use the `translatex` or `translatey` functions:

```
-webkit-transform: translatex(45px);
-moz-transform: translatex(45px);
-ms-transform: translatex(45px);
-o-transform: translatex(45px);
transform: translatex(45px);

-webkit-transform: translatey(-45px);
-moz-transform: translatey(-45px);
-ms-transform: translatey(-45px);
-o-transform: translatey(-45px);
transform: translatey(-45px);
```

For our ad, let's say we want to move the word "dukes" over to the right when the user hovers over it, as if it had been punched by our mustachioed pugilist. In the markup, we have:

```
<h1>Put your <span>dukes</span> up sire</h1>
```

Let's apply the style whenever the `h1` is hovered over. This will make the effect more likely to be stumbled across than if it was only triggered by hovering over the span itself:

```
                                        css/styles.css (excerpt)

#ad3 h1:hover span {
  color: #484848;
  -webkit-transform: translateX(40px);
  -moz-transform: translateX(40px);
  -ms-transform: translateX(40px);
  -o-transform:translateX(40px);
  transform: translateX(40px);
}
```

This works in most browsers, but you may have noticed that WebKit's not playing along. What gives? It turns out that WebKit will only allow you to transform block-level elements; inline elements are off-limits. That's easy enough to fix—we'll just add `display: inline-block;` to our span:

```
                                                        css/styles.css (excerpt)
#ad3 h1 span {
  font-size: 30px;
  color: #999999;
  display:inline-block;
```

The result is shown in Figure 8.2.

Figure 8.2. The result of our translate transform

It's nice, but we can still do better! Let's look at how we can scale our text to make it bigger as well.

Scaling

The scale(x,y) function scales an element by the defined factors horizontally and vertically, respectively. If only one value is provided, it will be used for both the x and y scaling. For example, scale(1) would leave the element the same size, scale(2) would double its proportions, scale(0.5) would halve them, and so on. Providing different values will distort the element, as you'd expect:

```
-webkit-transform: scale(1.5,0.25);
-moz-transform: scale(1.5,0.25);
-ms-transform: scale(1.5,0.25);
-o-transform: scale(1.5,0.25);
transform: scale(1.5,0.25);
```

As with translate, you can also use the scalex(x) or scaley(y) functions. These functions will scale only the horizontal dimensions, or only the vertical dimensions. They are the same as scale(x,1) and scale(1,y), respectively.

A scaled element will grow outwards from or shrink inwards towards its center; in other words, the element's center will stay in the same place as its dimensions change. To change this default behavior, you can include the `transform-origin` property, which we'll be covering a bit later.

Let's add a `scale` transform to our span:

css/styles.css *(excerpt)*

```css
#ad3 h1:hover span {
  color: #484848;
  -webkit-transform: translateX(40px) scale(1.5);
  -moz-transform: translateX(40px) scale(1.5);
  -ms-transform: translateX(40px) scale(1.5);
  -o-transform: translateX(40px) scale(1.5);
  transform: translateX(40px) scale(1.5);
}
```

Note that there's no need to declare a new transform—you provide it with a space-separated list of transform functions, so we just add our `scale` to the end of the list.

It's also worth remembering that scaling, like translation, has no impact on the document flow. This means that if you scale inline text, text around it won't reflow to accommodate it. Figure 8.3 shows an example of how this might be a problem. In cases like this, you might want to consider simply adjusting the element's height, width, or font-size instead of using a scale transform. Changing those properties will change the space allocated to the element by the browser.

Figure 8.3. Using the `scale` function on inline text can have unwanted results

In our example, however, we want the text to pop out of the ad without reflowing the surrounding text, so the scale does exactly what we need it to do. Figure 8.4 shows what our hover state looks like with the scale added to the existing translation.

Figure 8.4. Our ad now has plenty of pop

It's looking good, but there's still more to add.

Rotation

The `rotate()` function rotates an element around the point of origin (as with `scale`, by default this is the element's center), by a specified angle value. Generally, angles are declared in degrees, with positive degrees moving clockwise and negative moving counter-clockwise. In addition to degrees, values can be provided in grads, radians, or turns—but we'll just be sticking with degrees.

Let's add a `rotate` transform to our "dukes":

```
#ad3 h1:hover span {
  color: #484848;
  -webkit-transform:rotate(10deg) translateX(40px) scale(1.5);
  -moz-transform:rotate(10deg) translateX(40px) scale(1.5);
  -ms-transform:rotate(10deg) translateX(40px) scale(1.5);
  -o-transform:rotate(10deg) translateX(40px) scale(1.5);
  transform:rotate(10deg) translateX(40px) scale(1.5);
}
```

We're rotating our `span` by ten degrees clockwise—adding to the effect of text that has just been dealt a powerful uppercut. We are declaring the rotation *before* the `translate` so that it's applied first—remember that transforms are applied in the order provided. Sometimes this will make no difference, but if an effect is behaving differently to what you'd like, it's worth playing with the order of your transforms.

The final transformed text is shown in Figure 8.5.

Figure 8.5. Our text has now been translated, scaled, and rotated—that's quite a punch

There's one more type of transform we're yet to visit. It won't be used on *The HTML5 Herald*, but let's take a look anyway.

Skew

The skew(x,y) function specifies a skew along the X and Y axes. As you'd expect, the x specifies the skew on the X axis, and the y specifies the skew on the Y axis. If the second parameter is omitted, the skew will only occur on the X axis:

```
-webkit-transform: skew(15deg, 4deg);
-moz-transform: skew(15deg, 4deg);
-ms-transform: skew(15deg, 4deg);
-o-transform: skew(15deg, 4deg);
transform: skew(15deg, 4deg);
```

Applying the above styles to a heading, for example, results in the skew shown in Figure 8.6.

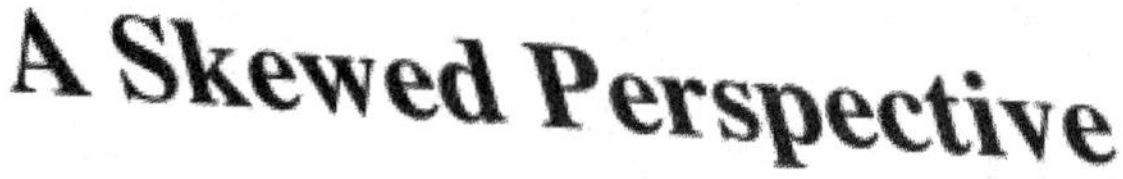

A Skewed Perspective

Figure 8.6. Some text with a skew transform applied

As with translate and scale, there are axis-specific versions of the skew transform: skewx() and skewy().

Changing the Origin of the Transform

As we hinted at earlier, you can control the origin from which your transforms are applied. This is done using the transform-origin property. It has the same syntax as the background-position property, and defaults to the center of the object (so that scales and rotations will be around the center of the box by default).

Let's say you were transforming a circle. Because the default transform-origin is the center of the circle, applying a rotate transform to a circle would have no visible effect—a circle rotated 90 degrees still looks exactly the same as it did before being rotated. However, if you gave your circle a transform-origin of 10% 10%, you would notice the circle's rotation, as Figure 8.7 illustrates.

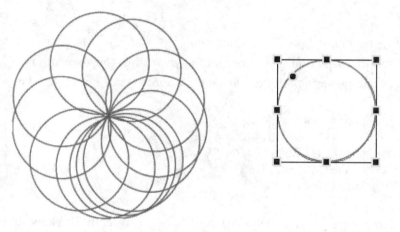

Figure 8.7. Rotating a circle only works if the transform-origin has been set

The transform-origin property is supported with vendor prefixes in WebKit, Firefox, and Opera:

```
-webkit-transform-origin: 0 0;
-moz-transform-origin: 0 0;
-o-transform-origin: 0 0;
transform-origin: 0 0;
```

Support for Internet Explorer 8 and Earlier

While CSS3 transforms are unsupported in IE6, IE7, or IE8, you can mimic these effects with other CSS properties, including filters. To "translate," use position: relative;, and top and left values:

```
.translate {
  position: relative;
  top: 200px;
  left: 200px;
}
```

You can also scale an element by altering its width and height. Remember, though, that while transformed elements still take up the space that they did before being scaled, altering a width or height alters the space allocated for the element and can affect the layout.

You can even use filters to rotate an element in Internet Explorer, but it's ugly:

```
.rotate {
  transform: rotate(15deg);
  filter: progid:DXImageTransform.Microsoft.Matrix(
      sizingMethod='auto expand', M11=0.9659258262890683,
      M12=-0.25881904510252074, M21=0.25881904510252074,
      M22=0.9659258262890683);
  -ms-filter: "progid:DXImageTransform.Microsoft.Matrix(
      M11=0.9659258262890683, M12=-0.25881904510252074,
      M21=0.25881904510252074, M22=0.9659258262890683,
      sizingMethod='auto expand')";
  zoom: 1;
}
```

This filter's syntax isn't worth going into here. If you want to rotate an element in Internet Explorer, go to http://css3please.com/ for cross-browser code for a given rotation. Just edit any of the `rotation` values, and the other versions will be updated accordingly.

Transitions

As much fun as it's been to have a feature work in IE9, it's time to again leave that browser behind. While Opera, Firefox, and WebKit all support CSS transitions, IE is once again left in the dust.

Transitions allow the values of CSS properties to change over time, essentially providing simple animations. For example, if a link changes color on hover, you can have it gradually fade from one color to the other, instead of a sudden change.

Likewise, you can animate any of the transforms we've just seen, so that your pages feel more dynamic.

Animation has certainly been possible for some time with JavaScript, but native CSS transitions require much less processing on the client side, so they'll generally appear smoother. Especially on mobile devices with limited computing power, this can be a lifesaver.

CSS transitions are declared along with the regular styles on an element. Whenever the target properties change, the browser will apply the transition. Most often, the change will be due to different styles applied to a hover state, for example. However, transitions will work equally well if the property in question is changed using JavaScript. This is significant: rather than writing out an animation in JavaScript, you can simply switch a property value and rely on the browser to do all the heavy lifting.

Here are the steps to create a simple transition using only CSS:

1. Declare the original state of the element in the default style declaration.

2. Declare the final state of your transitioned element; for example, in a hover state.

3. Include the transition functions in your default style declaration, using a few different properties: `transition-property`, `transition-duration`, `transition-timing-function`, and `transition-delay`. We'll look at each of these and how they work shortly.

The important point to note is that the transition is declared in the default state. Currently, the transition functions need to include the vendor prefixes `-webkit-`, `-o-`, and `-moz-`, for WebKit, Opera, and Firefox, respectively.

This may be a lot to grasp, so let's go over the various transition values. As we go, we'll apply a transition to the transforms we added to our ad in the last section, so that the word "dukes" moves smoothly into its new position when hovered.

transition-property

The `transition-property` lists the CSS properties of the element that should be transitioned. Properties that can be made to transition include background, border, and box model properties. You can transition font sizes and weights, but not font

families. The W3C last updated the list of properties that can be transitioned in August 2010:

- `background-color` and `background-position`
- `border-color`, `border-spacing`, and `border-width`
- `bottom`, `top`, `left`, and `right`
- `clip`
- `color`
- `crop`
- `font-size` and `font-weight`
- `height` and `width`
- `letter-spacing`
- `line-height`
- `margin`
- `max-height`, `max-width`, `min-height`, and `min-width`
- `opacity`
- `outline-color`, `outline-offset`, and `outline-width`
- `padding`
- `text-indent`
- `text-shadow`
- `vertical-align`
- `visibility`
- `word-spacing`
- `z-index`

More properties are available to transition in some browsers, including the transform functions, but they're not (yet) in the proposed specifications. Note also that not all browsers support transitions on all the above properties at the time of writing.

You can provide any number of CSS properties to the `transition-property` declaration, separated by commas. Alternatively, you can use the keyword `all` to indicate that every supported property should be animated.

In the case of our ad, we'll apply the transition to the `transform` property:

```
#ad2 h1 span {
  -webkit-transition-property: -webkit-transform;
  -moz-transition-property: -moz-transform;
```

```
  -o-transition-property: -o-transform;
  transition-property: transform;
}
```

Note that we need to specify the prefixed forms of properties—you can't animate `transform` in a browser that only understands `-moz-transform`, for example.

Because the list of properties that can transition is in flux, be careful what you include: it's possible that a property that doesn't animate at the time you're writing your page eventually will, so be selective in the properties you specify, and only use `all` if you really want to animate every property.

So far these styles will have no effect; that's because we still need to specify the duration of the transition.

transition-duration

The `transition-duration` property sets how long the transition will take. You can specify this either in seconds (`s`) or milliseconds (`ms`). We'd like our animation to be fairly quick, so we'll specify 0.2 seconds, or 200 milliseconds:

```
-webkit-transition-duration: 0.2s;
-moz-transition-duration: 0.2s;
-o-transition-duration: 0.2s;
transition-duration: 0.2s;
```

With those styles in place, our `span` will transition on hover. Notice that the "reverse" transition also takes place over the same duration—the element returns to its previous position.

Automatic Graceful Degradation

Although transitions are only supported in some browsers, the fact that they're declared separately from the properties that are changing means that those changes will still be apparent in browsers without support for transitions. Those browsers will still apply the `:hover` (or other) state just fine, except that the changes will happen instantly rather than being transitioned over time.

transition-timing-function

The `transition-timing-function` lets you control the pace of the transition in even more granular detail. Do you want your animation to start off slow and get faster, start off fast and end slower, advance at an even keel, or some other variation? You can specify one of the key terms `ease`, `linear`, `ease-in`, `ease-out`, or `ease-in-out`. The best way to familiarize yourself with them is to play around and try them all. Most often, one will just feel right for the effect you're aiming to create. Remember to set a relatively long `transition-duration` when testing timing functions—if it's too fast, you won't be able to tell the difference.

In addition to those five key terms, you can also describe your timing function more precisely using the `cubic-bezier()` function. It accepts four numeric parameters; for example, `linear` is the same as `cubic-bezier(0.0, 0.0, 1.0, 1.0)`. If you've taken six years of calculus, the method of writing a cubic Bézier function might make sense; otherwise, it's likely you'll want to stick to the five basic timing functions. You can also look at online tools that let you play with different values, such as http://www.netzgesta.de/dev/cubic-bezier-timing-function.html.

For our transition, we'll use `ease-out`:

```
-webkit-transition-timing-function: ease-out;
-moz-transition-timing-function: ease-out;
-o-transition-timing-function: ease-out;
transition-timing-function: ease-out;
```

This makes the transition fast to start with, becoming slower as it progresses. Of course, with a 0.2 second duration, the difference is barely perceptible.

transition-delay

Finally, by using the `transition-delay` property, it's also possible to introduce a delay before the animation begins. Normally, a transition begins immediately, so the default is 0. Include the number of milliseconds (`ms`) or seconds (`s`) to delay the transition:

```
-webkit-transition-delay: 250ms;
-moz-transition-delay: 250ms;
-o-transition-delay: 250ms;
transition-delay: 250ms;
```

Negative Delays

Interestingly, a negative time delay that is less than the duration of the entire transition will cause it to start immediately, but it will start partway through the animation. For example, if you have a delay of -500ms on a 2s transition, the transition will start a quarter of the way through, and will last 1.5 seconds. This might be used to create some interesting effects, so it's worth being aware of.

The `transition` Shorthand Property

With four transition properties and three vendor prefixes, you could wind up with 16 lines of CSS for a single transition. Fortunately, as with other properties, there's a shorthand available. The `transition` property is shorthand for the four transition functions described above. Let's take another look at our transition so far:

```
#ad2 h1 span {
  -webkit-transition-property: -webkit-transform, color;
  -moz-transition-property: -moz-transform, color;
  -o-transition-property: -o-transform, color;
  transition-property: transform, color;
  -webkit-transition-duration: 0.2s;
  -moz-transition-duration: 0.2s;
  -o-transition-duration: 0.2s;
  transition-duration: 0.2s;
  -webkit-transition-timing-function: ease-out;
  -moz-transition-timing-function: ease-out;
  -o-transition-timing-function: ease-out;
  transition-timing-function: ease-out;
}
```

Now let's combine all those values into a shorthand declaration:

```css
css/styles.css (excerpt)
#ad2 h1 span {
  -webkit-transition: -webkit-transform 0.2s ease-out;
  -moz-transition: -moz-transform 0.2s ease-out;
  -o-transition: -o-transform 0.2s ease-out;
  transition: transform 0.2s ease-out;
}
```

Note that order of the values is important and must be as follows (though you don't need to specify all four values):

1. `transition-property`
2. `transition-duration`
3. `transition-function`
4. `transition-delay`

Multiple Transitions

The transition properties allow for multiple transitions in one call. For example, if we want to change the color at the same time as changing the rotation and size, we can.

Let's say instead of just transitioning the rotation, we transition the text's `color` property as well. We'd have to first include a `color` property in the transitioned style declaration, and then either the `color` property in the `transition-property` value list, or use the key term `all`:

```css
transition-property: transform, color;
transition-duration: 0.2s;
transition-timing-function: ease-out;
```

You can also specify different durations and timing functions for each property being animated. Simply include each value in a comma-separated list, using the same order as in your `transition-property`:

```css
transition-property: transform, color;
transition-duration: 0.2s, 0.1s;
transition-timing-function: ease-out, linear;
```

The above properties will apply an `ease-out` transition over 0.2 seconds to the `transform`, but a `linear` transition over 0.1 seconds to the `color`.

It's possible to specify multiple transitions when using the shorthand `transition` property also. In this case, specify all the values for each transition together, and separate each transition with commas:

```
transition: color 0.2s ease-out, transform 0.2s ease-out;
```

If you want to change both properties at the same rate and delay, you can include both property names or, since you are transitioning all the properties listed in the hover state anyway, you can employ the `all` keyword.

When using the `all` keyword, all the properties transition at the same rate, speed, and delay:

```
-webkit-transition: all 0.2s ease-out;
-moz-transition: all 0.2s ease-out;
-o-transition: all 0.2s ease-out;
transition: all 0.2s ease-out;
```

If you don't want all your properties to transition at the same rate, or if you just want a select few to have a transition effect, include the various transition properties as a comma-separated list, including, at minimum, the `transition-property` and `transition-duration` for each.

Animations

Transitions animate elements over time; however, they're limited in what they can do. You can define starting and ending states, but there's no fine-grained control over any intermediate states. CSS animations, unlike transitions, allow you to control each step of an animation via **keyframes**. If you've ever worked with Flash, you're likely very familiar with the concept of keyframes; if not, don't worry, it's fairly straightforward. A keyframe is a snapshot that defines a starting or end point of any smooth transition. With CSS transitions, we're essentially limited to defining the first and last keyframes. CSS animations allow us to add any number of keyframes in between, to guide our animation in more complex ways.

At the time of this writing, only WebKit supports CSS animation. This means that support on the desktop is limited, but support on mobile devices is fairly good, as the default browsers on iOS and Android both run on WebKit. As we've already mentioned, the lack of powerful processors on many mobile devices make CSS animations a great alternative to weighty, CPU-intensive JavaScript animation.

Keyframes

To animate an element in CSS, you first create a named animation, then attach it to an element in that element's property declaration block. Animations in themselves don't do anything; in order to animate an element, you will need to associate the animation with that element.

To create an animation, use the @keyframes rule—or @-webkit-keyframes for current WebKit implementations—followed by a name of your choosing, which will serve as the identifier for the animation. Then, you can specify your keyframes.

For an animation called myAnimation, the @keyframes rule would look like this:

```
@-webkit-keyframes 'myAnimation'{
   /* put animation keyframes here */
}
```

Each keyframe looks like its own nested CSS declaration block. Instead of a selector, though, you use the keywords from or to, a percentage value, or a comma-separated list of percentage values. This value specifies how far along the animation the keyframe is located.

Inside each keyframe, include the desired properties and values. Between each keyframe, values will be smoothly interpolated by the browser's animation engine.

Keyframes can be specified in any order; it's the percentage values, rather than the order of the declarations, that determine the sequence of keyframes in the animation.

Here are a few simple animations:

```
@-webkit-keyframes 'appear' {
   0% {
      opacity: 0;
   }
```

```
    100% {
      opacity: 1;
    }
}

@-webkit-keyframes 'disappear' {
    to {
      opacity: 0;
    }
    from {
      opacity: 1;
    }
}

@-webkit-keyframes 'appearDisappear' {
    0%, 100% {
      opacity: 0;
    }
    20%, 80% {
      opacity: 1;
    }
}
```

The last animation is worth paying extra attention to: we've applied the same styles to 0% and 100%, and to 20% and 80%. In this case, it means the element will start out invisible (opacity: 0;), fade in to visible by 20% of the way through the duration, remain visible until 80%, then fade out.

We've created three animations, but they aren't attached to any elements. Once we have defined an animation, the next step is to apply it to one or more elements using the various animation properties.

Animation Properties

The animation properties supported by WebKit are as follows, with the -webkit- vendor prefix.

animation-name

This property is used to attach an animation (defined using the @keyframes syntax previously) to an element:

```
-webkit-animation-name: 'appear';
```

Note that the quotes around the animation name in both the property value and the @keyframe selector are optional. We recommend including them to keep your styles as legible as possible, and to avoid conflicts.

animation-duration

The animation-duration property defines the length of time, in seconds or milliseconds, an animation takes to complete one iteration (all the way through, from 0% to 100%):

```
-webkit-animation-duration: 300ms;
```

animation-timing-function

Like the transition-timing-function property, the animation-timing-function determines how the animation will progress over its duration. The options are the same as for transition-timing-function: ease, linear, ease-in, ease-out, ease-in-out, or cubic-bezier:

```
-webkit-animation-timing-function: linear;
```

animation-iteration-count

This property lets you define how many times the animation will play through. The value is generally an integer, but you can also use numbers with decimal points (in which case, the animation will end partway through a run), or the value infinite for endlessly repeating animations. If omitted, it will default to 1, in which case the animation will occur only once:

```
-webkit-animation-iteration-count: infinite;
```

animation-direction

When the animation iterates, you can use the animation-direction property with the value alternate to make every other iteration play the animation backwards. For example, in a bouncing ball animation, you could provide keyframes for the

falling ball, and then use `animation-direction: alternate;` to reverse it on every second play through:

```
-webkit-animation-direction: alternate;
```

The default is `normal`, so the animation will play forwards on each iteration.

When animations are played in reverse, timing functions are also reversed; for example, `ease-in` becomes `ease-out`.

animation-delay

Used to define how many milliseconds or seconds to wait before the browser begins the animation:

```
-webkit-animation-delay: 15s;
```

animation-fill-mode

The `animation-fill-mode` property defines what happens before the animation begins and after the animation concludes. By default, an animation won't affect property values outside of its runs, but with `animation-fill-mode`, we can override this default behavior. We tell the animation to "sit and wait" on the first keyframe until the animation starts, or stop on the last keyframe without reverting to the original values at the conclusion of the animation, or both.

The available values are `none`, `forwards`, `backwards`, or `both`. The default is `none`, in which case the animation proceeds and ends as expected, reverting to the initial keyframes when the animation completes its final iteration. When set to `forwards`, the animation continues to apply the values of the last keyframes after the animation ends. When set to `backwards`, the animation's initial keyframes are applied as soon as the animation style is applied to an element. As you'd expect, `both` applies both the `backwards` and `forwards` effects:

```
-webkit-animation-fill-mode: forwards;
```

animation-play-state

The `animation-play-state` property defines whether the animation is `running` or `paused`. A paused animation displays the current state of the animation statically.

When a paused animation is resumed, it restarts from the current position. This provides a simple way to control CSS animations from your JavaScript.

The Shorthand `animation` Property

Fortunately, there's a shorthand for all these animation properties. The `animation` property takes as its value a space-separated list of values for the longhand `animation-name`, `animation-duration`, `animation-timing-function`, `animation-delay`, `animation-iteration-count`, `animation-direction`, and `animation-fill-mode` properties:

```
.verbose {
  -webkit-animation-name: 'appear';
  -webkit-animation-duration: 300ms;
  -webkit-animation-timing-function: ease-in;
  -webkit-animation-iteration-count: 1;
  -webkit-animation-direction: alternate;
  -webkit-animation-delay: 5s;
  s-webkit-animation-fill-mode: backwards;
}

/* shorthand */
.concise {
  -webkit-animation: 'appear' 300ms ease-in 1 alternate 5s
➥backwards;
}
```

To declare multiple animations on an element, include a grouping for each animation name, with each shorthand grouping separated by a comma. For example:

```
.target {
  -webkit-animation:
    'animationOne' 300ms ease-in 0s backwards,
    'animationTwo' 600ms ease-out 1s forwards;
}
```

Moving On

With transforms, transitions, and animations, our site is looking more dynamic. Remember the old maxim, though: just because you can, doesn't mean you should. Animations were aplenty on the Web in the late nineties; a lot of us remember flashing banners and scrolling marquees, and to some extent, that problem still exists today. Use animations and transitions where it makes sense, enhancing the user experience—and skip it everywhere else.

We still have a few lessons to learn in CSS3 to make our website look more like an old-time newspaper. In the next chapter, we'll learn about creating columns without relying on `float`, and how to include fancy fonts that aren't installed by default on our users' computers.

Embedded Fonts and Multicolumn Layouts

We've added quite a lot of decoration to *The HTML5 Herald*, but we're still missing some key components to give it that really old-fashioned feel. To look like a real newspaper, the text of the articles should be laid out in narrow columns, and we should use some suitably appropriate fonts for the period.

In this chapter, we'll finish up the look and feel of our website with CSS3 columns and `@font-face`.

Web Fonts with `@font-face`

Since the early days of the Web, designers have been dreaming of creating sites with beautiful typography. But, as we all know too well, browsers are limited to rendering text in the fonts the user has installed on their system. In practical terms, this has limited most sites to a handful of fonts: Arial, Verdana, Times, Georgia, and a few others.

Over the years, we have come up with a number of clever workarounds for this problem. We created JPEGs and PNGs for site titles, logos, buttons, and navigation elements. When those elements required additional states or variants, we created even more images, or image sprites to ensure the page stayed snappy and responsive. Whenever the design or text changed, all those images had to be recreated.

This can be an acceptable solution for some elements on a page, but it's just unrealistic to expect a designer to handcraft the title of every new article in Photoshop and then upload it to the site. So, for key page elements that need to change frequently, we were stuck with those same few fonts.

To fill this typographic void, some very cool font embedding scripts were created, like sIFR, based on Flash and JavaScript, and the canvas-based Cufón. While these methods have been a great stopgap measure, allowing us to include our own fonts, they had severe drawbacks. Sometimes they were tricky to implement, and they required that JavaScript be enabled and, in the case of sIFR, the Flash plugin be installed. In addition, they significantly slowed the page's download and rendering.

Fortunately, there's now a better way: `@font-face` is a pure CSS solution for embedding fonts—and it's supported on every browser with any kind of market share, from IE6 on up.

We'll be including two embedded fonts on *The HTML5 Herald* site: League Gothic from The League of Movable Type,[1] and Acknowledgement Medium by Ben Weiner of Reading Type.[2] The two fonts are shown, respectively, in Figure 9.1 and Figure 9.2.

League Gothic

Figure 9.1. League Gothic

---

[1] http://www.theleagueofmoveabletype.com/
[2] http://www.readingtype.org/

ACKNOWLEDGEMENT

Figure 9.2. Acknowledgement Medium

We'll now look at how we can embed these fonts and use them to power any of the text on our site, just as if they were installed on our users' machines.

Implementing `@font-face`

`@font-face` is one of several CSS **at-rules**, like `@media`, `@import`, `@page`, and the one we've just seen, `@keyframes`. At-rules are ways of encapsulating several rules together in a declaration to serve as instructions to the browser's CSS processor. The `@font-face` at-rule allows us to specify custom fonts that we can then include in other declaration blocks.

To include fonts using `@font-face`, you have to:

1. load the font file onto your servers in a variety of formats to support all the different browsers

2. name, describe, and link to that font in an `@font-face` rule

3. include the font's name in a `font-family` property value, just as you would for system fonts

You already know how to upload a file onto a server, so we'll discuss the details of the various file types in the next section. For now, we'll focus on the second and third steps so that you can become familiar with the syntax of `@font-face`.

Here's an example of an `@font-face` block:

```
@font-face {
  font-family: 'fontName';
  src: source;
  font-weight: weight;
  font-style: style;
}
```

The font family and source are required, but the weight and style are optional.

You need to include a separate @font-face at-rule for every font you contain in your site. You'll also have to include a separate at-rule for each variation of the font—regular, thin, thick, italic, black, and so on. *The HTML5 Herald* will require two imported fonts, so we'll include two @font-face blocks:

css/styles.css (excerpt)

```
@font-face {
   ⋮
}

@font-face {
   ⋮
}
```

The font-family part of the @font-face at-rule declaration is slightly different from the font-family property with which you're already familiar. In this case, we're *declaring* a name for our font, rather than assigning a font with a given name to an element. The font name can be anything you like—it's only a reference to a font file, so it needn't even correspond to the name of the font. Of course, it makes sense to use the font's name to keep your CSS readable and maintainable. It's good to settle on a convention and stick to it for all your fonts. For our two fonts, we'll use camel case:

css/styles.css (excerpt)

```
@font-face {
   font-family: 'LeagueGothic';
}

@font-face {
   font-family: 'AcknowledgementMedium';
}
```

Declaring Font Sources

Now that we have a skeleton laid out for our @font-face rules, and we've given each of them a name, it's time to link them up to the actual font files. The src property can take several formats. Additionally, you can declare more than one source. If the browser fails to find the first source, it will try for the next one, and so on, until it either finds a source, or it runs out of options.

Let's add more formats to our League Gothic declaration:

```
css/styles.css (excerpt)

@font-face {
  font-family: 'LeagueGothicRegular';
  src: url('../fonts/League_Gothic-webfont.eot') format('eot'),
       url('../fonts/League_Gothic-webfont.woff') format('woff'),
       url('../fonts/League_Gothic-webfont.ttf') format('truetype'),
       url('../fonts/League_Gothic-webfont.svg#webfontFHzvtkso')
➥format('svg');
}
```

There are four font sources listed in the code block above. The first declaration is an EOT font declaration, a proprietary format for Internet Explorer, and the only file type understood by IE4–8.

Then we define the WOFF (Web Open Font Format, an emerging standard), OTF (OpenType), TTF (TrueType), and SVG (Scalable Vector Graphics) font files. While most desktop browsers will use one of the first three declarations, be sure to include the SVG format, which was originally the only format supported by the iPhone.[3]

Table 9.1 shows a breakdown of browser support for different formats. As you can see, there's no single format that's supported in every browser, so we need to provide a number of formats, as we did with video in Chapter 5.

Table 9.1. Browser support for font formats

	IE	Safari	Chrome	Firefox	Opera	iOS
@font-face	4+	3.1+	4+	3.5+	10+	3.2+
WOFF	9+	6+	6+	3.6+	11.1+	
OTF		3.1+	4+	3.5+	10+	4.2+
TTF	9+?	3.1+	4+	3.5+	10+	4.2+
SVG		3.1+	4+		10+	3.2+
EOT	4+					

[3] The iPhone recently expanded support to include OTF in 4.2, but it still makes sense to include SVG for the time being.

Adding these extra font formats ensures support for every browser, but unfortunately it will cause problems in versions of IE older than IE9. Those browsers will see everything between the first `url('` and the last `')` as one URL, so will fail to load the font. At first, it would seem that we've been given the choice between supporting IE and supporting every other browser, but fortunately there's a solution. Detailed in a FontSpring blog post,[4] it involves adding a query string to the end of the EOT URL. This tricks the browser into thinking that the rest of the `src` property is a continuation of that query string, so it goes looking for the correct URL and loads the font:

(excerpt)

```
@font-face {
  font-family: 'LeagueGothicRegular';
  src: url('../fonts/League_Gothic-webfont.eot?#iefix')
➥format('eot'),
      url('../fonts/League_Gothic-webfont.woff') format('woff'),
      url('../fonts/League_Gothic-webfont.ttf') format('truetype'),
      url('../fonts/League_Gothic-webfont.svg#webfontFHzvtkso')
➥format('svg');
}
```

This syntax has one potential point of failure: IE9 has a feature called **compatibility mode**, in which it will attempt to render pages the same way IE7 or 8 would. This was introduced to prevent older sites appearing broken in IE9's more standards-compliant rendering. However, IE9 in compatibility mode doesn't reproduce the bug in loading the EOT font, so the above declaration will fail. To compensate for this, you can add an additional EOT URL in a separate `src` property:

(excerpt)

```
@font-face {
  font-family: 'LeagueGothicRegular';
  src: url('../fonts/League_Gothic-webfont.eot');
  src: url('../fonts/League_Gothic-webfont.eot?#iefix')
➥format('eot'),
      url('../fonts/League_Gothic-webfont.woff') format('woff'),
      url('../fonts/League_Gothic-webfont.ttf') format('truetype'),
```

[4] http://www.fontspring.com/blog/the-new-bulletproof-font-face-syntax

```
            url('../fonts/League_Gothic-webfont.svg#webfontFHzvtkso')
➥format('svg');
}
```

This may be an unnecessary precaution, as generally a user would need to deliberately switch IE to compatibility mode while viewing your site for this issue to arise. Alternatively, you could also force IE out of compatibility mode by adding this `meta` element to your document's `head`:

```
<meta http-equiv="X-UA-Compatible" content="IE=Edge">
```

It's also possible to achieve the same result by adding an extra HTTP header; this can be done with a directive in your **.htaccess** file (or equivalent):

```
<IfModule mod_setenvif.c>
  <IfModule mod_headers.c>
    BrowserMatch MSIE ie
    Header set X-UA-Compatible "IE=Edge"
  </IfModule>
</IfModule>
```

Font Property Descriptors

Font property descriptors—including `font-style`, `font-variant`, `font-weight`, and others—can optionally be added to define the characteristics of the font face, and are used to match styles to specific font faces. The values are the same as the equivalent CSS properties:

```
@font-face {
  font-family: 'LeagueGothicRegular';
  src: url('../fonts/League_Gothic-webfont.eot');
  src: url('../fonts/League_Gothic-webfont.eot?#iefix')
➥format('eot'),
        url('../fonts/League_Gothic-webfont.woff') format('woff'),
        url('../fonts/League_Gothic-webfont.ttf') format('truetype'),
        url('../fonts/League_Gothic-webfont.svg#webfontFHzvtkso')
➥format('svg');
  font-weight: bold;
  font-style: normal;
}
```

Again, the behavior is different from what you'd expect. You are not telling the browser to make the font bold; rather, you're telling it that this *is* the bold variant of the font. This can be confusing, and the behavior can be quirky in some browsers.

However, there is a reason to use the `font-weight` or `font-style` descriptor in the `@font-face` rule declaration. You can declare several font sources for the same `font-family` name:

```
@font-face {
  font-family: 'CoolFont';
  font-style: normal;
  src: url(fonts/CoolFontStd.ttf);
}

@font-face {
  font-family: 'CoolFont';
  font-style: italic;
  src: url(fonts/CoolFontItalic.ttf);
}

.whichFont {
  font-family: 'CoolFont';
}
```

Notice that both at-rules use the same font-family name, but different font styles. In this example, the `.whichFont` element will use the **CoolFontStd.ttf** font, because it matches the style given in that at-rule. However, if the element were to inherit an italic font style, it would switch to using the **CoolFontItalic.ttf** font instead.

Unicode Range

Also available is the `unicode-range` descriptor, which is employed to define the range of Unicode characters supported by the font. If this property is omitted, the entire range of characters included in the font file will be made available.

We won't be using this on our site, but here's an example of what it looks like:

```
unicode-range: U+000-49F, U+2000-27FF, U+2900-2BFF, U+1D400-1D7FF;
```

Applying the Font

Once the font is declared using the `@font-face` syntax, you can then refer to it as you would any normal system font in your CSS: include it in a "stack" as the value of a `font-family` property. It's a good idea to declare a fallback font or two in case your embedded font fails to load.

Let's look at one example from *The HTML5 Herald*:

css/styles.css *(excerpt)*

```
h1 {
  text-shadow: #fff 1px 1px;
  font-family: LeagueGothic, Tahoma, Geneva, sans-serif;
  text-transform: uppercase;
  line-height: 1;
}
```

Our two embedded fonts are used in a number of different places in our stylesheet, but you get the idea.

Legal Considerations

We've included the markup for two fonts on our site, but we're yet to put the font files themselves in place. We found both of these fonts freely available online. They are both licensed as **freeware**—that is, they're free to use for both personal and commercial use. Generally, you should consider this the only kind of font you should use for `@font-face`, unless you're using a third-party service.

How is `@font-face` any different from using a certain font in an image file? By having a website on the Internet, your font source files are hosted on publicly available web servers, so in theory anyone can download them. In fact, in order to render the text on your page, the browser *has* to download the font files. By using `@font-face`, you're distributing the font to everyone who visits your site. In order to include a font on your website, then, you need to be legally permitted to distribute the font.

Owning or purchasing a font doesn't mean you have the legal right to redistribute it—in the same way that buying a song on iTunes doesn't grant you the right to throw it up on your website for anyone to download. Licenses that allow you to

distribute fonts are more expensive (and rarer) than licenses allowing you to use a font on one computer for personal or even commercial use.

However, there are several websites that have free downloadable web fonts with Creative Commons,[5] shareware, or freeware licensing. Alternatively, there are paid and subscription services that allow you to purchase or rent fonts, generally providing you with ready-made scripts or stylesheets that make them easy to use with @font-face.

A few sites providing web font services include Typekit,[6] Typotheque,[7] Webtype,[8] Fontdeck,[9] and Fonts.com[10].

Google's web fonts directory[11] has a growing collection of fonts provided free of charge and served from Google's servers. It simply provides you with a URL pointing to a stylesheet that includes all the required @font-face rules, so all you need to do is add a link element to your document in order to start using a font.

When selecting a service, font selection and price are certainly important, but there are other considerations. Make sure that any service you choose to use takes download speed into consideration. Font files can be fairly large, potentially containing several thousand characters. Good services allow you to select character subsets, as well as font-style subsets, to decrease the file size. Bear in mind, also, that some services require JavaScript in order to function.

Creating Various Font File Types: Font Squirrel

If you have a font that you're legally allowed to redistribute, there'll be no need for you to use any of the font services above. You will, however, have to convert your font into the various formats required to be compatible with every browser on the market. So how do you go about converting your fonts into all these formats?

---

[5] If you're unfamiliar with Creative Commons licenses, you can find out more at http://creativecommons.org/.

[6] http://typekit.com/

[7] http://www.typotheque.com/

[8] http://www.webtype.com/

[9] http://fontdeck.com/

[10] http://webfonts.fonts.com

[11] http://code.google.com/apis/webfonts/

One of the easiest tools for this purpose is Font Squirrel's @font-face generator.[12] This service allows you to select fonts from your desktop with a few clicks of your mouse and convert them to TTF, EOT, WOFF, SVG, SVGZ, and even a Base64 encoded version.[13]

By default, the **Optimal** option is selected for generating an @font-face kit; however, in some cases you can decrease the file sizes by choosing **Expert...** and creating a character subset. Rather than including every conceivable character in the font file, you can limit yourself to those you know will be used on your site.

For example, on *The HTML5 Herald* site, the Acknowledgement Medium font is used only in specific ad blocks and headings, so we need just a small set of characters. All the text set in this font is uppercase, so let's restrict our font to uppercase letters, punctuation, and numbers, as shown in Figure 9.3.

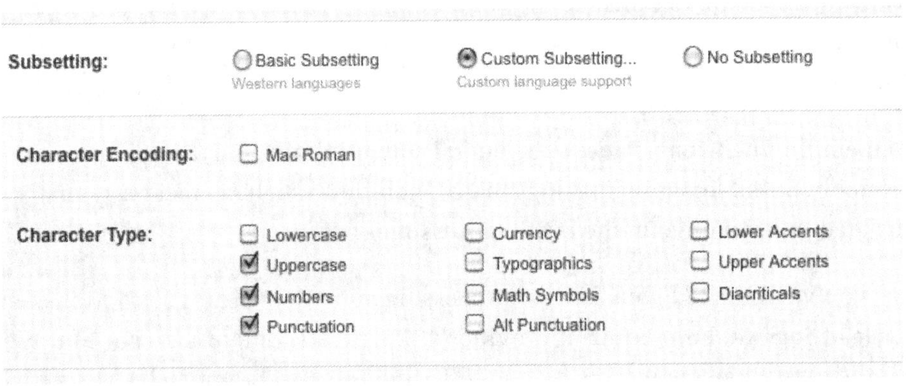

Figure 9.3. Selecting a subset of characters in Font Squirrel's @font-face generator

Figure 9.4 below shows how the file sizes of our subsetted fonts stack up against the default character sets. In our case, the uppercase-and-punctuation-only fonts are 25–30% smaller than the default character sets. Font Squirrel even lets you specify certain characters for your subset, so there's no need to include all the letters of the alphabet if you know you won't use them.

---

[12] http://www.fontsquirrel.com/fontface/generator

[13] Base64 encoding is a way of including the entire contents of a font file directly in your CSS file. Sometimes this can provide performance benefits by avoiding an extra HTTP request, but that's beyond the scope of this book. Don't sweat it, though—the files generated by the default settings should be fine for most uses.

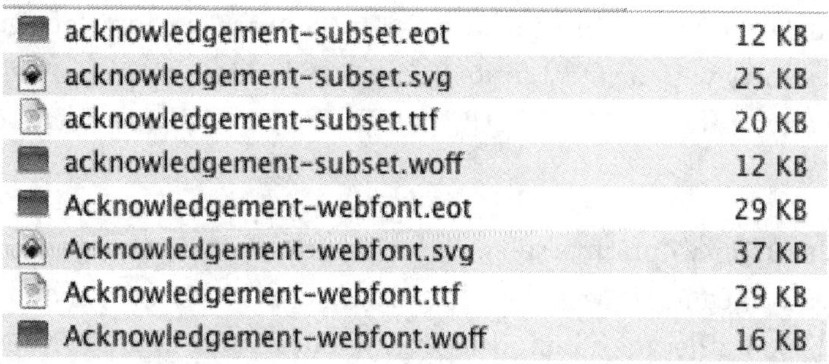

▣	acknowledgement-subset.eot	12 KB
◉	acknowledgement-subset.svg	25 KB
▢	acknowledgement-subset.ttf	20 KB
▣	acknowledgement-subset.woff	12 KB
▣	Acknowledgement-webfont.eot	29 KB
◉	Acknowledgement-webfont.svg	37 KB
▢	Acknowledgement-webfont.ttf	29 KB
▣	Acknowledgement-webfont.woff	16 KB

Figure 9.4. File sizes of subsetted fonts can be substantially smaller

For the League Gothic font, we'll need a more expanded character subset. This font is used for article titles, which are all uppercase like our ads, so we can again omit lowercase letters; however, we should consider that content for titles may include a wider range of possible characters. Moreover, users might use in-browser tools, or Google Translate, to translate the content on the page—in which case other characters might be required. So, for League Gothic, we'll go with the default **Basic Subsetting**—this will give you all the characters required for Western languages.

When employing @font-face, as a general rule minimize font file size as much as reasonably possible, while making sure to include enough characters so that a translated version of your site is still accessible.

Once you've uploaded your font for processing and selected all your options, press **Download Your Kit**. Font Squirrel provides a download containing: your font files with the extensions requested, a demo HTML file for each font face style, and a stylesheet from which you can copy and paste the code directly into your own CSS.

💡 Font Squirrel's Font Catalogue

In addition to the @font-face generator, the Font Squirrel site includes a catalog of hand-picked free fonts whose licenses allow for web embedding. In fact, both of the fonts we're using on *The HTML5 Herald* can also be found on Font Squirrel, with ready-made @font-face kits to download without relying on the generator at all.

To target all browsers, make sure you've created TTF, WOFF, EOT, and SVG font file formats. Once you've created the font files, upload the web fonts to your server. Copy and paste the CSS provided, changing the paths to point to the folder where

you've put your fonts. Make sure the font-family name specified in the `@font-face` rule matches the one you're using in your styles, and you're good to go!

Troubleshooting `@font-face`

If your fonts are failing to display in any browser, the problem could very well be the path in your CSS. Check to make sure that the font file is actually where you expect it to be. Browser-based debugging tools—such as the Web Inspector in WebKit, Dragonfly in Opera, or the Firebug Firefox extension—will indicate if the file is missing.

If you're sure that the path is correct and the file is where it's supposed to be, make sure your server is correctly configured to serve up the fonts. Windows IIS servers won't serve up files if they're unable to recognize their MIME type, so try adding WOFF and SVG to your list of MIME types (EOT and TTF should be supported out of the box):

```
.woff   application/x-font-woff
.svg    image/svg+xml
```

Finally, some browsers require that font files be served from the same domain as the page they're embedded on.

Browser–based Developer Tools

Safari, Chrome, and Opera all come standard with tools to help save you time as a web developer. Chrome and Opera already have these tools set up. Simply right-click (or control-click on a Mac) and choose **Inspect Element**. A panel will open up at the bottom of your browser, highlighting the HTML of the element you've selected. You'll also see any CSS applied to that element.

While Safari comes with this tool, it needs to be manually enabled. To turn it on, go to **Safari > Preferences**, and then click the **Advanced** tab. Be sure that you check the **Show Develop menu in menu bar** checkbox.

Firefox comes without such a tool. Luckily, there's a free Firefox plugin called Firebug that provides the same functionality. You can download Firebug at http://getfirebug.com/.

Other Considerations

Embedded fonts can improve performance and decrease maintenance time when compared to text as images. Remember, though, that font files can be big. If you need a particular font for a banner ad, it may make more sense (given the limited amount of text required) to simply create an image instead of including font files.

When pondering the inclusion of multiple font files on your site, consider performance. Multiple fonts will increase your site's download time, and font overuse can be tacky. Furthermore, the wrong font can make your content difficult to read. For body text, you should almost always stick to the usual selection of web-safe fonts.

Another factor worth considering is that browsers are unable to render the @font-face font until it has been downloaded entirely. They'll behave differently in how they display your content before the download is complete: some browsers will render the text in a system font, while others won't render any text at all.

This effect is referred to as a "flash of unstyled text," or FOUT, a term coined by Paul Irish.[14] To try to prevent this from happening (or to minimize its duration), make your file sizes as small as possible, Gzip them, and include your @font-face rules in CSS files as high up as possible in your markup. If there's a script above the @font-face declaration in the source, IE experiences a bug, whereby the page won't render *anything* until the font has downloaded—so be sure your fonts are declared above any scripts on your page.

Another option to mitigate @font-face's impact on performance is to defer the font file download until after the page has rendered. This may be unviable for your designer or client, however, as it may result in a more noticeable FOUT, even if the page loads faster overall.[15]

Of course, we don't want to scare you away from using @font-face, but it's important that you avoid using this newfound freedom to run wild without regard for the consequences. Remember that there are trade-offs, so use web fonts where they're appropriate, and consider the available alternatives.

---

[14] http://paulirish.com/2009/fighting-the-font-face-fout/

[15] For more on @font-face and performance, as well as an example of how to "lazy load" your font files, see http://www.stevesouders.com/blog/2009/10/13/font-face-and-performance/.

CSS3 Multicolumn Layouts

Nothing says "newspaper" like a row of tightly packed columns of text. There's a reason for this: newspapers break articles into multiple columns because lines of text that are too long are hard to read. Browser windows can be wider than printed books, and even as wide as some newspapers—so it makes sense for CSS to provide us with the ability to flow our content into columns.

You may be thinking that we've always been able to create column effects using the `float` property. But the behavior of floats is subtly different from what we're after. Newspaper-style columns have been close to impossible to accomplish with CSS and HTML without forcing column breaks at fixed positions. True, you could break an article into `divs`, floating each one to make it look like a set of columns. But what if your content is dynamic? Your back-end code will need to figure out where each column should begin and end in order to insert the requisite `div` tags.

With CSS3 columns, the browser determines when to end one column and begin the next without requiring any extra markup. You retain the flexibility to change the number of columns as well as their width, without having to go back in and alter the page's markup.

For now, we're mostly limited to splitting content across a few columns, while controlling their widths and the gutters between them. As support broadens, we'll be able to break columns, span elements across multiple columns, and more. Support for CSS3 columns is moderate: Firefox and WebKit have had support via vendor-prefixed properties for years, while Opera has just added support in 11.10 (without a vendor prefix), and IE still offers no support.

Almost all the content on the main page of *The HTML5 Herald* is broken into columns. Let's dig deeper into the properties that make up CSS3 columns and learn how to create these effects on our site.

The `column-count` Property

The `column-count` property specifies the number of columns desired, and the maximum number of columns allowed. The default value of `auto` means that the element has one column. Our leftmost articles are broken into three columns, and the article below the ad blocks has two columns:

```
                                        css/styles.css (excerpt)
#primary article .content {
   -webkit-column-count: 3;
   -moz-column-count: 3;
   column-count: 3;
}

#tertiary article .content {
   -webkit-column-count: 2;
   -moz-column-count: 2;
   column-count: 2;
}
```

This is all we really need to create our columns. By default, the columns will have a small gap between them. The total width of the columns combined with the gaps will take up 100% of the width of the element.

Yet, there are a number of other properties we can use for more granular control.

The `column-gap` Property

The `column-gap` property specifies the width of the space between columns:

```
                                        css/styles.css (excerpt)
#primary article .content,
#tertiary article .content {
   -webkit-column-gap: 10px;
   -moz-column-gap: 10px;
   column-gap: 10px;
}
```

Declare the width in length units, such as ems or pixels, or use the term `normal`. It's up to the browser to determine what `normal` means, but the spec suggests 1em. We've declared our gaps to be 10px wide. The resulting columns are shown in Figure 9.5.

Figure 9.5. Our leftmost content area has articles split over three columns

The `column-width` Property

The `column-width` property is like having a `min-width` for your columns. The browser will include as many columns of at least the given width as it can to fill up the element—up to the value of the `column-count` property. If the columns need to be wider to fill up all the available space, they will be.

For example, if we have a parent that is 400 pixels wide, a 10-pixel column gap, and the `column-width` is declared as `150px`, the browser can fit two columns:

(400px width – 10px column gap) ÷ 150px width = 2.6

The browser rounds down to two columns, making columns that are as large as possible in the allotted space; in this case that's 195px for each column—the total width minus the gap, divided by the number of columns. Even if the `column-count` were set to 3, there would still only be two columns, as there's not enough space to include three columns of the specified width. In other words, you can think of the `column-count` property as specifying the *maximum* column count.

The only situation in which columns will be narrower than the `column-width` is if the parent element itself is too narrow for a single column of the specified width. In this case, you'll have one column that fills the whole parent element.

It's a good idea to declare your `column-width` in ems, to ensure a minimum number of characters for each line in a column. Let's add a `column-width` of `9em` to our content columns:

css/styles.css *(excerpt)*

```
#primary article .content,
#tertiary article .content {
  ⋮
  -webkit-column-width: 9em;
  -moz-column-width: 9em;
  column-width: 9em;
}
```

Now, if you increase the font size in your browser, you'll see that the number of columns is decreased as required to maintain a minimum width. This ensures readability, as shown in Figure 9.6.

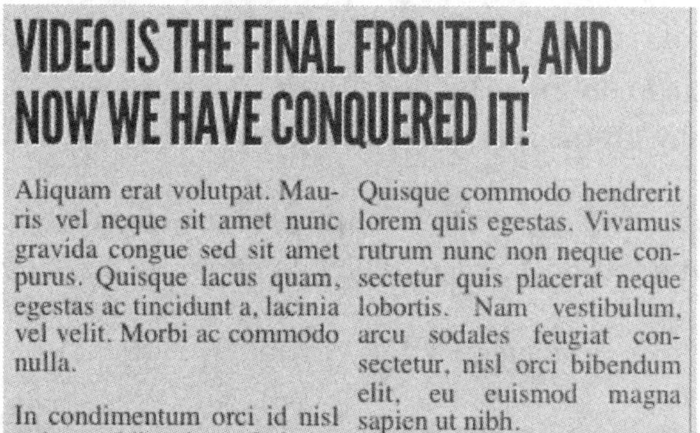

VIDEO IS THE FINAL FRONTIER, AND NOW WE HAVE CONQUERED IT!

Aliquam erat volutpat. Mauris vel neque sit amet nunc gravida congue sed sit amet purus. Quisque lacus quam, egestas ac tincidunt a, lacinia vel velit. Morbi ac commodo nulla.

In condimentum orci id nisl volutpat bibendum. Quisque commodo hendrerit lorem quis egestas. Vivamus rutrum nunc non neque consectetur quis placerat neque lobortis. Nam vestibulum, arcu sodales feugiat consectetur, nisl orci bibendum elit, eu euismod magna sapien ut nibh. Aliquam erat volutpat. Mauris vel neque sit amet nunc gravida congue sed sit amet purus.

Quisque commodo hendrerit lorem quis egestas. Vivamus rutrum nunc non neque consectetur quis placerat neque lobortis. Nam vestibulum, arcu sodales feugiat consectetur, nisl orci bibendum elit, eu euismod magna sapien ut nibh.

Neque sit amet nunc gravida congue sed sit amet purus. Quisque lacus quam, egestas ac tincidunt a, lacinia vel velit. Morbi ac commodo nulla. In condimentum orci id nisl volutpat bibendum. Quisque commodo hendrerit lorem quis egestas. Vivamus rutrum nunc non neque consectetur quis placerat neque lobortis. Nam vestibulum,

Figure 9.6. Declaring a `column-width` in ems ensures a minimum number of characters on each line

The `columns` Shorthand Property

The `columns` shorthand property is a composite of the `column-width` and `column-count` properties. Declare the two parameters—the width of each column and the number of columns—as described above.

At the time of this writing, this compound property is only supported in WebKit, so you will need to at least continue providing separate properties for the `-moz-` implementation:

```
                                                    css/styles.css (excerpt)

#primary article .content {
    -webkit-columns: 3 9em;
    -moz-column-count: 3;
    -moz-column-width: 9em;
    columns: 3 9em;
}
```

Rather than specifying different properties for `-webkit-` and `-moz-`, you might find it simpler to just stick with the separate `column-width` and `column-count` properties for now. It's up to you.

Columns and the `height` Property

With the above declarations—and no `height` specified on the element—browsers will balance the column heights automatically, so that the content in each column is approximately equal in height.

But what if a `height` is declared? When the `height` property is set on a multicolumn block, each column is allowed to grow to that height and no further before a new column is added. The browser starts with the first column and creates as many columns as necessary, creating only the first column if there is minimal text. Finally, if too little space is allocated, the content will overflow from the box—or be clipped if `overflow: hidden;` is set.

If you want to declare a `height` on your element, but would also like the content to be spread across your columns, you can use the `column-fill` property. When supported, and set to `balance`, the browser will balance the height of the columns as though there were no `height` declared.

> **Margins and Padding**
>
> Even with a `height` declared, columns may still not appear to have exactly the desired height, because of the bottom margins on paragraphs. WebKit currently splits margins and padding between columns, sometimes adding the extra spacing at the top of a following column. Firefox allows margins to go beyond the bottom of the box, rather than letting them show up at the top of the next column, which we think makes more sense.
>
> As with the `column-width`, you may also want to declare your `height` in ems instead of pixels; this way, if your user increases the font size, they are less likely to have content clipped or overflowing.

Other Column Features

Beyond the core `count`, `width`, and `gap` properties, CSS3 provides us with a few additional features for laying out multicolumn content, some of which are yet to be supported.

The `column-rule` Property

Column **rules** are essentially borders between each column. The `column-rule` property specifies the color, style, and width of the column rules. The rule will appear in the middle of the column gap. This property is actually shorthand for the `column-rule-color`, `column-rule-style`, and `column-rule-width` properties.

The syntax for the value is exactly the same as for `border` and the related `border-width`, `border-style`, and `border-color` properties. The width can be any length unit, just like `border-width`, including the key terms of `medium`, `thick`, and `thin`. And the color can be any supported color value:

css/styles.css (excerpt)

```
-webkit-column-rule: 1px solid #CCCCCC;
-moz-column-rule: 1px solid #CCCCCC;
column-rule: 1px solid #CCCCCC;
```

Column Breaks

There are three column-breaking properties that allow developers to define where column breaks should appear. The `break-before`, `break-after`, and `break-inside`

properties take a limited number of key terms as values to define whether a column break can and should occur before, after, or inside an element, respectively. Rather than being applied to the same element on which we defined our primary column properties, they're applied to other elements nested inside it.

The values available are the same as for page-break-after, page-break-before, and page-break-inside in CSS 2.1: auto, always, avoid, left, and right. CSS3 also adds a few new possible values for these properties: page, column, avoid-page, and avoid-column. The page and column values function like always, and will force a break. The difference is that page will only force page breaks and column applies only to columns. This gives you a bit more flexibility in how you manage breaks. avoid-page and avoid-column are similar, except that they function like avoid.

For example, you might want to avoid a column break occurring immediately after an h2 element in your content. Here's how you'd do that:

```
.columns {
  column-count: 3;
  column-gap: 5px;
}

.columns h2 {
  break-after: avoid;
}
```

The only browser engine that currently supports column breaks is WebKit. As well as being vendor-prefixed, the WebKit properties also take a different syntax from what's in the proposed specifications (note the addition of the word column to the property names):

```
-webkit-column-break-after: always;
-webkit-column-break-before: auto;
-webkit-column-break-inside: never;
```

Spanning Columns

The column-span property will make it possible for an element to span across several columns. If column-span: all; is set on an element, all content that comes *before* that element in the markup should be in columns *above* that element. All

content in columns appearing in the markup *after* the element should be in columns *below* the spanned element.

Currently, `column-span` is only supported in WebKit (as `-webkit-column-span`). Because it results in a very different appearance when it's unsupported, it's probably best to avoid using it for now—unless you can be sure that all your visitors will be using WebKit.

For example, for the first article on *The HTML5 Herald*, we could have applied the column properties to the `article` element rather than the `.content` div, and used `column-span` to ensure that the video spanned across the full width of the article. However, this would appear badly broken in browsers that support columns but not spanning—like Firefox—so we instead opted to separate the video from the column content.

Other Considerations

If you've been following along with our examples, you might notice that some of your blocks of text have ugly holes in them, like the one shown in Figure 9.7.

Figure 9.7. "Rivers" can appear in your text when your columns are too narrow

This problem occurs when text with `text-align: justify;` is set in very narrow columns—as we're doing for *The HTML5 Herald*. This is because browsers don't know how to hyphenate words in the same way that word processors do, so they space words out awkwardly to ensure that the left and right edges stay justified.

For *The HTML5 Herald*, we've used a JavaScript library called Hyphenator[16] to hyphenate words and keep our text looking tidy. This may, however be unnecessary for your site—our columns are extremely narrow, as we're trying to replicate an old-style newspaper. Few real-world sites would likely need justified columns that narrow, but if you ever come across this issue, it's good to know that there are solutions available.

Progressive Enhancement

While columns still have limited browser support, there's no harm including them in your sites unless your designer is a stickler for detail. Columns can be viewed as a progressive enhancement: making long lines easier to read. Those with browsers that lack support for columns will be none the wiser about what they're missing. For example, *The HTML5 Herald* will have no columns when viewed in Internet Explorer 9, as Figure 9.8 shows—but the site certainly doesn't look broken, it's simply adapted to the capabilities of the browser.

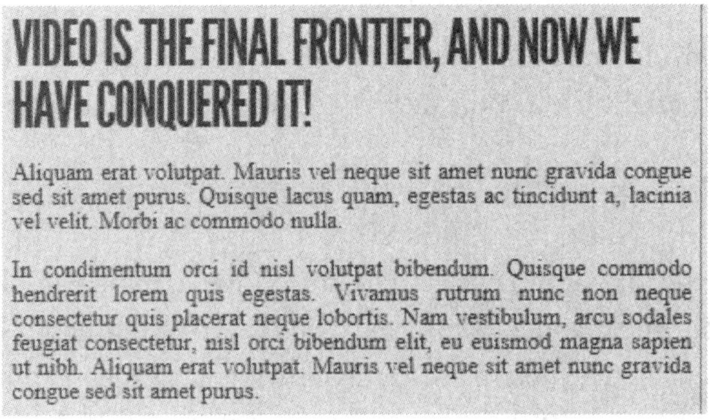

VIDEO IS THE FINAL FRONTIER, AND NOW WE HAVE CONQUERED IT!

Aliquam erat volutpat. Mauris vel neque sit amet nunc gravida congue sed sit amet purus. Quisque lacus quam, egestas ac tincidunt a, lacinia vel velit. Morbi ac commodo nulla.

In condimentum orci id nisl volutpat bibendum. Quisque commodo hendrerit lorem quis egestas. Vivamus rutrum nunc non neque consectetur quis placerat neque lobortis. Nam vestibulum, arcu sodales feugiat consectetur, nisl orci bibendum elit, eu euismod magna sapien ut nibh. Aliquam erat volutpat. Mauris vel neque sit amet nunc gravida congue sed sit amet purus.

Figure 9.8. Our site has no columns when viewed in IE9—but that's okay!

---

[16] http://code.google.com/p/hyphenator/

If, however, columns are an important feature of your design, and must be provided to all visitors, there are scripts that can help, such as Columnizer,[17] a jQuery plugin by Adam Wulf.

Media Queries

At this point, we've added a number of CSS3 enhancements to *The HTML5 Herald*. Along the way, we've filled in some knowledge gaps by presenting aspects of CSS3 that were outside the scope of our sample site. So while we're on the topic of columns, it's fitting that we introduce another CSS3 feature that's received much attention among designers targeting audiences on various devices.

In Chapter 1, we talked about the growth rate of mobile devices and the importance of considering the needs of mobile users. With CSS3 media queries, you can do just that—create a layout that resizes to accommodate different screen resolutions.

Media queries are at the heart of a recent design trend called **responsive web design**. This is when all page elements, including images and widgets, are designed and coded to resize and realign seamlessly and elegantly, depending on the capabilities and dimensions of the user's browser.

What are Media Queries?

Before CSS3, a developer could specify a media type for a stylesheet using the `media` attribute. So you might have come across a `link` element that looked like this:

```
<link rel="stylesheet" href="print.css" media="print">
```

Notice that the `media` type is specified as `print`. Acceptable values in addition to `print` include `screen`, `handheld`, `projection`, `all`, and a number of others you'll see less often, if ever. The `media` attribute allows you to specify which stylesheet to load based on the type of device the site is being viewed on. This has become a fairly common method for serving a print stylesheet.

With CSS3's media queries you can, according to the W3C spec, "extend the functionality of media types by allowing more precise labeling of style sheets." This is done using a combination of media types and expressions that check for the presence

---

[17] http://welcome.totheinter.net/columnizer-jquery-plugin/

of particular media features. So media queries let you change the presentation (the CSS) of your content for a wide variety of devices without changing the content itself (the HTML).

Syntax

Let's use the example from above, and implement a simple media query expression:

```
<link rel="stylesheet" href="style.css" media="screen and (color)">
```

This tells the browser that the stylesheet in question should be used for all screen devices that are in color. Simple—and it should cover nearly everyone in your audience. You can do the same using @import:

```
@import url(color.css) screen and (color);
```

Additionally, you can implement media queries using the @media at-rule, which we touched on earlier in this chapter when discussing @font-face. @media is probably the most well-known usage for media queries, and is the method you'll likely use most often:

```
@media handheld and (max-width: 380px) {
   /* styles go here */
}
```

In the example above, this expression will apply to all handheld devices that have a maximum display width of 380 pixels. Any styles within that block will apply only to the devices that match the expression.

Here are a few more examples of media queries using @media, so that you can see how flexible and varied the expressions can be. This style will apply only to screen-based devices that have a minimum device width (or screen width) of 320px and a maximum device width of 480px:

```
@media only screen and (min-device-width: 320px) and
➥(max-device-width: 480px) {
   /* styles go here */
}
```

Here's a slightly more complex example:

```
@media only screen and (-webkit-min-device-pixel-ratio: 1.5),
➥only screen and (min-device-pixel-ratio: 1.5) {
  /* styles go here */
}
```

In the above example, we use the only keyword, along with the and keyword in addition to a comma—which behaves like an or keyword. This code will specifically target the iPhone 4's higher resolution display, which could come in handy if you want that device to display a different set of images.

Flexibility of Media Queries

Using the above syntax, media queries allow you to change the layout of your site or application based on a wide array of circumstances. For example, if your site uses a two-column layout, you can specify that the sidebar column drop to the bottom and/or become horizontally oriented, or you can remove it completely on smaller resolutions. On small devices like smartphones, you can serve a completely different stylesheet that eliminates everything except the bare necessities.

Additionally, you can change the size of images and other elements that aren't normally fluid to conform to the user's device or screen resolution. This flexibility allows you to customize the user experience for virtually any type of device, while keeping the most important information and your site's branding accessible to all users.

Browser Support

Support for media queries is very good:

- IE9+
- Firefox 3.5+
- Safari 3.2+
- Chrome 8+
- Opera 10.6+
- iOS 3.2+
- Opera Mini 5+
- Opera Mobile 10+

▦ Android 2.1+

The only area of concern is previous versions of Internet Explorer. There are two options for dealing with this: you can supply these versions of IE with a "default" stylesheet that's served without using media queries, providing a layout suitable for the majority of screen sizes, or you can use a JavaScript-based polyfill. One such ready-made solution can be found at http://code.google.com/p/css3-mediaqueries-js/.

Thus, by taking advantage of CSS3 media queries, you can easily create a powerful way to target nearly every device and platform conceivable.

Further Reading

In a book like this, we can't possibly describe every aspect of media queries. That could be another book in itself—and an important one at that. But if you'd like to look into media queries a little further, be sure to check out the following articles:

▦ "Responsive Web Design" on *A List Apart*[18]

▦ "How to Use CSS3 Media Queries to Create a Mobile Version of Your Site" on *Smashing Magazine*[19]

▦ For a more critical perspective, "CSS Media Query for Mobile is Fool's Gold" on the Cloud Four blog[20]

---

[18] http://www.alistapart.com/articles/responsive-web-design/

[19] http://www.smashingmagazine.com/2010/07/19/how-to-use-css3-media-queries-to-create-a-mobile-version-of-your-website/

[20] http://www.cloudfour.com/css-media-query-for-mobile-is-fools-gold/

Living in Style

We've now covered all the new features in CSS that went into making *The HTML5 Herald*—and quite a few that didn't. While we haven't covered *everything* CSS3 has to offer, we've mastered several techniques that you can use today, and a few that should be usable in the very near future. Remember to check the specifications —as these features are all subject to change—and keep up to date with the state of browser support. Things are moving quickly for a change, which is both a great boon and an additional responsibility for web developers.

Up next, we'll switch gears to cover some of the new JavaScript APIs. While, as we've mentioned, these aren't strictly speaking part of HTML5 or CSS3, they're often bundled together when people speak of these new technologies. Plus, they're a lot of fun, so why not get our feet wet?

Chapter **10**

Geolocation, Offline Web Apps, and Web Storage

Much of what is loosely considered to be a part of "HTML5" isn't, strictly speaking, HTML at all—it's a set of additional APIs that provide a wide variety of tools to make our websites even better. We introduced the concept of an API way back in Chapter 1, but here's a quick refresher: an API is an interface for programs. So, rather than a visual interface where a user clicks on a button to make something happen, an API gives your code a virtual "button" to press, in the form of a method it calls that gives it access to a set of functionality. In this chapter, we'll walk you through a few of the most useful of these APIs, as well as give you a brief overview of the others, and point you in the right direction should you want to learn more.

With these APIs, we can find a visitor's current location, make our website available offline as well as perform faster online, and store information about the state of our web application so that when a user returns to our site, they can pick up where they left off.

Here There be Dragons

A word of warning: as you know, the P in API stands for Programming—so there'll be some JavaScript code in the next two chapters. If you're fairly new to JavaScript, don't worry! We'll do our best to walk you through how to use these new features using simple examples with thorough explanations. We'll be assuming you have a sense of the basics, but JavaScript *is* an enormous topic. To learn more, SitePoint's *Simply JavaScript* by Kevin Yank and Cameron Adams is an excellent resource for beginners.[1] You may also find the Mozilla Developer Network's JavaScript Guide useful.[2]

As with all the JavaScript examples in this book so far, we'll be using the jQuery library in the interests of keeping the examples as short and readable as possible. We want to demonstrate the APIs themselves, not the intricacies of writing cross-browser JavaScript code. Again, any of this code can just as easily be written in plain JavaScript, if that's your preference.

Geolocation

The first new API we'll cover is geolocation. Geolocation allows your visitors to share their current location.

Depending on how they're visiting your site, their location may be determined by any of the following:

- IP address
- wireless network connection
- cell tower
- GPS hardware on the device

Which of the above methods are used will depend on the browser, as well as the device's capabilities. The browser then determines the location and passes it back to the Geolocation API. One point to note, as the W3C Geolocation spec states: "No guarantee is given that the API returns the device's actual location."[3]

Geolocation is supported in:

---

[1] Melbourne: SitePoint, 2007

[2] https://developer.mozilla.org/en/JavaScript/Guide

[3] http://dev.w3.org/geo/api/spec-source.html#introduction

- Safari 5+
- Chrome 5+
- Firefox 3.5+
- IE 9+
- Opera 10.6+
- iOS (Mobile Safari) 3.2+
- Android 2.1+

Privacy Concerns

Not everyone will want to share their location with you, as there are privacy concerns inherent to this information. Thus, your visitors must opt in to share their location. Nothing will be passed along to your site or web application unless the user agrees.

The decision is made via a prompt at the top of the browser. Figure 10.1 shows what this prompt looks like in Chrome.

| ⊙ html5demos.com wants to track your physical location Learn more (Allow) (Deny) × |

Figure 10.1. Geolocation user prompt

Blocking of the Geolocation Prompt in Chrome

Be aware that Chrome may block your site from showing this prompt entirely if you're viewing your page locally, rather than from an internet server. If this happens, you'll see an icon in the address bar alerting you to it.

There's no way around this at present, but you can either test your functionality in other browsers, or deploy your code to a testing server (this can be a local server on your machine, a virtual machine, or an actual internet server).

Geolocation Methods

With geolocation, you can determine the user's current position. You can also be notified of changes to their position, which could be used, for example, in a web application that provided real-time driving directions.

These different tasks are controlled through the three methods currently available in the Geolocation API:

- `getCurrentPosition`
- `watchPosition`
- `clearPosition`

We'll be focusing on the first method, `getCurrentPosition`.

Checking for Support with Modernizr

Before we attempt to use geolocation, we should ensure that our visitor's browser supports it. We can do that with Modernizr.

We'll start by creating a function called called `determineLocation`. We've put it in its own JavaScript file, **geolocation.js**, and included that file in our page.

Inside the function, we'll first use Modernizr to check if geolocation is supported:

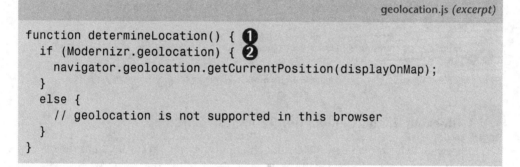

geolocation.js *(excerpt)*

```
function determineLocation() { ❶
  if (Modernizr.geolocation) { ❷
    navigator.geolocation.getCurrentPosition(displayOnMap);
  }
  else {
    // geolocation is not supported in this browser
  }
}
```

Let's examine this line by line:

❶ We declare a function called `determineLocation` to contain our location-checking code.

❷ We check the `Modernizr` object's `geolocation` property to see whether geolocation is supported in the current browser. For more information on how the `Modernizr` object works, consult Appendix A. If geolocation is supported, we continue on to line three, which is inside the `if` statement. If geolocation is unsupported, we move on to the code inside the `else` statement.

Let's assume that geolocation is supported.

Retrieving the Current Position

The `getCurrentPosition` method takes one, two, or three arguments. Here is a summary of the method's definition from the W3C's Geolocation API specification:[4]

```
void getCurrentPosition(successCallback, errorCallback, options);
```

Only the first argument, *successCallback*, is required. *successCallback* is the name of the function you want to call once the position is determined.

In our example, if the location is successfully found, the `displayOnMap` function will be called with a new `Position` object. This `Position` object will contain the current location of the device.

 Callbacks

A callback is a function that is passed as an argument to another function. A callback is executed after the parent function is finished. In the case of `getCurrentPosition`, the *successCallback* will only run once `getCurrentPosition` is completed, and the location has been determined.

Geolocation's `Position` Object

Let's take a closer look at the `Position` object, as defined in the Geolocation API. The `Position` object has two attributes: one that contains the coordinates of the position (`coords`), and another that contains the timestamp of when the position was determined (`timestamp`):

```
interface Position {
  readonly attribute Coordinates coords;
  readonly attribute DOMTimeStamp timestamp;
};
```

Interfaces

The HTML5, CSS3, and related specifications contain plenty of "interfaces" like the above. These can seem scary at first, but don't worry. They're just summarized descriptions of everything that can go into a certain property, method, or object. Most of the time the meaning will be clear—and if not, they're always accompanied by textual descriptions of the attributes.

But where are the latitude and longitude stored? They're inside the `Coordinates` object. The `Coordinates` object is also defined in the W3C Geolocation spec, and here are its attributes :

```
interface Coordinates {
  readonly attribute double latitude;
  readonly attribute double longitude;
  readonly attribute double? altitude;
  readonly attribute double accuracy;
  readonly attribute double? altitudeAccuracy;
  readonly attribute double? heading;
  readonly attribute double? speed;
};
```

The question mark after `double` in some of those attributes simply means that there's no guarantee that the attribute will be there. If the browser can't obtain these attributes, their value will be `null`. For example, very few computers or smartphones contain an altimeter—so most of the time you won't receive an `altitude` value from a geolocation call. The only three attributes that are guaranteed to be there are `latitude`, `longitude`, and `accuracy`.

`latitude` and `longitude` are self-explanatory, and give you exactly what you would expect: the user's latitude and longitude. The `accuracy` attribute tells you, in meters, how accurate is the latitude and longitude information.

The `altitude` attribute is the altitude in meters, and the `altitudeAccuracy` attribute is the altitude's accuracy, also in meters.

The `heading` and `speed` attributes are only relevant if we're tracking the user across multiple positions. These attributes would be important if we were providing real-time biking or driving directions, for example. If present, `heading` tells us, in degrees,

the direction the user is moving in relation to true north. And `speed`, if present, tells us how quickly the user is moving in meters per second.

Grabbing the Latitude and Longitude

Our *successCallback* is set to the function `displayOnMap`. Here's what this function looks like:

geolocation.js (excerpt)

```
function displayOnMap(position) {
  var latitude = position.coords.latitude;
  var longitude = position.coords.longitude;
  // Let's use Google Maps to display the location
}
```

The first line of our function grabs the `Coordinates` object from the `Position` object that was passed to our callback by the API. Inside the `Coordinates` object is the property `latitude`, which we store inside a variable called `latitude`. We do the same for `longitude`, storing it in the variable `longitude`.

In order to display the user's location on a map, we'll leverage the Google Maps JavaScript API. But before we can use this, we need to add a reference to it in our HTML page. Instead of downloading the Google Maps JavaScript library and storing it on our server, we can point to Google's publicly available version of the API:

geolocation.js (excerpt)

```
  ⋮
  <!-- google maps API -->
  <script type="text/javascript" src="http://maps.google.com/maps/
➥api/js?sensor=true">
  </script>
</body>
</html>
```

Google Maps has a *sensor* parameter to indicate whether this application uses a sensor (GPS device) to determine the user's location. That's the `sensor=true` you can see in the sample above. You must set this value explicitly to either `true` or `false`. Because the W3C Geolocation API provides no way of knowing if the information you're obtaining comes from a sensor, you can safely specify `false` for most

web applications (unless they're intended specifically for devices that you know have GPS capabilities, like iPhones).

Loading a Map

Now that we've included the Google Maps JavaScript, we need to, first, add an element to the page to hold the map, and, second, provide a way for the user to call our determineLocation method by clicking a button.

To take care of the first step, let's create a fourth box in the sidebar of *The HTML5 Herald*, below the three advertisement boxes. We'll wrap it inside an article element, as we did for all the other ads. Inside it, we'll create a div called mapDiv to serve as a placeholder for the map. Let's also add a heading to tell the user what we're trying to find out:

index.html (excerpt)

```html
<article id="ad4">
  <div id="mapDiv">
    <h1>Where in the world are you?</h1>
    <form id="geoForm">
      <input type="button" id="geobutton" value="Tell us!">
    </form>
  </div>
</article>
```

We'll also add a bit of styling to this new HTML:

css/styles.css (excerpt)

```css
#ad4 h1 {
  font-size: 30px;
  font-family: AcknowledgementMedium;
  text-align: center;
}

#ad4 {
  height: 140px;
}

#mapDiv {
```

```
    height: 140px;
    width: 236px;
}
```

Figure 10.2 reveals what our new sidebar box looks like.

Figure 10.2. The new widget that lets users tell us their location

The second step is to call `determineLocation` when we hit the button. Using jQuery, it's a cinch to attach our function to the button's click event:

js/geolocation.js *(excerpt)*

```
$('document').ready(function(){
  $('#geobutton').click(determineLocation);
});
```

 Document Ready

In the above code snippet, the second line is the one that's doing all the heavy lifting. The `$('document').ready(function(){ … });` bit is just telling jQuery not to run our code until the page has fully loaded. It's necessary because, otherwise, our code might go looking for the `#geobutton` element before that element even exists, resulting in an error.

This is a very common pattern in JavaScript and jQuery. If you're just getting started with front-end programming, trust us, you'll be seeing a lot of it.

With this code in place, `determineLocation` will be called whenever the button is clicked.

Now, let's return to our `displayOnMap` function and deal with the nitty-gritty of actually displaying the map. First, we'll create a `myOptions` variable to store some of the options that we'll pass to the Google Map:

```
js/geolocation.js (excerpt)

function displayOnMap(position) {
  var latitude = position.coords.latitude;
  var longitude = position.coords.longitude;

  // Let's use Google Maps to display the location
  var myOptions = {
    zoom: 14,
    mapTypeId: google.maps.MapTypeId.ROADMAP
  };
```

The first option we'll set is the zoom level. For a complete map of the Earth, use zoom level 0. The higher the zoom level, the closer you'll be to the location, and the smaller your frame (or viewport) will be. We'll use zoom level 14 to zoom in to street level.

The second option we'll set is the kind of map we want to display. We can choose from the following:

- `google.maps.MapTypeId.ROADMAP`
- `google.maps.MapTypeId.SATELLITE`
- `google.maps.MapTypeId.HYBRID`
- `google.maps.MapTypeId.TERRAIN`

If you've used the Google Maps website before, you'll be familiar with these map types. ROADMAP is the default, while SATELLITE shows you photographic tiles. HYBRID is a combination of ROADMAP and SATELLITE, and TERRAIN will display elements like elevation and water. We'll use the default, ROADMAP.

Options in Google Maps

To learn more about Google Maps' options, see the Map Options section of the Google Maps tutorial.[5]

---

[5] http://code.google.com/apis/maps/documentation/javascript/tutorial.html#MapOptions

Now that we've set our options, it's time to create our map! We do this by creating a new Google Maps object with new `google.maps.Map()`.

The first parameter we pass is the result of the DOM method `getElementById`, which we use to grab the placeholder `div` we put in our **index.html** page. Passing the results of this method into the new Google Map means that the map created will be placed inside that element.

The second parameter we pass is the collection of options we just set. We store the resulting Google Maps object in a variable called `map`:

js/geolocation.js *(excerpt)*

```
function displayOnMap(position) {
  var latitude = position.coords.latitude;
  var longitude = position.coords.longitude;

  // Let's use Google Maps to display the location
  var myOptions = {
    zoom: 16,
    mapTypeId: google.maps.MapTypeId.ROADMAP
  };

  var map = new google.maps.Map(document.getElementById("mapDiv"),
➥myOptions);
```

Now that we have a map, let's add a marker with the location we found for the user. A marker is the little red drop we see on Google Maps that marks our location.

In order to create a new Google Maps marker object, we need to pass it another kind of object: a `google.maps.LatLng` object—which is just a container for a latitude and longitude. The first new line creates this by calling new `google.maps.LatLng` and passing it the `latitude` and `longitude` variables as parameters.

Now that we have a `google.maps.LatLng` object, we can create a marker. We call new `google.maps.Marker`, and then between two curly braces (`{}`) we set `position` to the `LatLng` object, `map` to the map object, and `title` to `"Hello World!"`. The title is what will display when we hover our mouse over the marker:

```
function displayOnMap(position) {
  var latitude = position.coords.latitude;
  var longitude = position.coords.longitude;

  // Let's use Google Maps to display the location
  var myOptions = {
    zoom: 16,
    mapTypeId: google.maps.MapTypeId.ROADMAP
  };

  var map = new google.maps.Map(document.getElementById("mapDiv"),
➥myOptions);

  var initialLocation = new google.maps.LatLng(latitude, longitude);

  var marker = new google.maps.Marker({
    position: initialLocation,
    map: map,
    title: "Hello World!"
  });
}
```

The final step is to center our map at the initial point, and we do this by calling `map.setCenter` with the `LatLng` object:

```
map.setCenter(initialLocation);
```

You can find a plethora of documentation about Google Maps' JavaScript API, version 3 in the online documentation.[6]

A Final Word on Older Mobile Devices

While the W3C Geolocation API is well-supported in current mobile device browsers, you may need to account for older mobile devices, and support all the geolocation APIs available. If this is the case, you should take a look at the open source library geo-location-javascript.[7]

---

[6] http://code.google.com/apis/maps/documentation/javascript/
[7] http://code.google.com/p/geo-location-javascript/

Offline Web Applications

The visitors to our websites are increasingly on the go. With many using mobile devices all the time, it's unwise to assume that our visitors will always have a live internet connection. Wouldn't it be nice for our visitors to browse our site or use our web application even if they're offline? Thankfully, we can, with Offline Web Applications.

HTML5's Offline Web Applications allows us to interact with websites offline. This initially might sound like a contradiction: a web application exists online by definition. But there are an increasing number of web-based applications that could benefit from being usable offline. You probably use a web-based email client, such as Gmail; wouldn't it be useful to be able to compose drafts in the app while you were on the subway traveling to work? What about online to-do lists, contact managers, or office applications? These are all examples of applications that benefit from being online, but which we'd like to continue using if our internet connection cuts out in a tunnel.

The Offline Web Applications spec is supported in:

- Safari 4+
- Chrome 5+
- Firefox 3.5+
- Opera 10.6+
- iOS (Mobile Safari) 2.1+
- Android 2.0+

It is currently unsupported in all versions of IE.

How It Works: the HTML5 Application Cache

Offline Web Applications work by leveraging what is known as the **application cache**. The application cache can store your entire website offline: all the JavaScript, HTML, and CSS, as well as all your images and resources.

This sounds great, but you may be wondering, what happens when there's a change? That's the beauty of the application cache: your application is automatically updated every time the user visits your page while online. If even one byte of data has changed in one of your files, the application cache will reload that file.

> ### Application Cache versus Browser Cache
>
> Browsers maintain their own caches in order to speed up the loading of websites; however, these caches are only used to avoid having to reload a given file—and not in the absence of an internet connection. Even all the files for a page are cached by the browser. If you try to click on a link while your internet connection is down, you'll receive an error message.
>
> With Offline Web Applications, we have the power to tell the browser which files should be cached or fetched from the network, and what we should fall back to in the event that caching fails. It gives us far more control about how our websites are cached.

Setting Up Your Site to Work Offline

There are three steps to making an Offline Web Application:

1. Create a **cache.manifest** file.

2. Ensure that the manifest file is served with the correct content type.

3. Point all your HTML files to the **cache manifest**.

The HTML5 Herald isn't really an application at all, so it's not the sort of site for which you'd want to provide offline functionality. Yet it's simple enough to do, and there's no real downside, so we'll go through the steps of making it available offline to illustrate how it's done.

The cache.manifest File

Despite its fancy name, the **cache.manifest** file is really nothing more than a text file that adheres to a certain format.

Here's an example of a simple **cache.manifest** file:

```
CACHE MANIFEST
CACHE:
index.html
photo.jpg
main.js
```

```
NETWORK:
*
```

The first line of the **cache.manifest** file must read CACHE MANIFEST. After this line, we enter CACHE:, and then list all the files we'd like to store on our visitor's hard drive. This CACHE: section is also known as the explicit section (since we're explicitly telling the browser to cache these files).

Upon first visiting a page with a **cache.manifest** file, the visitor's browser makes a local copy of all files defined in the section. On subsequent visits, the browser will load the local copies of the files.

After listing all the files we'd like to be stored offline, we can specify an **online whitelist**. Here, we define any files that should never be stored offline—usually because they require internet access for their content to be meaningful. For example, you may have a PHP script, **lastTenTweets.php**, that grabs your last ten updates from Twitter and displays them on an HTML page. The script would only be able to pull your last ten tweets while online, so it makes no sense to store the page offline.

The first line of this section is the word NETWORK. Any files specified in the NETWORK section will always be reloaded when the user is online, and will never be available offline.

Here's what that example online whitelist section would look like:

```
NETWORK
lastTenTweets.php
```

Unlike the explicit section, where we had to painstakingly list every file we wanted to store offline, in the online whitelist section we can use a shortcut: the wildcard *. This asterisk tells the browser that any files or URLs not mentioned in the explicit section (and therefore not stored in the application cache) should be fetched from the server.

Here's an example of an online whitelist section that uses the wildcard:

```
NETWORK
*
```

All Accounted For

Every URL in your website must be accounted for in the **cache.manifest** file, even URLs that you simply link to. If it's unaccounted for in the manifest file, that resource or URL will fail to load, even if you're online. To avoid this problem, you should use the * in the NETWORK section.

You can also add comments to your **cache.manifest** file by beginning a line with #. Everything after the # will be ignored. Be careful to avoid having a comment as the first line of your **cache.manifest** file—as we mentioned earlier, the first line must be CACHE MANIFEST. You can, however, add comments to any other line.

It's good practice to have a comment with the version number of your **cache.manifest** file (we'll see why a bit later on):

```
CACHE MANIFEST
# version 0.1
CACHE:
index.html
photo.jpg
main.js

NETWORK:
*
```

Setting the Content Type on Your Server

The next step in making your site available offline is to ensure that your server is configured to serve the manifest files correctly. This is done by setting the content type provided by your server along with the **cache.manifest** file—we discussed content type in the section called "MIME Types" in Chapter 5, so you can skip back there now if you need a refresher.

Assuming you're using the Apache web server, add the following to your **.htaccess** file:

```
AddType text/cache-manifest .manifest
```

Pointing Your HTML to the Manifest File

The final step to making your website available offline is to point your HTML pages to the manifest file. We do that by setting the `manifest` attribute on the `html` element in each of our pages:

```
<!doctype html>
<html manifest="/cache.manifest">
```

Once we've done that, we're finished! Our web page will now be available offline. Better still, since any content that hasn't changed since the page has been viewed will be stored locally, our page will now load much faster—even when our visitors are online.

Do This for Every Page

Each HTML page on your website must set the `manifest` attribute on the `html` element. Ensure you do this, or your application might not be stored in the application cache! While it's true that you should only have one **cache.manifest** file for the entire application, every HTML page of your web application needs `<html manifest="/cache.manifest">`.

Getting Permission to Store the Site Offline

As with geolocation, browsers provide a permission prompt when a website is using a **cache.manifest** file. Unlike geolocation, however, not all browsers are required to do this. When present, the prompt asks the user to confirm that they'd like the website to be available offline. Figure 10.3 shows the prompt's appearance in Firefox.

Figure 10.3. Prompt to allow offline web application storage in the app cache

Going Offline to Test

Once we have completed all three steps to make an offline website, we can test out our page by going offline. Firefox and Opera provide a menu option that lets you work offline, so there's no need to cut your internet connection. To do that in Firefox, go to **File** > **Work Offline**, as shown in Figure 10.4.

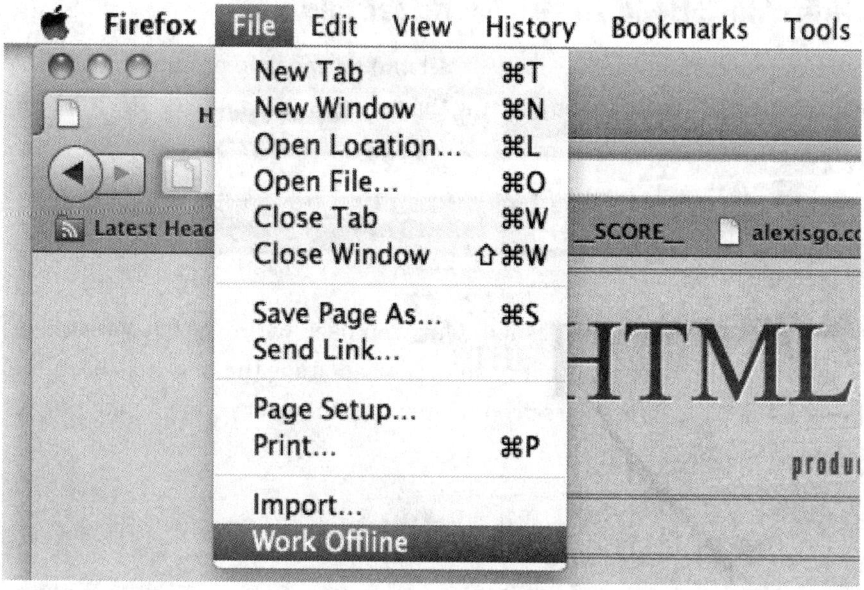

Figure 10.4. Testing offline web applications with Firefox's **Work Offline** mode

While it's convenient to go offline from the browser menu, it's most ideal to turn off your network connection altogether when testing Offline Web Applications.

Testing If the Application Cache Is Storing Your Site

Going offline is a good way to spot-check if our application cache is working, but for more in-depth debugging, we'll need a finer instrument. Fortunately, Chrome's Web Inspector tool has some great features for examining the application cache.

To check if our **cache.manifest** file has the correct content type, here are the steps to follow in Chrome (http://html5laboratory.com/s/offline-application-cache.html has a sample you can use to follow along):

1. Navigate to the URL of your home page in Chrome.

2. Open up the Web Inspector (click the wrench icon, then choose **Tools > Developer Tools**).

3. Click on the **Console** tab, and look for any errors that may be relevant to the **cache.manifest** file. If everything is working well, you should see a line that starts with "Document loaded from Application Cache with manifest" and ends

with the path to your **cache.manifest** file. If you have any errors, they will show up in the **Console**, so be on the lookout for errors or warnings here.

4. Click on the **Resources** tab.

5. Expand the **Application Cache** section. Your domain (www.html5laboratory.com in our example) should be listed.

6. Click on your domain. Listed on the right should be all the resources stored in Chrome's application cache, as shown in Figure 10.5.

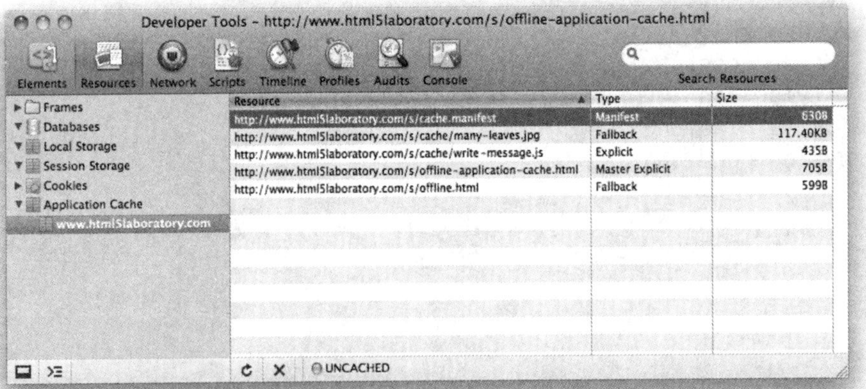

Figure 10.5. Viewing what is stored in Chrome's Application Cache

Making *The HTML5 Herald* Available Offline

Now that we understand the ingredients required to make a website available offline, let's practice what we've learned on *The HTML5 Herald*. The first step is to create our **cache.manifest** file. You can use a program like TextEdit on the Mac or Notepad on Windows to create it, but you have to make sure the file is formatted as plain text. If you're using Windows, you're in luck! As long as you use Notepad to create this file, it will already be formatted as plain text. To format a file as plain text in TextEdit on the Mac, choose **Format > Make Plain Text**. Start off your file by including the line CACHE MANIFEST at the top.

Next, we need to add all the resources we'd like to be available offline in the explicit section, which starts with the word CACHE:. We must list all our files in this section. Since there's nothing on the site that requires network access (well, there's *one*

thing, but we'll get to that in a bit), we'll just add an asterisk to the NETWORK section to catch any files we may have missed in the explicit section.

Here's an excerpt from our **cache.manifest** file:

```
                                                    cache.manifest (excerpt)
CACHE MANIFEST
#v1
index.html
register.html

js/hyphenator.js
js/modernizr-1.7.min.js
css/screen.css
css/styles.css
images/bg-bike.png
images/bg-form.png
⋮
fonts/League_Gothic-webfont.eot
fonts/League_Gothic-webfont.svg
⋮

NETWORK:
*
```

Once you've added all your resources to the file, save it as **cache.manifest**. Be sure the extension is set to **.manifest** rather than **.txt** or something else.

Then, if you're yet to do so already, configure your server to deliver your manifest file with the appropriate content type.

The final step is to add the manifest attribute to the html element in our two HTML pages.

We add the manifest attribute to both **index.html** and **register.html**, like this:

```
<!doctype html>
<html lang="en" manifest="cache.manifest">
```

And we're set! We can now browse *The HTML5 Herald* at our leisure, whether we have an internet connection or not.

Limits to Offline Web Application Storage

While the Offline Web Applications spec doesn't define a specific storage limit for the application cache, it does state that browsers should create and enforce a storage limit. As a general rule, it's a good idea to assume that you've no more than 5MB of space to work with.

Several of the files we specified to be stored offline are video files. Depending on how large your video files are, it mightn't make any sense to have them available offline, as they could exceed the browser's storage limit.

What can we do in that case? We could place large video files in the NETWORK section, but then our users will simply see an unpleasant error when the browser tries to pull the video while offline.

A better alternative is to use an optional section of the **cache.manifest** file: the fallback section.

The Fallback Section

This section allows us to define what the user will see should a resource fail to load. In the case of *The HTML5 Herald*, rather than storing our video file offline and placing it in the explicit section, it makes more sense to leverage the fallback section.

Each line in the fallback section requires two entries. The first is the file for which you want to provide fallback content. You can specify either a specific file, or a partial path like media/, which would refer to any file located in the **media** folder. The second entry is what you would like to display in case the file specified fails to load.

If the files are unable to be loaded, we can load a still image of the film's first frame instead. We'll use the partial path media/ to define the fallback for both video files at once:

cache.manifest *(excerpt)*

```
FALLBACK:
media/ images/ford-plane-still.png
```

Of course, this is a bit redundant since, as you know from Chapter 5, the HTML5 `video` element already includes a fallback image to be displayed in case the video fails to load.

So, for some more practice with this concept, let's add another fallback. In the event that any of our pages don't load, it would be nice to define a fallback file that tells you the site is offline. We can create a simple **offline.html** file:

offline.html

```html
<!doctype html>
<html lang="en" manifest="/cache.manifest">
  <head>
    <meta charset="utf-8">
    <title>We are offline!</title>
    <link rel="stylesheet" href="css/styles.css?v=1.0"/>
  </head>
  <body>
    <header>
      <h1>Sorry, we are now offline!</h1>
    </header>
  </body>
</html>
```

Now, in the fallback section of our cache manifest, we can specify /, which will match any page on the site. If any page fails to load or is absent from the application cache, we'll fall back to the **offline.html** page:

cache.manifest (excerpt)

```
FALLBACK:
media/ images/video-fallback.jpg
/ /offline.html
```

 Safari Offline Application Cache Fails to Load Media Files

There is currently a bug in Safari 5 where media files such as **.mp3** and **.mp4** won't load from the offline application cache.

Refreshing the Cache

When using a cache manifest, the files you've specified in your explicit section will be cached until further notice. This can cause headaches while developing: you might change a file and be left scratching your head when you're unable to see your changes reflected on the page.

Even more importantly, once your files are sitting on a live website, you'll want a way to tell browsers that they need to update their application caches. This can be done by modifying the **cache.manifest** file. When a browser loads a site for which it already has a **cache.manifest** file, it will check to see if the manifest file has changed. If it hasn't, it will assume that its existing application cache is all it needs to run the application, so it won't download anything else. If the **cache.manifest** file has changed, the browser will rebuild the application cache by re-downloading all the specified files.

This is why we specified a version number in a comment in our **cache.manifest**. This way, even if the list of files remains exactly the same, we have a way of indicating to browsers that they should update their application cache; all we need to do is increment the version number.

Caching the Cache

This might sound absurd, but your **cache.manifest** file may itself be cached by the browser. Why, you may ask? Because of the way HTTP handles caching.

In order to speed up performance of web pages overall, caching is done by browsers, according to rules set out via the HTTP specification.[8] What do you need to know about these rules? That the browser receives certain HTTP headers, including `Expire` headers. These `Expire` headers tell the browser when a file should be expired from the cache, and when it needs updating from the server.

If your server is providing the manifest file with instructions to cache it (as is often the default for static files), the browser will happily use its cached version of the file instead for fetching your updated version from the server. As a result, it won't re-download any of your application files because it thinks the manifest has not changed!

---

[8] http://www.w3.org/Protocols/rfc2616/rfc2616-sec13.html

If you're finding that you're unable to force the browser to refresh its application cache, try clearing the regular browser cache. You could also change your server settings to send explicit instructions not to cache the **cache.manifest** file.

If your site's web server is running Apache, you can tell Apache not to cache the **cache.manifest** file by adding the following to your **.htaccess** file:

.htaccess (excerpt)

```
<Files cache.manifest>
  ExpiresActive On
  ExpiresDefault "access"
</Files>
```

The `<Files cache.manifest>` tells Apache to only apply the rules that follow to the **cache.manifest** file. The combination of `ExpiresActive On` and `ExpiresDefault "access"` forces the web server to always expire the **cache.manifest** file from the cache. The effect is, the **cache.manifest** file will never be cached by the browser.

Are we online?

Sometimes, you'll need to know if your user is viewing the page offline or online. For example, in a web mail app, saving a draft while online involves sending it to the server to be saved in a database; but while offline, you would want to save that information locally instead, and wait until the user is back online to send it to your server.

The offline web apps API provides a few handy methods and events for managing this. For *The HTML5 Herald*, you may have noticed that the page works well enough while offline: you can navigate from the home page to the sign-up form, play the video, and generally mess around without any difficulty. However, when you try to use the geolocation widget we built earlier in this chapter, things don't go so well. This makes sense: without an internet connection, there's no way for our page to figure out your location (unless your device has a GPS), much less communicate with Google Maps to retrieve the map.

Let's look at how we can fix this. We would like to simply provide a message to users indicating that this functionality is unavailable while offline. It's actually very easy; browsers that support Offline Web Applications give you access to the

`navigator.onLine` property, which will be `true` if the browser is online, and `false` if it's not. Here's how we'd use it in our `determineLocation` method:

js/geolocation.js *(excerpt)*

```
function determineLocation(){
  if (navigator.onLine) {
    // find location and call displayOnMap
  } else {
    alert("You must be online to use this feature.");
  }
}
```

Give it a spin. Using Firefox or Opera, first navigate to the page and click the button to load the map. Once you're satisfied that it works, choose Work Offline, reload the page, and try clicking the button again. This time you'll receive a helpful message telling you that you'll need to be online to access the map.

Some other features that might be of use to you include events that fire when the browser goes online or offline. These events fire on the `window` element, and are simply called `window.online` and `window.offline`. These can, for example, allow your scripts to respond to a change in state by either synchronizing information up to the server when you go online, or saving data locally when you drop offline.

There are a few other events and methods available to you for dealing with the application cache, but the ones we've covered here are the most important. They'll suffice to have most websites and applications working offline without a hitch.

Further Reading

If you would like to learn more about Offline Web Applications, here are a few good resources:

- The WHATWG Offline Web Applications spec[9]
- HTML5 Laboratory's "Using the cache manifest to work offline"[10]
- Opera's Offline Application Developer's Guide[11]

---

[9] http://www.whatwg.org/specs/web-apps/current-work/multipage/offline.html#offline

[10] http://www.html5laboratory.com/working-offline.php

[11] http://dev.opera.com/articles/view/offline-applications-html5-appcache/

- Peter Lubbers' Slide Share presentation on Offline Web Applications[12]
- Mark Pilgrim's walk-through of Offline Web Applications[13]
- Safari's Offline Applications Programming Guide[14]

Web Storage

The Web Storage API defines a standard for how we can save simple data locally on a user's computer or device. Before the emergence of the Web Storage standard, web developers often stored user information in cookies, or by using plugins. With Web Storage, we now have a standardized definition for how to store up to 5MB of simple data created by our websites or web applications. Better still, Web Storage already works in Internet Explorer 8.0!

Web Storage is a great complement to Offline Web Applications, because you need somewhere to store all that user data while you're working offline, and Web Storage provides it.

Web Storage is supported in these browsers:

- Safari 4+
- Chrome 5+
- Firefox 3.6+
- Internet Explorer 8+
- Opera 10.5+
- iOS (Mobile Safari) 3.2+
- Android 2.1+

Two Kinds of Storage

There are two kinds of HTML5 Web Storage: session storage and local storage.

---

[12] http://www.slideshare.net/robinzimmermann/html5-offline-web-applications-silicon-valley-user-group

[13] http://diveintohtml5.org/offline.html

[14] http://developer.apple.com/library/safari/#documentation/iPhone/Conceptual/SafariJSDatabaseGuide/OfflineApplicationCache/OfflineApplicationCache.html

Session Storage

Session storage lets us keep track of data specific to one window or tab. It allows us to isolate information in each window. Even if the user is visiting the same site in two windows, each window will have its own individual session storage object and thus have separate, distinct data.

Session storage is not persistent—it only lasts for the duration of a user's session on a specific site (in other words, for the time that a browser window or tab is open and viewing that site).

Local Storage

Unlike session storage, local storage allows us to save persistent data to the user's computer, via the browser. When a user revisits a site at a later date, any data saved to local storage can be retrieved.

Consider shopping online: it's not unusual for users to have the same site open in multiple windows or tabs. For example, let's say you're shopping for shoes, and you want to compare the prices and reviews of two brands. You may have one window open for each brand, but regardless of what brand or style of shoe you're looking for, you're always going to be searching for the same shoe size. It's cumbersome to have to repeat this part of your search in every new window.

Local storage can help. Rather than require the user to specify again the shoe size they're browsing for every time they launch a new window, we could store the information in local storage. That way, when the user opens a new window to browse for another brand or style, the results would just present items available in their shoe size. Furthermore, because we're storing the information to the user's computer, we'll be able to still access this information when they visit the site at a later date.

Web Storage is Browser-specific

One important point to remember when working with web storage is that if the user visits your site in Safari, any data will be stored to Safari's Web Storage store. If the user then revisits your site in Chrome, the data that was saved via Safari will be unavailable. Where the Web Storage data is stored depends on the browser, and each browser's storage is separate and independent.

> **Local Storage versus Cookies**
>
> Local storage can at first glance seem to play a similar role to HTTP cookies, but there are a few key differences. First of all, cookies are intended to be read on the server side, whereas local storage is only available on the client side. If you need your server-side code to react differently based on some saved values, cookies are the way to go. Yet, cookies are sent along with each HTTP request to your server —and this can result in significant overhead in terms of bandwidth. Local storage, on the other hand, just sits on the user's hard drive waiting to be read, so it costs nothing to use.
>
> In addition, we have significantly more size to store things using local storage. With cookies, we could only store 4KB of information in total. With local storage, the maximum is 5MB.

What Web Storage Data Looks Like

Data saved in Web Storage is stored as key/value pairs.

A few examples of simple key/value pairs:

- key: *name*, value: *Alexis*
- key: *painter*, value: *Picasso*
- key: *email*, value: *info@me.com*

Getting and Setting Our Data

The methods most relevant to Web Storage are defined in an object called `Storage`. Here is the complete definition of Storage:[15]

```
interface Storage {
  readonly attribute unsigned long length;
  DOMString key(in unsigned long index);
  getter any getItem(in DOMString key);
  setter creator void setItem(in DOMString key, in any value);
  deleter void removeItem(in DOMString key);
  void clear();
};
```

---

[15] http://dev.w3.org/html5/webstorage/#the-storage-interface

The first methods we'll discuss are getItem and setItem. We store a key/value pair in either local or session storage by calling setItem, and we retrieve the value from a key by calling getItem.

If we want to store the data in or retrieve it from session storage, we simply call setItem or getItem on the sessionStorage global object. If we want to use local storage instead, we'd call setItem or getItem on the localStorage global object. In the examples to follow, we'll be saving items to local storage.

When we use the setItem method, we must specify both the key we want to save the value under, and the value itself. For example, if we'd like to save the value "6" under the key "size", we'd call setItem like this:

```
localStorage.setItem("size", "6");
```

To retrieve the value we stored to the "size" key, we'd use the getItem method, specifying only the key:

```
var size = localStorage.getItem("size");
```

Converting Stored Data

Web Storage stores all values as strings, so if you need to use them as anything else, such as a number or even an object, you'll need to convert them. To convert from a string to a numeric value, we can use JavaScript's parseInt method.

For our shoe size example, the value returned and stored in the size variable will actually be the string "6", rather than the number 6. To convert it to a number, we'll use parseInt:

```
var size = parseInt(localStorage.getItem("size"));
```

The Shortcut Way

We can quite happily continue to use getItem(key) and setItem(key, value); however, there's a shortcut we can use to save and retrieve data.

Instead of localStorage.getItem(key), we can simply say localStorage[key]. For example, we could rewrite our retrieval of the shoe size like this:

```
var size = localStorage["size"];
```

And instead of `localStorage.setItem(key, value)`, we can say `localStorage[key] = value`:

```
localStorage["size"] = 6;
```

There Are No Keys for That!

What happens if you request `getItem` on a key that was never saved? In this case, `getItem` will return `null`.

Removing Items and Clearing Data

To remove a specific item from Web Storage, we can use the `removeItem` method. We pass it the key we want to remove, and it will remove both the key and its value.

To remove *all* data stored by our site on a user's computer, we can use the `clear` method. This will delete all keys and all values stored for our domain.

Storage Limits

Internet Explorer "allows web applications to store nearly 10MB of user data."[16] Chrome, Safari, Firefox, and Opera all allow for up to 5MB of user data, which is the amount suggested in the W3C spec. This number may evolve over time, as the spec itself states: "A mostly arbitrary limit of five megabytes per origin is recommended. Implementation feedback is welcome and will be used to update this suggestion in the future." In addition, Opera allows users to configure how much disk space is allocated to Web Storage.

Rather than worrying about how much storage each browser has, a better approach is to test to see if the quota is exceeded before saving important data. The way you test for this is by catching the `QUOTA_EXCEEDED_ERR` exception. Here's one example of how we can do this:

---

[16] http://msdn.microsoft.com/en-us/library/cc197062%28VS.85%29.aspx

```
try
{
  sessionStorage["name"] = "Tabatha";
}
catch (exception)
{
  if (exception == QUOTA_EXCEEDED_ERR)
  {
    // we should tell the user their quota has been exceeded.
  }
}
```

Try/Catch and Exceptions

Sometimes, problems happen in our code. Designers of APIs know this, and in order to mitigate the effects of these problems, they rely on **exceptions**. An exception occurs when something unexpected happens. The authors of APIs can define specific exceptions to be thrown when particular kinds of problems occur. Then, developers using those APIs can decide how they'd like to respond to a given type of exception.

In order to respond to exceptions, we can wrap any code we think may throw an exception in a `try/catch` block. This works the way you might expect: first, you *try* to do something. If it fails with an exception, you can *catch* that exception and attempt to recover gracefully.

To read more about `try/catch` blocks, see the "try...catch" article at the Mozilla Developer Networks' JavaScript Reference.[17]

Security Considerations

Web Storage has what's known as **origin-based** security. What this means is that data stored via Web Storage from a given domain is only accessible to pages from that domain. It's impossible to access any Web Storage data stored by a different domain. For example, assume we control the domain html5isgreat.com, and we store data created on that site using local storage. Another domain, say, google.com, does not have access to any of the data stored by html5isgreat.com. Likewise, html5isgreat.com has no access to any of the local storage data saved by google.com.

---

[17] https://developer.mozilla.org/en/JavaScript/Reference/Statements/try...catch

Adding Web Storage to *The HTML5 Herald*

We can use Web Storage to add a "Remember me on this computer" checkbox to our registration page. This way, once the user has registered, any other forms they may need to fill out on the site in the future would already have this information.

Let's define a function that grabs the value of the form's `input` elements for name and email address, again using jQuery:

js/rememberMe.js *(excerpt)*

```
function saveData() {
  var email = $("#email").val();
  var name = $("#name").val();
}
```

Here we're simply storing the value of the email and name form fields, in variables called `email` and `name`, respectively.

Once we have retrieved the values in the two `input` elements, our next step is to actually save these values to `localStorage`:

js/rememberMe.js *(excerpt)*

```
function saveData() {
  var email = $("#email").val();
  var name = $("#name").val();

  localStorage["name"] = name;
  localStorage["email"] = email;
}
```

Let's also store the fact that the "Remember me" checkbox was checked by saving this information to local storage as well:

js/rememberMe.js *(excerpt)*

```
function saveData() {
  var email = $("#email").val();
  var name = $("#name").val();

  localStorage["name"] = name;
```

```
    localStorage["email"] = email;
    localStorage["remember"] = "true";
}
```

Now that we have a function to save the visitor's name and email address, let's call it if they check the "Remember me on this computer" checkbox. We'll do this by watching for the change event on the checkbox—this event will fire whenever the checkbox's state changes, whether due to a click on it, a click on its label, or a keyboard press:

js/rememberMe.js (excerpt)

```
$('document').ready(function() {
    $('#rememberme').change(saveData);
});
```

Next, let's make sure the checkbox is actually checked, since the change event will fire when the checkbox is unchecked as well:

js/rememberMe.js (excerpt)

```
function saveData() {
    if ($("#rememberme").attr("checked"))
    {
        var email = $("#address").val();
        var name = $("#register-name").val();

        localStorage["name"] = name;
        localStorage["email"] = email;
        localStorage["remember"] = "true";
    }
}
```

This new line of code calls the jQuery method attr("checked"), which will return true if the checkbox is checked, and false if not.

Finally, let's ensure that Web Storage is present in our visitor's browser:

```
function saveData() {
  if (Modernizr.localstorage) {
    if ($("#rememberme").attr("checked"))
    {
      var email = $("#address").val();
      var name = $("#register-name").val();

      localStorage["name"] = name;
      localStorage["email"] = email;
      localStorage["remember"] = "true";
    }
  }
  else
  {
    // no support for Web Storage
  }
}
```

Now we're saving our visitor's name and email whenever the checkbox is checked, so long as local storage is supported. The problem is, we have yet to actually do anything with that data!

Let's add another function to check and see if the name and email have been saved and, if so, fill in the appropriate input elements with that information. Let's also precheck the "Remember me" checkbox if we've set the key "remember" to "true" in local storage:

```
function loadStoredDetails() {
  var name = localStorage["name"];
  var email = localStorage["email"];
  var remember = localStorage["remember"];

  if (name) {
    $("#name").val(name);
  }
  if (email) {
    $("#email").val(name);
  }
  if (remember =="true") {
```

```
      $("#rememberme").attr("checked", "checked");
  }
}
```

Again, we want to check and make sure Web Storage is supported by the browser before taking these actions:

js/rememberMe.js *(excerpt)*

```
function loadStoredDetails() {
  if (Modernizr.localstorage) {
    var name = localStorage["name"];
    var email = localStorage["email"];
    var remember = localStorage["remember"];

    if (name) {
      $("#name").val(name);
    }
    if (email) {
      $("#email").val(name);
    }
    if (remember =="true") s{
      $("#rememberme").attr("checked", "checked");
    }
  } else {
    // no support for Web Storage
  }
}
```

As a final step, we call the loadStoredDetails function as soon as the page loads:

js/rememberMe.js *(excerpt)*

```
$('document').ready(function(){
  loadStoredDetails();
  $('#rememberme').change(saveData);
});
```

Now, if the user has previously visited the page and checked "Remember me on this computer," their name and email will already be populated on subsequent visits to the page.

Viewing Our Web Storage Values with the Web Inspector

We can use the Safari or Chrome Web Inspector to look at, or even change, the values of our local storage. In Safari, we can view the stored data under the **Storage** tab, as shown in Figure 10.6.

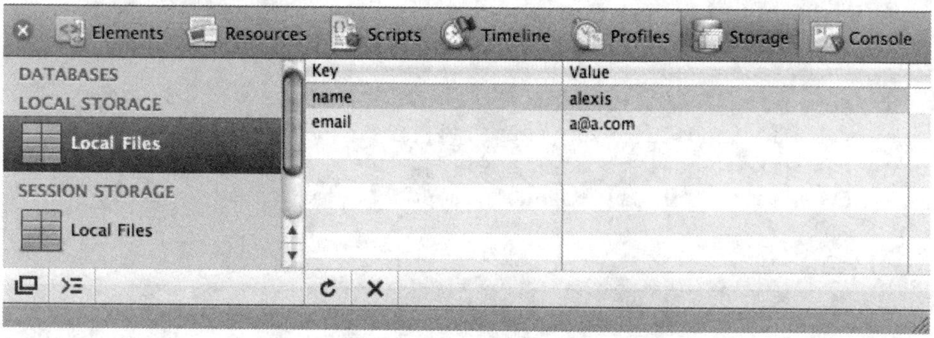

Figure 10.6. Viewing the values stored in local and session storage

In Chrome, the data can be viewed through the **Resources** tab.

Since the user owns any data saved to their hard drive, they can actually modify the data in Web Storage, should they choose to do so.

Let's try this ourselves. If you double-click on the "email" value in Web Inspector's **Storage** tab while viewing the **register.html** page, you can actually modify the value stored there, as Figure 10.7 shows.

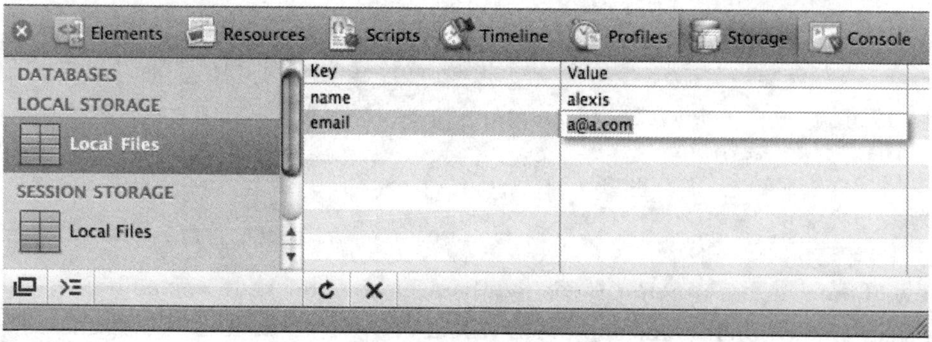

Figure 10.7. Modifying the values stored in Web Storage

There's nothing we as developers can do to prevent this, since our users own the data on their computers. We can and should, however, bear in mind that savvy users have the ability to change their local storage data. In addition, the Web Storage spec states that any dialogue in browsers asking users to clear their cookies should now also allow them to clear their local storage. The message to retain is that we can't be 100% sure that the data we store is accurate, nor that it will always be there. Thus, sensitive data should never be kept in local storage.

If you'd like to learn more about Web Storage, here are a few resources you can consult:

- The W3C's Web Storage specification[18]
- The Mozilla Developer Network's Web Storage documentation[19]
- Web Storage tutorial from IBM's developerWorks[20]

Additional HTML5 APIs

There are a number of other APIs that are outside the scope of this book. However, we'd like to mention them briefly here, to give you an overview of what they are, as well as give you some resources should you want to learn more.

Web Workers

The new Web Workers API allows us to run large scripts in the background without interrupting our main page or web app. Prior to Web Workers, it was impossible to run multiple JavaScript scripts concurrently. Have you ever come across a dialogue like the one shown in Figure 10.8?

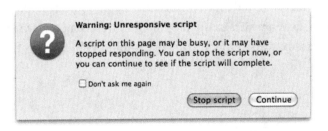

Figure 10.8. A script that runs for too long freezes the whole page

---

[18] http://dev.w3.org/html5/webstorage/#the-storage-interface

[19] https://developer.mozilla.org/en/DOM/Storage

[20] http://www.ibm.com/developerworks/xml/library/x-html5mobile2/

With Web Workers, we should see less of these types of warnings. The new API allows us to take scripts that take a long time to run, and require no user interaction, and run them behind the scenes concurrently with any other scripts that *do* handle user interaction. This concept is known as **threading** in programming, and Web Workers brings us thread-like features. Each "worker" handles its own chunk of script, without interfering with other workers or the rest of the page. To ensure the workers stay in sync with each other, the API defines ways to pass messages from one worker to another.

Web Workers are supported in:

- Safari 4+
- Chrome 5+
- Firefox 3.5+
- Opera 10.6+

Web Workers are currently unsupported in all versions of IE, iOS, and Android.

To learn more about Web Workers, see:

- HTML5 Rocks, "The Basics of Web Workers"[21]
- Mozilla Developer Network, "Using Web Workers"[22]
- The W3C Web Workers' specification[23]

Web Sockets

Web Sockets defines a "protocol for two-way communication with a remote host."[24] We'll skip covering this topic for a couple of reasons. First, this API is of great use to server-side developers, but is less relevant to front-end developers and designers. Second, Web Sockets are still in development and have actually run into some security issues. Firefox 4 and Opera 11 have disabled Web Sockets by default due to these issues.[25]

---

[21] http://www.html5rocks.com/tutorials/workers/basics/

[22] https://developer.mozilla.org/En/Using_web_workers

[23] http://dev.w3.org/html5/workers/

[24] http://www.w3.org/TR/websockets/

[25] See http://hacks.mozilla.org/2010/12/websockets-disabled-in-firefox-4/ and http://dev.opera.com/articles/view/introducing-web-sockets/ .

Web Sockets are supported in:

- Safari 5+
- Chrome 4+
- Firefox 4+ (but disabled by default)
- Opera 11+ (but disabled by default)
- iOS (Mobile Safari) 4.2+

Web Sockets are currently unsupported in all versions of IE and on Android.

To learn more about Web Sockets, see the specification at the W3C: http://dev.w3.org/html5/websockets/.

Web SQL and IndexedDB

There are times when the 5MB of storage and simplistic key/value pairs offered by the Web Storage API just aren't enough. If you need to store substantial amounts of data, and more complex relationships between your data, you likely need a full-fledged database to take care of your storage requirements.

Usually databases have been unique to the server side, but there are currently two database solutions proposed to fill this need on the client side: Web SQL and the Indexed Database API (called IndexedDB for short). The Web SQL specification is no longer being updated, and though it currently looks like IndexedDB is gaining steam, it remains to be seen which of these will become the future standard for serious data storage in the browser.

Web SQL is supported in:

- Safari 3.2+
- Chrome
- Opera 10.5+
- iOS (Mobile Safari) 3.2+
- Android 2.1+

Web SQL is currently unsupported in all versions of IE and Firefox. IndexedDB, meanwhile, is currently only supported in Firefox 4.

If you would like to learn more, here are a few good resources:

- Mark Pilgrim's summary of local storage in HTML5[26]
- The W3C's IndexedDB specification[27]
- The W3C's Web SQL specification[28]

Back to the Drawing Board

In this chapter, we've had a glimpse into the new JavaScript APIs available in the latest generation of browsers. While these might for some time lack full browser support, tools like Modernizr can help us gradually incorporate them into our real-world projects, bringing an extra dimension to our sites and applications.

In the next—and final—chapter, we'll look at one more API, as well as two techniques for creating complex graphics in the browser. These open up a lot of potential avenues for creating web apps that leap off the page.

---

[26] http://diveintohtml5.org/storage.html#future

[27] http://dev.w3.org/2006/webapi/IndexedDB/

[28] http://dev.w3.org/html5/webdatabase/

Chapter

Canvas, SVG, and Drag and Drop

The HTML5 Herald is really becoming quite dynamic for an "ol' timey" newspaper! We've added a video with the new `video` element, made our site available offline, added support to remember the user's name and email address, and used geolocation to detect the user's location.

But there's still more we can do to make it even more fun. First, the video is a little at odds with the rest of the paper, since it's in color. Second, the geolocation feature, while fairly speedy, could use a progress indicator that lets the user know we haven't left them stranded. And finally, it would be nice to add just one more dynamic piece to our page. We'll take care of all three of these using the APIs we'll discuss in this chapter: Canvas, SVG, and Drag and Drop.

Canvas

With HTML5's Canvas API, we're no longer limited to drawing rectangles on our sites. We can draw anything we can imagine, all through JavaScript. This can improve the performance of our websites by avoiding the need to download images off the network. With canvas, we can draw shapes and lines, arcs and text, gradients and patterns. In addition, canvas gives us the power to manipulate pixels in images

and even video. We'll start by introducing some of the basic drawing features of canvas, but then move on to using its power to transform our video—taking our modern-looking color video and converting it into conventional black and white to match the overall look and feel of *The HTML5 Herald*.

The Canvas 2D Context spec is supported in:

- Safari 2.0+
- Chrome 3.0+
- Firefox 3.0+
- Internet Explorer 9.0+
- Opera 10.0+
- iOS (Mobile Safari) 1.0+
- Android 1.0+

A Bit of Canvas History

Canvas was first developed by Apple. Since they already had a framework—Quartz 2D—for drawing in two-dimensional space, they went ahead and based many of the concepts of HTML5's canvas on that framework. It was then adopted by Mozilla and Opera, and then standardized by the WHATWG (and subsequently picked up by the W3C, along with the rest of HTML5).

There's some good news here. If you aspire to do development for the iPhone or iPad (referred to jointly as iOS), or for the Mac, what you learn in canvas should help you understand some of the basics concepts of Quartz 2D. If you already develop for the Mac or iOS and have worked with Quartz 2D, many canvas concepts will look very familiar to you.

Creating a canvas Element

The first step to using canvas is to add a canvas element to the page:

canvas/demo1.html *(excerpt)*

```
<canvas>
Sorry! Your browser doesn't support Canvas.
</canvas>
```

The text in between the canvas tags will only be shown if the canvas element is not supported by the visitor's browser.

Since drawing on the canvas is done using JavaScript, we'll need a way to grab the element from the DOM. We'll do so by giving our canvas an id:

canvas/demo1.html (excerpt)

```
<canvas id="myCanvas">
Sorry! Your browser doesn't support Canvas.
</canvas>
```

All drawing on the canvas happens via JavaScript, so let's make sure we're calling a JavaScript function when our page is ready. We'll add our jQuery document ready check to a script element at the bottom of the page:

canvas/demo1.html (excerpt)

```
<script>
$('document').ready(function(){
  draw();
});
</script>
```

The canvas element takes both a width and height attribute, which should also be set:

canvas/demo1.html (excerpt)

```
<canvas id="myCanvas" width="200" height="200">
Sorry! Your browser doesn't support Canvas.
</canvas>
```

Finally, let's add a border to our canvas to visually distinguish it on the page, using some CSS. Canvas has no default styling, so it's difficult to see where it is on the page unless you give it some kind of border:

css/canvas.css (excerpt)

```
#myCanvas {
  border: dotted 2px black;
}
```

Now that we've styled it, we can actually view the `canvas` container on our page —Figure 11.1 shows what it looks like.

Figure 11.1. An empty canvas with a dotted border

Drawing on the Canvas

All drawing on the canvas happens via the Canvas JavaScript API. We've called a function called `draw()` when our page is ready, so let's go ahead and create that function. We'll add the function to our `script` element. The first step is to grab hold of the `canvas` element on our page:

canvas/demo1.html *(excerpt)*

```
<script>
⋮
function draw() {
  var canvas = document.getElementById("myCanvas");
}
</script>
```

Getting the Context

Once we've stored our `canvas` element in a variable, we need to set up the canvas's context. The **context** is the place where your drawing is rendered. Currently, there's only wide support for drawing to a two-dimensional context. The W3C Canvas spec defines the context in the `CanvasRenderingContext2D` object. Most methods we'll be using to draw onto the canvas are methods of this object.

We obtain our drawing context by calling the `getContext` method and passing it the string `"2d"`, since we'll be drawing in two dimensions:

```
function draw() {
  var canvas = document.getElementById("myCanvas");
  var context = canvas.getContext("2d");
}
```

The object that's returned by `getContext` is a `CanvasRenderingContext2D` object. In this chapter, we'll refer to it as simply "the context object" for brevity.

 WebGL

WebGL is a new API for 3D graphics being managed by the Khronos Group, with a WebGL working group that includes Apple, Mozilla, Google, and Opera.

By combining WebGL with HTML5 Canvas, you can draw in three dimensions. WebGL is currently supported in Firefox 4+, Chrome 8+, and Safari 6. To learn more, see http://www.khronos.org/webgl/.

Filling Our Brush with Color

On a regular painting canvas, before you can begin, you must first saturate your brush with paint. In the HTML5 Canvas, you must do the same, and we do so with the `strokeStyle` or `fillStyle` properties. Both `strokeStyle` and `fillStyle` are set on a context object. And both take one of three values: a string representing a color, a `CanvasGradient`, or a `CanvasPattern`.

Let's start by using a color string to style the stroke. You can think of the **stroke** as the border of the shape you're going to draw. To draw a rectangle with a red border, we first define the stroke color:

```
function draw() {
  var canvas = document.getElementById("myCanvas");
  var context = canvas.getContext("2d");
  context.strokeStyle = "red";
}
```

To draw a rectangle with a red border and blue fill, we must also define the fill color:

```
                                               canvas/demo1.html (excerpt)
function draw() {
    ⋮
    context.fillStyle = "blue";
}
```

We can use any CSS color value to set the stroke or fill color, as long as we specify it as a string: a hexadecimal value like #00FFFF, a color name like red or blue, or an RGB value like rgb(0, 0, 255). We can even use RGBA to set a semitransparent stroke or fill color. Let's change our blue fill to blue with a 50% opacity:

```
                                               canvas/demo1.html (excerpt)
function draw() {
    ⋮
    context.fillStyle = "rgba(0, 0, 255, 0.5)";
}
```

Drawing a Rectangle to the Canvas

Once we've defined the color of the stroke and the fill, we're ready to actually start drawing! Let's begin by drawing a rectangle. We can do this by calling the fillRect and strokeRect methods. Both of these methods take the X and Y coordinates where you want to begin drawing the fill or the stroke, and the width and the height of the rectangle. We'll add the stroke and fill 10 pixels from the top and 10 pixels from the left of the canvas's top left corner:

```
                                               canvas/demo1.html (excerpt)
function draw() {
    ⋮
    context.fillRect(10,10,100,100);
    context.strokeRect(10,10,100,100);
}
```

This will create a semitransparent blue rectangle with a red border, like the one in Figure 11.2.

Figure 11.2. A simple rectangle—not bad for our first canvas drawing!

The Canvas Coordinate System

As you may have gathered, the coordinate system in the `canvas` element is different from the Cartesian coordinate system you learned in math class. In the canvas coordinate system, the top-left corner is (0,0). If the canvas is 200 pixels by 200 pixels, then the bottom-right corner is (200, 200), as Figure 11.3 illustrates.

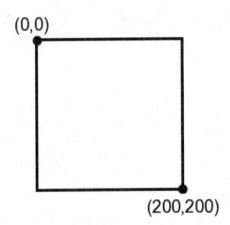

Figure 11.3. The canvas coordinate system goes top-to-bottom and left-to-right

Variations on `fillStyle`

Instead of a color as our `fillStyle`, we could have also used a `CanvasGradient` or a `CanvasPattern`.

We create a `CanvasPattern` by calling the `createPattern` method. `createPattern` takes two parameters: the image to create the pattern with, and how that image should be repeated. The repeat value is a string, and the valid values are the same as those in CSS: `repeat`, `repeat-x`, `repeat-y`, and `no-repeat`.

Instead of using a semitransparent blue `fillStyle`, let's create a pattern using our bicycle image. First, we must create an `Image` object, and set its `src` property to our image:

canvas/demo2.html *(excerpt)*

```
function draw() {
  ⋮
  var img = new Image();
  img.src = "../images/bg-bike.png";
}
```

Setting the `src` attribute will tell the browser to start downloading the image—but if we try to use it right away to create our gradient, we'll run into some problems, because the image will still be loading. So we'll use the image's `onload` property to create our pattern once the image has been fully loaded by the browser:

canvas/demo2.html *(excerpt)*

```
function draw() {
  ⋮
  var img = new Image();
  img.src = "../images/bg-bike.png";

  img.onload = function() {

  };
}
```

In our `onload` event handler, we call `createPattern`, passing it the `Image` object and the string `repeat`, so that our image repeats along both the X and Y axes. We store the results of `createPattern` in the variable `pattern`, and set the `fillStyle` to that variable:

canvas/demo2.html *(excerpt)*

```
function draw() {
  :
  var img = new Image();
  img.src = "../images/bg-bike.png";
  img.onload = function() {
    pattern = context.createPattern(img, "repeat");
    context.fillStyle = pattern;
    context.fillRect(10,10,100,100);
    context.strokeRect(10,10,100,100);
  };
}
```

Anonymous Functions

You may be asking yourself, "what is that `function` statement that comes right before the call to `img.onload`?" It's an **anonymous function**. Anonymous functions are much like regular functions except, as you might guess, they don't have names.

When you see an anonymous function inside of an event listener, it means that the anonymous function is being bound to that event. In other words, the code inside that anonymous function will be run when the `load` event is fired.

Now, our rectangle's fill is a pattern made up of our bicycle image, as Figure 11.4 shows.

Figure 11.4. A pattern fill on a canvas

We can also create a `CanvasGradient` to use as our `fillStyle`. To create a `CanvasGradient`, we call one of two methods: `createLinearGradient(x0, y0, x1, y1)` or `createRadialGradient(x0, y0, r0, x1, y1, r1)`; then we add one or more color stops to the gradient.

`createLinearGradient`'s *x0* and *y0* represent the starting location of the gradient. *x1* and *y1* represent the ending location.

To create a gradient that begins at the top of the canvas and blends the color down to the bottom, we'd define our starting point at the origin (0,0), and our ending point 200 pixels down from there (0,200):

canvas/demo3.html (excerpt)

```
function draw() {
  ⋮
  var gradient = context.createLinearGradient(0, 0, 0, 200);
}
```

Next, we specify our color stops. The color stop method is simply `addColorStop(offset, color)`.

The `offset` is a value between 0 and 1. An `offset` of 0 is at the starting end of the gradient, and an `offset` of 1 is at the other end. The `color` is a string value that, as with the `fillStyle`, can be a color name, a hexadecimal color value, an `rgb()` value, or an `rgba()` value.

To make a gradient that starts as blue and begins to blend into white halfway down the gradient, we can specify a blue color stop with an `offset` of 0 and a purple color stop with an `offset` of 1:

canvas/demo3.html (excerpt)

```
function draw() {
  ⋮
  var gradient = context.createLinearGradient(0, 0, 0, 200);
  gradient.addColorStop(0,"blue");
  gradient.addColorStop(1,"white");
  context.fillStyle = gradient;
  context.fillRect(10,10,100,100);
  context.strokeRect(10,10,100,100);
}
```

Figure 11.5 is the result of setting our `CanvasGradient` to be the `fillStyle` of our rectangle.

Figure 11.5. Creating a linear gradient with Canvas

Drawing Other Shapes by Creating Paths

We're not limited to drawing rectangles—we can draw any shape we can imagine! Unlike rectangles and squares, however, there's no built-in method for drawing circles, or other shapes. To draw more interesting shapes, we must first lay out the **path** of the shape.

Paths create a blueprint for your lines, arcs, and shapes, but paths are invisible until you give them a stroke! When we drew rectangles, we first set the `strokeStyle` and then called `fillRect`. With more complex shapes, we need to take three steps: lay out the path, stroke the path, and fill the path. As with drawing rectangles, we can just stroke the path, or fill the path—or we can do both.

Let's start with a simple circle:

```
                                      canvas/demo4.html (excerpt)

function draw() {
  var canvas = document.getElementById("myCanvas");
  var context = canvas.getContext("2d");

  context.beginPath();
}
```

Now we need to create an **arc**. An arc is a segment of a circle; there's no method for creating a circle, but we can simply draw a 360° arc. We create it using the `arc` method:

```
function draw() {
  var canvas = document.getElementById("myCanvas");
  var context = canvas.getContext("2d");

  context.beginPath();
  context.arc(50, 50, 30, 0, Math.PI*2, true);
}
```

The arguments for the `arc` method are as follows: `arc(x, y, radius, startAngle, endAngle, anticlockwise)`.

x and *y* represent where on the canvas you want the arc's path to begin. Imagine this as the center of the circle that you'll be drawing. *radius* is the distance from the center to the edge of the circle.

startAngle and *endAngle* represent the start and end angles along the circle's circumference that you want to draw. The units for the angles are in radians, and a circle is 2π radians. We want to draw a complete circle, so we will use 2π for the *endAngle*. In JavaScript, we can get this value by multiplying `Math.PI` by 2.

anticlockwise is an optional argument. If you wanted the arc to be drawn counterclockwise instead of clockwise, you would set this value to `true`. Since we are drawing a full circle, it doesn't matter which direction we draw it in, so we omit this argument.

Our next step is to close the path, since we've now finished drawing our circle. We do that with the `closePath` method:

```
function draw() {
  var canvas = document.getElementById("myCanvas");
  var context = canvas.getContext("2d");

  context.beginPath();
```

```
    context.arc(100, 100, 50, 0, Math.PI*2, true);
    context.closePath();
}
```

Now we have a path! But unless we stroke it or fill it, we'll be unable to see it. Thus, we must set a strokeStyle if we would like to give it a border, and we must set a fillStyle if we'd like our circle to have a fill color. By default, the width of the stroke is 1 pixel—this is stored in the lineWidth property of the context object. Let's make our border a bit bigger by setting the lineWidth to 3:

canvas/demo4.html (excerpt)

```
function draw() {
  var canvas = document.getElementById("myCanvas");
  var context = canvas.getContext("2d");

  context.beginPath();
  context.arc(50, 50, 30, 0, Math.PI*2, true);
  context.closePath();
  context.strokeStyle = "red";
  context.fillStyle = "blue";
  context.lineWidth = 3;
}
```

Lastly, we fill and stroke the path. Note that this time, the method names are different than those we used with our rectangle. To fill a path, you simply call fill, and to stroke it you call stroke:

canvas/demo4.html (excerpt)

```
function draw() {
  var canvas = document.getElementById("myCanvas");
  var context = canvas.getContext("2d");

  context.beginPath();
  context.arc(100, 100, 50, 0, Math.PI*2, true);
  context.closePath();
  context.strokeStyle = "red";
  context.fillStyle = "blue";
  context.lineWidth = 3;
  context.fill();
  context.stroke();
}
```

Figure 11.6 shows the finished circle.

Figure 11.6. Our shiny new circle

To learn more about drawing shapes, the Mozilla Developer Network has an excellent tutorial.[1]

Saving Canvas Drawings

If we create an image programmatically using the Canvas API, but decide we'd like to have a local copy of our drawing, we can use the API's toDataURL method to save our drawing as a PNG or JPEG file.

To preserve the circle we just drew, we could add a new button to our HTML, and open the canvas drawing as an image in a new window once the button is clicked. To do that, let's define a new JavaScript function:

canvas/demo5.html *(excerpt)*

```
function saveDrawing() {
  var canvas = document.getElementById("myCanvas");
  window.open(canvas.toDataURL("image/png"));
}
```

Next, we'll add a button to our HTML and call our function when it's clicked:

---

[1] https://developer.mozilla.org/en/Canvas_tutorial/Drawing_shapes

```
<canvas id="myCanvas" width="200" height="200">
Sorry! Your browser doesn't support Canvas.
</canvas>
<form>
  <input type="button" name="saveButton" id="saveButton"
➥value="Save Drawing">
</form>
⋮
<script>

$('document').ready(function(){
  draw();
  $('#saveButton').click(saveDrawing);
});
⋮
```

When the button is clicked, a new window or tab opens up with a PNG file loaded into it, as shown in Figure 11.7.

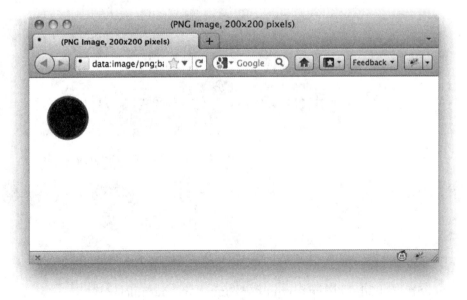

Figure 11.7. Our image loads in a new window

To learn more about saving our canvas drawings as files, see the W3C Canvas spec[2] and the "Saving a canvas image to file" section of Mozilla's Canvas code snippets.[3]

Drawing an Image to the Canvas

We can also draw images into the canvas element. In this example, we'll be redrawing into the canvas an image that already exists on the page.

For the sake of illustration, we'll be using the HTML5 logo[4] as our image for the next few examples. Let's start by adding it to our page in an img element:

canvas/demo6.html (excerpt)

```
<canvas id="myCanvas" width="200" height="200">
Your browser does not support canvas.
</canvas>
<img src="../images/html5-logo.png" id="myImageElem">
```

Next, after grabbing the canvas element and setting up the canvas's context, we can grab an image from our page via document.getElementById:

canvas/demo6.html (excerpt)

```
function draw() {
  var canvas = document.getElementById("myCanvas");
  var context = canvas.getContext("2d");
  var image = document.getElementById("myImageElem");
}
```

We'll use the same CSS we used before to make the canvas element visible:

css/canvas.css (excerpt)

```
#myCanvas {
  border: dotted 2px black;
}
```

Let's modify it slightly to space out our canvas and our image:

---

[2] http://www.w3.org/TR/html5/the-canvas-element.html#dom-canvas-todataurl
[3] https://developer.mozilla.org/en/Code_snippets/Canvas
[4] http://www.w3.org/html/logo/

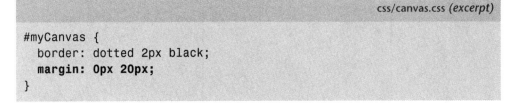

```css
#myCanvas {
  border: dotted 2px black;
  margin: 0px 20px;
}
```

Figure 11.8 shows our empty canvas next to our image.

Figure 11.8. An image and a canvas sitting on a page, not doing much

We can use canvas's `drawImage` method to redraw the image from our page into the canvas:

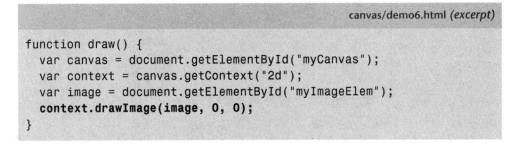

```javascript
function draw() {
  var canvas = document.getElementById("myCanvas");
  var context = canvas.getContext("2d");
  var image = document.getElementById("myImageElem");
  context.drawImage(image, 0, 0);
}
```

Because we've drawn the image to the (0,0) coordinate, the image appears in the top-left of the canvas, as you can see in Figure 11.9.

Figure 11.9. Redrawing an image inside a canvas

We could instead draw the image at the center of the canvas, by changing the X and Y coordinates that we pass to `drawImage`. Since the image is 64 by 64 pixels, and the canvas is 200 by 200 pixels, if we draw the image to (`68`, `68`),[5] the image will be in the center of the canvas, as in Figure 11.10.

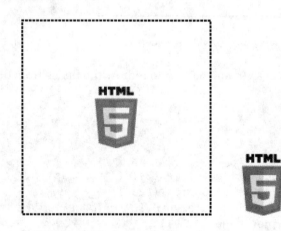

Figure 11.10. Displaying the image in the center of the canvas

Manipulating Images

Redrawing an image element from the page onto a canvas is fairly unexciting. It's really no different from using an `img` element! Where it does become interesting is how we can manipulate an image after we've drawn it into the canvas.

---

[5] Half of the canvas's dimensions minus half of the image's dimensions: (200/2) - (64/2) = 68.

Once we've drawn an image on the canvas, we can use the `getImageData` method from the Canvas API to manipulate the pixels of that image. For example, if we wanted to convert our logo from color to black and white, we can do so using methods in the Canvas API.

`getImageData` will return an `ImageData` object, which contains three properties: `width`, `height`, and `data`. The first two are self-explanatory, but it's the last one, `data`, that interests us.

`data` contains information about the pixels in the `ImageData` object, in the form of an array. Each pixel on the canvas will have four values in the `data` array—these correspond to that pixel's R, G, B, and A values.

The `getImageData` method allows us to examine a small section of a canvas, so let's use this feature to become more familiar with the data array. `getImageData` takes four parameters, corresponding to the four corners of a rectangular piece of the canvas we'd like to inspect. If we call `getImageData` on a very small section of the canvas, say `context.getImageData(0, 0, 1, 1)`, we'd be examining just one pixel (the rectangle from 0,0 to 1,1). The array that's returned is four items long, as it contains a red, green, blue, and alpha value for this lone pixel:

```
function draw() {
  var canvas = document.getElementById("myCanvas");
  var context = canvas.getContext("2d");
  var image = document.getElementById("myImageElem");
  // draw the image at x=0 and y=0 on the canvas
  context.drawImage(image, 68, 68);
  var imageData = context.getImageData(0, 0, 1, 1);
  var pixelData = imageData.data;
  alert(pixelData.length);
}
```

The alert prompt confirms that the data array for a one-pixel section of the canvas will have four values, as Figure 11.11 demonstrates.

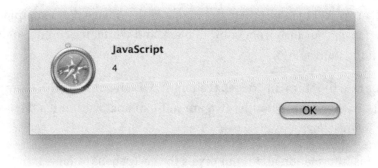

Figure 11.11. The data array for a single pixel contains four values

Converting an Image from Color to Black and White

Let's look at how we'd go about using getImageData to convert a full color image into black and white on a canvas. Assuming we've already placed an image onto the canvas, as we did above, we can use a for loop to iterate through each pixel in the image, and change it to grayscale.

First, we'll call getImageData(0,0,200,200) to retrieve the entire canvas. Then, we need to grab the red, green, and blue values of each pixel, which appear in the array in that order:

canvas/demo7.html *(excerpt)*

```
function draw() {
  var canvas = document.getElementById("myCanvas");
  var context = canvas.getContext("2d");
  var image = document.getElementById("myImageElem");
  context.drawImage(image, 68, 68);

  var imageData = context.getImageData(0, 0, 200, 200);
  var pixelData = imageData.data;

  for (var i = 0; i < pixelData.length; i += 4) {
    var red = pixelData[i];
    var green = pixelData[i + 1];
    var blue = pixelData[i + 2];
  }
}
```

Notice that our `for` loop is incrementing i by 4 instead of the usual 1. This is because each pixel takes up four values in the `imageData` array—one number each for the R, G, B, and A values.

Next, we must determine the grayscale value for the current pixel. It turns out that there's a mathematical formula for converting RGB to grayscale: you simply need to multiply each of the red, green, and blue values by some specific numbers, seen in the code block below:

canvas/demo7.html (excerpt)

```
for (var i = 0; i < pixelData.length; i += 4) {
  var red = pixelData[i];
  var green = pixelData[i + 1];
  var blue = pixelData[i + 2];

  var grayscale = red * 0.3 + green * 0.59 + blue * 0.11;
}
```

Now that we have the proper grayscale value, we're going to store it back into the red, green, and blue values in the `data` array:

canvas/demo7.html (excerpt)

```
for (var i = 0; i < pixelData.length; i += 4) {
  var red = pixelData[i];
  var green = pixelData[i + 1];
  var blue = pixelData[i + 2];

  var grayscale = red * 0.3 + green * 0.59 + blue * 0.11;

  pixelData[i] = grayscale;
  pixelData[i + 1] = grayscale;
  pixelData[i + 2] = grayscale;
}
```

So now we've modified our pixel data by individually converting each pixel to grayscale. The final step? Putting the image data we've modified back into the canvas

via a method called putImageData. This method does exactly what you'd expect: it takes image data and writes it onto the canvas. Here's the method in action:

```
function draw() {
  var canvas = document.getElementById("myCanvas");
  var context = canvas.getContext("2d");
  var image = document.getElementById("myImageElem");
  context.drawImage(image, 60, 60);

  var imageData = context.getImageData(0, 0, 200, 200);
  var pixelData = imageData.data;

  for (var i = 0; i < pixelData.length; i += 4) {
    var red = pixelData[i];
    var green = pixelData[i + 1];
    var blue = pixelData[i + 2];

    var grayscale = red * 0.3 + green * 0.59 + blue * 0.11;

    pixelData[i] = grayscale;
    pixelData[i + 1] = grayscale;
    pixelData[i + 2] = grayscale;
  }
  context.putImageData(imageData, 0, 0);
}
```

With that, we've drawn a black-and-white version of the validation image into the canvas.

Security Errors with getImageData

If you tried out this code in Chrome or Firefox, you may have noticed that it failed to work—the image on the canvas is in color. That's because in these two browsers, if you try to convert an image on your desktop in an HTML file that's also on your desktop, an error will occur in getImageData. The error is a security error, though in our case it's an unnecessary one.

The true security issue that Chrome and Firefox are attempting to stop is a user on one domain from manipulating images on another domain. For example, stopping me from loading an official logo from http://google.com/ and then manipulating the pixel data.

The W3C Canvas spec[6] describes it this way:

> Information leakage can occur if scripts from one origin can access information (e.g. read pixels) from images from another origin (one that isn't the same). To mitigate this, `canvas` elements are defined to have a flag indicating whether they are origin-clean.

This origin-clean flag will be set to `false` if the image you want to manipulate is on a different domain from the JavaScript doing the manipulating. Unfortunately, in Chrome and Firefox, this origin-clean flag is also set to `false` while you're testing from files on your hard drive—they're seen as files living on different domains.

If you want to test pixel manipulation using canvas in Firefox or Chrome, you'll need to either test it on a web server running on your computer (http://localhost/), or test it online on a real web server.

Manipulating Video with Canvas

We can take the code we've already written to convert a color image to black and white, and enhance it to make our color *video* black and white, to match the old-timey feel of *The HTML5 Herald* page. We'll do this in a new, separate JavaScript file called **videoToBW.js**, so that we can include it on the site's home page.

The file begins, as always, by setting up the canvas and the context:

js/videoToBW.js *(excerpt)*

```
function makeVideoOldTimey ()
{
  var video = document.getElementById("video");
  var canvas = document.getElementById("canvasOverlay");
  var context = canvas.getContext("2d");
}
```

Next, we'll add a new event listener to react to the `play` event firing on the `video` element.

We want to call a `draw` function when the video begins playing. To do so, we'll add an event listener to our video `element` that responds to the `play` event:

---

[6] http://dev.w3.org/html5/2dcontext/

```
                                                    js/videoToBW.js (excerpt)

function makeVideoOldTimey ()
{
  var video = document.getElementById("video");
  var canvas = document.getElementById("canvasOverlay");
  var context = canvas.getContext("2d");

  video.addEventListener("play", function(){
    draw(video,context,canvas);
  },false);
}
```

The draw function will be called when the play event fires, and it will be passed
the video, context, and canvas objects. We're using an anonymous function here
instead of a normal named function because we can't actually pass parameters to
named functions when declaring them as event handlers.

Since we want to pass several parameters to the draw function—*video*, *context*,
and *canvas*—we must call it from inside an anonymous function.

Let's look at the draw function:

```
                                                    js/videoToBW.js (excerpt)

function draw(video, context, canvas)
{
  if (video.paused || video.ended)
  {
    return false;
  }

  drawOneFrame(video, context, canvas);
}
```

Before doing anything else, we check to see if the video is paused or has ended, in
which case we'll just cut the function short by returning false. Otherwise, we
continue onto the drawOneFrame function. The drawOneFrame function is nearly
identical to the code we had above for converting an image from color to black and
white, except that we're drawing the video element onto the canvas instead of a
static image:

js/videoToBW.js *(excerpt)*

```
function drawOneFrame(video, context, canvas){
  // draw the video onto the canvas
  context.drawImage(video, 0, 0, canvas.width, canvas.height);

  var imageData = context.getImageData(0, 0, canvas.width,
➥canvas.height);
  var pixelData = imageData.data;
  // Loop through the red, green and blue pixels,
  // turning them grayscale
  for (var i = 0; i < pixelData.length; i += 4) {
    var red = pixelData[i];
    var green = pixelData[i + 1];
    var blue = pixelData[i + 2];
    //we'll ignore the alpha value, which is in position i+3

    var grayscale = red * 0.3 + green * 0.59 + blue * 0.11;

    pixelData[i] = grayscale;
    pixelData[i + 1] = grayscale;
    pixelData[i + 2] = grayscale;
  }

  imageData.data = pixelData;

  context.putImageData(imageData, 0, 0);
}
```

After we've drawn one frame, what's the next step? We need to draw another frame! The setTimeout method allows us to keep calling the draw function over and over again, without pause: the final parameter is the value for delay—or how long, in milliseconds, the browser should wait before calling the function. Because it's set to 0, we are essentially running draw continuously. This goes on until the video has either ended, or been paused:

js/videoToBW.js *(excerpt)*

```
function draw(video, context, canvas) {
  if (video.paused || video.ended)
  {
    return false;
  }
```

```
var status = drawOneFrame(video, context, canvas);

// Start over!
setTimeout(function(){ draw(video, context, canvas); }, 0);
}
```

The net result? Our color video of a plane taking off now plays in black and white!

Displaying Text on the Canvas

If we were to view *The HTML5 Herald* from a file on our computer, we'd encounter security errors in Firefox and Chrome when trying to manipulate an entire video, as we would a simple image.

We can add a bit of error-checking in order to make our video work anyway, even if we view it from our local machine in Chrome or Firefox.

The first step is to add a try/catch block to catch the error:

js/videoToBW.js *(excerpt)*

```
function drawOneFrame(video, context, canvas){
  context.drawImage(video, 0, 0, canvas.width, canvas.height);

  try {
    var imageData = context.getImageData(0, 0, canvas.width,
➥canvas.height);
    var pixelData = imageData.data;
    for (var i = 0; i < pixelData.length; i += 4) {
      var red = pixelData[i];
      var green = pixelData[i + 1];
      var blue = pixelData[i + 2];
      var grayscale = red * 0.3 + green * 0.59 + blue * 0.11;
      pixelData[i] = grayscale;
      pixelData[i + 1] = grayscale;
      pixelData[i + 2] = grayscale;
    }

    imageData.data = pixelData;
    context.putImageData(imageData, 0, 0);
  }
  catch (err) {
```

```
      // error handling code will go here
  }
}
```

When an error occurs in trying to call `getImageData`, it would be nice to give some sort of message to the user in order to give them a hint about what may be going wrong. We'll do just that, using the `fillText` method of the Canvas API.

Before we write any text to the canvas, we should clear what's already drawn to it. We've already drawn the first frame of the video into the canvas using the call to `drawImage`. How can we clear that out?

It turns out that if we reset the width or height on the canvas, the canvas will be cleared. So, let's reset the width:

js/videoToBW.js *(excerpt)*

```
function drawOneFrame(video, context, canvas){
  context.drawImage(video, 0, 0, canvas.width, canvas.height);

  try {
    ⋮
  }
  catch (err) {
    canvas.width = canvas.width;
  }
}
```

Next, let's change the background color from black to transparent, since the `canvas` element is positioned on top of the video:

js/videoToBW.js *(excerpt)*

```
function drawOneFrame(video, context, canvas){
  context.drawImage(video, 0, 0, canvas.width, canvas.height);

  try {
    ⋮
  }
  catch (err) {
    canvas.width = canvas.width;
```

```
    canvas.style.backgroundColor = "transparent";
  }
}
```

Before we can draw any text to the now transparent canvas, we first must set up the style of our text—similar to what we did with paths earlier. We do that with the fillStyle and textAlign methods:

js/videoToBW.js *(excerpt)*

```
videoToBW.js (excerpt)
function drawOneFrame(video, context, canvas){
  context.drawImage(video, 0, 0, canvas.width, canvas.height);

  try {
    ⋮
  }
  catch (err) {
    canvas.width = canvas.width;
    canvas.style.backgroundColor = "transparent";
    context.fillStyle = "white";
    context.textAlign = "left";
  }
}
```

We must also set the font we'd like to use. The font property of the context object works the same way the CSS font property does. We'll specify a font size of 18px and a comma-separated list of font families:

js/videoToBW.js *(excerpt)*

```
function drawOneFrame(video, context, canvas){
  context.drawImage(video, 0, 0, canvas.width, canvas.height);

  try {
    ⋮
  }
  catch (err) {
    canvas.width = canvas.width;
    canvas.style.backgroundColor = "transparent";
    context.fillStyle = "white";
    context.textAlign = "left";
```

```
        context.font = "18px LeagueGothic, Tahoma, Geneva, sans-serif";
    }
}
```

Notice that we're using League Gothic; any fonts you've included with `@font-face` are also available for you to use on your canvas. Finally, we draw the text. We use a method of the context object called `fillText`, which takes the text to be drawn and the (x,y) coordinates where it should be placed. Since we want to write out a fairly long message, we'll split it up into several sections, placing each one on the canvas separately:

js/videoToBW.js (excerpt)

```
function drawOneFrame(video, context, canvas){
    context.drawImage(video, 0, 0, canvas.width, canvas.height);

    try {
        ⋮
    }
    catch (err) {
        canvas.width = canvas.width;
        canvas.style.backgroundColor = "transparent";
        context.fillStyle = "white";
        context.textAlign = "left";
        context.font = "18px LeagueGothic, Tahoma, Geneva, sans-serif";
        context.fillText("There was an error rendering ", 10, 20);
        context.fillText("the video to the canvas.", 10, 40);
        context.fillText("Perhaps you are viewing this page from", 10,
➡70);
        context.fillText("a file on your computer?", 10, 90);
        context.fillText("Try viewing this page online instead.", 10,
➡130);

        return false;
    }
}
```

As a last step, we return `false`. This lets us check in the `draw` function whether an exception was thrown. If it was, we want to stop calling `drawOneFrame` for each video frame, so we exit the `draw` function:

```
function draw(video, context, canvas) {
    if (video.paused || video.ended)
    {
      return false;
    }

    var status = drawOneFrame(video, context, canvas);

    if (status == false)
    {
      return false;
    }
    // Start over!
    setTimeout(function(){ draw(video, context, canvas); }, 0);
}
```

Accessibility Concerns

A major downside of canvas in its current form is its lack of accessibility. The canvas doesn't create a DOM node, is not a text-based format, and is thus essentially invisible to tools like screen readers. For example, even though we wrote text to the canvas in our last example, that text is essentially no more than a bunch of pixels, and is therefore inaccessible.

The HTML5 community is aware of these failings, and while no solution has been finalized, debates on how canvas could be changed to make it accessible are underway. You can read a compilation of the arguments and currently proposed solutions on the W3C's wiki page.[7]

Further Reading

To read more about canvas and the Canvas API, here are a couple of good resources:

▦ "HTML5 canvas—the basics" at Dev.Opera[8]
▦ Safari's HTML5 Canvas Guide[9]

---

[7] http://www.w3.org/html/wg/wiki/AddedElementCanvas

[8] http://dev.opera.com/articles/view/html-5-canvas-the-basics/

[9] http://developer.apple.com/library/safari/#documentation/AudioVideo/Conceptual/HTML-canvas-guide/Introduction/Introduction.html

SVG

We already learned a bit about SVG back in Chapter 7, when we used SVG files as a fallback for gradients in IE9 and older versions of Opera. In this chapter, we'll dive into SVG in more detail and learn how to use it in other ways.

First, a quick refresher: SVG stands for Scalable Vector Graphics. SVG is a specific file format that allows you to describe vector graphics using XML. A major selling point of vector graphics in general is that, unlike bitmap images (such as GIF, JPEG, PNG, and TIFF), vector images preserve their shape even as you blow them up or shrink them down. We can use SVG to do many of the same tasks we can do with canvas, including drawing paths, shapes, text, gradients, and patterns. There are also some very useful open source tools relevant to SVG, some of which we will leverage in order to add a spinning progress indicator to *The HTML5 Herald*'s geo-location widget.

Basic SVG, including using SVG in an HTML `img` element, is supported in:

- Safari 3.2+
- Chrome 6.0+
- Firefox 4.0+
- Internet Explorer 9.0+
- Opera 10.5+

There is currently no support for SVG in Android's browser.

XML

XML stands for eXtensible Markup Language. Like HTML, it's a markup language, which means it's a system meant to annotate text. Just as we can use HTML tags to wrap our content and give it meaning, so can XML tags be used to describe the content of files.

Unlike canvas, images created with SVG are available via the DOM. This allows technologies like screen readers to see what's present in an SVG object through its DOM node—and it also allows you to inspect SVG using your browser's developer tools. Since SVG is an XML file format, it's also more accessible to search engines than canvas.

Drawing in SVG

Drawing a circle in SVG is arguably easier than drawing a circle with canvas. Here's how we do it:

```
<svg xmlns="http://www.w3.org/2000/svg" viewBox="0 0 400 400">
  <circle cx="50" cy="50" r="25" fill="red"/>
</svg>
```

The `viewBox` attribute defines the starting location, width, and height of the SVG image.

The `circle` element defines a circle, with `cx` and `cy` the X and Y coordinates of the center of the circle. The radius is represented by `r`, while `fill` is for the fill style.

To view an SVG file, you simply open it via the **File** menu in any browser that supports SVG. Figure 11.12 shows what our circle looks like.

Figure 11.12. A circle drawn using SVG

We can also draw rectangles in SVG, and add a stroke to them, as we did with canvas.

This time, let's take advantage of SVG being an XML—and thus text-based—file format, and utilize the `desc` tag, which allows us to provide a description for the image we're going to draw:

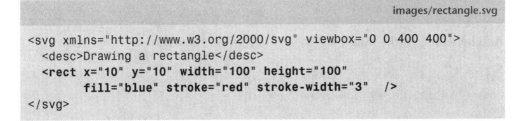

```
images/rectangle.svg (excerpt)

<svg xmlns="http://www.w3.org/2000/svg" viewbox="0 0 400 400">
  <desc>Drawing a rectangle</desc>
</svg>
```

Next, we populate the `rect` tag with a number of attributes that describe the rectangle. This includes the X and Y coordinate where the rectangle should be drawn, the width and height of the rectangle, the fill, the stroke, and the width of the stroke:

```
images/rectangle.svg

<svg xmlns="http://www.w3.org/2000/svg" viewbox="0 0 400 400">
  <desc>Drawing a rectangle</desc>
  <rect x="10" y="10" width="100" height="100"
        fill="blue" stroke="red" stroke-width="3"  />
</svg>
```

Figure 11.13 shows our what our rectangle looks like.

Figure 11.13. A rectangle drawn with SVG

Unfortunately, it's not always this easy. If you want to create complex shapes, the code begins to look a little scary. Figure 11.14 shows a fairly simple-looking star image from openclipart.org:

Figure 11.14. A line drawing of a star

And here are just the first few lines of SVG for this image:

```
<svg xmlns="http://www.w3.org/2000/svg"
  width="122.88545" height="114.88568">
<g
  inkscape:label="Calque 1"
  inkscape:groupmode="layer"
  id="layer1"
  transform="translate(-242.42282,-449.03699)">
  <g
    transform="matrix(0.72428496,0,0,0.72428496,119.87078,183.8127)"
    id="g7153">
    <path
      style="fill:#ffffff;fill-opacity:1;stroke:#000000;stroke-width
➥:2.761343;stroke-linecap:round;stroke-linejoin:round;stroke-miterl
➥imit:4;stroke-opacity:1;stroke-dasharray:none;stroke-dashoffset:0"
      d="m 249.28667,389.00422 -9.7738,30.15957 -31.91999,7.5995 c -
➥2.74681,1.46591 -5.51239,2.92436 -1.69852,6.99979 l 30.15935,12.57
➥796 -11.80876,32.07362 c -1.56949,4.62283 -0.21957,6.36158 4.24212
➥,3.35419 l 26.59198,-24.55691 30.9576,17.75909 c 3.83318,2.65893 6
➥.12086,0.80055 5.36349,-3.57143 l -12.10702,-34.11764 22.72561,-13
➥.7066 c 2.32805,-1.03398 5.8555,-6.16054 -0.46651,-6.46042 l -33.5
➥0135,-0.66887 -11.69597,-27.26175 c -2.04282,-3.50583 -4.06602,-7.
➥22748 -7.06823,-0.1801 z"
      id="path7155"
      inkscape:connector-curvature="0"
      sodipodi:nodetypes="ccccccccccccccc" />
    ⋮
```

Eek!

Using Inkscape to Create SVG Images

To save ourselves some work (and sanity), instead of creating SVG images by hand, we can use an image editor to help. One open source tool that you can use to make SVG images is Inkscape. Inkscape is an open source vector graphics editor that outputs SVG. Inkscape is available for download at http://inkscape.org/.

For our progress-indicating spinner, instead of starting from scratch, we've searched the public domain to find a good image from which to begin. A good resource to know about for public domain images is http://openclipart.org, where you can find images that are copyright-free and free to use. The images have been donated by the creators for use in the public domain, even for commercial purposes, without the need to ask for permission.

We will be using an image of three arrows as the basis of our progress spinner, shown in Figure 11.15. The original can be found at openclipart.org.[10]

Figure 11.15. The image we'll be using for our progress indicator

SVG Filters

To make our progress spinner match our page a bit better, we can use a filter in Inkscape to make it black and white. Start by opening the file in Inkscape, then choose **Filters > Color > Moonarize**.

You may notice if you test out *The HTML5 Herald* in Safari that our black-and-white spinner is still … in color. That's because SVG filters are a specific feature of SVG yet to be implemented in Safari 5, though it will be part of Safari 6. SVG filters are

---

[10] http://www.openclipart.org/people/JoBrad/arrows_3_circular_interlocking.svg

supported in Firefox, Chrome, and Opera. They're currently unsupported in all versions of Safari, Internet Explorer, the Android browser, and iOS.

A safer approach would be to avoid using filters, and instead simply modify the color of the original image.

We can do this in Inkscape by selecting the three arrows in the **spinner.svg** image, and then selecting **Object > Fill and Stroke**. The **Fill and Stroke** menu will appear on the right-hand side of the screen, as seen in Figure 11.16.

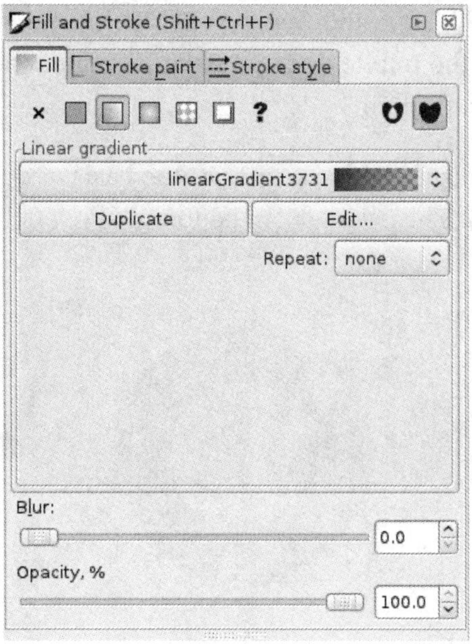

Figure 11.16. Modifying color using **Fill and Stroke**

From this menu, we can choose to edit the existing linear gradient by clicking the **Edit** button. We can then change the **Red**, **Green**, and **Blue** values all to 0 to make our image black and white.

We've saved the resulting SVG as **spinnerBW.svg**.

Using the Raphaël Library

Raphaël[11] is an open source JavaScript library that wraps around SVG. It makes drawing and animating with SVG much easier than with SVG alone.

Drawing an Image to Raphaël's Container

Much as with canvas, you can also draw images into a container you create using Raphaël.

Let's add a div to our main index file, which we'll use as the container for the SVG elements we'll create using Raphaël. We've named this div spinner:

css/styles.css (excerpt)

```
<article id="ad4">
  <div id="mapDiv">
    <h1 id="geoHeading">Where in the world are you?</h1>
    <form id="geoForm">
      <input type="button" id="geobutton" value="Tell us!">
    </form>
    <div id="spinner"></div>
  </div>
</article>
```

We have styled this div to be placed in the center of the parent mapDiv using the following CSS:

css/styles.css (excerpt)

```
#spinner {
  position:absolute;
  top:8px;
  left:55px;
}
```

Now, in our geolocation JavaScript, let's put the spinner in place while we're fetching the map. The first step is to turn our div into a Raphaël container. This is as simple as calling the Raphael method, and passing in the element we'd like to use, along with a width and height:

---

[11] http://raphaeljs.com/

```
                                              js/geolocation.js (excerpt)
function determineLocation(){
  if (navigator.onLine) {
    if (Modernizr.geolocation) {
      navigator.geolocation.getCurrentPosition(displayOnMap);

      var container = Raphael(document.getElementById("spinner"),
➥125, 125);
```

Next, we draw the spinner SVG image into the newly created container with the Raphaël method `image`, which is called on a Raphaël container object. This method takes the path to the image, the starting coordinates where the image should be drawn, and the width and height of the image:

```
                                              js/geolocation.js (excerpt)
var container = Raphael(document.getElementById("spinner"),125,125);
var spinner = container.image("images/spinnerBW.svg",0,0,125,125);
```

With this, our spinner image will appear when we click on the button in the geolocation widget.

Rotating a Spinner with Raphaël

Now that we have our container and the spinner SVG image drawn into it, we want to animate the image to make it spin. Raphaël has animation features built in with the `animate` method. Before we can use this method, though, we first need to tell it which attribute to animate. Since we want to rotate our image, we'll create an object that specifies how many degrees of rotation we want.

We create a new object `attrsToAnimate`, specifying that we want to animate the rotation, and we want to rotate by 720 degrees (two full turns):

```
                                              js/geolocation.js (excerpt)
var container = Raphael(document.getElementById("spinner"),125,125);
var spinner = container.image("images/spinnerBW.png",0,0,125,125);
var attrsToAnimate = { rotation: "720" };
```

The final step is to call the `animate` method, and specify how long the animation should last. In our case, we will let it run for a maximum of sixty seconds. Since `animate` takes its values in milliseconds, we'll pass it `60000`:

js/geolocation.js (excerpt)

```
var container = Raphael(document.getElementById("spinner"),125,125);
var spinner = container.image("images/spinnerBW.png",0,0,125,125);
var attrsToAnimate = { rotation: "720" };
spinner.animate(attrsToAnimate, 60000);
```

That's great! We now have a spinning progress indicator to keep our visitors in the know while our map is loading. There's still one problem though: it remains after the map has loaded. We can fix this by adding one line to the beginning of the existing `displayOnMap` function:

js/geolocation.js (excerpt)

```
function displayOnMap(position){
  document.getElementById("spinner").style.visibility = "hidden";
```

This line sets the `visibility` property of the spinner element to `hidden`, effectively hiding the spinner `div` and the SVG image we've loaded into it.

Canvas versus SVG

Now that we've learned about canvas and SVG, you may be asking yourself, which is the right one to use? The answer is: it depends on what you're doing.

Both canvas and SVG allow you to draw custom shapes, paths, and fonts. But what's unique about each?

Canvas allows for pixel manipulation, as we saw when we turned our video from color to black and white. One downside of canvas is that it operates in what's known as **immediate mode**. This means that if you ever want to add more to the canvas, you can't simply add to what's already there. Everything must be redrawn from scratch each time you want to change what's on the canvas. There's also no access to what's drawn on the canvas via the DOM. However, canvas does allow you to save the images you create to a PNG or JPEG file.

By contrast, what you draw to SVG is accessible via the DOM, because its mode is **retained mode**—the structure of the image is preserved in the XML document that describes it. SVG also has, at this time, a more complete set of tools to help you work with it, like the Raphaël library and Inkscape. However, since SVG is a file format—rather than a set of methods that allows you to dynamically draw on a surface—you can't manipulate SVG images the way you can manipulate pixels on canvas. It would have been impossible, for example, to use SVG to convert our color video to black and white as we did with canvas.

In summary, if you need to paint pixels to the screen, and have no concerns about the ability to retrieve and modify your shapes, canvas is probably the better choice. If, on the other hand, you need to be able to access and change specific aspects of your graphics, SVG might be more appropriate.

It's also worth noting that neither technology is appropriate for static images—at least not while browser support remains a stumbling block. In this chapter, we've made use of canvas and SVG for a number of such static examples, which is fine for the purpose of demonstrating what they can do. But in the real world, they're only really appropriate for cases where user interaction defines what's going to be drawn.

Drag and Drop

In order to add one final dynamic effect to our site, we're going to examine the new Drag and Drop API. This API allows us to specify that certain elements are **draggable**, and then specify what should happen when these draggable elements are dragged over or dropped onto other elements on the page.

Drag and Drop is supported in:

- Safari 3.2+
- Chrome 6.0+
- Firefox 3.5+ (there is an older API that was supported in Firefox 3.0)
- Internet Explorer 7.0+
- Android 2.1+

There is currently no support for Drag and Drop in Opera. The API is unsupported by design in iOS, as Apple directs you to use the DOM Touch API[12] instead.

There are two major kinds of functionality you can implement with Drag and Drop: dragging files from your computer into a web page—in combination with the File API—or dragging elements into other elements on the same page. In this chapter, we'll focus on the latter.

Drag and Drop and the File API

If you'd like to learn more about how to combine Drag and Drop with the File API, in order to let users drag files from their desktop onto your websites, an excellent guide can be found at the Mozilla Developer Network.[13]

The File API is currently only supported in Firefox 3.6+ and Chrome.

There are several steps to adding Drag and Drop to your page:

1. Set the `draggable` attribute on any HTML elements you'd like to be draggable.

2. Add an event listener for the `dragstart` event on any draggable HTML elements.

3. Add an event listener for the `dragover` and `drop` events on any elements you want to have accept dropped items.

Feeding the WAI-ARIA Cat

In order to add a bit of fun and frivolity to our page, let's add a few images of mice, so that we can then drag them onto our cat image and watch the cat react and devour them. Before you start worrying (or call the SPCA), rest assured that we mean, of course, computer mice. We'll use another image from OpenClipArt for our mice.[14]

The first step is to add these new images to our **index.html** file. We'll give each mouse image an `id` as well:

---

[12] http://developer.apple.com/library/safari/#documentation/AppleApplications/Reference/SafariWebContent/HandlingEvents/HandlingEvents.html

[13] https://developer.mozilla.org/en/Using_files_from_web_applications

[14] http://www.openclipart.org/detail/111289

```
                                              js/dragDrop.js (excerpt)

<article id="ac3">
  <hgroup>
    <h1>Wai-Aria? HAHA!</h1>
    <h2>Form Accessibility</h2>
  </hgroup>

  <img src="images/cat.png" alt="WAI-ARIA Cat">

  <div class="content">
    <p id="mouseContainer">
      <img src="images/computer-mouse-pic.svg" width="30"
➥alt="mouse treat" id="mouse1">
      <img src="images/computer-mouse-pic.svg" width="30"
➥alt="mouse treat" id="mouse2">
      <img src="images/computer-mouse-pic.svg" width="30"
➥alt="mouse treat" id="mouse3">
    </p>
  ⋮
```

Figure 11.17 shows our images in their initial state.

Figure 11.17. Three little mice, ready to be fed to the WAI-ARIA cat

Making Elements Draggable

The next step is to make our images draggable. In order to do that, we add the
draggable attribute to them, and set the value to true:

```
                                              js/dragDrop.js (excerpt)

<img src="images/computer-mouse-pic.svg" width="30"
➥alt="mouse treat" id="mouse1" draggable="true">
<img src="images/computer-mouse-pic.svg" width="30"
➥alt="mouse treat" id="mouse2" draggable="true">
<img src="images/computer-mouse-pic.svg" width="30"
➥alt="mouse treat" id="mouse3" draggable="true">
```

draggable Must Be Set

Note that draggable is *not* a Boolean attribute; you have to explicitly set it to true.

Now that we have set draggable to true, we have to set an event listener for the dragstart event on each image. We'll use jQuery's bind method to attach the event listener:

```
                                              js/dragDrop.js (excerpt)

$('document').ready(function() {
  $('#mouseContainer img').bind('dragstart', function(event) {
    // handle the dragstart event
  });
});
```

The DataTransfer Object

DataTransfer objects are one of the new objects outlined in the Drag and Drop API. These objects allow us to set and get data about the objects that are being dragged. Specifically, DataTransfer lets us define two pieces of information:

1. the type of data we're saving about the draggable element
2. the value of the data itself

In the case of our draggable mouse images, we want to be able to store the id of these images, so we know which image is being dragged around.

To do this, we first need to tell DataTransfer that we want to save some plain text by passing in the string text/plain. Then we give it the id of our mouse image:

```
                                            js/dragDrop.js (excerpt)
$('#mouseContainer img').bind('dragstart', function(event) {
  event.originalEvent.dataTransfer.setData("text/plain",
➥event.target.getAttribute('id'));
});
```

When an element is dragged, we save the `id` of the element in the `DataTransfer` object, to be used again once the element is dropped. The target property of a `dragstart` event will be the element that's being dragged.

dataTransfer and jQuery

The jQuery library's `Event` object only gives you access to properties it knows about. This causes problems when you're using new native events like `DataTransfer`; trying to access the `dataTransfer` property of a jQuery event will result in an error. However, you can always retrieve the original DOM event by calling the `originalEvent` method on your jQuery event, as we did above. This will give you access to any properties your browser supports—in this case that includes the new `DataTransfer` object.

Of course, this isn't an issue if you're rolling your own JavaScript from scratch!

Accepting Dropped Elements

Now our mouse images are set up to be dragged. Yet, when we try to drag them around, we're unable to drop them anywhere, which is no fun.

The reason is that by default, elements on the page aren't set up to receive dragged items. In order to override the default behavior on a specific element, we must stop it from happening. We can do that by creating two more event listeners.

The two events we need to monitor for are `dragover` and `drop`. As you'd expect, `dragover` fires when you drag something over an element, and `drop` fires when you drop something on it.

We'll need to prevent the default behavior for both these events—since the default prohibits you from dropping an element.

Let's start by adding an `id` to our cat image so that we can bind event handlers to it:

js/dragDrop.js *(excerpt)*

```
<article id="ac3">
  <hgroup>
    <h1>Wai-Aria? HAHA!</h1>
    <h2 id="catHeading">Form Accessibility</h2>
  </hgroup>

  <img src="images/cat.png" id="cat" alt="WAI-ARIA Cat">
```

You may have noticed that we also gave an id to the h2 element. This is so we can change this text once we've dropped a mouse onto the cat.

Now, let's handle the dragover event:

js/dragDrop.js *(excerpt)*

```
$('#cat').bind('dragover', function(event) {
  event.preventDefault();
});
```

That was easy! In this case, we merely ensured that the mouse picture can actually be dragged over the cat picture. We simply need to prevent the default behavior —and jQuery's preventDefault method serves this purpose exactly.

The code for the drop handler is a bit more complex, so let us review it piece by piece. Our first task is to figure out what the cat should say when a mouse is dropped on it. In order to demonstrate that we can retrieve the id of the dropped mouse from the DataTransfer object, we'll use a different phrase for each mouse, regardless of the order they're dropped in. We've given three cat-appropriate options: "MEOW!", "Purr ...", and "NOMNOMNOM."

We'll store these options inside an object called mouseHash. The first step is to declare our object:

js/dragDrop.js *(excerpt)*

```
$('#cat').bind('drop', function(event) {
  var mouseHash = {};
```

Next, we're going to take advantage of JavaScript's objects allowing us to store key/value pairs inside them, as well as storing each response in the mouseHash object, associating each response with the id of one of the mouse images:

js/dragDrop.js (excerpt)

```
$('#cat').bind('drop', function(event) {
  var mouseHash = {};
  mouseHash['mouse1'] = "NOMNOMNOM";
  mouseHash['mouse2'] = "MEOW!";
  mouseHash['mouse3'] = "Purr...";
```

Our next step is to grab the h2 element that we'll change to reflect the cat's response:

js/dragDrop.js (excerpt)

```
var catHeading = document.getElementById('catHeading');
```

Remember when we saved the id of the dragged element to the DataTransfer object using setData? Well, now we want to retrieve that id. If you guessed that we will need a method called getData for this, you guessed right:

js/dragDrop.js (excerpt)

```
var item = event.originalEvent.dataTransfer.getData("text/plain");
```

Note that we've stored the mouse's id in a variable called item. Now that we know which mouse was dropped, and we have our heading, we just need to change the text to the appropriate response:

js/dragDrop.js (excerpt)

```
catHeading.innerHTML = mouseHash[item];
```

We use the information stored in the item variable (the dragged mouse's id) to retrieve the correct message for the h2 element. For example, if the dragged mouse is mouse1, calling mouseHash[item] will retrieve "NOMNOMNOM" and set that as the h2 element's text.

Given that the mouse has now been "eaten," it makes sense to remove it from the page:

js/dragDrop.js (excerpt)

```
var mousey = document.getElementById(item);
mousey.parentNode.removeChild(mousey);
```

Last but not least, we must also prevent the default behavior of not allowing elements to be dropped on our cat image, as before:

js/dragDrop.js (excerpt)

```
event.preventDefault();
```

Figure 11.18 shows our happy cat, with one mouse to go.

Figure 11.18. This cat's already eaten two mice

Further Reading

We've only touched on the basics of the Drag and Drop API, to give you a taste of what's available. We've shown you how you can use `DataTransfer` to pass data from your dragged items to their drop targets. What you do with this power is up to you!

To learn more about the Drag and Drop API, here are a couple of good resources:

- The Mozilla Developer Center's Drag and Drop documentation[15]
- The W3C's Drag and Drop specification[16]

---

[15] https://developer.mozilla.org/En/DragDrop/Drag_and_Drop
[16] http://dev.w3.org/html5/spec/dnd.html

That's All, Folks!

With these final bits of interactivity, our work on *The HTML5 Herald* has come to an end, and your journey into the world of HTML5 and CSS3 is well on its way! We've tried to provide a solid foundation of knowledge about as many of the cool new features available in today's browsers as possible—but how you build on that is up to you.

We hope we've given you a clear picture of how most of these features can be used today on real projects. Many are already well-supported, and browser development is once again progressing at a rapid clip. And when it comes to those elements for which support is still lacking, you have the aid of an online army of ingenious developers. These community-minded individuals are constantly working at coming up with fallbacks and polyfills to help us push forward and build the next generation of websites and applications.

Get to it!

Appendix A: Modernizr

Modernizr is an open source JavaScript library that allows us to test for individual features of HTML5 in our users' browsers. Instead of testing just for a particular browser and trying to make decisions based on that, Modernizr allows us to ask specific questions like: "Does this browser support geolocation?" and receive a clear "yes" or "no" answer.

The first step to using Modernizr is to download it from the Modernizr site, at http://modernizr.com.

Once you have a copy of the script, you'll need to include the script file in your pages. We'll add it to the head in this example:

```
<!doctype html>
<html>
<head>
  <meta charset="utf-8">
  <title>My Beautiful Sample Page</title>
  <script src="modernizr-1.7.min.js"></script>
</head>
```

You can use Modernizr in two ways: with CSS, and with JavaScript.

Using Modernizr with CSS

When Modernizr runs, it will add an entry in the class attribute of the HTML <html> tag for every feature it detects, prefixing the feature with no- if the browser doesn't support it.

For example, if you're using Safari 5, which supports almost everything in HTML5 and CSS3, your opening <html> tag will look a little like this after Modernizr runs:

```
<html class=" js flexbox canvas canvastext no-webgl no-touch
geolocation postmessage websqldatabase no-indexeddb hashchange
history draganddrop websockets rgba hsla multiplebgs backgroundsize
borderimage borderradius boxshadow textshadow opacity cssanimations
csscolumns cssgradients cssreflections csstransforms csstransforms3d
csstransitions fontface video audio localstorage sessionstorage
webworkers applicationcache svg no-inlinesvg smil svgclippaths">
```

Here's what Modernizr adds to the `<html>` tag in Firefox 4:

```
<html class=" js flexbox canvas canvastext webgl no-touch
geolocation postmessage no-websqldatabase indexeddb hashchange
history draganddrop no-websockets rgba hsla multiplebgs
backgroundsize borderimage borderradius boxshadow textshadow opacity
no-cssanimations csscolumns cssgradients no-cssreflections
csstransforms no-csstransforms3d csstransitions fontface video audio
localstorage no-sessionstorage webworkers applicationcache svg
inlinesvg smil svgclippaths">
```

To make better use of this feature of Modernizr, we should first add the `class` `no-js` to our `html` element in our HTML source:

```
<html class="no-js">
```

Why do we do this? If JavaScript is disabled, Modernizr won't run at all—but if JavaScript *is* enabled, the first thing Modernizr will do is change `no-js` to `js`, as we saw in the Safari 5 and Firefox 4 samples above. This way, you'll have hooks to base your styles on the presence or absence of JavaScript.

You might be thinking, "That sounds pretty cool, but what am I actually supposed to do with this information?" What we can do is use these classes to provide two flavors of CSS: styles for browsers that support certain features, and different styles for browsers that don't.

Because the classes are set on the `html` element, we can use descendant selectors to target any element on the page based on support for a given feature.

Here's an example. Any element with an `id` of `#ad2` that lives inside an element with a `class` of `cssgradients` (in other words, the `html` element when Modernizr has detected support for gradients) will receive whatever style we specify here:

```
.cssgradients #ad2 {
  /* gradients are supported! Let's use some! */
  background-image:
    -moz-linear-gradient(0% 0% 270deg,
    rgba(0,0,0,0.4) 0,
    rgba(0,0,0,0) 37%,
    rgba(0,0,0,0) 83%,
    rgba(0,0,0,0.06) 92%,
```

```
    rgba(0,0,0,0) 98%);
  ⋮
}
```

But what if CSS gradients *aren't* supported? We could change the styling to use a simple PNG background image that recreates the same gradient look. Here's how we might do that:

```
.no-cssgradients #ad2 {
  background-image:
    url(../images/put_a_replacement_img_here.png)
}
```

Another way we could use the classes Modernizr adds to the `html` element is with Drag and Drop. We discussed Drag and Drop in Chapter 11, where we added several images of computer mice that can be dragged onto our cat picture to be eaten. These images are all stored in a `div` with an `id` of `mouseContainer`.

But in Opera, where Drag and Drop will fail to work, why even show the mouse images at all? We can use Modernizr to hide the `div` if Drag and Drop is unsupported:

css/styles.css (excerpt)

```
.no-draganddrop #mouseContainer {
  visibility:hidden;
  height:0px;
}
```

If Drag and Drop *is* supported, we simply align all the content in the `div` horizontally:

css/styles.css (excerpt)

```
.draganddrop #mouseContainer {
  text-align:center;
}
```

Using Modernizr with JavaScript

We can also use Modernizr in our JavaScript to provide some fallback if the visitor's browser lacks support for any of the HTML5 elements you use.

When Modernizr runs, as well as adding all those classes to your `<html>` element, it will also create a global JavaScript object that you can use to test for feature support. The object is called, appropriately enough, `Modernizr`. This object contains a property for every HTML5 feature.

Here are a few examples:

```
Modernizr.draganddrop;
Modernizr.geolocation;
Modernizr.textshadow;
```

Each property will be either `true` or `false`, depending on whether or not the feature is available in the visitor's browser. This is useful, because we can ask questions like "Is geolocation supported in my visitor's browser?" and then take actions depending on the answer.

Here's an example of using an `if`/`else` block to test for geolocation support using Modernizr:

```
if (Modernizr.geolocation) {
  // go ahead and use the HTML5 geolocation API,
  // it's supported!
}
else {
  // There is no support for HTML5 geolocation.
  // We may try another library, like Google Gears
  // (http://gears.google.com/), to locate the user.
}
```

Support for Styling HTML5 Elements in IE8 and Earlier

As mentioned in Chapter 2, IE8 and earlier versions will forbid unrecognized elements to be styled. We then introduced a solution by Remy Sharp, the "HTML5 shiv," that solves this problem. However, as we alluded to then, Modernizr also solves this problem for us!

As stated on the Modernizr documentation page: "Modernizr runs through a little loop in JavaScript to enable the various elements from HTML5 (as well as abbr) for styling in Internet Explorer. Note that this does not mean it suddenly makes IE support the audio or video element, it just means that you can use section instead of div and style them in CSS."

In other words, we now no longer need the HTML5 shiv for styling the new semantic elements in IE8 and below—if we're using Modernizr anyway, it will take care of that for us.

Location, Location, Location

If you're using Modernizr instead of the HTML5 shiv, it will need to be placed at the very top of the page. Otherwise, your elements will appear unstyled in IE until the browser has reached the location of the Modernizr script and executed it.

Further Reading

To learn more about Modernizr, see:

- Modernizr documentation: http://www.modernizr.com/docs/

- A fairly comprehensive and up-to-date list of polyfills for HTML5 and CSS3 properties that can be used in conjunction with Modernizr is maintained at https://github.com/Modernizr/Modernizr/wiki/HTML5-Cross-browser-Polyfills

- *A List Apart* article, "Taking Advantage of HTML5 and CSS3 with Modernizr": http://www.alistapart.com/articles/taking-advantage-of-html5-and-css3-with-modernizr/

Appendix B: WAI-ARIA

In Chapter 2 and Chapter 3, we covered considerable ground explaining the potential benefits of using HTML5's new semantic elements for greater accessibility and portability of our pages. Yet, improved semantics alone is sometimes insufficient to make a sophisticated web application fully accessible.

In order to have the content and functionality of our pages as accessible as possible for our users, we need the boost that WAI-ARIA provides, extending what HTML5 (or any markup language) already does.

We'll avoid going into an extensive discussion on WAI-ARIA here—that's a topic that could fill many chapters—but we felt it was important to mention it here so that you're aware of your options.

WAI-ARIA stands for Web Accessibility Initiative-Accessible Rich Internet Applications. The overview of WAI-ARIA on the W3C site explains it as:[1]

> [...] a way to make Web content and Web applications more accessible to people with disabilities. It especially helps with dynamic content and advanced user interface controls developed with Ajax, HTML, JavaScript, and related technologies.

Users who rely on screen reader technology, or who are unable to use a mouse, are often excluded from using certain website and web application functionality—for example, sliders, progress bars, and tabbed interfaces. With WAI-ARIA, you're able to deal with these shortcomings in your pages—even if the content and functionality is trapped in complex application architecture. Thus, parts of a website that would normally be inaccessible can be made available to users who are reliant on assistive technology.

How WAI-ARIA Complements Semantics

WAI-ARIA assigns **roles** to elements, and gives those roles properties and states. Here's a simple example:

---

[1] http://www.w3.org/WAI/intro/aria.php

```
<li role="menuitemcheckbox" aria-checked="true">Sort by Date</li>
```

The application might be using the list item as a linked element to sort content; yet without the `role` and `aria-checked` attributes, a screen reader would have no way to determine what this element is for. Semantics alone (in this case, a list item) tells it nothing. By adding these attributes, the assistive device is better able to understand what this function is for.

For semantic elements—for example `header`, `h1`, and `nav`—WAI-ARIA attributes are unnecessary, as those elements already express what they are. Instead, they should be used for elements whose functionality and purpose cannot be immediately discerned from the elements themselves.

The Current State of WAI-ARIA

The WAI-ARIA specification is new, as is HTML5, so these technologies are yet to provide all the benefits we would like. Although we've described the way that WAI-ARIA can extend the semantics of our page elements, it may be necessary to include WAI-ARIA roles on elements that *already* express their meaning in their names, because assistive technology doesn't support all the new HTML5 semantics yet. In other words, WAI-ARIA can serve as a sort of stopgap, to provide accessibility for HTML5 pages while the screen readers are catching up.

Let's look at a site navigation, for example:

```
<nav>
  <ul role="navigation">
    ⋮
  </ul>
</nav>
```

It would seem that we're doubling up here: the `nav` element implies that the list of links contained within it make up a navigation control, but we've still added the WAI-ARIA role `navigation` to the list. Because WAI-ARIA and HTML5 are new technologies, this sort of doubling up will often be necessary: some browsers and screen readers that may lack support for HTML5 *will* have support for WAI-ARIA —and the inverse is possible too.

Does this mean that WAI-ARIA will become redundant once HTML5 is fully supported? No. There are roles in WAI-ARIA without corresponding HTML5 elements; for example, the timer[2] role. While you might represent a timer using the HTML5 `time` element and then update it with JavaScript, you'd have no way of indicating to a screen reader that it was a timer, rather than just an indication of a static time.

For a screen reader to access WAI-ARIA roles, the browser must expose them through an accessibility API. This allows the screen reader to interact with the elements similarly to how it would access native desktop controls.

An article on *A List Apart*, published in late 2010, summarized WAI-ARIA support in browsers and assistive devices by saying:[3]

> Support for some parts of WAI-ARIA [...] is already quite good in later versions of browser and screen readers. However, many problems remain.

Finally, it's worth noting that not all users who could benefit from WAI-ARIA roles are utilizing them. In December, 2010, an organization called WebAIM (Web Accessibility In Mind) conducted their third screen reader user survey,[4] which revealed that more than 50% of participants didn't use WAI-ARIA features, nor knew they existed.

In short, there is some support for WAI-ARIA—and you won't hurt your HTML5 documents by including these attributes, as they validate in HTML5. Even though the full benefits are yet to be seen, they'll only increase over time.

Further Reading

As mentioned, a full primer on all of the WAI-ARIA roles is beyond the scope of this book, but if you're interested in learning more, we recommend the official specification[5] first and foremost. The W3C has also put together a shorter Primer[6] and an Authoring Practices guide.[7]

---

[2] http://www.w3.org/TR/wai-aria/roles#timer
[3] http://www.alistapart.com/articles/the-accessibility-of-wai-aria/
[4] http://webaim.org/projects/screenreadersurvey3/
[5] http://www.w3.org/TR/wai-aria/
[6] http://www.w3.org/TR/wai-aria-primer/
[7] http://www.w3.org/TR/wai-aria-practices/

Appendix C: Microdata

Microdata is another technology that's rapidly gaining adoption and support, but unlike WAI-ARIA, it's actually part of HTML5. The Microdata Specification[1] is still early in development, but it's worth mentioning this technology here, because it provides a peek into what may be the future of document readability and semantics.

In the spec, Microdata is defined as a mechanism that "allows machine-readable data to be embedded in HTML documents in an easy-to-write manner, with an unambiguous parsing model."

With Microdata, page authors can add specific labels to HTML elements to annotate them so that they are able to be read by machines or bots. This is done by means of a customized vocabulary. For example, you might want a script or other third-party service to be able to access your pages and interact with specific elements on the page in a certain manner. With Microdata, you can extend existing semantics (like `article` and `figure`) to allow those services to have specialized access to the annotated content.

This can appear confusing, so let's think about a real-world example. Let's say your site includes reviews of movies. You might have each review in an `article` element, with a number of stars or a percentage score for your review. But when a machine comes along, like Google's search spider, it has no way of knowing which part of your content is the actual review—all it sees is a bunch of text on the page.

Why would a machine want to know what you thought of a movie? It's worth considering that Google has recently started displaying richer information in its search results pages, in order to provide searchers with more than just textual matches for their queries. It does this by reading the review information encoded into those sites' pages using Microdata or other similar technologies. An example of movie review information is shown in Figure C.1.

---

[1] http://www.w3.org/TR/microdata/

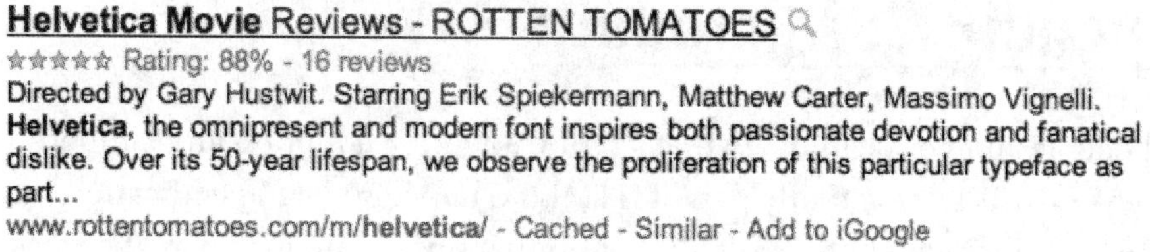

Helvetica Movie Reviews - ROTTEN TOMATOES 🔍
★★★★☆ Rating: 88% - 16 reviews
Directed by Gary Hustwit. Starring Erik Spiekermann, Matthew Carter, Massimo Vignelli.
Helvetica, the omnipresent and modern font inspires both passionate devotion and fanatical
dislike. Over its 50-year lifespan, we observe the proliferation of this particular typeface as
part...
www.rottentomatoes.com/m/**helvetica/** - Cached - Similar - Add to iGoogle

Figure C.1. Google leverages Microdata to show additional information in search results

By using Microdata, you can specify exactly which parts of your page correspond to reviews, people, events, and more—in a consistent vocabulary that software applications can understand and make use of.

Aren't HTML5's semantics enough?

You might be thinking that if a specific element is unavailable using existing HTML, then how useful could it possibly be? After all, the HTML5 spec now includes a number of new elements to allow for more expressive markup. But the creators of HTML5 have been careful to ensure that the elements that are part of the HTML5 spec are ones that will most likely be used.

It would be counterproductive to add elements to HTML that would only be used by a handful of people. This would unnecessarily bloat the language, making it unmaintainable from the perspective of a specification author or standards body.

Microdata, on the other hand, allows you to create your own custom vocabularies for very specific situations—situations that aren't possible using HTML5's semantic elements. Thus, existing HTML elements and new elements added in HTML5 are kept as a sort of semantic baseline, while specific annotations can be created by developers to target their own particular needs.

The Microdata Syntax

Microdata works with existing, well-formed HTML content, and is added to a document by means of name-value pairs (also called **properties**). Microdata does not allow you to create new elements; instead it gives you the option to add customized attributes that expand on the semantics of existing elements.

Here's a simple example:

```
<aside itemscope>
  <h1 itemprop="name">John Doe</h1>
  <p><img src="http://www.sitepoint.com/bio-photo.jpg"
➥alt="John Doe" itemprop="photo"></p>
  <p><a href="http://www.sitepoint.com" itemprop="url">Author's
➥website</a></p>
</aside>
```

In the example above, we have a run-of-the-mill author bio, placed inside an `aside` element. The first oddity you'll notice is the `itemscope` attribute. This identifies the `aside` element as the container that defines the **scope** of our Microdata vocabulary. The presence of the `itemscope` attribute defines what the spec refers to as an **item**. Each item is characterized by a group of name-value pairs.

The ability to define the scope of our vocabularies allows us to define multiple vocabularies on a single page. In the example above, all name-value pairs inside the `aside` element are part of a single Microdata vocabulary.

After the `itemscope` attribute, the next item of interest is the `itemprop` attribute, which has a value of `name`. At this point, it's probably a good idea to explain how a script would obtain information from these attributes, as well as what we mean by "name-value pairs."

Understanding Name–Value Pairs

A name is a property defined with the help of the `itemprop` attribute. In our example, the first property name happens to be one called `name`. There are two additional property names in this scope: `photo` and `url`.

The values for a given property are defined differently, depending on the element the property is declared on. For most elements, the value is taken from its text content; for instance, the `name` property in our example would get its value from the text content between the opening and closing `<h1>` tags. Other elements are treated differently.

The `photo` property takes its value from the `src` attribute of the image, so the value consists of a URL pointing to the author's photo. The `url` property, although defined on an element that has text content (namely, the phrase "Author's website"), doesn't

use this text content to determine its value; instead, it gets its value from the `href` attribute.

Other elements that don't use their associated text content to define Microdata values include `meta`, `iframe`, `object`, `audio`, `link`, and `time`. For a comprehensive list of elements that obtain their values from somewhere other than the text content, see the Values section of the Microdata specification.[2]

Microdata Namespaces

What we've described so far is acceptable for Microdata that's not intended to be reused, but that's a little impractical. The real power of Microdata is unleashed when, as we discussed, third-party scripts and page authors can access our name-value pairs and find beneficial uses for them.

In order for this to happen, each item must define a **type** by means of the `itemtype` attribute. Remember that an item in the context of Microdata is the element that has the `itemscope` attribute set. Every element and name-value pair inside that element is part of that item. The value of the `itemtype` attribute, therefore, defines the namespace for that item's vocabulary. Let's add an `itemtype` to our example:

```
<aside itemscope itemtype="http://www.data-vocabulary.org/Person">
  <h1 itemprop="name">John Doe</h1>
  <p><img src="http://www.sitepoint.com/bio-photo.jpg"
➥alt="John Doe" itemprop="photo"></p>
  <p><a href="http://www.sitepoint.com" itemprop="url">Author's
➥website</a></p>
</aside>
```

In our item, we're using the URL http://www.data-vocabulary.org/, a domain owned by Google. It houses a number of Microdata vocabularies, including Organization, Person, Review, Breadcrumb, and more.

---

[2] http://www.w3.org/TR/microdata/#values

Further Reading

This brief introduction to Microdata barely does the topic justice, but we hope it will provide you with a taste of what's possible when extending the semantics of your documents with this technology.

It's a very broad topic that requires reading and research outside of this source. With that in mind, here are a few links to check out if you want to delve deeper into the possibilities offered by Microdata:

- "Extending HTML5—Microdata" on HTML5 Doctor[3]
- The W3C Microdata specification[4]
- Mark Pilgrim's excellent overview of Microdata[5]
- Google's Rich Snippets Help[6]

---

[3] http://html5doctor.com/microdata/

[4] http://www.w3.org/TR/microdata/

[5] http://diveintohtml5.org/extensibility.html

[6] http://www.google.com/support/webmasters/bin/answer.py?hl=en&answer=99170

Index

Symbols